# Student Study Guide

to Accompany

# PSYCHOLOGY

Updated Seventh Edition

## John W. Santrock

*University of Texas at Dallas*

## Ruth Hallongren

*Triton College*

McGraw Hill

Boston   Burr Ridge, IL   Dubuque, IA   New York   San Francisco   St. Louis
Bangkok   Bogotá   Caracas   Kuala Lumpur   Lisbon   London   Madrid   Mexico City
Milan   Montreal   New Delhi   Santiago   Seoul   Singapore   Sydney   Taipei   Toronto

## Higher Education

*Study Guide to Accompany Psychology*
*Updated Seventh Edition*

ISBN 0-07-293782-3

Vice president and Editor-in-chief: *Emily Barrosse*
Publisher: *Stephen Rutter*
Sponsoring editor: *Michael Sugarman*
Development editor: *Sienne Patch*
Marketing manager: *Melissa Caughlin*
Senior supplement producer: *Louis Swaim*
Project manager: *Mel Valentín*
Compositor: *Noyes Composition and Graphics*
Typeface: *11 point Garamond*

http://www.mhhe.com

# Contents

Chapter 1    What Is Psychology?............................................................ 1

Chapter 2    Psychology's Scientific Methods ........................................ 31

Chapter 3    The Brain and Behavior ...................................................... 62

Chapter 4    Human Development............................................................ 86

Chapter 5    Sensation and Perception................................................... 115

Chapter 6    States of Consciousness..................................................... 140

Chapter 7    Learning............................................................................... 168

Chapter 8    Memory................................................................................ 196

Chapter 9    Thinking and Language...................................................... 226

Chapter 10   Intelligence.......................................................................... 256

Chapter 11   Motivation and Emotion .................................................... 287

Chapter 12   Personality........................................................................... 321

Chapter 13   Psychological Disorders..................................................... 351

Chapter 14   Therapies............................................................................. 386

Chapter 15   Stress, Coping, and Health................................................. 416

Chapter 16   Social Psychology............................................................... 443

# Chapter 1—What Is Psychology?

## Learning Goals

1. Explain what psychology is and how it developed.
2. Describe six contemporary approaches to psychology.
3. Describe two movements that reflect a positive approach to psychology.
4. Evaluate careers and areas of specialization in psychology.
5. Apply some strategies that will help you succeed in psychology.

*After studying Chapter 1, you will be able to:*

- Define psychology.
- Describe the influence that philosophy, biology, and physiology had on the beginnings of psychology as a science.
- Compare the two early scientific approaches in psychology: structuralism and functionalism.
- Describe the focus of each of the six contemporary approaches to psychology.
- Describe the positive psychology movement, and discuss why this movement recently emerged in psychology.
- Discuss career opportunities in psychology.
- Profile the main areas of specialization in psychology.
- Say how studying habits may be optimized.
- Understand how to be a critical thinker.

## CHAPTER 1: OUTLINE

- Psychology is a science dedicated to the study of behavior and mental processes. In this chapter you are introduced to the history of this science, a variety of contemporary perspectives in psychology, the positive psychology movement, and an overview of psychology-related careers. At the end of the chapter, the reader learns about the most effective methods of studying and learning.

- There are three concepts important to the definition of psychology: science, behavior, and mental processes. Psychologists use scientific methods to observe, describe, predict, and explain behaviors and mental processes. Behaviors are actions that can be directly observed, while mental processes are experiences that cannot be observed directly, such as thoughts and feelings.

- The history of psychology is rooted in philosophy, biology, and physiology. Rene Descartes and Charles Darwin strongly influenced the origins of psychology. Descartes contributed with his view of a separate mind and body, thus opening the door for studies focusing exclusively on the mind. Darwin proposed that humans are part of an evolutionary process he termed *natural selection*. This view led psychologists to consider the role of the environment and adaptation in psychology.

- In 1879, Wilhelm Wundt developed the first psychology laboratory. Wundt's approach, which emphasized the importance of conscious thought and classification of the mind's structures, was called *structuralism*. While structuralism focused inside the mind, William James emphasized the functions of the mind in adapting to the environment. James's approach was called *functionalism*.

- Structuralism and functionalism were the first two schools of thought in psychology; however, they are no longer followed. Contemporary psychologists approach the scientific study of behaviors and mental processes from a variety of perspectives, and each perspective offers an important piece of the psychology puzzle. As we study these perspectives, we should keep in mind that all the approaches are valid and each has advantages and disadvantages.

- Contemporary psychology perspectives can be classified into six approaches:

  1. Behavioral Approach:
     a. Behaviorism. The leaders of this perspective, which dominated psychology during the first half of the 20th century, were John Watson and B. F. Skinner. The focus is on observable responses and environmental determinants.
     b. Social Cognitive Theory. A more recent development of the behaviorist approach, researched by Albert Bandura, integrates the role of environmental factors and mental processes in understanding behaviors.
  2. Psychodynamic Approach. Sigmund Freud developed this perspective that focuses on the role of unconscious influences on how we think and act. Early life experiences are considered important determinants of adult psychology in this approach.
  3. Cognitive Approach. The focus here is on mental processes with an emphasis on attention, perception, memory, thinking, and solving problems.
  4. Behavioral Neuroscience Approach. This approach studies the biological basis of behavior and mental process, specifically focusing on the role of the nervous system.
  5. Evolutionary Psychology Approach. This perspective focuses on the adaptive aspects of our psychology, how adapting to the demands of our environment has shaped our repertoire of behaviors and mental processes.
  6. Sociocultural Approach. This perspective recognizes that social and cultural contexts influence our psychology—how we act, think, and feel.

- During the 20th century, psychology focused mostly on solving psychological problems, such as mental disorders and social disturbances. Most people associate psychologists with the changing of bad behaviors and problematic mental processes; however, psychologists also study and work with psychologically healthy people. The following two movements focus on the study of healthy psychology:

  1. Humanistic Psychology. An approach proposed in the middle of the 20th century. This movement was led by Maslow and Rogers. They emphasized the free will of people and their capacity for understanding and solving their own challenges.
  2. Positive Psychology. This movement emerged at the beginning of the 21st century, and it attempts to promote the study of positive psychological phenomena such as creativity, optimism, and effective social relations.

- A person with an undergraduate degree in psychology will be able to apply the knowledge of behaviors and mental processes to a variety of job possibilities in business, service areas, and research. However, having a graduate degree in psychology expands job opportunities and options.

- A student considering graduate studies in psychology has many areas of specialization from which to choose. Clinical and counseling psychologists are the areas we most commonly associate with psychology; they specialize in the diagnosis and treatment of psychological problems.

- An experimental psychologist uses the experiment research method to study basic psychology issues such as perception and thinking.

- Behavioral neuroscience and comparative psychology focuses on the biological basis of psychology, such as the role of the brain in behaviors.

- A developmental psychologist studies the process of human development across the lifespan, from childhood to late adulthood.

- Social psychology is dedicated to the study of social pressure, how we influence one another's behaviors and mental processes.

- Personality psychology explores the role of stable personality characteristics in our psychology.

- Health psychologists study the relationship between our psychological experience and our physical well-being or health; for example, they study how the psychological experience of stress is related to health problems.

- Community psychologists study the relationship between psychological well-being and the community. One of their areas of focus is the issue of proper access to psychological care services for the people in the community who need them.

- School and educational psychology are two separate areas, but they have in common the interest on the psychological experience of people in educational institutions. School psychologists are often found in schools working with behaviors and mental processes that interfere with a successful academic experience.

- Educational psychologists generally do research on the psychological factors involved in the academic experience.

- Industrial and organizational (I/O) psychologists study and deal with psychology in the workplace. An I/O Psychologist may help an organization design an optimal process for hiring new employees or may work inside a company, advising employees on how to improve their work environment and productivity.

- Environmental psychology studies the relationship between people and their physical environment. For example, an environmental psychologist might study the effect of the color of walls on the emotions of a person.

- Cross-cultural psychology explores the variations of behaviors and mental processes across cultures.

- The psychology of women focuses on the experiences of women and other factors that may explain gender differences in behaviors and mental processes.

- Forensic psychologists study the role of psychology in the legal system and may serve as consultants and expert witnesses in the courtroom.

- Sport psychologists explore the behaviors and mental processes involved in optimizing performance in sport events; they often advise athletes and develop strategies to enhance their performance.

- Getting the most out of this course will strongly depend on the studying strategies that you use. Based on psychological research, here are some strategies that make studying more effective. Chart monthly, weekly, and daily the class-related tasks, such as tests, and schedule the time that will be dedicated to studying. Distribute your study sessions across time—learning takes time. Minimize distractions while studying. Get an overall idea of the content of a chapter before you start reading the specifics. (It would be a good idea to read this section, The Big Picture: Chapter Overview in the Study Guide, before you start reading each chapter in the textbook.) Make an effort to apply the reading material to your personal experience, because these associations will increase the chances that you will remember the material in the future. Finally, review! Use alternative methods to revisit the material, such as doing the exercises at the end of the chapter, visiting the online resources that accompany the textbook, and testing yourself with the Study Guide exercises.

## Building Blocks of Chapter 1

### Clarifying some of the tricky points in Chapter 1
### and
### In Your Own Words
*To respond to the questions and exercises presented in the "In Your Own Words" section, please write your thoughts, perspectives, and reactions on a separate piece of paper.*

### *Exploring Psychology*
Psychology is the science of behavior and mental processes. Behaviors are everything that we do that can be directly observed. Mental processes refer to the thoughts, feelings, and motives that are not directly observable. Because psychology is a science, it uses systematic methods to observe, describe, predict, and explain behavior.

### In Your Own Words
*Please write your thoughts, perspectives, and reactions on a separate piece of paper.*
✓ *Mention five examples of behaviors and five examples of mental processes.*

### *Helpful Hints for Understanding Psychology*
### *Helpful Hint:*
*When we refer to a field as being "scientific" it simply means this profession adheres to the "scientific method" to collect and interpret its data. There are many scientific professions, such as biology, physics, and economics to name a few. Psychology is also a scientific profession.*

### In Your Own Words
*Please write your thoughts, perspectives, and reactions on a separate piece of paper.*
✓ *Put the definition of psychology into your own words.*

✓ *A friend of yours is talking with you about psychology. She claims that psychology is not a real science, at least not like biology. What's is your reasoned response to her?*

Psychology emerged as a science in the 19th century, and it was influenced by three fields: philosophy, biology, and physiology. Two influential figures on the origins of psychology were Rene Descartes and Charles Darwin. Descartes proposed that the body and the mind are separate entities. Darwin developed the concept of natural selection.

In 1879, Wilhelm Wundt developed the first scientific laboratory in psychology. His approach, which emphasized the importance of conscious thoughts and a classification of the mind's structure, became known as structuralism. William James, meanwhile, examined the mind's ability to adapt to the environment in an approach called functionalism.

### *Contemporary Approaches to Psychology*
There are seven contemporary approaches in psychology: *behavioral, psychodynamic, cognitive, behavioral neuroscience, evolutionary, sociocultural, and the humanistic movement and positive psychology.*

Two important figures in the *behavioral* approach were Watson and Skinner, who emphasized measuring overt behavior and rejected inferences about the conscious mind. In this approach, behavior is influenced by environmental determinants. Social cognitive theory, a further development of the behavioral perspective, stresses that thoughts or *cognitions* modify the effect of the environment on behavior. According to this perspective, *imitation* is an important process by which we learn about the world.

Freud believed that the key to understanding mind and behavior rested in the *unconscious* part of the mind; this perspective is known as the *psychoanalytic approach*. Freud argued that instincts, especially sexual and aggressive impulses, influence our psychology, that is, how we behave, think, and feel. Psychoanalytic and psychodynamic should not be confused. *Psychoanalytic* refers to Freud's theory; theorists who used Freud's idea of an unconscious and built on his theory are referred to as *psychodynamic*.

In the *cognitive* approach, there is an emphasis on mental processes involved in knowing. Within this approach, there is a perspective that studies how individuals process information. Generally, when you see the word *cognition*, think of "thinking" or "thoughts."

An approach that gives the brain the central nervous system primary roles in understanding behavior, thoughts, and emotions is called *behavioral neuroscience*, or neuropsychology.

The *evolutionary* approach examines the adaptive role of our psychology. According to this approach, *natural selection* favors behaviors and mental processes that increase the chances that we may reproduce and contribute to our genes passed on to future generations.

The *sociocultural* approach to psychology stresses the importance of culture, ethnicity, and gender in observing, describing, predicting, and explaining behaviors and mental processes.

It has been argued that in the 20th century psychology focused too much on negative aspects of life, such as aggression and psychological problems. Two movements define the current emphasis on a more positive psychology: the *humanistic approach* and *positive psychology*. The humanistic approach or movement emerged in the middle of the 20th century and stresses a person's capacity for personal growth, freedom of choice, and the positive qualities of people. At the beginning of the 21st century, psychologists *Seligman* and *Csikszentmihalyi* proposed a positive movement, one that would place stronger emphasis on positive psychological experiences, such as hope and optimism, creativity, and social responsibility. Humanistic approaches, such as the work of *Carl Rogers*, has added a great deal to our understanding of what constitutes effective therapy.

### In Your Own Words

*Please write your thoughts, perspectives, and reactions on a separate piece of paper.*

✓ *Consider the following questions and determine which psychological perspective(s) presented in Chapter 1 would be the most appropriate to address each issue. Explain in your own words why the perspective(s) you chose would be the best match for the question.*

- *How can I improve my memory and remember more of what I read?*
- *How can a person stop a nail-biting behavior?*
- *Can the personality of an individual be changed by a brain injury?*

- *Are all humans, regardless where in the world they live, able to experience happiness?*
- *In the long run, does it really make a difference how your parents treat you when you are a baby?*

## Correcting the Incorrect

Carefully read each statement. Determine if the statement is correct or incorrect. If the statement is incorrect, make the necessary changes to correct it. Then check the answer key at the end of the chapter for the correct statement and page reference in the textbook.

1. All psychologists work with people with psychological problems.
2. The three main terms contained in the definition of psychology are common sense, behaviors, and unconscious.
3. Psychology is the scientific study of people's psychological problems and how to help those people.
4. Mental processes include thoughts, feelings, and motives that cannot be observed directly.
5. Since mental processes are not directly observable, they are actually not real.
6. As a philosophy, psychology uses systematic methods to observe, describe, predict, and explain behavior.
7. Aristotle argued that the mind and the body are completely separate and contributed to psychology by focusing the attention on the study of the mind.
8. Sigmund Freud proposed the principle of natural selection.
9. Charles Darwin established the first psychological laboratory 1879.
10. Wundt and Titchener developed an approach called functionalism.
11. The most common method used in the functionalism approach was introspection.
12. Behaviorists, such as Freud and Rogers, would say that the environment determines behavior.
13. Social cognitive theory focuses on unconscious motives.
14. B. F. Skinner suggested psychology should study the mind.
15. Behaviorism emphasizes the scientific study of behavior and its environmental determinants.
16. The humanistic approach emphasizes the role that the unconscious mind plays in behavior, thought, and emotion.
17. Freud developed the psychodynamic approach.
18. The psychodynamic approach stresses how people have free will and can choose their own destiny.
19. The behavioral neuroscience perspective focuses on behaviors that increase organisms' reproductive success.
20. Natural selection states that organisms best adapted to their environment are likely to survive, reproduce, and pass on their characteristics to their offspring.
21. Behavioral neuroscientists study the memory of sea slugs.
22. Since psychology is a science, it readily accepts simple explanations of behavior.
23. Physiological psychology and neuroscience focus on providing accessible care for people with psychological problems.
24. Forensic psychology is the field of psychology that studies changes through the lifespan.
25. Psychology in the 20th century largely focused on the positive aspects of psychology.
26. The positive psychology movement is associated with an emphasis on psychological experiences such as hope, optimism, and happiness.
27. A person with an undergraduate degree in psychology can work as a psychotherapist.

28. Clinical psychologists can prescribe medication for a person with a psychological disorder because they also have a doctorate in medicine.

29. Experimental psychology focuses on basic research in sensation and perception, learning, and emotion.

30. One good studying strategy and a way to improve your memory is to study for many hours the day before the test.

31. Studying is more effective when distractions are minimized.

32. Reading is the process of thinking reflectively and productively, and evaluating the evidence.

33. There is significant scientific evidence that proves that telepathy, clairvoyance, and psychic healing exist.

## Practice Test 1

1. Psychology is best defined as the
   a. study of perception and memory.
   b. investigation of the human psyche.
   c. scientific study of conscious and unconscious processes.
   d. scientific study of behavior and mental processes.

2. As you read the definition of psychology you begin to think about examples. Of the following, which one is the best example of behavior?
   a. planning your weekend activities
   b. adding two numbers in your head
   c. a two-year-old boy coloring a picture
   d. thinking about this question

3. The definition of psychology is made up of three main concepts. Which concept refers to thoughts, feelings, and motives?
   a. scientific study
   b. behavior
   c. contexts
   d. mental processes

4. What is the main difference between philosophers and psychologists?
   a. the types of questions they ask about human behavior
   b. the causes they presume for human behavior
   c. the debate of the question how people acquire knowledge
   d. the methods they use for obtaining evidence

5. The British naturalist Charles Darwin is best known for his suggestion that
   a. organisms that are best adapted to their environment survive and pass on their characteristics to their offspring.
   b. conscious experience is made up of structure.
   c. psychology should focus only on observable behavior, not the mind.
   d. people have freedom to choose their own destiny.

6. A structuralist would have been most interested in studying
   a. the unconscious.
   b. dreams.
   c. conscious thought.
   d. behavior.

7. The mind's content is to Titchener as the mind's function is to
   a. Wundt.
   b. James.
   c. Watson.
   d. Darwin.

8. Structuralism is to _____ as functionalism is to _____.
   a. Wundt; Titchener
   b. Skinner; Wundt
   c. James; Bandura
   d. Wundt; James

9. You believe that the environment determines behavior. What approach would you be most likely to side with?
   a. psychodynamic
   b. humanistic
   c. behavioral neuroscience
   d. behavioral

10. What is the main difference between Bandura's approach and other behavioral theories?
    a. Bandura emphasizes the influence of the environment on behavior.
    b. Bandura acknowledges the importance of cognitive processes.
    c. Bandura insists that behavior has to be measurable.
    d. Bandura rejects the notion that behavior should be observed.

11. The _____ approach sees behavior as being influenced by the unconscious mind.
    a. cognitive
    b. humanistic
    c. psychodynamic
    d. evolutionary

12. Of the following, which best summarizes the humanistic approach?
    a. People are influenced by their unconscious mind and the conflict between their biological instincts and society's demands.
    b. Consciousness is understood by examining its basic elements.
    c. Ethnicity, gender, and culture are the primary determinants of behavior.
    d. People have the freedom to choose their own destiny.

13. Which of the following would make the best title for a presentation on humanistic psychology?
    a. Be all that you can be.
    b. The psychology of dancing tango.
    c. Explore your unconscious and you will find yourself.
    d. People are pawns of their environment.

14. Your professor says that memory, attention, problem-solving, and perception are key components of the _____ approach.
    a. cognitive
    b. sociocultural
    c. evolutionary
    d. functional

15. Which of the following approaches emphasizes the brain and nervous system?
    a. cognitive
    b. behavioral neuroscience
    c. information processing
    d. behavioral

16. Chemical changes in the brain associated with anxiety would be of most interest to a(n)
    a. evolutionary psychologist.
    b. cognitive psychologist.
    c. sociocultural psychologist.
    d. behavioral neuroscientist.

17. According to the evolutionary psychology approach, why does the mind have the capacity to achieve specific goals?
    a. the mind has evolved
    b. one's environment has shaped the mind
    c. the unconscious mind tends to create these goals
    d. because the person has so decided to achieve specific goals

18. Critical thinking involves all the following except which one?
    a. thinking reflectively
    b. thinking productively
    c. thinking impulsively
    d. evaluating evidence

19. What is the main difference between a clinical psychologist and a psychiatrist?
    a. their education
    b. their theoretical approach
    c. their research interests
    d. their number of publications

20. Dr. Chen is a community psychologist. What does he do?
    a. conducts basic research in the area of motivation
    b. provides accessible care for people with psychological problems
    c. prescribes medications to depressed patients
    d. helps companies select the best workers for the job

21. The most widely practiced specialization in psychology is
    a. experimental psychology.
    b. physiological psychology.
    c. forensic psychology.
    d. clinical and counseling psychology.

**Practice Test 2**

1. There are three key terms in the definition of psychology. Which of the three terms is the one defined as everything that we do that can be directly observed?
    a. thoughts
    b. science
    c. mental processes
    d. behaviors

2.    Which of the following statements is consistent with the theories and arguments of Rene Descartes?
      a.    Contemporary humans are part of an evolutionary process that has shaped their psychology.
      b.    Sensations and perceptions combine to form our thoughts.
      c.    The body and the mind are separate entities.
      d.    How we think and behave is determined by our body type.

3.    Which of the following fields is NOT historically associated with the origins of the science of psychology?
      a.    philosophy
      b.    physiology
      c.    biology
      d.    mathematics

4.    The conscious mental structures discovered by using the introspection method would be of most interest to a psychologist from the _____ perspective.
      a.    structuralism
      b.    functionalism
      c.    behavioral
      d.    psychodynamic

5.    "What we do is the ultimate test of who we are." This statement is consistent with the _____ perspective.
      a.    behavioral
      b.    cognitive
      c.    humanistic
      d.    psychodynamic

6.    Which of the following statements is consistent with social cognitive theory?
      a.    Our early life experiences are the major determinants of our behaviors and mental processes.
      b.    Imitation is one of the main ways we learn about the world.
      c.    Psychology should only focus on behaviors.
      d.    Unconscious influences are the most important factor in understanding psychology.

7.    Which of the following factors is NOT addressed is the psychodynamic perspective?
      a.    instincts
      b.    culture
      c.    parenting
      d.    unconscious

8.    Robert Esposito is a cognitive psychologist. Which of the following questions is more likely to be the focus of Dr. Esposito's research?
      a.    Which parts of the brain are activated when we run?
      b.    How effective is punishment in deterring behavior?
      c.    How can we improve our memory?
      d.    Does ethnicity influence social skills?

9.  Which of the contemporary approaches in psychology is more likely to be associated with the statement: "Memory is written in a chemical code"?
    a.  behavioral neuroscience
    b.  sociocultural
    c.  behavioral
    d.  evolutionary

10. Donna Hashmi is an evolutionary psychologist studying prejudice. Which of the following is more likely to be one of Dr. Hashmi's explanations?
    a.  Prejudice is learned.
    b.  Prejudice is more prevalent is some cultures than in others.
    c.  Prejudice is experienced by all humans because in some ways it help people adapt to the demands of their environments.
    d.  Prejudice happens unconsciously.

11. Latinos in the United States are facing a variety of challenges that are resulting in higher numbers of high school dropouts than other ethnic groups. Which contemporary perspective in psychology would be appropriate to study this tendency?
    a.  behavioral
    b.  cognitive
    c.  evolutionary
    d.  sociocultural

12. The humanistic perspective emerged in the middle of the 20th century and emphasized
    a.  the role of the psychotherapist in figuring out the psychological problems of others.
    b.  free will and the ability people have for self-understanding.
    c.  how external rewards determine what people do.
    d.  the role of unconscious determinants of our personality.

13. Seligman and Csikszentmihalyi, in an article published in the year 2000, proposed that in the 21st century psychology ought to focus more on positive psychological experiences. Which of the following questions is more likely to be studied under this movement?
    a.  What personality characteristics contributed to Picasso's lifelong creativity?
    b.  What is the relationship between self-esteem and eating disorders?
    c.  What is the psychological profile of a terrorist?
    d.  Are women more likely to experience depression than men?

14. The majority of psychologists have specialized in
    a.  personality psychology.
    b.  clinical and counseling psychology.
    c.  health psychology.
    d.  sport psychology.

15. Which of the following areas of specialization is more likely to use animals for research?
    a.  social psychology
    b.  industrial/organizational psychology
    c.  developmental psychology
    d.  behavioral neuroscience psychology

16. Lorna Durant did a study on the effect of family visits on the emotions of senior citizens residing in a nursing home. Dr. Durant is probably a
    a. developmental psychologist.
    b. personality psychologist.
    c. evolutionary psychologist.
    d. forensic psychologist.

17. A psychologist that develops an after school program to prevent kids from spending time alone at home in the afternoons is probably a(n)
    a. industrial/organizational psychologist.
    b. community psychologist.
    c. environmental psychologist.
    d. clinical psychologist.

18. If you want to be a forensic psychologist, you will probably take some classes on
    a. law.
    b. medicine.
    c. language.
    d. engineering.

19. You are a psychologist and you study self-concept, aggression, and inner directedness. You most likely specialize in
    a. school and educational psychology.
    b. cross-cultural psychology.
    c. personality psychology.
    d. clinical psychology.

20. The specialist who works at a secondary school and consults with teachers about children's school achievement problems is most likely in which field of specialization?
    a. learning and memory
    b. motivation and emotion
    c. school psychology
    d. biological psychology

## Practice Test 3

1. "A preference for physically attractive females has been favored by natural selection on heterosexual males." This statement is an argument likely to be made from the evolutionary psychology perspective, and it basically means that
    a. men who have mated with physically attractive women have been more likely to reproduce.
    b. physically attractive women are more likely to adapt.
    c. women would rather not be classified into attractive or not attractive.
    d. men mate only with attractive women.

2. Compared to other sciences, psychology is relatively young, because it is considered that modern psychology started approximately
    a. 50 years ago.
    b. 200 years ago.
    c. 100 years ago.
    d. 300 years ago.

3.	Using the research method of introspection, structuralists claimed to have uncovered the structure of the experience of emotions, referring to them as the three dimensions of feelings. Which of the following is NOT one of those three dimensions?
	a.	pleasure/displeasure
	b.	happiness/sadness
	c.	excitement/depression
	d.	tension/relaxation

4.	Which of the following contemporary approaches in psychology is reminiscent of the functionalist approach?
	a.	behavioral
	b.	cognitive
	c.	humanistic
	d.	evolutionary

5.	Which of the following approaches should we use if we want to learn about the meaning of dreams and other psychological experiences that occur when we are not conscious and aware?
	a.	psychodynamic
	b.	behavioral
	c.	sociocutural
	d.	evolutionary

6.	Structuralism is to _____ as functionalism is to _____.
	a.	purpose; parts
	b.	parts; purpose
	c.	unconscious; conscious
	d.	behaviors; mental processes

7.	Which of the following was the aspect of psychology most often studied during the first half of the 20th century?
	a.	thoughts
	b.	emotions
	c.	behaviors
	d.	motives

8.	Based on Bandura's social cognitive theory, we may wonder if
	a.	watching professional wrestling on TV could make children behave aggressively.
	b.	how we think about others influences how we think about ourselves.
	c.	the brain plays a role in learning.
	d.	a professional boxer has an aggression instinct that is stronger or more dominant than it is in the average person.

9.	The psychodynamic approach is to _____ as the cognitive approach is to

	_____.
	a.	mental processes; unconscious experience
	b.	Freud; Skinner
	c.	unconscious experience; mental processes
	d.	Rogers; Freud

10. The behavioral approach is to _____ as the psychodynamic approach is to _____.
    a. external factors; internal factors
    b. internal factors; external factors
    c. 20th century; 21st century
    d. 21st century; 20th century

11. Based on the studies performed by cognitive psychologists on eyewitness identification, we may predict that
    a. when a person is asked to pay attention, he or she will remember most things about the event accurately and in great detail.
    b. when a person is not asked to pay attention, he or she will remember most things about the event accurately and in great detail.
    c. even when a person is asked to pay attention, his or her memory of the event can be fairly inaccurate.
    d. even when a person is not asked to pay attention, his or her memory tends to be fairly accurate.

12. Which of the following statements is NOT consistent with Pinker's evolutionary explanation of the way the mind works?
    a. The mind computes.
    b. The mind was designed to compute by evolution.
    c. The computations of the mind are performed by brain systems favored by natural selection.
    d. The mind works differently depending on the culture of the person.

13. The behaviorist approach is to _____ as the humanistic approach is to _____.
    a. external control; environment
    b. environment; external control
    c. external control; free will
    d. free will; external control

14. When psychology was focusing too much on the psychological problems that are associated with traumatic and abusive early life experiences, the _____ approach emerged to emphasize that adults do not need to be victims and can choose to live a positive life.
    a. psychodynamic
    b. behavioral
    c. sociocultural
    d. humanistic

15. A forensic psychologist may be the best professional to consult if
    a. you are trying to figure out the psychology of a dead person.
    b. you are an M.D. specializing in forensic medicine.
    c. you are a defense attorney who needs to select a jury that will favor your client.
    d. you are a judge who needs psychological help.

16. "Does crowding have an effect on how people think and the decisions they make?" Which two areas of specialization in psychology could be combined to better address this question?
    a. personality and behavioral neuroscience
    b. social and environmental
    c. health and social
    d. community and environmental

17. Which area of psychology is more likely to be interested in the effects of eliminating driving tests in languages other than English (in the United States)?
    a. community psychology
    b. health psychology
    c. social psychology
    d. experimental psychology

18. Which of the following is NOT true about effective studying strategies?
    a. Having music in the background while studying helps memory.
    b. Studying many times for shorter periods is better than studying one time for a longer period.
    c. Reading a summary of a chapter before reading the chapter enhances the reading and improves memory.
    d. Critical thinking contributes to memory.

19. Which of the following questions will require critical thinking?
    a. Define psychology.
    b. Mention four of the contemporary approaches to psychology.
    c. Compare the behavioral, psychodynamic, and humanistic approaches to psychology.
    d. Describe Freud's approach to psychology.

20. Which of the following is NOT consistent with critical thinking?
    a. figuring out what "the real problem is"
    b. sticking to one approach to psychology
    c. being open-minded
    d. being skeptical

## Connections

*Take advantage of all the other study tools available for this chapter!*

| NAME OF CLIP | DESCRIPTION | KEY CONCEPTS AND IDEAS |
| --- | --- | --- |
| | | **Exploring Psychology** |
| | | **Contemporary Approaches to Psychology** |
| Freud's Contribution to Psychology | Video clip places Freud's contribution to psychology in a historical context. The origins of his perspective in the study of hysteria as well as his view of the brain are discussed. | History of psychology<br>Hysteria<br>Dream analysis<br>Manifest content of dreams<br>Repression |

| When Eyes Deceive | Video clip presents a classroom demonstration of an eyewitness identification experiment. Students at Brooklyn Law School witness a purse snatching, and the vulnerability of their memories is illustrated. | Eye witness identification<br>Memory |
|---|---|---|
| Evolutionary Psychology | "Evolutionary psychology" is an audio clip that offers an introduction to research on the universality of facial expressions. The work of Ekman on this subject is discussed. Jeff Cohn discussed how computers may be used in the future to determine if a person is depressed. | Universality of seven facial expressions<br>Emotions<br>Facial expressions |
| Identifying Psychological Perspectives | This interactivity allows users to apply and assess their knowledge of the different psychological perspectives. The interactivity involves the association of proverbs with the different perspectives. | Behavioral perspective<br>Psychodynamic perspective<br>Cognitive perspective<br>Behavioral neuroscience perspective<br>Evolutionary psychology perspective<br>Sociocultural perspective |
| Attraction | Video clip explores the relationship between biology and culture in determining mating preferences, including a discussion of the role of hormones in animal mating. Clip includes interviews with Alice Eagly and Davis Buss presenting the sociocultural and evolutionary perspectives on interpersonal attraction and mating. | Evolutionary perspective<br>Sociocultural perspective |

| | | A Positive Approach to Psychology |
|---|---|---|
| Self-Actualization | Adventure racers in the grueling Eco-Challenge are showcased. Participants share their motivations for engaging in this extreme sport. | Self-actualization Motivation |
| Positive Psychology | This audio clip is narrated by David Myers and presents a discussion of factors associated with happiness. The relationship between wealth and happiness is discussed. | Positive psychology Happiness |
| | | Psychology's Careers and Areas of Specialization |
| Culture and Self | This video clip starts with insights into what people in a conversation are thinking about themselves. The effect of culture on self-concept and how that definition of the self influences individual psychology are discussed. Experts Markus and Kitayama are interviewed and present their perspective on the role of culture in the definition of self, comparing American and Asian cultures. They discuss how we pass our cultural understandings through interactions. The video clip also presents a discussion of the relationship between the motivation for achievement and the definition of the self. The topics of conformity and persuasion and their relationship with definition of self are discussed. | Self-concept Culture Social psychology Cross-cultural psychology Independent vs. interdependent self Achievement motivation |

| | | **How to Get the Most Out of Psychology** |
|---|---|---|
| Mnemonic Strategies in Memory | U.S. Memoriad contest is showcased in this video clip. Champions share their extraordinary memory training tactics. | Memory<br>Mnemonic |

**Online Learning Center (www.mhhe.com/Santrockp7u)**

- Interact and make learning fun!
  - o **Interactive Exercise**
    - Psychological Perspectives
  - o **Interactive Review**
    - The Evolution of Psychological Theory
- Brush up on the Key Terms for this chapter by first reviewing the electronic **Glossary** (in English or Spanish) and then testing your retention using the **Flashcard** feature.
- "Notes"—This feature allows you to use the website as you would your text, inserting your own study notes and highlighting areas of particular importance.
- **Career Appendix**—Learn more about career opportunities in the field of psychology.

**In Your Text**

- Found throughout each chapter, the **Review and Sharpen Your Thinking** feature breaks the text into logical chunks, allowing you to process, review, and reflect thoughtfully on the information that you've just read. When going back to *study* the chapter, try reading the feature *before* the section of text to which it relates. In doing so, you will be able to focus your attention on important concepts *as* you encounter them. In this chapter, this feature can be found on the following pages: pp. 9, 16, 17, 25, and 33.

**Practice Quizzes**

- Test your knowledge of this chapter's material by taking the different practice quizzes found on your text's **Online Learning Center** and on the **In-Psych Plus CD-ROM** packaged with your text.

**ANSWER KEY**

## In Your Own Words

✓ Put the definition of psychology into your own words.
*This definition should include the following concepts: science, behavior, and mental processes.*

✓ Mention five examples of behaviors and five examples of mental processes.
*Examples of behaviors should be actions that are directly observable, while examples of mental processes should be psychological experiences that involve thoughts, emotions, and motives, which cannot be directly observed.*

✓ Think about the characteristics that men prefer in women and the characteristics that women prefer in men. What does a heterosexual man look for in a potential mate? What does a heterosexual woman look for in a potential mate? Use the Evolutionary Psychology approach to explain these preferences.
*Students are asked to consider their own experiences and ideas to answer the first part of this question. For example, one view is that men look for physical attractiveness in women and women look for resourcefulness ("can get things done") in men. The question then is how do these*

*preferences contribute to adaptation to the challenges of the environment. If the pattern of preferences is universal (found around the world) it may be argued that the preferences have been favored by natural selection.*

✓ Consider the following questions and determine which psychological perspective(s) presented in Chapter 1 would be the most appropriate to address each issue. Explain in your own words why the perspective(s) you chose would be the most appropriate to address each issue.
  - How can I improve my memory and remember more of what I read?
    o *Cognitive approach. This would be a question of interest to school and educational psychologists.*
  - How can a person stop a nail-biting behavior?
    o *Behavioral approach. Nail biting is an observable behavior and may be modified by manipulating aspects of the environment. A method commonly used it to "punish" the nail bitter by putting a bad tasting polish on the nails.*
  - Can the personality of an individual be changed by a brain injury?
    o *Behavioral neuroscience*
  - Are all humans, regardless of where in the world they live, able to experience happiness?
    o *This question can be addressed by various approaches, specifically sociocultural, evolutionary, humanistic, and positive psychology. The sociocultural psychologists could explore the role of culture in the experience of happiness and address the part of the question that reads "regardless of where in the world they live." If it is found that this is a universal experience, the evolutionary psychologists can address the question of why? What is the adaptation purpose of happiness? Finally, the positive psychological experience of happiness is of interest to both the humanistic approach and the positive movement.*
  - In the long run, does it really make a difference how your parents treat you when you are a baby?
    o *At least two of the contemporary approaches to psychology and one area of specialty in psychology could address this question. First, the psychodynamic perspective emphasizes the importance of the first few years of life on the psychology of the adult. Second, the behavioral perspective, including the social cognitive theory, emphasizes the role of external factors on our behaviors and mental process. The way in which parents treat their children is an external factor. Finally, developmental psychology is the area of specialization associated with this question.*

✓ Why is there a positive psychology movement? Describe two aspects of your life that would be of interest to a psychologist pursuing this focus on positive psychology.
*Positive psychology emerged as a response to the overwhelming focus on negative aspects of psychology that took place in the 20th century. Here the student is asked to consider positive aspects of his or her psychology, such as their experience of positive emotions, creativity, free will, and optimism, among many other positive aspects.*

✓ Chapter 1 discusses several specializations of psychology. Which one sounds most appealing to you? While you have learned about separate specializations in psychology, in practice psychologists may overlap, participate in, and contribute to more than one area. If you could create a new specialization in psychology, what would it be?
*One way of understanding psychology is realizing that our questions of interest are more important than fitting into any particular category of perspective or specialization. To a certain extent, a graduate degree in psychology prepares students to find their questions and find the best way to answer them. If a person is interested in the difference in brain activity between people who live near the equator and people who live near the North Pole, this person will have to virtually create his or her own specialization, a combination of behavioral neuroscience, with sociocultural, evolutionary, and experimental psychology.*

✓ Considering the studying strategies recommended in Chapter 1, describe five behaviors and/or mental processes that you could change in order to enhance your learning and improve your memory.

*This list should include reference to improved time management skills, improved reading skills, improved studying environment, and improved critical thinking skills.*

## Correcting the Incorrect

1. *Clinical* psychologists work with people with psychological problems. (p. 20)
2. The three main terms contained in the definition of psychology are *science*, behaviors, and *mental processes*. (p. 6)
3. Psychology is the scientific study of *behavior and mental processes*. (p. 5)
4. Mental processes include thoughts, feelings, and motives that cannot be observed directly. (p. 6)
5. Mental processes are not directly observable, *but they are nonetheless real*. (p. 6)
6. As a *science*, psychology uses systematic methods to observe, describe, predict, and explain behavior. (p. 6)
7. *Rene Descartes* argued that the mind and the body are completely separate and contributed to psychology by focusing the attention on the study of the mind. (p. 7)
8. *Charles Darwin* proposed the principle of natural selection. (p. 7)
9. *Wilhelm Wundt* established the first psychological laboratory in 1879. (p. 8)
10. Wundt and Titchener developed an approach called *structuralism*. (p. 8)
11. The most common method used in the *structuralism* approach was introspection. (p. 8)
12. Behaviorists, such as *Watson and Skinner*, would say that the environment determines behavior. (p. 10)
13. Social cognitive theory focuses on *how thoughts modify the effect of environment on behavior*. (p. 11)
14. B. F. Skinner suggested psychology should *not* study the mind. (p. 11)
15. Behaviorism emphasizes the scientific study of behavior and its environmental determinants. (p. 10)
16. The *psychodynamic* approach emphasizes the role that the unconscious mind plays in behavior, thought, and emotion. (p. 11)
17. Freud developed the psychodynamic approach. (p. 11)
18. The *humanistic* approach stresses how people have free will and can choose their own destiny. (p. 16)
19. The *evolutionary* perspective focuses on behaviors that increase organisms' reproductive success. (p. 13)
20. Natural selection states that organisms best adapted to their environment are likely to survive, reproduce, and pass on their characteristics to their offspring. (p. 13)
21. Behavioral neuroscientists study the memory of sea slugs. (p. 13)
22. Since psychology is a science, it *does not* readily accept simple explanations of behavior. (p. 6)
23. *Community* psychology focuses on providing accessible care for people with psychological problems. (p. 22)
24. *Developmental* psychology is the field of psychology that studies changes through the lifespan. (p. 21)
25. Psychology in the 20th century largely focused on the *negative* aspects of psychology. (p. 17)

26. The positive psychology movement is associated with an emphasis on psychological experiences such as hope, optimism, and happiness. (p. 16)

27. A person with a *graduate* degree in psychology can work as a psychotherapist. (p. 19)

28. *Psychiatrists* can prescribe medication for a person with a psychological disorder because they also have a doctorate in medicine. (p. 19)

29. Experimental psychology focuses on basic research in sensation and perception, learning, and emotion. (p. 21)

30. One good studying strategy and a way to improve your memory is to *distribute your studying sessions across time instead of cramming just before a test.* (p. 26)

31. Studying is more effective when distractions are minimized. (p. 26)

32. *Critical thinking* is the process of thinking reflectively and productively, and evaluating the evidence. (p. 29)

33. There is *no* significant scientific evidence to prove that telepathy, clairvoyance, and psychic healing exist. (p. 31)

## Practice Test 1

1. a. no; psychology is more than the study of just perception and memory
   b. sorry, this is not the best definition
   c. even though psychology does study conscious and unconscious processes, this is not the best answer
   d. THAT'S CORRECT; psychology is best defined as the scientific study of behavior and mental processes

p. 5

2. a. planning is an example of a mental process since it cannot be directly observed
   b. adding is an example of a mental process since it cannot be directly observed
   c. CORRECT; coloring a picture is behavior since it can be directly observed
   d. thinking is an example of a mental process since it cannot be directly observed

p. 6

3. a. scientific study refers to using systematic methods
   b. behavior is anything you do that is directly observable
   c. "contexts" is not a component of the definition
   d. YES; thoughts, feelings, and motives are examples of mental processes

p. 6

4. a. philosophers and psychologists often ask the same questions
   b. no; both may acknowledge the same causes of behavior
   c. no; both debate
   d. YES; philosophers think to obtain evidence; psychologists use the scientific method

p. 6

5. a. YES; this is the idea of natural selection
   b. this describes structuralism, not Darwinism
   c. focusing on observable behavior was Skinner's suggestion
   d. freedom to choose is a basic tenet of the humanistic approach

p. 7

6. a.  no; structuralism focused on conscious thought
   b.  no
   c.  YES; structuralism attempted to examine the structure of conscious thought
   d.  no; the emphasis of structuralism was on conscious thought, not behavior
   p. 8

7. a.  Wundt is associated with structuralism, as is Titchener
   b.  THAT'S RIGHT; William James studied how the mind adapted to the environment
   c.  Watson is related to behaviorism, which discounted the role of the mind
   d.  Darwin is best known for the theory of evolution
   p. 8

8. a.  both Wundt and Titchener are associated with structuralism
   b.  Skinner is associated with the behavioral approach; Wundt is associated with structuralism
   c.  James is associated with functionalism; Bandura is associated with social cognitive theory
   d.  THAT'S RIGHT; Wundt is associated with structuralism and James is associated with functionalism
   p. 8

9. a.  the psychodynamic approach focuses on unconscious influences
   b.  the humanistic approach says that people control their own lives, not the environment
   c.  the behavioral neuroscience approach argues that the brain and nervous system determine behavior
   d.  YES; environmental conditions determine behavior
   p. 10

10. a.  no; that is the main notion in the behavioral theories
    b.  THAT'S RIGHT; Bandura recognizes that thoughts influence the way the environment affects behavior
    c.  no; that's not a difference
    d.  no; in fact Bandura would argue that behavior should be observed
    p. 11

11. a.  the cognitive approach looks for the role of mental processes such as perception
    b.  the humanistic approach asserts that people, not the unconscious mind, choose who they are
    c.  RIGHT; the psychodynamicanalytic approach also focuses on biological instincts
    d.  the evolutionary approach focuses on the survival of the fittest
    p. 11

12. a.  this summary describes the psychodynamic approach
    b.  this summary describes structuralism
    c.  the sociocultural approach emphasizes ethnicity, gender, and culture
    d.  YES; this view sees people as having the freedom and the capacity for self-understanding
    p. 16

13. a.  GOOD; the humanistic perspective stresses growth and self-actualization
    b.  this sounds more like the sociocultural approach
    c.  the unconscious mind is the focus of the psychodynamic approach
    d.  this title would be best for the behavioral approach
    p. 16

14. a.  THAT'S CORRECT; the cognitive approach focuses on mental processes
    b.  the sociocultural view examines the role of ethnicity, culture, and gender
    c.  this approach stresses natural selection
    d.  the functional view examines how the mind adapts to the environment
    p. 12

15. a.  the cognitive approach emphasizes mental processes
    b.  YES; those in this approach examine how the physical structures of the brain and nervous system influence behavior, thoughts, and emotion
    c.  the information-processing approach focuses on attention, perception, and memory
    d.  this approach examines the relationship between the environment and behavior
    p. 12

16. a.  probably not, because evolutionary psychologists are more interested in how behavior allows organisms to adapt to the environment
    b.  a cognitive psychologist examines the role of mental processes
    c.  this psychologist would study the roles that culture, ethnicity, and gender play
    d.  SOUNDS GOOD; behavioral neuroscience studies how the brain and nervous system are important to behavior, thought, and emotion
    p. 12

17. a.  THAT'S RIGHT; it is theorized that the mind has evolved in ways that would have benefited hunters and gatherers
    b.  this option is best associated with the behavioral approach
    c.  the psychodynamic approach would suggest this role of the unconscious mind
    d.  this best describes the humanistic approach
    p. 13

18. a.  this is a component of critical thinking
    b.  critical thinking involves thinking productively
    c.  THAT'S RIGHT; critical thinking requires that we be reflective and not impulsive
    d.  critical thinking requires that we evaluate evidence
    p. 29

19. a.  YES; a psychiatrist holds a degree in medicine; a clinical psychologist does not
    b.  both are interested in helping people
    c.  both professionals help improve the lives of people, and their research reflects this
    d.  no; this is not important
    p. 20

20. a.  this describes an experimental psychologist
    b.  YES; that is the focus of community psychology
    c.  this sounds like a psychiatrist
    d.  this describes the focus on an industrial/organizational psychologist
    p. 22

21. a.  no
    b.  no
    c.  no
    d.  YES; clinical and counseling psychology is the most widely practiced specialization
    p. 20

## Practice Test 2

1. a.   thoughts are mental processes
   b.   science is one of the key terms, but it refers to the systematic methods of research used in psychology
   c.   mental processes cannot be directly observed
   d.   YES; behaviors can be directly observed and are an essential component in the definition of psychology.

   p. 6

2. a.   this statement is consistent with the arguments of Charles Darwin
   b.   this statement is consistent with the beliefs of Buddha
   c.   YES; Descartes argued that the body and the mind are separate entities
   d.   this statement is more consistent with ancient thinkers who sought to find links between the body and the mind

   p. 7

3. a.   philosophy did contribute to the origins of psychology; for example, consider the influence of Rene Descartes
   b.   physiology did contribute to the origins of psychology; for example, physiologists such as Muller were asking questions regarding the relationship between the brain and behaviors
   c.   biology did contribute to the origins of psychology; for example, Darwin's principle of natural selection opened the door for a new way of understanding the questions of psychology.
   d.   CORRECT; the field of mathematics is not associated with the origins of psychology; . however, in contemporary psychology, mathematics play a very important role

   p. 7

4. a.   YES; this was the focus of the work of Wundt and Titchner
   b.   no; functionalists were more interested in why we had a consciousness and how it helped us adapt to the demands of the environment than in the parts of the consciousness
   c.   no; behaviorists would even oppose the study of consciousness, as it is not observable
   d.   no; the psychodynamic perspective focused in the unconscious

   p. 8

5. a.   YES; Skinner emphasized this point
   b.   no; cognitive psychology actually focuses on how we think and how that influences who we are
   c.   no; humanistic psychologists would not limit who a person is to their observable behaviors
   d.   no; the psychodynamic perspective would argue that in order to really understand a person we have to go beyond what is observable and particularly explore their unconscious

   p. 11

6. a.   no; this statement is consistent with the psychodynamic perspective;. social cognitive theory and in general the behavioral approach consider life-long learning experiences
   b.   YES; Bandura argued that modeling and imitation are important ways of learning
   c.   no; this statement is more consistent with the traditional behavioristic perspective
   d.   no; this statement is consistent with the psychodynamic approach

   p. 11

7.  a.  instincts are important in the psychodynamic perspective
    b.  YES; the psychodynamic perspective has been criticized for not properly addressing the role of culture in psychology
    c.  parenting, particularly in the first few years of life, was one of the factors addressed in Freud's original theories
    d.  the unconscious is a concept central to the psychodynamic approach to psychology
    p. 11

8.  a.  this question may be of interest to a behavioral neuroscientist
    b.  this question may be of interest to a behavioral psychologist
    c.  YES; this question addresses memory, one of the psychological factors of interest to cognitive psychologists
    d.  this question may be of interest to a sociocultural psychologist
    p. 12

9.  a.  YES; behavioral neuroscience considers the biological basis of psychology; one of the areas of study is the nervous system and its chemical components
    b.  no; the sociocultural approach is more interested on broader social and cultural questions
    c.  no; memory is a mental process and thus is not likely to be studied by the behavioral
    d.  no; the evolutionary perspective focuses on the adaptive role of behaviors
    p. 12

10. a.  this explanation is more consistent with the behavioral approach
    b.  this explanation is more consistent with the sociocultural approach
    c.  YES; while a controversial argument, the evolutionary psychologist would try to uncover the relationship between prejudice and adaptation and survival
    d.  this explanation is more consistent with the psychodynamic approach
    p. 13

11. a.  no; the behavioral perspective is not associated with the study of ethnicity
    b.  no; the cognitive perspective is not associated with the study of ethnicity
    c.  no; the evolutionary perspective is not associated with the study of ethnicity; one of the main criticisms of this perspective is precisely that it does not account appropriately for cultural differences
    d.  YES; the sociocultural approach is dedicated to questions just like this, in which the relationship between culture, ethnicity, and a behavior (in this case, dropping out of high school) is studied
    p. 15

12. a.  no; this is more consistent with the psychodynamic perspective
    b.  YES; this is what distinguished the humanistic approach from other approaches such as the behavioral and the psychodynamic, which were dominating psychology during the first half of the 20th century
    c.  no; this issue is addressed by the behavioral perspective
    d.  no; this issue is addressed by the psychodynamic perspective
    p. 16

13. a.　YES; creativity should be one of the areas of study according to the positive psychology movement
    b.　this question focuses on the abnormal psychology of eating disorders, thus considered negative
    c.　this question focuses on terrorism, a phenomenon that involves negative behaviors such as aggression and violence
    d.　this question focuses on depression, a psychological disorder, thus considered negative
    p. 16

14. a.　no
    b.　YES
    c.　no
    d.　no; this is one of the most recent areas of specialization in psychology
    p. 20

15. a.　no; this area focuses on humans
    b.　no; this area focuses on humans in the workplace
    c.　no; this area focuses on the development, growth, and aging of humans
    d.　YES; this area focuses on the biological basis of psychology and many times research involves the systematic study of the nervous systems of animals
    p. 21

16. a.　YES; while we usually associate developmental psychology with children, this area of specialization considers psychological experiences of people across the lifespan, including the late adulthood years
    b.　a personality psychologist focuses on stable personality characteristics and not on specific age groups
    c.　an evolutionary psychologist would not be as interested on any specific age group
    d.　a forensic psychologist studies the psychology factors that play a role in the legal system, and the study of Dr. Durant does not address any legal issues
    p. 21

17. a.　no; I/O psychologists do not work with school and or children; they focus on adults in the workplace
    b.　YES; this is a job for a community psychologist, someone who has been trained to explore community services and how they relate to the psychological well-being of all members of the community, including children
    c.　no; an environmental psychologist studies the relationship between psychology and the physical environment
    d.　no; a clinical psychologist works with individuals who have psychological problems
    p. 22

18. a.　CORRECT; forensic psychology applies psychological principles to the legal system
    b.　no
    c.　no
    d.　no
    p. 24

19. a.　no; children's learning and adjustment in school take center stage in this specialization
    b.　no; cross-cultural psychology examines the role of culture
    c.　YES; these are examples of areas that a personality psychologist would study
    d.　no; a clinical psychologist studies and treats psychological problems
    p. 22

20. a. learning and memory are important in school, but this is not a field of specialization
    b. while important in school, "motivation and emotion" is not the name of a specialization
    c. CORRECT; school psychology is concerned about learning and adjustment in school
    d. biological psychology focuses on the relationships between brain and nervous and behavior, thought, and emotion
p. 22

## Practice Test 3

1. a. YES; arguing that a certain behavior is favored by natural selection is basically arguing that the particular behavior contributes to the reproductive success of the people who do the behavior
   b. no; the statement is making reference to the behavior of males, not females
   c. while this might be true, this statement is irrelevant to the issue of natural selection
   d. this statement is false
p. 7

2. a. no; by the 1950s there was already a great body of research in psychology
   b. no; modern psychology started later, in 1879, with the establishment of the first psychology laboratory by Wilhelm Wundt
   c. YES; about 120 years ago the first set of scientific studies in psychology were performed at the Leipzig, Germany laboratory founded by Wundt
   d. no; 300 years ago and even before then, the questions of psychology were being asked, but scientific methods were not being used in the process of answering the questions
p. 8

3. a. this is one of the dimensions
   b. CORRECT; this is NOT one of the dimensions of emotions proposed by structuralists
   c. this is another one of the dimensions of emotions that structuralists proposed
   d. this is another one of the dimensions of emotions that structuralists proposed
p. 8

4. a. no
   b. no
   c. no
   d. YES; the evolutionary approach, like functionalism, explores the question of the role of adaptation in psychology
p. 13

5. a. YES; the psychodynamic approach focuses on the unconscious ("when we are not conscious and aware")
   b. no; the behavioral perspective focuses on what can be observed, and dreams and other unconscious experiences cannot be directly observed
   c. no; this approach focuses on social and cultural factors of psychology
   d. no; in general, evolutionary psychology focuses on behaviors and mental processes that are common to most if not all humans, and the meaning of dreams is a very personal psychological experience
p. 11

6. a. no
   b. YES; structuralism focuses on the structure, dimensions, or "parts" of the mind, while functionalism asks what is the adaptive purpose of the mind and behaviors
   c. no
   d. no
p. 8

7. a. no; the behavioral perspective dominated psychology during the first half of the 20th century, and this perspective ignored the role of thoughts in psychology because they could not be directly observed
   b. no; for the same reason as item a
   c. YES; behaviors, which are everything that we do that is directly observable, were the main focus of behaviorists, who dominated psychology during the first half of the 20th century
   d. no; for the same reason as items a and b
   p. 10

8. a. YES; this question addresses the role of imitation, which is an important way of learning according to social cognitive theory
   b. no; this pertains to the domain of the cognitive approach
   c. no; this pertains to the domain of behavioral neuroscience
   d. no; this pertains to the domain of the psychodynamic approach
   p. 11

9. a. no; mental processes are the focus of cognitive psychology, while the unconscious is the focus of the psychodynamic approach
   b. no; Freud is associated with the psychodynamic perspective, but Skinner is associated with the behavioral perspective, not the cognitive approach
   c. YES; unconscious experiences are the focus of the psychodynamic perspective and mental process the focus of the cognitive approach
   d. no; Rogers is associated with the humanistic perspective and Freud with the psychodynamic
   pp. 11, 12

10. a. YES; the behavioral approach focuses on the environmental or external factors that shape our behaviors, while the psychodynamic approach focuses on internal factors such as instincts and the unconscious
    b. it is the opposite, as explained in the previous item
    c. actually, both the behavioral and the psychodynamic approach were developed and were widely popular during the first half of the 20th century
    d. incorrect, as both approaches were developed in the 20th century
    pp. 10, 11

11. a. no; in the study reported in Chapter 1, the participants were asked to pay attention, but their memory was not always accurate
    b. no; this statement is inconsistent with the study reported on Chapter 1
    c. YES; in the study reported in Chapter 1, even when the participants were asked to pay attention their memory was not completely accurate
    d. no; this statement is inconsistent with the study reported on Chapter 1
    p. 12

12. a. no; this is one of the principles proposed by Pinker
    b. no; this is the second principle proposed by Pinker
    c. no; this is the third principle proposed by Pinker
    d. CORRECT; this statement addresses the issue of culture; Pinker's evolutionary approach has been criticized for not properly addressing cultural differences
    p. 14

13. a.   no; while the behavioral approach is associated with the study of external factors that control behaviors and mental processes, the humanistic approach focuses more on internal factors, such as self-control, than on environmental or external explanations
    b.   no; this item is similar to item a but the order has been reversed; therefore, the explanation for item a also applies to item b
    c.   YES; the behavioral approach is associated with external or environmental controls on our psychology, whereas the humanistic approach emphasizes our free will and ability to control our behaviors and mental processes
    d.   no; this item presents the same concepts as in item c but in a reversed order; therefore, the item is incorrect; behaviorists do not focus on free will, humanists do
    pp. 10, 16

14. a.   no; the psychodynamic approach is associated with negative psychological experiences and psychological problems
    b.   no; the behavioral approach focuses on environmental factors and does not emphasize a person's free will and control over their life
    c.   no; the sociocultural approach studies cultural factors that shape how we act, think, and feel
    d.   YES; the humanistic approach emphasizes how people can overcome negative experiences because they have free will and the power to choose how to act, think, and feel
    p. 16

15. a.   while a doctor who has specialized in forensic medicine does work with dead bodies, for example, performing autopsies, forensic psychology has nothing to do with people who have passed away
    b.   no; forensic psychology and forensic medicine are not related fields
    c.   YES; in this case a forensic psychologist, someone who has specialized on the psychological factors involved in the legal system, would be a great resource in the process of selecting a jury
    d.   no; a judge with psychological problems would have to seek the assistance of a clinical psychologist
    p. 24

16. a.   no; in this example neither the individual's personality nor the role of the brain and nervous system is being studied
    b.   YES; social psychologists study how people make decisions when other people are present, and the environmental psychologist could offer insights on the issue of crowding as an environmental factor.
    c.   no; the question makes no direct reference to topics of health psychology
    d.   no; the question makes no direct reference to topics of community psychology
    pp. 21, 23

17. a.   YES; community psychologists are interested in the access that people have to important resources in their community; eliminating driving tests in languages other than English could potentially limit the access to driving privileges to one sector of the population
    b.   no; the question makes no direct reference to topics of health psychology
    c.   no; the question makes no direct reference to topics of social psychology
    d.   no; a study on this community-based topic is beyond the scope of the basic psychology of experimental psychology
    p. 22

18. a.  CORRECT; music may serve as a distraction, and distractions should be minimized when studying, thus this is not an effective strategy
    b.  distributing studying sessions across time contributes to the consolidation of the knowledge and enhances memory
    c.  having an idea of the order of the material and being aware of the goals of the chapter before reading it does make the reading and studying more effective
    d.  reflecting, being thoughtful and open-minded, does contribute to memory
    p. 27

19. a.  no; this just requires recollection of memorized material
    b.  no; this just requires recollection of memorized material
    c.  YES; comparing two perspectives requires understanding each perspective and a thoughtful consideration of comparable aspects of each approach
    d.  no; this just requires paraphrasing of memorized material
    p. 29

20. a.  finding "the real problem" requires thoughtfulness and attention; requires critical thinking
    b.  CORRECT; sticking to one approach is similar to being close-minded and therefore inconsistent with critical thinking
    c.  this is part of the definition of critical thinking
    d.  being skeptical sometimes requires questioning what other people don't question, and this is possible when the person is thinking critically
    p. 29

# Chapter 2—Psychology's Scientific Methods

## Learning Goals

1. Explain what makes psychology a science.
2. Discuss the three types of research that are used in psychology.
3. Distinguish between descriptive statistics and inferential statistics.
4. Discuss some research challenges that involve ethics, bias, and information.

*After studying Chapter 2, you will be able to:*

- Discuss the difference between science and information that is not scientific.
- Describe the four ideals or attitudes characteristic of the scientific approach.
- Say why collaboration is important in the scientific research.
- Explain what the scientific method is and discuss its steps.
- Define and describe the relationship among theories, hypotheses, and operational definitions.
- Describe the difference between a sample and a population.
- Discuss the purpose of descriptive research methods in psychology, and describe four types of descriptive methods.
- Understand the difference between findings of correlational research and findings of experimental research.
- Interpret a correlation coefficient, because you will know what the correlation coefficient measures, what is the meaning of the number, and what is the meaning of the sign in the correlation coefficient.
- Describe the difference between descriptive statistics and inferential statistics.

## CHAPTER 2: OUTLINE

- Psychology is a science; therefore, it relies on scientific research to study behaviors and mental processes. In comparison to personal observations and experiences, scientific research is systematic and usually requires collaboration among researchers. The scientific approach is characterized by four ideals: curiosity, skepticism, objectivity, and critical thinking. Embracing these ideals increases the likelihood that psychological research will result in reliable and objective scientific findings.

- Research in psychology is based on the scientific method and involves:

   1. <u>Conceptualizing a problem</u>. This step involves taking an issue that the researcher is curious or skeptical about and expressing it in terms of operational definitions and hypotheses.
   2. <u>Collecting data</u>. Based on the conceptualization of the problem, the researcher selects a research method that will be appropriate to explore the issue or test the proposed hypothesis or hypotheses. An important aspect of collecting data is selecting an appropriate sample that is representative of the population of interest. One of the options researchers have is to use a random sample, to increase the ability to generalize the results from the sample to the population. In psychology, generalizations often result from similar findings across a number of studies.

3. <u>Analyzing the data</u>. Based on what data was collected and how it was collected, the researcher will then proceed to analyze the data. Most research in psychology is analyzed using statistical procedures.

4. <u>Drawing conclusions</u>. Based on the results of the analysis of the data, the researcher develops explanations for the findings. These explanations involve the extent to which the findings confirm the theories and hypotheses that the study was addressing.

- In the process of conceptualizing the problem, the researcher chooses the research method that better addresses the research topic. Psychologists rely on three basic types of research methods to perform their studies of behaviors and mental processes: descriptive, correlational, and experimental.

- Descriptive methods involve systematic observations and recording of behaviors. The four types of descriptive methods discussed in Chapter 2 are observations, surveys and interviews, standardized tests, and case studies. Observations can take placed in natural settings or in laboratories.

- In <u>naturalistic observation</u>, the psychologist observes behavior in real-world settings and makes no attempt to manipulate or control the situation. However, many of the observations that take place in psychology occur in the laboratory, which gives the psychologist control over factors; for this reason, there are several drawbacks to this method, such as the unnatural behaviors that result from people knowing that they are being observed.

- An <u>interview</u> involves asking people questions to find out about their experiences and attitudes. One problem of interviewing people is the concern of participants to tell the interviewer what they think is socially acceptable or desirable.

- <u>Surveys</u> or questionnaires require subjects to read questions and mark their answers. Some psychologists observe behavior and mental processes by administering standardized tests. <u>Standardized tests</u> allow the researcher to measure some aspect of the participant's behaviors and/or mental processes and compare each individual's outcome to that of others who have also performed the same test.

- The last descriptive method discussed in Chapter 2 is the <u>case study</u>, which provides an in-depth examination of a single individual, from which the results may not be easily generalized to other people.

- The correlational method is basically a statistical procedure that allows the researcher to describe how strongly two or more events or characteristics are related. The correlation coefficient is a measure of the strength and direction of the relationship between the two factors. It is important to note that correlation does not equal causation but can allow us to make predictions.

- Unlike the correlational method, the experimental method allows psychologists to determine the causes of behaviors and mental processes. In an experiment, one or more factors are manipulated and all other factors held constant. The factor that is manipulated is called the *independent variable*. The behavior or mental process that is observed and measured in the experiment is called the *dependent variable*. In general terms, the goal of an experiment is to determine the extent to which the independent variable influences and causes the dependent variable.

- In experiments, researchers usually expose a number of participants to one level of the independent variable and others to another level. The group of participants whose experience is being manipulated is the known as the *experimental group*, while the comparison group is called the *control group*.

- In experimental research, participants are randomly assigned to experimental and control groups. One concern involves the experimenter's own bias influencing the outcome of the research; this is called *experimenter bias*. However, research may also be influenced by *participant bias*, whereby the research participants have beliefs about how they are expected to behave and behave according to their expectations. The research participant bias is also referred to as the *placebo effect*.

- To control for these expectations, an experiment may be designed as a double-blind experiment, whereby neither the participant nor the experimenter knows in which condition is the participant.

- In order to analyze the data collected in systematic research, psychologists rely on statistics, which are mathematical methods. There are two basic categories of statistics: descriptive and inferential.

- Descriptive statistics are used to summarize the information acquired in the study. Two types of descriptive statistics are discussed in Chapter 2: (1) measures of central tendency, which are used to assess the general tendencies or the "average" behavior or mental process that was observed in the study, and (2) measures of variability, which inform us as to the differences in behaviors and mental processes inside the sample that was studied.

- Once you understand the three most common types of measures of central tendency, you will understand the importance of measures of variability. The first measure of central tendency is the mean. This is what we commonly associate with an "average" response.

- The mean is calculated by adding all the scores and then dividing that total by the number of scores or participants.

- The median is the score that stands right in the middle of the series of scores. The third measure of central tendency is the mode, which is the most typical score in the series of scores—in other words, the most typical behavior observed in the study.

- While these three measures of central tendency do give us a summary or idea of the behaviors and mental processes observed in the participants of the study, they do not include information about the individuals in the study and the differences between the participants. Here is where the measures of variability play a very important role in psychological research.

- The range and the standard deviation give information about the differences between the people that participated in the study. The range is the distance between the highest and the lowest score. The standard deviation is a measure of, on average, how different individuals are from the mean or average behavior. The higher the standard deviation, the more difference was there between the mean score and the scores of individuals. In other words, the higher the standard deviation, the less descriptive or representative is the mean of the behaviors and mental processes of the individual participants.

- Inferential statistics are used to analyze the data collected in the study to test the hypotheses that guided the study. A hypothesis explains the expected relationship between the manipulated independent variable and the dependent variable.

- Inferential statistics inform the researcher regarding the extent to which the relationship between the independent variable and the dependent variable is real and significant or is due to chance.

- Psychologists only report an effect as significant if the inferential statistics indicate that the odds of the results being due to chance is equal or less than 5 out 100, or .05 statistical significance.

- Ethics and values are of great concern to psychologists. Values influence the types of questions psychological research poses. The American Psychological Association has developed a code of ethics for researchers that calls for researchers to provide subjects with informed consent, confidentiality, debriefing, the careful use of deception, and protection from physical and mental harm.

- Current controversies surround the values of psychology and use of animals in research. In recent years, psychologists have shown increasing interest in and sensitivity toward gender, cultural, and ethnic bias in psychological research.

- Learning to read journals can be of benefit regardless of one's career choice.

- Journal articles are often written with technical language and specialized terms since they are usually intended to be read by professionals in the field. Learning to be a wise consumer of information about psychology is very important. When reading information presented in the media, one needs to pay attention to overgeneralization based on a small sample and the acknowledgment that one study should not be taken as the final answer on a problem.

## Building Blocks of Chapter 2

### Clarifying some of the tricky points in Chapter 2
### and
### In Your Own Words
*To respond to the questions and exercises presented in the "In Your Own Words" section, please write your thoughts, perspectives, and reactions on a separate piece of paper.*

### *Exploring Psychology as a Science*
Science is not defined by the subject matter it studies, but by how it studies it. The four ideals or attitudes that are central to the scientific approach are: curiosity, skepticism, objectivity, and critical thinking. Science is essentially a collaborative effort because in order for a science to progress researchers must share information. The scientific method is an approach that can be used to discover accurate information and includes conceptualizing a problem, collecting data, analyzing the data, and drawing conclusions. A theory is a broad idea or set of closely related ideas that attempt to explain certain observations. To test theories, researchers develop hypotheses, which are specific predictions arrived at logically from theory that can be tested in research. An operational definition consists of an objective description of how a research variable is going to be observed and measured. A psychologist studying a group of subjects will want to be able to draw conclusions that will apply to a large group of people. A sample is a subset of the population. For the generalization to be accurate, the sample should be representative of the population. One of the ways in which researchers can make the sample more typical of the population is by using a random sample, a procedure that gives every member of the population equal chance of being a part of the sample.

### *Helpful Hint #1*
*The scientific method has four major steps to it, which fall in logical order: conceptualizing the problem, collecting the data, analyzing the data, and drawing conclusions. For example, let's say you observe that your roommates seem very cranky in the mornings before they have a cup of coffee. You are curious about this and wonder exactly what is going on to improve their moods. You decide you will conduct a scientific study. Before you can go any further you need to become educated on your topic. You study what others have found in their scientific studies about coffee and improved moods. Now you are in a position to state your hypothesis, which is an educated guess. Perhaps, your hypothesis would be "two cups of coffee in the a.m. improves one's mood for the day." The goal of your study is to either support your hypothesis or disprove it.*

*The next step would be to design your study, which means you account for every detail. You decide what a "cup of coffee" means (5 ounces or 10 ounces?) Is the coffee black or are cream and sugar added? How fast is the coffee consumed, and on and on. This is an important aspect referred to as "defining the parameters" of your study. At this point you are now prepared to collect the data. Perhaps when you defined the parameters of your study you decided you would give a pre- and a post-test: a short questionnaire before the participant had any coffee, and the same questionnaire after the participant had some coffee. In this step, you are administering the questionnaires and gathering the responses.*

*After you have collected your data, you can now analyze it. This is where statistics come in. In this step you are proving or disproving your hypothesis with the data you collected. Statistics are mathematical formulations that make sense of information for us.*

*Finally, the last step is to draw conclusions about your study and to share the results. Perhaps you found that two cups of coffee in the morning did not significantly improve people's moods. In your study you may discuss this. Most importantly, you share your findings with other researchers and practitioners in the field. This sharing helps the field grow and further our understanding of behaviors and mental processes.*

### In Your Own Words
*Please write your thoughts, perspectives, and reactions on a separate piece of paper.*
✓ *A friend of yours is talking with you about psychology. She claims that psychology is not a real science, at least not like biology. What's is your reasoned response to her?*

### *Types of Psychological Research*
Psychologists use three basic types of research methods: *descriptive, correlational, and experimental. Descriptive methods* have the purpose of observing and recording behavior and include observation, surveys and interviews, standardized tests, and case studies. *Naturalistic observation* means observing behaviors in real-world settings. However, much psychological research is conducted in a *laboratory*, a controlled setting that removes many complex real-world factors. Laboratory research has some drawbacks: participants are likely to know they are being studied; the laboratory setting is unnatural; and participants in university laboratory research are unlikely to represent diverse cultural backgrounds.

In an *interview*, a person is asked face-to-face questions about experiences and attitudes. A shortcoming of interviews occurs where participants are not willing to disclose socially unfavorable information about them. In a *survey*, the respondents read the questions and mark their answers on paper. Tests used to measure an aspect of a person's psychology and compare the individual's score with the scores of others are referred to as *standardized* tests. An in-depth look at a single individual is called a *case study*.

The goal of *correlational research* is to describe how strongly two or more events or characteristics are related. Remember that, just because two events may be correlated, it does not prove that one event causes the other. The *number* in the *correlation coefficient* indicates the strength of the relationship between the two factors, and the *sign* indicates the direction of the relationship. A *positive* sign in the correlation coefficient indicates that the two factors vary in the same direction, and a *negative* sign indicates that the factors vary in opposite directions.

A technique that does allow psychologists to determine the causes of behavior is called *experimental research*. In conducting an experiment, the researcher manipulates one variable to see the *effect* on behavior. The *independent* variable is the manipulated factor. The *dependent* variable is the factor that is measured in an experiment and changes as the independent variable is manipulated.

Subjects, whose experience is manipulated by the experimenter, are called the *experimental group*, while those who act as a comparison group are the *control group*. Subjects are assigned to groups by *random assignment*, which means that assignments are made by chance. Experimenter bias may occur in an experiment if the experimenter's own expectations influence the outcome of the research. Research participants have beliefs about how they should behave; this is known as *research participant bias*. To control for the influence of expectations, *double-blind* experiments are used in which neither experimenter nor participant is aware of which participants are in which groups.

### In Your Own Words
*Please write your thoughts, perspectives, and reactions on a separate piece of paper.*

✓ *One of the best ways to learn is by "doing." Explore the challenges of naturalistic observation by sitting at one of your favorite spots and systematically observing specific behaviors of others in that real-world setting. Based on your experience, list the advantages and disadvantages of this research method.*

✓ *How would you operationally define love?*

✓ *What is the difference between findings based on an experiment and findings from a correlational study?*

### Analyzing and Interpreting Data
Statistics are mathematical methods used to report data. There are two basic categories of statistics: descriptive and inferential statistics are used to summarize the data in meaningful ways, while descriptive statistics are used to draw conclusions about the data that has been collected, such as indicating whether there is sufficient support for the proposed hypothesis. One type of descriptive statistics uses the measures of central tendency. The mean is calculated by adding all the scores and dividing that total by the number of scores or participants. The median is the score that stands right in the middle of the ordered distribution of scores; unlike the mean, this measure of central tendency is not affected by extreme scores. The mode is the most typical score in the set of data. While the measures of central tendency provide summary information about the behaviors observed in the study, the measures of variability describe how much the scores in a sample are different from one another. The range is the distance between the highest and the lowest scores, and the standard deviation measures how much each scores varies on the average around the mean of the sample. This statistic informs the researcher of how close the participants were to the mean or typical behavior observed.

Inferential statistics, which are statistical methods used to draw conclusions about the data, rely on a probability assessment referred to as the level of statistical significance. A 5 out of 100, or .05 level, of statistical significance is considered the minimum level of probability to conclude that the effect of the independent variable on the dependent variable is real and significant.

### In Your Own Words
*Please write your thoughts, perspectives, and reactions on a separate piece of paper.*
✓ *Imagine that you are trying to explain some of the important concepts learned in this chapter*

*to a person who does not understand your language. Using drawings, describe the concepts independent variable, dependent variable, experimental group, and control group.*

✓ *To better understand the information that we get from the measures of central tendency, administer the following brief survey to 10 of your acquaintances and calculate/determine the mean, the median, and the mode for each of the questions. Question #1: What is your age? Question #2: How many close friends do you have? What kind of conclusions can you draw from the measures of central tendency for each of these questions? How informative would it be to also assess measures of variability on the answers to these questions?*

### Facing Up to Research Challenges

Three key reasons for studying the importance of ethics and values in psychological research are (1) we are active members of society in the age of information and technology; (2) we may participate in psychological research, so we need to know about our rights; and (3) students may themselves become researchers. The APA has developed ethical guidelines for psychologists. One guideline requires telling subjects about their participation and any potential risks. Researchers are responsible for keeping all the data gathered on individuals completely confidential and when possible completely anonymous. Informing participants of the purpose and methods used in a study when the study is completed is called informed consent. Subjects must not be harmed and must be debriefed as soon as possible in cases of deception. Regarding values, some psychologists believe that psychology should be value-free and morally neutral. For too long, the female experience was subsumed under the male experience; this illustrates gender bias. The use of an ethnic label in a way that makes a group seem more homogeneous than it is in actuality is called ethnic gloss.

Many times, when psychological research is reported by the media, it is sensationalistic and dramatic. A wise consumer of psychological information recognizes that most research focuses on groups, not individuals. The wise consumer also is aware of the effect that sample size has on generalizing the results of a study to a larger population. In addition, it is important to note that one study is not the final authority on the issue.

### In Your Own Words

*Please write your thoughts, perspectives, and reactions on a separate piece of paper.*

✓ *If you were a participant in a psychological research, what ethical concerns would you have? Describe the procedures that should take place in the study to guarantee your rights as a research participant.*

## Correcting the Incorrect

Carefully read each statement. Determine if the statement is correct or incorrect. If the statement is incorrect, make the necessary changes to correct it. Then check the answer key at the end of the chapter for the correct statement and page reference in the textbook.

1. Personal experience is objective, systematic, and testable.
2. Science is defined by what it investigates.
3. The four attitudes central to the scientific approach are skepticism, subjectivity, curiosity, and critical thinking.
4. Science is an individual effort.
5. An ideal definition is one that defines the concept precisely and in terms of observable events that can be measured.
6. The first step of the scientific method is collecting research information.
7. A hypothesis is a broad idea or set of closely related ideas that attempts to explain certain observations.
8. Essentially, the scientific method is a process of developing and testing theories.

9. Psychologists use research methods to collect data.

10. Random assignment is done when every member of the population has an equal chance of being selected to the sample.

11. The sample is the entire group of participants about which the researcher wants to draw conclusions.

12. The sample should be representative of the population.

13. In psychology, generalizations can be achieved only if the sample studied is random.

14. Descriptive research methods use carefully regulated procedures in which one or more factors are manipulated while other factors are held constant.

15. A naturalistic observation has the drawback that participants know they are being studied and may act unnaturally.

16. In an interview, the participant reads the questions and answers them on paper.

17. In a survey, an individual's score is compared to the scores of a large group of similar people to determine how the individual responded relative to others.

18. A case study consists of asking in-depth questions to a number of individuals that share the same problem or psychological characteristic.

19. In the laboratory, many of the complex factors of the real world are removed.

20. If a psychologist is conducting naturalistic observation, she is attempting to manipulate the behavior of the subjects.

21. Correlation equals causation.

22. A positive correlation indicates that the relationship between the two factors being studied is a good relationship.

23. The sign in the correlation coefficient is an indicator of the strength of the relationship between the two factors being studied.

24. If a psychologist is interested in determining behavior's causes, experimental research is the most appropriate method.

25. The dependent variable is the factor that is manipulated in an experiment.

26. The experimental group acts like a comparison group.

27. When using random sampling, the researcher assigns participants to experimental and control groups by chance.

28. Experiments should have experimental bias since it can improve the results.

29. A placebo effect occurs when the participant's expectations and not the experimental treatment produce a desired outcome.

30. In the double-blind experiment, the participant and the researcher both know which participants are in the experimental and placebo control groups.

31. The median is the measure of central tendency that is the score that occurs most often in the set of data.

32. The standard deviation is a measure of central tendency.

33. Descriptive statistics are used to draw conclusions about the data, such as indicating whether there is support for the proposed hypothesis.

34. The .10, or "10 out of 100," level of statistical significance is considered the minimum level of probability that scientists accept for concluding that there is significant support for the proposed hypothesis.

35. When the study is about to begin, the researcher informs the participants about the purpose and methods used in the study; this is called *debriefing*.

36. About 25% of the APA members use animals in their research.

37. The media tend to focus on sensationalistic and dramatic psychological findings.

38. As you read psychological information in the media, you should see how the research affects you as an individual.

39. One study is usually enough research on a particular topic or issue.

40. Sample size is not important to know when reading media reports of psychological information.

## Practice Test 1

1. Of the following, which best describes the role that mass media play in psychological research?
    a. Mass media tend to sensationalize psychological research.
    b. Mass media tend to accurately report most psychological research.
    c. Through its influence, mass media determine what type of research is funded.
    d. Mass media have had a profound effect on making us more knowledgeable about science and psychology.

2. _____ involves objective, systematic, and testable research.
    a. Philosophy
    b. The placebo effect
    c. Science
    d. Experimenter bias

3. Juan is engaged in a process to discover accurate information. He has followed several steps: conceptualizing a problem, collecting data, analyzing data, and drawing conclusions. Juan is using
    a. an operational definition of the dependent variable.
    b. a standardized test.
    c. the scientific method.
    d. a double-blind experiment.

4. What is the first step of the scientific method?
    a. draw conclusions
    b. analyze the data
    c. collect data
    d. conceptualize a problem

5. You have received feedback on your research proposal from your psychology professor. She has written, "You need to state your definitions more precisely and in terms of observable events that can be measured." What is she talking about?
    a. She is referring to including more references in your study.
    b. Her feedback is in regard to operational definitions.
    c. She is suggesting that readers will not understand what you mean by the placebo effect.
    d. You need to spell out in greater detail what statistical techniques you are proposing to use to analyze your data.

6. _____ are specific predictions that can be tested to determine their accuracy and are derived logically from theories.
    a. Correlations
    b. Experiments
    c. Observations
    d. Hypotheses

7. The use of statistical procedures allows researchers to
   a. conceptualize the problem.
   b. collect data.
   c. analyze the data.
   d. develop hypotheses.

8. A _____ is selected from the population.
   a. sample
   b. placebo
   c. dependent variable
   d. theory

9. Each of the following is a drawback of laboratory research, except
   a. participants know they are being studied.
   b. the laboratory setting might produce unnatural behavior.
   c. the participants are not likely to represent diverse cultural groups.
   d. laboratory settings do not permit control over complex real-world factors.

10. What is the main disadvantage of laboratory observation?
    a. The researcher cannot control the situation.
    b. The setting is too unpredictable.
    c. Subjects may not behave naturally because they know they are being observed.
    d. The variables cannot be defined in operational terms.

11. Ali and Michael are conducting a study in which they sit in the student center lobby and take notes on different students' hand gestures as they speak. What type of research method are they using?
    a. case study
    b. correlational study
    c. naturalistic observation
    d. experimental research

12. Caleb recently was asked by a researcher questions about his attitudes toward politics. Caleb participated in a(n) _____. He later admitted that he gave answers that he thought were what the researcher wanted to hear, which illustrates _____.
    a. questionnaire; the placebo effect
    b. interview; his desire to offer the answers he thought the researcher wanted to hear.
    c. experiment; experimenter bias
    d. experiment; informed consent

13. A research method typically used by clinical psychologists with unique individuals is called a(n)
    a. interview.
    b. random sample.
    c. experiment.
    d. case study.

14. Participants' tendency to respond in a way that is intended to create a good impression, rather than to provide true information, is one of the problems with
    a. experiments.
    b. correlational studies.
    c. surveys.
    d. naturalistic observations.

15. Standardized tests
    a. give every member of the population an equal chance to be tested.
    b. are used only by clinical psychologists.
    c. provide information about individual differences among people.
    d. involve making careful observations of people in real-world settings.

16. What is the main advantage of using standardized tests?
    a. They have very good external validity.
    b. They can determine cause and effect.
    c. They provide information about individual differences.
    d. They contain no biases.

17. The strength of the relationship between two or more events can be determined by
    a. experimental research.
    b. case study.
    c. physiological research.
    d. correlational research.

18. The research method that measures how much one characteristic is associated with another is known as
    a. classic experimentation.
    b. naturalistic observation.
    c. correlational strategy.
    d. standardized tests.

19. A researcher finds a strong positive correlation between work stress and high blood pressure. Based on this finding, which of the following statements is true?
    a. Work stress causes high blood pressure.
    b. High blood pressure causes people to perceive high levels of work stress.
    c. High blood pressure has nothing to do with stress.
    d. The higher the stress at work, the higher the blood pressure.

20. Which of the following research strategies allows for most control and precision?
    a. correlational
    b. naturalistic observation
    c. experimental
    d. interview

21. In a correlation coefficient, the _____ is the indicator of the direction of the relationship.
    a. number
    b. sign
    c. level of statistical significance
    d. statistic

22.    The _____ is the score that falls exactly in the middle of the distribution of scores after they have been arranged from highest to lowest.
    a.    mean
    b.    mode
    c.    median
    d.    range

## Practice Test 2

1.    If you conduct research in which you manipulate a variable while holding others constant and randomly assign participants to groups, what research method are you using?
    a.    case study
    b.    interview
    c.    correlational research
    d.    experimental research

2.    An experiment is being conducted to determine the effects of different teaching methods on student performance. The independent variable is _____, while the dependent variable is _____.
    a.    different teaching methods; number of students taking the test
    b.    student performance; grades on a test
    c.    different teaching methods; student performance
    d.    student performance; different teaching methods

3.    In an experiment, the _____ is the "cause" and the _____ is the "effect."
    a.    dependent; independent
    b.    independent; dependent
    c.    control; dependent
    d.    dependent; experimental

4.    In an experiment testing the effect of amphetamine on learning in rats, the amphetamine is the
    a.    dependent variable.
    b.    experimental variable.
    c.    independent variable.
    d.    extraneous variable.

5.    Manipulated factor is to _____ as measured factor is to _____.
    a.    experimental group; independent variable
    b.    control group; independent variable
    c.    dependent variable; experimental group
    d.    independent variable; dependent variable

6.    Experiments with people involve a comparison between at least two groups: a group that receives the special treatment and a group that receives a placebo or neutral treatment. This latter group is called the
    a.    control group.
    b.    representative sample.
    c.    experimental group.
    d.    random sample.

7.    Which of the following statements about psychological research methods is correct?
    a.    Only clinical psychologists are allowed to conduct experiments.
    b.    It would be inappropriate to combine observation and the correlational method.
    c.    Experiments usually involve standardized tests.
    d.    Correlational studies cannot be used to arrive at cause-and-effect conclusions..

8.    If you were a psychologist concerned about reducing gender bias in psychological inquiry, you would be least concerned about which of the following?
    a.    gender stereotypes
    b.    exaggeration of gender differences
    c.    gender of consumers of psychological research
    d.    selection of research topics

9.    Which of the following statements is NOT TRUE about the life and career of May Whiton Calkins?
    a.    This psychologist worked with William James.
    b.    Calkins became a faculty member at Wellesley, a women's college, in 1887.
    c.    In the 1890s Calkins established an experimental psychology program at Wellesley.
    d.    Unfortunately, Calkins was never recognized or achieved any recognition among her peers during her lifetime.

10.    Which of the following statements is TRUE about science?
    a.    Science is defined by what it investigates.
    b.    Science is defined by how it investigates.
    c.    Collaboration is not essential to the progress of science.
    d.    Objectivity is not necessary in science.

11.    Which of the following is NOT one of the ideals central to the scientific approach?
    a.    objectivity
    b.    curiosity
    c.    critical thinking
    d.    sensitivity

12.    Which of the following is NOT one of the ways in which scientists collaborate?
    a.    doing presentations in conferences
    b.    submitting their work for peer review and serving as peer reviewers themselves
    c.    avoiding replicating studies identical or similar to those that others have already done
    d.    publishing in professional journals

13.    Which of the following is NOT one of the basic steps of the scientific method?
    a.    publishing in a professional journal
    b.    collecting data
    c.    analyzing data
    d.    drawing conclusions

14.    The theory of _____ says that by expressing pent-up emotions, a person can eliminate the emotions and the physical symptoms of stress associated with the experience of the emotions.
    a.    the scientific method
    b.    statistics
    c.    random sampling
    d.    catharsis

15. In Pennebaker's study of catharsis, the operational definition of "health" was
    a.  if the participant got a cold or flu during the week following the study.
    b.  the number of times the participants had been seriously ill before attending college (and thus, before participating in the study).
    c.  the number of times the participants visited the heath center at the university.
    d.  the physical condition of the participants at the time of participating in the study.

16. In scientific studies, generalizations can be made only if the _____ is representative of the _____.
    a.  sample; random sample
    b.  random sample; sample
    c.  population; sample
    d.  sample; population

17. _____ is the extent to which a scientific research yields a consistent, reproducible result.
    a.  Generalizability
    b.  Reliability
    c.  Objectivity
    d.  Randomness

18. Which of the following is NOT one of the basic types of research in psychology?
    a.  correlational
    b.  descriptive
    c.  experimental
    d.  philosophical

19. A _____ is characterized by the unobtrusive observation of behaviors in real-world settings, such as parks, streets, and day care centers.
    a.  naturalistic observation
    b.  laboratory observation
    c.  correlational study
    d.  survey

20. The _____ is a measure of central tendency that is calculated by adding all the scores and dividing that total by the number of scores or participants.
    a.  mode
    b.  median
    c.  mean
    d.  range

21. The mode is the
    a.  score right in the middle of the distribution of scores.
    b.  "average" score as we commonly know it.
    c.  most common score.
    d.  difference between the highest and the lowest score.

## Practice Test 3

1.  When Mary Calkins and other female psychologists questioned the extent to which the theories proposed by male psychologists, which were tested with male participants, would apply to females, they were exercising the _____ ideal, which is central to the scientific approach.
    a.   curiosity
    b.   skepticism
    c.   objectivity
    d.   critical thinking

2.  In 1896 Mary Calkins did an experiment to find out whether people remember numbers better if they are linked with vivid colors. In this experiment, the independent variable was the
    a.   type of color linked to the numbers.
    b.   participants.
    c.   amount of numbers remembered.
    d.   memory of the participants.

3.  Michelle Russo is a cognitive psychologist who is curious about the effects of caffeine on memory. Her operational definition of caffeine is "ounces of caffeine," and memory is "number of details recalled after reading an essay." Of the following research methods, which would be most appropriate for this research question?
    a.   interview
    b.   case study
    c.   naturalistic observation
    d.   experiment

4.  If the correlation coefficient of the relationship between class attendance and final grade in a class is +.75, that means that
    a.   there is no relationship between going to class and the final grade.
    b.   going to class makes people get better grades.
    c.   the lower the class attendance, the lower the final grade in the class.
    d.   the less people attend class, the higher the final grade in the class.

5.  According to Pennebaker's study of emotions and catharsis, which of the following activities would you recommend to a person who is grieving the loss of a loved one?
    a.   The person should seek the assistance of a clinical psychologist.
    b.   The person should try to ignore the negative thoughts and focus on positive thoughts.
    c.   The person should write down what he/she is feeling and describe what he/she feels has been lost.
    d.   The person should exercise while listening to motivational tapes.

6.  Which of the following would be an appropriate sample if a researcher intends to generalize the results of the study to "all males"?
    a.   a sample of 100 members of the Knights of Columbus
    b.   a sample of 100 male freshman psychology students
    c.   a sample of 100 males, 50 from a university in Russia and 50 from a university in the U.S.
    d.   a sample of 100 American males who have been randomly selected from the draft registry

7. Why is it that surveys in magazines do not have good generalizability?
   a. Magazines can use random sampling.
   b. People who choose to buy the magazine and choose to send in their answers may have characteristics that are particular to and different from the characteristics of those who do not complete the survey.
   c. Surveys in magazines are poorly constructed and are about topics that cannot be generalized.
   d. Magazine articles are silly and meaningless.

8. Serena went to a clinical psychologist and was diagnosed with depression. She then decided to get a second opinion, and the second clinical psychologist also diagnosed her with depression. Serena can conclude that the diagnosis of depression is
   a. changeable.
   b. cathartic.
   c. reliable.
   d. correlated.

9. All the following are applications of Pennebaker's work on emotions, EXCEPT
   a. you should write about the most emotional trauma(s) in your life.
   b. you should just write and not worry about spelling or grammar.
   c. write when you feel like writing.
   d. do not plan to share your writing with others.

10. What is the main difference between naturalistic observation and experiments?
    a. In naturalistic observation, the researcher manipulates the environment to see what happens and then describe it.
    b. In experimental methods, the researcher tried to be as unobtrusive as possible.
    c. In naturalistic observation, the independent variable cannot be manipulated.
    d. In experimental methods, the researcher actively manipulates the environment of the participant.

11. Which of the following is a valid criticism of standardized tests?
    a. They cannot be used to compare people.
    b. They may be biased and favor people from some cultures.
    c. They do not measure appropriately the performance of an individual.
    d. They are used to compare people, and this is not good.

12. An internet company in Virginia has the highest rate of success in its business sector, and most observers attribute this to the CEO of the organization. Which of the following would be the best research method to study the CEO and the success of this organization?
    a. correlational
    b. a laboratory experiment
    c. case study
    d. naturalistic observation

13. Which of the following would be consistent with a −.68 correlation coefficient?
    a. The colder it is outside, the less people go outside.
    b. The more hours I study, the better my grade is on the test.
    c. The lower the ice cream sales, the lower the number of assaults reported at the police station.
    d. The number of books a person owns has no relationship with how knowledgeable he or she is.

14. Dr. Redding did an experiment in which he interrupted people who were sleeping to ask them if they were dreaming. Some people would be awakened 1 hour after falling asleep, others after 3 hours, and others were not awakened until 8 hours had passed, which is considered a normal night of sleep. In this experiment, which was the independent variable?
    a.   dreaming
    b.   the participants
    c.   the time at which the participants were awakened
    d.   the participants who were not awakened until 8 hours had passed

15. Dr. Wright did an experiment in which some people were placed in a nice-smelling room; others were placed in a foul-smelling room and still others placed in a room with no particular odor. Once the participants were in the room for 10 minutes, the researcher measured their mood with a questionnaire. In this experiment, which was the dependent variable?
    a.   the mood
    b.   the odor
    c.   the room that smelled foul
    d.   the 10 minutes

16. In a correlation coefficient the _____ is an indicator of the strength of the relationship between the two factors being studied.
    a.   number
    b.   sign
    c.   level of statistical significance
    d.   statistic

17. Which of the following is NOT one of the drawbacks of doing psychological research in laboratories?
    a.   Participants may act unnaturally.
    b.   University samples, which are most likely to be used in laboratory experiments, may not be representative of the population of interest.
    c.   The researcher has great control over factors that are irrelevant to the independent variable(s) of interest.
    d.   Some aspects of psychology are difficult or even unethical to study in laboratories.

18. In political elections, which measure of central tendency would be more consistent with the method of determining who is elected?
    a.   mean
    b.   median
    c.   mode
    d.   standard deviation

19. The statistic that measures how closely the scores are clustered around the mean is the
    a.   mean.
    b.   range.
    c.   standard deviation.
    d.   mode.

20. _____ statistics are the mathematical methods used to draw conclusions and test hypotheses.
   a.   Descriptive
   b.   Inferential
   c.   Psychological
   d.   Mathematical

## Connections

*Take advantage of all the other study tools available for this chapter!*

| NAME OF CLIP | DESCRIPTION | KEY CONCEPTS AND IDEAS |
|---|---|---|
| | | **Exploring Psychology as a Science** |
| | | Go to interactivity "Samples and Populations" to participate in an exercise that compares the costs and benefits of random samples vs. convenience samples. |
| Samples and Populations | In-Psych – Chapter 2 | **Types of Research** |
| | | See video clip "Cultural Variations in Nonverbal Behavior" to see how naturalistic observation has been used to study nonverbal behaviors across cultures. |
| *Cultural Variations in Nonverbal Behavior | Discovery – videos | Go to interactivity "Self-Report Bias in Surveys" to learn more about the challenges of using self-reports in psychological research. |
| Self-Report Bias in Surveys | Discovery – interactivities | Go to interactivity "Correlational Research" for an overview of correlational research and to engage in a correlational study. Learn more about the meaning of correlations from your own results. |
| Correlational Research | In-Psych – Chapter 2 | **Analyzing and Interpreting Data** |
| | | In the interactivity "Independent and Dependent Variables" you get to be a track coach. Your task is to use the experimental method to find the most effective performance tips. In the process, learn more about the process of manipulating independent variables and measuring dependent variables. |
| Independent and Dependent Variables | In-Psych – Chapter 2 | **Facing Up to Research Challenges** |

## Online Learning Center (www.mhhe.com/Santrockp7u)
- Interact and make learning fun!
  - **Interactive Exercises**
    - Correlational Research
    - Independent & Dependent Variables
    - Reliability, Validity, & Variability
    - Samples & Populations
- Brush up on the Key Terms for this chapter by first reviewing the electronic **Glossary** (in English or Spanish) and then testing your retention using the **Flashcard** feature.

- **"Notes"**—This feature allows you to use the website as you would your text, inserting your own study notes and highlighting areas of particular importance.

**In Your Text**

- Found throughout each chapter, the **Review and Sharpen Your Thinking** feature breaks the text into logical chunks, allowing you to process, review, and reflect thoughtfully on the information that you've just read. When going back to *study* the chapter, try reading the feature *before* the section of text to which it relates. In doing so, you will be able to focus your attention on important concepts *as* you encounter them. In this chapter, this feature can be found on the following pages: pp. 47, 59, 62, and 71.

**Practice Quizzes**

- Test your knowledge of the scientific method by taking the different practice quizzes found on your text's **Online Learning Center** and on the **In-Psych Plus CD-ROM** packaged with your text.

## ANSWER KEY

## In Your Own Words

✓ A friend of yours is talking with you about psychology. She claims that psychology is not a real science, at least not like biology. What's is your reasoned response to her?

*This answer should include the definition of psychology: the science of behavior and mental processes. The student may also make reference to the attitudes associated with the scientific approach in psychology: objectivity, curiosity, skepticism, and critical thinking. Illustrations of how psychologists creatively use research methods to test hypotheses and create theories should help the student make the point that psychology is a rigorous science not to be confused with uninformed and potentially biased opinions.*

✓ How would you operationally define *love*?

*An operational definition is a precise description of the phenomenon to be studied in terms of how it is going to be observed and measured. In this question the phenomenon to be operationalized is love, a concept subject to many operationalizations, even when it has be "narrowed down" to the context of romantic relationships. Love may be operationalized in various measurable ways, from observable behaviors such as gestures of affection (which gestures?) to mental processes, such as how often does a person think about the other person, what do they think about?, how do they feel, specific emotions, and so on.*

✓ Imagine that you are trying to explain some of the important concepts learned in this chapter to a person who does not understand your language. Using drawings, describe the concepts independent variable, dependent variable, experimental group, and control group.

*In the question, the student is asked to be creative in visualizing in a graphic format these concepts. When "drawing" independent variable and experimental group, the student may make pictorial reference to the issues of control and manipulation. The dependent variable may be expressed in a way that makes reference to its dependence on the independent variable. The control group may be expressed by emphasizing that in this group the independent variable is absent or not manipulated, it is the base against which the experimental groups are compared. This exercise is all about thinking about the basic meaning of these concepts so as to avoid getting lost in long and complex definitions.*

✓ One of the best ways to learn is by "doing." Explore the challenges of naturalistic observation by sitting at one of your favorite spots and systematically observing specific behaviors of others in that real-world setting. Based on your experience, list the advantages and disadvantages of this research method.

*Naturalistic observation is a research method in with the investigator observes behaviors as they naturally occur and makes efforts to be as unobtrusive as possible. The student engaged in this activity will probably realize some of the challenges of this method, such as the difficulty of recording behaviors that may be distant, quick, and simultaneous (i.e., more than one person doing the behavior of interest at the same time). Also, the student may set out to observe a particular behavior and never get to observe it; for example, going to a coffee shop to observe the people who order a "double mocha soy milk latte" and never having someone show up to make that order during the observation time. The main advantage of this method is that the observed behavior is genuine and naturally occurring.*

✓ To better understand the information that we get from the measures of central tendency, administer the following brief survey to 10 of your acquaintances and calculate/determine the mean, the median, and the mode for each of the questions. Question #1: What is your age? Question #2: How many close friends do you have? What kind of conclusions can you draw from the measures of central tendency for each of these questions? How informative would it be to also assess measures of variability on the answers to these questions?

*The mean is calculated by adding all the scores, for example, adding the ages, and dividing them by the total number of observations, in this case, 10. The median is the number that is located right in the middle of the series of numbers that have been organized in an ascending order. The mode is the most typical score in the list of scores—in the case of age, the most common age in the group of people interviewed. The sample is short and simply representative of acquaintances of the researcher; therefore, the results cannot be generalized beyond that group. A correlation coefficient would tell us about the relationship between age and number of friends. If the correlation was negative it would suggest that the younger the person the more friends he or she has, if it was positive it would suggest that the older the person the more friends he or she has.*

✓ What is the difference between findings based on an experiment and findings from a correlational study?

*Correlational research points out patterns of relationships. It answers questions regarding the extent and direction of the relationship between two variables; however, it never is an indicator of cause-and-effect relationships. Only experiments can provide that type of evidence. In experiments in which extraneous variables are controlled and only the independent variable is allowed to influence the behaviors observed (i.e., dependent variable), the researcher concludes cause-and-effect relationships.*

✓ If you were a participant in a psychological research, what ethical concerns would you have? Describe the procedures that should take place in the study to guarantee your rights as a research participant.

*Participants should expect that each of the following procedures takes place: informed consent at the beginning of the study, with clear instructions regarding their ability to leave the study at any point; ethical procedures that include deception only if it is absolutely necessary for the purposes of the study and in no way harms the participants; debriefing at the end of the study, in which participants receive information about the real purpose of the study and contact information for the researcher in case they want more details about the study.*

## Correcting the Incorrect

1. Personal experience is subjective, not always systematic, and can be difficult to test scientifically.

2. Science is defined by *how* it studies (i.e., the scientific method) not by what it studies.

3. The four attitudes central to the scientific approach are skepticism, *objectivity*, curiosity, and critical thinking. (p. 40)

4. Science is a *collaborative* effort. (p. 42)

5. An *operational definition* is one that defines the concept precisely and in terms of observable events that can be measured. (p. 44)

6. The first step of the scientific method is *conceptualizing the problem*. (p. 42)

7. A *theory* is a broad idea or set of closely related ideas that attempts to explain certain observations. (p. 42)

8. Essentially, the scientific method is a process of developing and testing theories. (p. 43)

9. Psychologists use research methods to collect data. (p. 45)

10. Random *sampling* is done when every member of the population has an equal chance of being selected to the sample. (p. 45)

11. The *population* is the entire group of participants about which the researcher wants to draw conclusions. (p. 45)

12. The sample should be representative of the population. (p. 45)

13. In psychology, generalizations can be achieved if the sample studied is random, *but generalizations may also come from similar results across various studies on the same issue.* (p. 46)

14. *Experimental* methods use carefully regulated procedures in which one or more factors are manipulated while other factors are held constant. (p. 56)

15. A *laboratory* observation has the drawback that participants know they are being studied and may act unnatural. (p. 49)

16. In a *survey* or *questionnaire*, the participant reads the questions and answers them on paper. (p. 51)

17. In a *standardized test,* an individual's score is compared to the scores of a large group of similar people to determine how the individual responded relative to others. (p. 51)

18. A case study consists of asking in-depth questions to *one individual*. (p. 52)

19. In the laboratory, many of the complex factors of the real world are removed. (p. 49)

20. If a psychologist is conducting naturalistic observation, she *is not* attempting to manipulate the behavior of the subjects. (p. 50)

21. Correlation *does not* equal causation. (p. 55)

22. A positive correlation indicates that the relationship between the two factors being studied *is one in which the factors vary in the same direction, but this has nothing to do with the relationship being good or bad.* (p. 54)

23. The *number* in the correlation coefficient is an indicator of the strength of the relationship between the two factors being studied. (p. 53)

24. If a psychologist is interested in determining behavior's causes, experimental research is the most appropriate method. (p. 56)

25. The *independent* variable is the factor that is manipulated in an experiment. (p. 56)

26. The *control* group acts like a comparison group. (p. 56)

27. When using random *assignment*, the researcher assigns participants to experimental and control groups by chance. (p. 56)

28. Experiments should *avoid* experimental bias since it can skew the results. (p. 57)

29. A placebo effect occurs when the participant's expectations and not the experimental treatment produces a desired outcome. (p. 58)

30. In the double-blind experiment, the participant and the researcher both *do not* know which participants are in the experimental and placebo control groups. (p. 58)

31. The *mode*, a measure of central tendency, is the score that occurs most often in the set of data. (p. 60)

32. The standard deviation is a measure of *variability*. (p. 61)

33. *Inferential* statistics are used to draw conclusions about the data, such as indicating whether there is support for the proposed hypothesis. (p. 61)

34. The *.05, or "5 out of 100,"* level of statistical significance is considered the minimum level of probability scientists accept for concluding that there is significant support for the proposed hypothesis. (p. 62)

35. When the study is about to begin, the researcher informs the participants about the purpose and methods used in the study; this is called *informed consent.* (p. 64)

36. About *5%* of the APA members use animals in their research. (p. 66)

37. The media tend to focus on sensationalistic and dramatic psychological findings. (p. 69)

38. As you read psychological information in the media, it is important to see how the research affects you as an individual, *keeping in mind that the study was done on groups.* (p. 69)

39. One study is usually *not enough* research on a particular topic or issue. (p. 70)

40. Sample size *is* important to know when reading media reports of psychological information. (p. 70)

## Practice Test 1

1. a.  CORRECT; the mass media tend to report only the sensational and the dramatic
   b.  reports in the media tend to be too brief and leave out important details
   c.  deciding what research is funded is not the role of the mass media
   d.  actually, the mass media have made us less knowledgeable
   p. 69

2. a.  no, philosophy does not involve the systematic research required from a science (see Chapter 1).
   b.  the placebo effect refers to changes in behavior that are due to expectations
   c.  YES; science involves objective and systematic research.
   d.  experimenter bias occurs when the experimenter has expectations that influence the outcome of the research
   p. 41

3. a.  operational definitions are a part of the scientific method but do not have these steps described
   b.  a standardized test may be used to collect data but is not relevant to the other steps
   c.  YES, THAT'S CORRECT; these steps describe the scientific method
   d.  a double-blind experiment may be used by the experimenter to control for expectations during the data-collection step
   p. 42

4. a.  drawing conclusions is the last step
   b.  no; this is third step
   c.  no; collecting data is the second step
   d.  RIGHT; the first step in the scientific method is to conceptualize a problem
   p. 42

5. a.  the comment is not related at all to the references used in the study
   b.  RIGHT; your teacher is asking you to develop the operational definitions for the concepts in your research proposal
   c.  the placebo effect in not being addressed in the feedback from the professor
   d.  the comment is really the definition of an operational definition and does not relate to statistical techniques
   p. 44

6. a. correlations are statistical assessments, not predictions
   b. experiments are research methods, not predictions
   c. observations are part of the process of collecting data and are not predictions
   d. TRUE; a hypothesis is a specific assumption or prediction that can be tested
   p. 43

7. a. statistical procedures are not involved in conceptualizing research problems
   b. collecting data is accomplished through research methods
   c. THAT'S RIGHT; statistical methods help psychologists understand the meaning of data
   d. hypotheses are developed in the process of conceptualizing the problem, and thus before the data is analyzed with statistics
   p. 46

8. a. YES; a sample is a subset of the population
   b. a placebo is an inert treatment that has no real effect
   c. the dependent variable is the variable that is being measured
   d. a theory is a set of interrelated ideas
   p. 45

9. a. this is a drawback; participants will know they are being studied
   b. this is a drawback; being in a laboratory can cause participants to behave unnaturally
   c. this is a drawback
   d. CORRECT; the laboratory does in fact permit control over factors
   p. 49

10. a. the researcher can control the situation in laboratory observation
    b. since the researcher can control the laboratory observation, the setting is predictable
    c. THAT'S RIGHT; subjects may change their behavior if they think they are being watched
    d. operationally defined variables are necessary in laboratory observation
    p. 49

11. a. no; a case study involves an in-depth examination of one person
    b. no; a correlational study examines the relationships of two or more events or characteristics
    c. YES; this is the method by which behavior is observed in real-world settings
    d. no; experimental research consists of the manipulation of variables and groups of subjects
    p. 50

12. a. a questionnaire consists of the participant writing down responses; the placebo effect refers to the participant's expectations affecting the research
    b. THAT'S RIGHT; an interview involves the person being asked questions; some people may give only socially desirable or acceptable answers
    c. an experiment involves the manipulation of variables; experimenter bias refers to the experimenter holding expectations that influence the outcome of the study
    d. an experiment involves the manipulation of variables; informed consent is an ethical guideline that requires researchers to inform their research participants
    p. 51

13. a. no; an interview is a face-to-face method whereby the participant is asked questions
    b. no; a random sample is a sample that is selected from the population at random
    c. no; an experiment involves the manipulation of variables and subject groups
    d. YES; a case study is an in-depth look at a single individual
    p. 52

14. a.  no, this is usually not a problem in an experiment
    b.  no, this tendency is unrelated to correlational studies
    c.  YES, this is one of the problems of surveys
    d.  incorrect
    p. 51

15. a.  this option describes a random sample
    b.  standardized tests are used by several different types of psychologists
    c.  CORRECT; these tests provide information about individual differences
    d.  standardized tests are not given in real-world settings
    p. 51

16. a.  this may be true, but it is not the main advantage
    b.  only experimentation can determine cause and effect
    c.  THAT'S RIGHT; standardized tests give information about individual differences
    d.  standardized tests can be biased against certain groups of people
    p. 52

17. a.  experimental research consists of manipulation of variables and subject groups
    b.  case studies provide an in-depth look at an individual
    c.  physiological research studies the biological basis of behavior
    d.  TRUE; correlational research examines relationships
    p. 53

18. a.  the experiment determines cause-and-effect relationships
    b.  no, since naturalistic observation does not attempt to control variables
    c.  YES, THAT'S RIGHT; correlational research attempts to determine the relationship between variables
    d.  this is incorrect
    p. 53

19. a.  no; correlation does not indicate causation
    b.  no; correlation does not indicate causation
    c.  incorrect; while we cannot say that one causes the other, the correlation does indicate that there is a relationship
    d.  YES; a positive correlation indicates that these two factors vary in the same direction, even if we don't know which causes which or if there are other factors that could be contributing to this relationship
    p. 54

20. a.  correlational research only determines relationships among variables and it is usually used when the researcher cannot control the factors of interest
    b.  this method by definition does not have any control over the factors influencing the observations
    c.  RIGHT; experimental research can determine cause and effect between events because it controls factors and manipulates precisely the variables of interest
    d.  no; in an interview, the researcher chooses which questions to ask but does not seek to control every aspect of the procedure
    p. 56

21. a. no; the numbers of the correlation coefficient range from −1 to +1, and the farther away the number from 0, the stronger is the relationship between the two factors
    b. YES; the sign is the indicator of the direction of the relationship; if the sign is positive, the factors vary in the same direction, and if the sign is negative the factors vary in opposite directions
    c. no; the level of significance is a measure relevant to inferential statistics and is not used in correlations
    d. no; the correlation coefficient is a statistic, but placing the concept "statistic" at that point in the sentence does not make sense
    p. 53

22. a. no
    b. no
    c. YES
    d. no
    p. 60

## Practice Test 2

1. a. a case study consists of an in-depth analysis of a single individual
   b. an interview is a face-to-face questioning of another person
   c. in correlational research, we examine the relationship between two or more events
   d. CORRECT; the experiment can help psychologists determine the causes of behavior
   p. 56

2. a. partially correct; the different teaching methods are the independent variable, but the dependent variable is not the number of students the taking test, which is irrelevant
   b. partially correct; student performance is not the independent variable, but student performance could be measured by grades on a test
   c. TOTALLY CORRECT; the different teaching methods are being manipulated (cause), and student performance is the dependent variable (effect) (it is being measured)
   d. no; they arc backward
   p. 56

3. a. no; the dependent variable is being measured to detect change that the manipulation of the independent variable might have caused
   b. CORRECT; the cause is the independent variable and the effect is the dependent variable
   c. no; the control group acts as a comparison; the dependent variable is the effect that is being measured because of changes to it due to manipulation
   d. no; the dependent variable is being measured to detect change that the manipulation of the independent variable might have caused; the experimental group is the group that receives the manipulation
   p. 56

4. a. no; the dependent variable is learning
   b. no
   c. YES; the amphetamine is the "cause" that is being manipulated
   d. no
   p. 56

5. a.   the experimental group receives the manipulation; the measured factor is the dependent variable
   b.   the control group acts as a comparison group; the measured factor is the dependent variable
   c.   the manipulated factor is the independent variable; the experimental group receivesthe manipulation
   d.   THAT'S RIGHT; the experimenter manipulates the independent variable and determines what, if any, changes occurred in the dependent variable
   p. 56

6. a.   RIGHT; this is the control group
   b.   the sample that is selected from the population should be a representative sample
   c.   the experimental group receives the special treatment
   d.   both groups make up the random sample
   p. 56

7. a.   psychologists from all specializations conduct experiments
   b.   combining methods is something that is often done and is appropriate when required
   c.   experiments involve the independent variable and the dependent variable
   d.   correct, correlations do not indicate causation.
   p. 55

8. a.   no; this is a very important issue
   b.   gender differences are often exaggerated
   c.   YEAH; this is the least important
   d.   research topics often reflect a male bias
   p. 67

9. a.   this is true; while it took time and negotiations, Calkins did work with James at Harvard
   b.   this is true; Wellesley, like Smith, where she studied, were both schools committed to the higher education of women
   c.   this is true; after working with William James, Calkins established this program at Wellesley.
   d.   CORRECT ANSWER; Calkins's career lasted nearly 40 years and she was recognized by her peers by becoming the first female president of the American Psychological Association
   p. 40

10. a.   no; philosophers may address the same issues, but they are not subject to the scientific methods that define a science
    b.   YES; the way the information is collected, in other words, the methods used, are what define and distinguish a science from other approaches
    c.   incorrect; collaboration is very important in the development of a science
    d.   incorrect; objectivity is one of the four ideals that are central to the scientific approach
    p. 40

11. a.   this is central to a science
    b.   this is central to a science
    c.   this is central to a science
    d.   RIGHT ANSWER; while sensitivity may be considered a valuable characteristic in a person, it is not one of the attitudes central to the scientific approach; to a certain extent, sensitivity could be construed as bias, and this tendency goes against the ideal of objectivity
    p. 40

12. a. this is one of the best ways to collaborate, by sharing information and taking advantage of the feedback that they may receive during the conference
    b. this is also one of the main ways in which scientists collaborate
    c. RIGHT ANSWER; avoiding replicating the studies of others is not in the spirit of collaboration; . when scientists replicate the studies of others they add very important information that can serve to support or disprove the hypotheses and theories proposed by others
    d. this is also a common form of collaboration; however, publishing in a prestigious journal requires a lot of work on the part of the scientist
    p. 42

13. a. CORRECT; while this is an important activity that contributes to scientific collaboration, it is not an essential step of the scientific method
    b. this is the second step of the scientific method
    c. this is the third step of the scientific method
    d. this is the fourth and last step of the scientific method
    p. 42

14. a. this is not a theory but a general approach to scientific investigations
    b. while there are theories of statistics, this is a conceptual theory not a mathematical theory
    c. this is not a theory but a procedure of sample selection
    d. YES; the theory of catharsis, originally created by Freud, was further developed by Pennebaker.
    p. 44

15. a. incorrect; this would not have been a good idea, since a week's period is too brief
    b. incorrect; only assessing their health before the study would not have been useful in determining if the catharsis had any effect on health
    c. CORRECT; the researchers asked for the number of times the participants visited the health center before, during, and after they participated in the study
    d. incorrect; the physical condition at the time of the study may have influenced their performance in the study but would not have been informative regarding the longer term effects of catharsis on health
    p. 45

16. a. no
    b. no
    c. incorrect; the population is larger than the sample; therefore, the statement does not make sense
    d. CORRECT; in almost all scientific studies, the scientist cannot study the complete population of interest and therefore must select a sample; in order to generalize the findings to the population, however, the sample must be representative
    p. 45

17. a. no; generalizability is the extent to which the results of one study with a sample can be generalized to the population
    b. CORRECT
    c. no; objectivity is one of the four ideal approaches to science
    d. no; randomness refers to the extent to which an event is due to chance
    p. 47

18. a. no
    b. no
    c. no
    d. CORRECT; while philosophers may address many of the same issues as do psychologists, they do not use the scientific method in the same manner
    p. 47

19. a. CORRECT; notice that unobtrusive means that investigators try not exert any influence or effect on those that are being observed; instead, they try to blend into the situation
    b. no; in laboratories the observations are obtrusive, since the participants do know that they are being observed and studied
    c. no; data collected through naturalistic observation may be analyzed with the correlational statistical procedure, but the correlational method is not limited to the use of data collected in real-world settings or in unobtrusive manners
    d. no; surveys may be collected in real-world settings, such as the mall, but they are obtrusive, since the participant does know that they are being studied
    p. 50

20. a. no; this is the most common score
    b. no; this is the score right in the middle of the distribution of scores
    c. YES; this is what we commonly associate with an average score
    d. no; this is a measure of variability, not of central tendency
    p. 59

21. a. no; this is the median
    b. no; this is the mean
    c. YES; the mode is the most common or typical score.
    d. no; this is the range
    p. 60

## Practice Test 3

1. a. no
   b. YES; they were challenging what others took for granted, which was that the studies done by male researchers with male participants would apply to males and females
   c. no
   d. no
   p. 41

2. a. YES; the type of color, vivid versus subtle, was the independent variable
   b. no; the participants are neither the independent variable nor the dependent variable
   c. no; this is the dependent variable
   d. no; this is another way of expressing the dependent variable
   p. 56

3. a. no; while with an interview the researcher may be able to ask participants about their caffeine intake and even give an essay to ask for details, the tendency for social desirability is likely to have an influence on the recollection of information
   b. no; finding out information about caffeine intake and memory from one individual would not answer this researcher's general question about the effects of caffeine on memory
   c. no; with this method the researcher would not be very likely to collect the information she needs to make any conclusions about caffeine and memory
   d. YES; the experiment is the most appropriate method for this research question; in an experiment the researcher will be able to manipulate the amount of ounces of caffeine the

participants take, then have participants read the essay; then the researcher systematically measures the details the participants remember

p. 56

4. a. incorrect; a correlation coefficient of 0 means that there is no relationship
   b. incorrect; this statement suggests causation, which cannot be concluded from a correlation coefficient
   c. YES; the positive and strong correlation coefficient says that these two factors vary in the same direction; we could also say that the higher the attendance, the higher the final grade in the class
   d. incorrect; this statement is consistent with a negative correlation coefficient

p. 54

5. a. no; a person who is feeling bad as a result of the loss of a loved one does not necessarily need the help of a clinical psychologist, since it is normal to be upset and emotional under such circumstances
   b. no; this recommendation would not be consistent with Pennebaker's research on catharsis
   c. YES; Pennebarker found that when people write about their negative emotions they experience a type of catharsis that allows them to move on to a more positive experience
   d. no; this is similar to item b in that it does not address the research done by Pennebaker on catharsis

p. 44

6. a. no; this sample of adult males who are also Roman Catholic is not representative of all males
   b. no; while this would be the most common way to recruit participants for a study, this would not be a representative sample of all males
   c. no; while this option is better than option b because it integrates males from different cultures, it is still limited to males from universities in powerful countries
   d. YES; while this sample has only American males, the fact that it is randomly selected from a list that includes males older than 18 would allow the researchers to get participants of various ages and from all of the United States

p. 45

7. a. no; magazines are chosen by the reader and cannot use random sampling
   b. YES; generalizability to the people that did not complete the survey is compromised by the specific characteristics of those who did complete the survey
   c. no; surveys in magazines can be very good and about important topics, they are just not likely to get a representative sample, unless their population of interest is only the people that choose to answer the survey
   d. no; surveys in magazines can be very well constructed

p. 45

8. a. no; the observation that two clinical psychologists concluded the same diagnosis does not indicate that it is changeable or not
   b. no; catharsis may help depression, but it has nothing to do with the agreement in the diagnosis
   c. YES; reliability is the extent to which research (which is what clinical psychologists do when they interview a client) yields consistent, reproducible results
   d. no; a case study cannot be correlated with another study; correlations require many observations

p. 47

9. a. YES; this is the correct answer because you should write about what bothers you now and not focus on larger traumas that may be in the past
   b. no; this is one of the recommendations; you want to focus on getting the emotions out and not on the details of how it reads
   c. no; this is one of the recommendations, since you should not feel forced to explore your emotions
   d. no; this is one of the recommendations, since people might inhibit their expression if they are thinking that others will read their work
   p. 48

10. a. no; naturalistic observation does not manipulate the environment
    b. no; experimental methods are obtrusive
    c. no; there is no independent variable to be manipulated in naturalistic observation
    d. YES; experimental methods are characterized by this manipulation of the environment in which the observations take place
    pp. 50, 56

11. a. no; standardized tests are designed for the purpose of comparing people
    b. YES; unfortunately, if a test is standardized based on scores of individuals from one culture, the standardization may not apply to people from another culture
    c. no; standardized tests do measure appropriately the performance of an individual
    d. no; comparing people in psychological factors is a valid research endeavor
    p. 52

12. a. no; the question does not mention correlation of any two variables
    b. no; studying a real organization would not be very effective in a laboratory
    c. YES; a case study of the CEO would be very informative on psychological issues of leadership in organizations
    d. no; unless the researcher becomes an employee and is able to participate in meetings at high levels in the organization in order to observe the CEO, this would not be the best method
    p. 52

13. a. CORRECT; -.68 is a strong negative correlation between cold, which goes up, and people going outside, which goes down. Notice that the item does not make reference to measuring of temperature. Change the item to mean the same, but instead of using "cold" use the corresponding description of temperature, "lower temperature," and see how the correlation coefficient changes.
    b. no; this is a positive correlation
    c. no; this is a positive correlation
    d. no; this presents no correlation
    p. 53

14. a. no; this is the dependent variable
    b. no; the participants are not a variable
    c. YES; the time lapse is the independent variable
    d. no; this is not a variable, but rather a control group
    p. 56

15. a. CORRECT; this is what the researchers measured and wanted to see if the independent variable of odor would influence
    b. no; this is the independent variable
    c. no; this is one of the experimental conditions
    d. no; this is part of the procedure and may be considered an independent variable if the researcher also varied the time spent in the room before measuring the mood
    p. 56

16. a. YES; the numbers of the correlation coefficient range from −1 to +1, and the farther away the number from 0, the stronger the relationship between the two factors
    b. no; the sign is the indicator of the direction of the relationship
    c. no; the level of significance is a measure relevant to inferential statistics and is not used in correlations
    d. no; the correlation coefficient is a statistic, but placing the concept "statistic" at that point in the sentence does not make sense
    p. 53

17. a. this is one of the main problems with laboratory studies: participants, when they know they are being observed and studied, may modify their behaviors and act "unnaturally"
    b. this has been a longstanding criticism of research depending on university samples, which may not be as culturally diverse as the population of interest
    c. CORRECT; this is not a drawback, this is the main asset of laboratory research
    d. laboratories cannot be used to study all the issues of interest in psychology, because many aspects of psychology cannot and should not be controlled
    p. 49

18. a. no; in elections we don't average votes
    b. no; this measure would be irrelevant
    c. YES; the mode is the score that occurs most often in a set of data; each time a person votes for candidate A this can be considered a score for A and the same for candidate B, etc.; the score that occurs more often (A, B, or C) determines who wins
    d. no; this is irrelevant
    p. 60

19. a. no; this is a measure of central tendency, and the statement is asking about a measure of variability
    b. no; while this is a measure of variability, it does not assess the extent to which the scores vary from the mean
    c. YES; the standard deviation does measure how much on the average scores vary around the mean
    d. no; this is a measure of central tendency
    p. 61

20. a. no; descriptive statistics are not used to test hypotheses, just to summarize the data
    b. YES; these types of statistics are used to draw inferences and test if the proposed hypotheses are supported by the data collected
    c. no; while there are some statistical procedures that are almost exclusively used by psychologists, "psychological statistics" is not the same as inferential statistics
    d. no; "mathematical statistics" is a redundant and incorrect concept because statistics *are* mathematics
    p. 61

# Chapter 3—The Brain and Behavior

## Learning Goals

1. Discuss the nature and basic functions of the nervous system.
2. Explain what neurons are and how they process information.
3. Identify the brain's levels and structures, and summarize the functions of its structures.
4. State what the endocrine system is and how it affects behavior.
5. Explain how genetics and evolutionary psychology increase our understanding of behavior.

*After studying Chapter 3, you will be able to:*

- Describe what the nervous system is and discuss what the field of neuroscience is about.
- Explain how the nervous system is organized.
- Describe what neurons are and how they process information.
- Understand the role of glial cells in the nervous system.
- Describe the process through which neurons communicate with one another, including the role of neurotransmitters.
- Outline the structures and functions of the hindbrain, midbrain, and forebrain.
- Explain how the cerebral cortex is organized and discuss its functions.
- Understand the role of the endocrine system in psychology.
- State some basic ideas about heredity, the evolutionary perspective, and how genetics and the environment interact to influence behavior.

## CHAPTER 3: OUTLINE

- The brain is a complex, versatile, and flexible network that controls our behaviors and mental processes.

- The evolutionary psychology approach, which emphasizes the importance of adaptation, reproduction, and natural selection in explaining psychology, considers how the human nervous system has evolved to its complex present state.

- Most scientists believe that behavior is determined by the interaction of the environment and the organism's biological inheritance.

- The nervous system is made up of interconnected nerve cells that transmit information throughout the body. There are four defining characteristics of the nervous system: (1) it communicates via electrochemical transmission; (2) it is characterized by its complexity, since the brain alone is composed of billions of nerve cells; (3) it can integrate information from many sources and create a coherent psychological experience; and (4) it has a great capacity to adapt to changes in the environment and the body.

- The capacity of the brain to adapt is termed *plasticity.*

- Cells that carry input to the brain are called *sensory neurons;* those that carry output from the brain are called *motor neurons.* Most of the communication in the nervous system takes place through neural networks, which are nerve cells that integrate sensory input and motor output.

- The nervous system is divided into the central nervous system and the peripheral nervous system. The central nervous system consists of the brain and the spinal cord.

- The peripheral nervous system connects the brain and the spinal cord to the other parts of the body. The peripheral nervous system is divided into the somatic nervous system, which contains sensory and motor nerves, and the autonomic nervous system, which monitors the body's internal organs.

- There are two types of nerve cells: neurons and glial cells. The neurons are in charge of communication, and the glial cells support and nourish the neurons. A neuron is made of (1) a cell body, which regulates the cell's growth and maintenance; (2) dendrites, which collect information for the neuron; and (3) an axon, which carries information away from the cell body to other cells. Most axons are covered with a layer of fat cells called the *myelin sheath*, which insulates the axon and speeds up the impulse.

- Neurons send information down the axon in the form of waves of electricity called the *action potential*. The neuron has a cell membrane that allows certain substances to enter the cell and other substances to exit the cell. The action potential operates according to the all-or-none principle.

- Each axon branches out into numerous fibers that store substances called *neurotransmitters*. When the electrochemical wave arrives at the end of an axon, the neurotransmitter is released onto the synapse, the tiny gap between neurons. The neurotransmitters carry the message across the synapse to the receiving dendrite or cell body of the next neuron.

- Dendrites and some soma have receptor sites, which are neurotransmitter specific. The most common analogy is that of a lock and key. The neurotransmitter is the key and the receptor site is the lock.

- When the neurotransmitter latches onto a receptor site, it initiates an electrochemical wave in the receiving neuron. This is how neurons communicate! However, some neurotransmitters are inhibitory, which means that when they latch onto a receptor site, they keep the next neuron from starting an action potential. The neurotransmitters that stimulate other neurons to start the action potential are referred to as *excitatory*.

- Chapter 2 includes a discussion of six neurotransmitters that are very important in the human nervous system: acetylcholine, GABA, norepinephrine, dopamine, serotonin, and endorphins.

- Glial cells provide support and nutritive functions for neurons.

- The neural communication is the foundation of our psychology. Whenever we have an experience, say stepping on a sharp stone, a number of neurons are stimulated and neural communication takes place throughout the nervous system. Some of those neurons will control your movements as you retrieve your foot and regain your balance; they will communicate again in the future when you recall the event and when a similar experience occurs.

- The brain consists of the hindbrain, the midbrain, and the forebrain.

- The hindbrain is the lowest portion of the brain and consists of the medulla, the cerebellum, and the pons.

- The midbrain is an area where many nerve-fibers ascend and descend and relay information between the brain and the eyes and ears. An important structure of the midbrain is the reticular formation.

- The highest region of the brain is the forebrain. Its major structures include the limbic system, thalamus, basal ganglia, hypothalamus, and cerebral cortex. Each performs certain specialized functions involving emotion, memory, senses, movement, stress, and pleasure.

- The cerebral cortex consitutes the largest part of the brain and comprises two hemispheres (left and right) and four lobes (occipital, temporal, parietal, and frontal). The cerebral cortex consists of the sensory cortex, the motor cortex, and the association cortex. The two hemispheres are connected by the corpus callosum. No complex function can be assigned to one single hemisphere or the other. There is interplay between the two hemispheres.

- A number of important body reactions produced by the autonomic nervous system result from its action on the endocrine glands. The endocrine system is a set of glands (pituitary, thyroid, parathyroid, adrenal, pancreas, and the ovaries in women and the testes in men) that regulate the activities of certain organs by releasing hormones into the bloodstream. The anterior part of the pituitary is called the *master gland*; it is controlled by the hypothalamus. The adrenal glands play an important role in mood, energy, and stress.

- Our psychology has genetic and evolutionary foundations. The last part of Chapter 2 explores the basic concepts of genetics and heredity. The nucleus of each human cell contains 46 chromosomes (23 pairs) that contain DNA.

- Genes, the units of hereditary information, are short segments of chromosomes.

- Genes combine with other genes to determine our characteristics. There are dominant and recessive genes.

- Polygenic inheritance is the effect that multiple genes have on behaviors and mental processes.

- The study of genetics has progressed from the basic experiments of Mendel to molecular genetics and the development of genomes. The Human Genome Project strives to describe the complete set of instructions for making a human being. There are great expectations for this project to contribute to the understanding of physical disease and mental disorders. Genetic methods include selective breeding and behavior genetics.

- Psychologists now face the challenge of finding theoretical frameworks that successfully integrate the biological foundations of psychology and research in genetics and neuroscience with the wealth of psychological theories that explore the influences of the environment and experiences on human psychology.

## Building Blocks of Chapter 3

### Clarifying some of the tricky points in Chapter 3
### and
### In Your Own Words

*To respond to the questions and exercises presented in the "In Your Own Words" section, please write your thoughts, perspectives, and reactions on a separate piece of paper.*

### *The Nervous System*

The body's electrochemical communication circuitry is known as the *nervous system;* the field that studies this system is called *neuroscience.* The four characteristics of the nervous system are *complexity, integration, adaptability,* and *electrochemical transmission.* The capacity of the nervous system to adapt is reflected in *plasticity,* which is the capacity of the brain to modify and change. This means with experience our brain literally changes!

When neurons communicate with one another they use chemicals, called *neurotransmitters.* Our nervous system is divided into two parts: the *central nervous system (CNS)* and the *peripheral nervous system (PNS)*. The CNS consists of the *brain and spinal cord*; the PNS *connects the brain and spinal cord to other parts of the body.*

The peripheral nervous system consists of two major divisions: one, which contains both sensory nerves and motor nerves, is called the *somatic nervous system*. The other, which monitors breathing, heart rate, and digestion, is the *autonomic nervous system*. The autonomic nervous system is divided into the *sympathetic nervous system*, which helps arouse the body, and the *parasympathetic nervous system*, which helps calm the body.

### In Your Own Words

*Please write your thoughts, perspectives, and reactions on a separate piece of paper.*
✓ *What are some circumstances in which the sympathetic nervous system is activated? In these circumstances, what advantage does one gain from the sympathetic nervous system being activated?*

### Neurons

There are two types of cells in the nervous system: *neurons* and *glial cells*.

### Helpful Hints for Understanding Neuropsychology

#### Helpful Hint #1:

*Neurons are the cells that process information; the glial cells provide support and nutrition in the nervous system. Think of the glial cells as the caretakers of the neurons. There are many more glial cells in the human brain than there are neurons, so we know neurons need nutrition and support to function well.*

Neurons have three parts: *dendrites, cell body,* and *axon*. The part of the neuron that *receives information is the dendrite*; the part that *carries the information away* from the cell body is the *axon*.

Neurons send messages by creating a brief wave of electrical charge; this charge is called an *action potential*. The action potential abides by the *all-or-none principle*. Each axon branches out into numerous fibers that store those chemicals called *neurotransmitters*. These are chemicals that are released onto the *synapse,* the tiny gap between neurons.

*Acetylcholine* is a neurotransmitter involved in the actions of muscles, learning, and memory. *GABA* is a neurotransmitter that *inhibits* the firing of neurons. Too little of the neurotransmitter *norepinephrine* is associated with *depression*, and too much is linked to agitated, *manic* states. Low levels of the neurotransmitter *dopamine* are associated with *Parkinson's disease*. A neurotransmitter that is involved in the regulation of *sleep and attention is serotonin*. Finally, neurotransmitters that seem to function as *natural opiates* are called *endorphins*.

#### Helpful Hint #2:

*A release of endorphins is what runners experience when they say they have a "runners high." You may have experienced that same feeling after a workout at the gym or other physical exercise.*

### Structures of the Brain and Their Functions

There are three major divisions of the brain: *hindbrain, midbrain,* and *forebrain*. The hindbrain contains the *medulla*, which helps control *breathing*. The *cerebellum* is believed to help control *movement*. The *pons* is a *bridge* in the hindbrain involved in *sleep and arousal*.

The *midbrain* is involved in the *relay of information between the brain and the hindbrain and forebrain*. A midbrain structure called the *reticular formation* is involved in *stereotyped patterns of behavior*.

The *highest region* of the brain is called the *forebrain*. A forebrain structure that plays important roles in both memory and emotion is the *limbic system*. One main part of the limbic system is the *amygdala*, which is *important in the organism's survival and emotion*. Another part of the limbic system, the *hippocampus*, plays a role in the storage of *memory*. (Hint: if you saw a *hippo* walking across your *campus*, you would *remember* it!) A *forebrain structure* that serves mainly as a *relay station* is called the *thalamus*. The forebrain structure that *regulates eating, drinking, and sex* is called the *hypothalamus*. Olds and Milner's rat research in the 1950s pointed to the existence of a *pleasure center* in the hypothalamus. Their research has important implications for drug addiction.

The largest part if the brain in volume is the *cerebral cortex*, which is divided into two halves, called *hemispheres*. Each is half divided into four *lobes*. The *temporal* lobe processes visual information; hearing is associated with the *occipital* lobe; control of the voluntary muscles, personality and intelligence is associated with the *frontal* lobe. The parietal lobe is involved in body sensation.

The *corpus callosum* is a large bundle of axons connecting the two cerebral hemispheres. Speech and grammar are localized to the *left hemisphere*, which mainly controls this ability in most people. Understanding aspects of language such humor and metaphors is localized in the *right hemisphere*, which is involved in the processing of nonverbal information. Researchers believe that complex thinking involves both sides of the brain.

### In Your Own Words

*Please write your thoughts, perspectives, and reactions on a separate piece of paper.*
✓ *Imagine that an evil scientist kidnaps you to study your brain. In his diabolical investigation, he must destroy one part of your brain. He asks you, "What part of the brain are you willing to give up for my diabolical investigation?" So, what part of the brain would you give up and why?*

### The Endocrine System

The endocrine system is a set of *glands* that regulates the activities of organisms by releasing *hormones* into the *bloodstream*. Among the important endocrine glands are (1) the gland that sits at the base of the skull, called the *pituitary gland*, and (2) the *adrenal glands*, which secrete *epinephrine and norepinephrine* and which play an important role in our *moods, our energy level, and our ability to cope with stress*.

### Genetic and Evolutionary Blueprints of Behavior

The nucleus of each human cell has *46 chromosomes*. Chromosomes contain *DNA*, a complex molecule that contains genetic information. Short segments of chromosomes that carry hereditary information are termed *genes*. Each person has *two genes for each hereditary characteristic*.

According to the dominant-recessive genes principle, the *dominant* gene exerts its influence. A recessive gene exerts its influence only when the two genes of a pair are both *recessive*. The term *polygenic inheritance* refers to the influence of multiple genes on behavior.

Three of the fields dedicated to the study of genetics are *molecular genetics, selective breeding, and behavioral genetics*. The Human Genome Project is an effort to identify all the genes in human DNA and map them. *Selective breeding* is a genetic method in which organisms are selected for reproduction based on how much of a particular trait they have. *Behavior genetics* is the study of the degree to which heredity influences behavior. One form of behavior genetics is the study of twins. *Identical twins* develop from a single fertilized egg, whereas *fraternal twins* develop from separate eggs fertilized by separate sperm.

A contemporary view that emphasizes the importance of adaptation, reproduction, and the survival of the fittest in explaining behavior is called the *evolutionary psychology approach*. Scientists warn that while evolution has shaped our body structures and biological potential, it did not give us behavioral dictates.

### In Your Own Words
*Please write your thoughts, perspectives, and reactions on a separate piece of paper.*
✓ *Think of five possible applications for the Human Genome Project.*

## Correcting the Incorrect

Carefully read each statement. Determine if the statement is correct or incorrect. If the statement is incorrect, make the necessary changes to correct it. Then check the answer key at the end of the chapter for the correct statement and page reference in the textbook.

1. The human nervous system is made up of approximately one million cells.
2. In general, the brains of individuals with epilepsy do not work effectively between seizures.
3. Motor nerves are the ones that carry sensory information to the brain.
4. Neural networks integrate sensory information and motor instructions from the brain.
5. The two main parts of the nervous system are the central nervous system and the autonomic nervous system.
6. The parasympathetic nervous system consists of the brain and the spinal cord.
7. The somatic nervous system consists of sensory nerves.
8. The sympathetic nervous system is involved when we are in a relaxed state.
9. Nerves are the basic unit of the nervous system.
10. Glial cells transmit messages throughout the nervous system.
11. The neurons consist of a cell body, dendrites, and axon.
12. The wave of electricity within the axon is called the resting potential.
13. The gap between neurons is called the axon.
14. Neurotransmitters move across the synapse.
15. GABA, dopamine, and serotonin are examples of endorphins.
16. Neural networks, once created, are static and cannot be changed.
17. A structure in the hindbrain is the reticular formation.
18. The medulla plays important roles in motor behavior.
19. The thalamus plays an important role in memory and emotion.
20. A person suffering damage to the hippocampus would be unable to see.
21. The Olds studies have important implications for research on Alzheimer's disease.
22. The occipital lobe is involved in hearing.
23. The parietal lobe is involved in bodily sensation.
24. The large bundle of axons that connects the brain's two hemisphere is called the pons.
25. The left hemisphere is associated with humor.
26. Endocrine glands release their chemicals directly into the brain.

27. The pituitary gland regulates mood, energy levels, and the ability to cope with stress.
28. Chromosomes are made up of genes.
29. A recessive gene can exert influence even if only one gene is recessive.
30. Behavioral genetics involves the manipulation of genes using technology to determine their effects on behavior.
31. Evolutionary psychologists believe that the specialized brain functions evolved because they helped humans adapt to the challenges of the environment.

## Practice Test 1

1. The nervous system is made up of _____ of interconnected cells.
   a. approximately ten thousand
   b. billions
   c. approximately one million
   d. less than one million

2. Which of the following is NOT one of the characteristics of the nervous system?
   a. integration
   b. adaptability
   c. simplicity
   d. electrochemical transmission

3. _____ is the brain's capacity to modify and change.
   a. Plasticity
   b. Integration
   c. Electrochemical transmission
   d. Evolution

4. Which of the following types of nerves carry input to the brain?
   a. sensory nerves
   b. motor nerves
   c. interneurons
   d. foreneurons

5. The majority of the brain consists of which type of nerves?
   a. sensory nerves
   b. motor nerves
   c. neural networks
   d. axons

6. The brain and the spinal cord constitute the
   a. central nervous system.
   b. peripheral nervous system.
   c. autonomic nervous system.
   d. sympathetic nervous system.

7. When you accidentally touch a hot burner on a stove, which part of your nervous system carries the pain message from your skin to your brain?
   a. the autonomic nervous system
   b. the sympathetic nervous system
   c. the parasympathetic nervous system
   d. the somatic nervous system

8. The physiological arousal that you feel as you enter a classroom to take an exam is produced by the _____ nervous system.
   a. parasympathetic
   b. sympathetic
   c. somatic
   d. central

9. Messages from other neurons are collected by the _____ of the receiving neuron.
   a. axon
   b. synapse
   c. neurotransmitter
   d. dendrite

10. The part of the neuron that carries messages away from the cell body is called the
    a. nucleus.
    b. axon.
    c. dendrite.
    d. neurotransmitter.

11. The _____ is the brief wave of electrical change that races down the axon.
    a. action potential
    b. achievement potential
    c. all-or-none principle
    d. ion

12. A neurotransmitter associated with schizophrenia is
    a. GABA.
    b. acetylcholine.
    c. dopamine.
    d. norepinephrine.

13. If a person has a low level of dopamine, this would most likely cause which problem?
    a. The person would have difficulty with walking.
    b. The person would suffer from anxiety.
    c. The person would suffer from depression.
    d. The person would have sleep problems.

14. The hindbrain structure that helps to control our breathing is called the
    a. pons.
    b. reticular formation.
    c. medulla.
    d. cerebellum.

15. The _____ is the forebrain structure that monitors eating, drinking, and sexual behavior.
    a.    thalamus
    b.    hypothalamus
    c.    neocortex
    d.    cerebellum

16. A forebrain structure that plays an important role in the storage of memories is the
    a.    hippocampus.
    b.    amygdala.
    c.    thalamus.
    d.    limbic system.

17. Which of the following is not one of the lobes of the neocortex?
    a.    occipital
    b.    frontal
    c.    temporal
    d.    posterior

18. Research about various brain areas indicates that higher mental processes such as thinking and problem solving are located within the
    a.    association area.
    b.    parietal sulcus.
    c.    limbic system.
    d.    thalamic nuclei.

19. The two hemispheres are connected by which structure?
    a.    corpus callosum
    b.    thalamus
    c.    hypothalamus
    d.    reticular formation

20. Dr. Beenken is working on one of the largest scientific projects ever done. Her responsibility is to map out the 19th chromosome pair. She is working on
    a.    the evolutionary perspective.
    b.    the Mankato Nun study.
    c.    split brain research.
    d.    the Human Genome Project.

21. Genes are short segments of _____ that are composed of _____.
    a.    neurons; glial cells
    b.    chromosomes; dopamine
    c.    chromosomes; DNA
    d.    DNA; chromosomes

22. The dominant-recessive genes principle applies to all the following except which one?
    a.    A recessive gene exerts its influence only if both genes of a pair are recessive.
    b.    Dominant genes override the effect of a recessive gene.
    c.    If one gene of a pair is dominant and one is recessive, the dominant gene exerts its effect.
    d.    If both genes of a pair are dominant, the effect converts into a recessive trait.

23.     According to evolutionary psychology, fears and phobias are related to
        a.      the inheritance of recessive genes.
        b.      the inheritance of dominant genes.
        c.      successful survival and reproduction.
        d.      low rate of survival and reproduction.

## Practice Test 2

1.      The part of the nervous system that includes the brain and the spinal cord is the
        a.      central nervous system.
        b.      peripheral nervous system.
        c.      autonomous nervous system.
        d.      somatic nervous system.

2.      Glial cells
        a.      are fewer in number than neurons.
        b.      have dendrites just like neurons.
        c.      provide supportive and nutritive functions in the brain.
        d.      are specialized to send and receive information.

3.      Which division of the nervous system is the one involved in relaxation and the calming of the body?
        a.      somatic
        b.      central
        c.      sympathetic
        d.      parasympathetic

4.      Most neurons have _____ dendrites.
        a.      many
        b.      one
        c.      no
        d.      myelinated

5.      The tiny holes on the cell membrane of neurons are termed
        a.      dendrites.
        b.      channels.
        c.      axons.
        d.      cell bodies.

6.      The layer of fat cells that insulate most axons is the
        a.      myelin sheath.
        b.      cell body.
        c.      plasticity.
        d.      ion.

7.      Which neurotransmitter is the one that is involved in the action of muscles, learning, and memory?
        a.      dopamine
        b.      acetylcholine
        c.      GABA
        d.      norepinephrine

8.    Which of the parts of the hindbrain is the one that is involved in motor coordination?
      a.    medulla
      b.    cerebellum
      c.    pons
      d.    reticular formation

9.    This system in the midbrain is involved in the control of walking, sleeping, and turning to attend sudden noise.
      a.    pons
      b.    brain stem
      c.    reticular formation
      d.    hypothalamus

10.   The "pleasure center" discovered by Olds and Milner is found in the
      a.    thalamus.
      b.    midbrain.
      c.    hippocampus.
      d.    hypothalamus.

11.   The lobe that is associated with the control of voluntary muscles, intelligence, and personality is the _____ lobe.
      a.    frontal
      b.    occipital
      c.    temporal
      d.    parietal

12.   The association cortex constitutes _____% of the entire cerebral cortex.
      a.    10
      b.    50
      c.    75
      d.    99.9

13.   Which of the following functions has NOT been associated with the left hemisphere of the cerebral cortex?
      a.    speech
      b.    grammar
      c.    humor
      d.    mathematics

14.   The _____ controls growth and regulates other glands, and part of it is controlled by the hypothalamus.
      a.    adrenal gland
      b.    spinal cord
      c.    pituitary gland
      d.    thalamus

## Practice Test 3

1.    The hypothalamus can be described best as a(n)
      a.    screen.
      b.    subordinate.
      c.    regulator.
      d.    advisor.

2. Which of the following descriptions of the brain correspond to the characteristic of integration?
   a. The brain is composed of billions of brain cells.
   b. The brain has plasticity.
   c. Behaving in a coordinated way requires a lot of connections in your brain.
   d. The brain is powered by electrical impulses.

3. When people are unexpectedly tapped on the shoulder from behind, they usually turn around pretty quickly. This is not a reflex, but it requires some pretty fast neural transmissions. When the person senses the tapping on the shoulder, which nerves are the ones transmitting information to the brain?
   a. sensory nerves
   b. motor nerves
   c. movement nerves
   d. glial cells

4. Jack stayed up until 3:00 a.m. studying for a test the next day, but by that time he could barely keep a posture and was too sleepy to continue. Which division of the nervous system was the one that initiated the set of psychological experiences of Jack at 3:00 a.m.?
   a. the somatic nervous system
   b. the parasympathetic nervous system
   c. the sympathetic nervous system
   d. the spinal cord

5. The input is to the _____ as the output is to the _____.
   a. axon; dendrite
   b. cell body; dendrite
   c. dendrite; cell body
   d. dendrite; axon

6. Fernanda was bitten by a black widow spider while on a trek. Which of the following neural activities did she experience?
   a. The level of norepinephrine was reduced.
   b. The level of dopamine was increased.
   c. Acetylcholine overflowed the nervous system.
   d. GABA was increased.

7. Which of the following neurotransmitters is not involved in the regulation of sleeping patterns?
   a. endorphins
   b. serotonin
   c. norepinephrine
   d. acetylcholine

8. The drug morphine reduces pain because it mimics the effects of _____.
   a. GABA
   b. acetylcholine
   c. endorphins
   d. serotonin

9. The reason why a person feels relaxed and uninhibited after a couple of alcoholic drinks is because alcohol blocks the activity of
   a. endorphins.
   b. acetylcholine.
   c. GABA.
   d. serotonin.

10. The most common myth about hemispheric specialization is that
   a. speech and grammar are localized in the left hemisphere.
   b. the right hemisphere is more dominant in processing nonverbal information.
   c. humor is localized in the right hemisphere.
   d. the left hemisphere is logical and the right hemisphere is creative.

11. Which of the following statements is NOT true about chromosomes?
   a. The nucleus of each human cell contains 46 chromosomes, or 23 pairs.
   b. Each pair of chromosomes comes from one of the parents.
   c. Chromosomes contain DNA.
   d. Genes are short segments of chromosomes.

12. _____ is the genetic research method in which organisms are chosen for reproduction based on how much of a particular trait they display.
   a. Molecular genetics
   b. Behavioral genetics
   c. Selective breeding
   d. Evolution

## Connections

*Take advantage of all the other study tools available for this chapter!*

## Media Integration

| NAME OF CLIP | DESCRIPTION | KEY CONCEPTS AND IDEAS |
|---|---|---|
| | | **The Nervous System** |
| Neurons: How They Work | This video clip addresses the role of evolution in the development of the brain and discusses the lower parts of the human brain that are shared with other species. The functions of the cerebral cortex are discussed. The development of neural networks is shown, including animations and a video of live neurons under a microscope. Animation is used to illustrate the activity in the synaptic gap. | Brain<br>Evolution<br>Cerebral cortex<br>Neural networks<br>Neurons<br>Synapse |
| | | **Neurons** |
| Neural Functioning | Participants are asked to identify the parts of the neuron in an interactive matching exercise. An animation of the neural | Parts of the neuron<br>Axon<br>Axon terminal<br>Dendrite |

| | | |
|---|---|---|
| | transmission is presented, including detailed illustrations of the action potential and comparisons of the resting potential and action potential. An animation of transduction in the retina is used to illustrate the reason why we can experience different degrees of a stimulus even though the action potential is an all-or-none phenomenon. | Myelin sheath<br>Node of Ranvier<br>Nucleus<br>Synapse<br>Resting potential<br>Action potential<br>Terminal buttons<br>Synaptic vesicles<br>Presynaptic neuron<br>Postsynaptic membrane<br>Nerve impulse<br>Oscilloscope<br>Transduction |
| Functions of Neurotransmitters | This video clips illustrates the role of neurotransmitters in a variety of psychological phenomena, including aggression, detection of threats, pain, and mood disorders. | Neurotransmitter<br>Serotonin<br>Noradrenaline<br>Substance P.<br>Endorphins |
| Brain Development | This video clip presents an introduction to the brain. The relationship among genes, the environment, and brain development is discussed. The process of development of neural maps and networks is presented, as well as a discussion of the differences in brain elasticity of young and older brains. The relationship between experience and the strength of neural circuits is illustrated. | Brain<br>Nature vs. nurture<br>Neural maps<br>Neural networks<br>Brain elasticity |
| | | **Structures of the Brain and Their Functions** |
| Brain Structure and Imaging Methods | This video clip presents the scanning of an active brain as it processes visual information. Applications for brain mapping are discussed. | MRI<br>FMRI<br>Brain mapping |
| Parts of the Brain | This video clip provides an interactive three-dimensional tour of the brain, including descriptions of names, locations, and functions. | Brain<br>Temporal lobe<br>Parietal lobe<br>Occipital lobe<br>Frontal lobe<br>Brain stem<br>Lateral view<br>Sagittal view<br>Cerebellum<br>Cerebral cortex |

| | | Corpus callosum<br>Hypothalamus<br>Medulla oblongata<br>Midbrain<br>Olfactory tract<br>Pineal gland<br>Pituitary gland<br>Pons<br>Thalamus<br>Ventricle(s) |
|---|---|---|
| Sensorimotor Neural Circuits | This interactivity demonstrates with animation the neural coordination, including motor and sensory coordination, needed to perform the simple act of opening a jar of pickles and how it is far more complicated than it seems, involving various areas of the brain. A second interactive exercise allows participants to test their own visual reaction time and relate their results to methods of measuring decision-making effort. | Motor cortex<br>Sensory cortex<br>Information processing<br>Frontal lobe<br>Parietal lobe<br>Spinal cord<br>Somatosensory area |
| Brain Lateralization | This interactivity introduces students to the concept of brain hemispheres in a two-part simulation. The first part is a replication of the experiment by Dr. Jerry Levy that explores how emotions are perception and processing of emotions and their corresponding facial expressions. The second simulation involves a split-brain task. The interactivity introduces students to the differences between the functions of the brain hemispheres and the role of the corpus callosum in sharing information between the hemispheres. | Brain hemispheres<br>Experiment<br>Emotions<br>Facial expressions<br>Split-brain<br>Corpus callosum |
| Sensory Processes and Brain Integration | This video introduces students to the complexities of sensory integration. The question of whether or not there is a specific part of the brain that integrates sensory information is addressed. Students are also introduced to the process of creation of mental maps. | Sensory integration<br>Perception<br>Brain<br>Memory<br>Neural networks<br>Mental maps |

| | | The Endocrine System |
| | | **Brain Damage, Plasticity, and Repair** |
| Brain Plasticity | This video presents the case of Jodi Miller, a young girl who experienced epileptic seizures only on her right hemisphere. A hemispherectomy was performed; the video presents the extraordinary evidence of brain plasticity, demonstrating how half of the brain may be removed and still the person can function normally. | Epileptic seizures<br>Brain hemispheres<br>Hemispherectomy<br>Brain plasticity<br>Cerebral cortex |
| | | **Genetic and Evolutionary Blueprints of Behavior** |
| Nature and Nurture: The Study of Twins | This video clip presents the case of identical twins who manifest a variety of physical differences owing to unequal nourishment in the womb; however, twins are very similar in a variety of characteristics, including psychological characteristics such as intelligence and personality. | Identical twins<br>Environmental influences<br>Genetic potential |

**Online Learning Center (www.mhhe.com/Santrockp7u)**
- Interact and make learning fun!
  - **Interactive Exercises**
    - Neural Functioning
    - Sensorimotor Neural Circuits
    - Parts of the Brain
  - **Interactive Reviews**
    - Level of Analysis: Immune Functioning
    - Neuron Labeling
    - Brain Labeling
    - Brain Labeling II
    - Brain Labeling III
    - Metabolic Structures Labeling
    - Sensorimotor Neural Pathways
    - Neural Transmission
- Brush up on the Key Terms for this chapter by first reviewing the electronic **Glossary** (in English or Spanish) and then testing your retention using the **Flashcard** feature.
- **"Notes"**—this feature allows you to use the website as you would your text, inserting your own study notes and highlighting areas of particular importance.

**In Your Text**
- Found throughout each chapter, the **Review and Sharpen Your Thinking** feature breaks the text into logical chunks, allowing you to process, review, and reflect thoughtfully on the information that you've just read. When going back to *study* the

chapter, try reading the feature *before* the section of text to which it relates. In doing so, you will be able to focus your attention on important concepts *as* you encounter them. In this chapter, this feature can be found on the following pages: pp. 47, 53, 64, 65, and 71.

**Practice Quizzes**

- Test your knowledge of the connection between biology and behavior by taking the different practice quizzes found on your text's **Online Learning Center** and on the **In-Psych Plus CD-ROM** packaged with your text.

## ANSWER KEY

## In Your Own Words

✓ Imagine that an evil scientist kidnaps you to study your brain. In his diabolical investigation, he must destroy one part of your brain. He asks you, "What part of the brain are you willing to give up for my diabolical investigation?" So, what part of the brain would you give up and why?

*This question requires critical thinking about the specialized functions of parts of the brain and the hierarchy of values and priorities of the student. Some students may be willing to sacrifice motor control while others may think it less important to be able to do math.*

✓ Think of an activity that you have done in the last 24 hours. Describe the brain areas that were especially active as you performed the activity.

*To answer this question the student must be familiar with the specialization of the brain and be able to associate his or her everyday activities with electrochemical transmissions in the brain.*

✓ Think of five possible applications for the Human Genome Project.

*The Human Genome Project seeks to map the complete human genome. Some of the possible applications are (1) results can help determine the degree of genetic similarity between humans and other species predicted to be part of our evolutionary history; (2) link DNA with specific diseases and reactions to drugs; (3) prevention based on genetic information; and creation of genetic profiles; and many others.*

### Correcting the Incorrect

1. The human nervous system is made up of *billions of* cells. (p. 44)
2. In general, the brains of individuals with epilepsy *do work effectively* between seizures. (p. 45)
3. *Sensory* nerves are the ones that carry sensory information to the brain. (p. 46)
4. Neural networks integrate sensory information and motor instructions from the brain. (p. 46)
5. The two main parts of the nervous system are the central nervous system and the *peripheral* nervous system. (p. 46)
6. The *central* nervous system consists of the brain and the spinal cord. (p. 46)
7. The somatic nervous system consists of sensory nerves. (p. 46)
8. The *parasympathetic* nervous system is involved when we are in a relaxed state. (p. 47)
9. *Neurons* are the basic unit of the nervous system. (p. 48)
10. *Neurons* transmit messages throughout the nervous system. (p. 48)
11. The neurons consist of a cell body, dendrites, and axon. (p. 48)
12. The wave of electricity within the axon is called the *action* potential. (p. 49)
13. The gap between neurons is called the *synapse*. (p. 49)

14. Neurotransmitters move across the synapse. (p. 49)
15. GABA, dopamine, and serotonin are examples of *neurotransmitters*. (p. 50)
16. Neural networks are *not* static and *can* be changed. (p. 52)
17. A structure in the *midbrain* is the reticular formation. (p. 54)
18. The medulla plays important roles in *breathing and reflexes*. (p. 54)
19. *The limbic system* plays an important role in memory and emotion. (p. 55)
20. A person suffering damage to the hippocampus *would be unable to remember new memories*. (p. 56)
21. The Olds studies have important implications for research on *drug addiction*. (p. 57)
22. The *temporal* lobe is involved in hearing. (p. 58)
23. The parietal lobe is involved in bodily sensation. (p. 59)
24. The large bundle of axons that connects the brain's two hemisphere is called the *corpus callosum*. (p. 60)
25. The *right* hemisphere is associated with humor. (p. 61)
26. Endocrine glands release their chemicals directly into the *bloodstream*. (p. 64)
27. The *adrenal* gland regulates mood, energy levels, and the ability to cope with stress. (p. 65)
28. Chromosomes are made up of *DNA*. (p. 66)
29. A recessive gene can exert influence *only if both genes are recessive*. (p. 66)
30. *Molecular* genetics involves the manipulation of genes using technology to determine their effects on behavior. (p. 67)
31. Evolutionary psychologists believe that the specialized brain functions evolved because they helped humans adapt to the challenges of the environment. (p. 70)

## Practice Test 1

1. a. no; a single cubic centimeter of the human brain has well over 50 million nerve cells
   b. YES; the total number varies from person to person, but it is in the billions
   c. no; this would not account for even one cubic centimeter of the human brain
   d. no; this would not account for even one cubic centimeter of the human brain
   p. 44

2. a. no; this is an important characteristic of the nervous system
   b. no; this is an important characteristic of the nervous system
   c. CORRECT; the nervous system is characterized by its complexity, not simplicity
   d. no; electrochemical transmission is part of the foundation of the nervous system
   p. 45

3. a. YES; this is the correct term used to refer to the capacity of the brain to change
   b. no; this is the brain's capacity to organize complex information into integrated experiences
   c. no; this is the method of communication in the nervous system
   d. no; evolution may have caused changes in the brain across millions of years, but it is not the process of change and modification of the brain within a person's lifespan
   p. 45

4. a. YES; sensory nerves carry sensory information to the brain
   b. no; sensory nerves carry motor messages from the brain
   c. no; interneurons mediate sensory input and motor output
   d. no
   p. 46

5. a.   no; sensory nerves carry information to the brain
   b.   no; motor nerves carry the brain's output
   c.   YES; most of the brain comprises neural networks
   d.   no; an axon is a part of a neuron, not a nerve
   p. 46

6. a.   THAT'S RIGHT; the central nervous system is made up of the brain and the spinal cord
   b.   no; the peripheral nervous system is made up of the somatic nervous system and the autonomic nervous system
   c.   no; this is part of the peripheral nervous system
   d.   no; the sympathetic nervous system is part of the autonomic nervous system
   p. 46

7. a.   no; the autonomic nervous system regulates internal organs
   b.   no; while the sympathetic nervous system will likely be involved in your reaction to the pain, it is not involved in the sending of the sensory pain information to the brain
   c.   no; the parasympathetic nervous system calms the body
   d.   YES; the somatic nervous system contains sensory neurons
   p. 46

8. a.   no; the parasympathetic nervous system calms the body
   b.   THAT'S RIGHT; during stressful situations, the sympathetic nervous system increases the body's arousal
   c.   no; the somatic nervous system provides sensory information to the central nervous system
   d.   no; the central nervous system is made up of the brain and spinal cord
   p. 47

9. a.   no; the axon carries information away from the cell body to other cells
   b.   no; the synapse is the space between neurons
   c.   no; neurotransmitters are involved in the transmission but are not the recipients of the message
   d.   YES; the dendrites collect information
   p. 48

10. a.   no; the nucleus is part of the cell body
    b.   CORRECT
    c.   no; the dendrite receives information
    d.   no; neurotransmitters are not a part of the neuron
    p. 48

11. a.   YES; the action potential is caused by the exchange of ions across the neuron's membrane
    b.   no
    c.   no; the all-or-none principle describes the action potential
    d.   no
    p. 49

12. a.   no; GABA is related to anxiety
    b.   no; acetylcholine is associated with learning and memory
    c.   YES; high levels of dopamine are linked to schizophrenia
    d.   no; norepinephrine is implicated in depression and manic states
    p. 51

13. a.   YES; dopamine is involved in voluntary movement
    b.   no; the neurotransmitter GABA is involved with anxiety
    c.   no; depression and serotonin and norepinephrine are related
    d.   no; sleep problems are associated with serotonin
    p. 51

14. a.   no; the pons is a structure in the hindbrain that is involved in sleep and arousal
    b.   no; the reticular formation is involved in stereotyped behaviors
    c.   YES; the medulla controls breathing and other reflexes
    d.   no; the cerebellum plays a role in motor behavior
    p. 54

15. a.   no; the thalamus is not involved in these behaviors
    b.   CORRECT; the hypothalamus monitors eating, drinking, and sexual behavior
    c.   no; the cerebral cortex is another portion of the forebrain
    d.   no; the cerebellum is involved in motor behavior and is in the hindbrain
    p. 56

16. a.   RIGHT; this structure plays a role in the storage of memories
    b.   no; the amygdala plays a role in emotions
    c.   no; the thalamus serves as a rely station-like function for sensory information
    d.   no; the limbic system is a network of structures
    p. 56

17. a.   no
    b.   no
    c.   no
    d.   CORRECT; there is no posterior lobe in the neocortex
    p. 58

18. a.   YES; association areas are involved in the highest intellectual functions
    b.   no
    c.   no
    d.   no
    p. 60

19. a.   CORRECT; the corpus callosum, a large bundle of fibers, connects the hemispheres
    b.   no; the thalamus serves to relay sensory information
    c.   no; the hypothalamus is involved in eating, drinking, and sex
    d.   no; the reticular formation plays a role in stereotyped behaviors
    p. 60

20. a.   this is not related to mapping out human genes
    b.   this study has nothing to do with mapping out human genes
    c.   split brain research would not map out human genes
    d.   RIGHT; the Human Genome Project hopes to map out every human gene
    p. 67

21. a.   no
    b.   no; dopamine is a neurotransmitter
    c.   CORRECT
    d.   no; it is the other way around
    p. 66

22. a.  no; this statement is correct
    b.  no; this statement is correct
    c.  no; this statement is correct
    d.  YES; this statement is incorrect
   p. 66

23. a.  no
    b.  no
    c.  RIGHT; the evolutionary perspective focuses on natural selection, survival, and reproduction
    d.  no; fears and phobias are seen as being adaptive, leading to successful survival and reproduction
   p. 70

## Practice Test 2

1. a.  YES; the central nervous system includes the brain and spinal cord
   b.  no; the peripheral nervous system connects the brain and the spinal cord with the rest of the body and external stimuli
   c.  no; this is a division of the peripheral nervous system
   d.  no; this is a division of the peripheral nervous system
   p. 46

2. a.  no; there are more glial cells than neurons
   b.  no; glial cells do not have dendrites or axons
   c.  YES; these are the functions of glial cells
   d.  no; glial cells do not send and receive information
   p. 48

3. a.  no
   b.  no
   c.  no; this division of the autonomous nervous system is involved in arousal
   d.  YES; this is the division of the autonomous nervous system that calms the body
   p. 47

4. a.  YES; most neurons have numerous dendrites
   b.  no; most neurons have numerous dendrites
   c.  no; all neurons have at least one dendrite
   d.  no; axons are the part of the neuron covered by the myelin sheath
   p. 48

5. a.  no; these are parts of the neuron
   b.  YES; the channels allow certain substances to pass into and out of the neurons
   c.  no; the axons are parts of the neuron
   d.  no; the cell bodies are parts of the neuron
   p. 48

6. a.  YES; the myelin sheath speeds up transmissions
   b.  no; the cell body is a part of the neuron
   c.  no; plasticity is the capacity of the brain to modify and change
   d.  no; an ion is an electrically charged particle
   p. 48

7.  a.  no; while dopamine is associated with learning, it also affects sleep, mood, and attention
    b.  YES; these are some of the psychological factors associated with acetylcholine
    c.  no; GABA has been linked to anxiety
    d.  no; while this neurotransmitter works with acetylcholine, it is associated with depression and mania

p. 50

8.  a.  no; the medulla is involved in breathing and reflexes
    b.  YES; leg and arm movement is coordinated at the cerebellum
    c.  no; the pons is involved in sleep and arousal
    d.  no; this is a part of the midbrain

p. 54

9.  a.  no; this is a part of the hindbrain
    b.  no; while this is a part of the midbrain, it is involved in alertness, breathing, heartbeat, and blood pressure
    c.  YES; it is a diffuse collection of neurons associated with those functions
    d.  no; the hypothalamus is part of the forebrain

p. 54

10. a.  no; the thalamus relays sensory information to the appropriate areas of the brain
    b.  no; this "pleasure center" is in a part of the forebrain
    c.  no; the hippocampus is linked to memory
    d.  YES; the hypothalamus is involved in pleasurable feelings

p. 57

11. a.  YES; damage to the frontal lobe can affect personality, as in the case of Phineas T. Gage
    b.  no; this lobe is associated with the processing of visual information
    c.  no; this lobe is associated with the processing of auditory information
    d.  no; this lobe is associated with the processing of special location, attention, and motor control

p. 58

12. a.  no
    b.  no
    c.  YES; most of the cerebral cortex is dedicated to the processing of sensory information and integrating it with the motor output generated by the brain; this is where thinking and problem solving take place
    d.  no

p. 60

13. a.  no; speech is localized in the left hemisphere
    b.  no; grammar is localized in the left hemisphere
    c.  YES; our sense of humor resides in the right hemisphere
    d.  no; the left hemisphere participates more in the kind of logic used to prove geometric theorems

p. 61

14. a.  no; the adrenal gland regulates moods, energy level, and the ability to cope with stress
    b.  no; this is a part of the central nervous system, not a gland
    c.  YES; the anterior part of the pituitary gland is also referred to as the master gland
    d.  no; the thalamus is not a gland

p. 65

## Practice Test 3

1.  a.  no
    b.  no
    c.  YES; the hypothalamus regulates several behaviors by its interaction with the pituitary gland
    d.  no

    p. 56

2.  a.  no; this corresponds to the characteristic of complexity
    b.  no; this corresponds to the characteristic of adaptability
    c.  YES; this item makes reference to the issue of coordination and connections in the brain, required for an integrated psychological experience
    d.  no; this corresponds to the characteristic of electrochemical transmission

    p. 62

3.  a.  YES; the afferent or sensory nerves carry the information from the sensory organs (in this case the sense of touch is involved) to the brain
    b.  no; these nerves carry information from the brain to the different parts of the body
    c.  no
    d.  no; these are not nerves and do not engage in electrochemical transmission

    p. 46

4.  a.  no, this division does not initiate these relaxation psychological experiences
    b.  YES; the parasympathetic nervous system calms the body and prepares it for sleep, relaxation, and restoration
    c.  no, the sympathetic nervous system does the opposite, it works when we are in high alert
    d.  no, this is not a division of the nervous system but rather a part of the central nervous system

    p. 47

5.  a.  no; the opposite is true
    b.  no; while the cell body may initiate messages, the dendrites would not be the source of output
    c.  no; while dendrites do receive the message and can be considered "input," the cell body is an intermediary and not the sender of the message
    d.  YES; this analogy is the correct one

    p. 48

6.  a.  no
    b.  no
    c.  YES; and as a result, the person may experience violent spasms
    d.  no

    p. 51

7.  a.  YES; endorphins are associated with increasing pleasure and reducing pain
    b.  no; serotonin works with norepinephrine and acetylcholine to regulate the states of sleeping and wakefulness
    c.  no; norepinephrine works with serotonin and acetylcholine to regulate the states of sleeping and wakefulness
    d.  no; acetylcholine works with norepinephrine and serotonin to regulate the states of sleeping and wakefulness

    p. 51

8. a. no
   b. no
   c. YES
   d. no
   p. 52

9. a. no
   b. no
   c. no
   d. YES; alcohol blocks the inhibitory effects of serotonin
   p. 51

10. a. no; this is true
    b. no; this is true
    c. no; this is true
    d. YES; this is a myth—logic and creativity are really broad capabilities, and we can be logical and creative about many things; therefore, logic and creativity are involved in the activity of both hemispheres
    p. 61

11. a. no; this is true
    b. CORRECT ANSWER; in each pair of chromosomes, one member of each pair comes from each parent: one chromosome comes from the biological mother and the other chromosome comes from the biological father
    c. no; this is true
    d. no; this is true
    p. 66

12. a. no; this method involves the manipulation of genes using technology to determine their effect on behavior
    b. no; this method is the study of the degree to which nature influences behavior
    c. YES; selective breeding is what Mendel used in his study of pea plants
    d. no; this is not a research method
    p. 67

# Chapter 4—Human Development

## Learning Goals

1. Explain how psychologists think about development.
2. Describe children's development from conception to adolescence.
3. Identify the most important changes that occur in adolescence.
4. Discuss adult development and the positive dimensions of aging.

After studying Chapter 4, you will be able to:

- Explain what development is, including its processes.
- Discuss the debated issues and contrasting perspectives in developmental psychology.
- Describe prenatal development.
- Identify the changes that take place in children's cognitive development, including Piaget's theory.
- Discuss children's socioemotional development, including Erikson's theory, attachment, and parenting.
- Discuss the effects of divorce on children.
- Explain the characteristics of resilient children and the factors that support resilience in children.
- Describe the perspectives on the psychological experiences during adolescence.
- Discuss the physical, cognitive, and socioemotional changes in adolescence, including identity development.
- Discuss the physical changes that take place in adult development and the biological aspects of aging.
- Explain cognitive changes in adulthood.
- Describe the issues in socioemotional development in adulthood.

## CHAPTER 4: OUTLINE

- In psychology, *development* is defined as a pattern of change in human capabilities that begins at conception and continues throughout the life span. The growth involved in development is a product of physical processes, cognitive processes, and socioemotional processes. These three processes are related and influence one another.

- Some developmental psychologists argue that experiences during the first year or so of life create life-long effects, while other developmentalists argue that experiences later in life are just as important as early life experiences.

- The nature-nurture issue involves the extent to which behavior and development are influenced by heredity (nature) and the environment (nurture). Developmentalists agree that the complex human psychology results from intricate combinations of nature and nurture influences. Optimal experiences or optimal life themes are what developmentalists argue allow certain humans to go beyond the framework set by their heredity and environmental influences.

- The continuity view states that development involves gradual change, whereas the discontinuity view suggests that there are distinct developmental stages. The early-later experience issue centers on whether children are malleable throughout development and whether late experiences are just as important as early ones.

- Development can be organized into periods with approximate age ranges. The fertilized egg is called a *zygote*. The first 2 weeks after conception are referred to as the *germinal period*; the period from 3 to 8 weeks is the *embryonic period*. The *fetal period* begins 2 months after conception and lasts about the next 7 months. A full-term infant is born 38 to 42 weeks following conception. Preterm infants are at a higher risk for developmental problems and learning disorders than are full-term babies.

- Teratogens are agents that cause birth defects. Heroin and alcohol are examples of teratogens.

- Infants come into the world with a number of reflexes, including those associated with grasping, sucking, stepping, and startle.

- During the first 24 months of life, a human being develops at a faster pace than at any other point in the life span. At birth, the billions of neurons in the brain are scarcely connected, basically waiting for life's experiences to create the interconnections that will support future brain functioning and capacity. While the brain as a whole does not grow in size, the patterns and interconnections within it vary dramatically during infancy, childhood, and adolescence.

- Piaget's theory of cognitive development focuses on how children actively construct their cognitive world and the stages that they go through. Children use schemas, which are cognitive frameworks that organize and interpret information.

- Two cognitive processes used by children are assimilation and accommodation. In the process of assimilation, the individual adjusts to new information by incorporating it into existing schemas; in accommodation, the individual adjusts to new information by modifying the existing schemas.

- Piaget believed that humans pass through four cognitive stages, each representing a different way of understanding the world: sensorimotor, preoperational, concrete operational, and formal operational.

- Erik Erikson proposed an influential theory of development that focuses on psychosocial development. In each of the eight life-span stages in this theory, the individual is confronted with a crisis or challenge that must be resolved. The challenges of the four childhood stages are (1) trust versus mistrust, (2) autonomy versus shame, (3) initiative versus guilt, and (4) industry versus inferiority. According to Erikson, the more successfully the individual resolves each crisis, the more competent he or she is likely to become.

- Developmental psychologists have been interested in studying the process of attachment, the close emotional bond between an infant and its caregiver. In a study of attachment in monkeys, Harlow and Zimmerman found that the comfort of contact is more important than feeding in the process of attachment. Lorenz described attachment in animals by using the process of imprinting.

- Some infants have more positive attachment experience than others. Ainsworth has described how attachment differs in the degree to which the caregiver is sensitive to the infant's signals.

- Children can also differ in temperament, which is an individual's behavioral style and characteristic way of responding. There are three basic types of temperament in children: easy child, difficult child, and slow-to-warm-up child.

- Parenting styles describe how parents interact with their children. According to Baumrind, there are four basic styles: authoritarian, authoritative, neglectful, and indulgent. Divorce makes children more vulnerable to stress, aggressive behavior, and depression; however, the majority of children in divorced families adjust well.

- Positive parenting involves spending time with children, emotion-coaching, and raising moral children. Kohlberg's theory suggests that moral development involves internalization, a change from behavior that is externally controlled to behavior that is controlled by internal, self-generated standards and principles. He also believed that moral development progresses through three levels: preconventional, conventional, and postconventional.

- Gilligan, emphasizing the role of gender on moral development, has suggested that Kohlberg's theory underrepresents the care perspective in moral development and overrepresents the justice perspective. *Gender* refers to the social and psychological aspects of being female and male.

- According to evolutionary psychology, differences in gender have resulted from gradual genetic adaptations, while alternative approaches, such as the social roles view of gender, argue that social experiences create gender differences. Social experiences can influence gender behavior through gender roles and gender schemas.

- Resilient children tend to have positive individual, family, and/or extrafamiliar factors that help them overcome obstacles faced in at risk circumstances, such as poverty and lack of quality parenting. Children in such at-risk circumstances benefit from programs that facilitate the factors contributing to resiliency, such as prevention and intervention programs, which give them an opportunity to become competent.

- Adolescence is the developmental period between childhood and adulthood. While adolescence has long been characterized as a stage of developmental crisis, the majority of adolescents develop more positively that commonly believed.

- A significant physical event that occurs in adolescence is puberty. The hormones testosterone and estrogen reach high concentrations during puberty in boys and girls, respectively.

- According to Piaget, children between the ages of 11 and 15 develop the ability to think abstractly and logically and engage in hypothetical-deductive reasoning. Piaget called this stage *formal operational thought*. Adolescents experience a type of egocentrism characterized by the belief that they are unique, invincible, and the center of everyone's attention.

- During adolescence, individuals are developing their sense of identity, according to Erikson's stage of identity versus identity confusion. The search for identity can lead to adolescents wanting to gain independence from their parents at the same time they fear fearing making the wrong decisions. Exploration and commitment are two dimensions of identity.

- Developing an ethnic identity is an important process during adolescence, particularly for the youth of ethnic minority groups.

- The peak of our physical skills and health comes in early adulthood; however, this tends to be the life-span period when people tend to engage in damaging lifestyles such as increased smoking, drinking, and poor eating habits.

- During middle adulthood, when the signs of aging start becoming more evident, a concern with health and youthful appearance tends to emerge.

- The majority of women do not experience psychological or physical problems from menopause.

- Health in late adulthood can be enhanced with exercise and a sense of self-control.

- Alzheimer's disease is characterized by progressive, irreversible brain disorders that involve gradual deterioration of memory, reasoning, language, and physical functioning.

- During early adulthood, intellectual skills and fluid intelligence are strong. Later, during the middle adulthood years, crystallized intelligence increases and fluid intelligence decreases.

- Although older adults show decline in the speed of processing information, they tend to outperform younger adults in general knowledge and wisdom. Socioemotional development in adulthood is concerned with such issues as work, intimacy, and lifestyle choices.

- During midlife, many individuals reach the highest satisfaction in their careers.

- Successful marriages are characterized by the following principles: feelings of fondness and admiration for each other, having each other as friends, giving up some power, and solving problems together.

- According to Levinson, while experiencing a midlife crisis, a person is concerned with being old, constructive, attached, and being masculine or feminine; however, the majority of adults do not experience a negative midlife crisis.

- Research in the development of adulthood and aging is increasingly demonstrating that while there are declines in physical, cognitive, and socioemotional functioning, overall older adults can have a positive and productive psychology.

## Building Blocks of Chapter 4

### Clarifying some of the tricky points in Chapter 4
### and
### In Your Own Words

*To respond to the questions and exercises presented in the "In Your Own Words" section, please write your thoughts, perspectives, and reactions on a separate piece of paper.*

Psychologists use the term *development* to mean a pattern of movement or change that begins at *conception* and continues through the *life span*. Development is complex because it is a product of *physical, cognitive, and socioemotional processes. Physical processes* involve changes in an individual's *biological nature*. Changes in an individual's *thought, intelligence, and language involve cognitive processes. Socioemotional* processes include changes in an individual's r*elationships with other people, changes in emotion, and changes in personality.*

The *early experience* doctrine suggests that experiences that happen in the beginning of life become relatively fixed and permanently affect our psychology. In contrast, *later experience* developmentalists argue that later experiences can be as significant as early experiences.

Another debate for developmental psychologists is about whether development is primarily influenced by maturation or by experience—the *nature-nurture controversy.* "Nature" refers to the contribution of *heredity*; "nurture" refers to the role of the environment. *Optimal experiences* support the notion that people can go beyond simply adapting to the environment and to *actively constructing their lives.*

### Child Development

The fertilized egg, called a *zygote*, receives *half* of its chromosomes from each parent. The first 2 weeks after conception is referred to as the *germinal period*; the period from 3 to 8 weeks is the *embryonic period*. During this period there is an increase in *cell differentiation,* and the organs begin to appear. The *fetal period* begins 2 months after conception and lasts for about 7 months.

Scientists label any agent that causes birth defects a *teratogen*. Mothers who are heavy drinkers, for example, risk giving birth to children with *fetal alcohol syndrome*.

Infants born prior to 38 weeks after conception are called *preterm infants*. When these infants are very small they are more likely than their larger counterparts to have developmental problems.

A child is born with several *reflexes,* including coughing, sucking, and blinking. Although physical development slows during the childhood years, *motor development* becomes smoother and more coordinated.

The infant's brain has approximately 100 billion neurons with only minimal connections; the brain is waiting for experiences that will create the connections. In the study by Thompson and associates, in which scanned images of the brains of children 3–15 years old were studied, it was found that the overall *size* of the brain did not change, but local *patterns* of neural connections did change dramatically.

With regard to cognitive development, Jean Piaget stressed that children actively construct their own cognitive world. A *schema* is a concept or framework that is already present in a person's mind and is used to organize and interpret information.

Piaget believed that we adapt in two ways: when we incorporate new information into our existing knowledge, it is called *assimilation*. When we have to adjust to new information, it is called *accommodation*.

Piaget believed we pass through four stages in understanding the world. According to Piaget, the thinking in one stage is qualitatively different from thinking in another stage. The first stage of development, which lasts from birth to age 2, is called the *sensorimotor stage*. In this stage, infants realize that objects continue to exist even when they are not in sight; Piaget called this *object permanence*.

According to Piaget, preschool children have trouble understanding the concept of reversibility; they cannot perform *operations*. Children between the ages of 2 and 7 are in a stage Piaget referred to as *preoperational* thought. Children in this stage have not yet grasped the concept of *conservation*, which is the recognition that a quantity stays the same even though its shape has changed. Children in this stage are also unable to distinguish between their perspective and someone else's perspective, a quality Piaget called *egocentrism*. The thinking in this stage is more *symbolic* than the previous stage. Piaget also called preoperational thought *intuitive*.

Between the ages of 7 and 11, children are in a stage Piaget called *concrete operational*. In this stage, mental reversibility is possible, and intuitive thought is replaced by *logical reasoning*. Another important skill that characterizes concrete operational thought is the ability to classify or divide things and to consider their interrelations.

The final stage is called *formal operations*, when the thinking is more *abstract, idealistic, and logical*. People in this stage can develop hypotheses about ways to solve problems; this is called *hypothetical-deductive reasoning*.

**In Your Own Words**

*Please write your thoughts, perspectives, and reactions on a separate piece of paper.*

✓ *Think about the formal operations stage; what was the last decision you made for which you used hypothetical-deductive reasoning?*

Piaget's theory has been criticized by psychologists because he ignored individual differences in thinking. *Vygotsky*, a Russian psychologist, recognized that development must be understood in *sociocultural context*.

Erik Erikson proposed an influential theory of *psychosocial or socioemotional development*. Each of the eight stages in his theory confronts individuals with a *crisis* that must be resolved. The first year of life represents the stage of *trust versus mistrust*. Erikson believes that the focus of the second year of life is on *autonomy versus shame and doubt*. During the preschool years, children face the conflict of *initiative versus guilt*. Developing a sense of responsibility increases initiative. During the elementary school years, children are challenged by *industry versus inferiority*. Erikson's theory has been criticized because he relied mostly on the case studies research method and because the stages are too narrow in focus.

In developmental psychology, *attachment* refers to a close emotional bond between an infant and its caregiver. Harlow and Zimmerman's research with infant monkeys illustrated the importance of *contact comfort*. Lorenz's research with goslings demonstrated the process of *imprinting*.

Bowlby and Ainsworth have suggested that, in humans, attachment to the caregiver during the first year provides an important foundation. Infants who are *securely attached* tend to have mothers who are responsive and accepting. Kagan has argued that genetics and temperament characteristics are important factors; other critics have pointed out that infants can attach to many people, not just their primary caretaker.

A child's behavioral style and characteristic way of responding is called *temperment*, of which there are three types: *easy child, difficult child,* and *slow-to-warm-up child.*

Baumrind has proposed a classification scheme for parenting styles. She refers to a restrictive, punitive style as *authoritarian* parenting. Children are encouraged to be independent but still have limits and controls on their actions in *authoritative* parenting. A parenting style characterized by lack of parental involvement is *neglectful* parenting. A style of parenting in which parents are highly involved with their children but place few demands on them are called *indulgent* parenting.

**In Your Own Words**

*Please write your thoughts, perspectives, and reactions on a separate piece of paper.*

✓ *What parenting style did your parent(s) use? If you are a parent, which parenting style do you use? Why? If you are not a parent, which parenting style do you think you would use? Why?*

During the experience of divorce, children are highly vulnerable to stress, yet 75–80% of children in divorced families do not have adjustment problems. Positive parenting takes time and effort.

Lawrence Kohlberg has identified three levels of *moral development*. The first, which shows no internalization of moral values, is the *preconventional level*. At the second level, called the *conventional level*, internalization is intermediate. At the highest level, called the *postconventional level*, morality is completely internalized. One criticism of Kohlberg's theory is that moral reasons are often a shelter for immoral behavior. Carol Gilligan has criticized

Kohlberg's approach because it doesn't adequately reflect concern with others; her view is the *care perspective*, in contrast with Kohlberg's *justice perspective*.

Carol Gilligan argued that *gender* is important in moral development. Gender refers to the social and psychological aspects of being *male* or *female*. Besides genetic and hormonal determinants of gender there are also social factors such as the *gender role*, which involves expectations of how females and males should behave, think, and feel.

Regardless of extremely negative life experiences, *resilient* children tend to have individual, family, and extrafamiliar factors that help them cope and overcome effectively.

### *Adolescence*
The transition from childhood to adulthood is called *adolescence*. Although adolescents are commonly portrayed as being rebellious and self-centered, most adolescents are competent human beings who are not experiencing deep emotional turmoil.

The rapid maturation that occurs mainly during early adolescence is called *puberty*. During adolescence there is a dramatic increase in the hormone *testosterone* in boys and in the hormone *estrogen* in girls.

In Piaget's theory, children between the ages of 11 and 15 are able to think abstractly; they are able to engage in *formal operational thought*. Adolescents are also able to think logically and engage in *hypothetical-deductive reasoning*. The belief that others are as *preoccupied* with the adolescent as he or she is with himself or herself, the belief that one is *invincible*, and the belief that one is *unique* are all components of *adolescent egocentrism*.

Erikson argued that adolescents experience a gap between the security of childhood and the autonomy of adulthood. Conflicts between adolescents and their parents involve the adolescent's desire to become *independent* from their parents. *Identity status* refers to the stage or place at which the person is in terms of the development of their identity. According to Erikson, the adolescent stage of development is characterized by identity versus *role confusion*. During this stage, according to Erikson, adolescents must determine who they are.

**In Your Own Words**
*Please write your thoughts, perspectives, and reactions on a separate piece of paper.*
✓ *When you were in eighth grade, what types of arguments did you have with your parents or other adults? Did the arguments revolve around your search for independence?*

Four identity statuses have been proposed in terms of the level at which the person has explored different identity possibilities and the extent to which the person is committed to a particular identity: (1) *identity diffusion* (no exploration and no commitment), (2) *identity foreclosure* (commitment without exploration), (3) *identity moratorium* (exploration but no commitment), and (4) *identity achievement* (exploration and commitment). *Ethnic identity* is also an important challenge for adolescents, particularly those belonging to minority groups.

### *Adult Development and Aging*
Most people reach their peak physical performance during *early adulthood*. During midlife, women experience *menopause*, when their menstrual periods cease completely.

A degenerative, irreversible brain disorder that impairs memory and social behavior is called *Alzheimer's disease*, which involves the neurotransmitter *acetylcholine*.

In middle adulthood, *crystallized intelligence* increases, while *fluid intelligence* starts to decline, a finding based on research done with the cross-sectional study research method.

The state of development that characterizes early adulthood is *intimacy versus isolation*. In middle adulthood, the stage is called *generativity versus stagnation*; in late adulthood, it is *integrity versus despair*.

**In Your Own Words**
*Please write your thoughts, perspectives, and reactions on a separate piece of paper.*
✓ *How might a middle-aged person help the next generation as it experiences generativity?*

Among older adults, speed of *processing information* is *slower* than in younger adults; however, *wisdom* may increase with age because of life experiences.

Concerns during adulthood include work and relationships. A successful marriage involves fondness, admiration, friendship, giving up power, and solving problems together.

Older adults become more *selective* about whom they associate with. Researchers have found that the psychological life of older adults is more positive than previously believed.

**In Your Own Words**
*Please write your thoughts, perspectives, and reactions on a separate piece of paper.*
✓ *Describe some biological, cognitive, and socioemotional changes that you have experienced in the past year.*

## Correcting the Incorrect

Carefully read each statement. Determine if the statement is correct or incorrect. If the statement is incorrect, make the necessary changes to correct it. Then check the answer key at the end of the chapter for the correct statement and page reference in the textbook.

1. Development refers to the changes that take place from conception through adolescence.
2. Physical processes include the development of the brain, height and weight, and motor skills.
3. An infant's smile in response to his mother's smile illustrates cognitive processes.
4. The nature and nurture theory refers to the influences of heredity and environment on behavior.
5. The stages of prenatal development are the germinal period, the embryonic period, and the fetal period.
6. *Teratogen* refers to the tip of the chromosome.
7. Object permanence is a concept or framework that already exists that organizes and interprets information.
8. A preterm infant is born prior to 40 weeks after conception.
9. In assimilation, the individual adjusts to new information.
10. Object permanence takes place in the preoperational stage.
11. Infants are more cognitively competent than Piaget thought.
12. The thinking of a child during the concrete operational stage is logical.
13. A person who can engage in hypothetical-deductive reasoning is most likely to be in the concrete operational stage.
14. Vygotsky ignored the role of culture in development.
15. Erikson proposed eight stages of psychosocial development.
16. Individuals during their 20s and 30s are in the identity versus identity-confusion stage, according to Erikson.

17. A parent who is restrictive and has a punitive style that demands obedience on the part of the child has an authoritative parenting style.

18. Testosterone is a hormone found in girls; it is responsible for the development of breasts, uterus, and skeleton.

19. An adolescent yells to her mother, "You just don't understand me!" This illustrates the preconventional stage of moral development.

20. During the conventional stage of moral thinking, the individual shows no internalization of moral values.

21. Moral development is completely internalized at the postconventional level of moral thinking.

22. Lawrence Kohlberg argued that people see their connectedness with others as important in moral thinking.

23. Most women who experience menopause report psychological problems or physical problems.

24. Parkinson's disease is characterized by the gradual deterioration of memory, reasoning, language, and, eventually, physical functioning.

## Practice Test 1

1. Psychologists define development as
    a. behavioral changes.
    b. patterns of movement or change.
    c. cognitive maturity.
    d. physical growth.

2. Which of the following is part of the term *development?*
    a. a pattern of movement or change
    b. continues throughout the life cycle
    c. begins at conception
    d. all of the above

3. Which of the following processes are involved in development?
    a. biological processes
    b. cognitive processes
    c. socioemotional processes
    d. all of the above

4. The debate over whether development is primarily a matter of heredity or experience is also known as the
    a. mechanics versus pragmatics controversy.
    b. storm and stress view.
    c. continuity/discontinuity problem.
    d. nature/nurture issue.

5. In the context if Piaget's theory of cognitive development, the concept *operations* means
    a. actions of the person.
    b. how the person feels.
    c. mental representations.
    d. accommodation.

6. Preoperational thinkers cannot yet do which of the following?
   a. think symbolically
   b. understand words
   c. reverse mental representations
   d. participate in "pretend" play

7. Children are able to grasp the principle of conservation in which stage of development?
   a. sensorimotor thought
   b. preoperational thought
   c. concrete operational thought
   d. none of the above

8. According to Erikson, the first psychosocial stage of development is called
   a. autonomy versus shame and doubt.
   b. industry versus inferiority.
   c. initiative versus guilt.
   d. trust versus mistrust.

9. According to Erikson, the final developmental stage is called
   a. generativity versus stagnation.
   b. intimacy versus isolation.
   c. integrity versus despair.
   d. ageism versus activity theory.

10. Authoritarian parents often have children who are
    a. overly self-confident.
    b. good communicators.
    c. socially incompetent.
    d. cognitively deficient.

11. A parenting style that encourages children to be independent but still places limits on their behavior is called
    a. authoritative.
    b. authoritarian.
    c. neglecting.
    d. indulgent.

12. The author of your text suggests that adolescence should be regarded as all of the following except which one?
    a. a time of evaluation
    b. a time of acute crisis
    c. a time of decision making
    d. a time of commitment

13. Adolescent egocentrism involves all of the following except which one?
    a. the perception of self as unique
    b. the perception of self as invincible
    c. the inability to see an issue from another's point of view
    d. the belief that others are aware of and watching one's every action

14. Which of the following characterizes adolescent cognitive development?
    a. formal operational thought
    b. hypothetical-deductive reasoning
    c. adolescent egocentrism
    d. all of the above

15. Individuals are able to engage in hypothetical-deductive reasoning after they achieve _____ thought.
    a. sensorimotor
    b. preoperational
    c. concrete operational
    d. formal operational

16. According to Kohlberg, at what level is moral development completely internalized and not based on others' standards?
    a. preconventional
    b. conventional
    c. postconventional
    d. justice

17. Kohlberg's theory of moral development has been criticized because
    a. it does not reflect the care perspective.
    b. it does not reflect the justice perspective.
    c. it is culturally biased.
    d. Kohlberg excluded males in his study.

18. People tend to become more concerned about their health status in
    a. early adulthood.
    b. adolescence.
    c. middle adulthood.
    d. late adulthood.

## Practice Test 2

1. Which of the following development processes is the one that involves changes in personality and relationships?
    a. physical processes
    b. socioemotional processes
    c. cognitive processes
    d. developmental processes

2. Nature is to _____ as nurture is to _____.
    a. genetics; environment.
    b. environment; genetics.
    c. phenotype; genotype.
    d. parenting; heredity.

3. The embryonic period of prenatal development
   a. runs from months 2 through 9; during this stage the organs mature to the point where life can be sustained outside the womb.
   b. occurs during weeks 1 and 2 after conception, when the zygote is created.
   c. is the time between weeks 38 and 40, when the baby is not at risk of being pre-term.
   d. occurs between weeks 3 and 8; by this time, arms, legs, and spinal cord are already in development.

4. Which of the following is NOT one of the abnormalities associated with the teratogen alcohol?
   a. small head
   b. below-average intelligence
   c. breathing problems
   d. defective limbs

5. Which of the following is NOT one of the reflexes that babies are born with?
   a. coughing
   b. sucking
   c. fear of water
   d. startle

6. By egocentrism, Piaget was referring to
   a. the selfish behaviors of some children.
   b. young children's inability to share.
   c. the inability to distinguish between one's own perspective and someone else's perspective.
   d. the psychology of adolescents.

7. According to Erikson, adolescents who experience identity confusion
   a. withdraw and isolate themselves from peers and family.
   b. eventually develop thoughts that are concrete and irrational.
   c. develop a sense of inferiority.
   d. develop postconventional level of moral thinking.

8. According to Erikson, the two stages of early and middle adulthood consist of intimacy versus isolation and
   a. integrity versus despair.
   b. identity versus identity confusion.
   c. generativity versus despair.
   d. generativity versus stagnation.

9. A parenting style in which parents are highly involved with their children but place few demands on them is called
   a. authoritative.
   b. authoritarian.
   c. neglecting.
   d. indulgent.

10. The relationship between two people in which each person does a number of things to continue the relationship is termed

    a.    attachment.
    b.    parenting.
    c.    development.
    d.    imprinting.

11. Which of the following is the temperament in which the child has a low activity level, shows low adaptability, and displays a low intensity of mood?

    a.    easy child
    b.    difficult child
    c.    slow-to-warm-up child
    d.    sociable child

12. Which of the following statements is consistent with the arguments Judith Harris made in her 1998 book "The Nurture Assumption"?

    a.    Parenting is essential in proper development.
    b.    Parents do not make a difference in children's behaviors.
    c.    Parents are more important than peers in development.
    d.    The genes are less important than parenting.

13. Which of the following activities is NOT associated with being an "emotion-coaching parent"?

    a.    ignoring when the child gets too emotional
    b.    monitoring their children's emotions
    c.    viewing their children's negative emotions as opportunities for teaching about emotions
    d.    providing guidance in how to deal with emotions effectively

14. Carol Gilligan criticized Kohlberg's theory of moral development on the basis that it did not address the role of this aspect of socioemotional development.

    a.    personality
    b.    emotions
    c.    gender
    d.    genetics

15. _____ is the period of rapid skeletal and sexual maturation that currently starts at around age 13.

    a.    Identity development
    b.    Puberty
    c.    Adolescence
    d.    Formal operational stage

16. According to the identity status approach, which status is the one in which the person has already explored various identities but has not yet committed to any one identity?

    a.    identity diffusion
    b.    identity foreclosure
    c.    identity moratorium
    d.    identity achievement

17. In a _____ study, the same participants are studied over a lengthy period, sometimes many years.
    a. cross-sectional
    b. longitudinal
    c. case
    d. cohort

## Practice Test 3

1. Fetal alcohol syndrome is a cluster of abnormalities that occur in children born to mothers who are heavy drinkers. This syndrome supports the notion that alcohol is
    a. bad for the mother.
    b. a teratogen.
    c. unrelated to birth defects.
    d. an appropriate beverage for pregnant women.

2. Maria is in her fifth week of pregnancy. Which prenatal stage is present?
    a. embryonic period
    b. germinal stage
    c. conception
    d. fetal period

3. Little Miranda screams with delight when she sees a horse. She yells to her dad, "See doggie." According to Piaget, what process has occurred?
    a. assimilation
    b. accommodation
    c. object permanence
    d. reversibility

4. Four-year-old Allison sees all the adults pitch in to clear the dinner table. Not wanting to be left out, she picks up a glass and carries it to the kitchen. Unfortunately, the glass slips out of her hand and breaks, just as she is trying to put it on the kitchen counter. According to Erikson's theory of psychosocial development, what would be the most appropriate response by Allison's mother?
    a. The mother should scold Allison severely.
    b. The mother should tell Allison that she is stupid and clumsy.
    c. The mother should ask Allison if she is OK and thank her for trying to help.
    d. The mother should make Allison clean up the mess.

5. Natalie is an infant who usually displays a sunny disposition, follows a regular sleep/wake schedule, and adjusts quickly to new routines and experiences. Natalie would most likely be classified as a(n)
    a. easy child.
    b. difficult child.
    c. slow-to-warm-up child.
    d. withdrawn child.

6. Karen, who is 52 years old, is going through menopause. This means that her
    a. children are leaving the home.
    b. menstrual periods are ceasing.
    c. ovaries are producing too much estrogen.
    d. cells are approaching the Hayflick limit.

7. Piaget's enduring contributions to the field of developmental psychology include all the following except which one?
   a. his view of children as active, constructive thinkers
   b. his extensive analysis of individual differences in cognitive development
   c. his focus on qualitative change in cognitive development
   d. his identification of an orderly sequence of cognitive development

8. Which of the following parenting styles corresponds with a parent who lets his kids smear food all over their faces and clothes in a restaurant because he doesn't want to stifle the kids' creativity?
   a. authoritarian
   b. neglectful
   c. authoritative
   d. indulgent

9. Which of the following parenting styles corresponds with a parent who expects a 5-year-old child to make the bed with corners tucked in and very neatly every morning before leaving for school; if the child does not comply, punishment is sure to follow.
   a. authoritarian
   b. neglectful
   c. authoritative
   d. indulgent

10. Which of the following social situations is associated with children experiencing stress, aggressiveness, and poor adjustment?
    a. grandparents babysitting
    b. divorce
    c. authoritative parenting
    d. starting school

11. The following are characteristics of positive parenting, EXCEPT
    a. parents are punitive.
    b. parents are supportive.
    c. parents model moral behavior.
    d. parents involve children in decision making.

12. Which of the following is the type of development involved in deciding whether or not to shoplift?
    a. physical development
    b. cognitive development
    c. social development
    d. moral development

13. Stephen decides not to shoplift because if his parents find out he knows he would receive a severe punishment. Which of the following Kohlberg levels corresponds to Stephen's moral development stage?
    a. preconventional level
    b. conventional level
    c. postconventional level
    d. preoperational level

14. April is a newborn who has an unnerving crying pattern. The pediatrician says that she probably has colic, but the new parents are at their wit's end. April hardly sleeps, and once she starts crying she can't seem to stop. April is likely to have been born with a(n) _____ temperament.
    a. easy
    b. difficult
    c. slow-to-warm
    d. changeable

15. _____ parents assume that if they interfere with their child's actions they would limit their psychological well-being.
    a. Authoritarian
    b. Neglectful
    c. Authoritative
    d. Indulgent

16. Which of the following is NOT one of the criticisms of Kohlberg's theory of moral development?
    a. Moral reasoning is not the same as moral behavior.
    b. The model does not reflect the concern for others in moral decision making.
    c. The theory is too focused on female morality and neglects male morality standards.
    d. The model ignores gender differences.

17. Which of the following principles is NOT associated with successful marriages?
    a. admiring each other
    b. having someone else as a best friend
    c. giving up some power
    d. solving conflicts together

18. Based on what we know about the cognitive development through the life span, which of the following age categories is more likely to be very good at Sunday's *New York Times* crossword puzzle (which is very hard)?
    a. adolescents
    b. middle adulthood
    c. late adulthood
    d. children

19. You will have reached your peak physical performance at age _____, and your physical skills will start declining by age _____.
    a. 16; 40
    b. 20; 30
    c. 20; 40
    d. 30; 20

## Connections

*Take advantage of all the other study tools available for this chapter!*

### Media Integration

| NAME OF CLIP | DESCRIPTION | KEY CONCEPTS AND IDEAS |
|---|---|---|
| | | **Exploring Human Development** |
| | | **Child Development** |
| Nature and Nurture: The Study of Twins | This video clip presents the case of identical twins who manifest a variety of physical differences owing to unequal nourishment in the womb; however, twins are very similar in a variety of characteristics, including psychological characteristics such as intelligence and personality. | Identical twins<br>Environmental influences<br>Genetic potential |
| Premature Babies | This audio clip discusses the behavioral, social, and cognitive delays in development of preterm children. Children who are born earlier and smaller than average are at greater risk of learning disabilities, ADHD, and school-related problems. | Preterm children<br>Learning disabilities<br>ADHD |
| Brain Development | This video clip presents an introduction to the brain. The relationship among genes, the environment, and brain development is discussed. The process of development of neural maps and networks is presented, as well as a discussion of the differences in brain elasticity between young and older brains. The relationship between experience and the strength of neural circuits is illustrated. | Brain<br>Nature vs. nurture<br>Neural maps<br>Neural networks<br>Brain elasticity |
| Formal Operational Thought | In this interactivity, students learn the rules associated with different levels of cognitive functioning. The level of cognitive processing required to make a decision such as looking for a job is discussed, and students engage in the balance beam task, which gives them feedback regarding their level of cognitive processing. The four Siegler rules are illustrated with the balance beam exercise. | Formal operational thought<br>Piaget stages of cognitive development<br>Siegler rules<br>Balance beam task |

| | | |
|---|---|---|
| Secure Attachment | This video clip presents the classic study by Harry Harlow in which monkeys are raised in isolation and given access to a terry cloth "mother" and a separate feeding "mother." The implications of the importance of attachment are discussed. | Attachment<br>Basic needs |
| Gender and Risk Taking | This audio clip presents the work of researcher Morrongiello, whose naturalistic observation studies have explored gender differences in risk-taking behaviors. Morrongiello argues that the tendency for boys to engage in more risky behavior than girls do is related to patterns of reinforcements provided by parents. | Gender differences<br>Reinforcement<br>Naturalistic observation |
| Neighborhood Violence | This audio clip presents evidence of the distressing effects on children of neighborhood violence. In a study of elementary school children, those living in violent neighborhoods manifested feeling less safe and having less trust in the police, as well as other psychological effects. The role of resiliency is also addressed. | Violence<br>Distress<br>Self-worth<br>Resiliency |
| | | **Adolescence** |
| Adolescent Brain | This video clip discusses in fascinating depth the differences between the adolescent brain and the adult brain, particularly in terms of the processing of information. The role of the amygdala in information processing in the adolescent brain and the implications of this pattern of brain activity are discussed. A gifted adolescent is studied with brain-imaging technology to demonstrate how his brain is cognitively adult, yet emotionally adolescent. | Adolescence<br>Brain<br>Amygdala<br>Frontal lobe<br>MRI<br>Information processing<br>Emotions<br>Intelligence<br>Maturity |

| | | |
|---|---|---|
| Alzheimer's Disease | In this video clip, a person with Alzheimer's disease is interviewed along with her daughter. Evidence of memory loss and personality changes, as well as the challenge of coping with the changes are presented. The person manifests amnesia for recent events while remembering old ones. | Alzheimer's disease<br>Memory<br>Amnesia |
| Dementia and Intelligence | This audio clip discusses the relationship between intelligence and dementia and the role of brain reserve. Also addressed is the role of engaging in regular activity over an extended period of time in delaying dementia. | Intelligence<br>Dementia |
| Cognitive Functioning in Centenarians | Using the brain has effects on brain connections. This video discusses the relationship between intelligence and experience. Testing of the mental abilities of centenarians is demonstrated. | Brain<br>Centenarians<br>Intelligence<br>Psychological testing |
| Aging and Memory | Deterioration of prospective memory in seniors is discussed, as well as a seven-session workshop designed to reverse the deterioration. The workshop includes cognitive strategies, relaxation, and memory tricks. | Memory<br>Prospective memory<br>Cognitive strategies<br>Relaxation<br>Visual associations |

**Online Learning Center (www.mhhe.com/Santrockp7u)**

- Interact and make learning fun!
  - o **Interactive Exercise**
    - ▪ Formal Operational Thought
  - o **Interactive Review**
    - ▪ Level of Analysis: Life-Span Development
- Brush up on the Key Terms for this chapter by first reviewing the electronic **Glossary** (in English or Spanish) and then testing your retention using the **Flashcard** feature.
- "Notes"—This feature allows you to use the website as you would your text, inserting your own study notes and highlighting areas of particular importance.

**In Your Text**

- Found throughout each chapter, the **Review and Sharpen Your Thinking** feature breaks the text into logical chunks, allowing you to process, review, and reflect thoughtfully on the information that you've just read. When going back to *study* the chapter, try reading the feature *before* the section of text to which it relates. In doing so, you will be able to focus your attention on important concepts *as* you encounter them. In this chapter, this feature can be found on the following pages: pp. 81, 104, 109, and 115.

**Practice Quizzes**

- Test your knowledge of human development by taking the different practice quizzes found on your text's **Online Learning Center** and on the **In-Psych Plus CD-ROM** packaged with your text.

## ANSWER KEY

## In Your Own Words

✓ Think about the formal operations stage; what was the last decision you made for which you used hypothetical-deductive reasoning?

*Hypothetical-deductive reasoning involves the creation of hypothesis and systematic deduction as a way of solving problems. It requires abstract and logical thinking. According to Piaget, in this process the individual thinks like a scientist does when he-she approaches a question, in a systematic and logical manner. This reasoning capacity is possible once the person reaches adolescence; therefore, it can be expected that students taking this course have engaged already in hypothetical-deductive reasoning.*

✓ What parenting style did your parent(s) use? If you are a parent, which parenting style do you use? Why? If you are not a parent, which parenting style do you think you would use? Why?

*This questions requires the student to understand and think critically about the four parenting styles discussed in the chapter: authoritarian, authoritative, neglectful, and indulgent.*

✓ When you were in eighth grade, what types of arguments did you have with your parents or other adults? Did the arguments revolve around your search for independence?

*This question requires integrated knowledge of Piaget's theory of cognitive development, Erikson's theory of socioemotional development, and the issues involved in adolescent egocentricity and the search for identity and interdependence.*

✓ How might a middle-aged person help the next generation as it experiences generativity?

*Erikson's 7th stage of socioemotional development involves a crisis between generativity and stagnation, and it occurs in middle adulthood. Generativity is the concern that develops during this age with assisting and guiding the younger generation in developing and leading useful lives. The feeling of having done nothing to help the next generation is stagnation. The answer to this question should include examples of ways in which an adult can engage in generativity, such as volunteering, coaching, working in child care, cooperating in fundraisers for the young, or donating to causes that benefit younger generations.*

✓ Describe some biological, cognitive, and socioemotional changes that you have experienced in the past year.

*This question requires students to understand the domains of physical, cognitive, and socioemotional processes as they may apply to their own development. Students in this class are expected to range in developmental stages from adolescence to adulthood; therefore, their answers should be consistent with the developmental changes corresponding to their developmental stage. Physical processes include changes in the individual's biological nature or maturation. Cognitive processes involve changes in an individual's mental processes, specifically thinking. Socioemotional processes include changes in individual's relationships, emotions, and personality.*

## Correcting the Incorrect

1. Development refers to the changes that take place from conception through the *life span*. (p. 79)

2. Physical processes include the development of the brain, height and weight, and motor skills. (p. 79)

3. An infant's smile in response to his mother's smile illustrates *socioemotional* processes. (p. 79)

4. The nature and nurture theory refers to the influences of heredity and environment on behavior. (p. 81)

5. The stages of prenatal development are the germinal period, the embryonic period, and the fetal period. (p. 82)

6. *Teratogen* refers to *any agent that causes a birth defect*. (p. 82)

7. A *schema* is a concept or framework that already exists that organizes and interprets information. (p. 86)

8. A preterm infant is born prior to *38* weeks after conception. (p. 83)

9. n *accommodation*, the individual adjusts to new information. (p. 86)

10. Object permanence takes place in the sensorimotor stage. (p. 87)

11. Infants are more cognitively competent than Piaget thought. (p. 91)

12. The thinking of a child during the concrete operational stage is logical. (p. 89)

13. A person who can engage in hypothetical-deductive reasoning is most likely to be in the *formal* operational stage. (p. 90)

14. Vygotsky *emphasized* the role of culture in development. (p. 91)

15. Erikson proposed eight stages of psychosocial development. (p. 91)

16. Individuals during their 20s and 30s are in the intimacy versus isolation stage, according to Erikson. (p. 113)

17. A parent who is restrictive and has a punitive style that demands obedience on the part of the child has an *authoritarian* parenting style. (p. 96)

18. *Estrogen* is a hormone found in girls; it is responsible for the development of breasts, uterus, and skeleton. (p. 105)

19. An adolescent yells to her mother, "You just don't understand me!" This illustrates adolescent *egocentrism*. (p. 106)

20. During the conventional stage of moral thinking, the individual shows *an intermediate level* of internalization of moral values. (p. 99)

21. Moral development is completely internalized at the postconventional level of moral thinking. (p. 100)

22. *Carol Gilligan* argues that people see their connectedness with others as important in moral thinking. (p. 101)

23. Most women who experience menopause *do not* report psychological problems or physical problems. (p. 110)

24. *Alzheimer's disease* is characterized by the gradual deterioration of memory, reasoning, language, and, eventually, physical functioning. (p. 111)

# Practice Test 1

1. a. no; development involves more than just behavior changes
   b. THAT'S RIGHT; development refers to pattern of movement or change
   c. no; development involves more than just cognitive maturity
   d. no; development involves more than just physical growth
   p. 79

2. a. no; but you're partially correct
   b. no; but you're partially correct
   c. no; but you're partially correct
   d. YES; development involves all the options
   p. 79

3. a. no; but biological processes are involved in development
   b. no; but cognitive processes are involved in development
   c. no; but socioemotional processes are involved in development
   d. THAT'S RIGHT; it involves biological, cognitive, and socioemotional processes
   p. 79

4. a. no
   b. no
   c. no; this refers to how the change occurs, suddenly or slowly
   d. YES; nature refers to heredity and nurture refers to experience
   p. 81

5. a. no; Piaget's theory is about cognitive development and does not focus on behaviors.
   b. no; this theory does not focus on emotions.
   c. YES; operations are mental representations that are reversible.
   d. no; while this concept is used in Piaget's theory it refers to the process of adjusting to new information.
   p. 87

6. a. these children can think symbolically; they can use language and can draw
   b. no; these children understand words
   c. RIGHT; preoperational thinkers (ages 2–7 years) cannot yet reverse their thinking
   d. no; these children can do "pretend" play
   p. 87

7. a. these children are not capable of conservation
   b. no; these children are not yet capable of conservation
   c. CORRECT; these children (ages 7–11 years) grasp conservation
   d. no
   p. 89

8. a. no; this is the second stage
   b. no; this is the fourth stage
   c. no; this is the third stage
   d. RIGHT; trust is built when the child's needs are met
   p. 92

9. a. no; this stage occurs in the 40s and 50s
   b. this stage occurs in early adulthood
   c. YES; this is the last stage, when people look back on their lives
   d. these are theories of aging and are not among Erikson's stages
   p. 113

10. a. no
    b. no
    c. CORRECT
    d. no
    p. 96

11. a. RIGHT; this style is characterized by limits and control and verbal give-and-take
    b. no; this style involves a restrictive, punitive style
    c. no; a neglecting style refers to a parent who is uninvolved in the child's life
    d. no; indulgent style entails involvement but few demands
    p. 96

12. a. no; adolescence is a time of evaluation
    b. CORRECT; for most adolescents, it is not a time of acute crisis
    c. no; adolescence is a time of decision making
    d. no; adolescence is a time of commitment
    p. 105

13. a. no; this is part of adolescent egocentrism
    b. no; this is part of adolescent egocentrism
    c. CORRECT; this is not the same as egocentrism in childhood
    d. no; this is part of adolescent egocentrism
    p. 106

14. a. no; but formal operational thought is part of cognitive development
    b. no; but this type of reasoning is part of cognitive development
    c. no; but egocentrism is one characteristic of cognitive development
    d. RIGHT; all are characteristics of adolescent cognitive development
    p. 106

15. a. no; this stage refers to nonsymbolic stage
    b. no; the child in this stage is capable of symbolic thinking
    c. no; the child in this stage engages in logical thinking about concrete events
    d. YES; in formal operational thought, people are able to engage in this reasoning
    p. 106

16. a. in this stage there is no internalization of moral values
    b. this is the intermediate level of internalization
    c. RIGHT; this is the highest level of moral thinking
    d. no; this is the type of orientation that Kohlberg takes
    p. 100

17. a. RIGHT; a care perspective considers people's connectedness
    b. no; Kohlberg's theory does take a justice perspective
    c. no; this is a criticism of Kohlberg's theory
    d. no; most of his research was with males
    p. 101

18. a. no
    b. no
    c. THIS IS CORRECT
    d. no; the concern starts earlier in middle adulthood
    p. 110

## Practice Test 2

1. a. no; these involve changes in biology and physiology
   b. YES; personality, relationship, and emotions all pertain to the socioemotional processes
   c. no; these involve changes in thinking
   d. no; too general
   p. 79

2. a. CORRECT; we are born with our genetics but are nurtured and modified by our environment
   b. no; the opposite would be true
   c. no; the phenotype is influenced by the environment while the genotype is not
   d. no; the opposite would be true
   p. 81

3. a. no; this is the fetal period
   b. no; this is the germinal period
   c. no
   d. YES; also, toward the end of this period the face starts to form and the intestinal tract appears
   p. 82

4. a. no; microencephaly is one of the effects of fetal alcohol syndrome
   b. no; this is also one of the effects of alcohol
   c. YES; this is a problem associated with the use of heroin during pregnancy
   d. no; this is also one of the effects of alcohol
   p. 83

5. a. no; this is a reflex that we are born with and that lasts throughout our life span
   b. no; this is a reflex that we are born with, initiated when the mouth of the infant is touched
   c. YES; we are not born with such fears, we learn them through experiences
   d. no; babies do have a reflexive way of responding to startling stimuli
   p. 83

6. a. no; egocentrism according to Piaget meant the inability to distinguish between one's own perspective and someone else's perspective
   b. no; young children can learn to share, they just can't think as if they were another person
   c. YES; this is the definition of egocentrism according to Piaget
   d. no; while adolescents do experience a type of egocentrism, Piaget used the concept to explain the psychology of children in the preoperational cognitive stage
   p. 88

7. a.   THAT'S CORRECT
   b.   no; just the opposite occurs; thoughts become more abstract and logical
   c.   no; inferiority is part of an earlier stage (6 years to puberty)
   d.   this is the highest level of moral thinking
   p. 107

8. a.   no; this occurs in late adulthood
   b.   this stage takes place in adolescence
   c.   no
   d.   YES; this stage occurs in the 40s and 50s
   p. 113

9. a.   no; this style is characterized by limits and control and verbal give-and-take
   b.   no; this style involves a restrictive, punitive style
   c.   no; a neglecting style refers to a parent who is uninvolved in the child's life
   d.   YES; indulgent style entails involvement but few demands
   p. 96

10. a.   YES; attachment results in a close emotional bond between the infant and its caregiver
    b.   no; unfortunately, parenting does not always involve a positive effort to continue the relationship
    c.   no; this concept is too broad
    d.   no; imprinting is a reflexive form of attachment
    p. 93

11. a.   no; this child adapts easily
    b.   no; this child tends to have higher levels of activity and high intensity of mood
    c.   YES; while somewhat negative in emotions, this child can adapt easier than the difficult child
    d.   no; this general description is not a temperament category
    p. 95

12. a.   no; Harris argued that what parents did was not an essential determinant of adult personality
    b.   YES; Harris argued that punishing or nurturing a child would not have a major effect on the child's adult personality
    c.   no; Harris argued that peers had a stronger impact on development
    d.   no; Harris argued that both genes and peers are stronger determinants of adult personality than parenting
    p. 98

13. a.   CORRECT; this is not consistent with good emotion-coaching parenting—they actually view their children's negative emotions as opportunities for teaching about emotions
    b.   no; this is one of the characteristics of emotion-coaching parenting
    c.   no; this is one of the characteristics of emotion-coaching parenting
    d.   no; this is one of the characteristics of emotion-coaching parenting
    p. 97

14. a. no; Gilligan did not argue that personality played a role in the development of morality
    b. no; Gilligan did not study the role of emotions in morality
    c. YES; Carol Gilligan argued that Kohlberg ignored the possibility that women and men have different criteria for morality
    d. no; genetics are not a socioemotional aspect of development
   p. 101

15. a. no; while this is crucial during adolescence, it is not a biological change
    b. YES; this is the correct term
    c. no; adolescence is the developmental period, thus a more general concept than just the biological processes of the period
    d. no; this refers to the cognitive processes during adolescence
   p. 105

16. a. no; during this status the person has neither explored nor committed to an identity
    b. no; during this status the person makes a commitment to an identity before exploring alternatives
    c. YES; as the concept moratorium suggests, the person has explored alternatives but is holding off on making a decision and commitment; this is common during college years
    d. no; during this status the person has already explored alternatives and made his or her commitment to an identity
   p. 108

17. a. no; in a cross-sectional study different people, of different ages, are assessed at the same time
    b. YES; longitudinal studies follow the same participants and assess them various times across a lengthy period
    c. no; the case study focuses only on one person
    d. no; cohort studies is another way of referring to cross-sectional studies
   p. 112

## Practice Test 3

1. a. no; fetal alcohol syndrome is proof that alcohol is very damaging to the child.
   b. YES; alcohol is an agent that causes birth defect.
   c. no; alcohol is a teratogen and mother intake is associated with birth defects.
   d. no; considering the serious effects of this teratogen it is not an appropriate beverage for pregnant women.
   p. 82

2. a. YES; the fifth week is in the embryonic period (three to eight weeks)
   b. no; the germinal stage is the first two weeks
   c. no; conception refers to the union of sperm and ovum
   d. no; the fetal period is 2 months to 9 months
   p. 82

3. a. YES; new information (horse) is adjusted to fit existing knowledge (doggie)
   b. no; the horse is perceived as a doggie
   c. no; object permanence is an understanding that objects exist even if they aren't seen
   d. no; this refers to the ability to think in reverse
   p. 86

4. a. no; this could lead to guilt over her willingness to help
   b. no; this could lead to guilt over her willingness to help
   c. RIGHT; she is in initiative versus guilt; she shows initiative in helping with the glass
   d. no; maybe, Allison's mother should do this, but not according to Erikson's theory of psychosocial development
   p. 93

5. a. RIGHT; Natalie has an easy child temperament
   b. a difficult child reacts negatively, cries frequently, and has an irregular routines
   c. this type involves low activity and shows low adaptability
   d. this is not a temperament type
   p. 95

6. a. no
   b. RIGHT
   c. no; in fact her ovaries are producing less estrogen
   d. no; the Hayflick limit is a theory of aging
   p. 110

7. a. this is an enduring contribution
   b. THAT IS CORRECT; Piaget focused on differences between groups of children
   c. no; this is an enduring contribution
   d. no; this is an enduring contribution
   p. 90

8. a. no; this parent would stop that behavior summarily
   b. no; this parent may let the kids do all that, not because of the concern with creativity, but rather because he just doesn't care
   c. no; this parent may allow this behavior at home but would probably modify the behavior of the children to be more appropriate in a social setting such as a restaurant
   d. YES; this is correct
   p. 96

9. a. YES; the authoritarian parenting style is adult centered, which means that parents expect the children to be able to do behaviors that adults can do and if they don't do them, punishment is used to modify the behavior
   b. no; this parent is not very likely to push consistently for an organized bedroom
   c. no; authoritative parents may train the child to make the bed every day, but the expectations would be consistent with the age of the child and they may be more likely to use rewards rather than punishment to mold behaviors
   d. no; this parent is not very likely to push consistently for an organized bedroom
   p. 96

10. a. no; this chapter reports no negative effects of grandparents babysitting
    b. YES; divorce has been associated with these experiences in children; however, the majority of children of divorce adjust properly
    c. no; the authoritative parenting style is a positive style
    d. no; starting school is not associated with these three experiences
    p. 97

11. a.  YES; this is not one of the characteristics of positive parenting; punitive refers to the use of punishment to modify behaviors
    b.  no; this is one of the characteristics of positive parenting
    c.  no; this is one of the characteristics of positive parenting
    d.  no; this is one of the characteristics of positive parenting
    p. 97

12. a.  no; this involves the maturation of the body
    b.  no; this involves the development of thinking; while it is associated, it is not the best answer
    c.  no; this involves the development of relationships in the person's life span
    d.  YES; moral development involves changes with age in thoughts, feelings, and behaviors regarding the principles and values that guide what people should do
    p. 98

13. a.  YES; during this level, people base morality on the probability of being rewarded or punished for the behavior; Stephen is probably a young child
    b.  No; during this level, people base morality on standards they have learned from others
    c.  No; during this level people base morality on their own personal moral code
    d.  No; this is a cognitive development stage, not a moral development stage
    p. 99

14. a.  no; the crying pattern of April is not consistent with the easy temperament
    b.  YES; the difficult child has a hard time developing a sleeping pattern and expresses more negative emotions that the other temperaments
    c.  no; the crying pattern of April is not consistent with the slow-to-warm temperament
    d.  no; April is clearly showing a difficult temperament pattern
    p. 95

15. a.  no; this belief is not consistent with the authoritarian parenting style
    b.  no; this belief is not consistent with the neglectful parenting style
    c.  no; authoritative parents interfere when they think it is in the child's best interest
    d.  YES; the indulgent parent sees total freedom as essential for psychological well-being
    p. 96

16. a.  no; this is one of the criticisms of the theory
    b.  no; this is one of the criticisms of the theory
    c.  YES; the opposite is true since Kohlberg studied only males
    d.  no; this is one of the criticisms of the theory
    p. 101

17. a.  no; this is one of the characteristics of successful marriages
    b.  YES; this is not a good idea, as people in successful marriages tend to turn to each other for friendship
    c.  no; this is one of the characteristics of successful marriages
    d.  no; this is one of the characteristics of successful marriages
    p. 114

18. a.  no
    b.  no; they tend to be better at fluid rather crystallized intelligence
    c.  YES; people in late adulthood may be slower but tend to have wisdom and a lot of
        information gathered throughout their life span; they may not be as effective at learning
        new things, but crossword puzzles usually require basic knowledge in many areas of life
    d.  no
    p. 115

19. a.  no; too young and too old
    b.  YES; this is the right range
    c.  no; decline starts by age 30
    d.  no; the opposite is true
    p. 109

# Chapter 5—Sensation and Perception

## Learning Goals

1. Discuss basic principles of sensation and perception.
2. Explain how the visual system enables us to see and, by communicating with the brain, to perceive the world.
3. Understand how the auditory system registers sound and how it connects with the brain to perceive it.
4. Know how the skin, chemical, and kinesthetic and vestibular senses work.

*After studying Chapter 5, you will be able to:*

- Define fine sensation and perception.
- Understand the role of thresholds in sensation and discuss different types of threshold.
- Discuss the visual stimulus and the eye.
- Explain how information is transmitted from the eye to the brain and what neural-visual processing is.
- Describe what sensory adaptation is.
- Explain about color vision, including different theories about it.
- Explain the principles involved in shape perception, depth perception, motion perception, and constancy perception.
- Discuss the nature of sound and how people experience it.
- Understand the ear's structure and functions.
- Describe the skin senses and chemical senses, as well as the kinesthetic and vestibular senses.

## CHAPTER 5: OUTLINE

- *Sensation* is the process of detecting and encoding stimulus energy in the world by our sense organs. Sensation is transformed into an action potential, and a neural impulse or message is delivered to the brain. In the brain, the stimulated areas produce what we refer to as *perception*. Perception refers to the process of organizing and interpreting sensory information to give it meaning.

- The process of sensation starts with sensory receptors, which are cells found in your sensory organs that are dedicated to receiving the stimulation and transmitting the stimulus information to the afferent nerves that will then take the message to the brain.

- There are three categories of sensory receptors: photreception (sight), mechanoreception (touch, hearing, balance), and chemoreception (smell and taste).

- Psychophysics studies the links between the physical properties of stimuli and a person's experience of them. One important question in psychophysics addresses how much stimulus is needed for the person to sense and perceive a stimuli. The answer is in the concept of threshold. An absolute threshold is the minimum amount of energy that we can detect 50% of the time.

- In psychophysics, *noise* is the term used to refer to irrelevant and competing stimuli. When a person senses something without being aware of this sensation, he or she has experienced a subliminal perception.

- The difference threshold is the smallest difference in stimulation needed to recognize that two stimuli are different from each other 50% of the time.

- Sensory adaptation happens because we tend to adapt to an average level of stimuli. If the level of stimili is changed, we will go through a process of readaptation.

- The visual system is dedicated to photoreception. Light is a form of electromagnetic energy that travels in waves. Light has different wavelengths, the distance from the peak of one wave to the peak of the next wave.

- We can see light with wavelengths between 400 and 700 nanometers, which is also the range of wavelengths emitted by the sun.

- The eye has different parts, all specialized in the process of photoreception. The main external structures of the eye include the sclera, iris, pupil, and cornea. Within the eye, the retina records the light information and converts it to neural impulses for processing in the brain.

- The retina is made up of light-sensitive receptors called *rods* and *cones*, which perform transduction. The fovea is a small area in the center of the retina where vision is at its best. The blind spot lacks receptors since it is where neural impulses exit the eye on the optic nerve. The optic nerve fibers cross and divide at the optic chiasm, resulting in visual information received on the left eye to be processed on the right side of the brain and vice versa.

- In the temporal lobe we process information about the color, form, and texture of the objects we see; in the parietal lobe we process information about the location, movement, and depth of the objects we see. Objects have color because they reflect only certain wavelengths of light. Two major theories of color vision are the trichromatic theory and the opponent-process theory.

- There are various dimensions to the process of perception. Some of these dimensions are shape, depth, motion, and constancy. The world is full of shapes, and our perception of them is influenced by the figure-ground relationship.

- Gestalt psychology describes how we tend to perceive according to certain patterns; a main principle is that the whole is different from the sum of its parts.

- Depth perception allows us to perceive objects three-dimensionally and involves binocular and monocular cues.

- In studying motor perception, psychologists examine apparent movement, stroboscopic motion, and movement aftereffects.

- Perceptual constancy includes size constancy, shape constancy, and brightness constancy.

- The auditory system is dedicated to one type of mechanoreception, audition. Sound waves vary from each other in frequency and amplitude. Timbre is the perceptual quality of a sound.

- The ear has different parts, all working together to capture auditory information and send it to the brain for interpretation. The ear is made up of the outer ear, middle ear, and inner ear.

- The outer ear consists of the pinna and the external auditory canal. The middle ear consists of the eardrum, hammer, anvil, and stirrup. The inner ear is made up of the oval window, cochlea, and the basilar membrane.

- Three theories that explain auditory processing are place theory, frequency theory, and the volley principle. The auditory nerve carries the neural impulses from the auditory system to the brain. The timing and intensity of a sound are important in the process of localizing the source of the sound. Excessive noise has been associated with poor reading skills, high blood pressure, and easy distraction from tasks.

- The skin senses are also dedicated to mechanoreception, specifically to the sensation of touch, temperature, and pain. Touch information goes to the thalamus, which relays information to the corresponding somatosensory areas of the parietal lobes.

- Females are more sensitive to touch than are males. Thermoreceptors are located under the skin and are dedicated to the reception of temperature. There are warm and cold thermoreceptors.

- Pain is the sensation that warns us of damage to our body. Some strategies used to reduce pain are distraction, focused breathing, and counterstimulation.

- Taste and smell are sensations based on chemoreception, thus they are also referred to as the *chemical senses*. Taste buds, which are located on the tongue, respond to sweet, sour, bitter, and salty qualities.

- The olfactory epithelium contains the chemoreceptors for smell. The kinesthetic sense provides information to the brain about movement, posture, and orientation, while the vestibular system provides information about balance and movement.

## Building Blocks of Chapter 5

### Clarifying some of the tricky points in Chapter 5
### and
### In Your Own Words

*To respond to the questions and exercises presented in the "In Your Own Words" section, please write your thoughts, perspectives, and reactions on a separate piece of paper.*

### *How We Sense and Perceive the World*

The process of detecting and encoding stimulus energy is called *sensation*. After environmental stimuli are detected and encoded, the physical energy is transformed into *electrochemical energy*. The process of organizing and interpreting sensory information to give it meaning is referred to as *perception*. The sense organs can be organized into three classes: (1) *photoreceptors*, dedicated to the reception of light, (2) *mechanoreceptors*, dedicated to the reception of touch, hearing, and balance, and (3) *chemorecptors*, dedicated to the reception of smell and taste.

### In Your Own Words

*Please write your thoughts, perspectives, and reactions on a separate piece of paper.*
  ✓ *Put the definitions of sensation and perception in your own words and give an example of each.*

The minimum amount of a stimulus an individual can detect 50% of the time is called *absolute threshold*. The term given to irrelevant and competing stimuli is *noise*. The difference threshold, or *just noticeable difference*, is the point at which a person detects the difference between two stimuli 50% of the time. According to Weber, regardless of their magnitude, two stimuli must differ by a constant proportion to be detected.

As we have see so far, factors such as threshold influence the extent to which sensed stimuli will be perceived. Other factors influencing sensation and perception are *attention* and *perceptual set*. *Selective attention* involves focusing on a specific aspect of the environment while ignoring others. *Perceptual set* refers to our predisposition to perceive things in ways that are consistent with what we have perceived before. Finally, another factor that influences sensation and perception is sensory *adaptation*, which is the change in responsiveness of the sensory system based on the average level of surrounding stimulation that the person has become accustomed to.

**In Your Own Words**

*Please write your thoughts, perspectives, and reactions on a separate piece of paper.*

✓ *Give an example of selective attention that you have recently experienced.*

### Visual System

Light is a form of *electromagnetic energy* that can be described in terms of *waves*. The distance from the peak of one wave of light to the next is a *wavelength*.

The white part of the eye, which helps maintain the shape of the eye and protects it from injury, is called the *sclera*. The colored part of the eye, which can range in color from light blue to dark brown, is the *iris*. The opening in the center of the iris is called the *pupil*. The clear membrane just in front of the eye is called the *cornea*. The transparent and flexible disklike structure is called the *lens*. The light-sensitive surface in the back of the eye is the *retina*.

The retina contains two kinds of light receptors, called *rods and cones*. Rods are active in *night vision* but are not useful for color vision. Cones are the receptors used for *color vision*.

In the center of the retina, where vision is the sharpest, is an area called the *fovea*. As a result of the placement of the rods on the retina, we are able to detect fainter spots of light on the *peripheral retina* than at the fovea.

Information is carried out of the eye toward the brain by the *optic nerve*. The place on retina where the optic nerve leaves the eye is the *blind spot*. After the optic nerve leaves the eye, most of its fibers divide and cross over to the other side at the *optic chiasm*. Therefore, what we see on the left side of our visual field ends up on the right side of the brain. Visual information is processed in the *visual cortex*, located in the *occipital lobe*.

Objects appear colored because they reflect certain *wavelengths* of light to our eyes. A theory of color vision that suggests that the retina responds to only one of three colors—red, blue, and green—is the *trichromatic theory*. Although the trichromatic theory helps explain color blindness, it cannot adequately explain *afterimages*. The phenomenon of afterimages led Hering to propose that the visual system treats colors as *complementary pairs*. The theory that cells in the retina respond to pairs of color is called the *opponent-process theory*.

Perception of visual stimuli can be organized in four dimensions: *shape, depth, motion,* and *constancy*. The principle that organizes our perceptual field into stimuli that stand out and those that do not stand out is called the *figure-ground relationship*. An area of psychology that studies how people organize their perceptions is called *gestalt psychology*.

The ability to perceive objects three-dimensionally is called *depth perception*. The cues that we use for depth perception are both *monocular and binocular*. People with vision in only one eye still see a world of depth because of *monocular cues*. An example of a monocular cue is *overlap*, whereby one object partially blocks another object. Monocular cues are especially intriguing to painters, who must create three-dimensional illusions on two-dimensional canvases.

We perceive three types of perceptual constancy. The recognition that an object remains the same size even though the retinal image changes is called *size constancy*. The perception that an object is the same even though its orientation to us changes is called *shape constancy*. The recognition that an object retains the same degree of brightness even though different amounts of light fall on it is called *brightness constancy*.

### Auditory System

Sound, or sound waves, are *vibrations* in the air that are processed by our auditory system. One way in which sound waves differ from one another is in *frequency*. The ear detects the frequency of a sound wave as *pitch*. Sound waves also vary in *amplitude*, which is the change of pressure created by sound waves. The amplitude of a sound wave is measured in *decibels*. The perception of a sound wave's amplitude is referred to as *loudness*. The blending of numerous sound waves is called *complexity*. We experience the different qualities of sound as *timbre*.

The outer ear is made up of the *pinna*, which helps us localize sounds, and the external auditory canal, which funnels sound to the *middle ear*. In the middle ear, the first structure touched by sound is the *tympanic membrane* (the eardrum). The eardrum's vibrations then touch the three tiny bone structures, *the mallus (hammer), the incus (anvil), and the stapes (stirrup)*. In the inner ear, sound waves travel from the *oval window* to the *cochlea*. Sensory receptors are stimulated by vibrations of the *cilia* (hair cells). These vibrations generate neural impulses.

How does the inner ear register the frequency of sound? According to the place theory, each frequency produces vibrations at a particular place on the *basilar membrane*. Another theory suggests that the perception of sound is tied to the frequency of the *auditory nerve* firing. This is called *frequency theory*. Another theory of hearing argues that neural cells can fire impulses in *rapid* succession; this is called the *volley principle*. Information travels from the cochlea to the lower portion of the brain by means of the *auditory nerve*. The difference in both *timing and intensity* helps us localize the source of the sound we are perceiving. Ultimately, auditory information is processed, integrated, and stored in the *temporal lobe* of the cerebral cortex.

### Other Senses

Our largest sensory system is the *skin*. The skin contains *mechanoreceptors for touch, temperature, and pain*. Receptors located under the skin that respond to increases and decreases in temperature are called *thermoreceptors*. The sensation that warns us that damage is occurring to our bodies is *pain*. Pain is affected by motivation as well as cultural variations. Strategies that can be used to reduce pain include *distraction, focused breathing, and counterstimulation.*

**In Your Own Words**

*Please write your thoughts, perspectives, and reactions on a separate piece of paper.*

✓  *If culture influences perception, list some ways that your culture has influenced your perception of clothing, behavior, music, or food.*

✓  *How would your life change if you lost your ability to experience the sense of pain?*

## Correcting the Incorrect

Carefully read each statement. Determine if the statement is correct or incorrect. If the statement is incorrect, make the necessary changes to correct it. Then check the answer key at the end of the chapter for the correct statement and page reference in the textbook.

1. Perception refers to the process of detecting and encoding stimulus energy in the world.
2. The minimum amount of energy that can be detected is called the difference threshold.
3. Signal is the term given to irrelevant and competing stimuli.
4. Selective attention allows us to focus on some aspects of the environment while ignoring others.
5. The pupil contains the rods and cones.
6. The visual receptors or photoreceptors are the rods and cones.
7. Rods provide color vision.
8. Perceptual constancy is the change in the sensory system's responsiveness based on the average level of surrounding stimulation.
9. A color's hue is based on its wavelength.
10. The three different cones are red, white, and yellow.
11. The opponent-process theory of color vision states that there are three types of receptors that are maximally sensitive to different but overlapping ranges of wavelengths.
12. The trichromatic and opponent-process theories are both correct.
13. The figure-ground relationship is the principle that explains depth perception.
14. Monocular cues provides us information about shape perception.
15. A binocular cue is overlapping.
16. We experience frequency of a sound wave as loudness.
17. The place theory of hearing adequately explains low-frequency sounds but not high-frequency sounds.
18. The auditory nerve carries neural impulses to the brain's auditory areas.
19. Smell, taste, and vision are our chemical senses.
20. The taste qualities include sweet and sour.
21. The sense that provides information about balance and movement is the kinesthetic sense.
22. The kinesthetic and vestibular senses are supplemented by information from hearing.

# Practice Test 1

1.  The process of detecting and encoding stimuli is called
    a.  sensation.
    b.  perception.
    c.  gestalt psychology.
    d.  accommodation.

2.  The minimum amount of energy that we can detect is called
    a.  the absolute threshold.
    b.  minimal threshold.
    c.  the difference threshold.
    d.  subliminal perception.

3.  Psychologists call the presence of competing and irrelevant stimuli
    a.  noise.
    b.  accommodation.
    c.  saturation.
    d.  subliminal perception.

4.  Wavelength is defined as the distance between
    a.  peak and valley of a light wave.
    b.  peak and peak of a light wave.
    c.  valley and amplitude of a light wave.
    d.  amplitude and peak of a light wave.

5.  In order to do its job, the pupil depends most on which other part of the eye?
    a.  lens
    b.  iris
    c.  cornea
    d.  retina

6.  The rods and cones are found in what part of the eye?
    a.  the sclera
    b.  the retina
    c.  the cornea
    d.  the fovea

7.  Why is vision sharpest in the fovea?
    a.  because it contains only cones
    b.  because it contains more cones than rods
    c.  because it contains both rods and cones
    d.  because it is located in the center of the retina

8.  After information passes the optic chiasm, images from the left side of our visual field end up
    a.  being reflected back to the blind spot.
    b.  being reflected back to the optic nerve.
    c.  on the right side of the brain.
    d.  on the left side of the brain.

9.    The visual cortex, which is responsible for processing visual information, is located in the
      _____ lobe.
      a.    occipital
      b.    parietal
      c.    temporal
      d.    frontal

10.   Which theory of color vision does the best job of explaining afterimages?
      a.    trichromatic theory
      b.    the opponent-process theory
      c.    the additive-subtractive theory
      d.    No theory currently explains afterimages.

11.   Your text states that the term *color blindness* is misleading. Which of the following terms
      would be the most appropriate replacement?
      a.    color vision deficit
      b.    green blindness
      c.    blue blindness
      d.    visually impaired

12.   Pitch is to frequency as loudness is to
      a.    amplitude.
      b.    Hertz.
      c.    wavelength.
      d.    pulsation.

13.   Which structures comprise the inner ear?
      a.    eardrum, oval window, and stirrup
      b.    pinna, external auditory canal, and eardrum
      c.    hammer, anvil, stirrup
      d.    oval window, cochlea, and the basilar membrane

14.   Which part of the ear is most important in the translation of sound?
      a.    the auditory nerve
      b.    the outer ear
      c.    the middle ear
      d.    the inner ear

15.   Which theory of hearing suggests that high-frequency tones are explained by cells firing in
      rapid succession?
      a.    place theory
      b.    frequency theory
      c.    volley theory
      d.    similarity theory

16.   What is the main difference between touch receptors and thermoreceptors?
      a.    sensitivity and speed
      b.    location and function
      c.    number and location
      d.    function and speed

17. The semicircular canals are found in
    a.    Venice.
    b.    the inner ear.
    c.    the outer ear.
    d.    the middle ear.

18. What do the sense of taste and the sense of smell have in common?
    a.    They are both mechanical senses.
    b.    They are both chemical senses.
    c.    They are both electromagnetic senses.
    d.    They are both electric senses.

19. What allows you to focus on this question while ignoring all the other stimulation in your environment?
    a.    perception
    b.    hue
    c.    selective attention
    d.    selective adaptation

## Practice Test 2

1. A change in the wavelength of light would result in a change in our perception of
    a.    hue.
    b.    saturation.
    c.    brightness.
    d.    timbre.

2. The principle by which we organize perception into those stimuli that stand out and those that are left over is called
    a.    figure-ground.
    b.    closure.
    c.    similarity.
    d.    proximity.

3. The tendency to mentally "fill in the spaces" in order to see figures as complete refers to the gestalt principle of
    a.    closure.
    b.    figure-ground.
    c.    proximity.
    d.    similarity.

4. When an object is partially concealed the concealing object is perceived as being closer. This monocular cue of depth is referred to as
    a.    linear perspective.
    b.    texture gradient.
    c.    shading.
    d.    overlap.

5.     Which of the following is the name for the process of sending sensory information to the brain for analysis and interpretation?
       a.     bottom-up
       b.     top-down
       c.     cognition to motor
       d.     brain to motor

6.     The cells that are dedicated to the reception and transmission of stimulus information are the
       a.     glial cells.
       b.     eyes.
       c.     ears.
       d.     sensory receptors.

7.     The sensory receptors in the eye are
       a.     photoreceptors.
       b.     mechanoreceptors.
       c.     chemoreceptors.
       d.     in the cornea.

8.     Which of the following monocular cues of depth is the one in which the cue involves how dense and fine are the images?
       a.     linear perspective
       b.     texture gradient
       c.     overlap
       d.     shading

9.     The _____ is the part of the forebrain that contributes to the perception of touch by relaying sensory information to the appropriate spot on the somatosensory areas of the parietal lobes.
       a.     hippocampus
       b.     hypothalamus
       c.     pons
       d.     thalamus

10.    Which of the following is NOT associated with the reduction of pain?
       a.     focused breathing
       b.     counterstimulation
       c.     distraction
       d.     overstimulation

11.    Which of the following is NOT one of the categories of taste detected by our taste buds?
       a.     salty
       b.     sour
       c.     pasty
       d.     bitter

12.    Feedback about the position of our limbs and body parts in relation to other body parts relies on the collaboration of these two senses.
       a.     kinesthetic and vestibular
       b.     vestibular and visual
       c.     kinesthetic and visual
       d.     visual and olfactory

13.    The retina is to the visual sense as the _____ are to the detection of head motion.
    a.    rods
    b.    eardrums
    c.    semicircular canals
    d.    cones

14.    All sensation begins with _____.
    a.    sensory receptors.
    b.    the brain.
    c.    perception.
    d.    chemoreceptors.

15.    What we sense in our left eye first goes to the right side of our brain and vice versa; however, the information is integrated in the
    a.    temporal lobe.
    b.    parietal lobe.
    c.    frontal lobe.
    d.    occipital lobe.

16.    The olfactory epithelium is to the sense of smell as the _____ are to the sense of taste.
    a.    retinas
    b.    papillae
    c.    semicircular canals
    d.    rods

17.    _____ perception is the ability to detect information below the level of conscious awareness.
    a.    Movement
    b.    Depth
    c.    Subliminal
    d.    Unconscious

## Practice Test 3

1.    The eye is to sensation as the brain is to
    a.    feeling.
    b.    perception.
    c.    impression.
    d.    hearing.

2.    A painter who is able to tell the difference between two similar shades of paint is demonstrating
    a.    the absolute threshold.
    b.    the difference threshold.
    c.    Weber's law.
    d.    sensory adaptation.

3.	You want to design a poster to advertise your company's new product. In order to entice people to pay attention to your poster and its message, you would design which of the following?
	a.	a large poster with much small print and a few standard graphics
	b.	a small poster with black and white text only
	c.	a medium sized poster with unique graphics and small print
	d.	a large poster with vivid colors, large print, and unique graphics

4.	An object that partially conceals another object is perceived as being closer, according to the monocular cue of
	a.	shadowing.
	b.	overlap.
	c.	texture gradient.
	d.	linear perspective.

5.	If you are driving on a foggy morning and get into an accident because you thought that the car in front of you was farther away than it really was, which depth perception cue was the one that contributed to the accident?
	a.	shadowing
	b.	overlap
	c.	texture gradient
	d.	linear perspective

6.	You are at a cocktail party and you hear the voice of someone you have been wanting to meet for a long time but fail to hear your annoying coworker calling your name across the room. Which perceptual phenomenon can explain this?
	a.	subliminal perception
	b.	selective attention
	c.	perceptual set
	d.	sensory adaptation

7.	Why is it that commercial ads on TV seem much louder than the TV program that we are watching?
	a.	sensory adaptation
	b.	perceptual set
	c.	selective attention
	d.	subliminal perception

8.	In the movie *Blair Witch Project*, the characters found themselves lost in the wilderness, and some of the more intense scenes took place in the night. During those scenes, the characters were able to see things based on the sensory reception work of the _____ on their retinas.
	a.	rods
	b.	cones
	c.	foveas
	d.	blind spots

9.	Which of the following is NOT true about color blindness?
	a.	Complete color blindness is rare.
	b.	There are different types of color blindness.
	c.	People with color blindness see in black and white.
	d.	Color blindness typically involves a malfunction of the green cone system.

10. The gestalt principles of visual perception may be applied to social perception. Which of the perceptual principles would explain the tendency to assume that a man and a woman walking together are a romantic couple?
   a. similarity
   b. closure
   c. proximity
   d. depth perception

11. Wendy is driving and has stopped at a red traffic light. Next to her is an enormous truck. Suddenly she perceives her own car moving backward and presses hard on the brakes, but it turns out that she was not the one moving, it was the truck that was moving slowly forward. Which perceptual phenomena can explain this?
   a. proximity
   b. similarity
   c. familiar size
   d. figure-ground

12. Recognizing your mother by seeing only the top of her head in a crowd demonstrates the
   a. brightness constancy.
   b. perceptual illusions.
   c. proximity.
   d. shape constancy.

13. Tone saturation is to _____ as wave's amplitude is to _____.
   a. timbre; loudness
   b. pitch; timbre
   c. loudness; pitch
   d. pitch; loudness

14. Place theory and frequency theory are two approaches to explaining
   a. how the outer ear collects sound waves.
   b. how the middle ear registers the amplitude of sound.
   c. how the inner ear registers the frequency of sound.
   d. why children get ear infections.

15. Which of the following factors is NOT involved in the process of echolocation used by bats to find their prey at night?
   a. light emitted by the prey
   b. timing of the sounds emitted by the prey
   c. intensity of the sounds emitted by the prey
   d. the frequency of the sound waves emitted by the prey

16. Which of the following is NOT true about the sense of touch?
   a. Newborn girls tend to be more sensitive to touch than male counterparts.
   b. The finger tips contain the highest densities of tactile receptors.
   c. There are specialized temperature receptors right under the skin.
   d. In terms of evolution, pain is unnecessary.

17. In preparation for the time of labor, expectant mothers are advised to plan for activities to kill time during the long hours leading to hard labor. Some hospitals provide video players and advise mothers to bring along a video of a favorite movie. This may also help reduce the perception of pain because it causes
    a. focused breathing.
    b. counterstimulation.
    c. distraction.
    d. pain control.

18. If an ear infection causes Malik to feel shaky and lose his balance, which sense is the one being disrupted?
    a. hearing
    b. kinesthetic
    c. tactile
    d. vestibular

## Connections

*Take advantage of all the other study tools available for this chapter!*

## Media Integration

| NAME OF CLIP | DESCRIPTION | KEY CONCEPTS AND IDEAS |
|---|---|---|
| | | **How We Sense and Perceive the World** |
| Perceptual Integration | The sensory organs of touch, taste, smell, and vision are illustrated and explained, including a discussion of how the senses are processed in the brain and integrated into a perception. The process of fragmenting visual information and rebuilding it into information we can understand is described. | Sensory organs<br>Touch<br>Taste<br>Smell<br>Vision<br>Perceptual integration |
| Sensory Processes and Brain Integration | This video introduces students to the complexities of sensory integration. The question of whether or not there is a specific part of the brain that integrates sensory information is addressed. Students are also introduced to the process of creation of mental maps. | Sensory integration<br>Perception<br>Brain<br>Memory<br>Neural networks<br>Mental maps |
| Weber's Law | This interactivity engages the participant in 20 trials of comparing volume (intensity) of pairs of tones. At the end participants are shown total percentage of correct answers and percentages of correct answers with high-volume sound pairs and low-volume sound pairs. Participants experience the Weber effect and see how the theory applies to their own experience. When the intensity of the original stimulus is high the difference is less noticeable and errors are more likely. | Weber's Law |

| | | |
|---|---|---|
| Stroop Effect | This interactivity is the classic Stroop effect study, in which participants are asked to determine the color of a stimuli presented, and their reaction time is measured. | Stroop effect<br>Reaction time |
| | | **The Visual System** |
| Vision | This is an animation of the parts of the eye. Rods and cones and illustrated, as well as the process of transduction. | Vision<br>Eye<br>Rods<br>Cones<br>Transduction |
| Visual Information Processing | This video clip presents a very detailed description of the process of visual perception. Reference is made to the brains efforts to compare the incoming visual information with stored information. | Vision<br>Visual perception<br>Memory |
| Phi Phenomenon | This interactivity is a study on the perception of apparent motion. | Perception<br>Apparent motion |
| Brightness Perception | This exercise allows participants to explore their own perception of brightness. Participants are able to manipulate brightness, objects, and explore the effects of shading, and motion. | Bightness perception<br>Shading<br>motion |
| | | **The Auditory System** |
| Hearing | This animation presents the effect of sound waves on the different parts of the ear. | Hearing<br>Sound waves<br>Ear<br>Outer ear<br>Middle ear<br>Inner ear<br>Ear canal<br>Ear drum<br>Tympanic membrane<br>Coclea |
| | | **Other Senses** |
| Tactile Information Processing | This video presents animation of the process of contralateral conduction. The detailed map of the body of the sensory cortex is illustrated. The effect of experiences on the brain's map of the body is discussed. | Sensory cortex |
| Sensorimotor Neural Circuit | This interactivity demonstrates with animation the neural coordination, including motor and sensory coordination, needed to perform the simple act of opening a jar of pickles and how it is far more complicated than it seems involving various areas of the brain. A second interactive exercise allows participants to test their own visual reaction time and | Motor cortex<br>Sensory cortex<br>Information processing<br>Frontal lobe<br>Parietal lobe<br>Spinal cord<br>Somatosensory area |

| | relate their results to methods of measuring decision-making effort. | |
|---|---|---|
| Taste | This animation illustrates how taste buds work and the process of taste sensation and perception. | Taste<br>Taste buds |
| Olfaction | This animation presents the process of olfactory sensation. | Olfaction |
| | | **Perception and Human Factors Psychology** |
| Human Factors: Keyboard Design | The QWERTY vs. DVORAK keyboards are compared. Participants are asked to type a paragraph with the QWERTY and then with the DVORAK. Participants have 60 seconds and are given feedback in terms of the number of words they typed in 60 seconds. QWERTY, while designed to slow down, tends to be faster because of familiarity. | Human factors<br>Familiarity |
| Human Factors: Designing Machines | This exercise, called "Biological Containment Room: Can you keep the Europidia alive?" engages participants in monitoring humidity, temperature, oxygen level, and lighting to keep an organism alive. The task is complex. Following the activity, participants are asked a series of questions to analyze their experience. Reference is made to stress and sympathetic activation. | Human factors<br>Stress<br>Sympathetic activation |

**Online Learning Center (www.mhhe.com/Santrockp7u)**
*Interact and make learning fun!*

- o **Interactive Exercises**
    - ▪ Target Practice I
    - ▪ Special FX
    - ▪ Brightness Perception
- o **Interactive Reviews**
    - ▪ Levels of Analysis: Pain Perception
    - ▪ Eye Labeling
    - ▪ Tongue Labeling
    - ▪ Auditory Labeling
    - ▪ Auditory Labeling II
    - ▪ Olfactory Labeling
- • Brush up on the Key Terms for this chapter by first reviewing the electronic **Glossary** (in English or Spanish) and then testing your retention using the **Flashcard** feature.
- • **"Notes"**—This feature allows you to use the website as you would your text, inserting your own study notes and highlighting areas of particular importance.

**In Your Text**

- • Found throughout each chapter, the **Review and Sharpen Your Thinking** feature breaks the text into logical chunks, allowing you to process, review, and reflect thoughtfully on the information that you've just read. When going back to *study* the chapter, try reading the feature *before* the section of text to which it relates. In doing so, you will be able to focus your attention on important concepts *as* you encounter them. In this chapter, this feature can be found on the following pages: pp. 131, 141, 146, and 153.

**Practice Quizzes**

- Test your knowledge of sensation and perception by taking the different practice quizzes found on your text's **Online Learning Center** and on the **In-Psych Plus CD-ROM** packaged with your text.

## ANSWER KEY

## In Your Own Words

✓ Put the definitions of sensation and perception in your own words and give an example of each.
*Sensation is the process of transforming information from the environment into the "language" of the brain in order for perception to take place. Perception is the process of interpreting the data that has been sensed.*

✓ Give an example of selective attention that you have recently experienced.
*Selective attention occurs all the time, and it refers to how we tend to focus on some things and not others. Motivation and interest influence our selective attention.*

✓ What did the gestalt psychologists mean when they said, "the whole is not equal to the sum of its parts"?
*This question should make the student think critically of the process of perception and how perception is different from sensation. Reference to the gestalt principles of visual perception can be used as illustrations.*

✓ On a separate piece of paper, draw a landscape that includes objects such as a house, a road, and trees. Give your drawing depth using monocular cues. Indicate which you have used and how.
*In this question, do not worry about being an artist as much as about practicing how the simple introduction of a few monocular cues of depth perception can significantly change the perception of a two-dimensional image.*

✓ If culture influences perception, list some ways that your culture has influenced your perception of clothing, behavior, music, or food.
*Cultures vary in the way that they use space and think of time. Cultures in geographic areas with year-round warm weather may have a different perceptual experience of space when compared to cultures in geographic areas with four annual seasons. Also, based on their priorities, time may be perceived as more or less structured. For example, a person growing up in an American suburban environment is likely to perceive space as highly organized (i.e., east, west, north, south, are all clear). They may have problems following directions in places where such cues are not used and seem irrelevant to the people, and directions are mostly based on landmarks. The American suburbanite will perceive this other space as disorganized and may not be able to process the information as effectively. Time is similarly highly structured and meaningful in the American culture and may even be perceived as an "object" to "stick" to. In other cultures the daily flow of events may be less tied to the 24-hour clock.*

✓ How would your life change if you lost your ability to experience the sense of pain?
*A person may find himself in dangerous situations if he could not sense or perceive pain.*

## Correcting the Incorrect

1.  *Sensation* refers to the process of detecting and encoding stimulus energy in the world. (p. 122)
2.  The minimum amount of energy that can be detected is called the *absolute* threshold. (p. 125)
3.  *Noise* is the term given to irrelevant and competing stimuli. (p. 126)
4.  Selective attention allows us to focus on some aspects of the environment while ignoring others. (p. 130)
5.  The *retina* contains the rods and the cones. (p. 133)
6.  The visual receptors or photoreceptors are the rods and the cones. (p. 133)
7.  *Cones* provide color vision. (p. 133)
8.  *Sensory adaptation* is the change in the sensory system's responsiveness based on the average level of surrounding stimulation. (p. 128)
9.  A color's hue is based on its wavelength. (p. 132)
10. The three different cones are *green, red, and blue.* (p. 136)
11. The *trichromatic* theory of color vision states that there are three types of receptors that are maximally sensitive to different but overlapping ranges of wavelengths. (p. 136)
12. The trichromatic and opponent-process theories are both correct. (p. 138)
13. The figure-ground relationship is the principle that explains *shape* perception. (p. 138)
14. Monocular cues provides us information about *depth* perception. (p. 138)
15. A *monocular* cue is overlapping. (p. 140)
16. We experience frequency of a sound wave as pitch. (p. 142)
17. The place theory of hearing adequately explains *high-frequency sounds but not low-frequency sounds.* (p. 144)
18. The auditory nerve carries neural impulses to the brain's auditory areas. (p. 145)
19. Smell and taste are our chemical senses. (p. 149)
20. The taste qualities include *sweet and sour, but also bitter, and salty.* (p. 150)
21. The sense that provides information about balance and movement is the *vestibular* sense. (p. 151)
22. The kinesthetic and vestibular senses are supplemented by information from sight. (p. 152)

## Practice Test 1

1. a.  RIGHT; this is sensation
   b.  no; perception refers to organizing and interpreting sensory information
   c.  gestalt psychology refers to the notion that perception follows certain patterns
   d.  accommodation is the lens changing its curvature
   p. 122

2. a.  YEAH
   b.  no
   c.  the difference threshold refers to the smallest difference required to discriminate two stimuli
   d.  subliminal perception is the ability to detect information below the level of conscious awareness
   p. 125

3. a. THAT'S RIGHT
   b. accommodation refers to the ability of the lens to change its curvature
   c. saturation is based on the color's purity
   d. subliminal perception is the ability to detect information below the level of conscious awareness

p. 126

4. a. no; this is not the correct definition
   b. CORRECT
   c. no
   d. no

p. 132

5. a. the lens focuses
   b. RIGHT; the iris is a muscle that controls the size of the pupil
   c. the cornea is clear membrane in front of the eye
   d. the retina contains the rods and cones and is located in the back of the eye

p. 132

6. a. no; the sclera is outer white part of the eye
   b. YES; the rods and cones are found in the retina
   c. no; the cornea is the clear membrane in the front of the eye
   d. no; the fovea is the area of the retina where vision is the most sensitive

p. 133

7. a. YES; cones are the receptors that provide us with fine detail
   b. no; it contains only cones
   c. no; the fovea contains only cones
   d. while the fovea is located in the center of the retina, the presence of cones is responsible for the sharp vision

p. 134

8. a. no
   b. no
   c. RIGHT; information crosses over to the other side
   d. no; information crosses over to the other side

p. 134

9. a. YES; the occipital lobe contains the visual cortex
   b. no
   c. no
   d. no

p. 134

10. a. no; the trichromatic theory says that there are three types of color receptors
    b. YES; the opponent-process theory suggests that if one member of the pair fatigues, the other member rebounds and gives an afterimage
    c. no
    d. no

p. 137

11. a. CORRECT; the old term suggests that a person cannot see color at all
    b. no
    c. no
    d. no
    p. 136

12. a. EXACTLY; loudness is determined by the sound's amplitude
    b. Hertz is a measurement of sound
    c. wavelength refers to the physical characteristic of sound
    d. no
    p. 142

13. a. no
    b. no
    c. no; these structures make up middle ear
    d. CORRECT; the inner is made up of these structures
    p. 143

14. a. this is important, but not in the actual translation of sound
    b. no
    c. no
    d. RIGHT
    p. 143

15. a. no; each frequency stimulates cells at particular places on the basilar membrane
    b. frequency theory says that how often cells fire is important
    c. YES, THAT'S RIGHT; the volley theory says that neural cells produce a volley of impulses
    d. no
    p. 144

16. a. no
    b. CORRECT
    c. no
    d. no
    p. 147

17. a. no
    b. YES
    c. no
    d. no
    p. 152

18. a. no
    b. THAT'S CORRECT
    c. no
    d. no
    p. 149

19. a.  although you are perceiving this question, perception does not allow you to focus on the question
    b.  no
    c.  THIS IS CORRECT; selective attention allows you to attend to one thing wile ignoring other things
    d.  no
p. 130

## Practice Test 2

1. a.  YEAH; hue is based on the color's wavelength
   b.  saturation is based on the color's purity
   c.  brightness refers to the intensity of light
   d.  timbre is the perceptual quality of sound
p. 132

2. a.  THAT'S RIGHT
   b.  no; closure refers to seeing incomplete figures as complete
   c.  no; we tend to perceive objects together that are similar to each other
   d.  no; we tend to group objects together that are near each other
p. 138

3. a.  YEAH
   b.  no; figure-ground illustrates how we divide our visual world
   c.  no; we tend to group objects together that are near each other
   d.  no; we tend to perceive objects together that are similar to each other
p. 138

4. a.  no; linear perspective is when two parallel lines appear to converge in the distance
   b.  no; texture gradient refers to how the texture changes as distance changes
   c.  no; shading involves changes in perception due to the position of the light and the position of the viewer.
   d.  CORRECT; this refers to one object partially blocking another object
p. 140

5. a.  YES; the bottom-up process is the one through which the senses send information up to the brain
   b.  no; this is the process of sending commands from the brain down to the rest of the body
   c.  no; this is not the name of a process, and in any case, the concepts are backward
   d.  no; this is not the name of a process, and in any case, the concepts are backward
p. 130

6. a.  no
   b.  no; the eyes contain sensory receptors, but they are not "a cell"
   c.  no; the ears contain sensory receptors, but they are not "a cell"
   d.  YES; this is the name of those cells
p. 124

7. a.  YES; the sensory receptors in the eye detect light
   b.  no; mechanoreceptors are involved in the touch, hearing, kinesthetic, and vestibular senses
   c.  no; mechanoreceptors are involved in smell and taste
   d.  no; photoreceptors are in the retina
p. 124

8. a.  no; this monocular cue relies on the amount of space the image takes on the retina
   b.  YES; the finer the texture, the farther away the object is perceived
   c.  no; this monocular cue relies on the partial covering of an object to figure out which object is closer
   d.  no; this monocular cue relies on the position of the light and the creation of shades to determine the depth
   p. 140

9. a.  no; the hippocampus is linked to memory
   b.  no; the hypothalamus is associated with pleasure
   c.  no; the pons is a part of the hindbrain
   d.  YES; the thalamus projects the map of the body's surface onto the somatosensory areas of the parietal lobes, and sends information to the appropriate spot
   p. 147

10. a.  no; this is a good technique practiced in Lamaze child birth
    b.  no; this works for pain, because causing another pain mutes the original pain
    c.  no; this works for pain, because focusing on something other than the source and place of pain mutes the original pain
    d.  YES; overstimulation will not reduce pain, it may contribute to more experience of pain as pain receptors continue to be stimulated
    p. 149

11. a.  no; this is one of the dimensions of taste
    b.  no; this is one of the dimensions of taste
    c.  YES; pasty may refer more to texture than to actual taste
    d.  no; this is one of the dimensions of taste
    p. 150

12. a.  YES
    b.  no
    c.  no
    d.  no
    p. 219

13. a.  no; these are sensory receptors found in the retina
    b.  no; the eardrum is in the ear but is not involved in the detection of head motion
    c.  YES; this structure is found in the inner ear
    d.  no; these are sensory receptors found in the retina
    p. 152

14. a.  YES; there are three types of sensory receptors: photoreceptors, mechanoreceptors, and chemoreceptors
    b.  no; sensations start with the activation of sensory receptors by stimulations from the environment
    c.  no; perception follows sensation
    d.  no; chemoreceptors are just one type of sensory receptors;. for this question, item a is the better answer
    p. 124

15. a. no; this lobe is associated with the integration of auditory information
    b. no; this lobe is associated with the integration of tactile information
    c. no; this lobe is associated with higher level processing
    d. YES; this lobe is associated with the processing of visual information
    p. 134

16. a. no; these correspond to the visual sense
    b. YES; the papillae, like the olfactory epithelium, hold the sensory receptors
    c. no; the sensory receptors in the semicircular canals determine the position of the head
    d. no; the rods are sensory receptors in the retina
    p. 150

17. a. no; we are aware of movement perception
    b. no; we are aware of depth perception
    c. YES; quickly flashing visual stimuli can result in a subliminal perception
    d. no; there is no unconscious perception
    p. 126

## Practice Test 3

1. a. no
   b. RIGHT; perception refers to the brain's process of organizing and interpreting sensory information
   c. no
   d. no
   p. 123

2. a. this is the minimum amount of energy that can be detected
   b. CORRECT; the difference threshold refers to the smallest difference required to discriminate two stimuli, in this case two shades of paint
   c. no
   d. sensory adaptation is the change of responsiveness to stimulation
   p. 128

3. a. no
   b. no
   c. no
   d. YES; size and color and novel objects influence our attention
   p. 130

4. a. no; the shadow of the objects provides information to its depth
   b. GOOD
   c. no; texture gradient refers to how the texture changes as distance changes
   d. no; linear perspective is when two parallel lines appear to converge in the distance
   p. 140

5. a. no; it was not the shadows of the car in front of you that confused you
   b. no; your car partially overlapped the one in front, so you knew that it was in front of you, but that was not the problem
   c. YES; the texture of the car in front seemed finer because of the fog; therefore, you perceived it to be farther away than it really was
   d. no; this was not the perceptual cue that caused the problem in perception
   p. 140

6. a.  no; this refers to the ability to detect information below the level of conscious awareness
   b.  YES; you hear the voice of the other person because you are motivated
   c.  no; this refers to the effect of expectations on perception
   d.  no; this refers to changes in sensation and the process of adapting to them
   p. 130

7. a.  YES; we get used to the volume of the program, and if the commercial is just slightly louder we are surprised and have to adapt to the new volume
   b.  no; this refers to the effect of expectations on perception
   c.  no; this refers to the effect of motivation on perception
   d.  no; this refers to the ability to detect information below the level of conscious awareness
   p. 128

8. a.  YES; the rods work best under conditions of low illumination
   b.  no; the cones need high illumination to work
   c.  no; the fovea does not have rods
   d.  no; the blind spots do not have rods (or cones)
   p. 133

9. a.  no; this is correct about color blindness
   b.  no; this is correct about color blindness
   c.  YES; this is incorrect; people with color blindness have problems sensing some color but not all colors
   d.  no; this is correct about color blindness
   p. 136

10. a.  no; the man and the woman may be very different
    b.  no; we are not adding/assuming another figure/person to the situation
    c.  YES; we perceive the two individuals as a whole, a couple
    d.  no; this is not one of the gestalt principles of perception
    p. 138

11. a.  no; this is not what caused the illusion
    b.  no; this is not what caused the illusion
    c.  no; this is not what caused the illusion
    d.  YES; Wendy, would usually perceive the landscape outside her car as the moving figures, but when the truck parked next to her she had her "background" changed; the truck became the background and her car became the figure; when the truck moved, she did not initially perceive the background moving (it is usually the figures that move), so she concluded that her car must be moving
    p. 138

12. a.  no; irrelevant to the question
    b.  no; this is not an example of a perceptual illusion, since the mother is correctly recognized (it is not a confusion)
    c.  no; this issue is not about two proximal stimuli
    d.  YES; based on the limited information of the "top of her head" you concluded that the rest of the body was there, and that corresponds to the mother
    p. 140

13. a. YES; timbre is tone saturation, and loudness is determined by the amplitude of the sound wave
    b. no; pitch is determined by the frequency of the sound wave
    c. no
    d. no
    p. 142

14. a. no; the pinna and external auditory canal, which compose the outer ear, channel the sounds into the interior ear
    b. no; the parts and functions of the middle ear have been clearly studied, and these theories are not addressing this
    c. YES; place theory says that each frequency of sound waves produces vibrations at specific spots on the basilar membrane, while frequency theory says that it all depends on how often the auditory nerve fires and sends information to the brain
    d. no; these theories don't address this
    p. 144

15. a. YES; bats are nocturnal animals and don't rely on their vision for hunting prey
    b. no; this is relevant to echolocation
    c. no; this is relevant to echolocation
    d. no; this is relevant to echolocation
    p. 146

16. a. no; this is true about the sense of touch
    b. no; this is true about the sense of touch
    c. no; this is true about the sense of touch
    d. YES; this is incorrect, pain is very important because it warns us of damage to our bodies, a capability most important for adaptation and survival
    p. 148

17. a. no; Lamaze child birth promotes focused breathing, but this is not what the question focuses on
    b. no; the movie does not cause direct counterstimulation
    c. YES; the movie may psychologically distract the mother and this way reduce the perception of pain
    d. no; the movie is not promoted as a pain-control object
    p. 149

18. a. no; the question does not address hearing loss
    b. no; while it is not easy to distinguish between the kinesthetic and the vestibular sense, this question makes reference to balance; therefore, the answer is not kinesthetic
    c. no; the question does not address problems with the sense of touch
    d. YES; the vestibular sense provides information about balance and movement and has receptors in the ear, which may be affected if there was an infection in the area
    p. 151

# Chapter 6—States of Consciousness

## Learning Goals

*After studying Chapter 6, you will be able to:*

- Discuss the nature of consciousness.
- Explain the nature of sleep and dreams.
- Describe hypnosis.
- Evaluate the uses and types of psychoactive drugs.

## CHAPTER 6: OUTLINE

- During much of the 20th century, consciousness was not considered for study in psychology, and the focus of the science was mainly on observable behaviors. *Consciousness* is awareness of both internal and external stimuli or events, including the self and thoughts about personal experiences.

- Awareness occurs at various levels: higher-level consciousness (the most alert state), lower-level consciousness (automatic processing and daydreaming), altered states of consciousness (e.g., drug induced, hypnosis, fatigue), subconscious awareness (subconscious creativity, sleep, and dreams), and no awareness (unconsciousness).

- Current neuroscience theories about consciousness argue that rather than having specific parts of the brain associated with consciousness, different parts and systems of the brain seem to work together simultaneously to produce consciousness.

- We dedicate more time to sleeping than to any other activity in our life span; approximately one-third of our lives is spent sleeping. Biological rhythms, such as the circadian rhythm, influence the daily patterns of sleeping and awake time. The daily rhythm is synchronized by our nervous system based on information such as daylight.

- We need sleep because it helps us restore, adapt, grow, and enhance memory, all positive effects that contribute to adaptation to the challenges of the environment. Sleep deprivation has been associated with many negative effects, among which are hallucinations, speech and movement problems, decreased brain activity, decreased alertness, impaired decision making, and ineffective communication skills.

- Developmental stages have been associated with differences in sleeping patterns. In late adolescents (16–18 years old) the biological clock automatically changes and delays the time of sleepiness to approximately one hour later than it is for younger adolescents. Later in life, during middle age, the biological clock moves sleepiness back to an earlier time.

- The sleep stages correspond to electrophysiological changes that can be measured using the EEG, a measure of the brain's electrical activity. When a person is awake, the EEG shows beta waves, which are high in frequency and low in amplitude. During relaxed or drowsy state, the EEG pattern is alpha waves, which are more synchronous than beta waves.

- When we sleep, we pass through four stages, from light sleep in stage 1 to deep sleep in stages 3 and 4. Sleep stages form a type of cycle, in which we go from stage 1 thru 4 (non-REM sleep) and proceeds to a more wakeful state; however, instead of going back to stage 1, we go into a stage characterized by rapid eye movement, referred to as REM sleep.

- Most dreaming occurs in REM sleep. We complete several sleep cycles nightly. The amount of REM sleep changes over the life span, raising questions about the purpose of REM sleep. During REM sleep, the brain carries out complex processes. Sleep disorders include insomnia, sleepwalking, sleeptalking, nightmares and night terrors, narcolepsy, and sleep apnea.

- Dreams have long been of interest, and several theories have been proposed to explain them. According to Freud's view, dreams reflect wish fulfillment of unmet needs and have manifest content and latent content. The cognitive view holds that dreams are related to information processing, memory, and problem solving. According to the activation-synthesis view, dreams are the brain's way of making sense out of neural activity while we are sleeping.

- *Hypnosis* is a psychological state of altered attention in which the individual is very receptive to suggestion. In the 18th century, Mesmer credited his success in curing his patients' problems to animal magnetism, but what was really occurring was a form of hypnotic suggestion.

- Hypnosis involves four steps: (1) minimization of distractions and comfort, (2) person is asked to concentrate on something specific, (3) expectations about the hypnotic state are shared with the person, and (4) suggestions begin with predictions of events that can be expected, such as "your eyes are getting tired," followed by suggestions that are then easily accepted by the person. That hypnosis is truly an altered state of consciousness has been challenged by the social cognitive behavior view of hypnosis, which argues that hypnotized people are basically acting as they believe hypnotized people act.

- Hypnosis is used in psychotherapy, medicine, and other areas in which having a person reach this level of relaxation and openness to suggestion could be of benefit for the person.

- Psychoactive drugs are drugs that alter consciousness. Users of psychoactive drugs may develop tolerance, physical dependence, or psychological dependence.

- The three main types of psychoactive drugs are depressants, stimulants, and hallucinogens. Alcohol is an extremely powerful drug and is a depressant. Alcoholism, a disorder that involves long-term uncontrollable excessive use of alcohol, is influenced by both genetics and environmental factors.

- Barbiturates (e.g., sleeping pills), tranquilizers (e.g., Valium), and opiates (e.g., morphine, heroin) are other depressants that are abused. Stimulants are drugs that increase activity in the central nervous system. A group of widely prescribed stimulants is amphetamines.

- Cocaine is also classified as a stimulant and is associated with a rush of euphoria; crack is an intensified form of cocaine and is usually smoked. MDMA (Ecstasy) is an illegal synthetic drug that has both stimulant and hallucinogenic effects and causes brain damage. Two stimulants that are widely used are caffeine and nicotine.

- Hallucinogens are drugs that modify an individual's perceptual experiences. LSD and marijuana, which produces its effect by disrupting neurons and neurotransmitters, are examples of hallucinogens.

- Addiction is characterized by an overwhelming involvement with using a drug and securing its supply. The disease model of addiction describes addiction as a lifelong disease characterized by loss of control and a requirement of treatment for recovery. Critics of this view see addiction as a habit and a source of gratification, not as a disease.

## Building Blocks of Chapter 6

### Clarifying some of the tricky points in Chapter 6
### and
### In Your Own Words

*To respond to the questions and exercises presented in the "In Your Own Words" section, please write your thoughts, perspectives, and reactions on a separate piece of paper.*

### The Nature of Consciousness

The awareness of both external and internal stimuli or events is called *consciousness*. William James described consciousness as a continuous flow called a *stream of consciousness*. Consciousness comes in different forms and levels. The most alert state of consciousness, in which individuals are actively focused on a goal, is referred to as *controlled processes*. Activities that require minimal attention are called *automatic processes*. Another form of consciousness that involves a low level of conscious effort is called *daydreaming*. A mental state that is noticeably different from normal awareness, produced by drugs, meditation, trauma, fatigue, hypnosis, or sensory deprivation, is called an *altered state of consciousness*. It has been argued that creative ideas can result from waking subconscious awareness. Sleep and dreams are also examples of low levels of consciousness. Freud believed that most of our thoughts are contained in a reservoir of unacceptable wishes; he referred to this as *unconscious thought*. In terms of the relationship between the brain and consciousness, the contemporary view is that a number of separate processing systems connect to produce consciousness.

### In Your Own Words
*Please write your thoughts, perspectives, and reactions on a separate piece of paper.*
✓ *Look at the definition of consciousness. Give some examples of external and internal awareness. Think of a behavior that you do regularly, such as driving, playing basketball, or writing e-mails. When you are engaged in that activity, which behaviors/thoughts/emotions are controlled processes? Which are automatic processes?*

### Sleep and Dreams

On the average, sleep takes up about one-third of our lives. Biological rhythms are periodic physiological fluctuations in the body that are controlled by biological clocks and play an important role in sleep. A circadian rhythm is a daily behavioral or physiological cycle. The suprachiasmic nucleus is a part of the brain that receives light information from the retina and synchronizes its rhythm based on the daily cycle of light and dark. This may explain why blind people tend to have lifelong problems with sleeping. These rhythms may become desynchronized when we fly cross-country or change our working hours. When all time and light cues are removed, the natural circadian rhythm averages 24 hours. Melatonin is the hormone that is increasingly produced at night; if taken as a supplement it can advance the circadian rhythm and help reduce the effects of jet lag. About 50% of the American population is sleep-deprived.

### In Your Own Words
*Please write your thoughts, perspectives, and reactions on a separate piece of paper.*
✓ *Imagine that you are a consultant who specializes in sleep and circadian rhythms. You have been hired by a large manufacturing company to guide them as they overhaul their shiftwork schedule. What advice do you give?*

We need sleep because it is a fundamental mechanism for survival. It has been argued that sleep restores our brains and bodies. In support of this notion, it has been observed that while we sleep, cells increase production and there is a reduction in the breakdown of proteins. Another explanation says that sleep helps keep us from wasting energy and from risking harm during those times for which we are not wasting. Some of the negative effects of sleep deprivation are decreased brain activity in the thalamus and prefrontal cortex, decline in alertness and cognitive performance. Sleep deprivation can also affect decision making, creativity, and communication.

The electroencephalograph allows researchers to measure changes in the brain's electrical activity. When we are awake but in a relaxed state, we produce an EEG pattern called *alpha waves*. As we fall asleep, we begin to produce slow brain waves; these are characteristic of stage 1 sleep. During Stage 2 sleep, we periodically produce brief bursts of high-frequency waves called *sleep spindles*. During Stage 3 and Stage 4 sleep we produce large, slow EEG waves called *delta waves*. After 90 minutes of sleep, the sleeper enters REM sleep when dreams often occur. REM stands for rapid eye movement. The amount of deep (Stage 4) sleep is greater in the first half of a night's sleep, whereas the majority of REM sleep takes place during the second part of a night's sleep. The amount of REM sleep decreases over the life span. The sleep stages are associated with activity in the reticular formation, and damage to this part of the brain may result in coma and death.

A common sleep disorder, characterized by the inability to fall asleep, is insomnia. The hormone melatonin may play a role in sleep disorders. A sleep disorder in which individuals walk in their sleep is called somnambulism. A frightening dream that awakens a sleeper from REM sleep is called a *nightmare*. When individuals experience a sudden arousal from sleep and an intense fear, this is called a *night terror*. Some individuals have a sleep disorder in which they experience an overpowering urge to sleep; this is called *narcolepsy*. Some individuals may have a sleep disorder in which they stop breathing while they are asleep; this is called *sleep apnea*.

Throughout history, dreams have had historical, personal, and religious significance. According to psychoanalysts, the sexual and aggressive content of dreams represents wish fulfillment. The manifest content is the dream's surface content, while the latent content is the dream's hidden meaning. Freud suggested that we disguise our wish fulfillment through the use of symbols. According to the cognitive theory of dreaming, dreaming involves information processing, memory, and problem solving. A different view of dreaming suggesting that dreams have no inherent meaning is the activation-synthesis view. This view holds that dreams are the way in which the brain tries to make sense out of neural activity.

## In Your Own Words

*Please write your thoughts, perspectives, and reactions on a separate piece of paper.*

✓ *For a week, keep a journal of dreams. Before you go to bed, write down the approximate time when you expect to start sleeping; then in the morning record the time you wake up and any details of dreams you remember. At the end of the week, study your notes and consider if the sleeping and awakening times have any relationship with the amount of information you recall about dreams. Also, consider the theories of dreams presented in the chapter in order to explain the meaning of your dreams.*

✓ *Describe one of your dreams in terms of manifest content and latent content.*

## Hypnosis

A psychological state of altered attention in which the individual is very receptive to suggestions is called *hypnosis*. In the 18th century, physician Anton Mesmer credited his success in curing problems to "animal magnetism"; we sometimes refer to a hypnotized person as being "mesmerized."

The four steps of hypnotic suggestion are (1) the subject is made to feel comfortable; (2) the subject is told to concentrate on one specific thing; (3) the subject is told what to expect; (4) the hypnotist suggests that certain events are to occur. Individuals vary widely in their ability to be hypnotized. Psychotherapy, medicine, dentistry, criminal investigations, and sports have all made use of hypnosis.

### *Psychoactive Drugs*

Drugs that act on the nervous system to alter our state of consciousness, modify our perceptions, and alter our moods are called *psychoactive drugs*. The users of many psychoactive drugs find that they need increasing amounts of the drug for its effect to be produced; they have developed tolerance. The physical need for a drug that is accompanied by unpleasant withdrawal symptoms is called *physical dependence*. The psychological need to take a drug is called *psychological dependence*.

The three main types of psychoactive drugs are stimulants, depressants, and hallucinogens. Examples of depressants are alcohol, barbiturates, tranquilizers, and opiates. A special concern among college students is binge drinking. A disorder involving long-term, repeated, compulsive, and extensive use of alcohol is called *alcoholism*. Family studies of alcoholism find a higher frequency of the disorder in first-degree relatives of alcoholics.

Two examples of barbiturates are Nembutal and Seconal. When heroin addicts share needles, they are at increased risk for contracting HIV.

Drugs that increase activity in the central nervous system are referred to as *stimulants*. A group of widely used stimulants that people use to boost energy, stay awake, and lose weight are amphetamines. A stimulant derived from the coca plant is cocaine. A highly addictive, intensified form of cocaine is called *crack*. Treating cocaine addiction has been relatively unsuccessful. Caffeine is a psychoactive drug that is found in soft drinks and chocolate. Caffeine activates the pleasure centers of the brain.

Psychoactive drugs that modify a person's perceptual experiences and produce visual images that are not real are called *hallucinogens*. One hallucinogen that produces striking perceptual changes, even in low doses, is LSD. LSD acts primarily on the neurotransmitter serotonin, though it can affect dopamine as well. Marijuana produces its effects by disrupting the membranes of neurons and affecting the functioning of a variety of neurotransmitters and hormones. Among the physiological effects of marijuana, users experience increases in pulse rate and blood pressure, reddening of the eye, coughing, and dryness of the mouth. Psychological effects include excitation, depression, and mild hallucinations.

Addiction is a pattern of behavior characterized by an overwhelming involvement with using a drug and securing its supply. A view of addictions that sees them as biologically based, lifelong diseases is called the *disease model of addiction*. Critics of this view argue that the biological origins of addiction have not been adequately identified, that seeing addiction as a disease keeps people from developing self-control, and that addiction is not necessarily lifelong.

### In Your Own Words
*Please write your thoughts, perspectives, and reactions on a separate piece of paper.*

✓ *Describe in a story format the biological effects and the psychological experience of a smoker or a smokeless tobacco user as he/she introduces the psychoactive drug nicotine into the body.*

## Correcting the Incorrect

Carefully read each statement. Determine if the statement is correct or incorrect. If the statement is incorrect, make the necessary changes to correct it. Then check the answer key at the end of the chapter for the correct statement and page reference in the textbook.

1. Consciousness is awareness of both external and internal stimuli or events.
2. An unconscious thought is what the individual experiences while in an altered state of consciousness.
3. If you are doing a task that requires minimal attention, then you are experiencing a controlled process.
4. Drugs, meditation, fatigue, and hypnosis can produce daydreaming.
5. A 24-hour behavioral or physiological cycle is called an *alpha rhythm*.
6. When deprived of all time and light cues, the circadian rhythm is about 28 to 29 hours.
7. Sleep spindles occur in Stage 1 sleep.
8. REM sleep is a stage of sleep during which dreaming occurs.
9. The hormone dopamine may be effective in reducing insomnia.
10. Sleep apnea is the formal term for sleepwalking.
11. Night terrors occur in REM and are really just bad dreams.
12. The overpowering urge to fall asleep is called *sleep apnea*.
13. A dream's true meaning is called the *manifest content*.
14. The activation-synthesis theory of dreaming suggests that dreaming may allow us to solve problems.
15. Dreams reflect the brain's efforts to make sense out of neural activity that takes place during sleep, according to the activation-synthesis theory.
16. Mesmer cured his patients using psychoactive drugs.
17. Ernest Hilgard proposed that hypnosis involved a state of complete lack of awareness.
18. Psychoactive drugs do not produce tolerance.
19. The strong desire and craving to repeat the use of a drug is called *psychological dependence*.
20. Alcohol is a stimulant.
21. Barbiturates are stimulant drugs that are used medically to induce sleep.
22. Tranquilizers include morphine and heroin.
23. Crack is an intensified form of caffeine.
24. MDMA (Ecstasy) is an illegal synthetic drug with both stimulant and depressant properties.
25. The nicotine in cigarettes is a depressant.
26. Marijuana affects the functioning of one neurotransmitter.
27. Critics of the disease model of addiction argue that addiction is a lifelong pattern.

## Practice Test 1

1. If you are aware of both external and internal stimuli, you are in a(n)
   a. altered state.
   b. conscious state.
   c. REM state.
   d. narcoleptic state.

2.  A form of consciousness that requires minimal attention is
    a.    controlled processes.
    b.    automatic processes.
    c.    stream of consciousness.
    d.    unconscious thought.

3.  Circadian rhythm refers to
    a.    a popular Latin dance.
    b.    a daily cycle.
    c.    the brain's level of activity when taking a psychoactive drug.
    d.    an abnormal biological rhythm associated with jet lag

4.  Which of the following is a circadian rhythm?
    a.    the stream of consciousness
    b.    the four stages of sleep
    c.    hypnosis
    d.    the sleep/wake cycle

5.  Delta waves are produced in which stage of sleep?
    a.    REM sleep
    b.    Stage 1 sleep
    c.    Stage 2 sleep
    d.    Stage 4 sleep

6.  A person who usually sleeps 8 hours completes an average of how many sleep cycles per night?
    a.    2
    b.    3
    c.    4
    d.    5

7.  What is the **main** difference between REM sleep and non-REM sleep?
    a.    number of times a person wakes up
    b.    hypnagogic level
    c.    degree of brain activity
    d.    number of sleep stages included

8.  Joe was upset when his date kept suddenly falling asleep, until she explained that she is
    a.    circadian.
    b.    bored.
    c.    somnambulistic.
    d.    narcoleptic.

9.  Another name for somnambulism is
    a.    sleepwalking.
    b.    hallucination.
    c.    insomnia.
    d.    bed-wetting.

10.    Bethany, a 2-year old, experiences sudden arousal from sleep and intense fear. She experiences
   a.    night terrors.
   b.    insomnia.
   c.    sleep apnea.
   d.    narcolepsy.

11.    The cognitive view of dreaming asserts that dreams
   a.    help dissipate problematic sexual and aggressive energy.
   b.    are the conscious equivalent of innate instincts.
   c.    are the conscious interpretation of relatively random neural activity.
   d.    are used to review daily events and orient toward future goals.

12.    According to the activation-synthesis view,
   a.    dreams represent wish fulfillment.
   b.    dreams have no inherent meaning.
   c.    dreams are a way to solve problems and think creatively.
   d.    dreams have manifest and latent content.

13.    The standard hypnosis session involves a hypnotist swinging a pocket watch or a pendulum in front of the subject to be hypnotized. The hypnotist does this because she wants the subject to
   a.    concentrate.
   b.    fall asleep.
   c.    lose control.
   d.    hallucinate.

14.    When hypnosis is induced, the hypnotist
   a.    tries to keep the subject distracted.
   b.    discourages the subject from concentrating on anything specific.
   c.    suggests to the subject what will be experienced in the hypnotic state.
   d.    is careful to prevent posthypnotic amnesia.

15.    Which of the following statements about hypnosis is correct?
   a.    Hypnosis is an unconscious state of awareness.
   b.    The majority of the population can be easily hypnotized.
   c.    Hypnosis tends to enhance people's memory.
   d.    Some people are more easily hypnotized than others.

16.    What do caffeine and cocaine have in common?
   a.    They are stimulants.
   b.    They are depressants.
   c.    They are hallucinogens.
   d.    They are opiates.

17.    Which of the following is a stimulant?
   a.    marijuana
   b.    alcohol
   c.    cocaine
   d.    LSD

18. Each of the following is a criticism of the disease model of addiction except
    a. it discourages people from developing self-control.
    b. it stigmatizes people with labels.
    c. it is not consistent with the approach taken by the medical profession
    d. it prescribes a rigid program of therapy.

19. No awareness is the same as the concept of _____ developed by Freud.
    a. daydreaming
    b. subconscious
    c. lower-level awareness
    d. unconscious

20. The part of the brain that keeps the biological clocks synchronized is the
    a. suprachiasmic nucleus.
    b. thalamus.
    c. hindbrain.
    d. frontal lobe.

## Practice Test 2

1. At the beginning of his lecture class, Mike, a student, finds that he is alert, attentive, and focused on the lecture. In which state of consciousness is Mike?
    a. controlled processes
    b. automatic processes
    c. hypnotized
    d. stream of consciousness

2. William James described the mind as a
    a. blank slate.
    b. confusing aspect that should not be studied by psychologists.
    c. stream of consciousness.
    d. lack of awareness.

3. A person who is daydreaming about an upcoming job interview is engaged in
    a. higher-level awareness.
    b. lower-level awareness.
    c. an altered state of consciousness.
    d. subconscious awareness.

4. Most experts argue that consciousness is
    a. located and processed in a very small area of the frontal lobe.
    b. located and processed in the hypothalamus.
    c. processed in numerous areas distributed across the whole nervous system.
    d. processed in numerous areas distributed across the brain.

5. Which of the following is NOT one of the reasons we need sleep?
    a. restoration
    b. dreams
    c. adaptation
    d. growth

6.  Which of the following neurotransmitters is not decreased as the sleep cycles progress from stages 1 to 4?
    a.  epinephrine
    b.  Serotonin
    c.  GABA
    d.  acetylcholine

7.  Which of the following is NOT TRUE about the relationship between sleep and disease?
    a.  People with depression tend to have sleep problems.
    b.  When we have an infectious disease, we have a harder time falling asleep.
    c.  Asthma attacks are more likely during the night, probably because of biological changes associated with sleep.
    d.  People with Alzheimer's disease tend to experience sleep problems.

8.  One of the gender differences in the manifest content of dreams is that
    a.  males dream more about the relationships in their lives than females.
    b.  females are more likely to dream about aggression than males.
    c.  females dream more about friends than males.
    d.  males dream more about friends than women.

9.  The theory of dreams that says dreams provide alternative ways for solving problems is called the
    a.  cognitive theory of dreams.
    b.  I-got-it dream approach.
    c.  activation-synthesis theory.
    d.  manifest content theory.

10. Which of the following is NOT one of the areas in which hypnosis has been applied?
    a.  medicine
    b.  studies of controlled processing
    c.  psychotherapy
    d.  dentistry

11. Soon after one of her parents died, Samantha dreamed about the house in which she grew up, and in her dream she saw the house crumble to the ground. In this dream, the manifest content would be
    a.  the parent.
    b.  the house in which they grew up crumbling to the ground.
    c.  the recent death of the parent.
    d.  her sadness and sense of loss.

12. Which of the following is not one of the characteristics of hypnosis?
    a.  While hypnotized, people present in an EEG patterns of brain activity different from those recorded when they are not hypnotized.
    b.  During the hypnotic state, the EEG shows a predominance of delta waves.
    c.  The EEG of a hypnotized person resembles those of a person in a relaxed waking state.
    d.  To begin hypnosis, distractions are minimized.

13. The use of psychoactive drugs for personal gratification and temporary adaptation can result in the all of the following, EXCEPT
    a.    an ability to know when to stop to prevent addiction.
    b.    drug dependence.
    c.    personal disarray.
    d.    predisposition to serious, sometimes fatal, diseases.

14. The difference between physical dependence and psychological dependence is that
    a.    psychological dependence does not cause addiction.
    b.    physical dependence does not cause addiction.
    c.    physical dependence is associated with the direct cause of withdrawal symptoms.
    d.    psychological dependence is not related to stress.

15. Psychoactive drugs increase the neurotransmitter _____ in the brain's reward pathways.
    a.    serotonin.
    b.    acetylcholine.
    c.    GABA.
    d.    dopamine.

16. The reason why a person "loosens up" after a few drinks is because
    a.    alcohol is a stimulant that makes people feel happy.
    b.    alcohol is a hallucinogen that makes things look different.
    c.    alcohol slows down the areas of the brain involved in inhibition.
    d.    alcohol, like cocaine, is a depressant.

17. The following are characteristics of alcoholism, EXCEPT
    a.    uncontrolled use of alcoholic beverages.
    b.    compulsive use of alcoholic beverages.
    c.    short-term use of alcoholic beverages.
    d.    repeated use of alcoholic beverages.

18. Based on the rates of alcohol consumption, which of the following countries may have the lowest number of cases of alcoholism?
    a.    China
    b.    Russia
    c.    France
    d.    United States

19. Which of the following statements demonstrates an environmental factor associated with alcohol consumption?
    a.    Alcohol increases the concentration of GABA.
    b.    Chronic binge drinking is more common among males who live in fraternity houses than among females and other students living away from home.
    c.    Family studies consistently find a high frequency of alcoholism in the first-degree relatives of alcoholics.
    d.    Alcohol use affects the areas of the frontal cortex involved in judgment and impulse control.

20.    Which of the following are psychoactive drugs associated with increased energy?
    a.    opiates
    b.    marijuana
    c.    amphetamines
    d.    alcoholic beverages

## Practice Test 3

1.    You can talk, eat a Big Mac, or listen to music while driving an automobile because
    a.    driving an automobile has become an automatic process.
    b.    you have developed an altered state of consciousness.
    c.    you have the special ability to concentrate on several things at one time.
    d.    driving an automobile has become a controlled process.

2.    Which of the following would be least likely to induce an altered state of consciousness?
    a.    meditation
    b.    hypnosis
    c.    caffeine
    d.    cocaine

3.    Which of the following air travelers would require the most time to recover from jet lag?
    a.    Michael, who is traveling east from Chicago to Paris
    b.    Carla, who is traveling west from Paris to Chicago
    c.    Karen, who is traveling north from Lima to Chicago
    d.    Benjamin, who is traveling south from Chicago to Lima

4.    While your father is napping on the couch, you notice his eyes moving around under his closed eyelids. If you wake your father up at this time, he is likely to
    a.    claim that he was really awake.
    b.    report that he was dreaming.
    c.    describe the presence of a "hidden observer."
    d.    report seeing slow-wave movement.

5.    When he first started using drugs, Ben needed only a small amount to feel euphoric. Now, six months later, he requires almost three times as much to have the same feeling. Ben
    a.    is addicted.
    b.    has developed psychological dependence.
    c.    has developed tolerance.
    d.    is a narcoleptic.

6.    Kathy drinks three cups of strong coffee a day. If in a particular day, she had only one cup in the morning, by 3:00 p.m. Kathy is likely to be experiencing all these symptoms, EXCEPT
    a.    headache.
    b.    boost in energy.
    c.    difficulties concentrating.
    d.    lethargy.

7. These are all treatments that have been applied to the sleep disorder of insomnia, EXCEPT
   a. reduction of melatonin.
   b. light therapy.
   c. sleeping pills.
   d. altering the circadian rhythm.

8. During what age are nightmares more frequent?
   a. newborns
   b. late adulthood
   c. childhood
   d. early adulthood

9. According to the psychoanalytic approach, when the story in a dream shifts suddenly in midstream, it means that
   a. a person is going to die.
   b. the dreamer is going to die.
   c. the dreamer is eluding a taboo.
   d. the level of neural activation has changed.

10. The following are characteristics of the sleep stages, EXCEPT
   a. the stages of sleep correspond to electrophysiological changes in the brain.
   b. when a person is sleeping he/she shows beta waves in an EEG.
   c. the first stage of sleep is characterized by the presence of electrical waves that are slow in frequency and great in amplitude.
   d. sleep spindles show up in stage two of sleep.

11. Which of the following waves of electrical brain activity is the one consistent with the deepest sleep?
   a. theta
   b. beta
   c. delta
   d. alpha

12. Martha is participating in a sleep study. When she is awakened by the researcher, she feels groggy and disoriented. It takes a few seconds for her to remember that she is in a sleeping lab. During which stage of sleep was Martha awakened?
   a. the theta waves stage
   b. the sleep spindles stage
   c. REM sleep
   d. the second delta waves stage or stage 4

13. Which of the following is NOT true about REM sleep?
   a. It does not take a long time in REM sleep for the person to report a long and complex dream.
   b. Infants spend most of their sleeping time in REM sleep.
   c. There is rapid eye movement during REM sleep.
   d. During REM sleep, the brain waves are similar to alpha waves.

14. The activation-synthesis theory proposed that dreams are
    a. symbolic expressions of what we wish would happen in our lives.
    b. predictions of the future.
    c. a result of brain activity.
    d. based on our childhood troubles.

15. Which brain waves are most common in the brain of a hypnotized person?
    a. alpha and delta
    b. theta and beta
    c. delta and beta
    d. alpha and beta

16. Which percentage of alcoholics is expected to have a genetic predisposition for the disorder?
    a. 10%
    b. 25%
    c. 50%
    d. 90%

17. Which of the following statements presents correctly one of the differences between barbiturates and tranquilizers?
    a. Barbiturates are more likely to be addictive than tranquilizers.
    b. Tranquilizers are given to induce sleep.
    c. Barbiturates are more likely to be prescribed than tranquilizers.
    d. An overdose of barbiturates is unlike to be dangerous or lethal.

18. Of the following alternatives, which is believed to be the most addictive drug?
    a. crack
    b. heroin
    c. barbiturates
    d. alcohol

19. Which of the following is NOT true about Ecstasy?
    a. It is a stimulant.
    b. It is a hallucinogenic.
    c. It is an illegal drug that comes from a bean.
    d. It causes brain damage.

20. Marijuana is a
    a. barbiturate.
    b. hallucinogen.
    c. stimulant.
    d. depressant.

21. Which of the following scenarios does NOT present a person experiencing an altered state of consciousness?

    a.    Jack is recuperating from a marathon run and he is lethargic, dehydrated, and disoriented.

    b.    Maya has been studying for four straight days, getting approximately four hours of sleep at night and studying every single hour of her time awake. She is now experiencing an inability to concentrate and feels that her body is about to fall asleep without her being able to control it.

    c.    Tim is on his third cup of coffee this morning; his mind is going a million miles a minute and he's feeling jittery.

    d.    Therese is at work but she is so bored with her task that she starts visualizing her upcoming vacation to the Bahamas.

## Connections

*Take advantage of all the other study tools available for this chapter!*

### MEDIA INTERGRATION

| NAME OF CLIP | DESCRIPTION | KEY CONCEPTS AND IDEAS |
| --- | --- | --- |
| | | **The Nature of Consciousness** |
| Sensory Processes and Brain Integration | This video introduces students to the complexities of sensory integration. The question of whether or not there is a specific part of the brain that integrates sensory information is addressed. Students are also introduced to the process of creation of mental maps. | Sensory integration<br>Perception<br>Brain<br>Memory<br>Neural networks<br>Mental maps |
| | | **Sleep and Dreams** |
| Stages of Sleep | Animated slides show the brain waves characteristic of the stages of sleep. | Stages of sleep<br>Beta waves<br>REM |
| REM Sleep | This video shows sleep laboratory studies and how electrodes are used to measure brain waves. The Freudian and REM perspectives are compared. A REM researcher suggests that REM sleep research does not necessarily render Freud's theory of dreams untenable. The controversial role of Freud in the history of psychology is discussed. | REM<br>Sigmund Freud |
| Sleep Stages | Animated slides show the brain waves characteristic of the stages of sleep. | Stages of sleep<br>Beta waves<br>REM |

| Freudian Interpretation of Dreams | This video clip is an introduction to Freud's theory of dream analysis. The concept of dream work and its processes are discussed. Common themes in Freudian dream analysis are also discussed. | Dreams<br>Dream work<br>Displacement<br>Condensation<br>Symbolization<br>Projection<br>Ego<br>Manifest dream<br>Latent dream |
|---|---|---|
| | | **Hypnosis** |
| | | **Psychoactive Drugs** |
| Neurochemical Basis of Addiction | This video clip presents the neurochemical basis of addiction and can be used to illustrate the role of classical conditioning in addiction. The presentation includes a description of a medicine that has been used to treat heroine addicts and now is being used to treat alcoholism. The drug blocks the receptors in opiates, reducing the effect of pleasure often associated with the intake of these drugs. | Neurotransmitters<br>Addiction<br>Cravings<br>Opiates |
| Effects of Alcohol | Alcohol is the drug of choice for American youth. Social psychologist McDonald discusses the disinhibition theory vs. alcohol myopia theory, which predicts that a person's behaviors depend on the most prominent cues available to them. An experiment is discussed that lends support to the alcohol myopia theory. Applications of this theory include making dangers more obvious, so that intoxicated people make better decisions. | Alcohol<br>Disinhibition theory<br>Alcohol myopia theory |
| Alcohol Addiction | The effects of withdrawal on persons with alcoholism are discussed including Delirium Tremens. A case study looks at the process detoxification. Physiological and psychological addictions are | Alcoholism<br>Delirium tremens<br>Detox<br>Physiological addiction<br>Psychological addiction |

| | | |
|---|---|---|
| | compared. The positive effects of psychotherapy and treatment for alcoholism are discussed. | |
| Substance Abuse | Bobby, a 31-year-old woman, describes a pattern of starting with alcohol and marijuana and leading to abuse of cocaine, LSD, and heroine. Bobby was introduced to heroine by her mother. She started smoking at 12; by age 21 she was a heroine addict. Bobby describes the experience of heroine addiction, including a pattern of drug use and prostitution. Bobby is HIV positive. While she has been clean for 2 years, she still thinks of herself as an addict and shares that sometimes she still craves the euphoria of heroine. | Drug addiction <br> Substance abuse <br> Heroine <br> HIV |

**Online Learning Center (www.mhhe.com/Santrockp7u)**

- Interact and make learning fun!
    - **Interactive Exercises**
        - Circadian Rhythms
        - Stages of Sleep
    - **Interactive Review**
        - Level of Analysis: Drug-Induced States of Consciousness
- Brush up on the Key Terms for this chapter by first reviewing the electronic **Glossary** (in English or Spanish) and then testing your retention using the **Flashcard** feature.
- **"Notes"**- this feature allows you to use the website as you would your text, inserting your own study notes and highlighting areas of particular importance.

**In Your Text**

- Found throughout each chapter, the **Review and Sharpen Your Thinking** feature breaks the text into logical chunks, allowing you to process, review, and reflect thoughtfully on the information that you've just read. When going back to *study* the chapter, try reading the feature *before* the section of text to which it relates. In doing so, you will be able to focus your attention on important concepts *as* you encounter them. In this chapter, this feature can be found on the following pages: pp. 232, 246, 249, and 261.

**Practice Quizzes**

- Test your knowledge of states of consciousness by taking the different practice quizzes found on your text's **Online Learning Center** and on the **In-Psych Plus CD-ROM** packaged with your text.

# ANSWER KEY

## In Your Own Words

✓ Look at the definition of consciousness. Give some examples of external and internal awareness. Think of a behavior that you do regularly, such as driving, playing basketball, or writing e-mails. When you are engaged in that activity, which behaviors/thoughts/emotions are controlled processes? Which are automatic processes?

*In this answer the student should demonstrate understanding of the difference between controlled and automatic processes and how they may occur simultaneously, especially for tasks that demand a lot of coordinated psychological activities. For example, in playing basketball, the person must be able to automatically process body movement to dribble, dunk, and perform any other behaviors associated with the sport. Also, skilled players process automatically the rules of the game and follow them without being highly aware of them. They don't step out of the line, not because they are purposefully making that decision at a controlled level, but because that is "just how it is done." However, in order to play effectively, a player must engage in controlled processing of the positions and actions of the other players, strategies and sudden shifts in behaviors.*

✓ Imagine that you are a consultant who specializes in sleep and circadian rhythms. You have been hired by a large manufacturing company to guide them as they overhaul their shiftwork schedule. What advice do you give?

*The student must make reference to the effects of interrupting the circadian rhythm and recommendations for restoring it.*

✓ For a week, keep a journal of dreams. Before you go to bed, write down the approximate time when you expect to start sleeping, then in the morning record the time you wake up and any details of dreams you may remember. At the end of the week, study your notes and consider if the sleeping and awakening times have any relationship with the amount of information you recall about dreams. Also, consider the theories of dreams presented in the chapter in order to explain the meaning of your dreams.

*This question integrates the physiological and psychological aspects of sleeping and dreaming. The time of sleep and awakening can influence the sleep cycle, and with this journal the student may become aware of the relationship between recalling dreams and the stage in the sleep cycle in which one is awakened.*

✓ Describe one of your dreams in terms of manifest content and latent content.

*The distinction between manifest and latent content is a simple one: manifest is the story that you recall, latent is what it was really about. What is more challenging is letting go of the images in the dream and exploring the possible symbolic meaning. If we dream about a person we know we tend to think that the dream was really about that person and not about what that person evokes or how he or she makes us feel.*

✓ Describe in a story format the biological effects and the psychological experience of a smoker or a smokeless tobacco user as he/she introduces the psychoactive drug nicotine into the body.

*The student should describe the behaviors involved in introducing nicotine to the body, either through smoking or through smokeless tobacco. The student may address the motivational state of the person: why does he or she use tobacco, or why aren't the warnings and dangers a deterrent? The story then should move into the body and describe how nicotine stimulates the reward centers by raising dopamine levels. Some of the psychological effects of nicotine withdrawal include irritability, cravings, inability to focus, and sleep disturbance.*

## Correcting the Incorrect

1. Consciousness is awareness of both external and internal stimuli or events. (p. 228)
2. *According to Freud*, unconscious thought refers to *a reservoir of unacceptable wishes, feelings, and thoughts*. (p. 231)
3. If you are doing a task that requires minimal attention, then you are experiencing an *automatic* process. (p. 230)
4. Drugs, meditation, fatigue, and hypnosis can produce *altered states of consciousness*. (p. 230)
5. A 24-hour behavioral or physiological cycle is called a *circadian rhythm*. (p. 233)
6. When deprived of all time and light cues, the circadian rhythm is about *24* hours long. (p. 234)
7. Sleep spindles occur in *Stage 2 of sleep*. (p. 238)
8. REM sleep is a stage of sleep during which dreaming occurs. (p. 239)
9. The hormone *melatonin* may be effective in reducing insomnia. (p.242)
10. *Sonambulism* is the formal term for sleepwalking. (p. 242)
11. *Nightmares* occur in REM and are really just bad dreams. (p. 243)
12. The overpowering urge to fall asleep is called *narcolepsy*. (p. 243)
13. A dream's true meaning is called the *latent content*. (p. 244)
14. The *cognitive theory of dreaming* suggests that dreaming may allow us to solve problems. (p. 244)
15. Dreams reflect the brain's efforts to make sense out of neural activity that takes place during sleep, according to the activation-synthesis theory. (p. 245)
16. Mesmer cured his patients using hypnosis. (p. 247)
17. Ernest Hilgard proposed that hypnosis involved a *state of divided consciousness in which a part of the person is like a hidden observer who is aware of the events*. (p. 248)
18. Psychoactive drugs *do* produce tolerance. (p. 251)
19. The strong desire and craving to repeat the use of a drug is called *psychological dependence*. (p. 251)
20. Alcohol is a depressant. (p. 252)
21. Barbiturates are *depressant* drugs that are used medically to induce sleep. (p. 255)
22. *Opiates* include morphine and heroin. (p. 255)
23. Crack is an intensified form of *cocaine*. (p. 256)
24. MDMA (Ecstasy) is an illegal synthetic drug with both stimulant and *hallucinogenic* properties. (p. 256)
25. The nicotine in cigarettes is a *stimulant*. (p. 257)
26. Marijuana affects the functioning of *many neurotransmitters*. (p. 258)
27. Critics of the disease model of addiction argue that addiction is *not necessarily* a lifelong pattern.(p. 261)

## Practice Test 1

1. a. no; this state refers to a state that is noticeable different from normal awareness
   b. YES; this is the definition of consciousness
   c. no; REM is rapid eye movement that occurs in sleep
   d. no

p. 228

2.  a.   no; controlled processes require much attention and focus
    b.   CORRECT; automatic processes require minimal attention
    c.   no; this refers to the continuous flow of sensations and thoughts
    d.   no; unconscious thought refers to the reservoir of unconscious wishes and feelings
    p. 230

3.  a.   no; not even close
    b.   YES; a circadian rhythm is a daily behavioral or physiological cycle
    c.   no; circadian rhythm is not related to drug use
    d.   no; jet lag is the result of rhythms being out of sync
    p. 233

4.  a.   no; the stream refers to the ever-changing thoughts, sensations, and images
    b.   no; the four stages of sleep are not necessarily a daily cycle
    c.   no; hypnosis is a change in consciousness
    d.   YES; this is an example of a circadian rhythm
    p. 233

5.  a.   no; in REM we experience fast waves
    b.   no
    c.   no; in stage 2 sleep there are sleep spindles
    d.   YES
    p. 238

6.  a.   no
    b.   no
    c.   no
    d.   RIGHT; the cycles of sleep last about 90 minutes
    p. 240

7.  a.   no; this is not relevant
    b.   no; this is not a difference
    c.   THAT'S CORRECT; the stages of sleep correspond to changes in brain activity
    d.   no; while this is a difference, it is not a main difference
    p. 239

8.  a.   no
    b.   no; at least probably not
    c.   no; somnambulism refers to sleepwalking
    d.   YES; she has narcolepsy and experiences the overpowering urge to sleep
    p. 243

9.  a.   CORRECT; somnambulism is the formal term for sleepwalking
    b.   no
    c.   no
    d.   no
    p. 242

10. a.   YES; Bethany has night terrors that occur in non-REM sleep
    b.   no; insomnia is the inability to sleep
    c.   no; sleep apnea is a condition in which a person stops breathing while sleeping
    d.   no; narcolepsy is the overpowering urge to sleep
    p. 243

11. a. no; this option sounds Freudian
    b. no
    c. no; this answer summarizes the activation-synthesis theory
    d. YES; it focuses on information processing, memory, and problem solving
    p. 244

12. a. no; Freud would argue this option
    b. YUP; dreams are the brain's effort to make sense of neural activity
    c. no; the cognitive theory is consistent with this option
    d. no; Freud's theory includes manifest and latent content
    p. 245

13. a. RIGHT; concentration is an important element in hypnosis
    b. no; falling asleep does not occur in hypnosis
    c. no; the subject does not lose control, but only becomes more suggestible
    d. no; using a pocket watch or pendulum does not lead to hallucinations
    p. 247

14. a. no; in fact, concentration and focus are very important
    b. no; concentrating and focusing on something specific are very important
    c. CORRECT; when the experience occurs, the person will believe it was suggested
    d. no; the hypnotist may actually desire posthypnotic amnesia to occur
    p. 247

15. a. no; the person remains very conscious and aware during hypnosis
    b. no; only about 10–20% are very susceptible to hypnosis
    c. no; hypnosis does not dramatically improve accuracy of memory
    d. RIGHT; people differ in their susceptibility to hypnosis
    p. 247

16. a. YES, THAT'S RIGHT; both caffeine and cocaine are stimulants
    b. no
    c. no
    d. no
    p. 256

17. a no; marijuana is a hallucinogenic drug
    b. no; alcohol is a depressant
    c. YES; cocaine is classified as a stimulant
    d. no; LSD is a hallucinogenic drug
    p. 256

18. a. no; the model does discourage people from developing self-control
    b. no; the labels are "addict" and "alcoholics"
    c. YES; the approach is consistent with the medical profession
    d. no; programs are very rigid and not flexible
    p. 261

19. a. no; daydreaming occurs at a conscious lower-level awareness
    b. no; sleeping and dreaming are examples of subconscious experiences
    c. no; in lower-level awareness the person is still aware
    d. YES; the unconscious is out of a person's awareness
    p. 231

20. a.   YES; this little structure in the hypothalamus registers light and uses it to synchronize our biological clocks; this is why blind people tend to have problems with their biological clocks, because they cannot perceive light and the information does not get to the suprachiasmic nucleus
    b.   no; the thalamus is not involved in this function
    c.   incorrect; the hindbrain is not involved in this function; the suprachiasm nucleus is in the hypothalamus, which in turn is in the forebrain
    d.   incorrect
p. 233


## Practice Test 2

1. a.   THAT'S RIGHT; Mike is experiencing a controlled processes with attention
   b.   no, automatic processes require minimal attention
   c.   no; hypnosis involves a heighten suggestibility
   d.   no; this refers to the continuous flow of sensations and thoughts
p. 229

2. a.   no; James did not see the mind as a static blank slate
   b.   no; James did consider the study of the mind a worthy topic for psychologists
   c.   YES; James thought of the mind as a dynamic continuous flow of sensations, images, thoughts, and feelings
   d.   no; James understood the mind as conscious
p. 228

3. a.   no; this occurs when we are engaged in controlled processing and we are very alert of what we are doing and thinking
   b.   YES; daydreaming is a type of lower-level awareness, in which we may be in automatic processing
   c.   no; daydreaming is not an altered state of consciousness, such as those induced by drugs, trauma, fatigue, and other factors
   d.   no; sleeping and dreaming are examples of subconscious awareness
p. 230

4. a.   no; consciousness is not processed in any specific or small area of the brain
   b.   no; consciousness is not processed in any specific or small area of the brain
   c.   no; remember that the nervous system runs throughout our body; only areas inside the brain are engaged in the production of consciousness
   d.   CORRECT; experts agree that consciousness is produced through the integrated and coordinated processing of many areas in the brain
p. 232

5. a.   no; this is one of the most important functions of sleep
   b.   YES; while there are various theories of dreams, none argues that dreaming is the reason we sleep; however, the type of deep sleep we are in when we dream is very important
   c.   no; adaptation seems to be an important reason to sleep; after all, we need the rest to face the challenges presented by our environment
   d.   no; growth also is enhanced by sleep
p. 235

6. a. no; levels of epinephrine do decrease as sleep progresses from stages 1 to 4
   b. no; levels of serotonin do decrease as sleep progresses from stages 1 to 4
   c. YES; a decrease in GABA is not observed as the sleep stages progress from 1 to 4
   d. no; levels of acetylcholine do decrease from stages 1 to 4 and begin increasing when REM starts
   p. 241

7. a. no; this statement is correct
   b. YES; this statement is incorrect, when we are fighting an infectious disease we tend to get sleepy, probably due to the work of the chemicals called cytokines
   c. no; this statement is true
   d. no; this statement is true
   p. 241

8. a. no; the opposite is true
   b. no; the opposite is true
   c. YES; females do report dreaming about friends more frequently than men
   d. no; the opposite is true
   p. 244

9. a. YES; this theory argues that while dreaming we are engaging in the same cognitive processes as when we are awake and among those processes features problem solving
   b. no; while this may seem like a trick item it is not; first of all, there is no theory called the *I-got-it dream approach*, but more importantly, theories in psychology are usually named with meaningful concepts, such as "cognitive"; remember that theories are broad and the names of theories are expected to carry a lot of meaning
   c. no; this theory focuses on the role of brain activity in the generation of dreams
   d. no; while manifest content is a concept relevant in the study of dreams, it is not a theory
   p. 244

10. a. no; hypnosis has been used in medicine
    b. YES; hypnosis would not be useful in studying the higher-level consciousness of controlled processing
    c. no; hypnosis is used in psychotherapy
    d. no; hypnosis has been used in dentistry
    p. 248

11. a. no; the parent is not in the dream; however, the parent may be symbolized in the house
    b. YES; this is the "story" of the dream, what she remembers; therefore, this is the manifest content
    c. no; the death may be symbolized in the crumbling of the house, but "death" is not part of the dream
    d. no; her psychological state can be expected to influence the content of her dreams, but she did not dream about a sense of loss but rather about a house crumbling
    p. 244

12. a. no; this statement is true
    b. YES; this is incorrect because during the hypnotic state the EEG shows a predominance of alpha and beta waves
    c. no; this statement is correct
    d. no; minimizing distractions is the first step in the process of hypnosis
    p. 247

13. a.  CORRECT; using psychoactive drugs does not give people a special ability to know when to stop using it and prevent addiction
    b.  no; this can be caused even if the use is casual
    c.  no; changing our psychology, that is, our behaviors and mental processes, with drugs, can have a serious effect on our lives
    d.  no; using psychoactive drugs can open the door for serious diseases
    p. 251

14. a.  no; this statement is false
    b.  no; this statement is false
    c.  YES; physical dependence is associated with the experience of withdrawal symptoms
    d.  no; this statement is incorrect, as some people may become psychologically dependent because the drug reduces stress
    p. 251

15. a.  no
    b.  no
    c.  no
    d.  YES; while different drugs have different mechanisms of action, each drug increases the activity of the reward pathway by increasing dopamine transmission
    p. 252

16. a.  no; alcohol is a depressant
    b.  no; alcohol is not an hallucinogenic
    c.  YES; alcohol is a depressant that slows down brain activity in various areas, including the one involving inhibition
    d.  no; while alcohol is depressant, cocaine is not, it is a stimulant
    p. 253

17. a.  no; this is one of the characteristics of alcoholism
    b.  no; this is one of the characteristics of alcoholism
    c.  YES; alcoholism involves a long-term use of alcoholic beverages
    d.  no; this is one of the characteristics of alcoholism
    p. 254

18. a.  YES; consumption of alcohol in China is low, particularly in comparison with the other three countries listed
    b.  no; alcohol consumption in France is so significant that about 30% of French adults have health problems associated with alcohol
    c.  no; Russia does have a high rate of alcohol consumption
    d.  no; after caffeine, alcohol is the next most widely used drug in the United States
    p. 254

19. a.  no; this is true but it is a biological factor
    b.  YES; this statement is true and presents at least two environmental factors: gender and residence
    c.  no; this is true but it is a genetic factor
    d.  no; this is true but it is a biological factor
    p. 254

20. a.   no; these are depressants, not stimulants
    b.   no; marijuana is a hallucinogen; it does not provide a boost in energy
    c.   YES; amphetamines are stimulants that are used to boost energy, stay awake, and lose weight
    d.   no; alcohol is a depressant
  p. 256


## Practice Test 3

1. a.   YES; driving requires minimal attention and doesn't interfere with ongoing activities
   b.   no; altered states refer to a state that differs from normal awareness
   c.   no; this is not a special ability
   d.   no; driving is not a controlled since it doesn't interfere with ongoing activities
  p. 230


2. a.   no; this is very likely to cause an altered state of consciousness
   b.   no; this is very likely to cause an altered state of consciousness
   c.   YES; caffeine is a stimulant and will not likely induce an altered state
   d.   no; this is very likely to cause an altered state of consciousness
  p. 230


3. a.   THAT'S RIGHT; Michael is travel east and this direction is difficult to adjust to
   b.   no; traveling west is easy on our sleep/wake cycle
   c.   no; traveling north is easy on our sleep/wake cycle
   d.   no; traveling south is easy on our sleep/wake cycle
  p. 234


4. a.   no; this is not likely
   b.   CORRECT; dad is experiencing REM, indicating that dreaming is occurring
   c.   no; the idea of the "hidden observer" is used in explaining hypnosis
   d.   no; slow-wave movement cannot be seen
  p. 239


5. a.   no; the description does not imply addiction
   b.   no; psychological dependence is the strong desire and craving to use a drug
   c.   YES; tolerance occurs when more of the drug is needed to produce an effect
   d.   no; this refers to narcolepsy, which is a sleep disorder
  p. 251


6. a.   no; this is one of the symptoms of caffeine withdrawal
   b.   YES; this is incorrect, caffeine boosts energy, but the opposite experience would occur if the person is in withdrawal
   c.   no; this is one of the symptoms of caffeine withdrawal
   d.   no; this is one of the symptoms of caffeine withdrawal
  p. 257


7. a.   YES; giving melatonin supplements has been tested as a therapeutic approach to insomnia
   b.   no; this has been tested as a therapeutic approach to insomnia
   c.   no; this has been tested as a therapeutic approach to insomnia
   d.   no; this has been tested as a therapeutic approach to insomnia
  p. 242

8. a.   no; a newborn is unlikely to have specific images to symbolize danger, the usual topic of nightmares.
   b.   no
   c.   YES; nightmares peak at 3 to 6 years of age and then decline
   d.   no; college students tend to have only 4 to 8 nightmares a year
   p. 243

9. a.   no; the question does not address any particular story or theme, and even if the dream is about death, psychoanalysts would argue that it just symbolizes something else
   b.   no; the question does not address any particular story or theme, and even if the dream is about death, psychoanalysts would argue that it just symbolizes something else
   c.   YES; the psychoanalytic approach was the one developed by Freud, and he believed that when the story line reached a taboo issue, the dream would shift into something less psychologically threatening
   d.   no; this would be a prediction of the activation-synthesis theory
   p. 246

10. a.   no; this is correct about sleep stages
    b.   YES; beta waves are characteristic of wakefulness and are highest in frequency and lowest in amplitude
    c.   no; this is correct about sleep stages
    d.   no; this is correct about sleep stages
    p. 238

11. a.   no; these are characteristic of the first stage
    b.   no; these are characteristic of being awake
    c.   YES; these are the waves that are characteristic of our deepest sleep; they are the slowest and the highest in amplitude
    d.   no; these are characteristic of being relaxed but awake
    p. 238

12. a.   no; this is the first stage of sleep
    b.   no; this is the second stage of sleep
    c.   no; during this stage people are more likely to be dreaming and they are not as likely to experience the disorientation that Martha experienced
    d.   YES; the deepest sleep occurs during the fourth stage of sleep
    p. 239

13. a.   YES; this is incorrect because the longer the period of REM sleep, the more likely the person will report dreaming
    b.   no; this is correct about REM sleep; older adults spend in REM sleep about one-eighth of the time an infant spends in REM sleep
    c.   no; this is correct about REM sleep
    d.   no; this is correct about REM sleep
    p. 239

14. a.   no; this would be more consistent with the psychoanalytic view of Freud
    b.   no; psychologists do not believe that dreams are predictions of actual future events
    c.   YES; according to this view, dreams are generated when the cerebral cortex synthesizes neural signals resulting from activity in the lower part of the brain
    d.   no; this is not consistent with the activation-synthesis theory
    p. 245

15. a.  no
    b.  no
    c.  no
    d.  YES; this suggests that hypnosis, in terms of brain activity, is no different from being deeply relaxed yet awake
    p. 247

16. a.  no; while environmental factors are important they do not account for 90% of the cases of alcoholism
    b.  no; while environmental factors, such as friends and culture, are important they do not account for 75% of the cases of alcoholism
    c.  YES; an estimated 50–60% of those who become alcoholics are believed to have a genetic predisposition
    d.  no; genetics are important factors but they do not account for 90% of the cases of alcoholism
    p. 255

17. a.  YES; this is true and one of the main reasons why tranquilizers have largely replaced barbiturates in the treatment of insomnia
    b.  no; barbiturates are given to induce sleep while tranquilizers are usually given to calm an anxious and nervous individual
    c.  no; the opposite is true
    d.  no; this is grossly incorrect; barbiturates are the most common drug used in suicide attempts because of the lethal effects of overdoses
    p. 255

18. a.  YES; crack is a potent form of cocaine, consisting of chips of pure cocaine that are usually smoked, and it is believed to be more addictive than heroin, barbiturates, or alcohol
    b.  no
    c.  no
    d.  no
    p. 256

19. a.  no; this is true about Ecstasy
    b.  no; this is also true about Ecstasy, it is a stimulant and a hallucinogenic
    c.  YES; this is incorrect because Ecstasy is a synthetic drug; it does not come from a bean or a plant
    d.  no; Ecstasy can cause brain damage, especially to neurons that use serotonin to communicate with other neurons
    p. 256

20. a.  no
    b.  YES; marijuana has a mild hallucinogenic effect
    c.  no
    d.  no
    p. 258

21. a.   no; Jack is experiencing the effects of fatigue, and this can produce an altered state of consciousness
    b.   no; Maya is experiencing the effects of sleep deprivation, and this can produce an altered state of consciousness
    c.   no; Tim is experiencing the altered state of consciousness caused by the intake of the psychoactive drug caffeine
    d.   YES; Therese is simply daydreaming and this is not an altered state of consciousness, it is a conscious manipulation of thoughts

p. 230

# Chapter 7—Learning

## Learning Goals

1. Explain what learning is.
2. Describe classical conditioning.
3. Discuss operant conditioning.
4. Understand observational learning.
5. Explain the role of cognition in learning.
6. Identify biological and cultural factors in learning.

*After studying Chapter 7, you will be able to:*

- Explain what learning is.
- Compare the two types of learning: observation learning versus associative learning.
- Discuss Pavlovian classical conditioning.
- Explain what extinction, generalization, and discrimination are in classical conditioning.
- Describe classical conditioning in humans.
- Evaluate classical conditioning.
- Discuss what operant conditioning is and how it differs from classical conditioning.
- Understand the predictions of Thorndike's law of effect.
- Discuss Skinner's operant conditioning and principles.
- Understand what the concepts *positive* and *negative* mean in the context of operant conditioning and think of examples for positive reinforcement, negative reinforcement, positive punishment, and negative punishment.
- Describe some applications of operant conditioning.
- Explain the role of expectations and cognitive maps in learning.
- Describe what latent learning is.
- Understand insight learning.
- Discuss biological factors that influence learning.
- Describe cultural factors in learning.

## CHAPTER 7: OUTLINE

- *Learning* is a relatively permanent change in behavior due to experience. There are two general types of learning: observational and associative. *Conditioning* is the process of learning associations. There are two types of conditioning: classical and operant. Classical conditioning occurs when the person learns to associate two stimuli; operant conditioning occurs when the person associates a behavior with a consequence.

- Pavlov discovered the principle of classical conditioning as he was investigating digestion in dogs. He found that dogs could be conditioned to salivate to various stimuli (e.g., a bell) in anticipation of eating meat powder. In this type of learning, an organism learns an association between an unconditioned stimulus and a conditioned stimulus.

- Before an association is learned, the unconditioned stimulus automatically produces an unconditioned response; in other words, it if is unconditioned, it is not learned. In Pavlov's study, the meat powder automatically produced the salivation. After an association has been established, the conditioned stimulus alone elicits a conditioned response.

- Extinction, spontaneous recovery, generalization, and discrimination are involved in classical conditioning. Many psychologists believe that, in humans, phobias and certain physical complaints are explained by classical conditioning.

- The case of little Albert illustrates how a fear of rats could be classically conditioned. Counterconditioning is a procedure for weakening a classically conditioned association.

- Classical conditioning can also explain associations with pleasant emotions. Since automatic body reactions and activities can become classically conditioned, a number of health problems can be produced owing to the presence (or lack of) a conditioned stimuli. For example, for an alcoholic, the bar, the drinking buddies, the drinking glass, and other stimuli that are associated with drinking can trigger the body's reactions in anticipation of the excessive alcohol drinking that the body expects.

- Classical conditioning is also used by advertisers when they want their audience to associate certain positive emotions and experiences with their product.

- In operant conditioning, the consequences of behavior produce changes in the probability of its occurrence. It is called *operant conditioning* because the behavior operates on the environment and then the environment operates back to the behavior.

- Thorndike's law of effect states that behaviors followed by good consequences are more likely to be repeated than are behaviors followed by bad consequences. *Shaping* is the process of rewarding approximations of desired behaviors. *Reinforcement* is the process of increasing the probability that a behavior will be repeated.

- While reinforcements are always desirable for the recipient, they can be classified as positive or negative. In the context of operant conditioning, *positive* refers to the offering or giving of something, whereas *negative* refers to the removal or taking away of something. A positive reinforcement increases the probability that the behavior will be repeated, because the behavior is followed by the offering of a desirable consequence. A negative reinforcement also increases the probability that the behavior will be repeated, but in this case through the removal of undesirable stimuli. Reinforcements can also be classified as primary (innate) or secondary (learned).

- Other important concepts in operant conditioning are time interval, shaping, and schedules of reinforcement (i.e., fixed-ratio, variable-ratio, fixed-interval, variable-interval). Like classical conditioning, the principles of operant conditioning also include extinction, generalization, and discrimination.

- Punishment refers to a consequence that decreases the probability of a behavior occurring since it weakens the behavior. Like reinforcement, punishment can also be classified as positive or negative, but remember that punishment is always undesirable for the recipient. Positive punishment refers to an undesirable consequence that results from giving an unpleasant stimulus, whereas in negative punishment a pleasant stimulus is removed.

- Reinforcement is usually recommended over punishment to change behavior. Some of the reasons why intense punishment should be avoided are that the parent is modeling inappropriate behavior; it might instill fear, rage and avoidance; and it can be abusive. In applied behavior analysis (or behavior modification), the principles of operant conditioning are used to change behavior.

- Observational learning is also called *imitation* or *modeling*. According to Bandura, the following processes influence an observer's behavior after viewing a model: attention, retention, production, and reinforcement. Many contemporary psychologists believe that learning involves more than stimulus-response connections and that cognitive factors play a role in learning.

- Tolman argued that it is necessary to study entire sequences of behaviors to understand the learning process and the role of purposiveness. He argued that expectancies and cognitive maps are alternatives to the conditioning explanations of behaviors.

- *Latent learning* is learning that is not reinforced and that does not manifest immediately in behavior, but that may show up later when an appropriate reinforcement is offered. *Insight learning* is a form of problem solving in which the organism develops a sudden understanding of a problem's solution.

- Learning is also influenced by biological and cultural factors. Biological factors include instinctive drift, preparedness and taste aversion. While the learning processes discussed here are considered to be universal, culture can influence the degree to which these learning processes occur and often determine the content of learning.


## Building Blocks of Chapter 7

### Clarifying some of the tricky points in Chapter 7
### and
### In Your Own Words
*To respond to the questions and exercises presented in the "In Your Own Words" section, please write your thoughts, perspectives, and reactions on a separate piece of paper.*

### Helpful Hints for Understanding Learning
### Helpful Hint #1:
*Many students find the chapter on Learning to be difficult, and they give up. Try NOT to do that! Understanding the tenets of learning theory can help you in you own life. You will understand what keeps people doing what they are doing and what changes if they stop a behavior. It is an extremely helpful tool. However, it takes a little practice to get it down. So, do just that, PRACTICE! Pay attention to your own and other's behaviors and try to figure out, according to learning theory, what is going on. First of all, when studying this chapter, think of it as learning a new language. Even though many of the words used in learning theory are English words that we think we understand, they DO NOT always mean the same thing in learning theory.*

### Types of Learning
Learning is a relatively permanent change in *behavior* that occurs through *experience*. There are two general types of learning: *observational learning*, in which a person learns by watching others, and *associative learning*, in which a connection is made between two events. *Conditioning* is the process of learning associations. There are two types of conditioning: *classical conditioning*, in which associations between two stimuli are learned, and *operant conditioning*, in which an association between a behavior and its consequence is learned.

### Classical Conditioning
Ivan Pavlov described the principle of *classical conditioning*. Classical conditioning consists of the following components: the *unconditioned stimulus (UCS)*, which is a stimulus that produces a response without prior learning; an unlearned response, called the *unconditioned response (UCR)*; a previously neutral stimulus that eventually elicits the conditioned response, called the *conditioned stimulus (CS)*; and a learned response called a *conditioned response (CR)*.

The time interval between the conditioned stimulus and the unconditioned stimulus is important because it helps define the degree of association, or *contiguity*, of the stimulus. When a new stimulus similar to the CS produces a similar CR, this is called *generalization*. When an organism is conditioned to respond to one stimulus and not another, this is called *discrimination*.

A weakening of the CR in the absence of the US is called *extinction*. When a CR recurs without further conditioning, this is called *spontaneous recovery*.

Many psychologists believe that, in humans, irrational, intense fears, or *phobias*, are caused by classical conditioning. A procedure for weakening a classically conditioned fear response is called *counterconditioning*. Behaviors associated with health problems or mental disturbances can involve *classical conditioning*. However, classical conditioning does not only contribute to the experience of negative emotions—for example, we may also become conditioned to respond with positive *emotions* to stimuli associated with sex, such as mood music. Consumer psychologists use classical conditioning in advertisements designed to induce associations between the product and positive emotional arousal.

## In Your Own Words

*Please write your thoughts, perspectives, and reactions on a separate piece of paper.*
✓ *Can you give an example of generalizations that Pavlov's dogs might have experienced?*

✓ *How would you classically condition a baby to like classical music? Make sure you indicate the unconditioned stimulus, unconditioned response, conditioned stimulus, and conditioned response.*

### Operant Conditioning

A form of learning in which the consequences of behavior lead to changes in the probability of the behavior's occurrence is called *operant conditioning*. In classical conditioning, the association is made between two *stimuli*. In operant conditioning, the association is between a *behavior* and its *consequences*.

The concept of operant conditioning was developed by *Thorndike*. According to Thorndike, behavior followed by positive outcomes is *strengthened*, and behavior followed by negative outcomes is *weakened*. Thorndike referred to these predictions as the *Law of Effect*. The stimuli that govern classically conditioned behavior *precede* the behavior, but in operant conditioning the stimuli that govern behavior *follow* the behavior.

Skinner used the term *operant* to describe the behavior of the organism. According to Skinner, consequences that increase the probability that a behavior will occur are called *reinforcement*; consequences that decrease a behavior's probability are labeled *punishment*.

When the frequency of a behavior increases because it is followed by the offering of a desired consequence (e.g., giving money), it is a *positive reinforcement*. Negative reinforcement increases the frequency of a response either by *removing* an undesirable stimuli or consequence (e.g., eliminating a curfew). Skinner extensively studied animals in the laboratory, in the belief that the principles of learning are the same for all species.

Skinner's ideas for a utopian society are spelled out in his novel *Walden Two*. Skinner developed an apparatus for studying animals that has become known as the *Skinner box*. Several factors affect the effectiveness of operant conditioning; for example, learning is more efficient under *immediate* rather than delayed consequences. Also, behaviors are learned more rapidly if approximations to the desired behavior are rewarded; this is called *shaping*.

Positive reinforcements that are innately rewarding are called *primary reinforcements*; those reinforcements that acquire their positive value through experience are called *secondary reinforcements*. Money and other objects that can be exchanged for another reinforcer eventually acquire reinforcing value themselves; these are referred to as *token reinforcers*.

Often, reinforcements do not follow every occurrence of a response. This is called *partial reinforcement* and occurs in four different *schedules* of reinforcement. Generally, behaviors are learned most rapidly on *continuous reinforcement schedules*. When a behavior must occur a set number of times before it is rewarded, it is referred to as a *fixed-ratio schedule*. However, slot machines give out rewards on a *variable-ratio schedule*. Behaviors that are rewarded after the passage of a fixed amount of time are on *fixed-interval schedules*, whereas behaviors that are rewarded after differing amounts of time are referred to as *variable-interval schedules*. In operant conditioning, a decrease in the tendency to perform a response that is brought about by no longer reinforcing the response is called *extinction*. Giving the same response to similar stimuli is called *generalization*.

*Punishment* is a consequence that decreases the likelihood a behavior will be repeated. In *positive punishment*, a behavior decreases when it is followed by an unpleasant stimulus. In *negative punishment*, a behavior decreases when a positive stimulus is removed. Applying the principles of operant conditioning to changing human behavior is called *behavior modification*.

Behavior modification can be used for learning self-control, and this process can be divided into five steps: (1) define the problematic behavior in *specific and concrete* terms; (2) make a commitment to *change*; (3) collect *data* about the behavior; (4) design a self-control *program*; and (5) set *maintenance goals*. One of the ways in which operant conditioning has been applied to education is with the *Premack principle*, which refers to the use of a *high-probability* activity to reinforce a *low-probability* activity.

### In Your Own Words
*Please write your thoughts, perspectives, and reactions on a separate piece of paper.*
- ✓ *You are trying to teach your pet a new trick, and you've decided to use operant conditioning. In anticipation of the behavior modification, you will develop a list of stimuli/consequences you may use in the process. List two of each of the following: positive reinforcement, negative reinforcement, positive punishment, and negative punishment.*

### Observational Learning
When an individual learns by imitation or modeling, psychologists refer to this as *observational learning*. Observational learning allows us to learn without having to go through the tedious *trial and error*. Bandura proposes that the following processes influence an observer's behavior after being exposed to a model: *(1) attention, (2) retention, (3) production, and (4) reinforcement or incentive conditions.*

## In Your Own Words

*Please write your thoughts, perspectives, and reactions on a separate piece of paper.*

✓ *How has observational learning affected your behavior? Discuss two examples of behaviors that you have acquired through observational learning. Consider both adaptive, positive behaviors and maladaptive, negative behaviors.*

### Cognitive Factors in Learning

According to Tolman, when classical and operant conditioning occur, the organism acquires *expectations*, therefore, much of behavior is *goal-directed*. Tolman wrote that individuals select information from the environment and develop a *cognitive map* of their world. Cognitive maps are also involved in *latent learning*, an unreinforced learning that is not immediately reflected in behavior. Another psychologist who worked on the role of cognitive factors in learning was Wolfgang Köhler, whose work with apes led him to conclude that humans and other animals engage in *insight learning*, a form of problem solving in which the organisms develop a sudden insight or understanding of a problem's solution.

### Biological and Cultural Factors in Learning

When animals are being trained, they tend to revert to instinctive behavior, a concept called *instinctive drift*. Organisms also bring a biological background to the learning context. An example of this is called *preparedness*, which refers to why some animals learn readily in one situation but have great difficulty in others. Culture can influence the *degree* to which learning processes occur and the *content* of learning.

## In Your Own Words

*Please write your thoughts, perspectives, and reactions on a separate piece of paper.*

✓ *A marketing company has hired you as a consumer psychology consultant. They want to know how they can use both observational and associative learning to sell a new model of a sport utility vehicle. Choose a type of learning and list at least five recommendations.*

## Correcting the Incorrect

Carefully read each statement. Determine if the statement is correct or incorrect. If the statement is incorrect, make the necessary changes to correct it. Then check the answer key at the end of the chapter for the correct statement and page reference in the textbook.

1. Learning is a relatively permanent change in behavior that occurs through maturation.
2. Skinner is best remembered for his work in classical conditioning.
3. In classical conditioning, the unconditioned stimulus becomes associated with a meaningful stimulus and acquires the capacity to elicit a similar response.
4. Reflexes play a role in operant conditioning.
5. An unconditioned stimulus is a stimulus that produces a response only after prior learning.
6. The conditioned stimulus elicits the unconditioned response.
7. In classical conditioning, the learned association is between the conditioned stimulus and unconditioned stimulus.
8. Classical conditioning is a form of operant conditioning.
9. After a period of extinction, contingency recovery may occur.
10. If an organism shows generalization after being classically conditioned, it will respond to certain stimuli and not to others.
11. Little Albert was conditioned to fear a snake.

12. In counterconditioning, the conditioned stimulus is weakened.
13. In operant conditioning, the conditioned stimulus and the conditioned response are paired.
14. In positive reinforcement, the frequency of a response is increased because it is followed by a reward stimulus.
15. In negative reinforcement, the behavior is punished.
16. Through the process of generalization, approximations of the desired behavior are reinforced.
17. Primary reinforcers are learned reinforcers.
18. A fixed-ratio schedule is a timetable in which reinforcement is given after a certain amount of time has passed.
19. A variable-interval schedule is a timetable in which reinforcement is given after a variable amount of time has passed.
20. In positive punishment, a behavior decreases when a positive stimulus is removed from it.
21. Punishment decreases the likelihood that behavior will be repeated.
22. Observational learning is also called *imitation* or *modeling*.
23. The four processes involved in observational learning are extinction, discrimination, generalization, and discrimination.
24. Köhler found that apes show insight learning.
25. In instinctive drift, animals tend to revert to instinctive behavior.
26. Discrimination refers to species-specific biological predispositions to learn in certain ways but not others.
27. Insight learning is when an unreinforced behavior is learned, yet not immediately manifested.
28. The content of learning is influenced by heredity.

## Practice Test 1

1. Each of the following is a part of the definition of learning except
   a. relatively permanent.
   b. change in behavior.
   c. maturation.
   d. experience.

2. As the term has been used in traditional psychology, learning refers to
   a. any relatively permanent change in behavior brought about by experience.
   b. changes in behavior, including those associated with fatigue and maturation.
   c. most changes in behavior, except those caused by brain damage.
   d. all permanent changes in behavior, including those caused by heredity.

3. In Pavlov's experiment, the bell was a previously neutral stimulus that became a(n)
   a. conditioned stimulus.
   b. conditioned response.
   c. unconditioned response.
   d. unconditioned stimulus.

4.  Jennifer is desperately afraid of snakes. Her psychologist believes that her fear of snakes may have been classically conditioned. If her psychologist is correct, Jennifer's fear is the
    a.   unconditioned stimulus.
    b.   unconditioned response.
    c.   conditioned stimulus.
    d.   conditioned response.

5.  You volunteer to participate in an experiment in classical conditioning, and the experimenter conditions your eye-blink reflex to the sound of a bell. The next day, you notice that you blink whenever the phone rings. You are not upset because you know that
    a.   this UR will extinguish soon.
    b.   discrimination will readily develop.
    c.   spontaneous recovery is not dangerous or long-lasting.
    d.   without the US, extinction will naturally occur.

6.  The classical conditioning process by which a conditioned response can recur after a time delay without further conditioning is called
    a.   extinction.
    b.   generalization.
    c.   spontaneous recovery.
    d.   discrimination.

7.  In Watson and Rayner's study, little Albert was conditioned to fear a white rat. Later, Albert showed a fear of similar objects, such as a white rabbit, balls of cotton, and a white stuffed animal. This is an example of stimulus
    a.   generalization.
    b.   substitution.
    c.   discrimination.
    d.   inhibition.

8.  The term *counterconditioning* best describes which of the following procedures?
    a.   presenting the conditioned stimulus by itself
    b.   reintroducing the conditioned stimulus after extinction has occurred
    c.   pairing a fear-provoking stimulus with a new response incompatible with fear
    d.   reinforcing successive approximations of the goal response

9.  Which approach to learning represents the view that people learn from the consequences of their actions?
    a.   response cost theory
    b.   operant conditioning
    c.   observational learning
    d.   classical conditioning

10. In operant conditioning, the association is between a _____ and its _____.
    a.   reinforcer; stimulus
    b.   behavior; response
    c.   consequence; punisher
    d.   behavior; consequences

11. According to Thorndike's law of effect,
    a.    a conditioned stimulus ultimately produces a conditioned response.
    b.    behaviors followed by positive outcomes are strengthened.
    c.    behavior learned on variable-interval schedules is difficult to extinguish.
    d.    reinforcers should be given immediately after a desired response.

12. Shaping is defined as the process of
    a.    reinforcing every avoidance response an organism makes.
    b.    reinforcing successive approximations of the target behavior.
    c.    directing an organism toward a specific stimulus target.
    d.    changing a primary reinforcer into a secondary reinforcer.

13. Which schedule of reinforcement is most resistant to extinction?
    a.    fixed-interval
    b.    fixed-ratio
    c.    variable-ratio
    d.    variable-interval

14. If you wanted to encourage a child to work hard in order to get good grades, which would be your best choice of reinforcement schedule?
    a.    variable-interval
    b.    variable-ratio
    c.    fixed-interval
    d.    fixed-ratio

15. Which of the following sets of terms best describes the difference between secondary and primary reinforcers?
    a.    learned; unlearned
    b.    hidden; observable
    c.    positive; negative
    d.    psychological; physical

16. When an animal responds only to stimuli associated with reinforcement, it shows that it has the ability to
    a.    discriminate.
    b.    extinguish.
    c.    generalize.
    d.    modify.

17. Little Noelle has learned to throw a temper tantrum in front of Dad (who often gives in). Noelle has learned, however, that this same behavior is not effective with Mom. Noelle has demonstrated
    a.    discrimination.
    b.    instinctive drift.
    c.    generalization.
    d.    superstitious behavior.

18.  Scott is 6 years old. His parents received a note from his teacher complaining about Scott's use of some inappropriate language in the classroom. Scott's parents are puzzled and wonder how to deal with this situation. Given your knowledge about observational learning principles, what advice would you give Scott's parents?
     a.  They should ignore the teacher's note; boys will be boys.
     b.  They should closely examine the language they use when Scott is around.
     c.  They should punish Scott by taking away his favorite activity.
     d.  They should take Scott to see a psychologist.

19.  Observational learning can occur
     a.  in less time than operant conditioning.
     b.  whether or not a model is reinforced.
     c.  only if a model is reinforced.
     d.  only with young children.

20.  Wolfgang Köhler is did experiments with apes on the issue of
     a.  classical conditioning.
     b.  insight learning.
     c.  latent learning.
     d.  learned helplessness.

## Practice Test 2

1.  Sandra had a bad car accident a few months ago. Now, every time she has to pass the location where the accident occurred, she gets very anxious. The best explanation for Sandra's anxiousness is
     a.  classical conditioning.
     b.  extinction.
     c.  exhibition of an unconditioned stimulus.
     d.  generalization.

2.  _____ learning involves watching what other people do, whereas _____ learning involves making connections between two events.
     a.  Operant; classical
     b.  Classical; operant
     c.  Associative; observational
     d.  Observational; associative

3.  Which of the following pairs of concepts presents two concepts that mean virtually the same?
     a.  conditioning/learning
     b.  operant/observational
     c.  behavior/mental process
     d.  unconditioned stimulus/conditioned stimulus

4.  In Pavlov's classical conditioning studies, the bell before the conditioning is referred to as the
     a.  unconditioned stimulus.
     b.  neutral stimulus.
     c.  conditioned stimulus.
     d.  conditioned response.

5. Unconditioned is to conditioned as _____ is to _____.
   a. learned; reflex
   b. classical; operant
   c. reflex; learned
   d. operant; classical

6. Jonathan has an extreme fear of swimming, which he acquired as a result of a near-drowning experience when he was 5 years old. Phobias such as Jonathan's are developed through classical conditioning. In this case, which of the following may be considered the unconditioned response?
   a. swimming
   b. the inability to breath (when he nearly drowned)
   c. the fear he experienced as a result of nearly drowning
   d. the fear he experiences now when he gets in a pool

7. _____ in classical conditioning occurs when a person learns to be afraid of being in a pool but not afraid of being in a bathtub full of water.
   a. Generalization
   b. Spontaneous recovery
   c. Extinction
   d. Discrimination

8. _____ occurs when a baby learns to get stressed when approached by all blond women, because once a blond woman who was holding her screamed and made her cry.
   a. Generalization
   b. Spontaneous recovery
   c. Extinction
   d. Discrimination

9. Which of the following is NOT one of the health issues associated with classical conditioning?
   a. Classical conditioning can be involved in the proper working of the immune system.
   b. Classical conditioning explains why people repeat risky health behaviors, such as smoking, because they are immediately rewarding.
   c. Classical conditioning can cause the body to react in anticipation to receiving a drug when the person is exposed to stimuli that have become associated with the use of the drug.
   d. Classical conditioning can contribute to asthma through the association with certain stimuli that cause stress and thus make the person more vulnerable to asthma attacks.

10. _____ is a form of associative learning in which the consequences of behavior produce changes in the probability of a behavior's occurrence.
    a. Operant conditioning
    b. Classical conditioning
    c. Observational learning
    d. Insight learning

11. Which of the following is NOT one of the predictions of Thorndike's law of effect?
    a. If a behavior is followed by a bad consequence, then it is less likely that it will be repeated.
    b. If an unconditioned stimuli is associated with a neutral stimuli, after a number of associations, the neutral stimuli will become a conditioned stimuli.
    c. If a behavior is followed by a good consequence, then it is less likely that it will be repeated.
    d. If a behavior is followed by a good consequence, then it is more likely that it will be repeated.

12. In his book, *Walden Two*, Skinner presented
    a. the basic principles of classical conditioning.
    b. the role of cognition in operant conditioning.
    c. a utopia created on the principles of operant conditioning.
    d. a utopia created on the principles of observational learning.

13. Sandi is trying to potty train her toddler. She plans to give her five M&Ms when the child first sits at the potty. After the child dominates this behavior, Sandi plans to give her the five M&Ms only when she sits and goes at the potty. What process of learning is Sandi planning to use?
    a. shaping
    b. observational learning
    c. classical conditioning
    d. extinction

14. Which of the following is an example of a primary reinforcer?
    a. sexual pleasure
    b. money
    c. a pat on the back
    d. an award

15. Thomas has a one-year contract, and he gets paid every two weeks. What is Thomas's schedule of reinforcement?
    a. fixed-ratio
    b. variable-ratio
    c. fixed-interval
    d. variable-interval

16. _____ in operant conditioning occurs when a previously reinforced behavior is no longer reinforced.
    a. Discrimination
    b. Generalization
    c. Punishment
    d. Extinction

17. Which of the following is an example of a negative punishment?
    a. removing an undesired chore, such as folding clothes
    b. giving a desired stimulus, such as candy
    c. removing a desired object, such as a favorite toy
    d. giving an undesired task, such as mowing the lawn

18. Which of the following issues is NOT associated with the positive punishment of spanking?

   a. Spanking by parents is associated with children's antisocial behaviors.
   b. When spanking, the adult is presenting a model of a person dealing with anger in a controlled manner.
   c. Children who are spanked are more likely to become bullies in school.
   d. Children who are spanked tend to be more disobedient than children who are not spanked.

19. Which of the following countries does NOT have anti-spanking laws?

   a. Sweden
   b. Austria
   c. Germany
   d. France

20. Learning is more efficient in operant conditioning if the reward is _____ and not _____.

   a. delayed; immediate
   b. negative; positive
   c. immediate; delayed
   d. positive; negative

## Practice Test 3

1. Lisa was very shy and would not play with her fellow first-graders. If the teacher praised her only when Lisa was interacting with her classmates, the teacher would be attempting to use

   a. positive reinforcement.
   b. shaping.
   c. negative reinforcement.
   d. extinction.

2. Which of the following illustrates negative reinforcement?

   a. teaching a dog to "shake hands" by giving him a biscuit every time he does so
   b. punishing a 3-year-old child for writing on the wall with crayons
   c. getting home early form a date to avoid getting yelled at by your parents
   d. developing a phobic response to anyone who looks like your mean third-grade teacher

3. Which reinforcement schedule helps explain the popularity of gambling?

   a. fixed-ratio
   b. variable-ratio
   c. fixed-interval
   d. variable-interval

4. The frequency of little Johnny's temper tantrums decreased sharply after his parents began to ignore the behavior. In the language of operant conditioning, Johnny's behavior was undergoing

   a. generalization.
   b. extinction.
   c. discrimination.
   d. all of the above

5.  If you wanted a group of kids to learn from your example or modeling of behavior, you would first have to make sure of which of the following?
    a.  that they can imitate the behavior
    b.  that they remember what I tell them
    c.  that they are paying attention
    d.  that they get reinforced

6.  Which of the following statements presents an aspect of the relationship between classical conditioning and addiction?
    a.  Because drugs are rewarding, they involve classical conditioning.
    b.  Classical conditioning helps explain addiction because the rewarding experience follows shortly after the drug intake.
    c.  Classical conditioning helps explain addiction because the punishing qualities, such as hangovers, occur hours after the drug intake.
    d.  Classical conditioning can cause the body to react in anticipation of receiving a drug.

7.  How can culture influence learning?
    a.  Classical and operant conditioning are not used in some cultures.
    b.  Culture can influence the degree to which operant and classical conditioning are used.
    c.  Culture often determines the content of learning.
    d.  both b and c

8.  A fetishist who become sexually aroused at the sight of red high heels is likely to have learned this through
    a.  observational learning.
    b.  operant conditioning.
    c.  classical conditioning.
    d.  latent learning.

9.  When a child with cancer is scheduled to receive a chemotherapy treatment, which tends to cause a lot of nausea and discomfort, the medical staff and parents avoid giving the child the foods she really likes right before the treatment. The reason for this is that they do not want the food she will eat with pleasure to become associated with and later cause nausea and discomfort. What type of learning is the medical staff and parents concerned about?
    a.  classical conditioning
    b.  operant conditioning
    c.  latent learning
    d.  observational learning

10. Shawna and Wayne are very unhappy with the latest school grades of their teenage son. In response, they have taken away their son's driving privileges. Which of the following are Shawna and Wayne using?
    a.  positive punishment
    b.  negative reinforcement
    c.  positive reinforcement
    d.  negative punishment

11.　　Suzy is trying to get her boyfriend to be more affectionate in public. Every time that he hold her hand or puts his arm around her shoulder, she tells him that he is really wonderful. Which schedule of reinforcement is Suzy using?
    a.　　fixed-ratio
    b.　　continuous
    c.　　fixed-interval
    d.　　variable-ratio

12.　　Which of the following combinations of reinforcements and punishments contribute to the health risk of obesity?
    a.　　a delayed reinforcement with a delayed punishment
    b.　　a delayed punishment with an immediate reinforcement
    c.　　an immediate reinforcement and also an immediate punishment
    d.　　an immediate punishment and a delayed punishment

13.　　Which of the following learning methods is the one that makes reference to the person using the behavior as an instrument to obtain the consequence?
    a.　　classical conditioning
    b.　　observational learning
    c.　　latent learning
    d.　　operant conditioning

14.　　Which of the following is NOT one of the steps of an operant conditioning behavior modification program?
    a.　　determining the neutral stimuli that will be used to associate with the unconditioned stimuli
    b.　　creating an operational definition of the behavior that will be changed and what it will be changed to
    c.　　measuring the behavior as it is at the beginning and throughout the behavior modification program
    d.　　determining the reinforcements that will be used to make the program last

15.　　Nicole is 3 years old and her parents are having a very hard time when they bring her along to Wal-Mart. As soon as she walks into the store she starts demanding toys and candy. The parents say no and Nicole promptly throws a tantrum. After 10–15 minutes of nagging, screaming, running down halls, and overall very bad behavior, in an effort to get her to calm down, the parents give her a piece of candy and give her a toy to be purchased. Without realizing it, the parents are teaching Nicole to throw tantrums at Wal-Mart. Which learning method is contributing to this dysfunctional learning?
    a.　　classical conditioning
    b.　　latent learning
    c.　　operant conditioning
    d.　　insight learning

16.　　According to Tolman, in classical conditioning, the conditioned stimulus has informational value because it signals the upcoming
    a.　　conditioned response.
    b.　　unconditioned stimulus.
    c.　　unconditioned response.
    d.　　neutral stimulus.

17. _____ occurs when the reinforcement offered for behavior A is not as strong as the innate urge to do behavior B, and thus behavior B is performed and behavior A is not performed.
    a.    Instinctive drift
    b.    Preparedness
    c.    Classical conditioning
    d.    Insight learning

18. During the early 20th century, an expert in child development would have suggested that
    a.    if children behave badly they should not be punished.
    b.    positive behaviors will automatically develop in good children and are not learned.
    c.    an infant could be shaped into any child the parents wanted.
    d.    children should not be allowed to cry themselves out.

19. Jeremy used to play the trumpet when he was in high school and was even a member of the school's marching band. He used to practice every day. Now that he's attending college he practices the trumpet once or twice a week and simply does not find playing the trumpet as enjoyable as he used to. We can predict that Jeremy's trumpet playing is in the process of
    a.    discrimination.
    b.    generalization.
    c.    punishment.
    d.    extinction.

20. In observational learning, the learner acquires a behavior by imitating the behavior of a model. Which of the following is NOT one of the characteristics of a model that would promote observational learning?
    a.    The model is different from others.
    b.    The model is a powerful figure.
    c.    The model is intimidating and cold.
    d.    The model is nice and warm.


## Connections

*Take advantage of all the other study tools available for this chapter!*

## Media Integration

| NAME OF CLIP | DESCRIPTION | KEY CONCEPTS AND IDEAS |
|---|---|---|
| | | **Types of Learning** |
| | | **Classical Conditioning** |
| Classical Conditioning 1 | This interactivity will help participants in understanding the process of the classic classical conditioning experiment by Ivan Pavlov. The concepts of acquisition, extinction, generalization, and | Classical conditioning<br>Acquisition<br>Extinction<br>Generalization<br>Discrimination |

| | | |
|---|---|---|
| | discrimination and demonstrated. | |
| Classical Conditioning 2 | This interactivity helps the participant review the elements of classical conditioning and applies the concepts to human learning. The experiences of habituation with sounds and generalizations with foods are illustrated. | Classical conditioning<br>Unconditioned stimulus<br>Unconditioned response<br>Neutral stimulus<br>Conditioned stimulus<br>Conditioned response<br>Habituation<br>Generalization |
| | | **Operant Conditioning** |
| Operant Conditioning | This interactivity assists participants in understanding and applying the concepts of operant conditioning, illustrating the concepts of reinforcement and punishment, including positive and negative reinforcement and punishment. Definitions, characteristics, and examples of the different reinforcement schedules are presented. | Operant conditioning<br>Reinforcement<br>Punishment<br>Positive reinforcement<br>Negative reinforcement<br>Positive punishment<br>Negative punishment<br>Reinforcement schedules |
| Classical vs. Operant Conditioning | In this interactivity participants compare classical and operant conditioning. For a series of examples of learned behaviors participants are asked to distinguish between classical and operant conditioning. | Classical conditioning<br>Operant conditioning |
| | | **Observational Learning** |
| | | **Cognitive Factors in Learning** |
| | | **Biological and Cultural Factors in Learning** |

**Online Learning Center (www.mhhe.com/Santrockp7u)**
- Interact and make learning fun!
  - ○ **Interactive Exercises**
    - ▪ Classical Conditioning
    - ▪ Invaders Video Game

- Target Practice II
- Partial Ratio Reinforcement
  o **Interactive Review**
    - Level of Analysis: Learning
- Brush up on the Key Terms for this chapter by first reviewing the electronic **Glossary** (in English or Spanish) and then testing your retention using the **Flashcard** feature.
- **"Notes"**—This feature allows you to use the website as you would your text, inserting your own study notes and highlighting areas of particular importance.

### In Your Text

- Found throughout each chapter, the **Review and Sharpen Your Thinking** feature breaks the text into logical chunks, allowing you to process, review, and reflect thoughtfully on the information that you've just read. When going back to *study* the chapter, try reading the feature *before* the section of text to which it relates. In doing so, you will be able to focus your attention on important concepts *as* you encounter them. In this chapter, this feature can be found on the following pages: pp. 270, 276, 291, 292, 296, and 299.

### Practice Quizzes

- Test your knowledge of the psychology of learning by taking the different practice quizzes found on your text's **Online Learning Center** and on the **In-Psych Plus CD-ROM** packaged with your text.


## ANSWER KEY

## In Your Own Words

✓ Can you give an example of generalizations that Pavlov's dogs might have experienced? *Generalization in classical conditioning occurs when a new stimulus that is similar to the original conditioned stimulus elicits a response that is similar to the conditioned response. The student should present examples of stimuli to which the effect of the conditioned bell might have been generalized.*

✓ How would you classically condition a baby to like classical music? Make sure you indicate the unconditioned stimulus, unconditioned response, conditioned stimulus, and conditioned response.
*The point is to associate classical music with something the baby innately likes, such as the touch of a familiar caregiver, caresses, loving looks and smiles, holding, and feeding, among other possibilities.*

✓ You are trying to teach your pet a new trick and you've decided to use operant conditioning. In anticipation of the behavior modification, you will develop a list of stimuli/consequences you may use in the process. List two of each of the following: positive reinforcement, negative reinforcement, positive punishment, and negative punishment.
*Positive reinforcement is when something good is given to the pet (e.g., a treat); negative reinforcement is when something bad is taken away from the pet (e.g., a leash); positive punishment is when something bad is given to the pet (e.g., yelling); and, negative punishment is when something good is taken away from the pet (e.g., a favorite toy or treat).*

✓ How has observational learning affected your behavior? Discuss two examples of behaviors that you have acquired through observational learning. Consider both adaptive, positive behaviors and maladaptive, negative behaviors.
*Observational learning is also called imitation or modeling and it occurs when a person observes and imitates someone's behavior. One of the keys to understanding observational learning is on*

*the nature of the consequences of the observed behavior. If the observed behavior has good consequences for the person, we are more likely to imitate it and if it has bad consequences for the person, we are less likely to imitate it.*

✓ A marketing company has hired you as a consumer psychology consultant. They want to know how they can use both observational and associative learning to sell a new model of a sport utility vehicle. Choose a type of learning and list at least five recommendations.
*This question requires that the student think critically about observational learning and the two types of associative learning and how they may be applied to practical issue such as marketing. Each of the three methods of learning can be used to maximize the effect of an advertisement, and they can be used simultaneously.*

## Correcting the Incorrect

1. Learning is a relatively permanent change in behavior that occurs through *experience*. (p. 269)
2. *Pavlov* is most remembered for his work in classical conditioning. (p. 270)
3. In classical conditioning, a neutral stimulus becomes associated with a meaningful stimulus and acquires the capacity to elicit a similar response. (p. 270)
4. Reflexes play a role in *classical* conditioning. (p. 271)
5. A *conditioned stimulus* is a stimulus that produces a response only after prior learning. (p. 271)
6. The conditioned stimulus elicits the *conditioned response*. (p. 271)
7. In classical conditioning, the learned association is between the conditioned stimulus and unconditioned stimulus. (p. 271)
8. Classical conditioning is a form of *associative* conditioning. (p.)
9. After a period of extinction, *spontaneous recovery* may occur. (p. 272)
10. If an organism shows *discrimination* after being classically conditioned, it will respond to certain stimuli and not to others. (p. 272)
11. Little Albert was conditioned to fear *a rat*. (p. 274)
12. In counterconditioning, the *conditioned response* is weakened. (p. 274)
13. In operant conditioning, *a response and its consequences are paired*. (p. 277)
14. In positive reinforcement, the frequency of a response is increased because it is followed by a reward stimulus. (p. 281)
15. In negative reinforcement, the behavior is *reinforced*. (p. 281)
16. Through the process of *shaping*, approximations of the desired behavior are reinforced. (p. 279)
17. *Secondary* reinforcers are learned reinforcers. (p. 281)
18. A *fixed-interval schedule* is a timetable in which reinforcement is given after a certain amount of time has passed. (p. 282)
19. A variable-interval schedule is a timetable in which reinforcement is given after a variable amount of time has passed. (p. 282)
20. In negative punishment, a behavior decreases when a positive stimulus is removed from it. (p. 284)
21. Punishment decreases the likelihood that behavior will be repeated. (p. 284)
22. Observational learning is also called *imitation* or *modeling*. (p. 291)
23. The four processes involved in observational learning are *attention, retention, production, and reinforcement*. (p. 292)
24. Köhler found that apes show insight learning. (p. 295)

25.    In instinctive drift, animals tend to revert to instinctive behavior. (p. 296)
26.    *Preparedness* refers to species-specific biological predispositions to learn in certain ways but not others. (p. 297)
27.    *Latent* learning is when an unreinforced behavior is learned, yet not immediately manifested. (p. 295)
28.    The content of learning is influenced by *culture*. (p. 298)

## Practice Test 1

1. a.    no; this is part of the definition of learning
   b.    no; this is part of the definition of learning
   c.    YES; the change in observable behavior is due to experience, not maturation
   d.    no; this is part of the definition of learning
   p. 269

2. a.    CORRECT; this is the definition of learning
   b.    no; in fact, changes in behavior owing to fatigue and maturation is not learning
   c.    no; this is not the definition of learning
   d.    no; the behavior change is relatively permanent and is due to experience
   p. 269

3. a.    CORRECT; the neutral stimulus becomes the conditioned stimulus since it can elicit the conditioned response
   b.    no; a stimulus never becomes a response
   c.    no; a stimulus never becomes a response
   d.    no; a UCS is never a previously neutral stimulus
   p. 271

4. a.    no; fear is a response, not a stimulus
   b.    no; a UCR is unlearned response; Jennifer's fear is learned or conditioned
   c.    no; her fear is a response, not a stimulus
   d.    RIGHT; since the fear is classically conditioned, it is a CR
   p. 271

5. a.    no; your eye blink is not a UCR
   b.    no; discrimination occurs when you eye blink to only specific stimuli
   c.    no; you are not showing any spontaneous recovery
   d.    YES; over time your eye blink will disappear or extinguish
   p. 272

6. a.    no; extinction in classical conditioning involves the weakening of the association.
   b.    no; generalization involves stimuli similar to the original stimulus eliciting the same response.
   c.    YES; spontaneous recovery occurs after extinction
   d.    no; discrimination in classical conditioning is the process of learning to respond to certain stimuli and not to others.
   p. 272

7. a.    GOOD; his fear was generalized from a white rate to other similar objects
   b.    no; the CS is not substituting for the UCS
   c.    no; in discrimination, the response is seen only for specific stimuli
   d.    no
   p. 272

8. a. no; this would cause extinction, but the CS is associated with fear
   b. no; this would have little effect on the fear
   c. GOOD; the CS is paired with a new response that is pleasant
   d. no; this describes shaping
   p. 274

9. a. no
   b. CORRECT; consequences that follow behavior affect the probability of it repeating
   c. no; observational learning involves modeling the behaviors of others.
   d. no; two stimuli are paired in classical conditioning
   p. 277

10. a. no; although a reinforcer could be a consequence
    b. no; these terms refer to the same thing
    c. no; these terms refer to the same thing
    d. RIGHT; in operant conditioning the learning involves associating the behavior with its consequence.
    p. 277

11. a. no; this option refers to classical conditioning
    b. YES; the law of effect includes this option
    c. no; while the law of effect does involve behavior, it does not involve schedules
    d. no; the law of effect does not refer to timing of consequences
    p. 278

12. a. no
    b. YES, THAT'S CORRECT; this is the definition of shaping
    c. no
    d. no
    p. 279

13. a. no; when the reward is given is unpredictable
    b. no; when the reward is given is unpredictable
    c. YES; when the reward is given is unpredictable
    d. no; behavior is slow and consistent
    p. 282

14. a. no; this schedule leads to behavior that is less resistant to extinction
    b. RIGHT; variable-ratio scheduling results in behavior that is very resistant to extinction
    c. no; this schedule leads to behavior that is less resistant to extinction
    d. no; this schedule leads to behavior that is less resistant to extinction
    p. 282

15. a. YES; primary reinforcers are unlearned and secondary reinforcers are learned
    b. no
    c. no; reinforcers are considered to be positive (or pleasant)
    d. no; both primary and secondary reinforcers can be psychological or physical
    p. 281

16. a. RIGHT; this occurs when there is response to stimuli that signal reinforcement
    b. no; this is not extinction
    c. no; there is no responding to a similar stimulus
    d. no
    p. 284

17. a. YES; she has learned that Dad reinforces her behavior, while Mom does not
    b. no; this refers to the biological influences on learning
    c. no; this means that the same response is given to similar stimuli
    d. no
    p. 284

18. a. no
    b. YES; this option underscores learning by imitation
    c. no; this may work, but it does not address observational learning; if the parents use the inappropriate language, Scott would still be hearing it
    d. no
    p. 291

19. a. no
    b. YES; the model does not have to be reinforced for observational learning to occur
    c. no; the model does not have to be reinforced for observational learning to occur
    d. no; observational learning takes place in people of different ages
    p. 291

20. a. no
    b. YES; Köhler used the stick problem and box problem to study insight learning
    c. no
    d. no
    p. 296

## Practice Test 2

1. a. YES; her anxiousness is associated with the location
   b. no; extinction refers to the weakening of an association
   c. no
   d. no; generalization refers to the tendency of a new similar stimulus to elicit a conditioned response
   p. 270

2. a. no; both are types of associative learning
   b. no; both are types of associative learning
   c. no; the opposite is true
   d. YES; observational learning happens through seeing others behave, while associative learning involves associations between stimuli or events
   p. 269

3. a. YES; conditioning is another way of referring to learning, particularly associative learning
   b. no; operant refers to acting on the environment and being directly influenced by the environment, while observational refers to a vicarious experience
   c. no; these are basic concepts to psychology that are different in meaning
   d. no; these concepts are clearly different
   p. 269

4. a. no; the bell is never unconditioned, because dogs don't have a reflex associated with the sounding of a bell
   b. YES; before conditioning, the bell is neutral, which means that it does not have any particular effect
   c. no; the bell will be the conditioned stimulus, but only after conditioning has occurred
   d. no; the bell is never a response, only a stimulus
   p. 271

5. a. no; the opposite is true
   b. no; classical and operant are different types of associative learning and would not fit in this analogy
   c. YES; something that is unconditioned is not learned; therefore, it is either a reflex, an instinct, or some other process that is innate
   d. no; the order does not matter; classical and operant are different types of associative learning and would not fit in this analogy
   p. 271

6. a. no; swimming is not an unconditioned response; we are not innately wired to swim
   b. no; this may be considered an unconditioned stimulus
   c. YES; if our survival is at risk, our body will automatically respond to rescue us from the situation, and experiencing fear prepares us to escape the danger; fear as a result of nearly drowning is not learned and can be considered as the unconditioned response in this learned phobia
   d. no; this would be the conditioned response, because it refers to a fear he has learned and that he experiences even if his life is not in danger
   p. 274

7. a. no; generalization would occur if the person did not distinguish from being in a pool versus being in a bathtub
   b. no; this example does not address the issue of a learned behavior reappearing
   c. no; this example does not address the issue of a learned behavior disappearing
   d. YES; this is the process of learning to respond to certain stimuli and not to others
   p. 284

8. a. YES; the baby has generalized to fear other stimuli that are similar to the one that caused the original fear
   b. no; this example does not address the issue of a learned behavior reappearing
   c. no; this example does not address the issue of a learned behavior disappearing
   d. no; the opposite is true
   p. 283

9. a. no; this is one of the ways in which classical conditioning contributes to health problems
   b. YES, this item corresponds to how operant conditioning can contribute to health problems
   c. no; this is one of the ways in which classical conditioning contributes to health problems
   d. no; this is one of the ways in which classical conditioning contributes to health problems
   p. 288

10. a. YES; this is the definition of operant conditioning
    b. no; classical conditioning is based on associations between stimuli
    c. no; observational learning is not a form of associative learning
    d. no; insight learning is not dependent on consequences of behavior, as it is spontaneous
    p. 277

11. a. no; this is one of the predictions of Thorndike's law of effect
    b. YES; while this statement is true, it pertains to classical conditioning, and Thorndike's law of effect refers to operant conditioning
    c. no; this is one of the predictions of Thorndike's law of effect
    d. no; this is one of the predictions of Thorndike's law of effect
    p. 278

12. a. no; Skinner did not work on classical conditioning
    b. no; Skinner did not study cognition
    c. YES; the book is a novel in which the principles of operant conditioning are used to shape and design a utopian society
    d. no; Skinner did not work on observational learning
    p. 278

13. a. YES; Sandi plans to reward approximations of the desired behavior
    b. no; Sandi is not planning on modeling to her toddler how to go to the potty
    c. no; potty training is a complex behavior and it would be hard to use classical conditioning; however, you do want the child to associate being in the potty with a positive emotion, not with stress and anger from the parent
    d. no; Sandi is trying to foster a new behavior, not eliminate one
    p. 279

14. a. YES; we do not need to learn to like sexual pleasure, it is innately a good experience
    b. no; money is a secondary reinforcer
    c. no; a pat on the back is a secondary reinforcer
    d. no; an award is a secondary reinforcer
    p. 281

15. a. no; this is a schedule in which the person gets rewarded based on a fixed amount of responses
    b. no; this is a schedule in which the person gets rewarded based on a variable amount of responses
    c. YES; Thomas gets paid every 2 weeks, therefore his reinforcer is given after a fixed amount of time has elapsed (2 weeks)
    d. no; this a schedule in which the person gets rewarded based on a variable amount of elapsed time
    p. 282

16. a. no; discrimination refers to responding to stimuli which signal that a behavior will be reinforced or will not be reinforced
    b. no; this means giving the same response to similar stimuli
    c. no; the absence of reinforcement does not imply punishment
    d. YES; this is the definition of extinction
    p. 284

17. a. no; this is a negative reinforcement
    b. no; this is a positive reinforcement
    c. YES; this is an example of a negative punishment
    d. no; this is a positive punishment
    p. 284

18. a. no; this is true
    b. YES; this is incorrect, as it is more likely than not that the parent is presenting a model of a person dealing with stress in a uncontrolled manner
    c. no; this is one of the findings of a correlational study
    d. no; this is one of the findings of a correlational study
    p. 287

19. a.   no; Sweden was the first (1979) of a series of countries to pass an anti-spanking law; very positive effects were observed in Swedish society after the law's passage
   b.   no; Austria, along with Finland, Denmark, Norway, Cyprus, Latvia, Croatia, Germany, and Israel, has passed anti-spanking laws
   c.   no; Germany, along with Finland, Denmark, Norway, Cyprus, Latvia, Croatia, Austria, and Israel, has passed anti-spanking laws
   d.   YES; France is not included in the countries that have passed anti-spanking laws; the United States also has not passed such laws
  p. 287

20. a.   no; the opposite is true
   b.   no; negative and positive reinforcers can be equally effective
   c.   YES; a reward that immediately follows a behavior is more effective than a reward that is delayed
   d.   no; negative and positive reinforcers can be equally effective
  p. 286

## Practice Test 3

1. a.   RIGHT; the teacher was presenting something pleasant (i.e., praise)
   b.   no; there is nothing in the question that refers to rewarding approximations
   c.   no; negative reinforcement refers to withdrawing something unpleasant
   d.   no; in extinction, a previously reinforced behavior is longer reinforced
  p. 281

2. a.   no; this is positive reinforcement where a pleasant stimulus is presented
   b.   no; this option describes an example of punishment
   c.   YES; the response (getting home early) removed the unpleasant stimulus (yelling)
   d.   no; this sounds more like an example of classical conditioning
  p. 281

3. a.   no; this refers to an unchanging number of responses to get reinforced
   b.   YES; the number of responses necessary to obtain reinforcement keeps changing
   c.   no; this refers to reinforcement given after passage of an unchanging amount of time
   d.   no; this refers to reinforcement given after passage of a changing amount of time
  p. 282

4. a.   no; there is no response is being made to similar stimuli
   b.   YES; the previously reinforced behavior is no longer reinforced
   c.   no; Johnny is not responding to a stimuli that signals availability of reinforcement
   d.   no
  p. 284

5. a.   no; important, but not of primary importance
   b.   no; important, but not of primary importance
   c.   CORRECT; the first step in observational learning is for the model to pay attention
   d.   no; important, but not of primary importance
  p. 291

6. a. no; this is one of the reasons operant conditioning contributes to addiction
   b. no; this is one of the reasons operant conditioning contributes to addiction
   c. no; this is one of the reasons operant conditioning contributes to addiction
   d. YES; through classical conditioning, stimuli that are associated with the intake of the drug can themselves initiate an anticipatory preparation of the body for the impact of the drug.
   p. 275

7. a. no; classical and operant conditioning are universal
   b. no; but you are half right
   c. no; but you are half right
   d. YES; both degree and content of learning are influenced by culture
   p. 298

8. a. no; this is an association of an object with a basic biological process, and observational learning does not address that type of learning
   b. no; this is an association of an object with a basic biological process, and operant conditioning does not address that type of learning
   c. YES; classical conditioning is the better method to explain this connection between the red high heels and sexual arousal
   d. no; this is an association of an object with a basic biological process, and latent learning does not address that type of learning
   p. 270

9. a. YES; the concern is that the food may become a conditioned stimulus because of its association with the upcoming chemotherapy treatment; since the nutrition of a child with a disease is a serious concern, medical staff and parents want to make sure that whatever the child enjoys eating will continue to be pleasurable
   b. no; the issue here is not reinforcements or punishments
   c. no; the example shows learning by association
   d. no; the example shows learning by association
   p. 270

10. a. no; while this is a punishment, it is not a positive punishment
    b. no
    c. no
    d. YES; Shawna and Wayne have taken away something that their teenage son enjoys (driving privileges)
    p. 284

11. a. no
    b. YES; Suzy is rewarding with praise every desired response
    c. no
    d. no
    p. 282

12. a. no
    b. no
    c. no
    d. YES; the immediate reinforcement of great-tasting food and the delayed punishment of obesity contribute to the problem; the immediate reinforcement can be more powerful than the concern about obesity
    p. 286

13. a.   no; this is learning associations between stimuli
    b.   no; in this learning the learner sees somebody else use behavior as an instrument to obtain a consequence
    c.   no
    d.   YES; operant conditioning is learning by acting on the environment to obtain a desired consequence
    p. 277

14. a.   YES; this would be appropriate if the behavior modification program was going to use classical conditioning
    b.   no; this corresponds to step 1 of a behavior modification program
    c.   no; this corresponds to step 3 of a behavior modification program
    d.   no; this corresponds to step 5 of a behavior modification program
    p. 288

15. a.   no; Nicole is not learning associations between stimuli
    b.   no; Nicole's actions at Wal-Mart are not latent
    c.   YES; the parents are offering positive reinforcements for the inappropriate behavior
    d.   no; Nicole did not learn this on her own and spontaneously
    p. 277

16. a.   no
    b.   YES; in classical conditioning the learner associates the conditioned stimulus with the unconditioned stimulus; Tolman argued that the association created an expectation; therefore, classical conditioning involves cognition
    c.   no
    d.   no
    p. 294

17. a.   YES; instinctive drift is the tendency of animals to revert to instinctive behavior that interferes with learning
    b.   no; preparedness refers to a biological predisposition to learn in certain ways and not others
    c.   no
    d.   no
    p. 296

18. a.   no; the opposite was recommended
    b.   no; during this period the conditioning approaches were very popular and the general idea was that parents should teach their children to be however they wanted them to be
    c.   YES; experts in child development proposed that genetics were not that important and that learning and the environment were really the most important determinants of behavior
    d.   no; the opposite was recommended
    p. 298

19. a.   no
    b.   no
    c.   no
    d.   YES; extinction occurs when a previously reinforced behavior is no longer reinforced and there is a decreased tendency to perform the behavior
    p. 284

20. a.   no; this promotes observational learning
    b.   no; this promotes observational learning
    c.   YES; this is not a characteristic of a model that would contribute or facilitate observational learning
    d.   no; this promotes observational learning
    p. 291

# Chapter 8—Memory

## Learning Goals

1. Identify three domains of memory.
2. Explain how memories are encoded.
3. Discuss how memories are stored.
4. Summarize how memories are retrieved.
5. Describe how encoding and retrieval failure are involved in forgetting.
6. Evaluate study strategies based on an understanding of memory.

*After studying Chapter 8, you will be able to:*

- Define memory and describe its three domains.
- Explain how memory gets encoded, including the role of level of processing and elaboration.
- Discuss the Atkinson-Shiffrin theory of memory and the three memory time frames it proposes.
- Describe the four approaches to how memory is organized, when it is stored, and the implications for retrieval involved in each of these four approaches.
- Distinguish and illustrate declarative versus nondeclarative memory.
- Describe the neurobiological basis of memory, including the specific parts of the brain that have been associated with memory.
- Discuss how people retrieve memory and the variables that influence this process such as serial position and retrieval cues.
- Describe autobiographical memory and the role of emotions in memories.
- Discuss the research on the problems in accuracy of eyewitness testimony.
- Understand why people forget information and can relate forgetting to failures in encoding and retrieval.
- Explain what amnesia, as well as the different manifestations of this memory disorder.
- Understand how the research on the three domains of memory can be applied to improve studying strategies.

## CHAPTER 8: OUTLINE

- *Memory* is the retention of information over time; it involves three domains: encoding, storage, and retrieval.

- *Encoding* is the process of getting information into memory. Selective attention explains why we may encode some stimuli and not others. Encoding is also affected by divided attention, which occurs when a person is paying attention to more than one thing at the same time.

- There are different levels at which we may encode: shallow level, intermediate level, and deepest level. The more in-depth our processing of the information, the more likely we are to place it in memory. Encoding also depends on elaboration, which refers to how extensively the information is processed at any given depth in memory. Encoding information in images, as illustrated in this chapter's opening story, can also improve our recollection of information.

- *Storage* consists of retention of information over time and the representation of information in memory. According to the popular Atkinson-Shiffrin theory, we can accumulate information in three main stores that vary according to time frames: sensory memory, short-term memory, and long-term memory.

- Information is stored very briefly in sensory memory. Visual sensory memory is called *iconic memory*, whereas auditory sensory memory is referred to as *echoic memory*.

- Short-term memory has a limited capacity of 7 ± 2 items, which can be illustrated by memory span. The capacity of short-term memory can be expanded with chunking. Short-term memory lasts up to 30 seconds, but this can also be expanded by maintenance rehearsal.

- In a revision of the Atkinson-Shiffrin model, psychologist Alan Baddeley proposed the concept of working memory, a system that holds information while we are thinking. From this perspective, working memory has three components: phonological loop, visuospatial working memory, and the central executive.

- Long-term memory can retain enormous amounts of information up to a lifetime, and we can efficiently retrieve information from long-term memory.

- Long-term memory has been classified into many types of memories, based on the content and purpose of the information. Information in long-term memory that can be verbally communicated is called *declarative memory* or *explicit memory*. *Episodic memory* is the retention of information about the where and when of life's happenings; *semantic memory* is a person's knowledge about the world. *Prospective memory* involves remembering information about doing something in the future, while *retrospective memory* refers to remembering the past. *Nondeclarative memory*, also called *implicit memory*, refers to memory in which behavior is affected by prior experience without that experience being consciously recollected.

- Three types of implicit memory are procedural, priming, and classical conditioning. Four main theories describe how long-term memory is organized: hierarchies, semantic networks, schemas, and connectionist network. The hierarchies approach argues that memory is organized on a hierarchy from general to specific types of things.

- The semantic networks approach claims that long-term memory is organized in a network of interconnected concepts. While the original semantic networks approach was hierarchical, more recent versions argue that concepts are organized in irregular networks of concepts connected based on the meaning and the relationships that we have learned through experiences. New material is placed in the network by connecting it to appropriate nodes.

- The schema approach suggests that our memories are not precise and that we reconstruct our past. A schema framework already exists in a person's memory, and that framework influences how new information is interpreted and integrated into memory.

- The connectionist networks view takes into consideration the role of the brain in memory and argues that memory is stored throughout the brain in connections between neurons, several of which may work together to process a single memory. Long-term potentiation contributes to memory at the level of the neurons. Brain structures that have been associated with memory include the hippocampus, the amygdala, and the cerebellum.

- *Retrieval* is the process of getting information out of memory. Much of the interest in retrieval has focused on long-term memory. The serial position effect refers to how recall is superior for items at the beginning (primacy effect) and at the end of the list (recency effect). Retrieval is also influenced by the presence of cues and the nature of the task.

- Two different types of memory retrieval are recall and recognition. *Recall* is a memory measure whereby information must be retrieved from previously learned information, whereas in *recognition* one has to identify only learned items. The encoding specificity principle states that associations formed at the time of encoding or learning tend to be effective retrieval cues.

- Retrieval also is influenced by priming, which involves activating particular connections or associations in memory. Research on the tip-of-the-tongue phenomenon suggests that good retrieval cues are helpful in retrieving information from memory.

- *Context-dependent memory* is the process through which people remember better when they try to recall information in the same context in which they learned it. *Autobiographical memory* consists of a person's recollections of his or her life experiences. *Emotional memories* may be flashbulb memories, which are memories of emotionally significant events that people often recall with more accuracy and vivid imagery than everyday events.

- Many people have flashbulb memories of personal events; their accuracy is far more durable and accurate than memories of everyday events. Memory of personal trauma is usually more accurate than memory for ordinary events; however, personal trauma can also result in the repression of the memory, a process of pushing the event into the unconscious mind. The recall of repressed memories is a controversial issue in psychology because research indicates that memories may be implanted, especially using hypnosis.

- *Forgetting* may occur because of interference and decay. *Proactive interference* occurs when material learned earlier interferes with the recall of material learned later. *Retroactive interference* occurs when material learned later interferes with material learned earlier. Decay theory suggests that a memory trace, formed when something new is learned, can disintegrate with the passage of time. Anterograde amnesia affects memory for new information, whereas retrograde amnesia is memory loss for a segment of the past.

- *Optimal studying strategies* may be developed based on memory research. To improve encoding, the strategies include managing study time effectively, paying attention and minimizing distraction, understanding the material rather than simply memorizing it, asking yourself questions, taking good notes, and using mnemonic strategies.

- *Mnemonics* are techniques for improving memory and include the method of loci, acronyms, and the keyword method. To enhance the storage of the information studied, it is recommended to consciously organize the information being memorized and spread out the study sessions. To improve the retrieval of the material studied, retrieval cues and the PQ4R method are recommended.

## Building Blocks of Chapter 8

### Clarifying some of the tricky points in Chapter 8
### and
### In Your Own Words
*To respond to the questions and exercises presented in the "In Your Own Words" section, please write your thoughts, perspectives, and reactions on a separate piece of paper.*

### The Nature of Memory
Memory is the retention of *information* over *time*. Psychologists study how information is *encoded* into memory, how it is stored, and how it is later *retrieved*. People do not

save information objectively like computers; memory is recognized as being *subjective* in nature and researchers even study how we *reconstruct* our own versions of the past.

### Memory Encoding

Getting information into memory is a process called *encoding*. Encoding is influenced by *selective* attention, which involves focusing on some aspects of the situation and ignoring others, as well as by *divided* attention, which refers to paying attention to several things simultaneously.

Besides attention, the *level* at which the information is processed also affects encoding. The *levels of processing* theory states that encoding is on a continuum from shallow to deep processing. According to this theory, the physical or sensory features of information are analyzed at the *shallow* level, the stimulus is recognized and objects are labeled at *intermediate* level, and information is processed semantically at the *deepest* level. The *deeper* the level of processing, the better the memory. Memory improves as it is processed more extensively. This process is called *elaboration*. Researchers have found that memory can also be improved through the use of *imagery*, which involves encoding the information in images.

### In Your Own Words

*Please write your thoughts, perspectives, and reactions on a separate piece of paper.*

✓ *When you read the textbook for this class, you may process the information at the shallow, intermediate, or deep level. Describe the processing of textbook information at each of these levels of encoding.*

### Memory Storage

According to the Atkinson and Shiffrin theory, memory involves a sequence of three stages: *sensory* memory, *short-term* memory, and *long-term* memory. *Sensory* memory holds information from our senses from a fraction of a second to several seconds. *Short-term* memory lasts approximately 30 seconds and it can retain 7±2 items.

Two ways of improving short-term memory are *chunking*, the grouping of information, and *rehearsal*, the conscious repetition of information. Alan Baddeley proposed the concept of *working* memory to refer to the system that temporarily holds information while the person is performing other *cognitive* tasks.

### In Your Own Words

*Please write your thoughts, perspectives, and reactions on a separate piece of paper.*

✓ *List some examples of how businesses and organizations use chunking in their 1-800 numbers.*

There are three components to working memory: (1) the *phonological* loop, which stores information about the sounds of the language; (2) the *visuospatial* working memory, which stores images; and (3) the *central* executive, which integrates the information from the previous two components.

The relatively permanent memory system that holds information for long periods of time is called *long-term* memory. Information in long-term memory that can be verbally communicated is called *explicit* or *declarative* memory.

### In Your Own Words

*Please write your thoughts, perspectives, and reactions on a separate piece of paper.*

✓ *What declarative memories have you retrieved in the last hour? What nondeclarative memories have you retrieved in the last hour?*

One type of declarative memory that focuses on the where and when of events is called *episodic* memory; another type, which reflects our general knowledge about the world, is called *semantic* memory.

Remembering things from the past is referred to as *retrospective* memory, while remembering information about doing something in the future is *prospective* memory. Information that cannot be verbalized or consciously recalled is called *nondeclarative* or implicit memory.

Four approaches have been advanced to explain the organization or representation of knowledge in memory: *hierarchies, semantic networks, schemas, and connectionist networks*. The hierarchies approach says that in memory information is organized from *general* to *specific* classes. In the semantic networks approach, memory is seen as being organized in a complex network of *nodes* that stand for concepts. Schemas are preexisting frameworks that help people *organize* and *interpret* information. According to the schema approach, our long-term memory search is not very exact, and we *reconstruct* the past.

A schema for an event is called a *script*. The connectionist networks approach considers the *biological* basis of memory. Connectionism or *parallel distributed* processing is the idea that memory is stored throughout the brain in connections between neurons, several of which may work *together* to process a single memory.

### In Your Own Words
*Please write your thoughts, perspectives, and reactions on a separate piece of paper.*
✓  *Compare the semantic networks approach and the schemas approach to the storage of memories.*

The past several decades have seen extensive investigation of the biological basis of memory. Long-term *potentiation* refers to the association between two neurons being activated at the same time and their corresponding memory being strengthened.

Some neuroscientists have focused on specific *brain* structures that appear to be responsible for memory. For example, the *hippocampus*, the temporal lobes in the cerebral cortex, and other areas of the *limbic* system are involved in explicit memory, whereas the cerebellum is involved in implicit memory used in doing various skills.

### Memory Retrieval
The process we use to get information out of memory storage is called *retrieval*. The superior recall for items at the beginning of a list is called the *primacy* effect, whereas the superior recall at the end of the list is called the *recency* effect.

Generally, items in the middle of a list produce a *low* level of recall. Collectively, this pattern is called the *serial position* effect. Two other important factors involved in retrieval are (1) the *nature* of the cues and (2) the retrieval *task* required. A memory measure that requires retrieval of previously learned information is called *recall*.

By contrast, a memory measure that requires only identification is called *recognition*. Associations formed at encoding tend to be effective retrieval cues, according to the *encoding specificity principle*. *Priming* is a form of implicit memory that *involves* the recall of information better and faster when it is preceded by similar information.

If someone is confident that he/she knows the answer to a question but has a hard time recalling it, it is said that he/she is experiencing the *tip-of-the-tongue phenomenon*. The *TOT* state arises because a person can retrieve some but not all of the information.

Another variable that influences the retrieval of memories is *context*, since we tend to recall information better in the same place in which we learned it; this process is referred to as *context-dependent* memory. Autobiographical memory is a form of *episodic* memory. There are various levels of autobiographical memories: *life time* periods, general events, and *event-specific* knowledge.

Memories of emotionally significant events that are often recalled more accurately and more vividly are known as *flashbulb memories*. The memory of personal trauma tends to be more *accurate* and long lasting than everyday events, and in some cases it may involve a mental disorder called *post-traumatic stress disorder*. If a memory is too traumatic the person may *repress* it, which basically means that the memory is pushed into the unconscious mind and the person cannot easily retrieve it.

## In Your Own Words
*Please write your thoughts, perspectives, and reactions on a separate piece of paper.*
✓ *Describe a flashbulb memory you have. Why are emotional memories easier to remember?*

### Forgetting
Ebbinghaus used *nonsense syllables* to study forgetting. Two kinds of *interference* are *proactive* and *retroactive*. When material that has been learned earlier interferes with the recall of material learned later, this is called *proactive interference*; when material learned later interferes with material learned earlier, it is termed *retroactive interference*.

Decay theory suggests that, when something is learned, a *memory trace* is formed. With the passage of time, however, the memory trace disintegrates. *Motivated forgetting* occurs when people forget something because it is too painful. The loss of memory is referred to as *amnesia*. A type of amnesia that affects the retention of new information is called *anterograde amnesia*. A type of amnesia involving memory loss for a segment of the past but not for new events is called *retrograde amnesia*.

### Memory and Study Strategies
The three domains of memory, *encoding, storage* and *retrieval*, influence the effectiveness of specific studying strategies. Encoding may be improved with effective time management, minimizing distractions, taking good notes, and using mnemonic strategies, among other approaches. Specific techniques designed to make memory efficient are called *mnemonic strategies*. Storage strategies include organizing your memory and spreading out the study sessions. Retrieval strategies include the use of good retrieval cues and the *PQ4R method*, which helps students remember information they are studying and involves several steps including *Preview and Review*.

## In Your Own Words
*Please write your thoughts, perspectives, and reactions on a separate piece of paper.*
✓ *Think of the last test that you took in this class. If you did not get a perfect score, explain why you got the wrong answer(s). There are possibly different reasons for different questions, but consider the possible encoding and retrieval failures that could explain the wrong answer(s).*

## Correcting the Incorrect

Carefully read each statement. Determine if the statement is correct or incorrect. If the statement is incorrect, make the necessary changes to correct it. Then check the answer key at the end of the chapter for the correct statement and page reference in the textbook.

1. Memory is defined as remembering declarative and nondeclarative information.
2. The three domains of memory include encoding, retrieval, and remembering.
3. If you focus on the meaning of a word, you are processing it at the deepest level.
4. As you think of examples of the concepts you are learning, you are practicing elaboration.
5. Elaboration is helpful because it adds to the primacy of the information.
6. Chunking involves taking information and packaging it into higher-order units that can be remembered as single units.
7. According to the Atkinson-Shiffrin theory, the three memory systems are sensory memory, iconic memory, and long-term memory.
8. Echoic memory refers to information from the auditory sense in sensory memory.
9. Information can last as long as 30 seconds in sensory memory.
10. Capacity in short-term memory is about 12 items.
11. The capacity of long-term is about 16 gigabytes.
12. Implicit memory is the conscious recollection of information.
13. Semantic memory refers to the retention of information about the where and when of life's happenings.
14. According to the schemas approach to the storage of memory, information is stored in a system in which items are organized from general to specific classes.
15. According to semantic network theory, we add new material by relating it to appropriate nodes.
16. Storage is a concept or framework that already exists in a person's mind that organizes and interprets information.
17. According to the semantic networks theories, we have a tendency to reconstruct our memories.
18. There are no specific memory centers in the brain.
19. The cerebellum is involved in explicit memory.
20. In the serial position effect, we tend to remember items in the middle of a list of items.
21. In recall, the individual has to identify only learned items, such as in a multiple choice quiz.
22. The associations made at the time of encoding tend to be effective retrieval cues.
23. Flashbulb memories are typically inaccurate.
24. Memory for traumatic events is usually less accurate than is memory for ordinary events.
25. Repression's main function is to protect the person from harm.
26. It is very difficult to create false memories, even using hypnosis.
27. Eyewitness memories are constructions that don't always match what really happened.
28. In proactive interference, material learned later disrupts retrieval of information learned earlier.
29. The decay theory suggests that when something new is learned, a neurochemical memory trace is formed.
30. A person who suffers from anterograde amnesia will have problems retaining new information or events.
31. In the Cornell Method of taking notes, the notes are written and rewritten, and the person reads the notes into a tape recorder.
32. The PQ4R stands for Preview, Question, Read, Reflect, Recite, and Review.

## Practice Test 1

1. Which of the following is the correct definition of memory?
   a. the retention of information over time
   b. the retention of time through conditioning
   c. the conditioning of thoughts via observation
   d. the neural processing of subconscious material

2. The encoding of memory refers to how information is
   a. retained.
   b. retrieved.
   c. placed into memory.
   d. all of the above

3. Storage is the memory process primarily concerned with
   a. getting information into memory.
   b. retaining information over time.
   c. taking information out of storage.
   d. registering information with our senses.

4. Thinking of examples of a concept is a good way to understand the concept. This approach is referred to as
   a. deep processing.
   b. storage.
   c. imagery.
   d. elaboration.

5. A teacher who wants to help students with long-term retention should present information in which manner?
   a. organized randomly
   b. without any specific order
   c. organized alphabetically
   d. organized logically or hierarchically

6. The capacity of working memory can be expanded by grouping information into higher-order units. This technique is called
   a. rehearsal.
   b. eidetic imagery.
   c. chunking.
   d. the phonological loop.

7. Which memory system can retain information in its original form for only an instant?
   a. sensory memory
   b. working memory
   c. long-term memory
   d. short-term memory

8. According to the Atkinson-Shiffrin theory of memory, the best way to move information into long-term memory is to
   a. rehearse the information and keep it in short-term memory as long as possible.
   b. move the information directly from sensory memory into long-term memory.
   c. rehearse the information in sensory memory as long as possible.
   d. move complex information directly to long-term memory.

9.   Which of the following statements about sensory memory is incorrect?
   a.   Information does not stay in sensory memory for very long.
   b.   Sensory memory processes more information than we may realize.
   c.   Sensory memory retains information from our senses.
   d.   Information in sensory memory is resistant to decay.

10.   Visual images that are stored in the sensory registers are called _____ memory.
   a.   iconic
   b.   echoic
   c.   semantic
   d.   nondeclarative

11.   Auditory information that is stored in the sensory memory is referred to as
   a.   iconic memory.
   b.   echoic memory.
   c.   nondeclarative memory.
   d.   memory span.

12.   You are reading a book, and your friend Rachel asks you a question. By the time you say, "Sorry, what did you say?" you "hear" her question in your head. This is due to
   a.   echoic memory.
   b.   long-term sensory memory.
   c.   working memory.
   d.   iconic memory.

13.   You have just looked up a phone number in a phone book. Which of the following strategies would be the most effective for remembering this phone number longer than 30 seconds?
   a.   transferring the phone number to short-term memory
   b.   processing the phone number in sensory memory
   c.   thinking of as many phone numbers as possible
   d.   rehearsing the phone number

14.   Which of the following can store information for up to 30 seconds?
   a.   sensory memory
   b.   working memory
   c.   long-term memory
   d.   iconic memory

15.   The storage capacity of working memory is _____ units of information.
   a.   12
   b.   $7 \pm 2$
   c.   $2.8 \times 10^{20}$
   d.   .45

16.   Declarative memory is subdivided into
   a.   procedural and virtual memory.
   b.   episodic and semantic memory.
   c.   echoic and iconic memory.
   d.   automatic and deliberate memory.

17. Early semantic network theories of memory were primarily criticized for
    a. underestimating the complexity of human memory.
    b. being too abstract.
    c. including too many hierarchical levels.
    d. focusing exclusively on semantic memory.

18. Which of the following theories is most consistent with reconstructive memory?
    a. network theories
    b. schema theories
    c. script theories
    d. none of the above

19. Experiments with sea slugs led to the speculation that memories are related to activity of
    a. the hippocampus.
    b. the amygdala.
    c. brain chemicals.
    d. the cell nucleus.

20. Your brother gives you a list of items he wants you to pick up at the grocery store on your way home from work. You glanced over the list during your lunch hour but inadvertently left the list on your desk when you left work. When you get to the grocery store, which items on the list are you most likely to remember?
    a. the items at the beginning of the list
    b. the items at the end of the list
    c. the items in the middle of the list
    d. the items at the beginning and end of the list

## Practice Test 2

1. The typical serial position effect pattern shows which of the following?
    a. stronger recency effect than primacy effect
    b. stronger primacy than recency effect
    c. equal strength for primacy and recency effect
    d. weaker recency effect than primacy effect

2. Essay questions measure which type of memory?
    a. recognition
    b. recall
    c. serial position
    d. none of the above

3. An essay examination is to recall as a multiple-choice test is to
    a. recognition.
    b. reconstruction.
    c. reorganization.
    d. restructuring.

4. According to _____, associations formed at the time of encoding tend to be effective retrieval cues.
    a. recall
    b. the serial position effect
    c. PQ4R
    d. the encoding specificity principle

5. Adam took a Spanish course during his first semester at college; during his second semester, he took a French course. Retroactive interference would suggest that Adam
   a. should now consider taking German.
   b. is going to have a difficult time learning French.
   c. is not going to remember his Spanish very well.
   d. is going to have a difficult time with both Spanish and French.

6. Which theory suggests that forgetting is caused by a fading memory trace?
   a. reconstruction theory
   b. repression
   c. decay
   d. interference theory

7. In retrograde amnesia, there is memory loss
   a. only for new information.
   b. only for segments of new information.
   c. for the complete past.
   d. only for a segment of the past.

8. Which of the following is not an effective study strategy?
   a. rehearse and memorize information by rote
   b. pay attention and minimize distraction
   c. organize what you put into memory
   d. use mnemonic strategies

9. The idea that memories are stored throughout the brain in connections between neurons is referred to as the
   a. serial position effect.
   b. interference theory.
   c. parallel distributed processing theory.
   d. dual-code hypothesis.

10. A schema for an event, such as the checkout procedure at your local supermarket, is referred to as
    a. implicit memory.
    b. nondeclarative memory.
    c. working memory.
    d. script.

11. _____ is a type of nondeclarative memory that involves information that is already in memory aiding in the retrieval of new information.
    a. Priming
    b. Procedural memory
    c. Prospective memory
    d. Semantic memory

12. Remembering that you have a doctor's appointment later today required the activity of
    a. semantic memory.
    b. implicit memory.
    c. retrospective memory.
    d. prospective memory.

13. Being able to recite the Pledge of Allegiance involves
    a. priming.
    b. explicit memory.
    c. nondeclarative memory.
    d. procedural memory.

14. The component of working memory that is involved in the storage of the sounds of language is the
    a. central executive.
    b. visuospatial working memory.
    c. phonological loop.
    d. sensory memory.

15. Chunking is used to improve which memory time frame?
    a. sensory memory
    b. short-term memory
    c. working memory
    d. long-term memory

16. Which of the following factors does not affect encoding?
    a. priming
    b. selective attention
    c. level of processing
    d. divided attention

17. Which of the following theories is the one that considers the biological basis of memory?
    a. schema theory
    b. hierarchies theories
    c. connectionism
    d. semantic networks theories

18. Which of the following brain structures is involved in procedural memory?
    a. hippocampus
    b. amygdala
    c. cerebellum
    d. limbic system

19. There are three levels of autobiographical memories. Which of the following would be the one involved in your memory of what you did last summer?
    a. life time periods
    b. general events
    c. event-specific knowledge
    d. flashbulb memories

20. Which of the following is the way of improving short-term memory that involves the conscious repetition of information?
    a. chunking
    b. recall
    c. recognition
    d. rehearsal

## Practice Test 3

1. A person who repeats 20 times the definition of psychology, until the exact words in the definition are memorized, is engaging in elaboration at the
   a. shallow processing level.
   b. intermediate processing level.
   c. definition processing level.
   d. deepest processing level.

2. When an eyewitness to a crime is asked to pick the suspect from a lineup, he or she will engage in which of the following memory tasks?
   a. recall
   b. encoding
   c. storage
   d. recognition

3. Which of the following memories can be expected to be the least accurate of the options?
   a. resurfaced repressed memories
   b. eyewitness recount right after the event
   c. flashbulb memory
   d. remembering a personal trauma

4. Which of the following statements does not represent one of the three domains of memory?
   a. paying attention to and processing information to memorize
   b. the process of saving information in memory for later retrieval
   c. the process of making a decision based on memorized information
   d. the process of taking information out of memory

5. Which of the following statements is NOT true about elaboration?
   a. Elaboration makes memory codes more unique or distinctive.
   b. Elaboration is associated with brain activity in the occipital lobe.
   c. Greater elaboration is linked with neural activity.
   d. The more information is stored, the more distinguishable is the code; thus, the information is easier to retrieve.

6. Based on the dual-code hypothesis, which of the following would produce a better memory?
   a. a drawn map of directions from school to your new job
   b. a verbal description of the route from school to your new job
   c. the definition of psychology
   d. the rhythm of salsa music

7. People who claim they can memorize whole pages of text by just looking briefly at the pages are said to have
   a. episodic memory.
   b. implicit memory.
   c. echoic memory.
   d. eidetic memory.

8.  The following are examples that involve implicit memory, EXCEPT
    a.  making an egg omelet.
    b.  feeling good after smelling the perfume used by someone you love.
    c.  giving someone your phone number.
    d.  doing macramé.

9.  Which of the following theories proposes that your memory of operant conditioning (from Chapter 7) should be organized as follows: operant conditioning is based on consequences; consequences may be reinforcements or punishers; reinforcements may be positive or negative; and so forth?
    a.  hierarchies
    b.  semantic networks
    c.  schemas
    d.  connectionist networks

10. Which of the following theories of memory storage would argue that people will notice and thus remember better things that are consistent with the information they already have stored in memory?
    a.  hierarchies
    b.  semantic networks
    c.  schemas
    d.  connectionist networks

11. Activity in the hippocampus may occur when experiencing the following memories, EXCEPT
    a.  remembering how to swing a golf club.
    b.  remembering the date of your birthday.
    c.  remembering your address.
    d.  remembering where you left the keys.

12. First impressions tend to be very important. It seems that we more clearly remember details we learn about a person during that first encounter. This tendency is explained by the
    a.  encoding specificity principle.
    b.  recency effect.
    c.  recognition memory task.
    d.  primacy effect.

13. When you meet an acquaintance in a school hall and can't remember his name, but you remember that he is a friend of your roommate, you are experiencing the
    a.  recency effect.
    b.  primacy effect.
    c.  tip-of-the-tongue phenomenon.
    d.  dual-code effect.

14. Which of the following is an example of an encoding failure?
    a.  failing to recall your old cell phone number
    b.  failing to recognize that B. F. Skinner is associated with operant conditioning, because you were not paying attention the day that was covered in class
    c.  recalling the old cell phone number but failing to recall the new number
    d.  failing the recall the details of a traumatic car accident

15. Renee was hit by lightning. As a result of this accident, she was unable to recognize her husband and children but had no problem remembering the names and faces of the doctors and staff that treated her at the hospital. When the psychologist or psychiatrist examines her, Renee is likely to be diagnosed with
    a. motivated forgetting.
    b. anterograde amnesia.
    c. repression.
    d. retrograde amnesia.

16. These are all good studying strategies, EXCEPT
    a. creating your own study guide.
    b. eating a snack before studying.
    c. studying at least five straight hours the day before the test.
    d. studying five hours across two weeks, dedicating approximately 20 minutes a day.

17. When LaToya studies and watches TV at the same time, she is engaging in divided attention. The memory of the studied material will probably be affected. Which memory domain would explain this deficit in memory?
    a. encoding
    b. storage
    c. retrieval
    d. forgetting

18. Siobhra is a teacher who routinely asks her students to come up with examples of the concepts discussed in class. Having the students think of examples promotes
    a. elaboration at the intermediate level.
    b. processing at the intermediate level.
    c. elaboration at the shallow level of processing.
    d. processing at the deepest level.

19. A friend calls on the phone and says that she just drove by your home, waved at you, but that you totally ignored her. "What's up?" she asks. You reply, "Well, there were so many cars passing by that even though I was looking at the road I did not see you!" Your friend's car and her wave were probably processed in
    a. short-term memory.
    b. sensory memory.
    c. working memory.
    d. long-term memory.

20. Which of the following is an example involving semantic memory?
    a. the nervousness Jon gets every time he goes to an ATM after he was robbed at one
    b. reciting your favorite poem
    c. remembering where you where on September 11, 2001
    d. knitting

## Connections

*Take advantage of all the other study tools available for this chapter!*

**MEDIA INTERGRATION**

| NAME OF CLIP | DESCRIPTION | KEY CONCEPTS AND IDEAS |
|---|---|---|
| | | **The Nature of Memory** |
| | | **Memory Encoding** |
| | | **Memory Storage** |
| Iconic Memory | Iconic memory is the conventional name for visual memory. This interactivity engages participants in the classic Sperling experiment of sensory store. The task involves the recall of letters presented in grid and the recall of letters and tones. Sperling established that iconic memory can hold most of the information in an array of 12 letters presented in three rows of four letters. | Iconic memory<br>Recall |
| Short-term Memory | The concepts of short-term memory and working memory are used interchangeably in this interactivity. The activity involves a self-test of digit span, a chunking test, and a short-term memory duration test. The task involves a list of three letters followed by number then the participants have to count backward in intervals of 3. | Short-term memory<br>Working memory<br>Chunking |
| Chunking in Memory | The exercise demonstrates that chunking improves memory; USADNAFBICNN illustrates that familiar stimuli are easier to remember. In this experiment, the value of breaking long lists of items into smaller components is demonstrated. | Chunking<br>Memory |

| Working Memory | In this interactive exercise, a working memory experiment is simulated. The focus of the activity is on the duration of working memory, but it also illustrates the method for measuring this type of memory. Emphasis in the questions that follow the activity is on the importance of rehearsing information in order to preserve it in working memory until needed. | Working memory |
|---|---|---|
| Aging and Memory | Deterioration of prospective memory in seniors is discussed, as well as a seven-session workshop designed to reverse the deterioration. The workshop includes cognitive strategies, relaxation, and memory tricks. | Memory<br>Prospective memory<br>Cognitive strategies<br>Relaxation<br>Visual associations |
| When Eyes Deceive | Video clip presents a classroom demonstration of an eye-witness identification experiment. Students at Brooklyn Law School witness a purse snatching, and the vulnerability of their memories is illustrated. | Eyewitness identification<br>Memory |
| | | **Memory Retrieval** |
| Serial Position Effect | A graphic and description are used to explain the classic Ebbinghaus study. The primacy and recency effects are illustrated. Activities include nonsense syllables to recall and a sound file with series of nouns to recall. The results and effects are explained. | Serial position effect<br>Primacy effect<br>Recency effect |
| Post Traumatic Stress Disorder | Carl, a 46-year-old Vietnam veteran describes his experiences with PTSD. Carl's graphic descriptions of his traumatic experiences in Vietnam bring to life the psychological horror of people with PTSD. Carl discusses how feelings of isolation, anger, and pain contributed to symptoms. He describes how nobody around him could understand what he went through and | Post traumatic stress disorder<br>Flashbacks<br>Coping |

| | morns the loss of innocence. He expresses great anger because of lack of social support he experienced. His flashbacks would include perceptions that did not correspond to current sensory experience, such as smelling gun powder. Carl also discusses how he has coped with the disorder and how the onset of symptoms is related to stress. | |
|---|---|---|
| Eye Witness Memory | Elizabeth Loftus is featured in this video clip discussing the misinformation effect. Leading questions and participation in conversations can lead to the adoption of erroneous information. Gary Wells discusses guidelines for the treatment of eyewitnesses. A dramatic case of mistaken identity is presented. | Eyewitness memory Misinformation effect |
| Eyewitness Testimony | Researcher Gary Wells discusses his work with eyewitness testimony. Eyewitnesses often identify the wrong person. Based on research, Wells proposed in 1999 to the Department of Justice a series of guidelines to make eyewitness testimony more effective. Among the recommendations were presenting lineup individuals one at a time, using open-ended questions and avoiding interrupting the witnesses as they answer. This exercise focuses on how eyewitness testimony and identification can be improved. Listeners will learn some of the guidelines that can make the process more fair and effective. | Eyewitness testimony |

| | | Forgetting |
| | | Memory and Study Strategies |
|---|---|---|
| Mnemonic Strategies in Memory | U.S. Memoriad contest is showcased in this video clip. Champions share their extraordinary memory-training tactics. | Memory<br>Mnemonic |

*Take advantage of all the other study tools available for this chapter!*

**Online Learning Center (www.mhhe.com/Santrockp7u)**

- Interact and make learning fun!
  - o **Interactive Exercises**
    - Iconic Memory
    - Short-Term Memory
    - Just the Facts, Please
    - In One Ear, Out the Other
    - Serial Position Effect
  - o **Interactive Review**
    - Level of Analysis: Forgetting
- Brush up on the Key Terms for this chapter by first reviewing the electronic **Glossary** (in English or Spanish) and then testing your retention using the **Flashcard** feature.
- **"Notes"**—This feature allows you to use the website as you would your text, inserting your own study notes and highlighting areas of particular importance.

**In Your Text**

- Found throughout each chapter, the **Review and Sharpen Your Thinking** feature breaks the text into logical chunks, allowing you to process, review, and reflect thoughtfully on the information that you've just read. When going back to *study* the chapter, try reading the feature *before* the section of text to which it relates. In doing so, you will be able to focus your attention on important concepts *as* you encounter them. In this chapter, this feature can be found on the following pages: pp. 307, 311, 326, 335, 339, and 343.

**Practice Quizzes**

- Test your knowledge of memory by taking the different practice quizzes found on your text's **Online Learning Center** and on the **In-Psych Plus CD-ROM** packaged with your text.

**ANSWER KEY**

**In Your Own Words**

✓ When you read the textbook for this class, you may process the information at the shallow, intermediate, or deep level. Describe the processing of textbook information at each of these levels of encoding.

*We may encode information at three levels of processing: shallow, intermediate, and deep. The shallow level of processing involves paying attention to the physical features of the stimuli. When reading a textbook, if you focus on the look and sound of words you are processing information at the shallow level. For example, if you read the definition of psychology: "Psychology is the science of behavior and mental processes" and you focus only on the look and sound of the words together in this definition, you are processing information at the shallow level. At the intermediate level of processing you may recognize that set of words as a unit that represents the definition of psychology; however, you may memorize the definition as presented in the textbook and not really understand what it means. This would also make it difficult for you to recognize the following definition of psychology as correct: "Psychology involves the systematic investigation of actions, thoughts, and emotions," which is virtually the same definition but with synonymic concepts. Because it does not look or sound like the definition that you memorized, you may fail to recognize it as correct. Ultimately, the better way to encode information to ensure retrieval is by using the deepest level of processing, which involves processing information based on what it means and creating associations with other information we already have in our memory. At the deepest level, the reader understands the definition of psychology based on the understanding of each of the concepts that constitute the definition. A person who processes the definition at this level would have no problem recognizing the alternate definition of psychology presented above. Concepts such as "science" and "systematic investigation" are recognized as equivalent.*

✓ List some examples of how businesses and organizations use chunking in their 1-800 numbers.
*Businesses and organizations often use the letter equivalents of numbers on telephones to aid the retrieval of the number in potential clients. They may use their company name or slogan as a phone number to facilitate the memory of the number. A national example in the United States is 1-800-CALL ATT, to make collect calls using the ATT service. Basically, a person needs to recall only three pieces of information: (1) 1-800, (2) CALL, and (3) ATT. Considering that we can keep 7 ± 2 items in our short-term memory, it should be relatively easy to recall these three units of information.*

✓ What declarative memories have you retrieved in the last hour? What nondeclarative memories have you retrieved in the last hour?
*Declarative memories involve the recollection of information such as facts or events that can be verbally communicated, and these include episodic and semantic memory. However, nondeclarative or implicit memories involve skills and sensory perceptions rather than consciously remembering facts. For example, if you are typing a homework assignment in which you have to discuss the difference between classical and operant conditioning, the actual definitions and examples of each of these learning methods are part of your declarative memory, but the movement of your fingers over the keyboard (if you are just a little bit skilled at it) involves implicit memory.*

✓ Compare the semantic networks approach and the schemas approach to the storage of memories.
*While these two approaches assume a network of interconnected concepts in our memory, the semantic networks theory assumes that these concepts are clearly and logically linked to one another. By contrast, the schema theory suggests that our memory is a lot more flexible, and we tend to reconstruct it and fill in the gaps of our memory.*

✓ Describe a flashbulb memory you have. Why are emotional memories easier to remember?
*Flashbulb memories are memories of emotionally significant events that people often recall with more accuracy and vivid imagery than everyday events. It has been argued that this tendency for accurate recall of emotional events is adaptive because it allows us to revisit the memory later in order to interpret it and analyze it. Emotions contribute to the durability of the memory. The emotional arousal may contribute to making the memories more vivid.*

✓ Think of the last test that you took in this class. If you did not get a perfect score, explain why you got the wrong answer(s). There are possibly different reasons for different questions, but consider the possible encoding and retrieval failures that could explain the wrong answer(s).
*If the studying strategies were not optimal, that could explain in great part the problem(s) in the test, but even when we study hard we may have problems remembering everything that we read and studied. Encoding failure is forgetting because the information was never entered into long-*

*term memory. Retrieval failure of study material could involve proactive interference, retroactive interference, decay, or transience.*

## Correcting the Incorrect

1. Memory is defined as *the retention of information over time.* (p. 306)
2. The three domains of memory include encoding, storage, and retrieval. (p. 306)
3. If you focus on the meaning of a word, you are processing it at the deepest level. (p. 309)
4. As you think of examples of the concepts you are learning, you are practicing elaboration. (p. 309)
5. Elaboration is helpful because it adds to the *distinctiveness* of the information. (p. 310)
6. Chunking involves taking information and packaging it into higher-order units that can be remembered as single units. (p. 313)
7. According to the Atkinson-Shiffrin theory, the three memory systems are sensory memory, *short-term memory*, and long-term memory. (p. 312)
8. Echoic memory refers to information from the auditory sense in sensory memory. (p. 312)
9. Information can last as long as 30 seconds in *short-term memory.* (p. 312)
10. Capacity in short-term memory is about *7 ± 2 items.* (p. 313)
11. The capacity of long-term *is virtually unlimited.* (p. 315)
12. *Declarative memory* is the conscious recollection of information. (p. 316)
13. *Episodic memory* refers to the retention of information about the where and when of life's happenings. (p. 316)
14. According to the *hierarchies* approach to the storage of memory, information is stored in a system in which items are organized from general to specific classes. (p. 320)
15. According to semantic network theory, we add new material by relating it to appropriate nodes. (p. 320)
16. *A schema* is a concept or framework that already exists in a person's mind that organizes and interprets information. (p. 321)
17. According to the *schema theory of memory*, we have a tendency to reconstruct our memories. (p. 322)
18. There *are* specific memory centers in the brain. (p. 325)
19. The cerebellum is involved in *implicit* memory. (p. 325)
20. In the serial position effect, we tend to remember items *at the beginning and end of a list of items.* (p. 327)
21. In *recognition*, the individual has to identify only learned items, such as in a multiple choice. (p. 328)
22. The associations made at the time of encoding tend to be effective retrieval cues. (p. 328)
23. Flashbulb memories are typically *accurate.* (p. 331)
24. Memory for traumatic events is *usually more accurate* than is memory for ordinary events. (p. 332)
25. Repression's main function is to protect the person from harm. (p. 333)
26. It is *easy* to create false memories, *especially* using hypnosis. (p. 333)
27. Eyewitness memories are constructions that don't always match what really happened. (p. 334)
28. In *retroactive interference*, material learned later disrupts retrieval of information learned earlier. (p. 337)
29. The decay theory suggests that when something new is learned, a neurochemical memory trace is formed. (p. 337)
30. A person who suffers from anterograde amnesia will have problems retaining new information or events. (p. 338)

31. In the Cornell Method of taking notes, the notes are written into two columns. (p. 341)
32. The PQ4R stands for Preview, Question, Read, Reflect, Recite, and Review. (p. 343)

## Practice Test 1

1. a. RIGHT
   b. no; this is not the correct definition of memory
   c. no; this is incorrect
   d. no; memory is not defined in this way
   p. 306

2. a. no; how information is retained refers to storage
   b. no; this sounds like retrieval
   c. YES; encoding refers to how information gets into memory
   d. no
   p. 307

3 . a. no; this option defines encoding
   b. YES; storage consists of retention of information over time
   c. no; this describes retrieval
   d. no; this option best relates to encoding
   p. 307

4. a. no; although at deep processing the stimulus' meaning is processed
   b. no; storage refers to retaining information over time
   c. no; imagery is the use of mental images and may or may not involve examples
   d. RIGHT; thinking of examples increases the extensiveness of processing information
   p. 309

5. a. no; this would also reduce long-term retention since it lacks organization
   b. no; in fact, this would decrease long-term retention
   c. no; but only if there is a more logical organization
   d. YES; when information is presented in an logically organized way, memory is helped
   p. 320

6. a. no; rehearsal is the conscious repetition of information
   b. no; this is a type of photographic memory
   c. CORRECT; chunking packs information into higher-order units
   d. no; the phonological loop is a subsystem of working memory
   p. 313

7. a. THAT'S RIGHT; sensory memory holds information for only a short time
   b. no
   c. no
   d. no
   p. 312

8. a. YES; this is correct, according to the Atkinson-Shiffrin theory
   b. no; the model includes short-term memory located between sensory and long-term
   c. no; information lasts for only a short time in sensory memory
   d. no; complex memory must first go through sensory and short-term memory
   p. 312

9. a.   no; this statement is correct
   b.   no; this statement is correct
   c.   no; this statement is correct
   d.   YES; information in sensory memory decays very rapidly
   p. 312

10. a.   CORRECT; iconic memory refers to visual images
    b.   no; echoic memory refers to auditory stimuli
    c.   no; semantic memory is memory of the meanings of words
    d.   no; nondeclarative memory refers to implicit memory
    p. 312

11. a.   no; iconic memory refers to visual images
    b.   YES; the word echoic includes the word echo
    c.   no; this term refers to memory that cannot be verbalized or consciously recalled
    d.   no; memory span describes the storage capacity of working or short-term memory
    p. 312

12. a.   YES; this demonstrates echoic memory or auditory information in sensory memory
    b.   no; this is not long-term sensory memory
    c.   no; working memory would not cause this experience
    d.   no; iconic memory refers to visual images, not auditory information
    p. 312

13. a.   no; the information is already in short-term memory
    b.   no; remember, information in sensory memory decays very rapidly
    c.   no; this would cause interference, and you would forget the correct phone number
    d.   THAT'S CORRECT; by rehearsal, the number will last longer in working memory
    p. 313

14. a.   no; in fact, information in sensory memory lasts for a very short time
    b.   YES; working memory (short-term) stores information for up to 30 seconds
    c.   no; information in long-term memory can be stored for a lifetime
    d.   no; iconic memory is visual information in sensory memory
    p. 313

15. a.   no; but that is close
    b.   THAT'S CORRECT
    c.   no; this is the estimated storage capacity of long-term memory
    d.   no; not even close
    p. 313

16. a.   no
    b.   RIGHT
    c.   no; these refer to the types of information found in sensory memory
    d.   no
    p. 316

17. a.   THAT'S RIGHT; hierarchical networks are too simple
    b.   no; if anything, network theories are too concrete
    c.   no; that is not a primary criticism
    d.   no; this is not a primary criticism
    p. 320

18. a. no; network theories are not consistent with reconstructive memory
    b. YES; schema are used when we reconstruct information
    c. no; there are script theories, but a script is a schema for an event
    d. no
    p. 321

19. a. no; the hippocampus is involved in human memory
    b. no; the amygdala is involved in human memory
    c. CORRECT; in particular, serotonin may play a role in memory
    d. no
    p. 324

20. a. no; although this is half correct
    b. no; although this is half correct
    c. no; these items would not likely be remembered
    d. YES; the primacy and the recency effect would be observed
    p. 327

## Practice Test 2

1. a. YES; this describes the typical serial position effect pattern
   b. no; this does not describes the typical serial position effect
   c. no; the typical pattern is stronger recency effect than primacy effect
   d. no; this is just the opposite of the typical serial position effect
   p. 327

2. a. no; multiple-choice questions involve recognition
   b. CORRECT; in recall, the study must retrieve learned information
   c. no; serial position refers to the pattern of information remembered
   d. no
   p. 328

3. a. YES; multiple-choice tests require the learner to recognize learned items
   b. no; recognition is the type of retrieval used in multiple-choice tests
   c. no; reorganization is not involved in multiple-choice tests
   d. no; this is not correct
   p. 328

4. a. no; recall is a type of retrieval in which information must be retrieved from previously learned information
   b. no; this describes how retrieval is affected by the position of information in a list
   c. no; PQ4R is a study method
   d. CORRECT; this describes the encoding specificity principle
   p. 328

5. a. no; the question makes no reference to taking German
   b. no; this would describe proactive interference of old information disrupting new
   c. YES; retroactive interference occurs when new information disrupts old
   d. no; retroactive interference would predict problems remembering Spanish
   p. 337

6. a. no; reconstruction describes how we remember information
   b. no; repression blocks memories from the conscious
   c. YES; decay theory says that the neurochemical memory trace disintegrates
   d. no; interference theory says memories are forgotten because of other information
   p. 337

7. a. no; this more accurately describes anterograde amnesia
   b. no; this more accurately describes anterograde amnesia
   c. no; only segments of the past are forgotten in retrograde amnesia
   d. THAT'S RIGHT; this is the definition of retrograde amnesia
   p. 339

8. a. YES; instead, you should try to understand the material
   b. no; this is an effective strategy
   c. no; this is an effective strategy
   d. no; this is an effective strategy
   p. 340

9. a. no; this refers to the tendency to remember better items at the beginning and the end of lists
   b. no; this refers to proactive and retroactive interference
   c. YES, this theory also says that several neurons may work together to process or produce a single memory
   d. no; this refers to the better recall of images over words
   p. 323

10. a. no; you could explain verbally the procedure to check out at a supermarket
    b. no; same as item a
    c. no; working memory is a temporary memory site
    d. YES; a script is the framework of expectations we have about events; you know what to expect at the checkout in a supermarket
    p. 322

11. a. YES; priming occurs when information in memory is activated to help in the retrieval of new information
    b. no; while this is also an implicit memory, it refers to memory for skills
    c. no; this refers to remembering information about doing something in the future
    d. no; this refers to the conceptual knowledge we have about the world
    p. 329

12. a. no; this refers to remembering concepts and their meaning
    b. no; nondeclarative memory is not involved here
    c. no; this refers to remembering the past
    d. YES; prospective memory involves remembering things that have to do with expected future activities
    p. 318

13. a. no; reciting is a conscious verbal behavior and requires declarative memory
    b. YES; explicit or declarative memory would be involved the this recitation
    c. no; reciting is a conscious verbal behavior and requires explicit memory
    d. no; reciting the Pledge of Allegiance requires the recollection of the words in the appropriate order, and not any particular procedure or set of actions
    p. 316

14. a. no; this component integrates the information stored in the phonological loop and the visuospatial working memory
    b. no; this component stores images
    c. YES; this component involves an acoustic code and rehearsal
    d. no; this is not one of the components of working memory
    p. 314

15. a. no; sensory memory lasts from only fractions of a second to a few seconds
    b. YES; chunking can improve short-term memory by packing down extensive information into chucks that fit the 7 $\pm$ 2 items limit of this time frame
    c. no; this concept was not applied in the theories of working memory
    d. no; long-term memory does not require chunking for improvement
    p. 313

16. a. YES; priming does not take place until after the information has been encoded and stored
    b. no; selective attention, which involves focusing on some stimuli and not others, does affect encoding, since we will encode what we attend to
    c. no; the level at which we process the information does have an effect on encoding
    d. no; divided attention also affects encoding; this happens when we have to pay attention to various things at the same time
    p. 329

17. a. no; schema theory looks at the cognitive basis and reconstructive nature of memory
    b. no; hierarchies theories argue that information is highly organized in memory
    c. YES; connectionism, connectionist networks, or parallel distributed processing theories consider the role of neurons and parts of the brain in memory
    d. no; these are also cognitive approaches to memory
    p. 323

18. a. no; this part is involved in explicit memory
    b. no; this part is involved in emotions such as fear and anger
    c. YES; the cerebellum is involved in the implicit memory required to perform skills
    d. no; the limbic system is involved in explicit memory
    p. 325

19. a. no; this is the most abstract and general level and it refers to general periods of your life, such as childhood
    b. YES; what you did last summer would classify under this level of autobiographical memories
    c. no; this level is much more specific; remembering how crowded it was at that lawn concert you went to, for example, would classify at this level
    d. no; this is not one of the levels of autobiographical memories
    p. 330

20. a. no; while chunking does improve short-term memory, it involves the grouping of information to fit the 5–9 items limit
    b. no; this is a memory task, not a way of improving short-term memory
    c. no; this is a memory task, not a way of improving short-term memory
    d. YES; rehearsal is basically repeating the information to keep it in short-term memory
    p. 313

## Practice Test 3

1. a. no; shallow processing would involve merely reading over the words without even tying then together as a definition
   b. YES; elaboration can occur at any level of processing; in this case, elaboration is taking place at the intermediate level, in which the person is focusing on the look and sound of the words in the definition and recalling how the words go together in the sentence
   c. no; this is not one of the levels of processing
   d. no; the elaboration presented in the question is not characteristic of the deepest level of processing

p. 309

2. a. no; recall would be involved if the eyewitness is asked to describe the offender to a sketch artist
   b. no; at the time of picking out the suspect from a lineup, the encoding of the suspect's information will have occurred previously
   c. no; at the time of picking out the suspect from a lineup, the storage of the suspect's information will have occurred previously
   d. YES; the eyewitness will have to recognize the suspect from various options, much like in a multiple-choice test

p. 328

3. a. YES; the accuracy of a suddenly remembered repressed memory has been challenged not only in courts of justice but also in research; memories may be implanted, especially using hypnosis
   b. no; while eyewitness testimony may not always be accurate, the shorter the time span between the event and the recall the more accurate it may be
   b. no; flashbulb memories tend to be highly accurate
   c. no; the memories of personal traumas tend to be highly accurate

p. 332

4. a. no; this statement represents the memory domain of encoding
   b. no; this statement represents the memory domain of storage
   c. YES; making a decision is a thinking process that usually depends on previously memorized information, but it is not one of the domains of memory
   d. no; this statement represents the memory domain of retrieval

p. 306

5. a. no; this is correct
   b. YES; this is incorrect, elaboration is associated with neural activity in the brain's left frontal lobe; as we learned in Chapter 3, the occipital lobe is mainly associated with the processing of visual information
   c. no; studies with MRI have demonstrated this relationship
   d. no; this is correct about elaboration

p. 309

6. a. YES; images, such as maps, are stored as both an image and a verbal code, thus they produce a better memory
   b. no; a verbal description would be stored only in a verbal code
   c. no; a definition is no different from a verbal description
   d. no; the dual-code hypothesis does not address the memorizing of auditory stimuli

p. 311

7. a.   no; episodic memory refers to memory of events
   b.   no; implicit memory cannot be described verbally
   c.   no; echoic memory involves the memories of auditory stimuli
   d.   YES; eidetic memory is also known as photographic memory; this phenomenon is very rare and some psychologists doubt it even exists

   p. 313

8. a.   no; the procedure of making an omelet would involve nondeclarative memory
   b.   no; the good feeling resulting from perceiving the familiar perfume is also implicit since the association is likely to have been established through classical conditioning
   c.   YES; this involves declarative or explicit memory
   d.   no; doing macramé is a manual procedure that would involve implicit memory

   p. 318

9. a.   YES; this example presents a hierarchy of information, from general to specific
   b.   no; this organization is not based on meaning but rather on hierarchy
   c.   no; the memory in the example is highly organized, unlike what the schema approach would propose
   d.   no; the connectionist networks theory considers the biological basis of memory

   p. 320

10. a.   no; the hierarchies approach assumes that all information may be attended to and added to the hierarchy at the appropriate spot
    b.   no; semantic networks theories propose that information is organized based on their meaning, but it does not suggest that if something is not consistent with the nodes already in memory that it will not be encoded
    c.   YES; according to this approach, schemas are frameworks that influence how we encode, make inferences, and retrieve information; previous schemas may influence what we pay attention to and thus what gets stored in memory
    d.   no; the connectionist networks approach considers the biological basis of memory

    p. 321

11. a.   YES; this is an example of implicit memory, which is associated with activity in the cerebellum
    b.   no; this is an example of explicit memory, which involves the hippocampus
    c.   no; this is an example of declarative memory, which involves the hippocampus
    d.   no; this is an example of explicit memory, which involves the hippocampus

    p. 325

12. a.   no; the encoding specificity principle states that information present at the time of encoding tends to be effective as a retrieval cue
    b.   no; this is the tendency for the latest information we have experienced to be remembered better
    c.   no; this memory task is a process not an effect
    d.   YES; the primacy effect states that information learned at the beginning of a series of information will be remembered better; the same principle that applies to remembering early items in a list applies to remembering better information from early in a relationship, such as the first impression

    p. 327

13. a. no; this is the tendency for information learned later in a list to be remembered better
    b. no; this is the tendency for information learned earlier in a list to be remembered better
    c. YES; you remember some aspects of the stimuli but not others
    d. no; actually, it is called the dual-code hypothesis, and it refers to the tendency for images to be remembered easier than conceptual information
    p. 329

14. a. no; this is an example of retroactive interference, which is a retrieval failure
    b. YES; this example demonstrates an encoding failure because the information was never stored in memory
    c. no; this is an example of proactive interference, which is a retrieval failure
    d. no; this is motivated forgetting, which is a retrieval failure
    p. 336

15. a. no; the question does not suggest that Renee has any reason or motivation to forget her family
    b. no; anterograde amnesia would be diagnosed if she was unable to remember new information, such as the doctor's name
    c. no; the question does not suggest that Renee's family was being the source of distress and unpleasant memories
    d. YES; retrograde amnesia involves memory loss for a segment of the past but not for new events
    p. 339

16. a. no; this is a good strategy, discussed in the textbook as "as yourself questions"
    b. no; this is a good strategy, discussed in the textbook under "storage strategies"
    c. YES; while this is fairly common, cramming before a test tends to produce short-term memory that is processed in a shallow rather than a deep manner
    d. no; this is a good strategy; while 20 minutes might seem brief, spreading out the study sessions contributes to the consolidation of the memories, making them better for future retrieval
    p. 342

17. a. YES; if the attention is divided, part of the studied material will not be encoded
    b. no; what is encoded will possibly be stored, but the deficit starts at encoding
    c. no; what is stored will possibly be retrievable, but the deficit starts at encoding
    d. no; this is not one of the domains of memory
    p. 308

18. a. no; the intermediate level is limited to recognizing and labeling stimuli; elaboration at this level would involve more of this, but not processing at a deeper level
    b. no; the intermediate level is limited to recognizing and labeling stimuli
    c. no; shallow level processing focuses on the physical features of the stimuli
    d. YES; examples and associations are characteristic of the deepest level of processing
    p. 309

19. a. no; in order for a stimuli to make it into short-term memory, we must first pay attention to it
    b. YES; it probably went through sensory memory ignored
    c. no; in order for a stimuli to make it into working memory, we must first pay attention to it
    d. no; information goes into long-term memory after it has been in short-term memory
    p. 312

20. a.  no; this involves implicit memory acquired through classical conditioning
    b.  YES; the poem involves conceptual knowledge
    c.  no; this involves episodic memory
    d.  no; this involves implicit memory of the procedural type

  p. 316

# Chapter 9—Thinking and Language

## Learning Goals

1. Characterize the "cognitive revolution" in psychology.
2. Explain concept formation.
3. Describe the requirements for solving problems.
4. Discuss the main factors in thinking critically, reasoning, and making decisions.
5. Identify the possible connections between language and thought.
6. Summarize how language is acquired and develops.

*After studying Chapter 9, you will be able to:*

- Describe psychology's cognitive revolution.
- Discuss how people form concepts.
- Explain how to apply the steps of problem solving.
- Describe common obstacles to problem solving.
- Understand what critical thinking is and how to engage in critical thinking.
- Discuss how people reason inductively and deductively.
- Understand decision making and the different biases that influence this process.
- Explain what language and the four rule systems are.
- Describe biological and environmental influences on language.
- Discuss the extent to which animals, particularly apes, can use language.
- Understand the concept of critical periods in language development.
- Describe linkages between language, culture, and thought.
- Be aware of the reasons why some people favor and others oppose bilingual education.
- Explain the two main methods used to teach reading.

## CHAPTER 9: OUTLINE

- Williams syndrome, a genetic disorder that involves impaired reading and writing but enhanced verbal and interpersonal skills, offers insights into the factors involved in thinking and language, the topic of this chapter.

- Thinking was not considered an appropriate area of studies in psychology until the second half of the 20th century. The first half of the 20th century was dominated by the behavioral perspective in psychology, but during the 1950s a cognitive revolution emerged in psychology. The cognitive focus was strongly encouraged by the invention of the computer and the information processing questions it raised and could potentially answer. Although some cognitive psychologists draw an analogy between human cognition and the functioning of computers, important differences exist; however, the role of computers in cognitive psychology has given rise to a field called artificial intelligence.

- The basic units of thinking are *concepts*, which are categories that help us to make sense of information in the world. Concepts allow us to generalize and to associate experiences and objects; they also enhance our memory and guide our behaviors.

- Three models of how concepts are created have been proposed: (1) the classical model, (2) the prototype model, and (3) the exemplar model.

- According to the classical model, concepts are categories of objects that share defining properties. This model has been criticized because we also have concepts that include objects that don't possess all the defining properties. The prototype model says that we introduce new objects into established concepts based on their similarity of the new object to the most typical object or the prototype of that concept.

- Concepts are also important in problem solving. Effective problem solving is characterized by a four-step process: (1) finding and framing the problem, (2) developing problem-solving strategies such as subgoaling, algorithms, and heuristics, (3) evaluating the solutions, and (4) redefining the problems and solutions over time.

- Some of the obstacles to optimal problem solving are functional fixedness, mental set, lack of motivation, poor emotional control, and lack of expertise. Some ways in which experts differ from novices in their problem-solving skills include having more and better organized knowledge about the issue, better memory on their area of expertise, more effective problem-solving strategies, and experience and practice at problem solving.

- Another area of thinking studied in psychology is *critical thinking*, which involves thinking reflectively and productively, then evaluating the evidence.

- Being mindful is one of the characteristics of critical thinkers. A mindful person is creative, open to new information, and aware of more than one perspective. Students of psychology who engage in critical thinking are expected to use questions as tools to gain quality information that will aid them in making good judgments and decisions.

- *Reasoning* is the mental activity of transforming information to reach conclusions. *Inductive reasoning* is reasoning from the specific to the general; analogies draw on inductive reasoning. Reasoning from the general to the specific is called *deductive reasoning*.

- Evaluating alternatives and making choices among them is called *decision making*. There are a number of biases that influence the decision-making process. Some of the biased tendencies in our thinking are the confirmation bias, belief perseverance, overconfidence bias, hindsight bias, availability heuristic, and the representativeness heuristic.

- *Language* is a form of communication based on a system of symbols that can be spoken, written, or signaled. All human languages have infinite generativity based on a limited set of rules, including phonology (basic sounds of a language), morphology (word formation rules), syntax (rules of combinations of words), and semantics (meaning of words).

- The relationship between language and thinking is an important question in psychology. Most agree that language (that is, words) plays an important role in memory and thinking, but Whorf suggested that language determines the way we think. Whorf's critics argue that language reflects rather than determines thinking.

- Studies with deaf children and individuals with Williams syndrome have demonstrated that thinking and language are not completely dependent on each other. Interest in studying the extent of the relationship between thinking and language has sparked interest in the use of language by animals. Apes are able to learn sign language; however, questions remain regarding their ability to understand the meaning of the symbols and their ability to learn the rules of language. There is evidence supporting both cognitive abilities in apes.

- The case of the "wild child" in France, who as a result of spending six years alone in the wilderness was unable to communicate effectively, raises important questions regarding the roles of nature and nurture in language.

- From the nature perspective, Noam Chomsky argues that humans are biologically pre-wired to learn language at a certain time and in a certain way. In support of this view is the evidence that children all over the world acquire language milestones at about the same time developmentally and in about the same order. There is also evidence associating brain activity and development with language milestones.

- Behaviorists have argued strongly for the nurture perspective, pointing out that reinforcement and imitation may also play a role in language development. While the reinforcement and imitation hypotheses have not been well supported by research, it is important for developing children to interact with skilled language users, as evidenced in the case of the "wild child."

- Research has shown that exposure to language and thus language development varies by socio economic background and level of maternal speech. Children learn morphological rules such as word endings to indicate plural nouns. A critical period for language acquisition is a span of time during which the child is ready to learn a certain aspect of language. Beyond the critical period, learning the corresponding aspect of language becomes difficult or even impossible.

- The unfortunate case of Genie illustrates the critical period for language acquisition. Language development proceeds from babbling in infants, to two-word statements, then to telegraphic speech. These language milestones, achieved usually by age 2, are then followed by structured school education and language rules.

- Two controversial issues on the role of schools in language development are bilingualism and the teaching of reading skills. There is considerable controversy regarding the best way to educate children whose first language is not English. Bilingualism attempts to teach academic subjects to immigrant children while slowly and simultaneously adding English instruction.

- Another controversy centers on the best way to teach children to read. The basic-skills-and-phonetics approach emphasizes that reading instruction should stress phonetics and its basic rules for translating written symbols into sounds, whereas the whole-language approach stresses that reading instruction should parallel children's natural language learning.

## Building Blocks of Chapter 9

### Clarifying some of the tricky points in Chapter 9
### and
### In Your Own Words
*To respond to the questions and exercises presented in the "In Your Own Words" section, please write your thoughts, perspectives, and reactions on a separate piece of paper.*

### *The Cognitive Revolution in Psychology*
An approach that seeks to explain behavior by investigating mental processes and structures that cannot be directly observed is called *cognitive* psychology. The increased focus on the cognitive approach in psychology took place in the *second* half of the 20th century, and this movement is referred to as the *cognitive revolution* in psychology. The cognitive revolution was fueled by the invention of the *computer* in the 1950s and the questions it raised about the processing of information. In recent years, the continued interest in computers has contributed to the development of the field of *artificial* intelligence, the science of creating machines capable of performing activities that require intelligence when performed by people. Human *thinking* involves forming concepts, solving problems, critical thinking, reasoning, and making decisions.

## Concept Formation

*Concepts* are mental categories that are used to group *objects,* events, and characteristics. We have concepts because they allow us to *generalize* from specific objects to many other similar objects. They also allow us to associate *experiences* and objects. Concepts also make memory more *efficient,* and they provide *clues* about how to react to a particular object or experience. Three models of how concepts are structured have been proposed: the *classical* model, the *prototype* model, and the *exemplar* model. According to the classical model of the structure of concepts, concepts are categories of objects that share *defining properties.* The prototype model proposed that we introduce new objects into established concepts based on their similarity of the new object to the *prototype* of that concept.

## Problem Solving

Problem solving is defined as an attempt to find an appropriate way of reaching a *goal* when it is not readily available. The steps of problem solving include finding and framing *problems,* developing good problem-solving strategies, evaluating *solutions,* and rethinking and redefining problems and solutions. Setting intermediate goals is called *subgoaling.*Two general strategies that people engage in while trying to solve problems are heuristics and *algorithms.* Heuristics are rules of thumb that can suggest a solution but do not *guarantee* a solution. A procedure that guarantees a solution is called an *algorithm.* One trap that may be experienced in solving a problem is *fixation,* which is using a prior strategy without considering a new perspective. *Functional* fixedness refers to when we fail to solve a problem because we view it in terms of its usual functions. Psychologists use the term *mental* set when individuals try to solve a problem in a particular way that has worked in the past. Experts differ in various ways from novices in their *problem-solving* skills. For example, compared to novices, experts tend to have a broader and highly organized *knowledge* base, are better at remembering information in their *domain* of expertise, have more effective *strategies* to solve problems, and engage in a conscious effort to *practice* their problem-solving skills.

## Critical Thinking, Reasoning, and Decision Making

*Critical thinking* is defined as thinking reflectively and productively and evaluating the evidence. According to Brooks and Brooks, schools should place greater emphasis on getting students to *expand* their thinking. A mindful person creates new ideas, is *open* to new information, and is aware of more than one *perspective.* One of the main characteristics of critical thinkers is that they ask *good questions.*

*Reasoning* is the mental activity of transforming information to reach conclusions. The process of deriving abstract principles, concepts, or hypotheses from specific observations is called *inductive* reasoning. Reasoning from the general to the specific is called *deductive* reasoning. *Analogies* draw on inductive reasoning. If a student is evaluating alternatives and making choices among them, she is engaged in *decision making* When we make decisions, we are prone to *biases* and flawed *heuristics*. If you seek out and use information that supports your ideas rather than refutes them, you are being influenced by the *confirmation bias*. When we have a hard time letting go of a belief, we are biased due to the tendency of belief *perseverance*. In making decisions, we often tend to be more confident than correct; this is called *overconfidence* bias. Psychologists study the tendency that people have of falsely reporting that they accurately predicted an event, but only after the event has occurred. These psychologists study *hindsight* bias. We evaluate the probability of an event based on the ease with which prior occurrences come to mind; this is called the *availability* heuristic. The tendency to arrive at incorrect conclusions about a person, an object, or an event because of how closely it matches a prototype that we have in our memory is called the *representativeness* heuristic.

## In Your Own Words

*Please write your thoughts, perspectives, and reactions on a separate piece of paper.*
✓ *Stereotypes are concepts about social groups. Explain the role of inductive reasoning and deductive reasoning in the development and use of stereotypes.*

### Language and Thought

Language is a form of *communication* that consists of a system of *symbols*. It allows individuals to produce an endless number of sentences from a finite set of rules, a quality called *infinite generativity*. All human languages are characterized by *four main rule systems:* (1) *phonology*, which is the study of the sound systems of language; (2) *morphology*, the rules of how words are formed; (3) *syntax*, the rules of the way in which words are combined; and (4) *semantics*, which refers to the actual meaning of words and sentences in the language.

The relationship between language and cognition is one that has created significant debate. It is known that *memory* is stored not only in sounds and images but also in words and that *language* helps us think. However, this basic relationship was taken a step further by Whorf, who said that language determines the structure of our *thinking* and shapes our basic ideas. Although the hypothesis is controversial, many researchers would agree that language can influence thought but probably does not *thinking* it. *Cognition* is considered an important foundation for language, but their relationship is not completely interdependent. For example, research has demonstrated that mental retardation (affected cognition) is not always accompanied by poor *language skills*, such as in *Williams syndrome*. Also, studies with deaf children have shown that not having command of written or *sign language* does not affect the ability of the children to engage in *problem solving*. All the evidence suggests that language and cognition evolved as *separate modular, biologically prepared components of the mind.*

Another way of exploring the relationship between *language* and *cognition* is by studying animal language. The debate about chimpanzees' ability to use language focuses on whether they can understand the meaning of *symbols* and whether they can learn the mechanics and rules of language, called *syntax*. While researchers agree that animals can communicate with one another and that some can *manipulate* languagelike symbols, their language abilities do not show the same degree of *complexity* as those required by human language.

### Language Acquisition and Development

Although many theorists stress the biological basis of language, others suggest that language is shaped more by environment and biological factors. Noam Chomsky believes that language is strongly related to biological factors. Chomsky argues that humans are *prewired* to acquire language. Among those who propose that language is shaped by the environment are B. F. Skinner, who argued that language is acquired through *reinforcement*, and Bandura, who proposed that language is acquired through *imitation*.

Language researcher Roger Brown has concluded that a child's ability to learn grammar is not based on reinforcement because parents reinforce both well-constructed and poorly constructed sentences. However, the extensiveness of the language acquired by the child is influenced by the extensiveness of the language used by the parents. Children from middle-income families and professional parents have a *greater (larger) vocabulary* than do children from disadvantaged families. Based on these studies, the following strategies are recommended for parents in talking to their babies: be an *active* conversational partner, talk as if the infant *understands* what you are saying, and use a language style in which you feel *comfortable*. The research on language acquisition illustrates that *biological* and *environmental* factors play roles.

A period in which there is a learning readiness, beyond which learning is different or impossible, is called a *critical period*. After conducting research on atypical populations, Lenneberg concluded that language development during the preschool years is the result of *maturation*. The stunted language development of "wild child" Genie and other similarly deprived children supports the *critical period* hypothesis.

Early language development in infants consists of *babbling*, which even deaf babies do, suggesting *biological* readiness. When children reach 18 to 24 months, they utter *two-word* statements, a capacity described as *telegraphic speech*.

An important debate in many school districts in the United States regards the issue of *bilingual* education, which involves teaching and learning in two languages. One group prefers delaying the mainstreaming of bilingual children until they have mastered their *native* language. This has usually involved from less than a year up to five years of education in the native language before moving on to English immersion classes. Opponents of this approach favor teaching the child in English from the beginning.

Another language issue in education involved reading. The *whole-language* approach stresses that reading instruction should be parallel to children's natural language learning. In this approach, reading is *integrated* with listening, writing, subjects, and real-world activities. The *basic-skills-and-phonetics* approach stresses that reading instruction should emphasize phonetics and the rules for translating written patterns into *sounds* . Research indicates that a *combined* approach is the best strategy.

## In Your Own Words

*Please write your thoughts, perspectives, and reactions on a separate piece of paper.*

✓ *The debate of the relationship between language and cognition is similar to the question of which came first, the chicken or the egg? However, it is a valid question, and in this chapter you are presented with evidence and theories on both sides. Draw a table with two columns. One column is called "language came first" and the other "cognition came first." List evidence and theories supporting each statement in the corresponding columns.*

## Correcting the Incorrect

Carefully read each statement. Determine if the statement is correct or incorrect. If the statement is incorrect, make the necessary changes to correct it. Then check the answer key at the end of the chapter for the correct statement and page reference in the textbook.

1.  Cognitive psychology challenged behaviorism.
2.  The cognitive revolution was prompted by the invention of the electroencephalograph.
3.  Cognitive psychologists use animals as an analogy to explain the relationship between cognition and the brain.
4.  Mentally manipulating information is referred to as *language*.
5.  Concepts are solutions we use to solve problems.

6. In real life, concepts are well defined.
7. The least typical item of a category is used as the prototype.
8. The first step in problem solving is to develop good problem-solving strategies.
9. If you are using a heuristic, you are using a strategy that is guaranteed to solve a problem.
10. Functional rigidity is a term used to describe the situation in which an individual fails to solve a problem by viewing it in terms of its usual functions.
11. According to Brooks & Brooks, schools already spend the right amount of time on teaching critical thinking.
12. A mindless person creates new ideas, is open to new information, and is aware of more than one perspective.
13. Inductive reasoning involves reasoning from general to specific; deductive reasoning is reasoning from specific to general.
14. If you seek out information that supports your own ideas rather than refutes them, you are engaging in the overconfidence bias.
15. People tend to falsely report that they accurately predicted an event; this is called the *availability heuristic.*
16. The tendency to hold on to a belief even in the face of contradictory evidence is belief perseverance.
17. The representativeness heuristic says that we can produce an endless number of meaningful sentences using a finite set of words and rules.
18. Language is based on a system of symbols.
19. Syntax refers to the way words are combined to form acceptable phrases and sentences.
20. Morphology refers to a language's sound system, and phonology refers to the meaning of words.
21. Memory is just stored in terms of words.
22. Thought can direct language, but language does not direct thought.
23. Chimps cannot understand symbols.
24. The idea that language determines the structure of thinking and shapes our basic ideas was proposed by Noam Chomsky.
25. B. F. Skinner suggested that we are biologically prewired to learn language.
26. Telegraphic speech is also known as babbling.
27. To say there is a critical period in language acquisition means that there is learning readiness during a particular period.
28. A child is learning to read using a method that parallels natural language learning; this is called the *whole-anguage approach.*

## Practice Test 1

1. When comparing the computer to the human brain, which statement is incorrect?
    a. Computers perform complex numerical calculations faster than the human brain.
    b. Computers apply rules more consistently than the human brain.
    c. Computers can develop more sophisticated learning goals than the human brain.
    d. Computers can represent complex mathematical patterns better than the human brain.

2. Which of the following was the most important in stimulating the growth of cognitive psychology?
    a. the development of MRI scan
    b. the development of the computer
    c. a study done by B. F. Skinner supporting cognitive psychology
    d. the case of Genie

3. Artificial intelligence systems have been used successfully in all of the following areas except which one?
   a. resolving interpersonal conflicts
   b. playing chess
   c. diagnosing medical illness
   d. evaluating loan applicants

4. The ability to form concepts helps us with all of the following cognitive activities except which one?
   a. generalizing experiences
   b. relating experience and objects
   c. feeling tired after a workout
   d. remembering associations

5. The use of concepts allows us to
   a. avoid the hindsight bias.
   b. extend the critical learning period for language.
   c. make memory less efficient.
   d. make generalizations.

6. You are watching a professional basketball game; most of the players are over 6' 6" tall. You are surprised to see a player under 6' tall. You are surprised because this player does not match your idea of a professional basketball player. Which of the following best describes your experience?
   a. prototype matching
   b. infinitive generativity
   c. syntax
   d. mental set

7. Your text describes the experiences of Fred Smith. who asked, "Why can't there be reliable overnight mail service?" His question represents which problem-solving step?
   a. rethinking and redefining the problem
   b. evaluating the solutions
   c. employing good problem-solving strategies
   d. finding and framing the problem

8. A good strategy for subgoaling is to
   a. work without a specific plan.
   b. work backward in establishing subgoals.
   c. set no more than three subgoals.
   d. work randomly in establishing subgoals.

9. In order to complete your algebra homework, you would be using which problem-solving strategy?
   a. heuristics
   b. trial-and-error
   c. algorithms
   d. subgoaling

10. An algorithm is
   a. a rule of thumb that does not a guarantee a solution.
   b. a rule of thumb that guarantees a problem.
   c. a strategy that guarantees a solution.
   d. a strategy for framing problems.

11. "A paper clip is used for attaching papers together and nothing more." This person is most likely experiencing
   a. inductive reasoning.
   b. mindfulness.
   c. functional fixedness.
   d. hindsight bias.

12. A person who has just used a penny to tighten a screw has
   a. solved an anagram.
   b. overcome functional fixedness.
   c. learned that heuristics can be ill defined.
   d. demonstrated proper use of language.

13. According to Brooks and Brooks, schools should focus more on teaching what kind of thinking skills?
   a. operational thinking skills
   b. heuristic thinking skills
   c. critical-thinking skills
   d. all of the above

14. According to Ellen Langer, a mindful person is characterized by all of the following except which one?
   a. continues to create new ideas
   b. engages in automatic behavior
   c. is open to new information
   d. is aware of more than one perspective

15. Inductive reasoning may be related to
   a. confirmation bias.
   b. analogies.
   c. overconfidence bias.
   d. belief perseverance.

16. A specific conclusion derived from general information involves
   a. representative heuristics.
   b. simulation heuristics.
   c. inductive reasoning.
   d. deductive reasoning.

17. Dwayne just got a promotion to a new department, but he has been told that his new supervisor is a cranky, disagreeable, critical person. According to the confirmation bias, what will Dwayne most likely do on his first day in the new supervisor's department?
   a. He will forget about the things he has been told about his new supervisor.
   b. He will look for positive behaviors on part of his supervisor.
   c. He will tell the new supervisor what he was told.
   d. He will look for negative behaviors on part of the supervisor.

18. "I knew it all along" is an example of
    a.   the availability heuristic.
    b.   the simulation heuristic.
    c.   the representativeness heuristic.
    d.   hindsight bias.

19. The heuristic that involves judging the probability of an event by how well it matches a prototype is the
    a.   availability heuristic.
    b.   similarity heuristic.
    c.   representativeness heuristic.
    d.   subgoaling strategy.

20. A system of symbols that can be spoken, written, or signed is considered a
    a.   transfer set.
    b.   language.
    c.   method.
    d.   signal.

21. According to advocates of bilingual education,
    a.   teaching immigrants in their native language leaves them behind in the workplace.
    b.   teaching immigrants in their native language increases their self-esteem.
    c.   the whole-language approach is flawed.
    d.   the whole-language approach is the best strategy to teach immigrants English.

## Practice Test 2

1.  All human languages have the capacity to create an endless number of meaningful sentences using a finite set of words and rules. This is called
    a.   functional fixedness
    b.   heuristics.
    c.   semantics.
    d.   infinite generativity.

2.  Language is made up of basic sounds called
    a.   morphemes.
    b.   syntax.
    c.   semantics.
    d.   phonemes.

3.  The meaning of words and sentences is called
    a.   morphology.
    b.   semantics.
    c.   syntax.
    d.   infinitive generativity.

4.  How do children convey meaning in their telegraphic speech?
    a.   with the words only
    b.   with rapid expression
    c.   with eye contact and volume
    d.   with gestures, tone, and context

5.  A _____ period is when there is learning readiness for language acquisition.
    a.  critical
    b.  sensitive
    c.  primary
    d.  secondary

6.  Which of the following is true regarding chimpanzees' ability to use language?
    a.  Evidence suggests that chimps can understand symbols.
    b.  Researchers agree that chimps can learn syntax.
    c.  Researchers agree that chimps can use language to create fairly complex sentences.
    d.  all of the above

7.  According to theWhorf's view of language,
    a.  language determines our thoughts.
    b.  thinking determines our language.
    c.  language influences but does not determine thought.
    d.  language can create an endless number of sentences.

8.  Which of the following is NOT one of the functions of concepts?
    a.  They impair memory.
    b.  They allow us to generalize.
    c.  They provide us with clues to figure out how to react in specific situations.
    d.  They allow us to associate experiences and objects.

9.  The _____ model of the structure of concepts proposes that concepts are categories of objects that share all the defining properties.
    a.  classical
    b.  prototype
    c.  exemplar
    d.  biased

10. There are various steps involved in optimal problem solving. Which of the following is the step in which we explain what the problem actually is?
    a.  developing strategies
    b.  evaluating solutions
    c.  framing the problem
    d.  subgoaling

11. A(n) _____ is a problem-solving strategy that involves extensive trial-and-error sessions; all possible strategies are tested until the right one is found.
    a.  heuristic
    b.  algorithm
    c.  mnemonic
    d.  mental set

12. The following factors facilitate problem solving, EXCEPT
    a.  being internally motivated to solve the problem.
    b.  being an expert in the domain of the problem.
    c.  having a mental set.
    d.  being a critical thinker when it comes to the framing of the problem.

13. Which of the following is NOT one of the questions we would expect of psychology students who engage in critical thinking of psychological issues?
    a.    I wonder why that person did that?
    b.    Is there another way of explaining that behavior?
    c.    What is the evidence to back up your explanation of that behavior?
    d.    Which theory of thinking is the correct one?

14. If you conclude that it must be fall because there are a few brown leaves on the ground, you are engaging in _____ reasoning.
    a.    inductive
    b.    critical
    c.    deductive
    d.    confirmatory

15. Ashley claims that she knew beforehand who was going to win an election; she is engaging in the
    a.    confirmation bias.
    b.    availability heuristic.
    c.    representativeness heuristic.
    d.    hindsight bias.

16. Sentences in English that contain double negatives are unacceptable and ambiguous. This is one of the _____ rules of the language.
    a.    phonology
    b.    morphology
    c.    syntax
    d.    semantic

17. According to Benjamin Whorf, _____ determines _____.
    a.    language; cognition
    b.    thinking; cognition
    c.    language; communication
    d.    cognition; language

18. Which of the following is NOT a recommendation of how parents should talk to their babies?
    a.    Talk as if the infant understands what you are saying.
    b.    Do not talk to your baby in a voice different from the one you use with others, such as talking to your baby in a high-pitched voice.
    c.    Use a language style with which you feel comfortable.
    d.    Be an active conversational partner.

19. The following statements refer to the language milestones that humans seem to have. All the statements are true, EXCEPT
    a.    babies babble before speaking.
    b.    until age two, kids can distinguish sounds from many different languages with equal effectiveness.
    c.    a child's first words are usually uttered between age 10 and 13 months.
    d.    telegraphic speech is used around age 2.

20. Which statement best describes reading experts' consensus on the most effective method of reading instruction?
   a. The whole language approach works best for most children.
   b. Reading instruction should focus exclusively on the basic-skills-and-phonetics approach.
   c. The best approach is to combine the whole language and the basic-skills-and-phonetics approach.
   d. The basic-skills-and-phonetics approach works better with younger readers.

## Practice Test 3

1. Joe has a problem with one of the back tires on his car. About every three weeks he finds it low and needing air. Whenever Joe realizes that the tire is low, he stops at the gas station and fills it with air. This strategy is not solving the problem, because approximately every three weeks he has to refill the tire with air. Which of the following problem-solving obstacles is the one affecting Joe?
   a. mental set
   b. functional fixedness
   c. confirmation bias
   d. overconfidence bias

2. Skinner is to _____ as Chomsky is to _____.
   a. imitation; reinforcement
   b. reinforcement; biology
   c. biology; reinforcement
   d. reinforcement; imitation

3. A 15-month-old child pounds the tray of her high chair with a cup and firmly says, "My milk." As a student of psychology, you recognize this use of language as
   a. generative speech.
   b. telegraphic speech.
   c. babbling
   d. the heuristic property of language.

4. When a stand-up comedian makes a joke that requires the audience to understand the double meaning of certain words, the comedian is manipulating the language rules of
   a. phonology.
   b. morphology.
   c. syntax.
   d. semantics.

5. Which of the following statements presents the dilemma presented by the psychology of Williams syndrome?
   a. People with Williams syndrome have a high intelligence, yet they can't communicate effectively with others.
   b. People with Williams syndrome have a good mastery of language, but they cannot relate well to others.
   c. People with Williams syndrome have mental retardation, yet they can use language effectively.
   d. People with Williams syndrome are cognitively very capable, yet their language skills are very limited.

6. According to the _____ model of concept structure, we would have a hard time concluding that a penguin is a bird, because penguins don't fly.
   a. classical
   b. prototype
   c. exemplar
   d. cognitive

7. Which of the following is the problem-solving strategy used by a student who is concerned about the upcoming finals week and makes a list of all the tasks she must complete before that week arrives?
   a. algorithm
   b. heuristic
   c. analogy
   d. subgoaling

8. Henrietta has been struggling with weight loss for many years. She has dieted, exercised, dieted and exercised, done yoga and karate, and even tried one of those all-liquid diets. Of all these approaches, the one that really helped her lose weight was when she dieted and exercised. Henrietta found a solution thanks to the _____ strategy of problem solving.
   a. heuristic
   b. mental set
   c. algorithmic
   d. functional

9. Which of the following is not one of the strategies we can expect experts to use in problem solving?
   a. using their broad and highly organized knowledge base
   b. using their memory skills
   c. engaging in a mental set
   d. practicing their problem-solving skills

10. Which of the following is an illustration of mindfulness?
    a. the office administrator who always communicates with the boss with handwritten messages
    b. the individual who resides in a nursing home and does not make any decisions during the course of a day, since all instructions come from the staff (This person does not have a physical or psychological condition that would impede decision making.)
    c. the person who plans to stop at the supermarket before getting home but finds himself in his driveway, having completely forgotten the planned stop
    d. the student who has always used a PC but tries a Mac to see if it fits her better

11. When a stereotype is established, it usually involves one or two experiences with few members of the group, from which we then generalize to all the members of the group. The creation of stereotypes involves
    a. inductive reasoning.
    b. heuristics.
    c. deductive reasoning.
    d. algorithms.

12. Jonathan, a high school junior, has just been informed by his mom that she won't be able to drive him to school but that Mrs. Schilling (the senior citizen who lives next door) will be driving him instead. Jonathan, simply put, fears for his life. While he has never been in the same car with Mrs. Schilling, he is sure that she is a danger on the road, like all other seniors who drive. Jonathan has a stereotype of seniors who drive, and when he applies this stereotype to Mrs. Schilling he is engaging in
    a.    inductive reasoning.
    b.    mental set.
    c.    deductive reasoning.
    d.    algorithms.

13. Rashid has always been told by friends and family that he is funny, but since he moved to the United States, whenever he tries to make a joke in English he is met with confused faces. Yet, regardless of the inconsistent feedback, he still sees himself as a funny guy. Which thinking bias is Rashid demonstrating here?
    a.    overconfidence bias
    b.    confirmation bias
    c.    belief perseverance
    d.    hidsight bias

14. When news about the tampering of over-the-counter drugs is reported in the media, the sales of such drugs, particularly the brands that were tampered with, tend to drop dramatically. This shift in the behavior of consumers is partly due to the
    a.    hindsight bias.
    b.    representativeness heuristic.
    c.    confirmation bias.
    d.    availability heuristic.

15. Here's a riddle: *A man and his son are in a car accident and are brought into the emergency room. The doctor who is going to attend to the boy says, "I can't take care of this patient, he is my son!" What is going on here?* People tend to take pause at this situation, since it seems that there are two fathers claiming the same son. The solution is simple: the doctor is the mother! Why is this a riddle at all? In other words, which of the following biases is playing a role here?
    a.    hindsight bias
    b.    confirmation bias
    c.    representativeness heuristic
    d.    availability heuristic

16. The observation by Edward Sapir that the Inuit of Alaska have over a dozen words to describe snow has been used to support the view that _____ determines _____.
    a.    thinking; language
    b.    language; thinking
    c.    thinking; cognition
    d.    cognition; language

17. Which of the following cannot be done by a chimpanzee?
    a.    speak
    b.    kiss
    c.    learn sign language
    d.    understand symbols

18. Damage to a certain area of the brain can result in speech impairments; the person may be able to think what he or she wants to say but may be unable to speak. Which area of the brain does this statement refer to?
    a.    Wernicke's area
    b.    the occipital lobe
    c.    the right hemisphere
    d.    Broca's area

19. Which of the following statement is NOT true about the critical periods of language acquisition?
    a.    According to Lenneberg, a first language must be acquired by age 5, or it may not be learned at all.
    b.    The brain plasticity in children has been associated with their ability to learn language.
    c.    Genie, the 13 year-old who had been kept in isolation, was able to learn some rudimentary language after rehabilitation.
    d.    Children with damage to the left hemisphere are able to recover their language skills.

20. A child is trying to tell her mother where the toy that she wants is. She looks at her mother and says, "Elmo there." The child is likely to be
    a.    1 year old.
    b.    2 years old.
    c.    4 years old.
    d.    mentally retarded.

## Connections

*Take advantage of all the other study tools available for this chapter!*

## Media Integration

| NAME OF CLIP | DESCRIPTION | KEY CONCEPTS AND IDEAS |
|---|---|---|
| | | **The Cognitive Revolution in Psychology** |
| Neurons: How They Work | This video clip addresses the role of evolution in the development of the brain and discusses the lower parts of the human brain that are shared with other species. The functions of the cerebral cortex are discussed. The development of neural networks is shown, including animations and video of live neurons under a microscope. Animation is used to illustrate the activity in the synaptic gap. | Brain<br>Evolution<br>Cerebral cortex<br>Neural networks<br>Neurons<br>synapsis |

| Brain Structure and Imaging Methods | This video clip presents the scanning of an active brain as it processes visual information. Applications for brain mapping are discusses. | MRI<br>FMRI<br>Brain mapping |
|---|---|---|
| | | **Concept Formation** |
| Hypothesis Testing | The activity is called "The Nautilus: Exploring an Underwater Maze"; it involves finding clues to get to the surface. Symbols are used in ways that are unusual. This is an exercise in concept formation. The prototype model is compared to classical model of forming concepts. | Concept formation<br>Prototype model<br>Classical model |
| | | **Problem Solving** |
| Solving Cryptograms | Cryptograms are language puzzles in which a code is used. The code involves one letter standing for another, and the key is in finding the patterns. Four cryptograms are presented. Results are given in terms of how many cryptograms were solved and the average solution time. Post-activity analysis questions have participants consider the types of heuristics they may have used in solving the cryptograms. | Cryptograms<br>Heuristics<br>Representativeness heuristic<br>Anchoring<br>Framing<br>Problem solving |
| Mental Set | "Anagrams: A Test of Your Problem-Solving Abilities" is an exercise that explores anagrams that follow heuristics versus those that do not follow heuristics.The work of Abraham Luchins in the | Anagrams<br>Mental set<br>Heuristics |

| | | |
|---|---|---|
| | formation of mental sets is discussed. | |
| | | **Critical Thinking, Reasoning, and Decision Making** |
| Cognitive Functioning in Centenarians | Using the brain has effects on brain connections. This video discusses the relationship between intelligence and experience. Testing of the mental abilities of centenarians is demonstrated. | Brain<br>Centenarians<br>Intelligence<br>Psychological testing |
| | | **Language and Thought** |
| Cultural Variations in Nonverbal Behavior | This video clip presents how the naturalistic observation method has been used to conduct cross-cultural research of nonverbal behaviors. Video of public speakers in London's Hyde Park is used to illustrate how nonverbal language can be used to control audiences and convey emotions and specific messages. | Naturalistic observation<br>Cross-cultural research<br>Sociocultural perspective<br>Language |
| Language of the Face | This video clip discusses the evolution of facial expressions, covering the characteristics of the aggression/anger face, fear face, smile face. Similarities between fear and smile face are discussed. | Evolution<br>Facial expressions<br>Anger<br>Fear<br>Smile |
| | | **Language Acquisition and Development** |
| Brain Lateralization | This interactivity introduces students to the concept of brain hemispheres in a two-part simulation. The first part is a replication of the experiment by Dr. Jerry Levy that explores how emotions are perception and | Brain hemispheres<br>Experiment<br>Emotions<br>Facial expressions<br>Split-brain<br>Corpus callosum |

| | processing of emotions and their corresponding facial expressions. The second simulation involves a split-brain task. The interactivity introduces students to the differences between the functions of the brain hemispheres and the role of the corpus callosum in sharing information between the hemispheres. | |
|---|---|---|
| It's Not What You Say | This interactivity focuses on the nonverbal component of speech, specifically tone and sounds. | Nonverbal behavior |

### Online Learning Center (www.mhhe.com/Santrockp7u)

- Interact and make learning fun!
    - **Interactive Exercises**
        - Solving Cryptograms
        - Mental Set
        - Hypothesis Testing
- Brush up on the Key Terms for this chapter by first reviewing the electronic **Glossary** (in English or Spanish) and then testing your retention using the **Flashcard** feature.
- **"Notes"**—This feature allows you to use the website as you would your text, inserting your own study notes and highlighting areas of particular importance.

### In Your Text

- Found throughout each chapter, the **Review and Sharpen Your Thinking** feature breaks the text into logical chunks, allowing you to process, review, and reflect thoughtfully on the information that you've just read. When going back to *study* the chapter, try reading the feature *before* the section of text to which it relates. In doing so, you will be able to focus your attention on important concepts *as* you encounter them. In this chapter, this feature can be found the following pages: pp. 353, 356, 361, 367, 373, and 381.

### In Your Text

- Test your knowledge of thinking and language by taking the different practice quizzes found on your text's **Online Learning Center** and on the **In-Psych Plus CD-ROM** packaged with your text.


### ANSWER KEY

### In Your Own Words

✓ Why is Williams syndrome of interest to cognitive psychologists? Compose two questions about the relationship between thinking and language that are raised or suggested by the characteristics of this disorder.

*Williams syndrome, a genetic disorder that involves impaired reading and writing but enhanced verbal and interpersonal skills, offers insights into the factors involved in thinking and language.*

*Why do people with Williams syndrome have problems with some aspects of verbal skills but not others? Do people with Williams syndrome think better about social stimuli (people) than they think about other stimuli (a math problem)? What processes are involved in reading and writing that are not involved in speaking?*

✓ Using your own words, narrate the history of the cognitive revolution in psychology. *This narrative should include reference to the dominance of the behavioral view in the first half of the 20th century, how it influenced the definition of psychology, and how the invention of the computer enhanced the creativity of psychologists. It should also make references to the types of questions that were being asked in the mid-1950s and after about psychology.*

✓ Think of a problem that you are currently experiencing. Describe how you would approach this problem using the four steps for optimal problem solving. Consider framing the same problem in different ways, and discuss how following the steps would change depending on the way the problem is framed.
*This exercise is designed to illustrate the importance of critical thinking in the process of framing a problem. Many times people are unable to fix a problem because they insist in framing in a way that leads to no solution. Here is an example. Sue has credit problems and never has enough money. Creditors keep calling on the phone, and she feels harassed. How can she frame this problem? (1) I spend money I don't have; (2) I have too many credit cards; (3) I don't make enough money; (4) Other people make me spend money; (5) The problem is the creditors that keep harassing; etc. Sue's framing of the problem is version #5. Solution? She buys a caller ID so she can screen the calls and not answer if it is a creditor. See, framing makes all the difference!*

✓ Stereotypes are concepts about social groups. Explain the role of inductive reasoning and deductive reasoning in the development and use of stereotypes.
*Inductive reasoning is the process of making decisions about general categories based on information of specific instances. The process of development of a stereotype is consistent with inductive reasoning. We have one experience with a person of another group, and based on that one instance we make generalizations and arrive at conclusions about the whole group to which that person belongs. Once the stereotype is established, deductive reasoning then influences the application of the stereotype. Deductive reasoning is involved when a person makes a decision about a specific instance based on generalizations.*

✓ The debate of the relationship between language and cognition is similar to the question of which came first, the chicken or the egg? However, it is a valid question, and in this chapter you are presented with evidence and theories on both sides. Draw a table with two columns. Once column is called "language came first" and the other "cognition came first." List evidence and theories supporting each statement in the corresponding columns.
*The relationship between language and thinking is an important issue in psychology. Most agree that language (that is, words) plays an important role in memory and thinking, but Whorf suggested that language determines the way we think ("language came first"). Whorf's critics argue that language reflects rather than determines thinking ("cognition came first"). Studies with deaf children and individuals with Williams syndrome have demonstrated that thinking and language are not completely dependent on each other. Interest in studying the extent of the relationship between thinking and language has sparked interest in the use of language by animals. Apes are able to learn sign language; however, questions remain regarding their ability to understand the meaning of the symbols and their ability to learn the rules of language. There is evidence supporting both cognitive abilities in apes.*

## Correcting the Incorrect

1. Cognitive psychology challenged behaviorism. (p. 351)
2. The cognitive revolution was prompted by the invention of the *computer*. (p. 351)
3. Cognitive psychologists use *the computer* as an analogy to explain the relation between cognition and the brain. (p. 351)
4. Mentally manipulating information is referred to as *thinking*. (p. 353)
5. Concepts are *mental categories that we use to group objects, events, and characteristics.* (p. 353)
6. In real life, concepts are *not* well defined. (p. 355)
7. The *most* typical item of a category is used as the prototype. (p. 355)
8. The first step in problem solving is to *find and frame problems*. (p. 356)
9. If you are using *an algorithm*, you are using a strategy that is guaranteed to solve a problem. (p. 357)
10. *Functional fixedness* is a term used to describe the situation in which an individual fails to solve a problem by viewing it in terms of its usual functions. (p. 358)
11. According to Brooks and Brooks, schools *probably do not spend the right amount of time* on teaching critical thinking. (p. 362)
12. A *mindful* person creates new ideas, is open to new information, and is aware of more than one perspective. (p. 363)
13. Inductive reasoning involves reasoning from specific to general; deductive reasoning is reasoning from general to specific. (pp. 363–364)
14. If you seek out information that supports your own ideas rather than refutes them, you are engaging in the *confirmation* bias. (p. 365)
15. People tend to falsely report that they accurately predicted an event; this is called the *hindsight bias*. (p. 366)
16. The tendency to hold on to a belief even in the face of contradictory evidence is belief perseverance. (p. 366)
17. *Infinite generativity* says that we can produce an endless number of meaningful sentences using a finite set of words and rules. (p. 368)
18. Language is based on a system of symbols. (p. 368)
19. Syntax refers to the way words are combined to form acceptable phrases and sentences. (p. 368)
20. *Phonology* refers to a language's sound system, and *semantics* refers to the meaning of words. (p. 368)
21. Memory is stored in terms of *words, sounds,* and *images*. (p. 369)
22. Thought can direct language, and language can direct thought. (p. 370)
23. Chimps *can* understand symbols. (p. 371)
24. The idea that language determines the structure of thinking and shapes our basic ideas *was proposed by Benjamin Whorf.*
25. *Noam Chomsky* suggested that we are biologically prewired to learn language. (p. 373)
26. Telegraphic speech is also known as the *use of short and precise words*. (p. 378)
27. To say there is a critical period in language acquisition means that there is learning readiness during a particular period. (p. 376)
28. A child is learning to read using a method that parallels natural language learning; this is called the *whole-language approach*. (p. 380)

## Practice Test 1

1. a.  no; this statement is correct
   b.  no; this statement is correct, humans have a number of biases that computers do not have
   c.  YES; this statement is incorrect, the complexity of the human brain allows us to plan complex and sophisticated learning goals, something a computer cannot do on its own
   d.  no; this statement is correct

p. 352

2. a.  no; the development of the MRI scan is less important
   b.  THAT'S RIGHT; computers provide information about how the brain might work
   c.  no; in fact Skinner would never support cognitive psychology
   d.  no; the case of Genie is more important in linguistics

p. 351

3. a.  YES; AI systems cannot resolve conflicts between people
   b.  no; AI systems have played chess
   c.  no; AI systems are able to diagnose medical illness
   d.  no; AI systems evaluate loan applicants

p. 352

4. a.  no; concepts allow us to make generalizations
   b.  no; concepts allow us to relate experiences and objects
   c.  RIGHT; concepts do not make us feel tired after a workout
   d.  no; concepts allow us to remember associations

p. 353

5. a.  no; the hindsight bias occurs independently of our use of concepts
   b.  no; the critical learning period is not related to our use of concepts
   c.  no; in fact, concepts make memory more efficient
   d.  YES; generalizations are possible because of concepts

p. 353

6. a.  CORRECT; we use prototypes to decide if something belongs to a category
   b.  no; this refers to one of the characteristics of language
   c.  no; syntax is the way we combine words to form phrases and sentences
   d.  no; this refers to a fixation in a problem solving method.

p. 355

7. a.  no; identifying the problem must occur first
   b.  no; identifying the problem must occur first
   c.  no; identifying the problem must occur first
   d.  THAT'S RIGHT; the problem must be recognized first

p. 356

8. a.  no; a plan is needed
   b.  RIGHT; this is a good strategy in establishing subgoals
   c.  no; maybe, but this can limit our thinking
   d.  no; subgoals must be ordered and logical, not random

p. 357

9. a. no; heuristics do not guarantee a solution to a problem
   b. no; this can be time consuming and ineffective
   c. YES; an algorithm is a strategy that always produces a solution, and this is desired
   d. no; an algorithm is the better strategy
   p. 357

10. a. no; this describes heuristics
    b. no; the problem has already been identified; you don't need to identify again
    c. YES; this is the definition of algorithms
    d. no, asking questions is effective for framing problems
    p. 357

11. a. no; inductive reasoning is reasoning from specific to general
    b. no; mindfulness is similar to critical thinking, which this person appears to lack
    c. YES; functional fixedness is failing to see other uses of an object
    d. no; hindsight bias is thinking that you knew it all along
    p. 358

12. a. no; this is not an anagram
    b. CORRECT; the penny is being used in an unusual function
    c. no; heuristics are rules of thumb
    d. no, this involves a cognitive not a language challenge
    p. 358

13. a. no
    b. no
    c. THAT'S CORRECT; schools focus now on lower skills, not critical skills
    d. no
    p. 362

14. a. no; this is part of mindfulness
    b. YES; a mindful person thinks about what he or she is doing
    c. no; this is part of mindfulness
    d. no; this is part of mindfulness
    p. 363

15. a. no; in this bias we seek out information that confirms our beliefs
    b. GOOD; analogies draw on inductive reasoning
    c. no; in this bias we show too much confidence in our decisions
    d. no; this is the tendency to hold on to a belief when there is contradictory evidence
    p. 364

16. a. no; in this heuristic we use prototypes to make decisions
    b. no
    c. no; inductive reasoning is going from specific to general
    d. YES; this is the definition of deductive reasoning
    p. 364

17. a. no; the confirmation bias would not predict this
    b. no; on the contrary, the bias would say he would seek out negative behaviors
    c. no; this is not the confirmation bias
    d. RIGHT; the bias predicts that people seek out information that fits their ideas
    p. 365

18. a.  no; this heuristic focuses on recalling the frequency of past occurrences
    b.  no
    c.  no; this bias says that we use prototypes to make decisions
    d.  YES; the hindsight bias says that people falsely report an event after it has occurred
    p. 366

19. a.  no; this heuristic focuses on recalling the frequency of past occurrences
    b.  no
    c.  YES; this defines the representativeness heuristic
    d.  no; this is a problem-solving strategy
    p. 367

20. a.  no
    b.  THAT'S RIGHT; this is how language is defined
    c.  no
    d.  no
    p. 368

21. a.  no; in fact, this is a criticism of bilingual education
    b.  CORRECT; also, they claim that bilingual education values others' culture
    c.  no; the whole language approach is an approach to teaching children to read
    d.  no; the whole language approach is an approach to teaching children to read
    p. 379

## Practice Test 2

1. a.  no; this is a type of fixation that interrupts optimal problem solving.
   b.  no; heuristics are rules of thumb that do not guarantee solutions to problems
   c.  no; semantics refers to the meaning of words and sentences
   d.  YES; using finite sets of words and rules, we can create infinite sentences
   p. 368

2. a.  no; all words are made up of one or more morphemes
   b.  no; syntax refers to how words are combined to form phrases and sentences
   c.  no; semantics refers to the meaning of words and sentences
   d.  YES; a phoneme is a basic sound
   p. 368

3. a.  no; morphology refers to word formation
   b.  YES; semantics refers to the meaning of words and sentences
   c.  no; syntax refers to how words are combined to form phrases and sentences
   d.  no; using finite sets of words and rules, we can create infinite sentences
   p. 368

4. a.  no; children convey meaning in other ways besides words
   b.  no
   c.  no; maybe, but this is not the entire story
   d.  YES; in addition to words, children convey meaning in these other ways as well
   p. 378

5. a. THAT'S CORRECT; the critical period is when there is learning readiness
   b. no
   c. no
   d. no
   p. 376

6. a. no; but the answer is partially correct
   b. no; but the answer is partially correct
   c. no; but the answer is partially correct
   d. RIGHT; all have been found
   p. 371

7. a. YES; this is correct
   b. no; actually this is the opposite of what Whorf argued.
   c. no; but this is what the research on Whorf's ideas has found
   d. no; this sounds more like infinitive generativity
   p. 369

8. a. YES; this is incorrect; concepts actually enhance memory
   b. no; this is one of the functions of concepts
   c. no; this is one of the functions of concepts
   d. no; this is one of the functions of concepts
   p. 353

9. a. YES; the classical model is actually criticized because sometimes we include objects in concepts even if they don't share all the defining properties
   b. no; this model argues that we use the most typical case of the category in establishing the concept
   c. no
   d. no; there is no such thing as a biased model of structure of concepts
   p. 355

10. a. no; this takes place after we explain what the problem is
    b. no; this takes place after strategies have been tested
    c. YES; framing the problem is precisely considering different ways in which the problem may be explained and understood
    d. no; this is a type of problem-solving strategy
    p. 356

11. a. no; in this strategy only the most commonly used method is used
    b. YES; an algorithm guarantees a solution because it involves trying all possible strategies
    c. no; a mnemonic is a memory-enhancing device
    d. no; a mental set is an obstacle to problem solving
    p. 357

12. a. no; this does facilitate problem solving
    b. no; being an expert does facilitate problem solving
    c. YES; a mental set is a fixation with solving problems in one particular way and ignoring other ways
    d. no; this is one of the most effective tools in problem solving
    p. 359

13. a. no; this is a good critical-thinking question, asking about motivations
    b. no; this is also a good critical-thinking question, considering more than one perspective
    c. no; this is also a good critical-thinking question, asking for research evidence
    d. YES; this is not a good critical-thinking question, as it assumes that only one perspective must have the right answer
   p. 362

14. a. YES; the person is making an observation about a few leaves and concluding that all other members of that category (leaves) must be getting ready to turn brown and fall; thus it must be fall
    b. no; there is not a concept used in this chapter that is referred to as critical reasoning (not to be confused with critical thinking)
    c. no; deductive reasoning involves making conclusions about specific issues from generalizations that we have in our memory
    d. no; there is not a concept used in this chapter that is referred to as confirmation reasoning (not to be confused with the confirmation bias)
   p. 363

15. a. no; Ashley is not seeking confirmation, she is just affirming that she knew all along
    b. no; in this instance, the availability of the information is not influencing Ashley's certainty
    c. no; in this instance, the representativeness heuristic is irrelevant
    d. YES; this is the bias we have to tend to think and claim that we knew things even when it was impossible to know them
   p. 366

16. a. no; the question does not address the appropriateness of certain sounds in the language
    b. no; the question does not address how correctly the words were constructed
    c. YES; this question addresses the rules of sentence construction; if the sentence contains more than one negative, we may not be able to understand its true and intended message
    d. no; the question does not address the meaning of the words in the sentence
   p. 368

17. a. YES; Whorf proposed that the content of our language determines our capacity to think
    b. no; these two concepts are virtually the same
    c. no; language does affect communication but this is not what Whorf theorized about
    d. no; the opposite is true
   p. 369

18. a. no; this is one of the recommendations
    b. YES; the opposite is recommended; parents should talk to their babies in a way in which they feel comfortable, and that may include using a high-pitched voice
    c. no; this refers to the point made in item b; this is one of the recommendations
    d. no; this is one of the recommendations
   p. 375

19. a. no; this statement is correct
    b. YES; this is incorrect because the universal linguist capacities of a child tend to become more specialized after 6 months of age
    c. no; this statement is correct
    d. no; this statement is correct
   p. 377

20. a. no; this does not best describe the experts' consensus
    b. no; this does not best describe the experts' consensus
    c. YES; a combination of the two approaches is best
    d. no; this does not best describe the experts' consensus
p. 381

## Practice Test 3

1. a. YES; he is trying to fix the problem with the same method that "worked" before, but he is not really solving the problem
   b. no; the issue is not about being able to use the air pump or tire in another way
   c. no; while this could be an obstacle to problem solving, it does not apply here
   d. no; while this could be an obstacle to problem solving, it does not apply here
p. 359

2. a. no; it was Bandura who emphasized imitation
   b. CORRECT; Skinner emphasized reinforcement in language acquisition, Chomsky emphasized prewired biological predispositions
   c. no; close, but it is actually the other way
   d. no; Chomsky focused on biological predispositions
pp. 373-374

3. a. no
   b. YES; short sentences are characteristic of telegraphic speech
   c. no; babbling is repeating sounds and syllables
   d. no
p. 378

4. a. no; this would apply if the comedian were playing around with the sounds of the words
   b. no; this would apply if the comedian were playing around with the way the words are constructed (such as referring to a female doctor as a doctorette—incorrect and for some offensive, but a play with how the words are constructed that some might find funny)
   c. no; this would apply if the comedian were playing around with the way the words are combined; comedians do this often if they are making fun of an English-speaking person who is trying to communicate in another language (for example, by constructing a sentence with Spanish words with English syntax or vice versa)
   d. YES; playing around with semantics is the same as playing around with the meaning of words
p. 368

5. a. no; the opposite is true, they tend to be low in intelligence, yet they can communicate effectively
   b. no; they do have a good mastery of language, but they can also communicate effectively
   c. YES; this is the main issue; their cognitive skills are poor, showing mental retardation, yet they communicate and use language well within the normal range of skills for people without the disorder
   d. no; the opposite is true
p. 370

6. a. YES; the classical model assumes that all instances of a concept (all birds) share all the characteristics of birds
   b. no; this model accounts for exceptions, such as penguins
   c. no
   d. no; all these models are cognitive, but no specific one is referred to as the cognitive model of concept structure

p. 355

7. a. no; she is trying only one approach
   b. no; while this could very well be her common way of approaching this problem, the question is suggesting a more specific strategy
   c. no; she is not using an analogy
   d. YES; she is subgoaling, listing the tasks that she needs to complete to finish the term

p. 357

8. a. no; if she had used heuristics she would not have tried different methods
   b. no; if she had been influenced by a mental set she would not have tried different methods
   c. YES; she basically used an algorithm, trying many different methods until she found the right one
   d. no; we did not discuss a "functional strategy," not to be confused with functional fixedness, which in any case is an obstacle to problem solving

p. 357

9. a. no; this is one of the advantages of being an expert
   b. no; memory of the knowledge domain tends to be enhanced in experts
   c. YES; a mental set may sound like something good, but it is actually an obstacle to problem solving that involves always going back to the same method of solving a problem
   d. no; this is one of the tendencies in problem-solving skills that separate experts from novices

p. 360

10. a. no; this office administrator is being mindless, since there are many other ways of communication (e.g., e-mail) that could be more effective
    b. no; this person is being extremely mindless, since possibly not even simple decisions, such as waking time, are being made by the individual
    c. no; this is also mindlessness, since the person drove in "automatic mode" and forgot a simple plan that was not part of the common trajectory home
    d. YES; this involves mindfulness; using computers involves developing a number of skills, and the more familiar you are with the equipment and interface the easier it is to use; therefore, changing the type of computer used requires being open to new information, being mindful

p. 363

11. a. YES; inductive reasoning involves reasoning from the specific to the general
    b. no; stereotypes are a type of heuristic, but the concept does not fit well in the statement.
    c. no; deductive reasoning is reasoning from the general to the specific
    d. no; using an algorithm in this context would involve meeting as many people as possible before establishing a stereotype

p. 363

12. a.    no; inductive reasoning was involved in the creation of this stereotype
    b.    no; mental set does not apply in this context
    c.    YES; deductive reasoning involves reasoning from the general (the stereotype) to the specific (Mrs. Schilling)
    d.    no; algorithms do not apply in this context
    p. 364

13. a.    no; the overconfidence bias is the tendency to think you are correct more often than could be reasonably expected
    b.    no; this is the tendency to look for confirmation to the belief and this is not addressed in the question
    c.    YES; Rashid is intent in believing he is funny, even when the feedback is inconsistent with that belief (notice that effectively using a second language in a humorous way is likely to require a lot of experience in manipulating the rules of the language)
    d.    no; this bias is irrelevant in this question
    p. 366

14. a.    no; the consumers are not engaging in an "I knew it all along" thinking
    b.    no; the consumers are not making their judgments based on representativeness
    c.    no; the confirmation bias is not influencing this tendency
    d.    YES; the consumers believe that because it was reported in the media that tampering is very likely to happen; therefore, they tend to reduce their consumption of the named product
    p. 367

15. a.    no; while the people figuring out the riddle may later say that they knew it all along, it does not apply to the question
    b.    no; the confirmation bias is the tendency to look for confirmation of beliefs
    c.    YES; the prototype of a doctor for many people is male; therefore, when the riddle mentions a doctor, people tend to immediately get the image of a male
    d.    no; the availability heuristic does not play a role here, at least not in the way that the question was phrased
    p. 367

16. a.    no; the opposite is true, since these findings have been considered consistent and supportive of Whorf's theory that language determines thinking
    b.    YES; this is correct; Sapir was a student of Whorf's
    c.    no; both concepts are virtually the same
    d.    no; the opposite is true
    p. 369

17. a.    YES; while they can communicate, they do not have the vocal mechanisms to speak like humans
    b.    no; they can do this
    c.    no; they can do this
    d.    no; they can do this
    p. 371

18. a. no; Wernicke's area is associated with understanding language
    b. no; the occipital lobe is associated with the processing of visual information (Chapter Three)
    c. no; the right hemisphere is too broad of an area, but in any case, language is associated with activity in the left hemisphere
    d. YES; Broca's area is associated with the production of speech
    p. 374

19. a. YES; actually Lenneberg said that a first language should be learned between 18 months and puberty, a much wider time span
    b. no; this is correct
    c. no; this is correct
    d. no; this is correct
    p. 376

20. a. no; by this time they are usually using single words
    b. YES; by this age they can communicate in this format, also referred to as *telegraphic speech*
    c. no; by age 4 the child is communicating in complete sentences
    d. no; the question does not mention the age of the child; therefore, there is no reference point to diagnose a mental retardation
    p. 378

# Chapter 10—Intelligence

## Learning Goals

1. Describe what intelligence is.
2. Explain how intelligence is measured and what the limitations of intelligence tests are.
3. Identify four neuroscience approaches to intelligence.
4. Evaluate theories of multiple intelligences.
5. Discuss characteristics of mental retardation, giftedness, and creativity.
6. Analyze the contributions of heredity and environment to intelligence.

*After studying Chapter 10, you will be able to:*

- Give the general definition of intelligence.
- Explain how intelligence is measured.
- Compare in general terms the Binet tests and the Wechsler scales.
- Discuss the multiple intelligences approaches of Spearman, Thurstone, Gardner, and Sternberg.
- Describe the uses and misuses of intelligence tests.
- Discuss the contributions of neuroscience to understanding intelligence.
- Discuss mental retardation.
- Explain what giftedness is, including the characteristics of gifted children.
- Evaluate what creativity is, including steps in the creative process, characteristics of creative thinkers, and strategies for living a more creative life.
- Understand the genetic and the environmental influences on intelligence.

## CHAPTER 10:  OUTLINE

- Defining *intelligence* is the source of significant controversy in psychology. In general terms, intelligence is the ability to solve problems and to adapt and learn from experience.

- Research in intelligence has focused primarily on the individual differences and in the ways in which intelligence may be measured. Early psychologists, such as Sir Francis Galton, defined intelligence in terms of simple sensory, perceptual, and motor responses, as opposed to higher mental processes such as thinking and problem solving. Galton's main contribution was that he raised questions about individual differences in intelligence and how it should be assessed.

- One of the first significant efforts to measure intelligence was the work of Alfred Binet and his student Theofile Simon, who developed the concept of mental age to measure the individual's level of mental development relative to others. Using Binet's concepts and calculations, William Stern developed the intelligence quotient (IQ).

- The IQ is a calculation that determines the intelligence of a person by comparing the mental age with the chronological age. If the mental age is the same as the chronological age, the person is assessed at an average level of intelligence. If the mental age is more than the chronological age, the person is said to have an intelligence above average, and if the mental age is less than the chronological age, the person is believed to be below average in intelligence. Binet believed that intelligence was determined by the ability of a person to engage in complex cognitive processes.

- The current version of the original IQ test is called the Stanford-Binet and it can be administered as early as age 2 and through adulthood. It has been revised to assess abilities in four areas: verbal reasoning, quantitative reasoning, abstract/visual reasoning, and short-term memory. Extensive testing with the Stanford-Binet test has shown that the distribution of IQ scores in the population approximates a normal curve.

- Besides the Stanford-Binet, the most widely used intelligence testing device is the Wechsler scales, which in addition to assessing IQ also provides other verbal and nonverbal assessments.

- There are also tests that can be administered to groups of individuals, such as the SAT, which is used to predict success in college education. The SAT has been criticized for the possible effects of private coaching and gender bias.

- On the issue of intelligence testing, psychologists distinguish between aptitude tests, which are designed to predict an individual's ability to learn a skill, and achievement tests, which are designed to measure what has been learned.

- Psychometrists specialize in psychological testing and work on issues such as the development, administration, and interpretation of the tests. Three concepts that are central to the work of psychometrists and that are very important in the testing of intelligence are validity, reliability, and standardization.

- *Validity* is the extent to which a test measures what it is intended to measure and includes content validity and criterion validity. Two types of criterion validity are concurrent validity and predictive validity. *Reliability* refers to the consistency of scores on a test. *Standardization* refers to the development of uniform procedures for the administration and scoring of a psychological test. *Norms* are established standards of performance on the test and are created by giving the test to a large group of individuals who are representative of the population.

- Cultural fairness is a challenge in all psychological testing but is particularly important in intelligence testing, because of the possible consequences of scoring low in an intelligence test.

- Intelligence tests have a history of cultural bias that has resulted in extensive revisions of the tests. Two of the procedures that are done in order to make tests less culturally biased are to use questions that can be equally understood and applied by people from different cultures and socioeconomic backgrounds and to include questions that are not verbal to assess the intelligence of people who do not understand the language of the test.

- The misuse of intelligence test scores can lead to stereotypes and unfair expectations. This information should be used with care and considered along with other psychological assessments, particularly in the academic setting.

- Using the latest technology, research has uncovered various relationships between intelligence and brain characteristics and activity. Regarding the biological basis of intelligence, correlational studies have revealed that a larger brain size is associated with higher intelligence. It has also been found that individuals with higher intelligence process information faster than those with lower scores in traditional IQ tests. Another set of correlational studies has uncovered that high intelligence is associated with faster evoked potential, the electrical activity in the sensory area of the brain caused by external stimulation. Intelligence has also been associated with the patterns of consumption of glucose in the brain.

- Psychologists have long debated whether intelligence is composed of one general ability or a number of specific abilities. Using the statistical procedure of factor analysis,

Spearman developed the two-factor theory of intelligence, in which he proposed that there was a general (g) intelligence and a number of specific abilities (s).

- Thurstone also used factor analysis and concluded that there was no general intelligence; rather, he proposed a multiple-factor theory. According to Thurstone, intelligence consists of seven mental abilities: verbal comprehension, number ability, word fluency, spatial visualization, associative memory, reasoning, and perceptual speed.

- A recent classification of intelligence, proposed by Howard Gardner, includes eight types of intelligence: verbal skills, mathematical skills, spatial skills, bodily-kinesthetic skills, musical skills, interpersonal skills, intrapersonal skills, and naturalistic skills. Project Spectrum is a program designed to apply the principles of Gardner's theory in the classroom.

- Another multiple intelligences approach was developed by Robert Sternberg. Sternberg's triarchic theory emphasizes three essential components: analytical intelligence, creative intelligence, and practical intelligence. Sternberg's approach has also been applied to the classroom, where he recommends that instruction should be balanced with respect to the three types of intelligence.

- Salovy and Mayer have developed the concept emotional intelligence to refer to the interpersonal, intrapersonal, and practical aspects of intelligence. Goleman proposes that emotional intelligence involves four areas: emotional awareness, management of emotions, reading emotions, and handling relationships. The multiple-intelligences approaches have been mostly criticized for taking the divisions of intelligence too far and possibly including abilities that are different from intelligence.

- Extreme forms of intelligence include mental retardation and giftedness. Mental retardation is a condition of limited mental ability (usually an IQ of below 70) and difficulty in adaptive behavior. There are several classifications of mental retardation: mild, moderate, severe, and profound. The two main causes of mental retardation are organic, which involves genetic disorder or brain damage, and cultural-familial, involving no evidence of organic brain damage.

- A gifted individual has a well-above-average IQ and/or a superior talent in a certain area. There are three criteria describing gifted children: precocity, learning in qualitatively different ways from those of ordinary children, and a passion to master. While gifted people tend to be socially well adjusted and excel in their chosen careers, only a few become extremely creative and revolutionary in their domains of interest. This points out that there is a difference between intelligence and creativity.

- *Creativity* is the ability to think about something in a novel and unusual way and to come up with unconventional solutions to problems. *Convergent thinking* refers to producing one correct answer, and this is the type of thinking required in conventional intelligence tests. In contrast, *divergent thinking* produces many answers to the same question and is more characteristic of creativity.

- The creative process can be organized in five steps: preparation, incubation, insight, evaluation, and elaboration; however, as might be expected, creative thinkers don't always follow the steps in order. Creative thinkers share several characteristics such as flexibility, inner motivation, risk taking, and objectively evaluating their creative work. Csikszentmihalyi recommends different ways in which we may all become more creative. Some of his recommendations are being open to new things every day, presenting others with new experiences every day, keeping notes of what surprises you, and following your interests.

- There is specific evidence of a genetic foundation for intelligence. Arthur Jensen has sparked debate with his thesis that intelligence is primarily inherited and that the differences in average intelligence between groups, races, nationalities, and social classes are therefore due to genetics. A concept used to figure out the extent to which intelligence is determined by genetics or the environment is *heritability*, which is a correlational statistic that indicates the fraction of the variance in IQ in a population that is attributed to genetics. The heritability of intelligence by late adolescence has been determined to be about .75, which reflects a strong genetic influence. An interesting observation is that heritability increases with age. Today's experts view intelligence as being determined by both genetics and the environment.

- Intelligence can be modified by providing an intellectually stimulating environment. In the controversial book, *The Bell Curve*, Herrnstein and Murray argue that a large underclass in America is developing that is unable to meet the needs of future employers. In response, psychologists have attempted to develop culture-fair tests since many early intelligence tests were culturally biased. Other debatable differences in intelligence are found when the scores of males are compared to the scores of females.

## Building Blocks of Chapter 10

### Clarifying some of the tricky points in Chapter 10
### and
### In Your Own Words

*To respond to the questions and exercises presented in the "In Your Own Words" section, please write your thoughts, perspectives, and reactions on a separate piece of paper.*

### The Nature of Intelligence

The only way we can study a person's intelligence is *indirectly*. According to the author, intelligence consists of problem-solving skills and the ability to *adapt* to and *learn* from life's everyday experiences. The consistent and stable ways we are different from one another are called *individual differences*.

### Intelligence Testing

Sir Francis *Galton,* considered the father of mental tests, believed that intelligence involved simple *sensory*, *perceptual*, and *motor* processes. In France in 1904, the French Ministry of Education commissioned Alfred *Binet* to create a test to assess which students would profit from a typical school education. Binet worked with the school system. His work led to the development of the concept of *mental* age. In 1912 William Stern devised the *intelligence quotient*. This calculation consists of a person's *mental* age divided by the person's *chronological* age and multiplied by 100. It has been found that intelligence as measured by the Binet test approximates a *normal* distribution, which means that the scores in the distribution are symmetrical, with a majority of cases falling in the middle ranges. The current Stanford-Binet test can be given to individuals from the age of 2 through *adulthood*. In addition to the Stanford-Binet, another widely used series of individual intelligence tests are the *Wechsler* scales. These tests allow an examiner to obtain separate *verbal* and *nonverbal* scores.

### Helpful Hints for Understanding Intelligence
### Helpful Hint #1:

*The Stanford-Binet and the Wechsler scales (for adults and children) are both used today, but the Wechsler more often. Typically, psychologists will choose to use the Stanford-Binet with individuals with below-average IQ. The scores on the S-B assess much lower and therefore can give a clearer picture of what the individual's strengths are.*

Group intelligence tests are more *convenient* and *economical* than individual intelligence tests, but they offer a disadvantage: an examiner cannot establish *rapport* with, or determine anxiety levels of, the subjects being tested. A group test that many students take is the *Scholastic Aptitude Test*. In recent years, a controversy has developed over whether *private coaching* can raise SAT scores. Another controversy is the discovery that some items on the SAT favor *males*.

Psychologists distinguish between tests designed to predict an individual's ability to learn a skill, called *aptitude* tests, and those designed to measure what has already been learned, called *achievement* tests.

*Psychometrists* are people dedicated to the study of the development, administration, and interpretation of psychological testing. Three issues that they study are reliability, validity, and standardization.

*Reliability* is how consistently an individual performs on a test. Reliability can be measured by giving an individual the *same test* on two different occasions. A second form involves giving *alternative* forms of the same test on two different occasions. The extent to which a test measures what it is intended to measure is called *validity*. One way of testing validity is by using two tests for the same quality that is being studied. When the scores on the two measures overlap substantially, it is said that the test has high *criterion* validity. Tests developed with uniform procedures for giving and scoring them are *standardized*. The test constructor also develops established standards of performance, called *norms*.

### Helpful Hint #2:
*Reliability and validity can be difficult to understand at first. Let's say I give you a new IQ test today that I have been developing. Today, your full-scale IQ (FSIQ) score is 110. However, when I give you the same exact test next week your FSIQ is 70. That's reliability (and my IQ test would have none). The question reliability asks is, Can I give you the same test at different times and have you score the same each time?*
*Validity, in contrast, looks at what I am testing. Assume I administer the same new IQ test I am developing. But, I insist that everyone who takes this test does it in a room with the heat is turned up to 105 degrees Fahrenheit. When you score low on this test because you could not concentrate because the room was so hot, that's validity! Validity concerns whether the test is testing what it aims to. A valid IQ test measures IQ, not stress levels.*

Many of the early intelligence tests were culturally *biased*. In response to this problem, psychologists have developed *culture-fair* tests. Two types of culture-fair tests have been devised. One type includes items that are *familiar* to individuals from all socioeconomic and ethnic backgrounds; the other type has all the *verbal* items removed. A single IQ score may lead to *stereotypes* and *expectations* about an individual. The use of intelligence tests as the sole indicator of intelligence is an example of the *misuse* of intelligence tests.

### Neuroscience and Intelligence
Modern neuroscience technology has opened the door for new and innovative research on the biological basis of intelligence. In a study associating the size of the head and brain with intelligence it was found that the *larger* the head and brain, the *higher* the intelligence. Another study focused on reaction time and found that the *speed* at which individuals process information is an important aspect of *intelligence*. At the level of electrical activity in the brain, it has been found that faster evoked *potential* is associated with higher intelligence. Finally, patterns of consumption of energy in the brain have also been associated with intelligence, such that people who are high in intelligence show *increased* energy consumption while resting but use *less* energy when actively processing information than do individuals with lower intelligence. Apparently, they have *more* energy available and also use it *more* efficiently.

### Theories of Multiple Intelligences

Given a number of notable exceptions to the traditional way of defining intelligence as a general ability, a number of multiple *intelligences* models have been proposed. Using *factor analysis*, Charles Spearman developed the two-factor theory of intelligence. In this theory, Spearman argued that we have a general ability, which he called *g,* and a number of specific abilities, which he called *s.*

Thurstone's theory, called the *multiple-factor* theory of intelligence, proposed the existence of seven *primary mental* abilities. A more recent attempt to classify intelligence, proposed by Howard Gardner, suggests that intelligence comprises of *eight* components, including musical, kinesthetic, and naturalistic skills. Project Spectrum is an application of *Gardner's* theory of multiple intelligences to the classroom.

### In Your Own Words
*Please write your thoughts, perspectives, and reactions on a separate piece of paper.*
✓ *Look at Gardner's eight types of intelligences. Give examples of famous contemporary people who illustrate intelligence of each type. Consider people you personally admire.*

Another multiple-intelligences approach was developed by Sternberg, who proposed the *triarchic* theory. According to Sternberg, intelligence consists of three factors: (1) *analytical* intelligence, which is composed of analytical thinking and abstract reasoning, (2) *creative* intelligence, which consists of insightful and creative thinking, and (3) *practical* intelligence, which involves "street smarts." This theory has also been applied in *classrooms*.

A type of intelligence that has received a lot of attention in recent years is *emotional* intelligence, which refers to the ability to monitor one's own and other's feelings, to *discriminate* among them, and to use the information to *guide* how one thinks and behaves. *Multiple*-intelligences theories have been criticized for going too far with the classification and subdivisions of intelligence. Even Howard Gardner criticized the introduction of *emotional* intelligence, as he considers feelings to be out of the realm of intelligence.

### The Extremes of Intelligence and Creativity

Limited mental ability, an IQ score below 70, and difficulty in adapting to everyday life are characteristic of *mental retardation*. Most mentally retarded individuals fall into the *mild* category. The causes of mental retardation include those associated with genetic disorders or brain damage, called *organic* retardation, and those with no evidence of organic retardation, referred to as *cultural-familiar* retardation.

### Helpful Hint #3:
*A diagnosis of mental retardation is NEVER made on IQ scores alone. How well the individual can adapt to and function in everyday life is of primary concern.*

Having above-average IQ and/or a superior talent in one area is referred to as *giftedness*. Despite a commonly held belief, there is no relationship between giftedness and *mental disorders*. Gifted people tend to have positive social lives but are not necessarily revolutionarily *creative* in their domains of interest. Creativity is defined as the ability to think in a *novel* and unusual way and to come up with *unconventional* solutions to problems. With regard to creativity, most researchers believe that it is not the same thing as *intelligence*. Creative people tend to think in *divergent* as opposed to convergent ways. The type of thinking that produces one correct answer is called *convergent* thinking, and the type that produces many answers and is associated with creativity is called *divergent* thinking. The steps in the creative process include *preparation*, incubation, insight, evaluation, and *elaboration*. Some of the activities involved in living a more *creative* life are inviting surprises into our lives, increasing our awareness of our interests, and setting goals and planning how to reach them.

## In Your Own Words
*Please write your thoughts, perspectives, and reactions on a separate piece of paper.*
✓ *Describe one problem and how you have been creative in solving it. Does the example fit the definition of creativity offered in the textbook?*

### *The Influence of Heredity and Environment*

Arthur Jensen sparked controversy with his thesis that intelligence is primarily *inherited (genetic)*. Other experts in the field of intelligence suggest that genetics do not determine intelligence to the extent Jensen thought. The *heritability* factor is a measure of the extent to which intelligence is determined by genetics. One of the criticisms of the use of the heritability factor is that most studies have been done using the traditional *IQ* test. Interestingly, it has been found that heritability *increases* from childhood to adulthood. Other factors that influence intelligence are *environmental* influences and group influences. Among the environmental influences, it has been found that the *more* the parents talk to a child, the *higher* the intelligence of the child. Overall, education seems to *increase* intelligence. Regarding group influences, it has been observed that cultures define *intelligence* differently. Ethnic differences in intelligence were discussed in the controversial book The *Bell Curve* by Herrnstein and Murray. In this book they argued that the *impoverished* in America, who tend to score *lower* in IQ tests, will not be able to meet the needs of most employers.

This book and its implications are strongly criticized by those who consider the traditional IQ test inappropriate to assess intelligence in all *ethnic* groups and socio-economic *classes*. It has also been noted that the gap in scores that Herrnstein and Murray based their commentary on has begun to *narrow,* especially in college, where students of all ethnic groups are influenced by a common environment. Finally, another social aspect that influences intelligence is gender. *Males* are more likely than females to have *extremely high* or *extremely low* scores. Males also tend to score better in *nonverbal* areas and *spatial* reasoning, whereas *females* tend to excel in *verbal* areas.

## In Your Own Words
*Please write your thoughts, perspectives, and reactions on a separate piece of paper.*
✓ *Consider the arguments of Herrnstein and Murray in their book* The Bell Curve. *Write a logical reply opposing their views.*

✓ *Imagine you are a developmental psychologist. You are an expert on the relationship between environment and intelligence. Recently you have been called to Washington, D.C., to give testimony to the Congress on what parents and schools can do to enhance the intelligence of children. List five recommendations you would make to Congress.*

## Correcting the Incorrect

Carefully read each statement. Determine if the statement is correct or incorrect. If the statement is incorrect, make the necessary changes to correct it. Then check the answer key at the end of the chapter for the correct statement and page reference in the textbook.

1.    A person's intelligence can be directly measured.
2.    Intelligence is defined by doing well on IQ tests.
3.    Arthur Jensen used simple sensory, perceptual, and motor responses to measure intelligence.

4. Reliability refers to the extent that a test yields a consistent, reproducible measure of performance.

5. The standards of performance of a test are known as norms.

6. If you take a test that involves uniform procedures for the administration and scoring of it, the test has been normed.

7. Binet developed the concept of mental age (MA).

8. Average mental age scores correspond to chronological age (CA).

9. In a normal distribution, there are a few scores in the middle and many toward the extremes.

10. IQ scores around 100 are considered average.

11. Intelligence as measured by the Stanford-Binet test approximates a normal distribution.

12. Achievement tests can predict if a person can learn a skill.

13. Smaller head and brain have been associated with higher intelligence.

14. Spearman proposed that intelligence is made up of two factors: g and s.

15. Howard Gardner developed a theory of intelligence that describes seven components.

16. A component of Sternberg's triarchic theory of intelligence is musical skill.

17. According to Sternberg, academically smart students usually are those who have high creativity.

18. Naturalistic intelligence refers to a person's ability to monitor one's own and other's feelings and emotions and to use this information to guide how one thinks and acts.

19. Intelligence is determined by genetic influences.

20. All cultures define intelligence the same way.

21. A type of culture-fair test involves removing all verbal questions.

22. Scores on intelligence tests alone are recommended as sufficient information to place a child in a special education class.

23. The sole determinant of mental retardation is below average intelligence.

24. Most mentally retarded individuals can be classified as having moderate mental retardation.

25. Down syndrome is a form of cultural-familial retardation.

26. A person who is gifted has an IQ of 100 or higher.

27. Convergent thinking is an important type of thinking in creativity.

28. Creativity is the ability to think about something in novel and unusual ways.

29. IQ is the fraction of the variance in intelligence in a population that is attributed to genetics.

## Practice Test 1

1. Which of the following represents the least comprehensive definition of intelligence?
   a. being original
   b. having problem-solving skills and the ability to adapt to and learn from everyday experiences
   c. becoming immersed in one's domain
   d. having verbal ability

2. Which of the following is NOT a component of the definition of intelligence?
   a. ability to learn from experiences
   b. problem-solving skills
   c. adapting to everyday experiences
   d. musical ability

3. Galton was one of the pioneers in the study of intelligence. What was his primary contribution to the field?
   a. He developed the first standardized intelligence test.
   b. He established a standard definition of intelligence.
   c. He started the tradition of studying individual differences in intelligence.
   d. He operationalized intelligence in terms of sensory and motor processes.

4. Which of the following theories of intelligence emphasizes the importance of "g"?
   a. Spearman's two-factor theory
   b. Thurstone's multiple-factor theory
   c. Sternberg's triarchic theory
   d. Wechseler's applied theory

5. Intelligence consists of seven factors, according to the theory proposed by
   a. Thurstone.
   b. Galton.
   c. Spearman.
   d. Sternberg.

6. If a person was given an intelligence test, and later given the same test again, the scores on the two test administrations should be close to identical if the test is
   a. reliable.
   b. standardized.
   c. normalized.
   d. valid.

7. When a test measures what it is intended to measure, it is
   a. valid.
   b. reliable.
   c. standard.
   d. psychometric.

8. You want to establish norms for a newly developed test. What would be your most appropriate strategy?
   a. give the test many times to a small group
   b. make sure the test measures what it is supposed to measure
   c. administer the test to a large representative group
   d. write up a series of standardized instructions

9. In terms of intelligence testing, chronological age (CA) means
   a. years in school.
   b. actual age of the child in years.
   c. number of years until school is finished.
   d. predicted mental age of the child.

10. According to the IQ test score calculation developed by Stern, a child with a mental age of 8 and a chronological age of 10 would have an IQ of
    a. 80.
    b. 125.
    c. 100.
    d. 95.

11. If IQ scores form a normal distribution, it means that
    a. the scores are symmetrical.
    b. most scores fall at the extremes.
    c. most scores fall in the middle range.
    d. all scores are below average.

12. Which child would probably perform better on the Wechsler scales than the Stanford-Binet?
    a. ten-year-old Jose, who has spoken English only for the past two years
    b. ten-year-old Austin, who always has high grades in language arts
    c. twelve-year-old Elizabeth, who likes to read and write
    d. fifteen-year-old Tasha, who scored very high on the SAT

13. Which of the following statements about group intelligence tests is incorrect?
    a. Group intelligence tests do not allow the examiner to establish rapport with the examinees.
    b. If many individuals are being tested, group intelligence tests are more convenient and economical.
    c. The Army Alpha Test was the first group intelligence test.
    d. Schools are advised to use group intelligence tests to make special education placement decisions.

14. Which of the following issues has been raised regarding the SAT?
    a. whether there is a correlation between SAT scores and scores on other achievement tests
    b. whether certain items are gender-biased
    c. security issues regarding the test
    d. the effects of computerizing the SAT

15. Which of the following statements is true about Gardner's concept of multiple intelligences?
    a. Gardner's eight intelligences are merely revisions of Thurstone's seven primary mental abilities.
    b. Most experts reject Gardner's concept of multiple intelligences.
    c. The problem with Gardner's multiple intelligences is that they are difficult to apply.
    d. Gardner views each of his eight intelligences as involving unique cognitive skills.

16. Both the ability to analyze the world spatially and musical intelligence are important components in the theory of intelligence proposed by
    a. Thurstone.
    b. Galton.
    c. Sternberg.
    d. Gardner.

17. According to Sternberg, a person who is street smart and gets along well with other people most likely has high
    a. creative intelligence.
    b. practical intelligence.
    c. analytical intelligence.
    d. visuo-spatial intelligence.

18. Which element in Sternberg's theory of intelligence is commonly measured by intelligence tests?
    a. analytical
    b. practical intelligence
    c. creative
    d. all of the above

19. When compared to the correlation of intelligence scores for identical twins raised apart, the correlation of intelligence scores for identical twins raised together is usually
    a. lower.
    b. no different.
    c. higher.
    d. not comparable.

20. According to Jensen, which of the following factors is most important in the determination of intelligence?
    a. culture
    b. genetics
    c. family environment
    d. quality of education

## Practice Test 2

1. The finding that African-American schoolchildren score, on average, 10 to 15 points lower on standardized intelligence tests than do White American schoolchildren indicates
    a. poor standardization of intelligence tests.
    b. cultural bias of intelligence tests.
    c. poor reliability of intelligence tests.
    d. inconsistency of intelligence tests.

2. What do the Raven Progressive Matrices Test and the SOMPA have in common?
    a. Both are entirely nonverbal.
    b. Both represent efforts to develop culture-fair intelligence tests.
    c. Both are designed for children from low-income families.
    d. Both have strict time limits.

3. Down syndrome is associated with
    a. cultural-familiar retardation.
    b. organic retardation.
    c. giftedness in certain, specific areas.
    d. all of the above.

4. If your psychology teacher held up a piece of string, a candle, a match, and a spoon and asked you to find as many ways as possible to involve all these objects in a cake recipe, she would be asking you to use
    a. convergent thinking.
    b. associative convergence.
    c. divergent thinking.
    d. construction intuition.

5. The kind of thinking associated with creativity is called
   a. divergent thinking.
   b. convergent thinking.
   c. critical thinking.
   d. none of the above

6. Which of the following is NOT one of the areas in which we may find a psychometrist working?
   a. using the findings of a psychological test in the treatment and therapy of a person with a psychological disorder
   b. administering group intelligence tests in schools
   c. helping organizations design assessments to help them find the best fitting employees
   d. researching the validity of tests used to diagnose depression

7. Which of the following is not one of the main characteristics of highly creative people?
   a. They can think about something in a novel way.
   b. They think differently to others.
   c. They tend to have an IQ of 120 or higher.
   d. They come up with unconventional solutions to problems.

8. What does mental age mean?
   a. a period of development in which the person focuses more on thinking and feeling
   b. intelligence
   c. the relationship between how old a person is and the level at which he or she thinks
   d. the level of mental development of a person as compared to others

9. Which of the following is NOT one of the areas *extensively* assessed in the Stanford-Binet intelligence test?
   a. verbal reasoning
   b. nonverbal abilities
   c. quantitative reasoning
   d. short term memory

10. The Army Beta Test was one of the first
    a. tests to measure nonverbal abilities.
    b. intelligence tests administered to illiterate individuals.
    c. tests to measure mental age.
    d. tests used to recruit people in the Army.

11. Which of the following is NOT one of the criticisms and controversies surrounding the use of SAT scores?
    a. SAT scores may be improved with private coaching.
    b. There is a gender gap in SAT scores.
    c. SAT scores are not good predictors of performance in college education.
    d. SAT scores are different for men and women.

12. _____ tests are designed to assess the amount of knowledge a person has in his or her memory or the skills that the person has mastered.
    a. Intelligence
    b. Achievement
    c. Aptitude
    d. Mental age

13. The extent to which a test measures what it is intended to measure is referred to as
    a. validity.
    b. reliability.
    c. standardization.
    d. norms.

14. If an intelligence test is given to a 4-year-old and it is repeated when the person is 6 years old, and the results are equivalent or the same, it can be said that that intelligence test has
    a. validity.
    b. reliability.
    c. standardization.
    d. norms.

15. The following are all ways of measuring reliability of a test, EXCEPT
    a. administering the same test at two or more different points in time.
    b. administering alternate forms of the same test on two different occasions.
    c. administering parallel forms of the same test with items and procedures that are similar but not identical.
    d. comparing different tests that are designed to measure the same factor.

16. During middle school and high school years, students take a variety of achievement and aptitude assessments. Students are usually given a limited amount of time and are asked to use a #2 pencil, and there might even be measured breaks, such as 15 minutes between part 1 and part 2 of the test. Children in all schools that administer the test follow the same procedures. These procedures are part of the
    a. validity of the test.
    b. reliability of the test.
    c. standardization of the test.
    d. norming of the test.

17. Which of the following is NOT consistent with culture-fair testing?
    a. including questions that address aspects of everyday life that children should know, such as what time of the year do we rake leaves; the answer: fall
    b. including questions that are familiar to people from all socioeconomic backgrounds
    c. including nonverbal questions
    d. including questions that are familiar to people from all ethnic backgrounds

18. The SOMPA is
    a. a part of the brain that is associated with intelligence.
    b. the Sensitive Overall Multiple Practical Assessment.
    c. a test designed to measure intelligence in children from low-income families.
    d. a system of operations in the brain associated with intelligence.

19. The electrical activity in the sensory area of the brain that is caused by external stimulation is referred to as the
    a. nerve conduction velocity.
    b. action potential.
    c. resting potential.
    d. evoked potential.

20. Which of the following is NOT one of the intelligences proposed by Thurstone in his multiple-factor theory?
    a. verbal comprehension
    b. number ability
    c. naturalistic skills
    d. associative memory

## Practice Test 3

1. In testing intelligence, Galton focused on _____, whereas Binet focused on _____.
    a. higher mental processes; sensory, perceptual, and motor processes
    b. mental age; chronological age
    c. sensory, perceptual, and motor processes; higher mental processes
    d. chronological age; mental age

2. Based on the normal distribution of Stanford-Binet intelligence test scores, which of the following statements is incorrect?
    a. There are more people with an IQ of 100 than any other IQ.
    b. There are fewer people with an IQ of 130 than there are people with an IQ of 90.
    c. There are fewer people with an IQ of 75 than there are people with an IQ of 140.
    d. There are fewer people with an IQ of 70 than there are people with an IQ of 100.

3. The following are examples of what an aptitude test would measure, EXCEPT
    a. a person's ability to apply old knowledge to new situations.
    b. a person's ability to make analogies.
    c. a person's ability to remember the definition of science.
    d. a person's ability to engage in deductive reasoning.

4. If a test designed to diagnose depression is effective and actually measures and predicts well the symptoms of the disorder, it is said that the test has
    a. validity.
    b. reliability.
    c. standardization.
    d. norms.

5. The statistical procedure used in test development that allows researchers to test an extensive number of items and then tells researchers which items are correlated and are clustered together is the
    a. experiment.
    b. factor analysis.
    c. correlation.
    d. IQ.

6. Which of the following types of intelligences/skills proposed by Gardner would be the ones that we can expect Michael Jordan to be very high in?
   a. naturalistic; spatial
   b. bodily-kinesthetic; musical
   c. spatial; bodily-kinesthetic
   d. intrapersonal; mathematical

7. Which of the following statements is NOT true about Gardner's theory of multiple intelligences?
   a. People with autism may be high in one or more intelligence types.
   b. The intelligence types are not associated with brain activity.
   c. Intrapersonal skills have to do with a person's ability to understand himself or herself.
   d. A person with mental retardation may be high on one or more intelligence types.

8. These are descriptions of each of the three intelligences proposed by Sternberg, EXCEPT:
   a. scoring high in the IQ test.
   b. being creative.
   c. having musical ability.
   d. getting along with people.

9. Emotional intelligence, as described by Daniel Goleman, involves four areas. Which of the following situations is NOT consistent with emotional intelligence?
   a. keeping things that bother you to yourself, and then finally sharing them with anger
   b. keeping to yourself some good news that you know may make the other person feel bad
   c. knowing exactly when to stop a discussion because other people are getting upset
   d. being in long-term relationships that go through ups and downs but continue

10. Mental retardation is likely to be diagnosed in which of the following individuals?
    a. James: 14 years of age; IQ of 120; no apparent cognitive deficits
    b. Barbara: 16 years of age; IQ of 100; has a reading disability
    c. Andrew: 18 years of age; IQ of 80; has difficulty when several instructions are given at once
    d. Julia: 8 years old; IQ below 70; has difficulty adapting to changes in everyday situations.

11. Which of the following areas of specialization in psychology is most likely to include research on organic retardation? (This question makes reference to material learned in Chapter 1.)
    a. counseling psychology
    b. social psychology
    c. health psychology
    d. neuroscience

12. Children with cultural-familial retardation have a mental deficit without an organic foundation. Which of the following situations is NOT consistent with this type of mental retardation?
    a. A child with cultural-familial retardation tends to become an adult who is unable to function in society.
    b. Cultural-familial retardation may be initially detected by a teacher during the grade school years.
    c. Giving money to a child with cultural-familial retardation is more effective to get him to do something than giving him a hug.
    d. A child with cultural-familial retardation can get very upset if the teacher does not recognize his efforts in the same way that he recognizes the efforts of others in the classroom.

13. People who are gifted are
    a. highly creative.
    b. more likely to have mental problems than people with lower intelligence.
    c. socially well adjusted.
    d. able to consider many things at the same time, which also makes them less likely to be able to focus effectively.

14. Which of the following questions is likely to encourage divergent thinking?
    a. What is the difference between mental age and chronological age?
    b. How could we use the experimental method to study the differences between human and chimpanzee intelligence?
    c. What is the definition of psychology?
    d. How can we calculate the IQ of a psychologist?

15. Csikszentmihalyi recommends a number of activities that lead to a more creative life. Which of the following activities is NOT consistent with his recommendations?
    a. Keep a diary to make sure that you do all the things that you are supposed to do.
    b. Bring flowers to your secretary for no particular reason (Secretary's Day excluded).
    c. Spend time in places in which you feel creative.
    d. Follow your interests.

16. Which of the following concepts are we less likely to find in a publication of Arthur Jensen?
    a. heritability
    b. genetics
    c. intelligence
    d. reinforcers

17. One of the problems with the heritability factor is that
    a. it cannot be used with the scores of the IQ test.
    b. it quantifies genetic and environmental influences separately.
    c. it is based on the correlation statistic.
    d. it is used to measure the genetic basis of intelligence and other psychological factors.

18. Which of the following is NOT true about the relationship between the environment and intelligence?
    a. Verbal communication between parents and children has a positive correlation with intelligence.
    b. Going to day care has been associated with increases in IQ for children of low-income families.
    c. There is a world-wide negative correlation between intelligence and education.
    d. There is a negative correlation between length of time of being deprived of formal education and intelligence.

19. Which of the following environmental factors has not been associated with intelligence assessments?
    a. ethnicity
    b. workplace
    c. socioeconomic class
    d. gender

20. For which of the following job positions would it be less relevant to test for interpersonal intelligence?
    a. biology teacher
    b. clinical psychologist
    c. engineer
    d. doctor

## Connections

*Take advantage of all the other study tools available for this chapter!*

## Media Integration

| NAME OF CLIP | DESCRIPTION | KEY CONCEPTS AND IDEAS |
|---|---|---|
| | | **The Nature of Intelligence** |
| | | **Intelligence Testing** |
| Reliability, Validity, and Variability | This exercise illustrates the differences between physical measurements and measuring psychological concepts. Participants engage first in measuring depth of water and in a second activity engage in measuring speed of information processing. The roles of reliability, validity, and variance in both physical and psychological concepts are illustrated. | Reliability Variance Validity Reaction time |

| | | Neuroscience and Intelligence |
|---|---|---|
| | | **Theories of Multiple Intelligences** |
| Asperger Syndrome | Asperger Syndrome has been associated with autism; symptoms include impaired and mechanical speech and difficulty understanding emotions and reading facial expressions. This video clip features a sister and a brother who have Asperger and showcases both the functional and dysfunctional aspects of the disorder. | Asperger syndrome |
| | | **The Extremes of Intelligence and Creativity** |
| Beautiful Minds: An Interview with John Nash and Son | This video features a description of the career trajectory of John Nash as well as the list of treatments he has received for schizophrenia. Dr. Nash is described as being able to "at will" move from insanity to sanity. The schizophrenia experienced by his son is also characterized by patterns of recovering intellectual capacity with recurring psychosis. During the interview the son manifests anger and denial, which in many cases of schizophrenia tend to make treatment more difficult. | Schizophrenia<br>Heredity |
| | | **The Influence of Heredity and Environment** |
| Nature and Nurture: The Study of Twins | This video clip presents the case of identical twins who manifest a variety of physical differences owing to unequal nourishment in the womb; however, twins are very similar in a variety of | Identical twins<br>Environmental influences<br>Genetic potential |

| | characteristics, including psychological characteristics such as intelligence and personality. | |
|---|---|---|
| Music and Intelligence | Music instruction and the positive effect it has on cognitive development are discussed. Children that receive training in music show improvements in spatial-temporal reasoning strategies as measured by Stanford-Binet. The parental involvement is important. Music instruction requires several mental processes at the same time, and active participation is the key ingredient. | Intelligence<br>Music<br>Stanford-Binet |
| Intelligence and Racial Differences | This audio clip discusses the achievement gap between racial groups. Wendy Williams discusses how a race gap has been evident since the 1920s. There have been trends across decades of decrease and stagnation of the gap and their signs of progress in the 1970s but the progress has remained stagnant since the late 1980s. Hugh Price, president of the Urban League, discusses how the findings are disturbing and unacceptable. The racial gap is not due to genetics, testing, or socioeconomic variables. An interesting finding has been that in the United States, the gap is lowest at | Racial differences<br>Intelligence |

| | | |
|---|---|---|
| | Pentagon schools. Military schooling and parental involvement, as well as teacher quality may help explain this trend. | |

**Online Learning Center (www.mhhe.com/Santrockp7u)**

- Interact and make learning fun!
  - o **Interactive Review**
    - ▪ Level Analysis: Intellectual Functioning
- Brush up on the Key Terms for this chapter by first reviewing the electronic **Glossary** (in English or Spanish) and then testing your retention using the **Flashcard** feature.
- **"Notes"**—This feature allows you to use the website as you would your text, inserting your own study notes and highlighting areas of particular importance.

**In Your Text**

- Found throughout each chapter, the **Review and Sharpen Your Thinking** feature breaks the text into logical chunks, allowing you to process, review, and reflect thoughtfully on the information that you've just read. When going back to *study* the chapter, try reading the feature *before* the section of text to which it relates. In doing so, you will be able to focus your attention on important concepts *as* you encounter them. In this chapter, this feature can be found on the following pages: pp. 389, 397, 399, 405, 412, and 417.

**Practice Quizzes**

- Test your knowledge of intelligence by taking the different practice quizzes found on your text's **Online Learning Center** and on the **In-Psych Plus CD-ROM** packaged with your text.

**ANSWER KEY**

**In Your Own Words**

✓ Look at Gardner's eight types of intelligences. Give examples of famous *contemporary* people who illustrate intelligence of each type. Consider people you personally admire.
*Gardner's eight types of intelligences are verbal skills, mathematical skills, spatial skills, bodily-kinesthetic skills, musical skills, interpersonal skills, intrapersonal skills, and naturalistic skills. The focus is on contemporary figures who could be good examples of each intelligence type. For some people it is challenging to move beyond the classic examples of Beethoven for musical skills, even if they couldn't tell Beethoven from Mozart. Students are encouraged to think of the people they admire to explore the different intelligences. Interesting examples are Tupac Shakur for verbal skills, Oprah Winfrey for interpersonal skills, and Cirque de Soleil performers for bodily-kinesthetic skills.*

✓ Describe one problem and how you have been creative in solving it. Does the example fit the definition of creativity offered in the textbook?
*Creativity is the ability to think about something in novel and unusual ways and come up with unconventional solutions to problems. Every day we face tasks that could be enhanced by using some creativity, not only by doing the task more effectively but also by making it more enjoyable. The definition of creativity in the book is broad enough to include simple tasks, such as doing laundry, or more life-changing things, such as choosing a career. However, most people tend to*

*think that only the brilliant inventors are creative. For example, stretching out pizza dough under plastic wrap is a creative solution to a messy, often frustrating task.*

✓ Consider the arguments of Herrnstein and Murray in their book *The Bell Curve*. Write a logical reply opposing their views.

*The scientific tone of the arguments in* The Bell Curve *has made this book a must-read among those who oppose an integrated and diverse society. However, there are a number of problems with Herrnstein and Murray's arguments, and they are not that difficult to figure out. Two important points are mentioned in the textbook: (1) The book is based on data collected on the IQ test. All the criticisms of the IQ test weaken the conclusions of Herrnstein and Murray. If the test is not valid (across ethnic groups) it cannot be used to fairly compare different performance between groups. (2) The environments of the groups are fairly similar (all in the United States); therefore, it can be expected that the effect of the environment is going to be weak. The differences between ethnic groups in the United States are more likely than not caused by a history of racism and discrimination that has unequally influenced the access to resources such as optimal education.*

✓ Imagine you are a developmental psychologist. You are an expert on the relationship between environment and intelligence. Recently you have been called to Washington, D.C., to give testimony to the Congress on what parents and schools can do to enhance the intelligence of children. List five recommendations you would make to Congress.

*As an expert, you would want to point out to Congress that there is more than one definition of intelligence and that there is currently a lot of interest in a multiple-intelligences approach. It would be a good idea to emphasize that we need to be aware of how we as a culture define intelligence. However, Congress will most likely be interested in the general definition of intelligence: the ability to solve problems and to adapt and learn from experience. While this ability seems to have a significant genetic component, environmental factors such as socioeconomic class, ethnicity, and culture have been associated with intelligence. You would want to emphasize that testing must continue to develop to be increasingly sensitive and fair in assessments across different social groups. Congress can create and support programs that target different intelligences. They can also create and support programs that expose parents of all socioeconomic backgrounds to ways of enhancing and stimulating early childhood experiences, such as talking to the children. You would also want to emphasize the clear and positive association between education and intelligence.*

## Correcting the Incorrect

1. A person's intelligence can be *only indirectly* measured. (p. 389)
2. Intelligence is defined *as the ability to solve problems and the ability to adapt and learn.* (p. 389)
3. *Francis Galton* used simple sensory, perceptual, and motor responses to measure intelligence. (p. 390)
4. Reliability refers to the extent that a test yields a consistent, reproducible measure of performance. (p. 394)
5. The standards of performance of a test are known as norms. (p. 395)
6. If you take a test that involves uniform procedures for the administration and scoring of it, the test has been *standardized*. (p. 394)
7. Binet developed the concept of mental age (MA). (p. 390)
8. Average mental age scores correspond to chronological age (CA). (p. 390)
9. In a normal distribution, there are *a few scores toward the extremes and many in the middle*. (p. 391)

10. IQ scores around 100 are considered average. (p. 390)
11. Intelligence as measured by the Stanford-Binet test approximates a normal distribution. (p. 391)
12. *Aptitude* tests can predict if a person can learn a skill. (p. 393)
13. *Larger* head and brain have been associated with higher intelligence. (p. 398)
14. Spearman proposed that intelligence is made up of two factors: g and s. (p. 400)
15. Howard Gardner developed a theory of intelligence that describes *eight* components. (p. 400)
16. A component of *Gardner's eight intelligences* is musical skill. (p. 400)
17. According to Sternberg, academically smart students usually are those who have *high analytical intelligence*. (p. 402)
18. *Emotional* intelligence refers to a person's ability to monitor one's own and other's feelings and emotions and to use this information to guide how one thinks and acts. (p. 404)
19. Intelligence is determined by *both genetic and environmental influences*. (p. 413)
20. All cultures *do not* define intelligence the same way. (p. 415)
21. A type of culture-fair test involves removing all verbal questions. (p. 395)
22. Scores on intelligence tests alone are *not* recommended as sufficient information to place a child in a special education class. (p. 397)
23. The *determinants of mental retardation are below-average intelligence, difficulty in adapting to everyday life, and being under 18 years of age.* (p. 406)
24. Most mentally retarded individuals can be classified as having *mild* mental retardation. (p. 406)
25. Down syndrome is a form of *organic* retardation. (p. 406)
26. A person who is gifted has an IQ of 120 or higher. (p. 406)
27. *Divergent* thinking is an important type of thinking in creativity. (p. 408)
28. Creativity is the ability to think about something in novel and unusual ways. (p. 408)
29. *Heritability* is the fraction of the variance in intelligence in a population that is attributed to genetics. (p. 413)

## Practice Test 1

1. a. no; this includes multiple intelligences
   b. no; this is a rather comprehensive definition
   c. no; this includes several intelligences
   d. YES; this is the least comprehensive definition of intelligence
   p. 389

2. a. no; this is a component of the definition of intelligence
   b. no; this is a component of the definition of intelligence
   c. no; this is a component of the definition of intelligence
   d. YES; musical ability is not part of the general definition of intelligence; however, it is included as one of the types of intelligences proposed by Howard Gardner.
   p. 400

3. a. no; he used different measures that were not standardized
   b. no; this was not his primary contribution
   c. YES; he believed that individual differences had to be measured
   d. no; but he believed these processes were at the heart of intelligence
   p. 390

4. a. YES; Spearman's two-factor theory included g (general intelligence) and s (specific intelligences)
   b. no; Thurstone's theory included seven primary mental abilities
   c. no; Sternberg's theory included componential, experiential, and contextual
   d. no
   p. 400

5. a. CORRECT; Thurstone proposed seven primary mental factors
   b. no
   c. no; Spearman proposed a general intelligence (g) and specific intelligences (s)
   d. no; Sternberg proposed a triarchic theory of intelligence
   p. 400

6. a. YES; reliability refers to the extent to which scores are consistent
   b. no; standardization refers to developing uniform procedures for giving and scoring
   c. no; norms are established standards of performance for a test
   d. no; validity refers to the extent to which a test measures what it is suppose to measure
   p. 394

7. a. YES; validity refers to the extent to which a test measures what it is supposed to measure
   b. no; reliability refers to the extent to which scores are consistent
   c. no; standardization refers to developing uniform procedures for giving and scoring
   d. no; this is a reliability examining consistency in scores from two test versions
   p. 394

8. a. no; the small group would not be representative of the entire population
   b. no; validity is important, but it is more a characteristics of a test that a way to norm it
   c. YES; this is done to determine what are the "normal" responses
   d. no; standardization is important, but it will not identify the norms
   p. 395

9. a. no
   b. RIGHT
   c. no
   d. no
   p. 390

10. a. YES; MA/CA x 100; 8/10 x 100 = 80
    b. no; MA/CA x 100
    c. no; MA/CA x 100
    d. no; MA/CA x 100
    p. 390

11. a. no
    b. no; there are few scores at the extremes
    c. YES; a normal distribution is shaped like a bell with few scores on the ends
    d. no; that would not be a normal distribution
    p. 391

12. a. YES; the Stanford-Binet reports just one IQ score; the Wechsler scales report both verbal and nonverbal IQ scores
    b. no; Austin would do equally well on both tests
    c. no; Elizabeth would do equally well on both tests
    d. no; Tasha would do equally well on both tests
    p. 391

13. a. no; this is correct
    b. no; this is correct
    c. no; this is correct
    d. YES; group intelligence testing does not allow decisions to be made about individuals
    p. 392

14. a. no
    b. YES; the issue is whether there are some questions that favor one gender or the other
    c. no
    d. no
    p. 393

15. a. no; Gardner's eight types are very different from Thurstone's seven categories
    b. no; however, more research needs to be completed
    c. no; Gardner's multiple intelligences are being applied in education
    d. YES; this is correct about Gardner's theory of multiple intelligences
    p. 400

16. a. no
    b. no
    c. no; Sternberg proposed the analytical, creative, and practical intelligences
    d. YES; these are among Gardner's eight types of intelligences
    p. 400

17. a. no; this refers to solving problems in innovative ways
    b. YES; this refers to getting along in the world
    c. no; this is related to storing and retrieving information and to solving problems
    d. no; this is one of Gardner's types of intelligence
    p. 402

18. a. YES; this is related to storing and retrieving information and to solving problems
    b. no; this refers to getting along in school and in the world
    c. no; this refers to solving familiar problems in more automatic ways
    d. no; only the analytical
    p. 402

19. a. no
    b. no
    c. YES; this suggests that there is some genetic contribution to intelligence
    d. no
    p. 412

20. a. no; this is an environmental factor, which Jensen downplayed
    b. YES; Jensen stated that intelligence is primarily inherited
    c. no; this is an environmental factor, which Jensen downplayed
    d. no; this is an environmental factor, which Jensen downplayed
    p. 412

## Practice Test 2

1.  a.   no; intelligence tests are very well standardized
    b.   YES; intelligence tests tend to favor certain backgrounds and classes
    c.   no; intelligence tests have good reliability
    d.   no; intelligence tests have good reliability or consistency
    p. 395

2.  a.   no; there is a verbal component on the SOMPA
    b.   YES
    c.   no; both tests can measure intelligence in children from different backgrounds
    d.   no
    p. 395

3.  a.   no; Down syndrome is not due to cultural or familiar factors
    b.   YES; Down syndrome is a genetic condition
    c.   no; people with Down syndrome are not gifted
    d.   no
    p. 406

4.  a.   no; convergent thinking refers to producing one correct answer
    b.   no
    c.   YES; divergent thinking produces many answers and is related to creativity
    d.   no
    p. 408

5.  a.   YES; divergent thinking produces many answers and is related to creativity
    b.   no; convergent thinking refers to producing one correct answer
    c.   no
    d.   no
    p. 408

6.  a.   YES; while the testing may have been done by a psychometrist, the applications in therapy are done by a clinical psychologist
    b.   no; administering and designing procedures for administration of tests is one of the areas in which psychometrists work
    c.   no; psychometrists do work with organizations in designing testing for hiring
    d.   no; this is also one of the most common tasks of psychometrists, doing statistical analysis to study the validity and reliability of psychological testing
    p. 393

7.  a.   no; this is part of the definition of being creative
    b.   no; this is part of the definition of being creative
    c.   YES; this is one of the characteristics of gifted people, but not all gifted people are highly creative
    d.   no; this is part of the definition of being creative
    p. 409

8.  a.   no; in Chapter 4, the chapter on development, no such stage was discussed
    b.   no; mental age is part of the IQ calculation of intelligence, but they are not the same
    c.   no; this is a paraphrasing of the IQ calculation
    d.   YES; this is how Binet defined this concept
    p. 390

9.  a.   no; this is measured in the Stanford-Binet, along with quantitative, abstract/visual, and short-term memory
    b.   YES; while the Stanford-Binet does have a few nonverbal items, this dimension of intelligence is measured extensively in the Wechsler scales
    c.   no; this is measured in the Stanford-Binet, along with verbal, abstract/visual, and short-term memory
    d.   no; this is measured in the Stanford-Binet, along with verbal, quantitative, and abstract/visual
    p. 390

10.  a.   no; this test was administered orally, but still required verbal proficiency
     b.   YES; this test was given to recruits who could not read or write
     c.   no; the Binet tests were the ones designed to do this
     d.   no; the Army tests were administered after the person had been recruited
     p. 392

11.  a.   no; this is a criticism; however, the improvement is minimal
     b.   no; this is a criticism, men tend to outscore women by 42 points
     c.   YES; this is NOT a criticism, because SAT scores do predict the performance of students in college fairly effectively
     d.   no; this is one of the criticisms, especially since the predictions of success of men and women seem to be inconsistent with the actual success of the students in the first year
     p. 393

12.  a.   no; intelligence is more than what this statement is presenting
     b.   YES; achievement tests are similar to the tests you take in a class that are used to measure how much you learned
     c.   no; aptitude tests are used to predict future performance
     d.   no; mental age is an aspect of the measure of IQ
     p. 393

13.  a.   YES; validity is the extent to which a test measures what it is intended to measure
     b.   no; reliability is the extent to which a test yields a consistent, reproducible measure of performance
     c.   no; standardization involves developing uniform procedures for administering and scoring a test
     d.   no; norms are the performance standards for a test
     p. 394

14.  a.   no; validity is the extent to which a test measures what it is intended to measure
     b.   YES; reliability is the extent to which a test yields a consistent, reproducible measure of performance
     c.   no; standardization involves developing uniform procedures for administering and scoring a test
     d.   no; norms are the performance standards for a test
     p. 394

15.  a.   no; this is one of the most typical ways of measuring reliability
     b.   no; this is also another way of measuring reliability
     c.   no; this item is virtually the same as item b
     d.   YES; this would be an approach for measuring validity
     p. 394

16. a. no; these procedures are part of the standardization of the test
    b. no; these procedures are part of the standardization of the test
    c. YES; standardizing the procedures makes the scores comparable
    d. no; these procedures are part of the standardization of the test
    p. 394

17. a. YES; these types of items are the most widely criticized, because the "everyday life" is likely to be very different from children of different socioeconomic and ethnic backgrounds
    b. no; this is one of the ways in which culture-fair tests are developed
    c. no; this is one of the ways in which culture-fair tests are developed
    d. no; this is one of the ways in which culture-fair tests are developed
    p. 395

18. a. no; neuroscience research has not associated any specific part of the brain with intelligence; in any case, the SOMPA is not a part of the brain
    b. no; while the abbreviation fits, this is a made up set of words
    c. YES; the System of Multicultural Pluralistic Assessment is designed to be sensitive to the conditions of low-income children
    d. no; yet another made up set of words; but more importantly, there is no system of brain parts that is directly responsible for intelligence
    p. 396

19. a. no; this is the speed at which electrical impulses are transmitted along nerve fibers and across synapses
    b. no; this is a concept from Chapter 3 that refers to the state of the neuron when it is communicating
    c. no; this is a concept from Chapter 3 that refers to the state of the neuron when it is not communicating
    d. YES; faster evoked potential has been associated with higher intelligence
    p. 398

20. a. no; this is one of the seven factors, along with number ability, word fluency, spatial visualization, associative memory, reasoning, and perceptual speed
    b. no; this is one of the seven factors, along with verbal comprehension, word fluency, spatial visualization, associative memory, reasoning, and perceptual speed
    c. YES; this is one of the eight intelligences proposed by Gardner
    d. no; this is one of the seven factors, along with number ability, word fluency, spatial visualization, verbal comprehension, reasoning, and perceptual speed
    p. 400

## Practice Test 3

1. a. no; the opposite is true
   b. no; these concepts were developed after Galton worked on intelligence
   c. YES; Galton focused on simple processes, whereas Binet defined intelligence in terms of thinking and problem solving
   d. no; whereas Binet developed the concept mental age, Galton did not use the concept of chronological age
   p. 390

2. a. no; this is correct: 100 is the average scored, right in the middle of the range
   b. no; this is correct, 130 is 30 points removed from the center, whereas 90 is only 10 points removed; therefore, there are more with an IQ of 90 than with an IQ of 130
   c. YES; this is incorrect; 75 IQ is 25 points removed from the center, whereas 140 is further away, 40 points removed; this means that there are more people with an IQ of 75 than there are people with an IQ of 140
   d. no; this is correct; see reply for item a
   p. 391

3. a. no; this can be used to predict an individual's ability to learn a skill or what the individual can accomplish with training, the purpose of aptitude tests
   b. no; this can be used to predict an individual's ability to learn a skill or what the individual can accomplish with training, the purpose of aptitude tests
   c. YES; this assessment would be more appropriate in an achievement test, whose purpose is to test what a person has learned—what he or she has in memory
   d. no; this can be used to predict an individual's ability to learn a skill or what the individual can accomplish with training, the purpose of aptitude tests
   p. 393

4. a. YES; validity is the extent to which a test measures what it is intended to measure
   b. no; reliability is the extent to which a test yields a consistent, reproducible measure of performance
   c. no; the question does not address the issue of standardization
   d. no; while the test may have norms, that is not addressed in the question
   p. 394

5. a. no; the experiment is a research method, not a statistical procedure
   b. YES; the factor analysis was used by Spearman in the creation of the two-factor model
   c. no; correlations are used in factor analysis, but the question was addressing a more complex statistical procedure
   d. no; the IQ is a mathematical calculation, but it is not the one referred to in the question
   p. 400

6. a. no; while he may be high in naturalistic skills, based on what the general public knows about him, we cannot conclude that this is true
   b. no; while we can expect him to be high in bodily-kinesthetic intelligence, we don't know of his musical abilities; therefore, we cannot conclude that this is true
   c. YES; both spatial and bodily-kinesthetic intelligence can be expected to be high in such a successful basketball player; spatial skills would be important for the captain of the team to be able to visualize the players during the course of the game and direct the activities on the court
   d. no; while he may be high on both skills, the general public does not have access to this information; therefore, we cannot conclude that this is true
   p. 400

7. a. no; Gardner did argue that this can occur, such as in the case portrayed in the movie *Rain Man*
   b. YES; this is incorrect since Gardner did argue that each of the eight intelligences can be destroyed by brain damage
   c. no; this is a correct definition of intrapersonal intelligence
   d. no; this is one of Gardner's predictions
   p. 400

8. a. no; this is consistent with the analytical intelligence
   b. no; this is consistent with the creative intelligence
   c. YES; this is not one of the types proposed by Sternberg; this type belongs in Gardner's categories
   d. no; this is consistent with the practical intelligence
   p. 402

9. a. YES; this is not consistent with high emotional intelligence; the person is letting the emotion control the communication
   b. no; being sensitive to others, even when it is about sharing good news, is a sign of emotional intelligence—even if it bothers you that the other person cannot share in your joy
   c. no; reading the emotions of others is a sign of emotional intelligence
   d. no; being able to handle relationships and deal with positive and negative situations is a sign of emotional intelligence
   p. 404

10. a. no; James's IQ is above average
    b. no; Barbara's IQ is average
    c. no; Andrew's IQ does not meet the cut-off of an IQ of 70 or below
    d. YES; Julia's case fits the definition of mental retardation
    p. 406

11. a. no; counselors deal with psychological problems that are generally mild in nature and do not engage in the type of biological research that is involved in studies of organic retardation
    b. no; social psychologists deal with issues of social influence and do not engage in the type of biological research that is involved in studies of organic retardation
    c. no; health psychologists work on issues that relate psychological factors with health and illness, but they do not engage in the type of biological research that is involved in studies of organic retardation
    d. YES; neuroscientists are the most likely to engage in the type of biological research required to study organic retardation, the mental retardation caused by a genetic disorder or by brain damage
    p. 406

12. a. YES; this is inconsistent with the findings about individuals with this condition; actually, adults with this disorder tend to become "invisible," which also possibly means that they become integrated into society; perhaps these people don't become doctors, but they may be able to hold jobs and have families
    b. no; cultural-familial retardation is usually detected in school
    c. no; tangible rewards do tend to be more effective with these children
    d. no; children with cultural-familial retardation are very sensitive to what others think about them and their expectations, so they could become upset if they feel that they are being treated differently
    p. 406

13. a. no; this is not true about all gifted people; creativity seems to be different and separate from intelligence
    b. no; the gifted are not more likely to have mental problems than others
    c. YES; gifted people do tend to have positive social lives
    d. no; the gifted have a great ability to focus, even if they have many interests
    p. 407

14. a. no; there is only one right answer . . . and by now you should know it!
    b. YES; the experimental method is a framework for studying issues, but there are infinite combinations of independent variables, operational definitions, and dependent variables that can be studied with that method and on the issue of human versus animal intelligence
    c. no; there is one right answer, with a few variations, but those would not account for divergent thinking
    d. no; we would measure the IQ of a psychologist just as we would measure the IQ of anybody else, clearly taking into consideration that the individual might be more knowledgeable of the methods; basically, though, there is one right answer here also

    p. 408

15. a. YES; while Csikszentmihalyi does recommend keeping a diary, he recommends that the person use it to find new patterns and interests, not as a tool to keep track of "to-do lists"
    b. no; this would qualify as offering a surprise to someone else, and that is one of the recommendations
    c. no; this is one of the recommendations
    d. no; this is one of the recommendations

    pp. 410–411

16. a. no; this concept is central to his arguments that ethnic differences in intelligence are due to genetics
    b. no; this concept is central to his arguments that ethnic differences in intelligence are due to genetics
    c. no; intelligence is the main topic of much of his work
    d. YES; the concept of reinforcers pertains to the area of environmental influences; Jensen discards environmental influences as important, so he is less likely to be interested and dedicate space in his publications to this concept

    p. 412

17. a. no; actually the heritability evidence is almost exclusively based on IQ scores, which turns out to be one of the main reasons of criticism of the concept as it is applied to intelligence
    b. YES; this is a serious problem, because the heritability factor requires two different and separate measures for each of these two components; it basically assumes that they can be separated, and many psychologists argue that genetics and the environment are interdependent and thus cannot be effectively mathematically separated
    c. no; this is correct and is not a problem with the concept itself
    d. no; this is true and not a problem with the concept itself

    p. 413

18. a. no; the more verbal communication between parents and children, the higher the intelligence of the child, so this is correct
    b. no; this is correct
    c. YES; the correlation between intelligence and education is positive
    d. no; the longer a person is deprived of a formal education, the lower the intelligence, therefore the statement is correct

    p. 414

19. a.  no; this has been associated and has sparked significant controversy regarding the validity of intelligence tests
    b.  YES; the workplace, which at least in our society involves adult labor, has not been studied in terms of its possible effect on intelligence assessments (at least no such studies are reported in this chapter)
    c.  no; this has been associated and has sparked significant controversy regarding the validity of intelligence tests
    d.  no; this has been associated and has sparked significant controversy regarding the validity of intelligence tests

p. 414

20. a.  no; teachers are more effective if they are high in interpersonal intelligence
    b.  no; a clinical psychologist should be high in interpersonal intelligence in order to be empathic and effective in therapy
    c.  YES; the engineer is likely to work with others, but the topics are very technical while communications can be simple and straight to the point; it is probably more important for an engineer to be high in mathematical and spatial skills
    d.  no; doctors work with people who are vulnerable and sensitive, since they are likely to have an illness or be concerned about their health; so high interpersonal intelligence is a great skill for a doctor to have

p. 400

# Chapter 11—Motivation and Emotion

## Learning Goals

1. Describe psychological approaches to motivation.
2. Explain the physiological basis of hunger and the nature of eating behavior.
3. Discuss the motivation for sex.
4. Characterize the social cognitive motives and how they influence behavior.
5. Summarize views of emotion.

*After studying Chapter 11, you will be able to:*

- Explain what the concept motivation means.
- Understand why evolutionary psychologists focus on the role of instincts in motivations.
- Discuss the predictions of drive reduction theory and understand the difference between this theory and the optimum arousal theory of motivation.
- Understand the cognitive approach to motivation.
- Explain the hierarchy of needs proposed by Maslow.
- Discuss the biological, environmental, and cognitive factors in hunger.
- Evaluate eating and weight, including ideas about obesity and dieting.
- Compare anorexia nervosa and bulimia nervosa.
- Discuss the biological, environmental, and cognitive factors in sexual motivation.
- Discuss the human sexual response cycle and sexual dysfunctions.
- Understand the concept of sexual orientation and discuss the psychological research on this topic.
- Describe the motivations of achievement, affiliation, and well-being.
- Explain the effects of happiness.
- Understand the emotion of anger, as well as the different positions on the relationship range between catharsis and anger.

## CHAPTER 11: OUTLINE

- Complex human experiences usually involve motivations and emotions that strengthen or weaken those motivations, such as in the incredible case of Lance Armstrong, a story of amazing success after taxing health problems. Motivation refers to the question of "why" we behave, think, and feel the way we do. Motivated behavior is energized, directed, and sustained.

- The Evolutionary Approach. This perspective emphasizes the role of instincts (unlearned patterns of behavior) in motivation. McDougall and Freud are associated with the early instinct theories of motivation. The contemporary view is that instincts do influence behaviors, particularly those behaviors that are common to all members of a species.

- Drive Reduction Theory. This perspective suggests that drives and needs motivate behavior. A *drive* is an aroused state that occurs because of a physiological need. *Need* is a lack or deprivation that energizes the drive to reduce that need. The goal of drive reduction is homeostasis, the body's tendency to maintain equilibrium. This theory has been criticized because many times people act in ways that increase rather than decrease drive.

- <u>Optimum Arousal Theory</u>. Rather than seeking some biologically based balance, the optimum arousal theory says that people are motivated to reach an optimal state of alertness or activation. Consistent with this perspective, the Yerkes-Dodson theory predicts that people perform better at a moderate level of arousal. Also related to this theory is the observation that people differ in the level at which they enjoy and seek stimulation. Sensation-seeking is a motivation to experience new and intense experiences.

- <u>The Cognitive Approach</u>. The previous three perspectives considered some form or another of a biological basis for motivation. The cognitive approach focuses on the rationality and decision-making capacities of humans. Motivations can be intrinsic (based on internal factors) or extrinsic (based on external incentives). For individuals with intrinsic motivation, receiving external rewards may actually reduce their motivation, because of the way in which they interpret the reward. Overall, intrinsic motivation is more effective than extrinsic motivation, particularly if the behaviors are part of complex and long-term goals.

- <u>Maslow's Hierarchy of Human Needs</u>. Maslow's theory views motivation as a hierarchy of needs that must be satisfied in the following order: physiological, safety, love and belongingness, esteem, and self-actualization. Self-actualization is the motivation to develop one's full potential as a human being.

- While these approaches separate biological, cognitive, and social influences, in reality all these factors are interrelated.

- Hunger is a motivation with a physiological basis; a number of processes and substances influence this motivation to eat. Cannon found that stomach contractions are related to hunger. A full stomach stimulates the hormone CCK to signal the brain to stop eating.

- The levels of glucose in the bloodstream and in the liver influence the brain signals that can initiate hunger. The hormone insulin influences the level of sugar in the bloodstream, and thus influences hunger. The protein leptin has been associated with obesity, because low levels of leptin lead to slow metabolism, overeating, and getting extremely fat. In the brain, the hypothalamus has what amounts to an on/off switch for hunger. Brain lesions of the ventromedial hypothalamus cause animals to become obese, while lesions of the lateral hypothalamus cause animals to stop eating.

- The genetic basis of obesity is predicted to be between 25% and 70%. The aging process, which involves a decline in the basal metabolism rate, contributes to obesity. Weight is also influenced by the set point (the weight maintained when no effort is made to gain or lose weight).

- Environmental influences on weight include socioeconomic class and culture. Some psychologists have studied dieting by examining restrained eaters, who are people who chronically restrict their food intake to control their weight. Many people on diets initially lose weight, but many gain it back. Programs that include an exercise component seem to be the most effective in weight loss and long-term effects. While some diets have been associated with health problems, people who diet and keep the weight loss reduce their risks for depression and health problems.

- Eating disorders include anorexia nervosa and bulimia nervosa. Anorexia nervosa, a disorder that involves starvation as a means to continually lose weight and gain control in a stressful life, can lead to death. Bulimia nervosa is characterized by a binge-and-purge eating pattern. While anorexia nervosa is associated with an observable extreme thinness (weighing less than 85% of what is considered normal for age and height), bulimia nervosa occurs in people with a normal weight range, therefore making it harder to detect and diagnose.

- Sexuality is another dimension of human behavior that is motivated by physiological as well as environmental factors. In the brain, the hypothalamus and the limbic system are associated with sexual behavior. Sexual arousal is moderated in the temporal lobe.

- Sexual motivation is characterized by a basic urge-reward-relief neural circuit; the reward element involves the rush of dopamine that occurs during an orgasm and, following the orgasm, the relief experience results from the release of the hormone oxytocin. Sexuality is influenced by hormones, specifically estrogens, which predominate in females, and androgens, which predominate in males.

- According to Masters and Johnson, the human sexual response pattern consists of four stages: excitement, plateau, orgasm, and resolution.

- Cognitive factors such as thoughts, imagery, and interpretation are important in sexuality as well. Sexual scripts influence sexual motivation and are stereotyped patterns of expectancies for how people should behave sexually; examples of scripts include the traditional religious script and the romantic script.

- Our senses and perceptions also play a role in sexual motivation. Pheromones are odorous hormones released in animals that are powerful attractants and aphrodisiacs are substances that supposedly arouse sexual desires and increase sexual capacity.

- Culture also influences significantly the manifestations of sexual motivations and behaviors. Some cultures are sexually repressed, while others are more permissive.

- Psychosexual dysfunctions are disorders that involve impairments in the sexual response pattern, either in the desire for gratification or in the inability to achieve it. Therapies that focus directly on each sexual dysfunction as opposed to traditional psychotherapy have been very effective.

- Contrary to the claims of an extremely permissive sexuality in America, largely based on improperly conducted research, Americans seem to be relatively conservative in their sexual behaviors. The current view on sexual orientation is that of a continuum from exclusive heterosexuality to exclusive homosexuality; the continuum includes bisexual orientation.

- Homosexuality is not a psychological disorder. An individual's sexual orientation is determined by a combination of genetic, hormonal, cognitive, and environmental factors.

- Both hunger and sexual motivations have a strong physiological component; however, many of our motivations do not have such a strong biological basis. Three motivations that have a strong social cognitive foundation are achievement, affiliation, and well-being.

- The motivation for achievement is the desire to accomplish something to reach a standard of excellence and to expend effort to excel. Attribution theory says that individuals are motivated to discover the underlying causes of behavior as they make sense of behavior. Goal-setting, planning, and self-monitoring are studied as important factors in achievement motivation.

- People in the United States are often more achievement-oriented than people in other countries, suggesting that there are cultural, ethnic, and socioeconomic effects. For studies involving ethnic minorities, socioeconomic status is a better predictor of achievement than ethnicity.

- The motivation of achievement plays an important role in the workplace and in sports. To increase achievement, goals should be set that are specific, proximal, and challenging.

- The need for affiliation is the motive to be with other people. There are individual as well as cultural variations in the need for affiliation. The motivation for well-being is subjectively determined, but it involves three factors: wanting to be competent, being able to be autonomous, and having affiliations.

- A positive psychological health can be achieved when the person has a purpose in life, has good relationships with others, feels good about himself, and is able to do things effectively.

- An emotion is made up of affect, physiological arousal, and behavioral expression. The physiological arousal associated with emotions is controlled in the nervous system. As discussed in Chapter 3, the autonomic nervous system is divided into the sympathetic nervous system, which is responsible for quick responses to stressors, and the parasympathetic nervous system, which calms the body.

- The emotion of anger is associated with activity in the sympathetic nervous system. Methods of measuring arousal include the polygraph, which monitors changes in the body believed to be influenced by emotional states to determine if someone is lying.

- Two emotion theories integrate the physiological component: the James-Lange theory and the Cannon-Bard theory. The James-Lange theory of emotion holds that we perceive a stimulus, our body responds, and we interpret the body's reaction as emotion.

- The Cannon-Bard theory suggests that we experience an emotion and bodily changes simultaneously. The amygdala is a part of the brain that controls our experience of fear. It receives danger information and sends out instructions to prepare the body.

- The amygdala is also involved in memory, and it is believed to be an important brain structure in explaining the long-term effects of extreme fear experiences. There is also some degree of hemisphere specialization in emotions. The left hemisphere is associated with emotions such as happiness, whereas the right hemisphere is more linked to emotions such as disgust.

- The two-factor theory of emotion developed by Schachter and Singer suggests that cognitive factors affect emotion. In this theory, emotions are determined by physiological arousal and cognitive labeling, as we look at the external word to explain the arousal and then label the emotion. In some situations, emotions come before cognition. An emotion emerges immediately and automatically as a response to the experience and then we think about the situation, such as when someone screams and scares you. However, in other situations, the way in which we think can determine how we feel about things, such as when a man thinks about a woman, starts by liking her, and then experiences feelings of love toward her. In this case, the emotion followed the cognition.

- Examining the behavioral expression of emotion, Ekman has found six basic emotions: happiness, anger, sadness, surprise, disgust, and fear. Facial expressions may also influence emotions, according to the facial feedback hypothesis. While there are strong universal, biological ties to the facial expression of emotion, there are cultural factors that influence it.

- Display rules are sociocultural standards that determine when, where, and how emotions should be expressed. The master stereotype of gender and emotion is that females are emotional and males are not. Researchers have not found differences between males and females with regard to experiencing emotions.

- In reality, the relationship between emotion and gender is more complex. Emotions often involve social contexts and relationships, and gender differences are more likely to occur in contexts that emphasize social roles and relationships. According to Plutchik, emotions have four dimensions: they are positive or negative, they are primary or mixed, many are polar opposites, and they vary in intensity.

- Another classifying theory is the two-dimensional approach, which focuses on positive versus negative affectivity. Positive emotions are associated with well-being, coping, and the elimination of negative emotions. An example of a negative emotion is anger.

- The psychodynamic perspective and the social cognitive theory have opposite views regarding the role of catharsis in controlling anger. The psychodynamic approach considers expressing anger as a cathartic experience that reduces the chances of future expressions of anger, while the social cognitive approach reports evidence that anger tends to breed anger.

- Some of the techniques recommended to manage anger are lowering the anger arousal by waiting, avoid sulking or getting upset over small matters, and exploring different perspectives. An example of a positive emotion is happiness. Some of the psychological factors associated with happiness are self-esteem, optimism, personal control, close relationships, having work and leisure, and faith. One view of happiness says that it boils down to the frequency of positive emotions and the infrequency of negative emotions.

## Building Blocks of Chapter 11

### Clarifying some of the tricky points in Chapter 11
### and
### In Your Own Words

*To respond to the questions and exercises presented in the "In Your Own Words" section, please write your thoughts, perspectives, and reactions on a separate piece of paper.*

### Approaches to Motivation
*Motivation* refers to why individuals behave, think, and feel the way they do. Behaviors that are not learned and are universal throughout a species are called *instincts*.

*Evolutionary* psychology is particularly interested in the role of *instincts* as the motivations of our behaviors.

A *drive* is an aroused state that occurs because of a physiological need. A *need* is a deprivation that energizes a drive. One theory of motivation suggests that, as a drive becomes stronger, we are motivated to reduce it; this is the *drive reduction* theory. Whereas drives pertain to a *psychological* state, needs involve a *physiological* state. The body's tendency to maintain a balanced equilibrium is called *homeostasis*. One weakness of this theory is that it doesn't explain well why many people behave in ways that increase rather than reduce a drive.

### *Helpful Hints for Understanding Motivation*
### *Helpful Hint #1:*
*Homeostasis is the goal of the drive reduction theory. Our bodies function in a narrow band. A good example is body temperature. Average body temperatures are 98.6 degrees. If you catch the flu and have a temperature of 100.1, you feel lousy, even though it is only 2 degrees different. Your body then works hard to reestablish homeostasis and return your body temperature to 98.6.*

## In Your Own Words

*Please write your thoughts, perspectives, and reactions on a separate piece of paper.*
✓ *Write a narrative of the sequence of events as we establish homeostasis according to the drive reduction theory.*

It seems that some people seek to stimulate their drives, and this may be explained by the *optimum* arousal theory. Consistent with this theory is the Yerkes-Dodson Law, which states that we perform better at a *moderate* level of arousal rather than at a *low* level or a *high* level. One individual difference that also addresses this issue of different levels of preferred arousal is *sensation seeking*. Sensation seekers tend to be motivated to engage in risky activities and enjoy a hedonistic life style.

## In Your Own Words

*Please write your thoughts, perspectives, and reactions on a separate piece of paper.*
✓ *How much of a sensation seeker are you? Describe how your sensation-seeking tendencies (low or high) influence different aspects of your life. For example, how do they influence your preferred activities, way of studying, way of relating to people, foods, music, etc.?*

How we think also plays a role in motivations, illustrated by the different effects of *intrinsic* versus extrinsic motivations. *Intrinsic* motivations involve doing things because we want to do them and we wish to put the effort into them. In contrast, *extrinsic* motivations involve external reasons, such as rewards and the expectations of acceptance by others once the action is performed.

## In Your Own Words

*Please write your thoughts, perspectives, and reactions on a separate piece of paper.*
✓ *Think of all the different behaviors you do in a typical day. Now consider which of those behaviors are intrinsically motivated and which are extrinsically motivated. Write down your reflections, based on your personal experience, on the difference between being intrinsically versus extrinsically motivated.*

External stimuli that motivate behavior are called *incentives*. Abraham Maslow's theory uses a *hierarchy* of needs. According to this theory, the main needs must be satisfied in the following order: *physiological, safety, love and belongingness, esteem,* and *self-actualization*. Three issues are important in understanding motivations: (1) *innate (unlearned) versus learned factors*, (2) *conscious (aware) versus unconscious motivations*, and (3) *internal versus external motivations*. The dimensions of motivations—biological, *cognitive*, and behavior/social/cultural processes—are often interrelated.

### Hunger

Biological factors involved in hunger include *stomach contractions* and *blood glucose (sugar) levels*. The stomach produces the hormone *CCK*, which signals the brain to stop eating. The protein *leptin* has been associated with obesity, because *low* levels lead to slow metabolism, overeating, and getting extremely fat. Insulin causes excess sugars in the blood to be stored in cells as *fats* and *carbohydrates*.

Two important areas of the hypothalamus involved in eating are the *lateral* hypothalamus and the *ventromedial* hypothalamus. The *ventromedial* hypothalamus is involved in reducing hunger, whereas the *lateral* hypothalamus stimulates eating. It has been argued that an important difference between obese and normal individuals is their response to *external* cues. The weight that is maintained without effort to lose or gain is called the *set point*. During adolescence and adulthood, the basal metabolism rate declines, leading to gradual weight increases over many years. Exercise burns calories but also lowers a person's set point and increases the metabolism rate following exercising.

### In Your Own Words

*Please write your thoughts, perspectives, and reactions on a separate piece of paper.*
✓ *Mention ten external cues to eat that you encounter on a regular basis.*

The eating disorder characterized by the pursuit of thinness through starvation is called *anorexia nervosa*. A person who is consistently following a binge-and-purge eating pattern may suffer from *bulimia nervosa*.

### Sexuality

Two parts of the brain have been closely linked to sexual motivation: the *hypothalamus* and the *limbic* system. Also, the *temporal* lobes of the cerebral cortex are involved in controlling sexual arousal.

Sexual motivation is characterized by a basic urge-*reward*-relief *neural* circuit; the reward element involves the rush of the neurotransmitter *dopamine* that occurs during an orgasm; following the orgasm, the relief experience results from the release of the hormone *oxytocin*. The sexual motivation is also influenced by hormones. Sex hormones are controlled by the *pituitary* gland. The class of sex hormones *estrogens* is more prevalent in females, whereas the class of sex hormones *androgens* is more prevalent in men. The pituitary gland monitors hormone levels, but it is regulated by the *hypothalamus*.

As identified by Masters and Johnson, the human sexual response pattern consists of *four* phases. Erotic responsiveness begins in the *excitement* phase; a continuing and heightening of sexual arousal occurs in the *plateau* phase; the third phase is *orgasm;* following orgasm, the individual enters the *resolution* phase. Men are more likely to *quickly* become sexually aroused compared to women. Women are more likely to become sexually aroused by *touch*.

Odorous substances released by animals that are powerful attractants are called *pheromones*. *Aphrodisiacs* are substances that increase sexual desire and sexual capacity.

There are *cultural* differences in sexuality that influence what is considered normal sexual behavior; examples of this are the culture of the island of Ines Beag and Mangaian culture. Sexual motivation is influenced by stereotyped expectancies of how people should behave sexually; these are called *scripts* and include the traditional *religious* script and the *romantic* script

Disorders that involve impairments in the sexual response cycle are called *psychosexual dysfunctions*. Although efforts at treating psychosexual dysfunctions have not been very successful, new treatments that focus directly on each *dysfunction* have led to greater success rates. The drug *Viagra* has helped men with impotence.

Kinsey conducted research on sexual behavior, but his samples were not *representative*. According to a 1994 survey of American sexual behavior, Americans' sexual lives are more *conservative* than previously believed. Many experts in the field of sexuality view sexual orientation as a *continuum*, ranging from exclusive heterosexuality to exclusive *homosexuality*. Some people are sexually attracted to people of both sexes and are *bisexual*. Researchers have explored the possible biological basis of homosexuality by examining genetic, hormonal, and anatomical factors. An individual's sexual orientation is most likely determined by a combination of *genetic, hormonal, cognitive,* and *environmental* factors.

## In Your Own Words

*Please write your thoughts, perspectives, and reactions on a separate piece of paper.*

✓ *As discussed in the chapter, sexual motivation can be influenced by cultural factors, but similar psychological mechanisms can influence sexual motivations at more proximate levels, such as communities, schools, fraternities, etc. In what ways do you think that your own community or school influences the sexual motivations of people? How do these "cultures" develop?*

### Social Cognitive Motives

Three motivations that have a strong social cognitive foundation are *achievement, affiliation,* and *well-being.* Our motivation to accomplish something and to reach a standard of excellence is called the need for *achievement.* People with high achievement motivation take *moderate* risks and persist with effort when tasks become difficult. We are motivated to understand the causes that underlie *difficult* behavior; this is the focus of *attribution* theory.

The best type of goal to set is one that is specific, short term, and *challenging.* People who are ego-involved will focus on how smart they will look and their ability to outperform others. Individuals who set *task-involved* goals focus on their ability and mastery of the task.

In *work-avoidant* goals, the individual will exert as little effort as possible on a task. People in the United States are often more *achievement* oriented than people in other countries. For studies involving ethnic minorities, *socioeconomic status* is a better predictor of achievement than ethnicity.

The need for *affiliation* is the motive to be with other people. The motivation for *well-being* is subjectively determined, but it involves three factors: wanting to be competent, being able to be autonomous, and having affiliations. *Positive* psychological health can be achieved when the person has a purpose in life, has good relationships with others, feels good about the self, and is able to do things effectively.

### Emotion

An *emotion* is a feeling, or affect, that involves a mixture of physiological arousal, conscious experience, and overt behavior. The *autonomic* nervous system regulates and monitors the body's internal organs and processes such as breathing and digestion. When the body needs to prepare for a response to a stressor, the *sympathetic* nervous system is activated. This quick response is sometimes referred to as the *fight-or-flight* response. It is the responsibility of the *parasympathetic* nervous system to calm the body to promote relaxation and healing.

Methods of measuring arousal include the *polygraph,* which monitors changes in the body that are believed to be influenced by emotional states to determine if someone is lying.

One theory of emotion holds that an individual perceives a stimulus in the environment, then the body responds, and the person interprets the body's reaction as emotion. This is *James-Lange* theory. A different view is the one proposed in the *Cannon-Bard* theory, which argues that *emotions* and *physiological* changes occur simultaneously.

The *amygdala,* a part of the limbic system, is involved in emotions. Cognitive theorists believe that both *physiological arousal* and *cognitive labeling* are involved in emotion, as in the two-factor theory. Schachter and Singer believe that after emotional events produce physiological arousal, we look to the *external* world and then *label* the emotion. While some psychologists believe that cognitive activity is a *precondition* for emotion, others believe that thoughts are the *result* of emotions.

Although much of the interest in emotion has focused on physiological and cognitive factors, emotions also have a *behavioral* component. Ekman's research has shown that the facial expressions of basic emotions are *universal* across cultures and include *happiness, anger, sadness, surprise, fear,* and *disgust*.

According to *facial feedback* theory, expressions influence emotions as much as emotions influence expressions. The *display rules* for emotion are not universal and determine when, where, and how emotions are expressed. The *master* stereotype suggests that females are more emotional than males. Researchers have found that females and males generally are *alike* in the way they experience emotion. Female-male differences in emotion are more likely to occur in contexts that highlight social roles and relationships.

According to Plutchik, emotions have four dimensions: (1) they are *positive or negative*, (2) they are *primary or mixed*, (3) *many are opposites*, and (4) *they vary in intensity*. Plutchik believes that some emotions, such as happiness and disgust, are *primary* emotions that can be mixed to form all other emotions.

Another classifying theory is the two-dimensional approach, which focuses on *positive* versus *negative* affectivity. *Positive* emotions are associated with well-being, coping, and the elimination of negative emotions. Research on lottery winners has indicated that having more money *does not* lead to greater happiness.

According to Diener, happiness is a reflection of the frequency of *positive* emotions and the infrequency of *negative* emotions. The release of anger by directly or vicariously engaging in anger or aggression is called *catharsis*. The psychodynamic catharsis hypothesis states that behaving angrily or watching others do so *reduces* subsequent anger. Although *psychoanalytic* theory promotes catharsis, social cognitive theory argues against this view.

Research has not supported the power of catharsis to reduce anger. Some recommended ways of controlling anger include (1) waiting, (2) coping with anger in other ways, (3) forming a self-help group, (4) taking action to help others, and (5) breaking out of your usual perspective.

### In Your Own Words

*Please write your thoughts, perspectives, and reactions on a separate piece of paper.*

✓ *In general terms, how happy are you? Use Diener's definition of happiness to estimate and interpret the current level of happiness in your life.*

## Correcting the Incorrect

Carefully read each statement. Determine if the statement is correct or incorrect. If the statement is incorrect, make the necessary changes to correct it. Then check the answer key at the end of the chapter for the correct statement and page reference in the textbook.

1. Motivated behavior is energized, directed, and instinctual.
2. Ekman argued that all human behavior involves instincts.
3. A need is an aroused state.
4. As a drive becomes stronger, we are motivated to reduce it.
5. A drive involves a psychological state, whereas a need involves an emotional state.
6. Self-actualization is found at the peak of Maslow's hierarchy of needs.
7. When the lateral hypothalamus of a rat is stimulated, the rat stops eating.
8. The set point is fixed and cannot be modified.
9. Few people with anorexia nervosa grow up in families with high achievement demands.

10. Estrogens include testosterone and are produced by the testes.
11. Hormones are more important in human females than human males with regard to sexual behavior.
12. Activity in the hypothalamus is associated with both hunger and sexual motivations.
13. Pheromones are substances that arouse a person's sexual desire and capacity for sexual activity.
14. In the romantic script for sexual behavior, sex is synonymous with lust.
15. The four phases of the human sexual response pattern are excitement, plateau, orgasm, and self-actualization.
16. Sexual orientation is best understood as an either/or proposition.
17. The need for affiliation refers to the desire to accomplish something, to reach a standard of excellence, and to expend effort to excel.
18. Emotion has three components: affect, behavioral, and physiological.
19. If you think someone is following you back to the dorm on a dark night, your parasympathetic nervous system is probably very active in preparing you for the fight-or-flight response.
20. The Yerkes-Dodson theory states that performance is best under conditions of low rather than moderate or high arousal.
21. In the James-Lange theory of emotion, emotion occurs after physiological reaction.
22. In the Cannon-Bard theory of emotion, physiological reaction occurs after emotion.
23. The two-factor theory states that physiological arousal and cognitive labeling determine emotion.
24. The facial feedback hypothesis predicts that happiness makes people smile.
25. Display rules are physiological standards of when, where, and how emotions are expressed.
26. Plutchik suggested that emotions have six dimensions.
27. According to the wheel model of emotion, some emotions are primary and can be mixed with others to form all other emotions.
28. Anger can be understood by examining the frequency of positive emotions and frequency of negative emotions.
29. An effective way to deal with anger is catharsis.
30. Well-being is objective and has three factors: competence, autonomy, and affiliation.

## Practice Test 1

1. "The question of why individuals behave, think, and feel the way they do" defines
   a. motivation.
   b. instinct.
   c. emotion.
   d. drive.

2. Psychologists who focus upon why people and organisms do what they do are studying
   a. association.
   b. cognition.
   c. emotion.
   d. motivation.

3. Which aspect of motivation was supported by Darwin and Freud?
   a. drives
   b. instincts
   c. needs
   d. incentives

4. A need is to a physiological state as a drive is to a(n)
   a. innate state.
   b. psychological state.
   c. physical state.
   d. biological state.

5. Which of the following is an example of homeostasis?
   a. An organism in pain cries out loudly.
   b. A cold organism shivers to reduce heat loss.
   c. A fearful organism huddles in the corner and cries.
   d. Two friends who have been separated for months greet each other with hugs.

6. The highest and most elusive of needs, according to Maslow, is
   a. self-esteem.
   b. self-actualization.
   c. love and belongingness.
   d. safety.

7. Which intervention would cause a rat to become obese?
   a. destroy the ventromedial hypothalamus
   b. stimulate the ventromedial hypothalamus
   c. enhance the ventromedial hypothalamus
   d. stimulate the mid-sagittal hippocampus

8. The minimal amount of energy an individual uses in a resting state is referred to as the
   a. set point
   b. basal metabolism rate
   c. gastric signals for hunger
   d. homeostasis

9. People's ability to control their sexual behavior relates most strongly to
   a. sensory factors.
   b. perceptual factors.
   c. social factors.
   d. cognitive factors.

10. A man is more likely than a woman to link sexual intercourse with
   a. love.
   b. conquest.
   c. commitment.
   d. attachment.

11. The treatment of sexual dysfunctions has been largely
   a. successful using traditional forms of psychotherapy.
   b. successful using treatments that focus directly on the dysfunction.
   c. unsuccessful regardless of the treatment.
   d. successful when they are treated as personality disorders.

12.    _____ is a drug that is designed to treat impotence.
    a.    Viagra
    b.    Prozac
    c.    Rogaine
    d.    none of the above

13.    If male homosexuals are given androgens, their sexual
    a.    desire for males decreases.
    b.    orientation changes.
    c.    orientation does not change.
    d.    desire for females increases.

14.    The desire to do a job well for its own sake is called
    a.    extrinsic motivation.
    b.    intrinsic motivation.
    c.    the Yerkes-Dodson law.
    d.    the Cannon-Bard theory.

15.    When both ethnicity and socioeconomic status are taken into account, the best predictor of achievement is
    a.    race.
    b.    socioeconomic status.
    c.    ethnicity.
    d.    none of the above

16.    Emotion is defined as
    a.    a feeling that involves physiological arousal, conscious experience, and behavioral expression.
    b.    a feeling that involves physiological arousal.
    c.    physiological arousal.
    d.    behavior that involves facial expressions.

17.    According to the Yerkes-Dodson theory, your performance on an exam will be best if you are
    a.    extremely aroused.
    b.    minimally aroused.
    c.    moderately aroused.
    d.    extremely happy.

18.    According to the James-Lange theory, an environmental stimulus
    a.    is perceived as emotional by the hypothalamus.
    b.    triggers emotional arousal, which is labeled by the brain.
    c.    is emotional because of cultural and social expectations.
    d.    causes arousal if it appears threatening.

19.    According to Schachter and Singer, the specific emotion we experience depends on the
    a.    rate of firing of fibers leading from the hypothalamus to the neocortex.
    b.    amount of serotonin released in the peripheral nervous system.
    c.    specific pattern of heart rate, blood pressure, and skin resistance.
    d.    environmental circumstances to which we attribute our arousal.

20. The Cannon-Bard theory predicts that after witnessing a shocking event, a person will
    a. first experience shock and then be motivated to turn away.
    b. be motivated to turn away and then will experience shock.
    c. experience cathartic shock as a release of anxiety.
    d. experience physical and emotional reactions simultaneously.

## Practice Test 2

1. When first-graders work hard on a project in order to collect praise and gold stars from their teacher, what kind of motivation are they demonstrating?
    a. achievement motivation
    b. competence motivation
    c. extrinsic motivation
    d. intrinsic motivation

2. Researchers have found universality in each of the following, EXCEPT
    a. facial expressions of happiness.
    b. facial expressions of fear.
    c. facial expressions of surprise.
    d. facial expression of contentment.

3. Bill was raised to believe that males should not cry in public except at an immediate relative's funeral, and he adheres strictly to these
    a. facial feedbacks.
    b. display rules.
    c. stereotypes.
    d. set points.

4. Plutchik suggests that our emotions can be classified according to four dimensions. Which of the following is not one of the four?
    a. Emotions are primary or mixed.
    b. Emotions are strong or weak.
    c. Emotions are bright or dull.
    d. Emotions are positive or negative.

5. According to Plutchik, mixing primary emotions leads to
    a. psychological difficulties.
    b. polar opposites.
    c. other emotions.
    d. negative emotions.

6. Anthony expected to get a nice raise after having had the most sales in his department for the past year. When Anthony found out the amount of his raise, he considered it "unfair." Anthony was most likely
    a. sad.
    b. happy.
    c. satisfied.
    d. angry.

7.  Which of the following is NOT one of the characteristics of motivated behavior?
    a.  energized
    b.  directed
    c.  sustained
    d.  random

8.  Which of the following theories of motivation predicts that a person drinks water because she has an uncomfortable lack of fluids in her body?
    a.  optimum arousal theory
    b.  the cognitive approach
    c.  drive reduction theory
    d.  hierarchy of human needs

9.  The deprivation that energizes the drive to eliminate or reduce the deprivation is referred as a(n)
    a.  instinct.
    b.  drive.
    c.  homeostasis.
    d.  need.

10. A sensation seeker is likely to be motivated to engage in the following behaviors, EXCEPT
    a.  watching TV for hours every night.
    b.  eating crunchy and spicy nachos.
    c.  working as a police officer.
    d.  participating in the Eco-Challenge (an extreme reality TV show).

11. Which of the following perspectives on motivation is the one that focuses on a person's ability to choose which behaviors they want to do?
    a.  drive reduction theory
    b.  evolutionary theory
    c.  optimum arousal theory
    d.  the cognitive approach

12. Which of the following is NOT an example of an extrinsic motivator to do a house chore?
    a.  the smile of a mother
    b.  the desire to do it
    c.  they keys to the parents' car
    d.  the allowance

13. Self-generated goals are important motivators. The following are examples of self-generated goals, EXCEPT
    a.  restoring homeostasis.
    b.  life tasks.
    c.  personal projects.
    d.  personal strivings.

14. The second level of needs in Maslow's hierarchy involves concerns with
    a.  love and belongingness.
    b.  self-actualization.
    c.  safety.
    d.  esteem.

15. Which of the following is NOT one of the three main issues in the studies of motivation?
    a. internal versus external motivations
    b. unlearned versus learned motivations
    c. conscious versus unconscious motivations
    d. behavioral vesus observable motivations

16. Which of the following biological factors is NOT associated with an increase in the hunger motivation?
    a. insulin injections
    b. the release of the hormone cholecystokinin (CCK)
    c. low levels of glucose in the brain
    d. low or no production of leptin

17. All of the following are symptoms of bulimia nervosa, EXCEPT
    a. extreme loss of weight.
    b. a binge-and-purge eating pattern.
    c. strong fear of becoming overweight.
    d. depression.

18. Oysters are believed to induce sexual motivations. In other words, oysters are believed to be
    a. hormonal.
    b. a cultural factor of sexuality.
    c. aphrodisiacs.
    d. pheromones.

19. The following factors are associated with happiness, EXCEPT
    a. being engaged by work and leisure.
    b. extreme happiness increases the experience of happiness in the future.
    c. having faith.
    d. being extroverted.

20. Which of the following theories of emotions is the one that argues that the way in which we explain our physiological arousal plays a central role in determining exactly which emotion we experience?
    a. the two-factor theory
    b. the James-Lange theory
    c. the Cannon-Bard theory
    d. the neural circuits explanation

## Practice Test 3

1. If you had to write a research paper on Maslow's hierarchy of motives, which of the following title would you choose to capture the essence of Maslow's theory?
    a. keep those reinforcements coming
    b. the power of the unconscious
    c. easy come, easy go
    d. be all that you can be

2. According to statistics, which of the following is at highest risk for anorexia nervosa?
   a. 21-year-old White college student who works 30 hours a week to pay for school
   b. 18-year-old African-American female whose parents are both teachers
   c. 16-year-old Hispanic female who works at a fast-food place after school
   d. 15-year-old White female whose parents are both lawyers

3. A child who cleans up his room every day so he can receive his two-dollar allowance on Saturday is
   a. self-actualizing.
   b. extrinsically motivated.
   c. intrinsically motivated.
   d. high in the affiliation motivation.

4. Which of the following theorists would be least interested in the role of instincts in motivations?
   a. Freud
   b. Maslow
   c. McDougall
   d. Buss

5. According to drive reduction theory, we eat to reduce
   a. food.
   b. homeostasis.
   c. instincts.
   d. arousal.

6. According to the Yerkes-Dodson theory, under which of the following conditions can we expect a novice dancer to perform best?
   a. at home in front of the mirror
   b. in front of for the selection committee at a highly prestigious art school
   c. at the dance studio where she works
   d. in a new show in her community

7. Which of the following motivators in the workplace is more likely to result in productivity and high quality work?
   a. a high salary
   b. a good and understanding boss
   c. the challenge presented by the task
   d. a good work environment

8. In Maslow's hierarchy of needs, when are people concerned with having friends and stable family lives?
   a. after they satisfy their basic physiological needs
   b. before they become concerned with having a positive self-image
   c. after they have become self-actualized
   d. before they are concerned with their own safety

9.  Which of the following situations is consistent with Maslow's motivation theory?
    a.   Pablo is a painter, and he is very motivated to develop his creativity even though he lives in a very dangerous neighborhood and does not have much money.
    b.   Pam is a woman in an abusive relationship; she continues in the relationship because she loves him even though her life may be in danger.
    c.   Cynthia is a mother who is concerned with making enough money to feed the family, even though she hates her very unfulfilling job.
    d.   Sebastian is a body builder who uses steroids. He is really concerned with being attractive, even though he might be damaging his health.

10. Which of the following biological factors does not contribute to overeating?
    a.   lower basal metabolism rate
    b.   heredity
    c.   damage to the ventromedial hypothalamus
    d.   having an average of 100 billion fat cells

11. Sexual orientation
    a.   can be categorized into two classes: heterosexual or homosexual.
    b.   is learned.
    c.   can't be changed with hormones.
    d.   that is not heterosexual can be classified as a psychological disorder.

12. Well-being is less likely if a person
    a.   gets to use his skills effectively.
    b.   is unable to get along with others.
    c.   gets to use her intelligence.
    d.   can do things independently.

13. Julia is watching *The Joy Luck Club*, a movie with many tragic scenes. As some horrific images are shown, she stops breathing for a second in shock and starts sobbing uncontrollably. After realizing that she's crying, Julia feels sadness. Which of the following theories of emotions is consistent with the order in which Julia experienced the components of her emotion?
    a.   the James-Lange theory
    b.   the Cannon-Bard theory
    c.   the two-factor theory
    d.   the neural circuitry approach

14. Which of the following facts explains why is it easier to acquire a fear than to get rid of the fear?
    a.   The amygdala participates in positive emotions.
    b.   There is a direct pathway involved in the communication of fear from the thalamus to the amygdala.
    c.   The amygdala sends more connections to the cerebral cortex than it gets back.
    d.   There is an indirect path involved in the communication of fear from the thalamus through the sensory cortex to the amygdala.

15. Lazarus argues that cognition comes before emotion while Zajonc argues that emotion is followed by cognition. What is the variable that explains why they are both correct?
    a. physiology
    b. time
    c. personality
    d. culture

16. Esther likes to study at night. When she has an important test coming up, she usually starts studying at 10:00 p.m. and tries to stay up until 2:00 a.m. Esther has a very hard time staying up after midnight, yet she fights her sleepiness and continues studying. Which of the following theories of motivation cannot explain very well why Esther stays up even if she is really sleepy?
    a. drive reduction theory
    b. optimum arousal theory
    c. cognitive approach
    d. humanistic approach

17. In Chapter 1 you learned about the main psychological perspectives. Which of the following perspectives would argue that we should study the fact that sometimes we do things and we don't really know why we do them?
    a. cognitive
    b. evolutionary
    c. sociocultural
    d. psychodynamic

18. Which of the following signs of emotional arousal is measured by a polygraph?
    a. blood pressure
    b. sweating
    c. heart rate
    d. body temperature

19. Happiness is to the _____ hemisphere of the brain as disgust is to the _____ hemisphere of the brain.
    a. left; occipital
    b. right; left
    c. left; right
    d. temporal; parietal

20. In some cultures, widows (who have just lost their husbands) express their sadness with very loud and uncontrollable crying, screaming, calling the name of the lost husband, and bouts of fainting. In other cultures, widows respond with a quiet sadness that is hardly interrupted by others. These differences are explained by the concept of
    a. universal emotions.
    b. display rules.
    c. facial feedback hypothesis.
    d. gender influences.

# Connections

*Take advantage of all the other study tools available for this chapter!*

## Media Integration

| NAME OF CLIP | DESCRIPTION | KEY CONCEPTS AND IDEAS |
|---|---|---|
| | | **Approaches to Motivation** |
| Self-Actualization | Adventure racers in the grueling Eco-Challenge are showcased. Participants share their motivations for engaging in this extreme sport. | Self-actualization<br>Motivation |
| | | **Hunger** |
| Teenage Dieting | This audio clip discusses trends of teenage dieting. Children see as many as 10,000 food commercials in a year, mostly for junk food. The CDC reports that obesity is higher among teens of lower income. A study with teenagers and dieting published in the *Journal of Consulting and Clinical Psychology* shows that teenagers who dieted tended to gain more weight and were more likely to become obese. Overweight teens may overeat without realizing it. Unsupervised or naturalistic diets tend to be ineffective. Healthy diet and exercise are effective in weight reduction. Teenagers should be discouraged to engage in naturalistic dieting, a practice that tends to lead to obesity and eating disorders. | Dieting<br>Obesity<br>Adolescence |
| Perception of Body Shape | The interactivity "The Body Beautiful: Hawaiian Adventure" explores the issues related to body images in women. The interactivity includes a self-assessment of body image, asking participants how satisfied they are with their bodies? There are separate assessments for men and women. The assessment asks female participants to rate | Body image |

| | | |
|---|---|---|
| | their body image based on four body types: ideal physique, current physique, and most attractive to men. After this assessment, they are asked for the male body types most attractive to them. Their results are presented in a scree plot, and they also see an overlay of the results of the study by Fallon and Rozin with undergraduates at University of Pennsylvania. At the end of the interactivity there is a comparison of men versus women. It is recommended that participants engage in the exercise for a second time from the point of view of the opposite sex. | |
| Bulimia Nervosa | This video clip presents the pattern of bulimia nervosa. Nancy, a woman who has had bulimia nervosa for 17 years describes how her mind is consumed with thoughts of food and her daily efforts to get through the day without food. Nancy describes how she has tried many different pseudo-scientific approaches to the disorder and nothing works, only therapy and self-awareness have helped her cope. | Bulimia nervosa Eating disorders |
| | | **Sexuality** |
| Transvestic Fetishism | The person showcased in this video interview describes his compulsion to dress in women's clothing. For a person with Transvestic fetishism, cross-dressing is essential to sexual gratification. | Transvestic fetishism Sexuality |
| Changing Genders | Angela is a man preparing for a sex change, or sex-reassignment surgery that will remove genitals and other male physical features. Angela used to be an Air | Sexuality Sex change Sex-reassignment surgery |

| | | Social Cognitive Motives |
|---|---|---|
| | Force pilot. She describes the changes in personality as a result of hormone therapy in transition. The concept of having a "female" brain is discussed, and the video tracks Angela's experience through the surgery, as well as including interviews with the wife. | |
| Need for Achievement | The interactivity "The ring toss game: How will you play a game in which you can set your own challenges?" addresses differences in the need for achievement. The rules of the game involve deciding the distance from which to toss, but the closer you are the fewer points you make (1–10 point range). For each toss the participant has to decide distance, force of throw, and direction of throw. A score is kept on current score, number of tosses so far, and percent of successful tosses. People high in need for achievement (nAch) tend to choose the middle distances, to have a balance between challenge and skill. Also, people high in nAch tend to be intrinsically motivated for success. Participants can print their results. | Need for achievement |
| Culture and Self | This video clip starts with insights into what people in a conversation are thinking about themselves. The effect of culture on self-concept and how that definition of the self influences individual psychology are discussed. Experts Markus and Kitayama are interviewed and present their perspective on the role of culture in the definition of self, comparing American and Asian cultures. They discuss how we pass our | Self-concept<br>Culture<br>Social psychology<br>Cross-cultural psychology<br>Independent vs. interdependent self<br>Achievement motivation |

| | | |
|---|---|---|
| | cultural understandings through interactions. The video clip also presents a discussion of the relationship between the motivation for achievement and the definition of the self. The topics of conformity and persuasion and their relationship with definition of self are discussed. | |
| Social Ostracism | Kipling Williams, an expert in social ostracism, discusses how humans need to belong, to have a sense of control, self-esteem, and a meaningful existence. Ostracism is a metaphor for death. Experiments that simulate ostracism are presented. Physiological arousal is experienced in those being ostracized. A response to ostracism may be frustration, leading to aggression. The case of the killers at Columbine High School is discussed. At the end of the video clip, Elliot Aronson discusses how the jigsaw classroom, by encouraging cooperation also has positive effects on intelligence, cognition, and motivation. | Social ostracism<br>Experimental method<br>Jigsaw classroom<br>Cooperation |
| | | **Emotion** |
| Detecting Deception | This video clip showcases a study in which microgestures are used to detect deception. Participants in the study are given the opportunity to lie, and an observer, an expert in microgestures, determines if the person is lying or not by focusing mainly on facial muscle movements related to fear and anxiety. | Deception<br>Microgestures |
| Brain Lateralization | This interactivity introduces students to the concept of brain hemispheres in a two-part simulation. The first part is a replication of the | Brain hemispheres<br>Experiment<br>Emotions<br>Facial expressions |

| | experiment by Dr. Jerry Levy that explores how emotions are perception and processing of emotions and their corresponding facial expressions. The second simulation involves a split-brain task. The interactivity introduces students to the differences between the functions of the brain hemispheres and the role of the corpus callosum in sharing information between the hemispheres. | Split-brain<br>Corpus callosum |
|---|---|---|
| Language of the Face | This video clip discusses the evolution of facial expressions, covering the characteristics of the aggression/anger face, fear face, smile face. Similarities between fear and smile face are discussed. | Evolution<br>Facial expressions<br>Anger<br>Fear<br>Smile |
| Evolutionary Psychology | "Evolutionary psychology" is an audio clip that offers an introduction to research on the universality of facial expressions. The work of Ekman on this subject is discussed. Jeff Cohn discussed how computers may be used to determine if a person is depressed. | Universality of seven facial expressions<br>Emotions<br>Facial expressions |
| Nonverbal Components of Speech | "It's not what you say" is an interactivity that focuses on the nonverbal component of speech, specifically tone and sounds. | Nonverbal behavior |
| Cultural Variations in Nonverbal Behavior | This video clip presents how the naturalistic observation method has been used to conduct cross-cultural research of nonverbal behaviors. Video of public speakers in London's Hyde Park is used to illustrate how nonverbal language can be used to control audiences and convey emotions and specific messages. | Naturalistic observation<br>Cross-cultural research<br>Sociocultural perspective<br>Language |

**Online Learning Center (www.mhhe.com/Santrockp7u)**

- Interact and make learning fun!
  - o **Interactive Exercises**
    - ▪ Sensation Seeking Scale
    - ▪ Perception of Body Shape
    - ▪ Need for Achievement (nAch)
    - ▪ Fixed Bowling
    - ▪ What Provokes You?
  - o **Interactive Reviews**
    - ▪ Level of Analysis: Eating
    - ▪ Hierarchy of Needs
- Brush up on the Key Terms for this chapter by first reviewing the electronic **Glossary** (in English or Spanish) and then testing your retention using the **Flashcard** feature.
- "Notes"—This feature allows you to use the website as you would your text, inserting your own study notes and highlighting areas of particular importance.

**In Your Text**

- Found throughout each chapter, the **Review and Sharpen Your Thinking** feature breaks the text into logical chunks, allowing you to process, review, and reflect thoughtfully on the information that you've just read. When going back to *study* the chapter, try reading the feature *before* the section of text to which it relates. In doing so, you will be able to focus your attention on important concepts *as* you encounter them. In this chapter, this feature can be found on the following pages: pp. 430, 437, 446, 454, and 469.

**Practice Quizzes**

- Test your knowledge of motivation and emotion by taking the different practice quizzes found on your text's **Online Learning Center** and on the **In-Psych Plus CD-ROM** packaged with your text.

## ANSWER KEY

### In Your Own Words

✓ Write a narrative of the sequence of events as we establish homeostasis according to the drive reduction theory.

*This narrative should include a description of a cycle of restoring homeostasis, the body's tendency to maintain equilibrium. The cycle should include the steps of satisfaction, need, drive, motivation, behavior, satisfaction, and starting over with need as the cycle is repeated. An example to illustrate the process is recommended.*

✓ How much of a sensation seeker are you? Describe how your sensation-seeking tendencies (low or high) influence different aspects of your life. For example, how do they influence your preferred activities, way of studying, way of relating to people, foods, music, etc.?

*Being a sensation seeker means that the person is likely to be motivated to engage in risky behaviors, is interested in highly active careers and activities, enjoys stimulation through eating and drinking, and has a hedonistic attitude toward relationships. A high sensation seeker may study while listening to music or watching TV and might prefer studying with others for the stimulating conversation. The preference for thrilling and exciting activities influence the types of things that these individuals are motivated to do.*

✓ Think of all the different behaviors you do in a typical day. Now consider, which of those behaviors are intrinsically motivated and which are extrinsically motivated. Write down your reflections, based on your personal experience, on the difference between being intrinsically versus extrinsically motivated.

*An intrinsic motivation is based in internal factors such as self-determination, curiosity, challenge, and effort, while an extrinsic motivation involves external incentives such as rewards and punishments. The same activities may be intrinsically motivating for a person but would be done by others only if an extrinsic motivator were offered. A typical day includes many routine behaviors, such as cooking, studying, working out, and taking a shower; each of these behaviors may be intrinsically or extrinsically motivated.*

✓ Mention ten external cues to eat that you encounter on a regular basis.
*External cues to eat include any stimuli that are associated with eating. The association is likely to have been established through classical or operant conditioning (from Chapter 7). Some examples are logos and jingles of fast-food places, the smell of food, time of the day, vending machines, and even studying.*

✓ In general terms, how happy are you? Use Diener's definition of happiness to estimate and interpret the current level of happiness in your life.
*Ed Diener defined happiness as the combination of the frequency of positive emotions and the infrequency of negative emotions. He proposed that people are likely to have both positive and negative emotions in their lives but that happiness is more an issue of long-term patterns of emotions (overall more good than bad).*

## Correcting the Incorrect

1. Motivated behavior is energized, directed, and *sustained*. (p. 425)
2. *McDougall* argued that all human behavior involves instincts. (p. 425)
3. A *drive* is an aroused state. (p. 425)
4. As a drive becomes stronger, we are motivated to reduce it. (p. 426)
5. A drive involves a *psychological state*, while a need involves a *physiological state*. (p. 426)
6. Self-actualization is found at the peak of Maslow's hierarchy of needs. (p. 429)
7. When the lateral hypothalamus of a rat is stimulated, the rat *begins* eating. (p. 432)
8. The set point is *not fixed and can be modified*. (p. 433)
9. Many people with anorexia nervosa grow up in families with high achievement demands. (p. 436)
10. *Androgens* include testosterone and are produced by the testes. (p. 438)
11. Hormones are *less important* in human females than human males with regard to sexual behavior. (p 438.)
12. Activity in the hypothalamus is associated with both hunger and sexual motivations. (p. 438)
13. Aphrodisiacs are substances that arouse a person's sexual desire and capacity for sexual activity. (p. 440)
14. In the romantic script for sexual behavior, sex is synonymous with *love*. (p. 440)
15. The four phases of the human sexual response pattern are excitement, plateau, orgasm, and *resolution*. (p. 438)
16. Sexual orientation is best understood as a *continuum*. (p. 442)
17. The need for *achievement* refers to the desire to accomplish something, to reach a standard of excellence, and to expend effort to excel. (p. 447)
18. Emotion has three components: affect, behavioral, and cognitive experience. (p. 455)
19. If you think someone is following you back to the dorm on a dark night, your *sympathetic nervous system* is probably very active in preparing you for the fight-or-flight response. (p. 455)

20. The Yerkes-Dodson theory states that performance is best under conditions of *moderate rather than low or high arousal.* (p. 426)

21. In the James-Lange theory of emotion, emotion occurs after physiological reaction. (p. 456)

22. In the Cannon-Bard theory of emotion, physiological reaction and emotion occur *simultaneously.* (p. 457)

23. The two-factor theory states that physiological arousal and cognitive labeling determine emotion. (p. 459)

24. The facial feedback hypothesis predicts *that smiling leads to feeling happiness.* (p. 462)

25. Display rules are *sociocultural* standards of when, where, and how emotions are expressed. (p. 464)

26. Plutchik suggested that emotions have *four* dimensions. (p. 465)

27. According to the wheel model of emotion, some emotions are primary and can be mixed with others to form all other emotions. (p. 465)

28. *Happiness* can be understood by examining the frequency of positive emotions and infrequency of negative emotions. (p. 469)

29. An *ineffective* way to deal with anger is catharsis. (p. 467)

30. Well-being is *subjective* and has three factors: competence, autonomy, and affiliation. (p. 453)

## Practice Test 1

1. a. YES, this is the definition of motivation; it energizes, directs, and sustains behavior
   b. no; an instinct is an innate, biological pattern of behavior
   c. no; an emotion is a feeling that has physiological and behavioral components
   d. no; a drive is an aroused state that occurs because of a need
   p. 425

2. a. no
   b. no
   c. no; an emotion is a feeling that has physiological and behavioral components
   d. YES; motivation is the question "why" behind behavior
   p. 425

3. a. no
   b. RIGHT; Darwin and Freud believed that instincts motivate behavior
   c. no
   d. no
   p. 425

4. a. no
   b. YES; a drive involves a psychological state
   c. no
   d. no
   p. 426

5.  a.   no; there is no indication that crying loudly leads to a return to a steady state
    b.   YES; homeostasis refers to the body's equilibrium or steady state
    c.   no; there is no reference that this behavior returns the organism to equilibrium
    d.   no; this does not involve a return to the body's equilibrium
    p. 426

6.  a.   no; this is second from the top of the hierarchy
    b.   YES, this refers to developing one's full potential and sits on top of the hierarchy
    c.   no; this is third from the top of the hierarchy
    d.   no; this is fourth from the top of the hierarchy
    p. 429

7.  a.   CORRECT; this area is involved in reducing hunger and restricting eating
    b.   no; to stimulate the area leads to a reduction in hunger and restriction of eating
    c.   no; the ventromedial hypothalamus is either destroyed or stimulated, not enhanced
    d.   no
    p. 432

8.  a.   no; the set point is the weight maintained when no effort is made to gain or lose weight.
    b.   YES; basal metabolism declines with age.
    c.   no; gastric signals refers to changes in hormone levels that signal hunger to an individual.
    d.   no; homeostasis is the body's tendency to maintain an equilibrium or balance.
    p. 433

9.  a.   no; sensory factors play a lesser role in our ability to control sexual behavior
    b.   no; perceptual factors play a role in sexual behavior but probably not in its control
    c.   no; while important, social factors are not most strongly related to control
    d.   YES; our ability to think about sexuality can control our sexual behavior
    p. 439

10. a.   no; females are more likely to link intercourse with love
    b.   YES; the script for men suggests that men emphasize sexual conquest
    c.   no
    d.   no
    p. 440

11. a.   no; these treatments have not been successful
    b.   YES; treatment that focuses directly on the dysfunction are very effective
    c.   no; there are successful treatments that focus directly on the dysfunction
    d.   these treatments are ineffective
    p. 442

12. a.   RIGHT; Viagra has a success rate of about 60–80%
    b.   no; Prozac is an antidepressant
    c.   no; Rogaine is a baldness remedy
    d.   no
    p. 442

13. a.   no; the opposite occurs
    b.   no; the orientation is not affected
    c.   YES, this suggests that the role of hormones in sexual orientation is unclear
    d.   no; actually their desire does increase, but not in a heterosexual orientation
    p. 445

14. a. no; extrinsic motivation refers to an external reward for a job well done
    b. YES, this illustrates intrinsic motivation since the desire is internal
    c. no; this refers to the relationship between performance and arousal
    d. no; this is an emotion theory
    p. 428

15. a. no
    b. YES; socioeconomic status seems to be a better predictor than ethnicity
    c. no
    d. no
    p. 450

16. a. RIGHT; these characteristics define emotion
    b. emotion includes other components
    c. no; but you're partially correct
    d. no; there's more to emotion that this option
    p. 455

17. a. too much arousal will impair your performance
    b. no; too little arousal will impair your performance
    c. THAT'S RIGHT; moderate arousal tends to maximize performance
    d. no; the Yerkes-Dodson theory describes arousal and performance, not happiness
    p. 426

18. a. the Cannon-Bard theory of emotion includes the hypothalamus
    b. RIGHT; emotional arousal is interpreted or labeled by the brain to create emotion
    c. no; this theory doesn't directly include cultural and social expectations
    d. no; the brain first interprets arousal before anything is perceived as threatening
    p. 456

19. a. no; this is not relevant in this theory
    b. no; Schachter and Singer do not consider serotonin
    c. no; the pattern of arousal is less important than the external cues for it
    d. THIS IS RIGHT; we look for reasons or external cues to explain our arousal
    p. 459

20. a. no
    b. no; this option sounds more like the James-Lange theory
    c. no
    d. RIGHT; this theory says that physiological arousal and the emotion are experienced at the same time
    p. 457

## Practice Test 2

1. a. while children may want to accomplish something, this is not the best option
   b. no
   c. YES; the children are receiving praise and gold stars, both of which are external
   d. no; the rewards are external
   p. 428

2. a. happiness is expressed in a universal way
   b. fear is expressed in a universal way
   c. surprise is expressed in a universal way
   d. RIGHT; contentment is not expressed in a universal way
   p. 462

3. a. no; the facial feedback hypothesis is not being addressed in this question
   b. YES; display rules are sociocultural standards that determine when, where, and how emotions should be expressed
   c. no; this concept is also not relevant in the question
   d. no; set point is a concept related to weight
   p. 464

4. a. emotions can be primary or mixed
   b. no; emotions can be strong or weak
   c. RIGHT; Plutchik does not classify emotions in this way
   d. no; emotions can be positive or negative
   p. 465

5. a. no
   b. no; this is one of the four dimensions
   c. CORRECT; mixing primary emotions leads to other emotions such disappointment
   d. no; mixing primary emotions may lead to negative or positive emotions
   p. 465

6. a. no; sadness is not likely
   b. no; Anthony is not likely to be happy
   c. no
   d. YES; anger is most likely the result of when we believe we have been treated unfairly or when expectations are violated
   p. 467

7. a. no; this is one of the characteristics of motivated behaviors
   b. no; this is one of the characteristics of motivated behaviors
   c. no; this is one of the characteristics of motivated behaviors
   d. YES; motivated behaviors are not random; even if they are instinctual, they respond to particular patterns in the body or the environment
   p. 425

8. a. no; this question simply states that a person has a need and behaves to reduce the drive; it does not address the person's particular level of optimal hydration
   b. no; the motivation is physiological
   c. YES; the behavior is done to reduce the drive, thirst
   d. no; while physiological needs are at the base, the best answer in this question is item c
   p. 426

9. a. no; an instinct is an unlearned pattern of behavior shared by a species
   b. no; a drive does not energize a drive
   c. no; homeostasis is restored when the need is eliminated
   d. YES; a need is a deprivation, a lack of something, that when provided will restore homeostasis
   p. 426

10. a. YES; TV programming is not necessarily very stimulating
    b. no; nachos are definitely stimulating
    c. no; working as a police officer is likely to offer daily interesting and stimulating opportunities
    d. no; the Eco-Challenge is a highly stimulating and risky activity
    p. 427

11. a. no; drive reduction is a biologically based theory
    b. no; evolutionary theory focuses on the role of instincts
    c. no; optimum arousal is a physiologically based theory
    d. YES; the cognitive approach focuses on how we think and consciously decide to engage in some behaviors and not in others
    p. 427

12. a. no; this is extrinsic, offered by the mother to the child
    b. YES; this is intrinsic, something that is internal
    c. no; this is a reward that is external
    d. no; this is a reward that is external
    p. 428

13. a. YES; restoring homeostasis is a biological process that is not self-generated
    b. no; life tasks are self-generated goals that involve problems the individual is currently working on
    c. no; personal projects are self-generated goals that range from trivial pursuits to life goals
    d. no; personal strivings are self-generated goals that represent what a person is typically trying to do, such as doing a good job, keeping the family together, making friends, etc.
    p. 428

14. a. no; this is the third level
    b. no; this is the fifth and last level
    c. YES; concerns for safety follow the physiological needs
    d. no; this is the fourth level, right before self-actualization
    p. 429

15. a. no; this is one of the main issues: to what degree are we internally or externally motivated?
    b. no; this is one of the main issues: to what degree are we motivated by innate or external factors?
    c. no; this is one of the main issues: to what degree are we aware of what motivates us?
    d. YES; this is not an issue: behavioral and observable are equivalent concepts and motivations are neither; motivations are internal influences that push us to behave, to engage in observable actions
    p. 430

16. a. no; this leads to hunger
    b. YES; CCK helps start digestion and travels to the brain through the bloodstream and signals you to stop eating; a contributor in this process is the neurotransmitter serotonin
    c. no; this increases hunger
    d. no; this increases hunger
    p. 431

17. a. YES; people with bulimia nervosa tend to keep a normal weight range, whereas people with anorexia nervosa tend to weigh less than 85% of what is considered normal for their age and height
    b. no; this is characteristic of bulimia nervosa
    c. no; this is characteristic of bulimia nervosa as well as of anorexia nervosa
    d. no; this is characteristic of bulimia nervosa as well as of anorexia nervosa
    p. 437

18. a. no; hormones are substances secreted by the endocrine system; estrogens and androgens are hormones that influence the sexual motivation
    b. no; while the belief may be culturally based, the question is addressing another aspect
    c. YES; aphrodisiacs are substances that supposedly arouse a person's sexual desire and increase the capacity for sexual activity
    d. no; pheromones are scented substances that are powerful attractants in some animals
    p. 440

19. a. no; this has been associated with happiness
    b. YES; actually, intense positive moments can diminish the sensation of future positive events
    c. no; this has been associated with happiness
    d. no; this has been associated with happiness
    p. 468

20. a. YES; the two-factor theory says that emotions are determined by physiological arousal and cognitive labeling; cognitive labeling is a process of explaining the physiological arousal
    b. no; this theory says that stimuli cause a physiological reaction, which in turn causes an emotion; however, it does not address the cognitive process
    c. no; this theory says that the processing of the physiological reaction and the emotion occurs simultaneously
    d. no; the neural circuits approach focuses on the role of certain parts of the brain, such as the amygdala, in receiving, processing, and sending out information about emotions
    p. 459

## Practice Test 3

1. a. no; this would be more appropriate for incentives
   b. no; the unconscious is emphasized in psychodynamic perspective
   c. no
   d. YES; we are motivated to become self-actualized
   p. 429

2. a. no; this person does not have the highest risk
   b. no; this person does not have the highest risk
   c. no; this person does not have the highest risk
   d. CORRECT; this person has the most risk factors (age, race, family background)
   p. 436

3. a. no; self-actualization refers to fulfilling one's potential
   b. THIS IS CORRECT; extrinsic motivation involves external rewards for doing a task
   c. no; intrinsic motivation involves internal rewards for a task
   d. no; while this could be true, the question does not address the child's affiliation tendencies
   p. 428

4.  a.  no; Freud did argue that we have instincts such as sex and aggression
    b.  YES; Maslow, a humanist, developed a theory of motivation that considered the behaviors that are controlled by the person
    c.  no; McDougall thought all behaviors are controlled by instincts
    d.  no; Buss is an evolutionary psychologist and as such he would be interested in instincts
    p. 429

5.  a.  no; unless you are in a hotdog eating competition
    b.  YES; the goal of drive reduction is homeostasis, the body's tendency to maintain equilibrium
    c.  no; instincts are not reduced, they motivate behavior in a different way
    d.  no; arousal is a state of alertness and is unrelated to drive reduction
    p. 426

6.  a.  no; this is likely to be a low arousal situation, and thus performance will not be peaked
    b.  no; this is likely to be a high arousal situation, and thus performance may be impaired
    c.  no; this, like item a, is likely to be a low arousal situation, and thus performance will not be peaked
    d.  YES; a new show for a novice dancer is likely to result in a moderate level of arousal, and thus result in the best performance, according to the Yerkes-Dodson theory
    p. 426

7.  a.  no; this is an extrinsic motivator that may actually diminish the achievement motivation
    b.  no; this is an extrinsic motivator
    c.  YES; this is an intrinsic motivator and thus it may be expected to have more positive outcomes than an extrinsic motivator
    d.  no; this is an extrinsic motivator
    p. 428

8.  a.  no; after the physiological need comes safety
    b.  YES; according to Maslow, people go on to be concerned with esteem needs once the love and belongingness needs are satisfied
    c.  no; self-actualization is the last level.
    d.  no; love and belongingness needs go after safety needs.
    p. 429

9.  a.  no; Pablo is placing self-actualization before safety and possibly physiological needs
    b.  no; Pam is placing love and belongingness before safety
    c.  YES; Cynthia is concerned with safety and love and belongingness and cannot be bothered yet with esteem or self-actualization
    d.  no; Sebastian is placing love and belongingness over safety and physiological needs
    p. 429

10. a.  no; this is associated with overeating and obesity
    b.  no; this is associated with overeating and obesity
    c.  YES; when this area has been destroyed in animal research, the animal eats profusely and quickly becomes obese
    d.  no; this is associated with overeating and obesity
    p. 432

11. a. no; sexual orientation is better understood as a continuum from exclusive heterosexuality to exclusive homosexuality
    b. no; external factors may contribute, but it is most likely determined by a combination of genetic, hormonal, cognitive, and environmental factors
    c. YES; this is correct; when male homosexuals are given androgens, their sexual orientation does not change; however, their sexual drive does increase.
    d. no; both the American Psychiatric Association and the American Psychological Association agree that homosexuality is not a psychological disorder

    p. 445

12. a. no; this is an example of competence, one of the three factors that need to be present for well-being
    b. YES; this is inconsistent with affiliation, one of the three factors that need to be present for well-being
    c. no; this is an example of competence, one of the three factors that need to be present for well-being
    d. no; this is an example of autonomy, one of the three factors that need to be present for well-being

    p. 453

13. a. YES; the James-Lange theory would predict that the stimulus (movie) caused a physiological reaction (crying) followed by the awareness of the emotion (sadness)
    b. no; the Cannon-Bard theory would predict that she would have started crying and realized that she was sad simultaneously
    c. no; the two-factor theory addresses the possibility that similar physiological reactions may be interpreted in more than one way; Julia was not experiencing a general arousal, she was expressing sadness and then realized that she was sad
    d. no; this approach considers the role of parts of the brain in emotions, and these were not addressed in this question

    p. 456

14. a. no; this is a fact, but positive emotions do not contribute to fears
    b. no; this is a fact, but it does not explain why it is easier to learn than to unlearn fears
    c. YES; this is a fact, and it explains why once a fear is learned and "saved" in the amygdala, this information can more easily influence how we think (amygdala sending out messages to cortex); however, when we try to unlearn something we are engaging in activation on the cerebral cortex and sending the information back to the amygdala; there are fewer pathways back into the amygdala, thus less opportunity for connections to be established
    d. no; this is a fact, but it does not explain why it is easier to learn than to unlearn fears

    p. 459

15. a. no; physiology is a component of emotion
    b. YES; time is the key; Lazarus refers to a relationship between cognition and emotion across an extended period of time, such as thinking that your partner does not love you followed by feeling sad; however, Zajonc referred to more immediate situations, such as being scared by a scream.;the emotion occurs immediately followed by an awareness and the thoughts of the situation.
    c. no; personality does not play a role in this issue
    d. no; culture plays no role in this issue; this is more likely to be explained in terms of brain circuitry

    p. 462

16. a. YES; drive reduction would predict that the sleepiness would signal the need for sleep and that the drive for resting would be initiated; however, Esther does not do what she needs to do to satisfy the need, which is sleep; she increases rather than reduces the drive

    b. no; this theory can explain in part why Esther stays up; she may prefer to work at that sleepiness level of arousal

    c. no; this approach can explain why Esther, who thinks of herself as a night person even when she has a time staying up, studies at night

    d. no; the humanistic approach or Maslow's hierarchy of needs (Chapter 1) would argue that Esther would want to sleep (physiological) instead of studying (esteem/self-actualization)

    p. 426

17. a. no; this perspective would focus on conscious motivations

    b. no; this perspective would focus on instincts as motivators; instincts are shared by all humans, and we engage in instinctual behavior because we are human

    c. no; this perspective focuses on broad social and cultural influences; we engage in those behaviors because of others

    d. YES; this perspective focuses on unconscious motivations

    p. 427

18. a. no; this is not measured by a polygraph

    b. no; don't confuse the polygraph with the galvanic skin response assessment, which measures the electrical conductivity of the skin when sweat glands increase activity

    c. YES; this is one of the measures taken by polygraphs, along with breathing and electrodermal response, an index detecting skin resistance to passage of a weak electrical current

    d. no; this changes with emotions but it is not measured by a polygraph

    p. 456

19. a. no; while happiness is associated with the left hemisphere, occipital refers to a lobe, not a hemisphere

    b. no; the opposite is true

    c. YES; the left hemisphere of the brain is associated with approach-related emotions, such as happiness, while the right hemisphere is associated with withdrawal-related emotions, such as disgust

    d. no; these are lobes of the hemispheres, not hemispheres themselves

    p. 459

20. a. no; while sadness is universal and crying is universally associated with sadness, the studies done by Ekman do not account for such dramatic differences in the expression of emotions

    b. YES; display rules are sociocultural standards that determine when, where, and how emotions should be expressed

    c. no; this hypothesis states that behavioral aspects of emotions can initiate the emotional experience

    d. no; the question is not about gender differences in the expression of sadness

# Chapter 12—Personality

## Learning Goals

1. Define personality, and identify the major issues in the study of personality.
2. Summarize the psychodynamic perspectives.
3. Explain the behavioral and social cognitive perspectives.
4. Describe the humanistic perspectives.
5. Discuss the trait perspectives.
6. Characterize the main methods of personality assessment.

*After studying Chapter 12, you will be able to:*

- Explain what personality is.
- Identify the three main issues in personality psychology.
- Describe the psychodynamic perspective, including Freud's theories, as well as the psychodynamic dissenters and revisionists.
- Distinguish between the behavioral and the social cognitive perspectives on personality.
- Understand the concept of reciprocal determinism.
- Evaluate the humanistic perspective, including Rogers's and Maslow's views.
- Define self-concept and self-esteem, and describe how self-esteem can be increased.
- Explain what the trait perspective is, as well as Allport's and Eysenck's contributions to this perspective.
- Describe each of the five main personality factors.
- Compare the interactionist and the situationist views of personality.
- Describe the advantages and the disadvantages of each of the four main perspectives in personality psychology.
- Explain what validity and reliability are in the context of personality assessments.
- Understand how projective tests measure personality.
- Evaluate the use of self-report tests to measure personality.
- Distinguish between behavioral and cognitive assessments of personality.
- Understand how personality assessments are used in the workplace.

## CHAPTER 12: OUTLINE

- *Personality* refers to our enduring, distinctive thoughts, emotions, and behaviors, which characterize how we adapt to our world. For example, a study of great American presidents found that they had in common openness to experiences, assertiveness, and extroversion, among other personality characteristics.

- Four perspectives are discussed in this chapter: psychodynamic, behavioral and social cognitive, humanistic, and trait. What separates these perspectives is how they answer the key questions in personality psychology: (1) Is personality innate or learned? (2) Is it conscious or unconscious? (3) Is it influenced by internal or external factors?

- The psychodynamic view sees personality as primarily unconscious, occurring in stages, and being linked to early experiences. Freud believed that much more of our mind is unconscious than conscious and that the unconscious is the key to understanding personality.

- According to Freud, personality has three structures: the id, the ego, and the superego. The id houses biological instincts, is completely unconscious, and operates according to the pleasure principle. The ego operates according to the reality principle. The superego is the moral branch of the personality. The conflicting demands of the personality structures produce anxiety.

- In response to the anxiety, the ego uses defense mechanisms as protective methods to resolve conflicts and reduce the anxiety. Defense mechanisms include repression, which is the most powerful and pervasive defense mechanism. When used in moderation or on a temporary basis, defense mechanisms can be helpful and healthy. Defense mechanisms are unconscious, and we are not aware of their use.

- Freud argued that we go through five psychosexual stages, and at each stage we have a distinct erogenous zone, a part of the body that causes pleasure more than others. Freud maintained that adult problems stem primarily from early childhood experiences and fixations owing to unsatisfactory progress through the psychosexual stages. The five psychosexual stages are oral, anal, phallic, latency, and genital. We can become fixated at any stage if we experience too much or too little stimulation of our erogenous zones.

- The main objections to Freud's theory are his overemphasis on sexuality and on the events of the first five years of life. Other objections are that sociocultural factors are more important than Freud believed and that the ego and conscious thought are more important.

- Karen Horney rejected the notion that "anatomy is destiny." She emphasized the need for security as a prime motivator. Jung, a contemporary of Freud's, emphasized the collective unconscious and archetypes or ideas and images. Alfred Adler believed that we can consciously monitor and direct our lives.

- The concepts of striving for superiority, inferiority complex, superiority complex, and compensation are important in Adler's individual psychology. Concepts in the psychodynamic perspective that seem to be validated are the importance of early experiences in shaping personality, understanding personality developmentally, and how we mentally transform environmental experiences. The main concepts of psychoanalysis have been difficult to test since they involve inference and interpretation.

- Behaviorism asserts that the observable behaviors of a person are in fact the personality and emphasize the importance of the environment in determining behaviors and thus personality. It follows that if the environment changes, the behavior changes, and so does the personality.

- Social cognitive theorists agree on the importance of the environment but emphasize the role of thinking and the capacity that individuals have to influence their environments. Social cognitive theory focuses on behavior, environment, and person/cognitive factors and how these three factors interact in determining personality; this process is called *reciprocal determinism*.

- The behavioral and social cognitive perspectives focus on the control people have over their behaviors and personalities because they can choose their environments.

- Two psychological factors that illustrate reciprocal determinism are personal control and optimism. Different levels of personal control are illustrated in delayed gratification, self-efficacy, and locus of control. *Optimism* refers to the tendency to explain bad events as external, unstable, and specific, whereas *pessimism* is characterized by a pattern of explaining bad events as internally caused, stable, and global.

- Optimism (a cognitive factor) has been associated with being more effective and being physically and mentally healthy, whereas pessimism has been associated with helplessness. One criticism of the behavioral perspective is its view that cognitive factors play no role in behavior, with too much emphasis placed on environmental factors. The behavioral and social cognitive points of view have been criticized for being too concerned with changes caused by the environment and for ignoring the relative stability of personality.

- The humanistic perspective stresses the importance of people's capacity for personal growth, freedom to choose their destinies, and for their positive qualities. Rogers' approach suggests that each of us is a victim of conditional positive regard (e.g., we are given love only if we behave according to the standards of others). As a result, our real self is not valued as positively as it should be. Rogers advocated unconditional positive regard to enhance our self-concept.

- A more positive self-concept can be achieved by showing unconditional positive regard, empathy, and genuineness. When our real self and ideal self are very different, we fail to become fully functioning people.

- According to Maslow, people strive for self-actualization. Maslow believed that human needs consist of several needs arranged in a hierarchy of motives, with self-actualization as the motivation to develop one's full potential as a human being. Maslow also emphasized that an important component of personality is self-esteem, which is a person's overall evaluation of his or her self-worth or self-image. Self-esteem can be improved through achievement and coping. While the humanistic perspective reminds us of the importance of the whole person, its concepts are difficult to test scientifically.

- Trait theories suggest that personality is best understood by studying the organization of traits within the person. *Traits* are broad dispositions that lead to characteristic responses. Three trait theories discussed in the chapter are Allport's, Eysenck's and the so-called "big five."

- Allport grouped traits into cardinal traits, central traits, and secondary traits depending on how influential they were on the individual. Eysenck proposed three dimensions to explain personality: introversion-extraversion, stable-unstable, and psychoticism. Recent analysis has revealed the existence of the big five factors of personality: openness, conscientiousness, extraversion, agreeableness, and neuroticism (acronym: OCEAN). These big five factors may be able to predict physical and mental health. The trait perspective argues that personality is consistent across situations and time.

- According to situationalism, personality often varies considerably from one context to another. A view of personality called *interactionism* suggests that both person and situation variables are necessary to understand personality.

- There are many popular ways of guessing personality, such as palmistry (reading the palm of the hand), but the assessments tend to be very general and trivial and are usually believed as a result of the Barnum effect (i.e., the descriptions are so general that they could apply to anybody). Psychology is a science and the personality assessments developed by psychologists are intended to be specific and accurate and are usually subjected to extensive validity and reliability analysis.

- Four types of personality assessment techniques are discussed in this chapter: projective tests, self-report tests, behavioral and cognitive assessment, and assessment in the selection of employees.

- Projective tests present the individual with an ambiguous stimulus and then ask for a description or story, and the expectation is that the person will project unconscious feelings and thoughts into the ambiguous stimuli, be it a picture or a story. Two projective tests are the Rorschach Inkblot Test and the Thematic Apperception Test. Rorschach inkblots are controversial because they have low reliability and validity, yet they are considered very useful by many clinical psychologists.

- Self-report tests are used to assess personality by asking individuals whether items describe their personality. Tests that select items that predict a particular criterion are called *empirically keyed tests* and are not based on face validity and an attempt to control social desirability. A widely used self-report test is the Minnesota Multiphasic Personality Inventory (MMPI). The MMPI-2 has four validity scales and ten clinical scales. The big five factors can also be assessed using self-report tests.

- In behavioral assessments, an individual's behavior is observed directly or the individual is asked to report observations of his or her own behaviors. Cognitive assessments are used to determine what thoughts underlie behavior. Psychological tests are also useful in predicting how well a person will perform in the workplace.

## Building Blocks of Chapter 12

### Clarifying some of the tricky points in Chapter 12
### and
### In Your Own Words
*To respond to the questions and exercises presented in the "In Your Own Words" section, please write your thoughts, perspectives, and reactions on a separate piece of paper.*

### *Theories of Personality*
The enduring, distinctive thoughts, emotions, and behaviors that characterize the way an individual adapts to the world is what psychologists call *personality*. The three main issues that distinguish different perspectives on personality are: (1) innate versus *learned,* (2) conscious versus *unconscious,* and (3) internal versus *external* factors. The four main perspectives on personality are *psychodynamic, behavioral* and social cognitive, *humanistic,* and *trait*

### In Your Own Words
*Please write your thoughts, perspectives, and reactions on a separate piece of paper*
 ✓ *Paraphrase the textbook's definition of personality.*

### *Psychodynamic Perspectives*
Personality from the *psychodynamic* perspective is seen as primarily unconscious and as occurring in stages. This perspective also views *early* life experiences as important. Sigmund Freud was a neurologist who developed his ideas for his theory from his work with *psychiatric* patients.

### *Helpful Hints for Understanding Personality*
#### *Helpful Hint #1:*
*Sigmund Freud's theory is termed "psychoanalytic theory"; theorists who based their work on his are termed "psychodynamic theorists." Obviously, there are many psychodynamic theories, but only one psychoanalytic theory. Whether one agrees with Freud or not, there is no refuting the influence his theory has had on psychology and modern Western Civilization.*

An interesting phenomenon that, according to Freud, is proof of unconscious influences is the *parapraxis,* or *Freudian slip*—a "slip of the tongue" or a misstatement that perhaps reveals unconscious thoughts. Freud also believed that *dreams* are unconscious representations of the conflicts and tension in our everyday lives.

According to the psychoanalytic perspective, personality has *three* structures. One, which is a reservoir of psychic energy and instincts and continually presses to satisfy our basic needs, is called the *id;* this structure works according to the *pleasure principle*. As a child experiences the demands and constraints of reality, a second personality structure called the *ego* is formed. The ego tries to bring pleasure to the individual within the boundaries of society, a concept called the *reality principle*. The third personality structure, the moral branch, is called the *superego*. The superego corresponds to our *conscience*. The demands for reality, the wishes of the id, and the constraints of the superego produce *conflict*.

One way to resolve these conflicts is by means of *defense* mechanisms. The most pervasive defense mechanism is *repression*. This works by pushing id impulses out of awareness into our *unconscious* mind. Defense mechanisms are unconscious and not necessarily unhealthy when used in *moderation*.

### Helpful Hint #2:
*For a defense mechanism to work, it has to remain unconscious to the person. However, defense mechanisms can be easily identified by others. The goal of psychoanalytic therapy (Chapter 13) is to make some of the unconscious, conscious! Then the person has a choice regarding his or her behaviors or mental processes, instead of unconsciously responding to them.*

Freud believed that individuals experience pleasure in different parts of the body at different stages of development; he called these body parts *erogenous zones*. If an individual's needs at any level of development are under- or overgratified, the result is *fixation*.

During the first 18 months of life, a child is in the *oral* stage of development; the most pleasurable activities at this stage center on the *mouth*. From age 1 1/2 to 3, the child is in the *anal* stage; the child's greatest pleasure centers around the *eliminative* function. During the next stage, the *phallic* stage, pleasure centers on the *genitals*. It is during this period that the *Oedipus complex* develops. From age 6 until puberty, the child represses all interest in sexual urges and is said to be in the *latency* stage. Finally, during the *genital* stage, which begins at puberty, the source of sexual pleasure becomes someone outside the family.

The key objections to Freud's theory are that (1) the pervasive force behind personality is not sexuality, (2) the first five years of life are not as powerful in shaping personality, (3) the ego and conscious thought play more important roles than Freud believed, and (4) sociocultural factors are more important than Freud believed.

Some of the most famous *revisionists* of the psychoanalytic perspective are Horney, Jung, and Adler (all *psychodynamic* theorists). Karen Horney's approach emphasized *sociocultural* factors in development. She also believed that the prime motive in human existence was *security,* not sexuality. She suggested that people usually develop one of the following strategies to cope with anxiety: they either move *toward* people, *away* from people, or *against* people.

Chodorow's feminist revision of psychodynamic theory emphasized that women are more likely than men are to define themselves in terms of their *relationships,* and that *emotions* are more important in women's lives.

Jung's approach involved the belief that the roots of our personality go back to the beginning of human existence. Jung called this common heritage the *collective unconscious,* and the impressions they have made in the mind were called *archetypes*. Two common archetypes are *anima* (female) and *animus* (male).

Adler's theory, which focused on the uniqueness of every person, is called *individual* psychology. He disputed Freud's emphasis on sexual motivation, believing we can *consciously* monitor our lives.

According to Adler, all individuals strive for *superiority*. In order to overcome real or imagined weaknesses, we use *compensation*. An exaggerated effort to conceal a weakness is called *overcompensation*. A person who exaggerates feelings of inadequacy has an inferiority complex, whereas a person who exaggerates self-importance to mask feelings of inferiority has a *superiority* complex.

Although many psychologists agree that early experiences are important determinants of personality and that personality should be studied developmentally, the main concepts of psychodynamic theories have been difficult to *test*. Another criticism of the psychodynamic perspective is that it portrays people in a *negative* light.

### Behavioral and Social Cognitive Perspectives

Behaviorists believe that psychology should examine only what can be directly *observed* and *measured*.

### Helpful Hint #3:
*Classic behaviorism is learning theory (Chapter 7).*

Skinner concluded that personality is the individual's *behavior*, which is determined by the *external environment*. Since personality is learned in the environment, behaviorists believe that changes in the environment can change an individual's personality.

Social cognitive theorists emphasize behavior, environment, and *cognition* as the key factors in determining personality. The way in which these three factors interact to determine personality is referred to as *reciprocal determinism*. Social cognitive theorists believe that we acquire much of our personality by *observing (imitating)* the behavior of others. They also believe that we can *regulate* our own behavior. The behavioral and social cognitive perspectives focus on the *control* people have over their behaviors and personalities because they can choose their environments.

### In Your Own Words
*Please write your thoughts, perspectives, and reactions on a separate piece of paper.*
✓ *Consider how reciprocal determinism has played a role in your personality. First, describe what is reciprocal determinism. Second, describe one aspect of your personality that has been shaped by choices that you have made.*

Two psychological factors that illustrate reciprocal determinism are *personal control* and *optimism*. Different levels of personal control are illustrated in *delayed gratification*, *self-efficacy*, and *locus of control*.

A prominent social cognitive theorist, Walter Mischel, believes that *delay of gratification* is important in understanding personality because it shows how people can control the reinforcers they receive from the environment.

*Optimism* refers to the tendency to explain bad events as external, unstable, and specific, whereas pessimism is characterized by a pattern of explaining bad events as internal, stable, and global. Optimism (a cognitive factor) has been associated with being more effective and being physically and mentally healthy, whereas pessimism has been associated with *helplessness*, which is a learned passiveness and unresponsiveness that results from experiencing uncontrollable negative events.

One criticism of the behavioral perspective is its view that *cognitive* factors play no role in behavior, with too much emphasis placed on environmental factors. The behavioral and social cognitive points of view have been criticized for being too concerned with changes caused by the environment and for ignoring the relative stability of personality.

## Humanistic Perspectives

An approach that stresses the importance of our personal growth, people's positive qualities, and our freedom is the *humanistic* approach. Carl Rogers, a humanistic psychologist, believed that love and praise often are not given unless we conform to *parental* or social standards. Through an individual's experiences of the world, a *self* emerges. *Self-concept* refers to individuals' overall perceptions of their abilities, behaviors, and personalities. According to Rogers, maladjustment results when there are large discrepancies between our *real* self and our *ideal* self. Rogers believed we should all be valued and feel accepted regardless of our behavior, a situation called *unconditional positive regard*.

### Helpful Hint #4:
*Rogers was not so naïve to believe that there should be no conditions put on relationships. One could not expect to stop showing up for work and receive the employee of the month award!*

Rogers also believed that individuals can develop a positive self-concept if others are *empathic* and *genuine*. Rogers stressed the importance of becoming a *fully functioning* person.

Abraham Maslow, who called the humanistic approach the *"third force,"* believed that people strive for self-actualization. According to Maslow, human needs are arranged in a *hierarchy* of needs, ranging from the most basic needs to *higher* needs. Self-*esteem* refers to our overall evaluation of our self-worth or self-image.

Four ways to improve self-esteem are identifying the causes of low self-esteem, experiencing support and approval, achievement, and coping. A weakness of the humanistic approach is that it is very difficult to test *empirically*. It has also been criticized for being too optimistic about human nature.

## Trait Perspectives

*Trait theories* suggest that personality consists of broad dispositions to respond in particular ways. According to Allport, each of us is unique because of our *personality traits*. Allport argued that traits could be grouped into *cardinal, central,* and *secondary*. Eysenck found that personality could be explained with three dimensions: *introversion-extraversion, stable-unstable,* and *psychoticism*.

Recent studies have revealed the existence of the *five main factors of personality*, which can be remembered via the acronym OCEAN. The five main factors are *openness, conscientiousness, extraversion, agreeableness,* and *neuroticism*. Research has also focused on the role of the five main factors in different cultures and in predicting health.

Many psychologists in the field today believe that both traits and situations have to be taken into account in understanding personality. This approach is called *interactionism*. Studies that have considered both factors have uncovered that the *narrower* the trait, the more likely it will predict behavior; that some people are *consistent* in some traits and other people are *consistent* in other traits; and that personality traits are more influential when situational influences are *less* powerful.

Cross-cultural psychologists go a step further and argue that there are various levels of situational influence. They suggest that personality is best understood by considering both the *immediate setting* and the broader *cultural context*.

Criticism of this view includes that traits can provide only a partial view of personality. The view that personality varies extensively from one context to another is called *situationism*.

### Personality Assessment

What seems like incredibly accurate explanations of personality by palmists and psychics are due to the *Barnum effect*, which results from offering predictions broad enough to describe any person. However, psychologists work hard at creating *personality assessments* that are valid and reliable. Also, most personality tests measure *stable (enduring) characteristics*.

Some tests present individuals with an ambiguous stimulus and then ask for a description or story. These tests are called *projective* tests. The purpose of projective tests is to elicit *unconscious* behaviors and conflicts.

A popular but controversial projective test is the *Rorschach Inkblot* test. While the test is widely used by clinical psychologists, it has been criticized for its low *validity* and *reliability,* when compared to other *objective* tests like the MMPI. Another projective test, which consists of a series of ambiguous pictures about which individuals are asked to tell a story, is the *Thematic Apperception Test.*

A projective test that uses handwriting analysis to determine individuals' personality traits by asking them about their traits is called a *graphology* test. Researchers have found graphology to have low *reliability* and *validity.*

Although many early self-report tests were constructed using *face* validity, these assume that individuals respond honestly. However, even if an individual is honest, he or she may be giving *socially desirable* answers.

Tests that select items that predict a particular criterion are called *empirically keyed tests*, or *objective tests*. A widely used self-report personality test used originally with mentally disturbed patients is the *Minnesota Multiphasic Personality Inventory (MMPI)*. Much research has found that the MMPI is able to improve the diagnosis of mentally disturbed individuals.

An assessment technique that observes an individual's behavior directly is called *behavioral assessment*. A test that asks an individual what her thoughts were before getting angry would be an example of *cognitive assessment*. An example of a cognitive assessment is the *locus* of *control scale* developed by Julian Rotter.

Finally, a common application of personality tests is in the process of *selection* of employees. These tests are designed to assess personality characteristics that can predict future *job performance.*

# Correcting the Incorrect

Carefully read each statement. Determine if the statement is correct or incorrect. If the statement is incorrect, make the necessary changes to correct it. Then check the answer key at the end of the chapter for the correct statement and page reference in the textbook.

1. Personality consists of a stable patter of behavior.
2. The key issues in psychology are innate versus learned and conscious versus unconscious.
3. The humanistic perspective argues that personality is primarily unconscious.
4. In developing his theory, Freud conducted scientifically rigorous and well-controlled studies.
5. According to Freud, our mind is more conscious than unconscious.
6. The id refers to the structure of personality that deals with the demands of reality.
7. Regression is the most powerful and pervasive defense mechanism.
8. Fixation occurs when the individual remains locked in a stage because needs are under-gratified or overgratified.
9. The order of the stages in the psychodynamic perspective is oral, phallic, anal, genital, and latency.
10. During the genital stage, young children may experience the Oedipus complex.
11. Research has found that sexuality is the pervasive underlying force behind personality.
12. Horney emphasized the role of the collective unconscious.
13. The superego is an emotionally laden idea or image in the collective unconscious.
14. Overcompensation, according to Jung, describes what a person does to overcome imagined or real inferiorities by developing one's abilities.
15. For Skinner, personality is behavior.
16. The behavioral perspective argues that unconscious motives determine personality.
17. In social cognitive theory, there are reciprocal influences of behavior, environment, and person/cognitive factors.
18. Optimism is characterized by explaining bad events as being caused by internal, stable, and global factors.
19. The humanistic perspective stresses the importance of observable behavior and environmental influences on personality.
20. Self-concept and self-esteem refer to the same thing—a person's overall perceptions of his or her abilities, behavior, and personality.
21. Self-actualization refers to the ability to satisfy the lower motives in Maslow's hierarchy of motives.
22. Cardinal traits are those that most people have and are limited traits that rarely are shown.
23. The situationist view argues that the situation has little effect on personality.
24. Mischel has attacked social cognitive theory, arguing that both person and situation variables are important in understanding personality.
25. The Barnum effect refers to the special ability that palmists have to accurately assess personality.
26. The type of assessment that involves ambiguous stimuli is referred to as objective tests.
27. Most psychologists agree that the Rorschach Inkblot test meets the criteria of reliability and validity.
28. The Rorschach Inkblot test and the Thematic Apperception Test are examples of empirically keyed tests.

29.     The test that was developed by giving many statements to both mental patients and normal people was the MMPI.

30.     Behavioral assessment focuses on directly observing an individual's behavior.

## Practice Test 1

1.     Which of the following concepts is not part of the definition of personality?
        a.     thoughts
        b.     emotions
        c.     behaviors
        d.     situations

2.     According to psychodynamic theorists, personality is primarily
        a.     unconscious.
        b.     shaped by self-actualization.
        c.     conscious.
        d.     acquired through reinforcement and punishment.

3.     According to Freud, which part of the personality is dominated by the pleasure principle?
        a.     the id
        b.     the conscience
        c.     the ego
        d.     the superego

4.     According to Freud, the executive branch of the personality is called the
        a.     ego.
        b.     superego.
        c.     id.
        d.     conscience.

5.     The moral branch of personality, according to the psychodynamic perspective, is
        a.     ego.
        b.     superego.
        c.     id.
        d.     regression.

6.     _____ are the ego's protective methods for reducing anxiety by unconsciously distorting reality.
        a.     Sublimations
        b.     Archetypes
        c.     Defense mechanisms
        d.     Cardinal traits

7.     During the Oedipus complex,
        a.     the child enters the anal stage.
        b.     the child develops an intense desire to replace the parent of the same sex.
        c.     the child represses all interest in sexuality.
        d.     the genital stage begins.

8.  During what Freudian stage of development does the child focus on social and intellectual skills?

    a.  the oral stage
    b.  the anal stage
    c.  the latency stage
    d.  the genital stage

9.  Which of the following is not a criticism of Freud's ideas about personality?

    a.  Sexuality is not the pervasive underlying force Freud believed it to be.
    b.  Experiences after 5 years of age are powerful in shaping adult personality.
    c.  Conscious thoughts play little role in our personality.
    d.  Sociocultural factors are much more important Freud argued.

10. If a person tries to conceal her weaknesses in an exaggerated way, she might be showing _____, according to Adler.

    a.  overcompensation
    b.  compensation
    c.  fixation
    d.  situationism

11. According to Jung, archetypes

    a.  are conscious events.
    b.  are responsible for hallucinations and delusions.
    c.  are derived from the collective unconscious.
    d.  cause inferiority and superiority complexes.

12. People cope with anxiety by moving either toward people, away from people, or against people, according to

    a.  Freud.
    b.  Jung.
    c.  Horney.
    d.  Adler.

13. An important difference between the behavioral and social cognitive perspectives relates to

    a.  the unconscious.
    b.  cognition.
    c.  early childhood events.
    d.  the collective unconscious.

14. "Personality is a collection of observable behavior." Who is most likely to have said that?

    a.  Freud
    b.  Adler
    c.  Skinner
    d.  Chodrow

15. Which perspective would be most likely to stress the importance of reinforcement and the environment in personality?

    a.  behaviorism
    b.  psychodynamic
    c.  humanistic
    d.  individual

16. Which personality theorists would place the most emphasis on cognitive factors mediating the environment's effects on the personality?
    a.  psychoanalysts
    b.  behaviorists
    c.  social cognitive theorists
    d.  humanists

17. Which of the following stresses the interaction between behavior, environment, and person/cognitive variables?
    a.  humanistic
    b.  psychodynamic
    c.  behavioral
    d.  social cognitive

18. According to Bandura, the belief that a person has mastery over a situation and the ability to produce positive outcomes is called
    a.  self-efficacy.
    b.  self-esteem.
    c.  self-concept.
    d.  self-actualization.

19. According to Walter Mischel, a key to understanding personality is the concept of
    a.  delay of gratification.
    b.  repression.
    c.  unconditional positive regard.
    d.  central traits.

20. According to Rogers, acceptance of another person regardless of the person's behavior is called
    a.  self-esteem.
    b.  unconditional positive regard.
    c.  self-actualization.
    d.  hierarchy of motives.

## Practice Test 2

1.  Rogers would describe a person who is open to experience, not very defensive, and sensitive to others as being
    a.  fixed in the anal stage.
    b.  receiving conditional positive regard.
    c.  a fully functioning person.
    d.  striving for superiority.

2.  A person's overall evaluation of his or her self-worth or self-image is referred to as
    a.  self-esteem.
    b.  self-worth.
    c.  self-efficacy.
    d.  all of the above

3. Unconditional positive regard and conditions of worth are important concepts in
   a. the behavioral perspective.
   b. the social cognitive perspective.
   c. the humanistic perspective.
   d. trait theory.

4. Each of the following is considered one of the five main factors in personality except
   a. extraversion.
   b. emotional stability.
   c. agreeableness.
   d. intellect.

5. Which of the following personality characteristics was found to be common to Abraham Lincoln, Franklin Roosevelt, George Washington, and other great American presidents?
   a. neuroticism
   b. pessimism
   c. openness to experience
   d. introversion

6. On the issue of innate versus learned, the position of psychodynamic psychologists is
   a. innate.
   b. learned.
   c. innate and learned.
   d. neither nor learned; this theory does not address this issue.

7. Which of the following is NOT one of the archetypes proposed by Carl Jung?
   a. anima (female)
   b. mandala (self)
   c. wheel (technology)
   d. animus (male)

8. The following are criticisms of the psychodynamic perspective, EXCEPT
   a. the perspective is too positive and optimistic.
   b. early life experiences are the most important in determining personality.
   c. the perspective has a largely male, Western bias.
   d. the main concepts of this theory are difficult to test.

9. Which of the following concepts is relevant to the social cognitive perspective of personality?
   a. fixation
   b. unconditional positive regard
   c. reciprocal determinism
   d. projective tests

10. Self-efficacy can be increased by
    a. ignoring old successes and focusing on the future.
    b. doing difficult tasks before easier tasks.
    c. doing something that you can expect to be able to do.
    d. choosing new and challenging projects.

11. An individual's belief about whether the outcomes of his actions depend on what he does or on events outside of his personal control is referred to as
    a. self-esteem.
    b. self-concept.
    c. delayed gratification.
    d. locus of control.

12. Optimism is associated with all the following, EXCEPT
    a. good physical health.
    b. coming up with stable explanations for bad events.
    c. coming up with external explanations for bad events.
    d. avoidance of depression.

13. The behavioral and social cognitive perspectives have been criticized on all these grounds, EXCEPT
    a. they have fostered a scientific climate for understanding personality.
    b. they are too concerned with change.
    c. they ignore the role of biology.
    d. they reduce personality to a few factors.

14. Carl Rogers argued that people need _____ positive regard, which was his term for accepting, valuing, and being positive toward another person regardless of the person's behavior.
    a. conditional
    b. unconditional
    c. unconditioned
    d. conditioned

15. According to the humanistic perspective, which of the following is not consistent with the fully functioning person?
    a. being very defensive
    b. being aware of and sensitive to the self
    c. being sensitive to the external world
    d. being open to experience

16. Based on research, there are a few strategies recommended to improve self-esteem. In the following list, find the one that is not one of those strategies.
    a. experiencing emotional support and approval
    b. going to therapy
    c. identifying the causes of self-esteem
    d. coping

17. The humanistic perspective has been criticized on all of the following grounds, EXCEPT
    a. some of its central concepts are difficult to test.
    b. it relies too much on the experimental method.
    c. it is too optimistic.
    d. its views may encourage narcissism.

18.   According to Allport's view of personality, traits that are limited in frequency and least important in understanding an individual's personality are referred to as _____ traits.

   a.   cardinal
   b.   secondary
   c.   central
   d.   lower

19.   Projective tests are more likely to be used by a psychologist from the

   a.   psychodynamic perspective.
   b.   behavioral perspective.
   c.   humanistic perspective
   d.   social cognitive perspective.

20.   Which of the following statements is consistent with an internal locus of control?

   a.   Getting a job is a matter of being in the right place at the right time.
   b.   I believe that people have a destiny waiting for them.
   c.   I'm not lucky; I just make things happen.
   d.   Doing well in a class depends on the teacher you get.

## Practice Test 3

1.   "This is a test of your imagination. I am going to show you some pictures, and I want you to tell me an interesting story about each one. What is happening, how did it develop, and how will it end?" These instructions are part of the preparation for the

   a.   Thematic Apperception Test.
   b.   Rorschach Inkblot test.
   c.   MMPI.
   d.   self-report test.

2.   A basic assumption of behavioral assessment is that

   a.   the unconscious always influences behavior.
   b.   personality cannot be evaluated apart from the environment.
   c.   traits are consistent even in varying situations.
   d.   personality is inherited.

3.   Which type of personality test is designed to elicit the individual's unconscious feeling?

   a.   self-report tests
   b.   the MMPI
   c.   NEO-PI-R
   d.   projective tests

4.   The major personality theories differ on their answers to the following questions, EXCEPT:

   e.   Is personality unique to humans or do animals have personalities?
   f.   Is personality unlearned or learned?
   g.   Are people aware of the causes of their personality?
   h.   Is personality influenced by internal or external factors?

5.   The behavioral perspective is to _____ factors as the humanistic perspective is to _____ factors.

   a.   innate; learned
   b.   external; internal
   c.   learned; unconscious
   d.   internal; external

6.    Fred intended to ask his date, "what do you want from the menu?" but instead he said, "what do you want with my money?" Poor Fred, he just

   a.    demonstrated his introversion.
   b.    made a Freudian slip.
   c.    showed his low self-esteem.
   d.    let her know that he is a neurotic.

7.    Todd brags all the time. He also insists on being called "The Toddmeister." If Adler considered Todd's tendencies, he would probably conclude that Todd has

   a.    an inferiority complex.
   b.    a fixation on the anal stage of psychosexual development.
   c.    a superiority complex.
   d.    managed his anxiety by moving away from people..

8.    Serena scored very high in optimism on the optimism scale developed by Martin Seligman. She just received a letter from her top-choice university saying that she was not admitted into the freshman class. Serena is likely to come up with the following explanation for the rejection letter:

   a.    I'm not smart enough for that university.
   b.    I'll never get into a good school.
   c.    This must have been a tough year to get into that university.
   d.    I knew I needed better SATs.

9.    Which of the following perspectives is the most optimistic regarding our ability to control our lives and basically choose our personalities?

   a.    psychodynamic
   b.    behavioral
   c.    humanistic
   d.    social cognitive

10.    According to Rogers, human relations must be based on all the following, EXCEPT

   a.    being a sensitive listener and understanding another's true feelings.
   b.    being open with our feelings and dropping pretenses and facades.
   c.    accepting others as long as they do the things that are considered right in our society.
   d.    unconditional positive regard.
   e.

11.    In the beginning of Chapter 12, you were asked to "write down six or seven personality traits that you think best describe you." According to Allport, you were being asked to list your

   a.    cardinal traits.
   b.    secondary traits.
   c.    central traits.
   d.    lower traits.

12.    According to Eysenck, a person who can't accept even constructive criticism and is highly emotional is likely to be

   a.    highly introverted.
   b.    high in psychoticism.
   c.    unstable in neuroticism.
   d.    highly extroverted.

13. Rhonda measures high in pessimism, yet her psychologist argues that the results of the personality assessment must be considered as they apply to specific situations. The psychologist then proceeds to ask Rhonda about her level of pessimism on school issues, home issues, and relationship issues. Rhonda's psychologist is likely to agree with the
    a. psychodynamic perspective.
    b. interactionist perspective.
    c. humanistic perspective.
    d. behavioral perspective.

14. Horoscopes and fortune cookies have in common that they take advantage of the
    a. situationist view.
    b. unconscious.
    c. naïve personality.
    d. Barnum effect.

15. Rorschach Inkblot tests
    a. when administered by two different psychologists result in the same personality assessment.
    b. are valued as good assessment tools by psychodynamic psychologists.
    c. give individuals four alternatives for each question.
    d. are often used by behavioral psychologists to measure personality.

16. Which of the following characteristics is associated with an external locus of control?
    a. very ready to explore their surroundings
    b. highly Perceptive
    c. shy about asking questions
    d. better problem-solving skills

17. Self-_____ is to the social cognitive perspective as self-_____ is to the humanistic perspective.
    a. esteem; concept.
    b. concept; esteem.
    c. esteem; efficacy.
    d. efficacy; esteem.

18. One of the main differences between the behavioral and the social cognitive perspectives is that
    a. social cognitive theorists emphasize the extent to which we can control our environments.
    b. behaviorists emphasize reciprocal determinism.
    c. social cognitive theorists focus on unconscious influences on personality.
    d. behaviorists define personality based on how people act, think, and feel.

19. One thing that the psychodynamic and the humanistic perspectives have in common is that
    a. both base some of their theories on studies with unrepresentative samples of normal healthy populations.
    b. both consider the importance of early life experiences.
    c. both value the power of the person to choose his or her destiny.
    d. both consider behaviors the main determinant of personality.

20.    Projective tests are designed to figure out

    a.    what happened in a person's early childhood that might not be consciously remembered.

    b.    a person's explanation of his or her personality.

    c.    the main characteristics of an individual's personality.

    d.    the extent to which a person wants to be liked by the researcher as reflected in socially desirable answers.

## Connections

*Take advantage of all the other study tools available for this chapter!*

## Media Integration

| NAME OF CLIP | DESCRIPTION | KEY CONCEPTS AND IDEAS |
|---|---|---|
| | | **Theories of Personality** |
| | | **Psychodynamic Perspectives** |
| Freud's Contribution to Psychology | Video clip places Freud's contribution to psychology in a historical context. The origins of his perspective in the study of hysteria as well as his view of the brain are discussed. | History of psychology<br>Hysteria<br>Dream analysis<br>Manifest content of dreams<br>Repression |
| Freudian Interpretation of Dreams | This video clip is an introduction to Freud's theory of dream analysis. The concept of dream work and its processes are discussed. Common themes in Freudian dream analysis are also discussed. | Dreams<br>Dream work<br>Displacement<br>Condensation<br>Symbolization<br>Projection<br>Ego<br>Manifest dream<br>Latent dream |
| Freudian Structures of the Mind | The video clip "Freudian structures of the mind" explains the id, ego, and superego and their development. The psyche is presented as being in an ongoing struggle. The concept of repression is introduced and a discussion of how repression occurs is presented. The concept of the unconscious is also explained. | Sigmund Freud<br>Id<br>Ego<br>Superego<br>Repression<br>Unconscious |
| | | **Behavioral and Social Cognitive Perspectives** |
| Operant Conditioning | This interactivity assists participants in understanding and | Operant conditioning<br>Reinforcement |

| | applying the concepts of operant conditioning, illustrating the concepts of reinforcement and punishment, including positive and negative reinforcement and punishment. Definitions, characteristics, and examples of the different reinforcement schedules are presented. | Punishment<br>Positive reinforcement<br>Negative reinforcement<br>Positive punishment<br>Negative punishment<br>Reinforcement schedules |
|---|---|---|
| | | **Humanistic Perspectives** |
| Self-Actualization | Adventure racers in the grueling Eco-Challenge are showcased. Participants share their motivations for engaging in this extreme sport. | Self-actualization<br>Motivation |
| | | **Trait Perspectives** |
| Styles of Responses | The interactivity "Styles of Responses" guides the participant in an assessment of his or her own response style. Four modes of response are discussed: passive, manipulative, aggressive, and assertive. | Response styles<br>Passive<br>Manipulative<br>Aggressive<br>Assertive |
| Culture and Self | This video clip starts with insights into what people in a conversation are thinking about themselves. The effect of culture on self-concept and how that definition of the self influences individual psychology are discussed. Experts Markus and Kitayama are interviewed and present their perspective on the role of culture in the definition of self, comparing American and Asian cultures. They discuss how we pass our cultural understandings through interactions. The video clip also presents a discussion of the relationship between the motivation for achievement and the definition of the self. The topics of | Self-concept<br>Culture<br>Social psychology<br>Cross-cultural psychology<br>Independent vs. interdependent self<br>Achievement motivation |

| | | Personality Assessment |
|---|---|---|
| | conformity and persuasion and their relationship with definition of self are discussed. | |
| Self-Report Bias in Surveys | This exercise demonstrates the problems associated with self-report bias in surveys. Participants are asked to rate the degree to which they are concerned about a series of social issues and to rate the degree to which others are concerned about those same social issues. The tendency for self-enhancing bias is illustrated. | Self-report bias<br>Self<br>Self-enhancing bias |

**Online Learning Center (www.mhhe.com/Santrockp7u)**

- Interact and make learning fun!
  - o **Interactive Exercises**
    - ▪ Response Styles
    - ▪ Shyness Inventory
  - o **Interactive Review**
    - ▪ Level of Analysis: Personality Differences
- Brush up on the Key Terms for this chapter by first reviewing the electronic **Glossary** (in English or Spanish) and then testing your retention using the **Flashcard** feature.
- **"Notes"**- this feature allows you to use the website as you would your text, inserting your own study notes and highlighting areas of particular importance.

**In Your Text**

- Found throughout each chapter, the **Review and Sharpen Your Thinking** feature breaks the text into logical chunks, allowing you to process, review, and reflect thoughtfully on the information that you've just read. When going back to *study* the chapter, try reading the feature *before* the section of text to which it relates. In doing so, you will be able to focus your attention on important concepts *as* you encounter them. In this chapter, this feature can be found on the following pages: pp. 478, 485, 490, 495, 500, and 510.

**Practice Quizzes**

- Test your knowledge of personality by taking the different practice quizzes found on your text's **Online Learning Center** and on the **In-Psych Plus CD-ROM** packaged with your text.

**ANSWER KEY**

**In Your Own Words**

✓ Paraphrase the textbook's definition of personality.

*In the textbook, personality is defined as a pattern of enduring, distinctive thoughts, emotions, and behaviors that characterize the way an individual adapts to the world. This question addresses the extent to which the student is able to independently define each of the concepts that form this definition. This definition includes key concepts such as pattern, endurance, thoughts, emotions, behaviors, characterize, individual, adapts, and world. Try using alternate concepts for each of these key concepts to discover new versions of the definition of personality.*

✓ Consider how reciprocal determinism has played a role in your personality. First, describe what is reciprocal determinism. Second, describe one aspect of your personality that has been shaped by choices that you have made.

*According to Albert Bandura, reciprocal determinism is the way behavior, environment, and person/cognitive factors interact to create personality. The main difference between this and the behavioral view is the emphasis on the importance of how the person perceives situations and his or her power to choose environments that in turn influence actions and thoughts. For example, a person who decides to go to college is choosing an environment that is likely to influence his or her behaviors and mental processes. The challenges of college may change a misfit into a creative student, or the other way around.*

✓ Based on the definition of optimism as an explanatory style—that is, how a person explains bad events—how optimistic are you? How do you think that this aspect of your personality influences your well-being?

*According to Martin Seligman, optimism is an explanatory style, a way of explaining things that happen in your life. When a bad thing happens, let's say, a bad grade on a test, the optimist explains the situation as caused by external factors ("The test was not fair"), as unstable ("I'm not like this, this is temporary"), and as specific ("It was just this test, I'll do better on the next one"). Pessimists tend to think the opposite. If a bad thing happens, the pessimist takes the blame (internal), thinks that he is always to be blamed (stable), and that he is to be blamed for everything (global). Optimism has been associated with physical and mental health, whereas pessimism has been associated with the psychological state of helplessness.*

✓ List some behaviors of others that exemplify conditional positive regard and unconditional positive regard toward you.

*Conditional positive regard, according to Rogers, is what most parents exhibit toward their children. They withdraw love and attention if the child does not behave according to their preferred standard of behaviors. Rogers recommends unconditional positive regard and argues that everybody, regardless of how annoying he or she is, deserves unconditional positive regard.*

## Correcting the Incorrect

1. Personality consists of a stable pattern of behavior *and mental processes.* (p. 477)
2. The key issues in psychology are *innate versus learned, conscious versus unconscious, and internal versus external influences.* (p. 477)
3. The *psychodynamic* perspective argues that personality is primarily unconscious. (p. 478)
4. In developing his theory, Freud *observed psychiatric patients.* (p. 478)
5. According to Freud, our mind is *more unconscious than conscious.* (p. 479)
6. The *ego* refers to the structure of personality that deals with the demands of reality. (p. 479)
7. *Repression* is the most powerful and pervasive defense mechanism. (p. 480)
8. Fixation occurs when the individual remains locked in a stage because needs are under-gratified or overgratified. (p. 481)
9. The order of the stages in the psychodynamic perspective is *oral, anal, phallic, genital, and latency.* (p. 481)
10. During the *phallic stage,* young children experience the Oedipus complex. (p. 481)

11. Research has found that *sexuality is not* the pervasive underlying force behind personality. (p. 482)

12. *Jung* emphasized the role of the collective unconscious. (p. 483)

13. *An archetype* is an emotionally laden idea or image in the collective unconscious. (p. 483)

14. *Compensation, according to Adler,* describes what a person does to overcome imagined or real inferiorities by developing one's abilities. (p. 484)

15. For Skinner, personality is behavior. (p. 486)

16. The behavioral perspective argues that *the environment determines personality.* (p. 486)

17. In social cognitive theory, there are reciprocal influences of behavior, environment, and person/cognitive factors. (p. 487)

18. *Pessimism* is characterized by explaining bad events as being caused by internal, stable, and global factors. (p. 489)

19. The humanistic perspective stresses *personal growth, freedom to choose, and positive qualities.* (p. 491)

20. *Self-concept and self-esteem do not refer to the same thing. Self-esteem refers to a person's overall perceptions of his or her abilities, behavior, and personality, whereas self-concept refers to the overall perception of abilities, behavior, and personality.* (pp. 491, 493)

21. Self-actualization refers to *the motivation to develop one's full potential.* (p. 493)

22. *Secondary traits* are those that most people have and are limited traits that rarely are shown. (p. 497)

23. The situationist view argues that the situation has a *great effect* on personality. (p. 500)

24. Mischel has attacked *trait theory,* arguing that both person and situation variables are important in understanding personality. (p. 500)

25. The Barnum effect refers to *broad predictions made by people such as palmists that are likely to be true for most people.* (p. 501)

26. The type of assessment that involves ambiguous stimuli is referred to as *projective tests.* (p. 501)

27. Most psychologists agree that the Rorschach Inkblot test *does not meet* the criteria of reliability and validity. (p. 502)

28. The Rorschach Inkblot test and the Thematic Apperception Test are examples of *projective tests.* (p. 501)

29. The test that was developed by giving many statements to both mental patients and normal people was the MMPI. (p. 506)

30. Behavioral assessment focuses on directly observing an individual's behavior. (p. 508)

## Practice Test 1

1. a. no; cognition is part of the definition of personality
   b. no; these mental processes are also part of the definition of personality
   c. no; actions are part of the definition of personality
   d. YES; situations is not a concept addressed in the definition of personality
   p. 477

2. a. YES; personality is shaped by unconscious processes
   b. no; this sounds too much like the humanistic perspective
   c. no; remember that personality is mostly out of awareness
   d. no; this option describes the behavioral viewpoint
   p. 478

3.  a.  YES; the id is dominated by the pleasure principle
    b.  no; the ego operates according to the reality principle
    c.  no; the ego operates according to the reality principle
    d.  no; the superego is often described as being our conscience
    p. 479

4.  a.  YES; the ego deals with the demands of reality
    b.  no; the superego is the moral branch of the personality
    c.  no; the id always seeks pleasure and avoids pain
    d.  no; this is not one of the three components of personality according to Freud
    p. 479

5.  a.  no; the ego deals with the demands of reality
    b.  YES; the superego is the moral branch of the personality
    c.  no; the id always seeks pleasure and avoids pain
    d.  no; this is not one of the three components of personality according to Freud
    p. 480

6.  a.  no; sublimation is an example of a defense mechanism
    b.  no; archetypes are emotion-laden ideas and images in the collective unconscious
    c.  YES; this is the definition of defense mechanism
    d.  no; cardinal traits are a type of trait proposed by Allport
    p. 480

7.  a.  no; the anal stage occurs earlier
    b.  YES; the child also has the desire to enjoy the affections of the opposite-sex parent
    c.  no; this describes the latency stage, which appears following the Oedipus complex
    d.  no; the genital stage is the fifth Freudian stage, appearing after the Oedipus complex
    p. 481

8.  a.  no; the mouth is center of pleasure in this stage
    b.  no; this is associated with pleasure regarding the eliminative function
    c.  YES; this is related to going to school
    d.  no; this coincides with puberty, where there is a sexual reawakening
    p. 481

9.  a.  no; this is a criticism
    b.  no; this is a criticism
    c.  YES; in fact, conscious thoughts play a large role in our personality
    d.  no; this is a criticism
    p. 482

10. a.  YES; this is the definition of overcompensation
    b.  no; the key is that she is trying to conceal her weakness, not trying to overcome
    c.  no; fixation refers to receiving too much or too little stimulation
    d.  no; situationism is the notion that personality changes according to the situation
    p. 484

11. a.  no; the opposite is true
    b.  no; they are unrelated to such experiences
    c.  YES; archetypes are emotion-laden ideas and images from collective unconscious; examples are the anima and the animus
    d.  no; they are not related to those aspects of personality
    p. 483

12. a. no; Freud did not address these social aspects of personality
    b. no; Jung focused more on the unconscious
    c. YES; according to Horney, these are ways that people cope with anxiety
    d. no; Adler did not consider these aspects of personality
    p. 483

13. a. no; neither places any weight on the unconscious
    b. CORRECT; social cognitive theory suggests that cognitive factors play a role
    c. no; this is not an important difference
    d. no; neither even refers to the collective unconscious
    p. 486

14. a. no; Freud stressed the role of the unconscious mind on personality
    b. no; Adler's focus is on striving for superiority
    c. YES; for Skinner, personality is behavior
    d. no; her focus is on how people define the self in terms of relationships
    p. 486

15. a. YES; behaviorism focuses on reinforcement and the environment
    b. no; the emphasis is on unconscious processes
    c. no; the humanistic perspective stresses personal growth and freedom to choose
    d. no; Adler stressed our need to strive for superiority
    p. 486

16. a. no; unconscious processes play the primary role in personality for psychoanalysts
    b. no; the behaviorists would say that cognitive factors play no role in personality
    c. YES; these theorists would say that behavior, environment, and cognitive factors interact with one another
    d. no; the humanists stress self-actualization, positive regard, and self-concept
    p. 487

17. a. no; the humanistic perspective stresses personal growth and freedom to choose
    b. no; unconscious processes play the primary role in personality for psychoanalysts
    c. no; this perspective focuses on the role of the environment in personality
    d. CORRECT
    p. 487

18. a. CORRECT; this defines self-efficacy, and it is one of the cognitive/person factors
    b. no; self-esteem is how we evaluate and feel about our self-concept
    c. no; this is an individual's overall perception of ability, behavior, and personality
    d. no; this term refers to the motivation to develop one's full potential
    p. 488

19. a. YES; this refers to the ability to defer immediate gratification for something better in the future
    b. no; repression is an example of a defense mechanism from the psychodynamic view
    c. no; unconditional positive regard is a concept from the humanistic perspective
    d. no; these are traits that are adequate enough to describe someone's personality
    p. 487

20. a.  no; self-esteem is the person's overall evaluation of his or her self-worth or self-image.
    b.  CORRECT
    c.  no; this term refers to the motivation to develop one's full potential
    d.  no; this is a way to order an individual's needs from physiological needs to self-actualization
    p. 492

## Practice Test 2

1. a.  no; this pertains to the psychodynamic perspective
   b.  no; while Rogers addressed this issue, the question refers to another aspect of his theories
   c.  CORRECT; these characterize the fully functioning person
   d.  no; this is a concept associated with the work of Adler
   p. 492

2. a.  CORRECT; this is the definition of self-esteem
   b.  no; this is only part of the definition of self-esteem
   c.  no; this is the belief that one can master a situation and produce desired outcomes
   d.  incorrect; even if a and b are close, self-efficacy refers to a different aspect of personality
   p. 493

3. a.  no; the behavioral perspective emphasizes reinforcement
   b.  no; this perspective underscores learning and cognitive processes
   c.  YES; these are important concepts in the humanistic perspective
   d.  no; traits stress broad dispositions that lead to characteristic responses
   p. 492

4. a.  no; this is one of the "big five"
   b.  no; this is one of the "big five"
   c.  no; this is one of the "big five"
   d.  YES; this is not among the "big five"
   p. 498

5. a.  no; however, they were attentive to their emotions
   b.  no; this was not part of the study
   c.  YES; openness to experience showed the highest correlation with greatness as an American president
   d.  no; actually, the opposite is true
   p. 498

6. a.  YES; the psychodynamic perspective argues that the structure of personality is innate and that there are a number of developmental stages to which we are predisposed
   b.  no; while there are a number of aspects to this theory that involve learning, the dominant position is an innate or deterministic view of personality
   c.  incorrect
   d.  incorrect
   p. 478

7. a.  no; this represents our feminine side
   b.  no; this is a figure within a circle and it has shown up in art through the ages
   c.  YES; the wheel is a specific technology and this is inconsistent with the concept of collective unconscious
   d.  no; this represents our masculine side
   p. 483

8. a. YES; this is not a criticism
   b. no; this is the position of this theory, for which is has been criticized
   c. no; this is one of the criticisms of this perspective
   d. no; this is a serious problem with this perspective; if it can't be tested, it can't be supported

   p. 484

9. a. no; this concept is associated with the psychodynamic perspective and the psychosexual stages of development
   b. no; this concept is associated with Rogers' humanistic perspective
   c. YES; this is a concept proposed by Bandura to describe the way behavior, environment, and cognitive factors interact to create personality
   d. no; projective tests measure unconscious influences, and these are not of interest to social cognitive psychologists

   p. 487

10. a. no; to increase self-efficacy, it is recommended that the person consider old successes
    b. no; to increase self-efficacy, the opposite is recommended
    c. YES; to increase self-efficacy, it is recommended that we engage in something at which we know we are likely to succeed
    d. no; before doing this, we are advised to do something we know we are able to do

    p. 488

11. a. no; self-esteem is the sense of self-worth that a person has
    b. no; self-concept involves the beliefs that a person has about his or her own abilities
    c. no; delayed gratification refers to the ability people have to choose how and when their behaviors will be reinforced
    d. YES; this concept and the scale to measure it were developed by Julian Rotter

    p. 488

12. a. no; this is associated with optimism; people who had been classified as optimistic at age 25 were healthier at ages 45 to 60 than those classified as pessimistic
    b. YES; this is actually consistent with pessimism
    c. no; this is consistent with the optimistic explanatory style
    d. no; this is one of the positive mental health factors associated with optimism

    p. 489

13. a. YES; this is actually one of the main contributions of these perspectives, their strong focus on research
    b. no; they have been criticized for focusing too much on the influence of a changing environment
    c. no; they have ignored the role of biology and instincts
    d. no; they have reduced personality to a few factors, such as in the reciprocal determinism approach that considers three forces shaping personality

    p. 490

14. a. no; conditional positive regard is when people may threaten to withhold their love unless we conform to their standards
    b. YES; this is the correct term
    c. no; while this may seem like a trick item, in psychology it is very important to distinguish between unconditional and unconditioned; *unconditioned* refers to something that has not been learned, as you recall from Chapter 7, classical conditioning
    d. no; this refers to something that has been learned, as reported in Chapter 7
    p. 492

15. a. YES; this is inconsistent, as the fully functioning person is not very defensive
    b. no; this is characteristic of the fully functioning person
    c. no; this is characteristic of the fully functioning person
    d. no; this is characteristic of the fully functioning person
    p. 492

16. a. no; this is one of the recommended strategies for increasing self-esteem
    b. YES; while this might help, it is not one of the recommended strategies
    c. no; this is one of the recommended strategies for increasing self-esteem
    d. no; this is one of the recommended strategies for increasing self-esteem
    p. 495

17. a. no; similar to the psychodynamic perspective, this view has a few concepts, such as self-actualization, that are hard to define and thus hard to test
    b. YES; the opposite is true; humanists actually scorn the experimental approach, in favor of conclusions based on clinical interpretations
    c. no; it has been argued that the view that humanists have of human psychology is unrealistic and simply too optimistic
    d. no; humanists are criticized for promoting excessive self-love and narcissism
    p. 495

18. a. no; cardinal traits are the most powerful and pervasive
    b. YES; examples of secondary traits would be the type of food or music a person likes
    c. no; central traits are usually adequate to describe most people's personalities
    d. no; this is not one of the categories of traits that Allport proposed
    p. 497

19. a. YES; this perspective focuses strongly on unconscious influences; therefore, projective tests would be of interest to a psychodynamic psychologist
    b. no; behaviorists would never use a projective test
    c. no; humanists might be curious, but they would rather ask directly the person to share his or her concerns, possibly through a self-report test
    d. no; social cognitive psychologists focus on conscious influences and that is not what projective tests measure
    p. 502

20. a. no; this is consistent with external locus of control
    b. no; destiny is out of a person's control; therefore, the statement is more consistent with external locus of control
    c. YES; the person asserts that it is not a matter of luck, but rather of personal control; this is consistent with internal locus of control
    d. no; this is consistent with external locus of control
    p. 488

## Practice Test 3

1. a.  CORRECT; the TAT is made up of pictures that elicit information about personality
   b.  no; this test involves asking individuals what they see in inkblots
   c.  no; the MMPI is a self-report test
   d.  no; these tests directly ask people whether items describe their personality or not
   p. 503

2. a.  no; in fact, this is not assumed in behavioral assessment, but is in psychodynamic
   b.  YES; this is an important assumption of behavioral assessment
   c.  no
   d.  no
   p. 508

3. a.  no; these tests directly ask people whether items describe their personality or not
   b.  no; the MMPI is an example of self-report test
   c.  no; this is an example of self-report test that assesses the five main factors
   d.  YES; these tests are designed to elicit unconscious feelings
   p. 501

4. a.  CORRECT; personality psychologists focus on humans; this is not an issue
   b.  no; this is one of the main issues that separate personality theories
   c.  no; this is one of the main issues that separate personality theories
   d.  no; this is one of the main issues that separate personality theories
   p. 477

5. a.  no; the behavioral perspective ignores innate factors, and humanists do not focus on learning and the environment
   b.  YES; behaviorists focus on environmental influences, whereas humanists consider how people control their personalities
   c.  no; while behaviorists do consider learning important, humanists are not interested in unconscious influences
   d.  no; the opposite is true
   pp. 486, 491

6. a.  no; the question does not present any particular evidence of introversion
   b.  YES; this is a misstatement that perhaps reveals Fred's unconscious concern with how much the dinner is going to cost
   c.  no; saying a Freudian slip is not necessarily associated with self-esteem
   d.  no; this question does not address Fred's level of neuroticism
   p. 479

7. a.  no; if he had an inferiority complex he would not be likely to tell others how they are supposed to address him
   b.  no; this would belong in Freud's theory and even in the context of that theory a fixation in the anal stage is not associated with these tendencies
   c.  YES; Todd is manifesting an exaggerated self-importance caused by his feelings of inferiority
   d.  no; this is more consistent with Horney's views within the psychodynamic perspective
   p. 484

8.  a.  no; this is an internal explanation for a bad event, an explanation more characteristic of pessimism
    b.  no; this is a stable explanation ("never") for a bad event
    c.  YES; this is a temporary/unstable explanation for a bad event, likely to be thought of by an optimistic person
    d.  no; this is also an internal explanation for the bad event
    p. 489

9.  a.  no; this perspective, it could be argued, is very pessimistic in this respect
    b.  no; this perspective argues that personality is shaped by the environment, not the individual
    c.  YES; this perspective views people as being innately good and able to self-actualize
    d.  no; the reciprocal determinism view characteristic of the social cognitive perspective strikes a compromise between person/cognitive, environmental, and behavioral influences
    p. 491

10. a.  no; this is the definition of empathy and Rogers considered this very important in human relations
    b.  no; this is the definition of genuine and Rogers considered this very important in human relations
    c.  YES; Rogers believed that people should be accepted and valued, even if they did things we didn't like
    d.  no; this is very important in human relations, according to Rogers
    p. 492

11. a.  no; we are not expected to have cardinal traits, since we are not likely to be known by others by one or two dominating traits
    b.  no; these would refer to traits that are not very informative about personality, such as your sense of fashion and preferred TV shows
    c.  YES; central traits, according to Allport, are precisely those few characteristics that best describe your personality
    d.  no; this is not one of the categories established by Allport
    p. 497

12. a.  no; this question does not address this dimension
    b.  no; this question does not say that the person is not in contact with reality
    c.  YES; this person seems to be moody, anxious, restless, and touchy, the description of being on the side of unstable in the neuroticism dimension
    d.  no; this question does not address this dimension
    p. 497

13. a.  no; the psychologist is not asking Rhonda to explore unconscious influences to her pessimism
    b.  YES; Rhonda's psychologist is insisting that Rhonda consider how personality traits may vary depending on the setting
    c.  no; a humanist psychologist would be more interested in Rhonda's ability to manage her pessimism and transform it into optimism
    d.  no; behaviorists would not be interested in measuring pessimism
    p. 499

14. a. no; the situationist view argues that situations have a strong effect on what we consider personality, but this is not the issue addressed in the question
    b. no; they do not take advantage of the unconscious
    c. no; getting a fitting description from a horoscope or a fortune cookies is not a matter of being naïve
    d. YES; this refers to making really broad statements that basically would apply to anybody who reads them

    p. 501

15. a. no; actually, the Rorschach Inkblot test has the problem of being low in reliability
    b. YES; this test is used to assess unconscious influences, of great interest to psychologists from the psychodynamic perspective
    c. no; they actually give people great freedom in their responses
    d. no; behaviorists are not interested the unconscious

    p. 503

16. a. no; this is associated with internal locus of control
    b. no; this is associated with internal locus of control
    c. YES; this is consistent with external locus of control
    d. no; this is associated with internal locus of control

    p. 488

17. a. no; both of these concepts are associated with the humanistic perspective
    b. no; see item a
    c. no; the opposite is true
    d. YES; self-efficacy is the belief that one can master a situation and produce a positive outcome; this concept is representative of the social cognitive view, because it refers to the person's belief that he or she can affect the environment, which in turn will affect the person; however, self-esteem, a concept important in the humanistic perspective, refers to a more general sense of self-worth that influences many aspects of a person's life

    pp. 488, 493

18. a. YES; behaviorists focus only on the effects of the environment, but social cognitive theorists add the aspect of personal control to understanding personality
    b. no; social cognitive theorists are the ones who emphasize reciprocal determinism
    c. no; the psychodynamic perspective is the one that focuses on the unconscious
    d. no; behaviorists focus only on actions

    p. 487

19. a. YES; Freud did studies with psychiatric patients, and Maslow studied extraordinarily successful people; these are unrepresentative samples of normal people
    b. no; this is consistent with the psychodynamic perspective but not with the humanistic perspective
    c. no; this is consistent with the humanistic perspective but not with the psychodynamic perspective
    d. no; this is consistent with the behavioral perspective

    pp. 478, 493

20. a. YES; projective tests consist of ambiguous stimuli
    b. no; the psychodynamic perspective emphasizes the unconscious
    c. no; projective tests do not allow self-reporting of traits
    d. no; social desirability is a flaw that should be avoided in personality assessment

    p. 501

# Chapter 13—Psychological Disorders

## Learning Goals

1. Discuss the characteristics and classifications of abnormal behavior.
2. Distinguish among the various anxiety disorders.
3. Describe the dissociative disorders.
4. Compare the mood disorders, and specify risk factors for depression and suicide.
5. Characterize schizophrenia.
6. Identify the behavior patterns typical of personality disorders.

*After studying Chapter 13, you will be able to:*

- Define abnormal behavior.
- Describe the criteria of abnormal behavior.
- Discuss the causes of psychological disorders and distinguish among biological, psychological, and sociocultural factors.
- Explain how abnormal behavior is classified, and discuss the advantages and disadvantages of the *DSM-IV* classifying system.
- Describe anxiety disorders, including generalized anxiety disorder, panic disorder, phobic disorder, obsessive-compulsive disorder, and post-traumatic stress disorder.
- Discuss the characteristics of dissociative disorders and distinguish among dissociative amnesia, dissociative fugue, and dissociative identity disorder.
- Understand mood disorders, including depressive disorders and bipolar disorder.
- Discuss the causes of mood disorders and the risk of suicide associated with these disorders.
- Understand what is schizophrenia and describe the different types of schizophrenia.
- Evaluate the causes of schizophrenia.
- Describe personality disorders and the three clusters of these disorders: odd/eccentric, dramatic/emotional, and chronic-fearful/avoidant.

## CHAPTER 13: OUTLINE

- About one-third of those who participated in a national survey said that they had experienced one or more psychological disorders in their lifetime. Twenty percent reported that they currently had an active disorder.

- *Abnormal behavior* is defined differently depending on the context; for example, in legal institutions *insanity* is a term used to refer a person's inability to understand the nature and quality or wrongfulness of his or her acts. From psychology's point of view, if the behavior is deviant, maladaptive, and/or personally distressing, it is considered abnormal behavior.

- The explanations for abnormal behavior come from various perspectives, including biological, psychological, and sociocultural.

- The biological approach explains psychological disorders in terms of internal and organic causes. For example, the medical model describes mental disorders as medical disorders with a biological origin. Biological explanations may be structural (e.g., problems in brain structures), biochemical (e.g., neurotransmitter imbalance), or genetic (e.g., presence of certain genetic markers associated with psychological disorders).

- The psychological approach is founded on the main psychological perspectives: psychodynamic, behavioral and social cognitive, and humanistic.

- From the psychodynamic point of view, psychological disorders are caused by unconscious conflicts.

- Behavioral and social cognitive psychologists argue that psychological disorders stem from rewards and punishments in the environment that promote the abnormal behaviors.

- The humanistic perspective focuses on factors that may limit a person's ability to fulfill his or her potential as the causes of psychological disorders.

- The sociocultural approach considers broader contextual variables that may contribute to psychological disorders, such as culture, socioeconomic background, and gender socialization.

- The interactionist, or biopsychosocial, approach suggests that the causes of normal as well as abnormal behaviors are a combination of biological, psychological, and sociocultural factors.

- The *DSM*, published by the American Psychiatric Association, is a widely used system for classifying mental disorders. The most recent version, the *DSM-IV-TR* (published in 2000), is a text revision of the 1994 *DSM-IV*, which included descriptions for over 200 specific disorders.

- The *DSM-IV* uses a multiaxial system, consisting of five dimensions for assessing individuals.

- Critics charge the *DSM-IV* with focusing too much on the medical model, categorizing everyday problems as mental disorders and overemphasizing problems or pathology. A study by Rosenhan illustrated the danger of overemphasizing pathology in diagnosis: eight normal college students instructed to present an incomplete pattern of abnormal behavior were diagnosed with schizophrenia and hospitalized from 3 to 52 days.

- Motor tension, hyperactivity, and apprehensive expectations and thoughts characterize anxiety disorders. Generalized anxiety disorder consists of persistent anxiety for at least one month without specific symptoms.

- *Etiology* refers to the investigation of the causes or significant antecedents of a mental disorder. The etiology of generalized anxiety disorders includes genetic predispositions and life stressors.

- Panic disorder involves recurrent and sudden onset of apprehension or terror and may include agoraphobia, a fear of being in public and being unable to escape or to get help if incapacitated.

- Phobic disorders involve an irrational, overwhelming, persistent fear of an object or a situation. An example is social phobia, an intense fear of being humiliated or embarrassed in public.

- Obsessive-compulsive disorder is a mental disorder characterized by obsessions (anxiety-provoking thoughts that won't go away) and compulsions (ritualistic behaviors performed in a stereotyped way). The most common compulsions include checking, cleaning, and counting.

- Post-traumatic stress disorder (PTSD) is an anxiety disorder that develops through exposure to a traumatic event such as combat, war-related traumas, sexual abuse, assault, or a catastrophic incident. The symptoms of PTSD include flashbacks, emotional numbness, excessive arousal, problems with memory and concentration, feelings of apprehension, and impulsivity. PTSD involves a course of increased symptoms followed by remission or decrease of symptoms; however, this disorder is characterized by the vivid quality of the flashback experiences, which can be triggered by ordinary events that serve as reminders of the traumatic event.

- Dissociative disorders involve a sudden memory loss or change of identity. The concept of hidden observer, developed to study hypnosis, has been theoretically associated with dissociative disorders. Dissociative amnesia is memory loss due to extensive psychological stress. Dissociative fugue is amnesia in addition to unexpected travel away from home and the assumption of a new identity.

- The most dramatic but rare dissociative disorder is dissociative identity disorder; an individual with this disorder has two or more distinct personalities or selves, each having its own memories, behaviors, and relationships. Many individuals with dissociative identity disorder have histories of sexual or physical abuse during early childhood.

- Mood disorders include depressive disorders and bipolar disorder.

- Major depressive disorder is a severe form of depression that involves experiencing unhappiness, fatigue, problems in thinking, and other symptoms for at least two weeks or longer.

- Another depressive disorder is dysthymic disorder, which tends to be longer-lasting with fewer and less severe symptoms than major depressive disorder.

- Bipolar depression is characterized by dramatic mood swings that include mania and depression. Biological explanations of mood disorders focus on heredity, brain processes, and neurotransmitter deregulation.

- Individuals with severe major depressive disorder show a decreased metabolic activity in the cerebral cortex, and depressed individuals experience less of the deep resting sleep. Psychosocial factors have also been suggested as causes of mood disorders. Freud described depression as the turning inward of aggressive instincts. Psychologists from the behavioral perspective argue that depression can be a result of learned helplessness.

- Depressed individuals have been found to resort to a ruminative coping style, which involves focusing on the sadness and hopelessness of their circumstances. From the cognitive perspective, Beck suggests that negative thoughts are the cause of depression. The attributional view of learned helplessness argues that optimistic thinking protects against depression, whereas pessimistic thinking contributes to depression.

- Another approach to understating depression, depressive realism, argues that people with the disorder are simply too realistic. Supporting this view is the observation that people without depression tend to overestimate the extent to which they can control things in their life.

- Among the sociocultural factors, according to Bowlby, is the attachment experience of the person. Bowlby suggests that insecure attachment between child and mother plays a role in depression. Individuals living in poverty are more likely to develop depression than are individuals in a higher socioeconomic status. It has also been argued that the fact that depression is more common and intense in some cultures supports the view that sociocultural factors play a role in this disorder. Another sociocultural factor, gender, has been associated with depression, since women are twice as likely as men to develop depression.

- Experiencing severe depression or other psychological disorders could prompt a person to consider suicide. Statistics indicate that women are more likely to threaten suicide but men are more likely to commit suicide. Suicide runs in families, suggesting a genetic factor. High stress and trauma have also been associated with suicide, as have cultural patterns and sociocultural factors such as economic hardship.

- Distorted thoughts and perceptions, odd communication, inappropriate emotion, abnormal motor behavior, and social withdrawal characterize the schizophrenic disorders. Many schizophrenics have delusions and hallucinations.

- Disorganized schizophrenia consists of delusions and hallucinations that have little or no recognized meaning. In catatonic schizophrenia, the individual engages in bizarre motor behavior, such as being in a completely immobile stupor.

- Paranoid schizophrenia is characterized by delusions of reference, grandeur, and persecution. In undifferentiated schizophrenia, the symptoms don't meet the criteria for the other types, or they meet the criteria for more than one type.

- Genetic factors have been examined as important in schizophrenia, with the disorder running in families. Imbalances in brain chemistry and distorted cerebral blood flow may also be related to schizophrenia. The diathesis-stress view emphasizes a combination of genetic predisposition and environmental stress as causes of schizophrenia.

- Personality disorders are chronic, maladaptive cognitive-behavioral patterns that are thoroughly integrated into the individual's personality. These disorders are grouped into three clusters: odd/eccentric, dramatic/emotionally problematic, and chronic-fearfulness/avoidant.

- The odd/eccentric cluster includes the paranoid, schizoid, and schizotypal personality disorders.

- The dramatic/emotionally problematic cluster includes histrionic, narcissistic, borderline, and antisocial personality disorders. The antisocial personality disorder has been associated with violent crimes and is much more common in males than females. Biological, psychological, and sociocultural factors contribute to the understanding of the antisocial personality disorder.

- The chronic-fearfulness/avoidant cluster includes the avoidant, dependent, passive-aggressive, and obsessive-compulsive personality disorders.

## Building Blocks of Chapter 13

### Clarifying some of the tricky points in Chapter 13
### and
### In Your Own Words
*To respond to the questions and exercises presented in the "In Your Own Words" section, please write your thoughts, perspectives, and reactions on a separate piece of paper.*

### Understanding Psychological Disorders
Behavior that is deviant, maladaptive, or personally distressful is called *abnormal* behavior.

## In Your Own Words
*Please write your thoughts, perspectives, and reactions on a separate piece of paper.*
✓ *Give two examples of each of the three criteria of abnormal behavior.*

The causes of abnormal behavior include *biological*, *psychological*, and *sociocultural* factors. An approach that views abnormal behavior as the result of a physical malfunction in the body is the *biological* approach, which is evident in the *medical* model.

There are three main categories of biological views for psychological disorders: (1) *structural* views, which focus on abnormalities in the functioning of brain structures; (2) *biochemical* views, which emphasize the role of neurotransmitters and hormones; and (3) *genetic* views, which argue that psychological disorders may be explained in terms of genetic foundations.

The *psychological* approach includes the psychodynamic, behavioral, social cognitive, and humanistic perspectives.

From the *psychodynamic* point of view, psychological disorders are caused by unconscious conflicts. Behavioral and social cognitive psychologists argue that psychological disorders are caused by *rewards* and *punishments* in the environment that promote the abnormal behaviors, and the *humanistic* perspective focuses on factors that may limit a person's ability to fulfill his or her potential as the causes of psychological disorders. The *sociocultural* approach focuses on the influence of larger social contexts on psychological disorders, including family, neighborhood, culture, and gender. Women tend to be diagnosed with *internalized* disorders, in particular *anxiety* disorders and *depression*. Men are more likely to have *externalized* disorders. Biological, psychological, and social factors interact to produce abnormal behavior, according to the *interactionist* or *biopsychosocial* approach.

## In Your Own Words
*Please write your thoughts, perspectives, and reactions on a separate piece of paper.*
✓ *Consider the psychological and sociocultural factors that contribute to psychological disorders. Can you find a pattern across disorders? In other words, what psychological and sociocultural factors seem to be associated with more than one psychological disorder? Explain why these factors contribute to psychological disorder.*

Classification systems for mental disorders allow psychologists to *communicate* with one another and do a better job of *predicting* psychological disturbances.

The first edition of the *Diagnostic and Statistical Manual (DSM)* was published in 1952 by the American Psychiatric Association; however, the most recent version is the *DSM-IV-TR*, published in 2000, is a text revision of the *DSM-IV* of 1994.

One of the main features of the *DSM-IV* is the comprehensive *multiaxial* system that it uses to diagnose psychological disorders.

### Helpful Hints for Understanding mental disorders
### Helpful Hint #1:
*The* DSM-IV *is used to classify and diagnosis mental disorders. It does not explain the etiology (causes) of disorders.*

The five axes of the *DSM-IV* are Axis I: all diagnostic categories except *personality* disorders and *mental retardation*; Axis II: personality disorders and *mental retardation*; Axis III: general *medical conditions*; Axis IV: *psychosocial* and *environmental* problems, and; Axis V: *current* level of functioning.

The main criticism of the *DSM* in all its versions is that it continues to foster a *medical* model of psychological disorders.

### In Your Own Words
*Please write your thoughts, perspectives, and reactions on a separate piece of paper.*
✓ *In what ways does the medical model influence the understanding of abnormal behaviors?*

### Anxiety Disorders
Disorders that are characterized by motor tension, hyperactivity, and apprehensive expectations and thoughts are called *anxiety* disorders.

### Helpful Hint #2:
*Anxiety is always future oriented. When we worry or feel anxious our feelings are always based in something that has not happened.*

*Generalized* anxiety disorder consists of persistent anxiety for at least one month, although the individual is unable to specify the reasons for the anxiety. When studying disorders such as generalized anxiety disorders, psychologists are interested in its *etiology,* which refers to the investigation of the causes or significant antecedents of a mental disorder.

Recurrent and sudden apprehension or terror characterize *panic* disorder. For some individuals, panic disorder may be associated with *agoraphobia,* a set of fears centered on being in public and being unable to escape or get help if incapacitated.

Irrational, overwhelming, and persistent fear of an object or a situation is found in *phobic* disorders. Psychodynamic theorists believe that phobias develop as *defense mechanisms,* whereas learning theorists suggest that classical conditioning and *observational* learning explain the development of phobias. Other researchers suggest a possible *biological* predisposition for phobias, since they find a greater incidence of the disorder among first-generation relatives.

An anxiety disorder that consists of anxiety-provoking thoughts that won't go away (called *obsessions)* and/or repetitive, ritualistic behaviors performed in a stereotyped way *(compulsions)* is referred to as *obsessive-compulsive disorder.*

### Helpful Hint #3:
*Obsessions are the thoughts (mental processes) and compulsions are the actions (behaviors) that help reduce the anxiety.*

A mental disturbance that develops through exposure to traumatic events is called *post-traumatic stress* disorder.

### Dissociative Disorders
Psychological disorders that involve sudden losses of memory or changes in identity are called *dissociative disorders.*

Memory loss that is due to extensive psychological stress is called *dissociative amnesia.* A loss of memory in which the individual unexpectedly travels away from home and assumes a new identity is called a *dissociative fugue.*

A dramatic but less common dissociative disorder is *dissociative identity* disorder, in which there are two or more distinct personalities. Many of these individuals have early childhood histories of *sexual* and/or *physical abuse*.

## Mood Disorders

*Mood* disorders are characterized by disturbance in moods. The *depressive* disorders involve depression without mania. In *major depressive* disorder, the mood is so severe that the person cannot function.

Dysthymic disorder is more *chronic* and has *fewer* symptoms than major depressive disorder. Depression is so widespread it is referred to as the *common cold* of mental disorders.

### In Your Own Words
*Please write your thoughts, perspectives, and reactions on a separate piece of paper.*
✓ *What is the difference between feeling depressed and being diagnosed with major depressive disorder?*

Dramatic mood swings characterize the mood disorder called *bipolar* disorder. *Biological* factors are important in bipolar disorder, considering the higher risk of developing bipolar disorder when a first-degree relative has the disorder. The *monoamine* neurotransmitters have also been implicated in mood disorders.

Aaron Beck suggests that *negative thoughts* shape the depressed person's experiences. Seligman argues that depressed people have developed *learned* helplessness, which has also been associated with a *ruminative* coping style that involves extensive focus on feelings of sadness and hopelessness.

Depressive *realism* refers to the tendency of people with depression to see their world accurately and realistically. People who don't have depression tend to *overestimate* the amount of control they have in their lives.

Severe *depression* and other psychological disorders can cause individuals to want to commit suicide.

### Helpful Hint #4:
*Never assume that because an individual is depressed, he or she is suicidal. The vast majority of people diagnosed with depression never become suicidal. However, the majority of suicidal individuals are depressed.*

Gender differences in suicide rates are reflected in the facts that *females* are more likely to threaten suicide but *males* are more likely to actually commit suicide. Regarding biological factors, the neurotransmitter *serotonin* has been found in low levels in postmortem analyses of people who have committed suicide.

## Schizophrenia

The *schizophrenic* disorders are characterized by distorted thoughts and perceptions, odd communication, inappropriate emotion, abnormal motor behavior, and social withdrawal. Many schizophrenics have false beliefs, called *delusions;* they also may hear or see things not there, called *hallucinations*.

They may communicate in incoherent, loose word associations called *word salad*.

A type of schizophrenia characterized by delusions and hallucinations that have little or no recognizable meaning is *disorganized schizophrenia*. Bizarre motor behavior is the central feature of *catatonic schizophrenia*. In a catatonic state, an individual may show *waxy flexibility*. The central theme of paranoid schizophrenia is complex, elaborate *delusions*.

The three main types of delusions are *grandeur*, *reference*, and *persecution*.

A fourth form of schizophrenia, characterized by disorganized behavior, hallucinations, delusions, and incoherence, is *undifferentiated schizophrenia*.

Genetic factors are strongly implicated as a cause of schizophrenia: an *identical* twin of a person with schizophrenia has a *46%* chance of developing the disorder. In other words, the more *similar* the genetic makeup, the higher the *risk* of developing the disorder. Other biological factors include enlarged *ventricles* in the brains of people with schizophrenia and higher-than-normal levels of the neurotransmitter *dopamine*. The *diathesis-stress* view suggests that a combination of environmental stress and *biogenetic* predisposition is involved in the disorder of schizophrenia. *Sociocultural* factors are also involved, because the type and the incidence of schizophrenia vary from culture to culture.

### *Personality Disorders*

When personality traits become inflexible and maladaptive, *personality disorders* develop. The different personality disorders are clustered around three types of characteristics.

Cluster A involves *odd or eccentric* behaviors; Cluster B involves *dramatic or erratic behaviors,* and a third involves *fear and avoidance.*

A pattern of crime, violence, and delinquency with little remorse typifies the *antisocial* personality disorder; people with this disorder were once called sociopaths or *psychopaths*. The disorder typically begins before the age of *15* and is more common in *males*. Since the disorder is more likely to appear in identical twins than in fraternal twins, *genetic* factors have been suggested. Parental behavior may also play a role in the disorder, since parents may be more *inconsistent* or *punitive* in their discipline.

**In Your Own Words**

*Please write your thoughts, perspectives, and reactions on a separate piece of paper.*

✓ *Select one of the mental disorders described in this chapter and create a fictitious case study of an individual with the disorder. Include appropriate background information that is consistent with the disorder.*

## Correcting the Incorrect

Carefully read each statement. Determine if the statement is correct or incorrect. If the statement is incorrect, make the necessary changes to correct it. Then check the answer key at the end of the chapter for the correct statement and page reference in the textbook.

1. Abnormal behavior is behavior that is strange or odd.
2. Once people have a mental disorder, they will never be able to get rid of it.
3. *Insanity* is a psychiatric term.
4. Maladaptive behavior is behavior that is atypical.
5. The medical model describes mental disorders as medical diseases.
6. The structural views of psychological disorders consider the role of neurotransmitters and hormones in the causes of mental disorders.
7. Ethnicity plays a stronger role in mental disorders than does socioeconomic status.
8. The main features of the anxiety disorders are motor tension, hyperactivity, and apprehensive expectations and thoughts.

9. In generalized anxiety disorder, the individual experiences flashbacks that are related to traumatic events.

10. Obsessions are ritualistic behaviors, and compulsions are anxiety-provoking thoughts.

11. The symptoms of post-traumatic stress disorder typically show up immediately after the person experiences the traumatic event or the oppressive situation.

12. The dissociative disorders involve distorted thoughts and perception and social withdrawal.

13. A person has memory loss, travels, and assumes a new identity in dissociative identity disorder.

14. Swings of mood from mania to depression typify depression.

15. There is a stronger family link for depressive disorder than for bipolar disorders.

16. Delusions include hearing, seeing, feeling, and smelling things that are not there.

17. In catatonic schizophrenia, the person suffers from delusions and hallucinations that have little or no meaning.

18. The brains of people diagnosed with schizophrenia show less alpha-wave activity than do those of normal individuals.

19. The personality disorders consist of chronic, maladaptive cognitive-behavioral patterns that are thoroughly integrated into the individual's personality.

20. Someone who has antisocial personality disorder shows behavior that is unstable, anxious, and irritable.

## Practice Test 1

1. Which of the following is not an important factor in psychological disorders?
   a. biological factors
   b. psychological factors
   c. sociocultural factors
   d. technological factors

2. Abnormal behavior is
   a. always bizarre.
   b. very different from normal behavior.
   c. treatable.
   d. easy to distinguish from normal behavior.

3. Babara's psychological disorder is keeping her from going to work. The fact that this disorder is interfering with her ability to function effectively means that her behaviors are
   a. deviant.
   b. maladaptive.
   c. personally distressing.
   d. atypical.

4. Each of the following is an axis on the *DSM* multiaxial system, EXCEPT
   a. personality disorders.
   b. psychological stressors in the individual's recent past.
   c. the individual's highest level of functioning in the past year.
   d. potential treatments for the individual.

5.  Martha has been sitting in a hunched-over position on her hospital bed for several hours. When you speak to her, her position remains unchanged, and she doesn't answer. When you lift her arm, she remains sitting motionless, with her arm in a raised position. Martha is most likely suffering from which type of schizophrenia?

    a.  paranoid
    b.  catatonic
    c.  disorganized
    d.  undifferentiated

6.  Which of the following is a criticism of the *DSM-IV*?

    a.  Five axes are not sufficient for the classification of all mental disorders.
    b.  The classification is not comprehensive enough.
    c.  The classification is not current enough.
    d.  Labels can become self-fulfilling prophecies.

7.  Mr. Dodge engages in very rigid and structured behavior. He is preoccupied with cleanliness. He washes his hands more than twenty times per day and brings two changes of underwear to work with him. He would probably be diagnosed as suffering from a(n)

    a.  conversion disorder.
    b.  schizophrenia.
    c.  generalized anxiety disorder.
    d.  obsessive-compulsive disorder.

8.  Stanley was fearful of developing cancer, which was the cause of the deaths of both of his parents. He avoided any situation in which someone might smoke, ate no processed meat or dairy products, and would not even speak with anyone who had been diagnosed with cancer. Wherever he was, he constantly had thoughts of wasting away with cancer. Stanley's thoughts were

    a.  obsessions.
    b.  compulsions.
    c.  a generalized anxiety disorder.
    d.  a dysthymic disorder.

9.  The fear cluster centered on public places and an inability to escape or find help should one become incapacitated is called

    a.  agoraphobia.
    b.  social phobia.
    c.  compulsion.
    d.  generalized anxiety disorder.

10. The fear-of-fear hypothesis refers to

    a.  agoraphobias being a fear of public places.
    b.  fear of death.
    c.  agoraphobias being a fear of having a panic attack in a public place.
    d.  fear of pain.

11. Which of the following phobias involves a fear of darkness?

    a.  mysophobia
    b.  xenophobia
    c.  nyctophobia
    d.  algophobia

12. A disorder characterized by unexpected travel away from home and a new identity is called
    a. dissociative identity disorder.
    b. dissociative amnesia.
    c. dissociative fugue.
    d. panic disorder.

13. Which of the following has not been associated with dissociative identity disorder?
    a. sexual abuse
    b. brain trauma
    c. rejecting mothers
    d. alcoholic fathers

14. Which of the following is NOT a type of mood disorder?
    a. bipolar disorder
    b. major depressive disorder
    c. dysthymic disorder
    d. obsessive-compulsive disorder

15. The "common cold" of mental disorders is
    a. schizophrenia.
    b. depression.
    c. the bipolar disorder.
    d. multiple personality.

16. Which of the following individuals is at highest risk for developing a mood disorder?
    a. Angela, whose aunt is often moody and withdrawn
    b. Fred, whose father is a diagnosed manic-depressive
    c. Roslyn, who is often in a bad mood
    d. Andrew, whose brother has a personality disorder

17. Which of the following refers to a biological cause of mood disorders?
    a. heredity
    b. learned helplessness
    c. personality factors
    d. childhood experiences

18. According to Aaron Beck, a depressed person is more likely than a nondepressed person to engage in
    a. productive thinking.
    b. creative thinking.
    c. catastrophic thinking.
    d. reactive thinking.

19. Which of the following is not a symptom of a schizophrenic disorder?
    a. hallucinations
    b. delusions
    c. bizarre motor behavior
    d. manipulation of people

20. _____ disorders are chronic, maladaptive cognitive-behavioral patterns that are thoroughly integrated into an individual's personality.
   a. Anxiety
   b. Personality
   c. Schizophrenic
   d. Dissociative

## Practice Test 2

1. An example of the personal distress criterion of abnormal behavior is
   a. Chad's inability to stop exercising even when he knows that there are other things he should be doing.
   b. Chad's schedule of exercising three hours a day, seven days a week.
   c. Chad's embarrassment and concern that people might find out that he always has to do his workout in the same order and if he can't he has to start all over again.
   d. Chad's insistence on wearing the exact same workout clothes everyday.

2. In legal terms, insanity means that the person
   a. is a schizophrenic.
   b. is unable to appreciate the nature and quality or wrongfulness of his/her acts.
   c. does not know right from wrong at the time of the trial.
   d. did not plan to commit the crime.

3. A person who behaves very differently from what the social norms indicate can be argued to fulfill the _____ criterion of abnormal behavior.
   a. personal distress
   b. deviance
   c. maladaptiveness
   d. disfunction

4. Which of the following is not one of the main categories of biological views on psychological disorders?
   a. medical views
   b. biochemical views
   c. genetic views
   d. structural views

5. Among the psychological factors of psychological disorders, the humanistic perspective argues that
   a. disorders are a result of unconscious conflict.
   b. disorders are caused by a person's inability to fill one's potential.
   c. disorders are caused by environmental factors such as rewards and punishments.
   d. disorders are caused by having a high self-concept.

6. Women are to _____ disorders as men are to _____ disorders.
   a. externalized; internalized
   b. unconscious; conscious
   c. internalized; externalized
   d. conscious; unconscious

7. In the study in which 20,000 people, who were randomly selected, answered questions about psychological disorders, approximately how many of them reported that they had experienced one or more psychological disorders in their lifetime?
    a.    10%
    b.    30%
    c.    75%
    d.    90%

8. The following are issues addressed in the axes of the *DSM-IV*, EXCEPT
    a.    general medical condition.
    b.    psychosocial issues.
    c.    environmental problems.
    d.    labeling problems.

9. Gerard is a professional chef. He has had a long career, but lately he has been unable to focus at work because he has been feeling very nervous most of the time and he is not sure exactly why. When he's not worried about the restaurant he is worried about his children or the weather. He even worries about food orders for the restaurant that have been reliable for years. If Gerard went to a psychologist, he would likely to be diagnosed as experiencing
    a.    a phobia.
    b.    depression.
    c.    generalized anxiety disorder.
    d.    panic disorder.

10. _____ involves an intense fear of being humiliated or embarrassed in social situations.
    a.    A social phobia
    b.    Generalized anxiety disorder
    c.    Schizophrenia
    d.    Obsessive-compulsive disorder

11. The following are symptoms of post-traumatic stress disorder (PTSD), EXCEPT
    a.    flashback memories.
    b.    impulsive behaviors, such as aggressiveness.
    c.    difficulties in concentration.
    d.    a fear of a specific object or situation.

12. The "hidden observer" concept has been used to explain _____ disorders.
    a.    somatoform
    b.    anxiety
    c.    dissociative
    d.    personality

13. Which type of schizophrenic disorder is characterized by a "waxy flexibility"?
    a.    disorganized schizophrenia
    b.    catatonic schizophrenia
    c.    paranoid schizophrenia
    d.    undifferentiated schizophrenia

14. Delusions of reference, grandeur, and persecution characterize which type of schizophrenia?
    a. disorganized
    b. catatonic
    c. paranoid
    d. undifferentiated

15. Which theory argues that a biogenetic disposition and stress cause schizophrenia?
    a. diathesis-stress view
    b. disorganized-stress theory
    c. dopamine hypothesis
    d. psychoanalytic theory

16. An individual who engages in stealing and vandalism, who cannot uphold financial obligations, and who shows no remorse after harming someone may be considered to have a(n)
    a. panic disorder.
    b. bipolar disorder.
    c. anxiety disorder.
    d. antisocial personality disorder.

17. Which of the following characterizes antisocial personality disorder?
    a. It usually begins in middle adulthood.
    b. It affects males and females equally.
    c. Most adolescents grow out of the disorder.
    d. Those with the disorder show no remorse when harming someone.

18. Andrea has an excessive need to be the center of attention. At work, she is highly competitive and gets very angry if anyone criticizes her. She constantly manipulates others, especially younger coworkers. With which personality disorder are these behaviors associated?
    a. paranoid
    b. borderline
    c. schizoid
    d. narcissistic

19. What is the main difference between schizophrenia and dissociative personality disorder?
    a. The schizophrenic has one personality that has disintegrated.
    b. The schizophrenic has one integrated personality.
    c. The schizophrenic never has more than one alternate personality.
    d. The schizophrenic always has more than two alternate personalities.

20. Which of the following statements is NOT true about the mania aspect of bipolar disorder?
    a. Fewer than 10% of bipolar individuals tend to experience manic-type episodes and not depression.
    b. A manic episode involves feelings of euphoria.
    c. During a manic episode, the person often experiences fatigue.
    d. Mania is associated with impulsiveness.

# Practice Test 3

1. Dr. Feerst concludes that his new patient, Anna, has a psychological disorder. One of the main indicators for Dr. Feerst was that Anna, who used to be able to handle the challenges of school and having a family, is now unable to continue her school work and deal with the demands of the family. Dr. Feerst is using the _____ criterion for abnormal behavior.
   a. deviance
   b. maladaptiveness
   c. distress
   d. danger

2. Which of the following is NOT a myth or misconception of psychological disorders?
   a. People with psychological disorders do things that normal people don't do.
   b. Abnormal behaviors are easy to detect because they are so weird.
   c. People with psychological disorders are dangerous.
   d. Psychological disorders can be inherited.

3. Dr. Chompra is the psychiatrist treating Therese. Dr. Chompra studies the biochemical etiology of Therese's depressive disorder. In other words, Dr. Chompra is studying
   a. possible abnormalities in the way Therese's brain works.
   b. the history of mental disorders in Therese's family.
   c. the role of neurotrasmitters or hormones in Therese's condition.
   d. the stressors in Therese's life.

4. Sergio's psychologist concludes that the reason he is experiencing a psychological disorder is because of the conflictive relationship he had with his parents during the first few years of life. The psychologist also notes that Sergio seems to be unaware of the importance of those issues in his current problem. Sergio's psychologist is likely to have been trained in the
   a. psychodynamic perspective.
   b. behavioral perspective.
   c. social cognitive perspective.
   d. humanistic perspective.

5. Statistically, a person diagnosed with an internalized disorder is more likely to be a (n) _____ than a(n) _____.
   a. man; woman
   b. woman; man
   c. ethnic minority; woman
   d. man; ethnic minority

6. When a mental health professional is using the *DSM-IV* to diagnose a disorder, he will ask a number of questions to the individual and/or family members to see where the individual stands in each of the five axes. Which of the following questions is unlikely to be asked by a mental health professional in the process of determining a diagnosis with the *DSM-IV*?
   a. Has the individual been previously diagnosed with a psychological disorder or mental retardation?
   b. What type of therapy would the individual prefer?
   c. How well is the individual functioning in comparison to previous levels of functioning?
   d. Does the individual have diabetes?

7. Labels can become self-fulfilling prophecies because
   a. labels encourage people to develop mental competence.
   b. labels are used only for the most severe psychological disorders.
   c. labels legitimize the belief that there is something wrong and permanent about having a psychological disorder.
   d. labels of psychological disorders are rarely associated with other personality characteristics.

8. Which of the following disorders is less likely to be diagnosed in a woman?
   a. agoraphobia
   b. antisocial personality disorder
   c. dissociative identity disorder
   d. depressive disorders

9. Which of the following psychological disorders has an etiology of sexual and physical abuse during early childhood?
   a. phobic disorder
   b. histrionic personality disorder
   c. paranoid schizophrenia
   d. dissociative identity disorder

10. Which of the following is not true about dissociative identity disorder?
    a. It is rare.
    b. It runs in families.
    c. Some psychologists believe that in the past it has been misdiagnosed as schizophrenia.
    d. Most of the people diagnosed with the disorder are adult males.

11. A person experiencing major depressive disorder is unlikely to
    a. be impulsive.
    b. lose weight.
    c. have a hard time concentrating.
    d. have problems sleeping.

12. Which of the following disorders has been associated with a decrease in metabolic activity in the cerebral cortex?
    a. catatonic schizophrenia
    b. panic disorder
    c. major depressive disorder
    d. narcissistic personality disorder

13. Marcus has been diagnosed with depression. One of the experiences he shared with his psychologist is that he has a very hard time getting rid of nagging negative thoughts. If he arrived late at work, he keeps visualizing the situation, how the boss looked at him, and thinking and rethinking about how awful he felt and how all is hopeless. According to Susan Nolen-Hoeksema, Marcus is using
    a. an excuse to show up late at work.
    b. an action-oriented coping style.
    c. a negative schema of the workplace.
    d. a ruminative coping style.

14. Thomas has been diagnosed with terminal cancer. He has also been manifesting a number of the symptoms of depression. While in therapy, Thomas simply states that he feels sad and hopeless because his physical condition is hopeless. The therapist may explain that Thomas's depression is due to
    a.  having few receptors of the neurotransmitter serotonin.
    b.  hormonal changes.
    c.  a turning inward of aggressive instincts.
    d.  depressive realism.

15. John Bowlby proposed that depression could be caused by a combination of an insecure attachment to the mother and a lack of love and affection as a child, among other factors. The factors mentioned in this question are _____ interpersonal experiences.
    a.  proximal
    b.  distal
    c.  positive
    d.  genetic

16. Esther has been diagnosed with schizophrenia. One of her cognitions involves the belief that when the light switches in her home are turned on, her neighbor to the north is able to hear what she is thinking. Esther's type of schizophrenia is
    a.  disorganized.
    b.  catatonic.
    c.  paranoid.
    d.  undifferentiated.

17. The case of the Genain quadruplets has been paid extraordinary attention because
    a.  it proved that schizophrenia is influenced by genetics.
    b.  it proved that strict parenting can contribute to schizophrenia.
    c.  it is unlikely to be repeated.
    d.  the children showed some of the structural/biological patterns characteristic of schizophrenia.

18. Habeeba has a very hard time connecting with other people. She is shy and has never shown much interest in an intimate friendship or romantic relationships; actually, most co-workers think of her as a cold person. Habeeba could possibly be diagnosed as experiencing
    a.  schizoid personality disorder.
    b.  depression.
    c.  schizotypal personality disorder.
    d.  antisocial personality disorder.

19. A father who is always late to his kids' little league games, often forgets when their school tuition is due, is not flexible with the children, and tends to look for excuses to avoid spending time with his wife and the kids may be diagnosed with _____ personality disorder.
    a.  antisocial
    b.  dependent
    c.  schizotypal
    d.  passive-aggressive

20. The causes of psychological disorders include the following, EXCEPT
    a. specific genes.
    b. insanity.
    c. a person's community.
    d. how a person thinks about the disorder.

## Connections

*Take advantage of all the other study tools available for this chapter!*

## Media Integration

| NAME OF CLIP | DESCRIPTION | KEY CONCEPTS AND IDEAS |
|---|---|---|
| | | **Understanding Psychological Disorders** |
| History of Mental Illness | Historical definitions of mental illness are discussed, including the beliefs that they were punishment from God and the inhumane treatments related with these definitions. The video focuses on schizophrenia, which was identified in the 20th century and is described as a fragmented mind. In 1951 drugs were discovered that could be used to treat schizophrenia. Schizophrenia is described as sensory overload, with a brain unable to distinguish real from unreal stimuli, unable to focus; unable to distinguish external experience from internal thought. The video helps viewers understand how a person with schizophrenia experiences the world. The FMRI has been used to study hallucinations and explain why people with schizophrenia experience hallucinations as real. | Mental illness<br>History of psychology<br>Schizophrenia<br>Drug treatment<br>Hallucinations<br>Sensory overload |
| ADHD | David is a 16 year-old with ADHD. Characteristic behaviors and cognitions as well as treatments are discussed. The controversy surrounding this diagnosis is addressed. Ritalin and the side effects associated with this medication are discussed. | ADHD<br>Ritalin |
| Asperger Syndrome | Asperger syndrome has been associated with autism; symptoms include impaired and mechanical speech and difficulty understanding emotions and reading facial expressions. This video clip features a sister and a | Asperger syndrome |

| | brother who have Asperger and showcases both the functional and the dysfunctional aspects of the disorder. | |
|---|---|---|
| Stigma of Mental Illness | People diagnosed with mental illnesses fear exclusion and often have to cope with stigmatized expectations that they are childlike and irresponsible. Patrick Corrigan and David Penn propose three strategies for reducing stigma: protests, such as when the National Alliance for the Mentally Ill protested media programming, which resulted in reduction in negative portrayal of mentally ill in the media; contact between those with and without mental illness; and public education, making sure that messages make sense to audiences and encouraging programs such as partnerships with MTV. The challenge for psychology is to integrate approaches, research, education, community, and media efforts. | Mental illness<br>Stigma<br>Strategies for reducing stigma |
| | | **Anxiety Disorders** |
| Measuring Anxiety | "How anxious are you? A test to assess your level of anxiety" is the topic of this interactivity. The activity includes a 10-item self-test. Each question has a 4-point scale: almost never, sometimes, often, almost always. At the end participants are given scores, between 10 and 40; the higher the score, the higher the anxiety level. Individuals scoring high on anxiety are asked to consider the foundation for the anxiety and referred to the textbook for more information on how to reduce anxiety. | Anxiety |
| Agoraphobia | Annie is a young woman who has been diagnosed with agoraphobia. Annie describes her experience with anticipatory anxiety as well as the physiological symptoms of panic attack. Annie is concerned with possible humiliation and feels sad because she is unable to do things she used to be able to do. | Agoraphobia<br>Panic attacks |

| | Annie also discusses therapies she has tried for anxiety disorders and states that in her experience drugs take away her creativity. She has not taken drugs for 2 years and is looking for alternative methods. | |
|---|---|---|
| Obsessive-Compulsive Disorder | Laura and Marla are friends, and both have been diagnosed with obsessive-compulsive disorder. Both mention how symptoms were already present in high school. They explain how some obsessions/compulsions bring shame and disturbing urges to hurt other people. Both have engaged in behavior therapy and medication. They describe the recurrent pattern of the disorder and their experience with depression. | Obsessive-compulsive disorder Depression Obsessions Compulsions |
| Post-Traumatic Stress Disorder | Carl, a 46-year-old Vietnam veteran, describes his experiences with PTSD. Carl's graphic descriptions of his traumatic experiences in Vietnam bring to life the psychological horror of people with PTSD. Carl discusses how feelings of isolation, anger, and pain contributed to symptoms. He describes how nobody around him could understand what he went through and mourns the loss of innocence. He expresses great anger because of lack of social support. His flashbacks include perceptions that did not correspond to current sensory experience, such as smelling gun powder. Carl also discusses how he has coped with the disorder and how the onset of symptoms is related to stress. | Post-traumatic stress disorder Flashbacks Coping |
| | | **Dissociative Disorders** |
| Personality Disorder | This video clip showcases Steven, a man with personality disorder with dissociative and borderline features. Steven describes one of his personalities and how he was not aware of what happened when the other personality was attacking someone else (he went to jail for that attack). He considers this | Personality disorder Dissociative identity disorder Depression Borderline personality disorder |

| | | |
|---|---|---|
| | personality very dangerous. Steven also describes how other people walk up to him and seem to be talking to another personality, so he had to guess what they were referring to or talking about. Another personality thought he had to die. Steven also has borderline personality disorder and depression. Each of the three disorders is described in separate vignettes with Steven. Difficulty in the process of diagnosis is discussed. | |
| | | **Mood Disorders** |
| Major Depression | Tara has been coping for 15 years with depression. She has recently been treated with electroconvulsive therapy and discusses the positive and negative aspects of this treatment for depression. Tara describes her patterns of negative affect and disturbed sleep. Pretending to be well is stressful and seems to lead to stronger feelings of depression. Describes persistent thoughts of death and dying. Tara has been committed to psychiatric institutions, and her depression has not responded to traditional psychotherapy and medication. She has responded better to electroconvulsive therapy. The video ends with suggestions for what to do if you are feeling depressed, including checking the Internet and talking to someone. | Depression Electroconvulsive therapy Suicide |
| Dysthymic Disorder | A comparison between major depression and dysthymic disorder is presented. Roberto, a man with dysthymic disorder is interviewed. He describes feeling no control over his life and feeling very small and insignificant. He devalues everything in his life. Roberto describes his daily activities and how he wants to change but feels unable to do so. | Dysthymic disorder Depression |
| Bipolar Disorder I | Bernie traces his first symptoms of bipolar disorder to the 11th grade and describes drastic changes in | Bipolar disorder Depression Mania |

| | his performance. Symptoms of mania are described, including getting in trouble, promiscuity, and getting arrested. When he starts the depression phase he gets very angry. Depression involves disturbed sleeping and eating patterns and alcohol drinking. Bernie discusses the types of therapies he has tried and how the depression cycles tend to last longer than the mania cycles. | |
|---|---|---|
| Bipolar Disorder II | This video clip presents a broad introduction to bipolar disorder, including a discussion of the pattern of cycles and the drug Lithium. Isolation is one of the main problems with the depression component of the disorder. Brain imaging is used to extract data and look at what chemicals are present and active in the brain of a person with depression. MRI scans are used to study the orbital frontal lobe, an area that controls moods and emotions. Coline is a substance that has been found in abnormally high levels in the brains of depressed teenagers. | Bipolar disorder<br>Depression<br>Lithium<br>Brain imaging<br>MRI<br>Coline<br>Self-help support groups |
| | | **Schizophrenia** |
| History of Mental Illness | Historical definitions of mental illness are discussed, including the beliefs that they were punishment from God and the inhumane treatments related with these definitions. The video focuses on schizophrenia, which was identified in 20th century and is described as a fragmented mind. In 1951 drugs were discovered that could be used to treat schizophrenia. Schizophrenia is described as sensory overload, with a brain unable to distinguish real from unreal stimuli, unable to focus; unable to distinguish external experience from internal thought. The video helps viewers understand how a person with schizophrenia experiences the world. The FMRI has been used to study hallucinations and explain | Mental illness<br>History of psychology<br>Schizophrenia<br>Drug treatment<br>Hallucinations<br>Sensory overload |

| | | |
|---|---|---|
| | why people with schizophrenia experience hallucinations as real. | |
| Paranoid Schizophrenia | Paranoid schizophrenia is a psychotic disorder that includes symptoms of delusions and hallucinations. Valerie has had schizophrenia for more than 20 years. Valerie describes how the disorder had an onset in her late 20s, which is one of the main symptoms of paranoid schizophrenia. She explains her fear of death, thoughts of martyrdom, and complex delusions. She experiences many religious-based delusions. She describes the cycle of stopping medicines because of side effects and remission. With treatment, Valerie is now functional. | Paranoid schizophrenia<br>Delusions<br>Hallucinations |
| Schizophrenia | This set of vignettes starts with a description of schizophrenia and the different types. Two types are showcased, disorganized and undifferentiated. Peter, a man with disorganized schizophrenia is interviewed. While his thought is incoherent he remains aware of social interactions. Isidore, a man with undifferentiated schizophrenia, shares how he has seen Jesus and since then has not been sick. He describes visual and auditory hallucinations and is confused with situations, not being fully aware of experiencing a psychological disorder. | Schizophrenia<br>Types of schizophrenia<br>Disorganized schizophrenia<br>Undifferentiated schizophrenia |
| Beautiful Minds: An Interview with John Nash and Son | This video features a description of the career trajectory of John Nash, as well as the list of treatments he has received for schizophrenia. Dr. Nash is described as being able to "at will" move from insanity to sanity. The schizophrenia experienced by his son is also characterized by patterns of recovering intellectual capacity with recurring psychosis. During the interview the son manifests anger and denial, which in many cases of schizophrenia tend to make treatment more difficult. | Schizophrenia<br>Heredity |

| | | **Personality Disorders** |
|---|---|---|
| Borderline Personality Disorder | Becky, a young woman diagnosed with borderline personality disorder describes her uncontrollable anger and how self-mutilation is calming. She has used mutilation as punishment for her own irrational thoughts. She describes how touching her scars leads to memories of a cutting episode and results in a cathartic calmness. Becky shares problems of trust and dilemmas between her public and private personas. | Borderline personality disorder |

**Online Learning Center (www.mhhe.com/Santrockp7u)**
- Interact and make learning fun!
  - o **Interactive Exercise**
    - ▪ Measuring Anxiety
  - o **Interactive Review**
    - ▪ Level of Analysis: Antisocial Behavior
- Brush up on the Key Terms for this chapter by first reviewing the electronic **Glossary** (in English or Spanish) and then testing your retention using the **Flashcard** feature.
- **"Notes"**—This feature allows you to use the website as you would your text, inserting your own study notes and highlighting areas of particular importance.

**In Your Text**
- Found throughout each chapter, the **Review and Sharpen Your Thinking** feature breaks the text into logical chunks, allowing you to process, review, and reflect thoughtfully on the information that you've just read. When going back to *study* the chapter, try reading the feature *before* the section of text to which it relates. In doing so, you will be able to focus your attention on important concepts *as* you encounter them. In this chapter, this feature can be found on the following pages: pp. 526, 534, 537, 547, 553, and 555.

**Practice Quizzes**
- Test your knowledge of psychological disorders by taking the different practice quizzes found on your text's **Online Learning Center** and on the **In-Psych Plus CD-ROM** packaged with your text.

**ANSWER KEY**

**In Your Own Words**

✓ Give two examples of each of the three criteria of abnormal behavior.
*The three criteria for abnormal behavior are as follows:*
- *Deviance – if the behavior is atypical and deviates from what is acceptable in the culture, the behavior may be considered abnormal. This criterion is to be considered carefully, since simply behaving differently does not mean that the person has a psychological disorder. When deviant behavior is accompanied by maladaptiveness and/or distress, then it is more likely that the person is experiencing a psychological disorder.*

- *Maladaptiveness – if the behavior interrupts the person's ability to function effectively, the person may be experiencing a psychological disorder. Think of examples that illustrate a maladaptiveness that was not there before. Usually a behavior is considered maladaptive if it keeps a person from doing something he or she used to be able to do.*
- *Distress – if the behavior makes the person feel uncomfortable, distressed, or guilty, the person may be experiencing a psychological disorder. For examples, consider behaviors that cause distress in one person but not another.*

✓ Consider the psychological and sociocultural factors that contribute to psychological disorders. Can you find a pattern across disorders? In other words, what psychological and sociocultural factors seem to be associated with more than one psychological disorder? Explain why these factors contribute to psychological disorder.

*Across the different categories of disorders discussed in Chapter 13, there are some psychological and sociocultural factors that repeat, such as stress and gender differences. High stress is associated with the manifestation of a number of psychological disorders, and women are more likely either to be diagnosed with certain disorders or to experience the disorder differently from men. Hypothesize as to why these factors seem to be associated with psychological disorders.*

✓ In what ways does the medical model influence the understanding of abnormal behaviors?
*The medical model of psychological disorders mainly comes from the practice of psychiatry. Psychiatrists, medical doctors, usually treat severe forms of psychological disorders and dedicate a great part of the treatment to the administration and monitoring of medications to control the symptoms of the disorders. While psychiatrists also engage in psychological therapy, their medical approach and dominant influence on the categorization of psychological disorders has resulted in a view of psychological disorders as illnesses and diseases. This approach implies an internal cause for disorders and overlooks external and environmental factors. The medical model also contributes to the bias toward finding something wrong with any person who is diagnosed. The person with the psychological disorder becomes a patient to be cured by the doctor. This approach keeps the person from being an effective agent in the process of working with the psychological disorder. The problems associated with labeling are also influenced by the mental model of psychological disorders.*

✓ Select one of the mental disorders described in this chapter and create a fictitious case study of an individual with the disorder. Include appropriate background information consistent with the disorder.
*The challenge in this question is to consider how the symptoms of a disorder may manifest on a daily basis. This exercise should also help the student understand the issue of levels of severity of the disorder. Many psychological disorders are characterized by episodes during which the symptoms are more severe but also periods during which the symptoms are not as maladaptive.*

✓ What is the difference between feeling depressed and being diagnosed with major depressive disorder?
*People often used the term* depression *to refer to their brief periods of feeling sadness or discontent with life. For most, the behavior and mental processes pattern of depression lasts a few hours, days, or even weeks, but it usually comes and goes and is particularly associated with external factors, such as romantic break-up or final exams. However, a person experiencing major depressive disorder experiences lethargy and the sense of hopelessness for at least two weeks or longer, and the depression is maladaptive. Also, at least five out of nine symptoms must be present in order for the diagnosis to be established. The symptoms of major depressive disorder are depressed mood most of*

*the day, reduced interest in activities, weight loss or gain, trouble sleeping, psychomotor agitation or retardation, fatigue, feeling worthless or guilty, problems thinking, and recurrent thoughts of death and suicide.*

## Correcting the Incorrect

1. Abnormal behavior is behavior that is *deviant, maladaptive, or distressful.* (p. 520)
2. *Most people can be successfully treated for a mental disorder.* (p. 519)
3. *Insanity* is a *legal* term. (p. 520)
4. *Deviant* behavior is behavior that is atypical. (p. 520)
5. The medical model describes mental disorders as medical diseases. (p. 520)
6. The *biochemical* views of psychological disorders consider the role of neurotransmitters and hormones in the causes of mental disorders. (p. 520)
7. *Socioeconomic status plays a stronger role in mental disorders than does ethnicity.* (p. 521)
8. The main features of the anxiety disorders are motor tension, hyperactivity, and apprehensive expectations and thoughts. (p. 527)
9. In *post-traumatic stress disorder*, the individual experiences flashbacks that are related to traumatic events. (p. 532)
10. *Compulsions* are ritualistic behaviors, and *obsessions* are anxiety-provoking thoughts. (p. 531)
11. The symptoms of post-traumatic stress disorder can show up immediately *or years after* the person experiences the traumatic event or the oppressive situation. (p. 532)
12. The dissociative disorders involve *loss of memory or change in identity.* (p. 535)
13. A person has memory loss, travels, and assumes a new identity in *dissociative fugue.* (p. 535)
14. Swings of mood from mania to depression typify *bipolar disorder.* (p. 539)
15. There is a stronger family link for *bipolar disorder than for depressive disorders.* (p. 540)
16. *Hallucinations* include hearing, seeing, feeling, and smelling things that are not there. (p. 548)
17. In *disorganized schizophrenia*, the person suffers from delusions and hallucinations that have little or no meaning. (p. 549)
18. The brains of people diagnosed with schizophrenia show less alpha-wave activity than do those of normal individuals. (p. 551)
19. The personality disorders consist of chronic, maladaptive cognitive-behavioral patterns that are thoroughly integrated into the individual's personality. (p. 553)
20. Someone who has antisocial personality disorder shows behavior that is *guiltless, exploitive, irresponsible, and self-indulgent.* (p. 554)

## Practice Test 1

1. a.  no; biological factors are important in psychological disorders
   b.  no; psychological factors also contribute to psychological disorders
   c.  no; sociocultural factors also contribute to psychological disorders
   d.  YES; technological factors are not a category of variables considered in the study of psychological disorders

   p. 520

2. a. no; this is a myth, because people diagnosed with a disorder often cannot be distinguished from normal people
   b. no; many times the problems is a poor fit between the behavior and the situation; however, the behaviors may be similar
   c. YES; most people diagnosed with psychological disorders can be successfully treated
   d. no; this statement is similar to item b
   p. 519

3. a. no; the question does not address the deviance criteria of abnormal behavior; her behaviors are not described as atypical or uncommon
   b. YES; Barbara used to be able to work and now she can't; therefore, the behaviors are maladaptive
   c. no; the question does not address Barbara's level of distress
   d. no; this is similar to item a, in the sense that *deviant* and *atypical* are equivalent concepts
   p. 520

4. a. no; personality disorders are placed on Axis II
   b. no; psychological stressors are indicated on Axis IV
   c. no; information on functioning is placed on Axis V
   d. YES; treatment options are not among the axes in the *DSM*
   p. 523

5. a. no; there is no indication of delusions
   b. YES; Martha shows bizarre motor behavior
   c. no; these symptoms do not fit a diagnosis of disorganized schizophrenia
   d. no; these symptoms do fit a particular type of schizophrenia
   p. 549

6. a. no; the more accurate the classifications, the better the diagnosis will be
   b. no; great effort has been put into making the classifications comprehensive
   c. no; the classifications have been revised in a timely manner
   c. YES; this is a criticism since the *DSM* does have a strong medical focus and looks more at pathology and problems than at other aspects of psychology
   p. 523

7. a. no; there are no physical symptoms
   b. no; Mr. Dodge is not experiencing hallucinations or other important symptoms of schizophrenia
   c. no; his concern is focused on cleanliness
   d. YES; obsessive-compulsive disorder includes the types of thoughts and rituals that Mr. Dodge is experiencing
   p. 531

8. a. YES; obsessions are thoughts that are anxiety-provoking
   b. no; while Stanley may have some compulsions (repetitive and ritualistic behaviors), the question is about thoughts
   c. no; he does not experience persistent anxiety—the problem is focused on cancer worries
   d. no; the question does not address symptoms of depression across an extended time span
   p. 531

9. a. YES; this is the definition of *agoraphobia*, often associated with panic disorder
   b. no; social phobias are intense fears of being embarrassed in social situations
   c. no; this is a phobia, not a pattern of behaviors
   d. no; the phobia is specific, not a generalized anxiety
   p. 528

10. a. no; the fear-of-fear hypothesis challenges this popular conceptualization of agoraphobia
    b. no; this is the definition for thanatophobia
    c. YES; this hypothesis proposes that agoraphobia is the fear of being afraid and experiencing a panic attack in a public situation
    d. no; this is the definition of *algophobia*
    p. 529

11. a. no; this is the fear of dirt
    b. no; this is the fear of strangers
    c. YES; this is the name for the fear of darkness
    d. no; this is the fear of pain
    p. 529

12. a. no; this is the current name for what used to be called *multiple personality disorder*
    b. no; dissociative amnesia is not associated with travel and change of identity
    c. YES; these are the characteristics of dissociative fugue
    d. no; these are not the symptoms or characteristics of panic disorder
    p. 535

13. a. no; this has been associated with dissociative identity disorder, since sexual abuse occurred in 56% of reported cases
    b. YES; brain trauma has not been associated with this disorder; it seems to have strong psychological contributors
    c. no; this is one of the patterns observed in individuals with dissociative identity disorder
    d. no; this is also one of the patterns observed in individuals with dissociative identity disorder
    p. 536

14. a. no; bipolar disorder is a mood disorder
    b. no; major depressive disorder is a mood disorder
    c. no; dysthymic disorder is a mood disorder and is more chronic
    d. YES; obsessive-compulsive disorder is an anxiety disorder and it is also a name used to refer to a particular pattern of personality disorder
    p. 531

15. a. no; this is an uncommon psychological disorder, diagnosed in approximately 1% of Americans
    b. YES; depression is so widespread that it has been called the "common cold" of mental disorders, with more than 250,000 individuals hospitalized every year for the disorder
    c. no; this is also a mood disorder, but not as common as depression
    d. no; this is an uncommon psychological disorder
    p. 538

16. a. no; in terms of genetics, the aunt is slightly removed and the moodiness and withdrawal by themselves are not a psychological disorder
    b. YES; the genetic factors of mood disorder would suggest that Fred is at risk
    c. no; a bad mood is too general a description for it to be considered a symptom
    d. no; having one disorder in the family does not necessarily result in higher risk for other disorders
    p. 540

17. a. CORRECT; heredity refers to genetics and is a biological cause of mood disorders
    b. no; learned helpless is a psychosocial explanation
    c. no; personality factors do not refer to biological causes
    d. no; childhood experiences are not related to biological causes
    p. 540

18. a. no; Beck does not make reference to productive thinking
    b. no; Beck does not make reference to creative thinking
    c. YES; Beck focuses on how negative thoughts shape person's experience
    d. no; Beck does not make reference to reactive thinking
    p. 543

19. a. no; this is a symptom of a schizophrenic disorder
    b. no; this is a symptom of a schizophrenic disorder
    c. no; this is a symptom of a schizophrenic disorder
    d. YES; this implies that the person is in control to manipulate others, and that does not apply to schizophrenic disorders
    p. 548

20. a. no; these involve motor tension, hyperactivity, and apprehensive expectations
    b. YES; this is the definition of personality disorders
    c. no; these disorders involve disturbances in thought, emotion, and motor behavior
    d. no; dissociative disorders involve changes in memory and identity
    p. 553

## Practice Test 2

1. a. no; this is an example of maladaptiveness
   b. no; this is an example of deviant behavior
   c. YES; he is aware that his behaviors are different, and this causes him stress
   d. no; this is an example of deviant behavior
   p. 520

2. a. no; this is a very specific diagnosis that is different from what is understood as insanity in the legal system
   b. YES; this is the definition of the term *insanity* in the legal system
   c. no; the issue is the mental state at the time of the crime
   d. no; a person who is legally insane may be able to plan a crime
   p. 520

3. a. no; this question does not address the person's level of distress caused by the behavior
   b. YES; deviant behavior is behavior that is different according to social standards such as norms
   c. no; the question does not address the functionality of the behavior
   d. no; the behavior is not described as dysfunctional or maladaptive
   p. 520

4. a.  CORRECT; while the medical model describes psychological disorders as medical diseases with a biological origin, there is not a specific medical view within the different biological views; it is a matter of organization—there is the medical model, and within that model there are different ways of looking at biological causes: biochemical, genetic, and structural
   b.  no; this is one of the biological views, along with genetic and structural
   c.  no; this is one of the biological views, along with biochemical and structural
   d.  no; this is one of the biological views, along with biochemical and genetic
   p. 520

5. a.  no; this is the view of the psychodynamic perspective
   b.  YES; this is consistent with what we learned about personality in Chapter 12
   c.  no; this is consistent with the behavioral perspective
   d.  no; humanists would argue that disorders may be caused by having a low self-concept
   p. 521

6. a.  no; the opposite is true; see item c
   b.  no; no evidence is presented in this chapter that suggests that there are gender differences on the issue of conscious versus unconscious influences
   c.  YES; women are more likely to suffer from anxiety disorders and depression, which have symptoms that are turned inward, whereas men are more likely to have externalized disorders that involve aggression and substance abuse
   d.  no; see explanation on 6b
   p. 521

7. a.  no; actually the number was much higher
   b.  YES; exactly 32%, and 20% said that they had an active disorder at the time of the interview
   c.  no; this number is too high; society would be unable to function
   d.  no; this would mean that being normal would be abnormal
   p. 518

8. a.  no; this information is collected in Axis III
   b.  no; this information is collected in Axis IV
   c.  no; this information is also part of Axis IV
   d.  YES; although being labeled with a diagnosis can have lasting effects, it is unlikely that those issues will be addressed in the process of determining the diagnosis
   p. 523

9. a.  no; his fears are not specific
   b.  no; the questions did not address Gerard's mood
   c.  YES; the nervousness and inability to pinpoint the source of anxiety are characteristic of generalized anxiety disorder
   d.  no; Gerard is not described as experiencing intense terrors
   p. 527

10. a.  YES; these individuals are often afraid of saying the wrong thing and may avoid public situations
    b.  no; in this question, the fear is focused
    c.  no; in a social phobia, the person is not experiencing hallucinations or delusions
    d.  no; while this is also an anxiety disorder, obsessive-compulsive disorder involves other fears and concerns
    p. 530

11. a.  no; this is one of the main symptoms of PTSD
    b.  no; this is also a symptom of PTSD
    c.  no; this is also a symptom of PTSD
    d.  YES; this is not a symptom of PTSD, it is a symptom of a phobic disorder, another type of anxiety disorder
    p. 532

12. a.  no; somatoform disorders involve the manifestation of a psychological problem in physical symptoms
    b.  no; the cognitive component of anxiety disorders involves apprehensive expectations and thoughts
    c.  YES; the hidden observer is a concept Hilgard used to explain hypnosis; it involves a person's ability to have a divided state of consciousness; it has been argued that people with dissociative disorders can effectively integrate the different dimensions of consciousness
    d.  no; personality disorders don't involve the issue of the hidden observer
    p. 535

13. a.  no; this disorder involves delusions and hallucinations with no meaning
    b.  YES; waxy flexibility is seen sometimes in people with catatonic schizophrenia
    c.  no; this type is characterized by delusions of reference, grandeur, and persecution
    d.  no; this type does not meet the criteria of any one or more than one disorder
    p. 549

14. a.  no; these delusions are not consistent with disorganized schizophrenia
    b.  no; catatonic schizophrenia symptoms involve bizarre motor behaviors
    c.  YES; these types of symptoms characterize paranoid schizophrenia
    d.  no; these symptoms can be associated with one specific type of schizophrenia
    p. 550

15. a.  YES; the diathesis refers to the disposition
    b.  no
    c.  no; but dopamine is a neurotransmitter that may play a role in schizophrenia
    d.  no
    p. 552

16. a.  no; this is an anxiety disorder
    b.  no; this disorder involves extreme moods such as mania and depression
    c.  incorrect
    d.  YES; these characterize antisocial personality disorder
    p. 554

17. a.  no; typically the disorder starts in adolescence
    b.  no; this disorder affects more males than females
    c.  no; in fact, people do not "grow out" of personality disorders
    d.  YES; people with this disorder show no remorse
    p. 554

18. a.  no; this disorder involves mistrust and suspiciousness
    b.  no; it refers to emotional instability and impulsiveness
    c.  no; schizoid personality disorder involves problems with social relationships
    d.  YES; Andrea shows an exaggerated sense of self-importance
    p. 554

19. a. YES; schizophrenia is not "split personality"
    b. no; in schizophrenia, the personality has disintegrated
    c. no; this is not an accurate description of schizophrenia
    d. no; this is not an accurate description of schizophrenia
    p. 548

20. a. no; this is correct, most cases of bipolar disorder involve the movement from one extreme to the other
    b. no; this is correct and the main symptom of mania
    c. YES; this is incorrect because fatigue is a symptom of depression; during manic episodes, a person feels full of energy
    d. no; this is correct and is one of the main reasons why people experiencing manic episodes can get in serious trouble as their behavior becomes more risky and impulsive
    p. 540

## Practice Test 3

1. a. no; Anna's behavior (i.e., not being able to handle school and family) when compared to other people is not necessarily deviant
   b. YES; Anna is now unable to function at something she used to be able to do
   c. no; the question does not address the issue of the personal distress that Anna may be experiencing
   d. no; the question does not address the issue of Anna being dangerous to herself or others
   p. 520

2. a. no; this is one of the myths, that normal and abnormal behaviors are very different
   b. no; this is one of the myths, that abnormal behaviors are bizarre
   c. no; this is one of the myths; with few exceptions, most psychological disorders don't make the person dangerous to others
   d. YES; this is not a myth; many psychological disorders have a strong genetic component, however, nature and nurture interact; therefore, having the genetic predisposition does not mean that the disorder will be manifested
   p. 519

3. a. no; abnormalities in brain structures pertain to the structural view of biological basis of psychological disorders
   b. no; a history of mental disorders in the family pertains to the genetic view of biological basis of psychological disorders
   c. YES; the biochemical view of biological basis considers possible imbalances in neurotransmitters or hormones in psychological disorders
   d. no; stressors are psychological factors
   p. 520

4. a. CORRECT; the focus of Sergio's psychologist is on early life experiences and the unconscious
   b. no; a psychologist from this perspective would not consider Sergio's lack of awareness of the causes of his current problem
   c. no; the social cognitive perspective would focus on how Sergio thinks to understand his current state of mind
   d. no; humanists may consider conflictive relationships with parents but only if the person is interested in exploring those issues; they would be more interested in Sergio's current ability to work through the psychological disorder
   p. 521

5. a. no; the opposite is true; men are more likely to be diagnosed with externalized disorders
   b. YES; women are more likely to be diagnosed with anxiety or depression, disorders characterized by symptoms that are turned inward
   c. no; in studies of sociocultural factors of psychological disorders presented in the chapter, these different categories (i.e., gender and ethnicity) were not compared across groups
   d. no; in studies of sociocultural factors of psychological disorders presented in the chapter, these different categories (i.e., gender and ethnicity) were not compared across groups

p. 521

6. a. no; this is an important question in reference to both Axes I and II
   b. YES; this is not a typical question in the process of diagnosis, since the mental health professional has not even classified the disorder yet
   c. no; this is an important question in reference to Axis V
   d. no; this is also an important question in reference to Axis III; a person with diabetes may be taking medication that could interact with possible treatment for a psychological disorder

p. 523

7. a. no; on the contrary, because of their negative connotations, labels motivate people to get rid of the bad aspects of the mental disorder but don't necessarily encourage the person to work with the disorder and develop mental competence even if the challenges of the disorder continue
   b. no; this is incorrect, labels have been developed even for mild problems, such as caffeine-use disorder, making the effect of labels even more pervasive
   c. YES; once people are labeled with a disorder they are more likely to give into the belief that a psychological disorder is a terrible thing that will not go away, and they may buy into the social stigma attached to psychological diagnosis
   d. no; being labeled as having a psychological disorder is usually associated with being incompetent, dangerous, and socially unacceptable

p. 525

8. a. no; this disorder is more common in women than in men
   b. YES; this disorder is more common in men than in women
   c. no; this disorder is more common in women than in men
   d. no; these disorders are more common in women than in men; however, bipolar disorder is equally common in men and in women

p. 554

9. a. no; phobic disorders involve extreme fears of specific objects or situations, and etiology studies reveal that most phobias can be associated with a traumatic experience but not of sexual or physical abuse
   b. no; this personality disorder involves an excessive desire of attention, and it is more common in women than in men
   c. no; the etiology of schizophrenic disorders indicates that they have a very strong genetic component
   d. YES; the etiology of the disorder that used to be called multiple personality indicates that this disorder is characterized by an inordinately high rate of sexual or physical abuse during early childhood

p. 536

10. a. no; this is true about this disorder.
    b. no; this is true about this disorder.
    c. no; this is true about this disorder.
    d. YES; most people diagnosed with this disorder are adult females.
  p. 536

11. a. YES; this is a characteristic of people experiencing mania
    b. no; this could happen, or gaining weight
    c. no; this is one of the characteristic problems in thinking
    d. no; this is one of the main symptoms of the disorder, possibly due to the lesser amount of slow-wave sleep and the faster arrival at REM that depressive individuals experience
  p. 538

12. a. incorrect
    b. incorrect
    c. YES; the metabolic activity in the cerebral cortex decreases during depression and, for bipolar individuals, increases during mania
    d. no
  p. 541

13. a. no; the symptoms of depression are not an excuse managed by the individuals experiencing the disorder
    b. no; Marcus is not thinking about a plan of how to deal with the symptoms of the disorder
    c. no; this may contribute to problems in the workplace, but it is not the problem with Marcus
    d. YES; Marcus is focusing intently on how he feels but is not trying to do anything about the feelings
  p. 542

14. a. no; while this contributes to depression, the therapist in the question has not measured that
    b. no; hormonal changes are not addressed in the question
    c. no; this would be the explanation of a psychodynamic psychologist, but there is nothing presented in the question to suggest this explanation
    d. YES; Thomas has a very serious problem, and he is realistically facing it; it has been found that nondepressed people tend to overestimate their control over situations such as terminal cancer
  p. 544

15. a. no; proximal interpersonal experiences are those that are recent
    b. YES; distal interpersonal experiences are those that are distant and took place earlier in time
    c. no; these experiences are clearly not positive
    d. no; experiences are not genetic
  p. 545

16. a. no; Esther is not described as being withdrawn
    b. no; Esther is not described as engaging in bizarre motor behavior
    c. YES; Esther has an elaborate delusion of persecution
    d. no; only one symptom was presented in the question, and it can be associated with the paranoid schizophrenia pattern
  p. 550

17. a.  no; one case could not prove this hypothesis; many other cases of identical twins along with the case of the Genain quadruplets lend support to this view
    b.  no; again, one case cannot prove this hypothesis, but it probably contributed to the onset of the disorder in the sisters
    c.  YES; the chance of quadruplets all developing schizophrenia happens only once in tens of billions of births, a figure much greater than the current world population
    d.  no; they did show such structural patterns, but that was not why they were so interesting to researchers

p. 551

18. a.  YES; the schizoid disorder is characterized by all the tendencies of Habeeba plus a difficulty expressing anger
    b.  no; the question does not address the emotional state of Habeeba
    c.  no; the schizotypal person tends to be hostile and overtly aggressive
    d.  no; antisocial individuals are guiltless, law-breaking, exploitive, irresponsible, self-indulgent, and intrusive

p. 553

19. a.  no; this man is not directly taking advantage of his family members or others
    b.  no; there is no evidence in this scenario that this person lacks self-confidence and needs others to make decisions for him
    c.  no; this man is not directly being hostile or aggressive
    d.  YES; this man is sabotaging the success of this family by doing things that make them less effective

p. 555

20. a.  no; there are specific genes that have been associated with specific disorders, such as the genetic markers for schizophrenia on chromosomes 10, 13, and 22
    b.  YES; insanity is a legal concept and not a cause of psychological disorder
    c.  no; a person's community can be a sociocultural contributor to psychological disorders
    d.  no; cognition is an important aspect of psychological disorders; how a person thinks about the disorder may contribute to the disorder

p. 520

# Chapter 14—Therapies

## Learning Goals

1. Describe the biological therapies.
2. Define psychotherapy, and characterize four types of psychotherapies.
3. Explain the sociocultural approaches and issues in treatment.
4. Evaluate the effectiveness of psychotherapy.

*After studying Chapter 14, you will be able to:*

- Explain what psychotherapy is.
- Describe the connections of psychotherapies with different personality theories.
- Describe the biological therapies, including drug therapy, electroconvulsion therapy, and psychosurgery.
- Name the three categories of psychological disorders in which drug therapy is used.
- Discuss the psychodynamic therapies, including Freud's psychoanalysis and some contemporary psychodynamic therapies.
- Explain the humanistic perspective, including client-centered therapy and Gestalt therapy.
- Discuss behavior therapies, including classical conditioning and operant conditioning approaches.
- Describe the cognitive therapies, including rational emotive behavior therapy and Beck's cognitive therapy.
- Discuss group therapies, including their nature, family/couple therapy, and self-help support groups.
- Evaluate the effectiveness of psychotherapy, including research on the topic, common themes in psychotherapy, and gender/ethnicity issues.
- Discuss therapy integration.
- Describe the effects of managed care on mental health services.
- Identify the behavioral and mental signs that could indicate that a person needs therapy.

## CHAPTER 14: OUTLINE

- There are several types of mental health professionals who vary in degree, education, and nature of training.

- Psychiatrists, who are medical doctors, can administer drugs as part of therapy. The theories of personality serve as the foundation for many forms of psychotherapy.

- This chapter is organized like previous chapters and explores biological therapy, psychotherapy, and sociocultural therapy.

- Psychotherapy is the process used by mental health professionals to help individuals recognize, define, and overcome their psychological and interpersonal difficulties and improve their adjustment.

- Biological therapies are designed to alter the way an individual's body functions in order to reduce or eliminate the symptoms of psychological disorders. The most common type of biomedical therapy is drug therapy.

386

- Drug therapy is mainly used for anxiety disorders, mood disorders, and schizophrenia. Antianxiety drugs are also knows as tranquilizers (e.g., Xanax, Valium, Librium). Antidepressant drugs regulate mood (e.g., Elavil, MAO inhibitors, Prozac, Paxil, lithium). A new antidepressant drug is being developed that targets an amino acid, substance P., and is expected help in the treatment of depression with fewer side effects. Antipsychotic drugs (e.g., neuroleptics, which block the activity of dopamine) are used for schizophrenia and reduce tension, hallucinations, and improve sleep and social behavior.

- Tardive dyskinesia is a major side effect of neurolpetic drugs and involves grotesque, involuntary movements of facial muscles and mouth. Another neuroleptic drug, Clozaril, has toxic effects on white blood cells in some patients.

- Electroconvulsive therapy (ECT) and psychosurgery are two extreme techniques that are used as last resorts. ECT is mainly used to treat severe depression and involves causing a seizure. Adverse side effects include memory loss or other cognitive impairments. Psychosurgery involves the removal or destruction of brain tissue to improve psychological adjustment.

- Psychotherapies can be classified into four perspectives: psychodynamic, humanistic, behavioral, and cognitive.

- Insight therapy is used by psychodynamic and humanistic psychologists with the goal of encouraging insight and self-awareness.

- The psychodynamic therapies stress the importance of the unconscious mind, the role of infancy and childhood experiences, and extensive interpretation by a therapist. Psychoanalysis is a well-known psychodynamic therapy.

- In psychoanalysis, the individual's unconscious thoughts are analyzed. Freud believed that mental disturbances are caused by unresolved unconscious conflicts, often involving sexuality, that originate in early childhood. The therapist may use free association, which is encouraging the patient to say out loud whatever comes to mind no matter how trivial or embarrassing; this would allow for emotional feelings to be released through catharsis. The therapist would also interpret free association, dreams, statements, and behaviors to search for the underlying symbolic meaning.

- In dream analysis, the therapist analyzes the dream's manifest content to determine its latent content. *Transference* refers to the person's relating to the therapist in ways that reproduce or relive important relationships. *Resistance* is a term used to describe unconscious defense strategies that prevent the analyst from understanding the person's problems.

- An important theme in contemporary psychodynamic theories is the development of the self in social contexts such as early relationships with attachment figures. Few contemporary psychodynamic therapists rigorously follow Freud's guidelines.

- In the humanistic therapies, clients are encouraged to understand themselves and to grow personally. The humanistic perspective focuses on conscious thoughts, the present, personal growth, and self-fulfillment.

- Client-centered therapy was developed by Carl Rogers and creates a warm, supportive atmosphere to improve the client's self-concept and to encourage the client to gain insight about problems. Unconditional positive regard, genuineness, and active listening are critical in creating this type of atmosphere.

- Fritz Perls developed Gestalt therapy to help clients become more aware of their feelings and to face their problems. Role playing and confrontation are often used in Gestalt therapy to help clients. Both the humanistic therapies encourage clients to take responsibility for their feelings and actions and to understand themselves.

- Behavior therapies are based on the principles of learning to reduce or eliminate maladaptive behavior. Behavior therapists assume that overt maladaptive symptoms are the problem and not unconscious conflicts or inaccurate perceptions.

- Behavior therapy is based on the learning principles of classical, operant, and social cognitive theories. Systematic desensitization, a technique that uses the principles of classical conditioning, has been used to treat phobias; anxiety is treated by getting the person to associate deep relaxation with increasingly intense anxiety-producing situations.

- Aversive conditioning is used to teach people to avoid such behaviors as smoking, overeating, and drinking. Aversive conditioning consists of repeated pairings of the undesirable behavior with aversive stimuli to decrease the behavior's rewards.

- Using operant conditioning is based on the idea that maladaptive behavior patterns are learned and, therefore, can be unlearned. Behavior modification is a therapy technique that uses operant conditioning. It is believed that many problem behaviors are caused by inadequate response consequences.

- In a token economy, behaviors are reinforced with tokens that can be exchanged for desired rewards.

- Cognitive therapists emphasize that an individual's cognitions, or thoughts, are the main sources of abnormal behavior.

- Cognitive therapies focus on changing the individual's thoughts or cognitions to change behaviors. Rational-emotive therapy is an example of cognitive therapy. In this type of therapy, the therapist disputes the individual's self-defeating beliefs and encourages the client to change his or her belief system.

- Beck's cognitive therapy tries to change the illogical thinking of depressed individuals. Beck's approach helps clients to make connections between logical errors and emotional responses.

- Cognitive behavior therapy consists of a combination of cognitive therapy to change self-defeating thoughts and behavior therapy to change behaviors. This approach considers self-efficacy the key to successful therapy. Self-instructional methods encourage individuals to change their own behavior. Cognitive therapy in conjunction with drug therapy has been effectively used to treat anxiety disorders. Studies have also shown that cognitive therapy is just as effective as drug therapy in the treatment of depression. Cognitive therapy is increasingly being used in the treatment of schizophrenia.

- Sociocultural therapies take into consideration that the individual is part of a social system and seek to treat the person within the context of those groups that he/she belongs to.

- Sociocultural therapies include group therapy, family/couple therapy, and self-help support groups. Other issues in this approach are community mental health and cultural perspectives in therapy.

- Group therapies stress that social relationships are important in successful therapy; therefore, group interaction may be more beneficial than individual therapy. Family therapy is group therapy with family members. Family therapy techniques include validation, reframing, structural change, and detriangulation.

- Self-help support groups are voluntary organizations of individuals who get together to discuss topics of common interest. Weight Watchers is an example of a self-help support group.

- Community psychology focuses on both prevention and treatment of mental disorders. Prevention takes one of three courses: primary (e.g., targeting high-risk populations), secondary (e.g., screening for early detection), and tertiary (e.g., halfway houses).

- From the cultural perspective, variables such as ethnicity and gender should be considered in the development of therapies.

- Much research has been conducted to determine whether or not psychotherapy is effective and if one approach is superior to another. Hans Eysenck concluded that psychotherapy is ineffective and found that neurotic individuals on a waiting list showed marked improvement even though they did not receive psychotherapy.

- Using meta-analysis, which statistically combines the results of many different studies, researchers found that psychotherapy is effective in general. When comparing different approaches, research has found that behavior therapy and insight therapies were superior to no treatment but did not differ from each other in effectiveness.

- Some therapies have been found to be more effective than others in treating some disorders. Behavior therapies have been most successful in treating phobias and sexual dysfunctions, whereas cognitive therapies are effective in treating depression and anxiety. Relaxation training is effective in treating anxiety disorders.

- The most effective psychotherapies have the common elements of expectations, mastery, and emotional arousal as well as a supportive therapeutic relationship.

- In the last two decades, psychologists have turned their attention to gender and ethnic concerns in psychotherapy.

- Most therapists take an eclectic or integrative approach to therapy. In this approach, the therapist is open to using various therapeutic techniques. An example of this is the use of psychotherapy in combination with drug therapy.

- Psychotherapy is expensive, which may contribute to the criticism that psychotherapists are more likely to offer their services to young, attractive, verbal, intelligent, and successful clients than to quiet, ugly, old, institutionalized, and different clients. Managed care has changed the mental health care delivery to control health care costs and has met with much criticism.

- Psychotherapy is practiced by clinical psychologists, psychiatrists, counselors, and other mental health professionals. Society controls individuals who practice psychotherapy through licensing and certification.

- A person seeking professional help for a psychological disorder should identify the professional credential of the mental health professional, give the therapy some time before judging how useful it is, and be a careful consumer of the services.

## Building Blocks of Chapter 14

### Clarifying some of the tricky points in Chapter 14
### and
### In Your Own Words

*To respond to the questions and exercises presented in the "In Your Own Words" section, please write your thoughts, perspectives, and reactions on a separate piece of paper.*

### Biological Therapies

Therapies designed to deal with psychological problems by altering the way an individual's body functions are called *biological* or *biomedical* therapies. A common type of biomedical therapy is *drug* therapy.

One group of drugs, commonly known as tranquilizers, are *antianxiety* drugs. Drugs used to diminish agitation, hallucinations, and delusions are the *antipsychotic* drugs. The most widely used antipsychotic drugs are the *neuroleptics,* which apparently block the *dopamine* system's action in the brain. A major side effect of the neuroleptics is a neurological disorder called *tardive dyskinesia*. Drugs that regulate mood are called *antidepressant* drugs. The three main classes of antidepressant drugs are *tricyclics, SSRI,* and *MAO* inhibitors. A drug that is widely used to treat bipolar disorder is *lithium*. A new type of drug being tested to treat depression targets an amino acid, *substance P*. This new drug is expected to have less serious side effects.

### Helpful Hints for Understanding Therapies
### Helpful Hint #1:

*Drug therapies are not a cure for a mental disorder. They help to manage the symptoms but do not eliminate the disorder. Most mental health professionals agree that drug therapy alone is treating only part of the problem.*

"Shock treatment," more formally known as *electroconvulsive* therapy (ECT), is used to treat severe *depression*. One treatment even more extreme than ECT involves removal or destruction of brain tissue to improve an individual's psychological adjustment. It is called *psychosurgery* and has become more precise.

### Psychotherapies

The goal of both psychodynamic and humanistic therapies is to encourage insight and awareness of self; therefore, they are called *insight* therapies.

The types of therapies that stress the importance of the unconscious mind, the role of the infant and childhood experiences, and extensive interpretation by a therapist are called *psychodynamic* therapies. A well-known psychodynamic approach was developed by Freud; it is called *psychoanalysis*. According to this approach, psychological problems can be traced to childhood experiences, often involving conflicts about *sexuality*. These conflicts are not *available* to the conscious mind.

Special therapeutic techniques help bring these conflicts into *awareness*. One technique, in which the patient lies on a couch and is encouraged to talk freely, is called *free association*. By talking freely, Freud felt that emotional tension could be released, a process called *catharsis*. The search for symbolic, hidden meanings in what the client says and does is called *interpretation*.

Psychoanalysts interpret a client's dreams in the technique called *dream analysis*. According to Freud, the conscious, remembered aspects of a dream are called the *manifest* content, whereas the unconscious, symbolic aspects of a dream are called the *latent* content. Often, patients relate to the therapist in ways that reproduce important relationships in the patient's life, a process called *transference*. The client's unconscious defense strategies that prevent an analyst from understanding the client's problems are called *resistance*. Showing up late for sessions or arguing with the psychoanalyst are examples of *resistance*. An important theme in contemporary psychodynamic theories is the development of the self in *social contexts*.

### Helpful Hint #2:
*The goal of psychodynamic therapies is to make part of the unconscious, conscious. Then the person has a choice in their behaviors and does not solely respond out of unconscious directives.*

Clients are encouraged to understand themselves and to grow personally in the *humanistic* psychotherapies. One type of humanistic psychotherapy, developed by Carl Rogers, is called *humanistic* therapy. According to Rogers, the positive regard we receive from others has strings attached, a situation he refers to as *conditions* of *worth*.

Rogers believes that therapists should create a warm and caring environment, a concept called unconditional *positive regard*. Additionally, Rogers believes that therapists must not hide behind a façade; in other word, therapists must be *genuine*. Also, therapists should restate and support what clients say and do, a process called *active listening*.

In another type of humanistic psychotherapy, therapists question and challenge clients to help them become aware of their *feeling*. This approach is called *Gestalt* therapy and was founded by *Perls*. In this technique, therapists set examples, encourage *congruence* between verbal and nonverbal behavior, and use *role* playing. Gestalt therapy is much more *directive* than client-centered therapy.

Behavior therapies use the principles of *learning* to reduce or eliminate maladaptive behavior. Two procedures deal with behaviors learned through *classical* conditioning. One procedure, which treats anxiety by getting clients to relax as they visualize anxiety-producing situations, is *systematic desensitization*. Research suggests that this technique is an effective way to treat a number of *phobias*.

A second technique that is based on classical conditioning repeatedly pairs undesirable behavior with an aversive stimulus; this is called *aversive conditioning*. Other behavior therapy techniques make use of *operant* conditioning in order to change the individual's behavior; this process is often called *behavior modification*.

A behavior therapy technique that allows individuals to earn tokens that can later be exchanged for desired rewards is called a *token economy*.

Cognitive therapists emphasize that the individual's cognitions or *thoughts* are the main source of abnormal behavior. Albert Ellis developed a cognitive therapy called *rational-emotive* behavior therapy. In this type of therapy, the therapist *examines* the individual's self-defeating beliefs and encourages him or her to change his or her *belief* system.

### In Your Own Words
*Please write your thoughts, perspectives, and reactions on a separate piece of paper.*
✓ *What irrational beliefs or logical thinking errors are you able to notice in yourself?*

The cognitive therapy of Aaron Beck focuses on treating a variety of dysfunctions, especially *depression*. Beck's approach helps the individual understand the connection between illogical thinking and *emotional responses*.

## In Your Own Words

*Please write your thoughts, perspectives, and reactions on a separate piece of paper.*

✓ *Make up titles of fictitious songs that could have been written by Freud, Rogers, and Ellis. The title of each song should be consistent with the therapeutic approaches of these individuals.*

## *Sociocultural Approaches and Issues in Treatment*

The following features make group therapy attractive: (1) the individual receives *information* from either the group leader or group members; (2) group members realize that others are suffering also, a feature called *information;* (3) group members can support one another, a feature termed *altruism;* (4) because a therapy group resembles a family, it provides corrective *recapitulation* of the family group; (5) feedback from other group members promotes development of *social* skills; and (6) the group offers a setting for *interpersonal* learning.

Group therapy with family members is called *family* therapy and stresses that an individual's psychological adjustment is related to a pattern of interaction within the family. Therapy with couples that focuses on their relationship is called *couple therapy.* Four widely used techniques in family systems therapy are (1) *validation,* (2) *reframing,* (3) *structural* change, and (4) *detriangulation.*

Groups that are run on a voluntary basis and without a professional therapist are called *self-help support* groups. One well-known self-help group is *Alcoholics Anonymous.*

## In Your Own Words

*Please write your thoughts, perspectives, and reactions on a separate piece of paper.*
✓ *If you were a mental health professional, what aspects of the different psychotherapies discussed in this chapter would you use to treat depression?*

## *The Effectiveness of Psychotherapy*

Is psychotherapy effective? One well-known study, which used a procedure called *meta-analysis* to evaluate many other investigations, found psychotherapies to be effective. If a study is using a *wait-list* control group, it means that there are individuals wanting to see a psychotherapist who have not yet received psychotherapy. Studies have found behavior therapies and cognitive therapies to be especially effective in treating *anxiety* disorders and *depressive* disorders.

Frank has concluded that effective psychotherapies have the common elements of *expectations,* mastery, and emotional arousal. In the past two decades, psychologists have become sensitive to the concerns of ethnicity and *gender* in psychotherapy. An important issue regarding females in therapy focuses on the appropriateness of *autonomy* as a therapy goal. Some have suggested that therapy goals for women should be *relatedness* and connection with others.

Ethnic minority individuals generally prefer to discuss problems with friends and *relatives* rather than with mental health professionals. Research also suggests that *ethnic minority* individuals are more likely to terminate therapy early when there is an ethnic mismatch between client and therapist.

Most therapists use a variety of approaches to therapy; that is, they are *eclectic (integrative).* In integrative therapy, the mental health professional uses various techniques and methods from diverse therapies. Therapy integrations are conceptually compatible with the *biopsychosocial* model of abnormal behavior. One approach to dealing with increasing mental health costs, involving the use of external reviewers to approve the treatments, is called *managed* care.

Mental health professionals differ in their degree and *training*. Society controls individuals who practice psychotherapy by *licensing* and *certification*.

## In Your Own Words

*Please write your thoughts, perspectives, and reactions on a separate piece of paper.*

✓ *Consider this scenario: You have a friend who seems troubled. What kinds of question would you ask him/her to help this friend figure out if he/she needs to seek help from a psychotherapist?*

## Correcting the Incorrect

Carefully read each statement. Determine if the statement is correct or incorrect. If the statement is incorrect, make the necessary changes to correct it. Then check the answer key at the end of the chapter for the correct statement and page reference in the textbook.

1. Drug therapy is often administered to patients by their psychologists.
2. MAO inhibitors are drugs that are most commonly used to treat bipolar disorder.
3. Drug therapy for a person with schizophrenia includes the use of a neuroleptic.
4. There are no significant side effects to electroconvulsive therapy.
5. The behavioral theories of Skinner were important in developing psychoanalysis.
6. Freud believed that problems could be traced back to childhood conflicts about sexuality.
7. In catharsis, the person is asked to say whatever comes to mind even if it is trivial or embarrassing.
8. The manifest content of a dream refers to its underlying, symbolic meaning.
9. Psychoanalysis tries to encourage resistance.
10. In client-centered therapy, the therapist creates an atmosphere with many conditions of worth.
11. The therapist's role in client-centered therapy is directive.
12. Perls developed Gestalt therapy to help people focus on their past.
13. Behavior therapies are based on Freud's theory.
14. In systematic desensitization, the person receives tokens for appropriate behavior.
15. Aversive conditioning associates some undesirable behavior with aversive stimuli.
16. An example of a procedure based on operant conditioning is free association.
17. A cognitive therapist focuses on how the environment influences her client's behavior.
18. Ellis argues that irrational and self-defeating beliefs play a role in psychological problems.
19. Beck's approach to therapy is much more directive and confrontational than Ellis's.
20. Group therapy takes advantage of relationships that may hold the key to an individual's problems.
21. Hans Eysenck provided evidence that psychotherapy is effective.
22. A meta-analysis examines one study in a very detailed way.
23. Cognitive therapies seem to be most successful with depression and anxiety.
24. The integrative therapy approach contradicts the biopsychosocial model of abnormal behavior.

**Practice Test 1**

1.  The process used by mental health professionals to help individuals recognize, define, and overcome their psychological and interpersonal difficulties is called
    a.  biological therapy.
    b.  drug therapy.
    c.  electroconvulsive therapy.
    d.  psychotherapy.

2.  Neuroleptics are widely used to reduce symptoms of
    a.  depression.
    b.  schizophrenia.
    c.  bipolar disorder.
    d.  multiple personality.

3.  Electroconvulsive therapy (ECT) is
    a.  the most effective treatment for major depressive disorder.
    b.  comparable in effectiveness to cognitive therapy and drug therapy.
    c.  more effective than cognitive therapy, but not as effective as drug therapy.
    d.  less effective than both cognitive therapy and drug therapy.

4.  Electroconvulsive therapy is used in treating severe
    a.  schizophrenic disorder.
    b.  bipolar disorder.
    c.  multiple personality.
    d.  depression.

5.  James dreamed that he went to his neighbor's house at midnight and made himself a sandwich. His psychoanalyst interpreted the dream to mean that James really wanted to go to bed with his neighbor's wife. Making the sandwich was the
    a.  symbolic content of the dream.
    b.  manifest content of the dream.
    c.  latent content of the dream.
    d.  resistant content of the dream.

6.  The psychoanalytic term to explain a client who suddenly begins missing appointments and becomes hostile in therapy sessions is
    a.  resistance.
    b.  transference.
    c.  free association.
    d.  catharsis.

7.  The release of emotional tension associated with reliving an emotionally charge experience is called
    a.  catharsis.
    b.  resistance.
    c.  free association.
    d.  unconditional positive regard.

8. Which of the following is not a focus of humanistic therapy?
    a. conscious thoughts
    b. past experiences
    c. personal growth
    d. self-fulfillment

9. According to Carl Rogers, client-centered therapy requires all of the following except which one?
    a. unconditional positive regard
    b. genuineness
    c. interpretation
    d. active listening

10. Gestalt therapy is similar to psychoanalytic therapy in that they both
    a. assume that problems stem from past unresolved conflicts.
    b. assume that the client can find solutions in the right atmosphere.
    c. expect resistance and transference to occur.
    d. deny the importance of dreams in understanding a person.

11. The term *insight therapy* applies to both psychodynamic therapy and
    a. behavior therapy.
    b. humanistic therapy.
    c. biomedical therapy.
    d. aversive conditioning.

12. Vigorously challenging and questioning clients about critical issues and forcing them to face their problems are techniques used in
    a. psychodynamic therapy.
    b. humanistic therapy.
    c. Gestalt therapy.
    d. client-centered therapy.

13. Your roommate Rachel has terrifying memories of having been bitten by a pit bull when she was a child. To this day, she gets extremely nervous if a dog is anywhere near her. In order to help Rachel overcome this fear of dogs, you have brought home a puppy and intend to use systematic desensitization. Which of the following best describes your procedure?
    a. bringing the puppy closer and closer to Rachel after she has been given time to completely relax
    b. keeping the puppy in a separate room where Rachel does not have to interact with it
    c. forcing Rachel to hold the dog because fear of a puppy is ridiculous
    d. letting young children handle the dog in front of Rachel

14. The principles of operant and classical conditioning are extensively used by practitioners of
    a. psychoanalysis.
    b. Gestalt therapy.
    c. group therapy.
    d. behavior therapy.

15. A technique of behavior therapy that pairs an undesirable behavior with an unpleasant stimulus is
    a. token economy.
    b. systematic desensitization.
    c. aversive conditioning.
    d. rational-emotion therapy.

16. Cognitive therapists are likely to be concerned with
    a. an individual's thoughts.
    b. unconditional positive regard.
    c. the manifest content of dreams.
    d. unconscious motives.

17. Which approach is most likely to be concerned with irrational and self-defeating beliefs?
    a. Beck's cognitive therapy
    b. Ellis' rational-emotional behavior therapy
    c. systematic desensitization
    d. operant therapy

18. The following are characteristics of Beck's cognitive therapy, EXCEPT
    a. this therapy tends to be confrontational.
    b. this therapy aims at getting individuals to reflect on their personal issues.
    c. this therapy encourages people to explore inaccuracies in their beliefs.
    d. this therapy involves an open dialogue between the therapist and the individual.

19. When a family systems therapist is using validation, a member of the family would hear the therapist
    a. expressing understanding to a family member.
    b. telling the family which member is correct about the nature of a problem.
    c. encouraging the parents to spend more time together.
    d. trying to encourage the family to have fewer conflicts.

20. What is the main advantage of an integrative approach to psychotherapy?
    a. It is usually more cost effective.
    b. It is usually less time consuming.
    c. It requires less formal training on part of the psychotherapist.
    d. It utilizes the strengths of a variety of approaches to meet the specific needs of the client.

## Practice Test 2

1. In family systems therapy, teaching family members to view individual problems as family problems is called
    a. validation.
    b. reframing.
    c. structural change.
    d. detriangulation.

2. Ann and the children feel that they are not getting enough of Jerry's attention. Ann complains that Jerry works too much. Their family therapist told them all that Jerry is not the problem and that they should not complain to or about him for 2 weeks. The therapist is using
   a. restructuring.
   b. detriangulation.
   c. something other than the systems approach.
   d. reframing.

3. Development of social skills is most immediately facilitated in which type of therapy approach?
   a. behavior therapy
   b. individual
   c. group
   d. client-centered

4. Based on the most current research, is psychotherapy effective?
   a. yes, overall
   b. no, not very effective
   c. only for those with schizophrenia
   d. only for those with phobias

5. An ethnic match between the therapist and the client appears to provide which main advantage for psychotherapy?
   a. professional similarity
   b. cultural commonality
   c. educational similarity
   d. socioeconomic commonality

6. There is _____ between number of therapy sessions and improvement in the psychological disorder.
   a. a negative correlation
   b. a positive correlation
   c. no correlation
   d. no relationship

7. If you were to consider seeking professional psychological help, you would do all of the following except which one?
   a. research the services offered by potential therapists
   b. identify the professional credentials of potential therapists
   c. pick a therapist from the *Yellow Pages* and make an appointment
   d. set specific therapy goals and frequently assess whether these goals are being met

8. A criticism of the managed health care system for providing psychotherapy is the
   a. emphasis on long-term psychotherapy.
   b. emphasis on short-term psychotherapy.
   c. development of explicit and measurable treatment plans.
   d. lack of certified practitioners.

9.  A _____ is a therapist who because of graduate training is able to prescribe medication for psychological disorders.
    a.  psychiatrist
    b.  clinical psychologist
    c.  social worker
    d.  counselor

10. The following are antianxiety drugs, EXCEPT
    a.  Xanax.
    b.  Valium.
    c.  Prozac.
    d.  Buspirone.

11. The use of benzodiazepines has been associated with
    a.  alertness.
    b.  birth defects.
    c.  agitation.
    d.  lack of addiction.

12. MAO (monoamine oxidase) inhibitors are used to treat
    a.  schizophrenia.
    b.  anxiety disorders.
    c.  mood disorders.
    d.  personality disorders.

13. Neuroleptics, the most widely used class of antipsychotic drugs, relieve the symptoms of schizophrenia because
    a.  they inhibit MAO.
    b.  they block the dopamine system's action in the brain.
    c.  they increase the level of norepinephrine and serotonin.
    d.  they bind to the receptor sites of neurotransmitters that become overactive during anxiety.

14. Which of the following is not a technique used in psychoanalysis?
    a.  dream analysis
    b.  systematic desensitization
    c.  free-association
    d.  catharsis

15. If a patient started treating the psychotherapist in the same way he treats his mother, a psychoanalyst would argue that the person is engaging in
    a.  catharsis.
    b.  resistance.
    c.  transference.
    d.  free-association.

16. Heinz Kohut is a contemporary psychoanalyst. Which of the following issues is not emphasized in Kohut's therapeutic approach?
    a.  having the person seek out appropriate relationships with others
    b.  early relationships with attachment figures
    c.  analysis of dreams by the psychotherapist
    d.  having people develop a realistic understanding of relationships

17. Client-centered therapy is an approach consistent with the _____ theory of personality.
    a. psychodynamic
    b. humanistic
    c. behavioral
    d. social cognitive

18. When a behavioral therapist is trying to help a person associate smoking with a bad thing, such as getting nauseous, the technique being used is
    a. systematic desensitization.
    b. token economy.
    c. aversive conditioning.
    d. operant conditioning.

19. The cognitive-behavior technique(s) that teach individuals how to modify their own behaviors are called
    a. psychoanalysis.
    b. rational-emotive behavior therapy.
    c. self-instructional methods.
    d. client-centered therapy.

20. Which of the following is the type of prevention that involves efforts made to reduce the number of new cases of psychological disorders?
    a. primary
    b. secondary
    c. tertiary
    d. psychological

21. Ellis's rational-emotive behavior therapy focuses on eliminating self-defeating beliefs. According to Ellis, individuals tend to have three basic demands for themselves. Which of the following is NOT one of the demands proposed by Ellis?
    a. My life conditions should not be frustrating but rather should be enjoyable.
    b. I expect other people to be mean and untrustworthy.
    c. I absolutely must perform well and win the approval of other people.
    d. Other people have to be fair to me.

## Practice Test 3

1. Which of the following is not one of the ways in which drug therapy improves the condition of people with mood disorders?
    a. reducing the level of serotonin
    b. increasing the level of norepinephrine
    c. inhibiting MAO
    d. targeting substance P

2. It may be argued that one of reasons people with schizophrenia stop drug treatment is because
    a. the symptoms usually don't reappear or become milder.
    b. these drugs keep them in the hospital longer than they want to be there.
    c. of their concern with developing tardive dyskinesia.
    d. they need the excess dopamine in the brain to feel good.

3. When psychosurgery is used today, it usually involves the lesioning of
   a. the area connecting the frontal lobe and the thalamus.
   b. a part of the limbic system.
   c. the prefrontal lobe.
   d. the frontal lobe of the cerebral cortex.

4. Which therapist is less likely to take the statements of a patient at face value?
   a. psychoanalyst
   b. behavioral therapist
   c. humanistic therapist
   d. Gestalt therapist

5. Cognitive therapists test the misinterpretations of people experiencing panic disorder by
   a. trying to change the behaviors associated with the panic disorder.
   b. asking the person to free-associate to explore the possible reasons for the panic disorder.
   c. inducing an actual panic attack.
   d. telling the patient to relax and get over it.

6. In the treatment of depression, cognitive therapy is just as effective as
   a. prescribing benzodiazepines.
   b. prescribing an antidepressant.
   c. prescribing neuroleptics.
   d. psychoanalysis.

7. Sociocultural approaches to therapy understand that the person
   a. benefits most from individual therapy.
   b. is part of a social system of relationships.
   c. is less likely to improve a psychological problem if he or she must share it with other people.
   d. should not be concerned with the credentials of the therapist.

8. One of the reasons group therapy is effective is because it helps people realize that they are not alone in their problem. This is a feature of group therapy referred to as
   a. altruism.
   b. information.
   c. corrective recapitulation.
   d. universalism.

9. The credibility of peers in the psychological problem contributes to the effectiveness of
   a. family therapy.
   b. cognitive therapy.
   c. self-help support groups.
   d. rational-emotive behavioral therapy.

10. Which of the following practices is not associated with the community mental health approach?
    a. training teachers and ministers on psychological issues
    b. preventing psychological disorders
    c. the use of mental health institutions as the primary source of psychological treatment
    d. deinstitutionalization

11. Karen is a psychologist who works in a daytime facility for individuals with severe psychological disorders. The individuals who attend this facility live at home and are brought in by a caregiver. Some come everyday, others come some days of the week. During the day, the individuals engage in group therapies and recreational activities. Karen's work is an example of
    a.    primary prevention.
    b.    secondary prevention.
    c.    tertiary prevention.
    d.    behavioral therapy.

12. A culturally sensitive therapist would not
    a.    wish a Merry Christmas to his patients with a nice card during the holidays.
    b.    keep abreast of political and economic world issues.
    c.    make an effort to learn a second language.
    d.    study the culture of his patients.

13. Psychologists who have studied gender issues in therapy recommend that when the client is a female the therapy should
    a.    focus on autonomy.
    b.    emphasize relatedness and connections with others.
    c.    focus on self-determination.
    d.    be cognitive instead of behavioral.

14. Which of the following is not one of the common elements in effective psychotherapies?
    a.    establishing a plan of expectations with the client
    b.    encouraging the client to take control of the therapeutic process
    c.    arousing of emotions that motivate the client
    d.    actively changing bad behaviors into more adaptive behaviors

15. Therapy integrations take place when
    a.    the client integrates the knowledge from the therapy into his or her life.
    b.    the therapist helps the person bring together the past and the present in the therapy.
    c.    the therapist uses an eclectic approach.
    d.    the therapist brings two or more clients together because they have issues in common.

16. Ling has been diagnosed with schizophrenia. She has a psychiatrist who monitors her drug therapy and a clinical psychologist whom she sees for cognitive therapy. Ling is engaged in
    a.    rational-emotive behavioral therapy.
    b.    integrative therapy.
    c.    managed care.
    d.    transference.

17. The following are all criticisms of how managed care has changed mental health services, EXCEPT
    a.  managed care organizations have less well-trained therapists doing the job that used to be done by psychiatrists and clinical psychologists.
    b.  managed care organizations use stringent screening procedures to figure out who needs help and who does not need help.
    c.  managed care encourages the use of traditional services, such as extended individual therapy.
    d.  managed care encourages and even limits psychotherapists to use lower-cost brief treatment options.

18. Which of the following is not recommended when seeking professional help?
    a.  Identify what exactly the therapist studied, what school the therapist attended, and the status of the therapist's license.
    b.  Try a couple of therapists before settling down with one. After one or two sessions, you should be able to figure out if it is going to work out for you.
    c.  Choose a therapist of your same gender, if that is important for you.
    d.  Find out what is the perspective of the therapist.

19. When evaluating whether you need a therapist, the following symptoms are good indicators that professional help would be useful, EXCEPT
    a.  if recently you have had trouble concentrating on school work.
    b.  if you have problems but feel that you can't talk to anyone about them.
    c.  if you are frightened of walking around at night in urban areas.
    d.  if your self-esteem is really low.

20. In the critical controversies section, we learned that recent research on antidepressant drugs finds them close in effectiveness to
    a.  behavioral therapy.
    b.  placebos.
    c.  humanistic therapy.
    d.  group therapy.

## Connections

*Take advantage of all the other study tools available for this chapter!*

## Media Integration

| NAME OF CLIP | DESCRIPTION | KEY CONCEPTS AND IDEAS |
|---|---|---|
| | | **Biological Therapies** |
| Functions of Neurotransmitters | This video clips illustrates the role of neurotransmitters in a variety of psychological phenomena, including aggression, detection of threats, pain, and mood disorders. | Neurotransmitter Serotonin Noradrenaline Substance P. Endorphins |
| Bipolar Disorder II | This video clip presents a broad introduction to bipolar disorder, including a discussion of the pattern of cycles and the drug Lithium. Isolation is one of the main problems with the depression | Bipolar disorder Depression Lithium Brain imaging MRI |

| | component of the disorder. Brain imaging is used to extract data and look at what chemicals are present and active in the brain of a person with depression. MRI scans are used to study the orbital frontal lobe, an area that controls moods and emotions. Coline is a substance that has been found in abnormally high levels in the brains of depressed teenagers. | Coline |
|---|---|---|
| Major Depression | Tara has been coping for 15 years with depression. She has recently been treated with electroconvulsive therapy and discusses the positive and negative aspects of this treatment for depression. Tara describes her patterns of negative affect and disturbed sleep. Pretending to be well is stressful and seems to lead to stronger feelings of depression, and she describes persistent thoughts of death and dying. Tara has been committed to psychiatric institution, and her depression has not responded to traditional psychotherapy and medication. She has responded better to electroconvulsive therapy. The video ends with suggestions for what to do if you are feeling depressed, including checking the internet and talking to someone. | Depression<br>Electroconvulsive therapy<br>Suicide |
| | | **Psychotherapies** |
| Electroconvulsive Therapy | This audio clip addresses the negative stigma associated with electroconvulsive therapy (ECT). ECT is now safer that it used to be and it is particularly useful with patients who do not respond to medication. May be the first choice of treatment for suicidal individuals. Many have benefited but some patients tend to experience memory problems. | Electroconvulsive therapy<br>Depression<br>Memory |
| Freud's Contribution to Psychology | Video clip places Freud's contribution to psychology in a historical context. The origins of his perspective in the study of hysteria as well as his view of the brain are discussed. | History of psychology<br>Hysteria<br>Dream Analysis<br>Manifest content of dreams<br>Repression |
| Freudian Interpretation of | This video clip is an introduction to Freud's theory of dream analysis. | Dreams<br>Dream work |

| Dreams | The concept of dream work and its processes are discussed. Common themes in Freudian dream analysis are also discussed. | Displacement<br>Condensation<br>Symbolization<br>Projection<br>Ego<br>Manifest dream<br>Latent dream |
|---|---|---|
| Classical Conditioning II | This interactivity helps the participant review the elements of classical conditioning and applies the concepts to human learning. The experiences of habituation with sounds and generalizations with foods are illustrated. | Classical conditioning<br>Unconditioned stimulus<br>Unconditioned response<br>Neutral stimulus<br>Conditioned stimulus<br>Conditioned response<br>Habituation<br>Generalization |
| Tourette's Syndrome | Tim is a young man with Tourette's syndrome. His disorder is controllable for a certain extent of time as long as he focuses on the control. His cognitive and emotional states influence the extent of his control. The more relaxed and focused he is, the more controlled the tics are. The disorder is embarrassing for Tim as he also copes with the challenges of adolescence. The symptoms of this disorder tend to become less prevalent with age. | Tourette's syndrome |
| Virtual Reality Therapy | This audio clip explains the innovative use of virtual reality technology for therapy, a behavior modification approach. About 25 million Americans are afraid of flying. Samantha Smith has recommended the use of virtual reality to treat people with fear of flying. The technology is used as part of an anxiety management training. In a study, one group received anxiety training at an airport and another received virtual reality treatment in a therapist's office. Both groups were comparable in results, showing improvements even 6 months. | Virtual reality therapy<br>Behavior modification<br>Fears<br>Anxiety |
| | | **Sociocultural Approaches and Issues in Treatment** |
| Bipolar Disorder II | This video clip presents a broad introduction to bipolar disorder, | Bipolar disorder<br>Depression |

| | | |
|---|---|---|
| | including a discussion of the pattern of cycles and the drug Lithium. Isolation is one of the main problems with the depression component of the disorder. Brain imaging is used to extract data and look at what chemicals are present and active in the brain of a person with depression. MRI scans are used to study the orbital frontal lobe, an area that controls moods and emotions. Coline is a substance that has been found in abnormally high levels in the brains of depressed teenagers. | Lithium<br>Brain imaging<br>MRI<br>Coline<br>Self-help support groups |
| | | **The Effectiveness of Psychotherapy** |

## Online Learning Center (www.mhhe.com/Santrockp7u)

- Interact and make learning fun!
    - o **Interactive Exercise**
        - ▪ My Friend the Spider
    - o **Interactive Reviews**
        - ▪ Level of Analysis: Therapeutic Behavior Change
        - ▪ Therapies for Psychological Disorders
- Brush up on the Key Terms for this chapter by first reviewing the electronic **Glossary** (in English or Spanish) and then testing your retention using the **Flashcard** feature.
- **"Notes"**—This feature allows you to use the website as you would your text, inserting your own study notes and highlighting areas of particular importance.

## In Your Text

- Found throughout each chapter, the **Review and Sharpen Your Thinking** feature breaks the text into logical chunks, allowing you to process, review, and reflect thoughtfully on the information that you've just read. When going back to *study* the chapter, try reading the feature *before* the section of text to which it relates. In doing so, you will be able to focus your attention on important concepts *as* you encounter them. In this chapter, this feature can be found on the following pages: pp. 568, 583, 589, and 595.

## Practice Quizzes

- Test your knowledge of therapies by taking the different practice quizzes found on your text's **Online Learning Center** and on the **In-Psych Plus CD-ROM** packaged with your text.

## ANSWER KEY

## In Your Own Words

✓  What irrational beliefs or logical thinking errors are you able to notice in yourself?
*Rational-emotive behavioral therapy focuses on the irrational beliefs that we have that keep us from being effective. Sometimes the expectations we have of ourselves are so unrealistic that they contribute to psychological problems. Think of yourself in all the settings you participate in: student, family member, friend, romantic partner, worker, and others. Consider your expectations*

*for each of these areas of your life. Are any of your expectations extreme or unrealistic? How do you think that they influence your emotions and behaviors?*

✓ Make up titles of fictitious songs that could have been written by Freud, Rogers, and Ellis. The title of each song should be consistent with the therapeutic approaches of these individuals. *Freud is associated with the unconscious, dreams, free-association, manifest and latent content of dreams, psychoanalysis, and catharsis, among many other concepts that you have learned in other chapters. Rogers, a humanist, is associated with the client-centered therapy, an approach that wants to encourage the client to find his or her own solutions. Concepts associated with Rogers are free-will, unconditional positive regard, empathy, and listening. Finally, Ellis, the creator of rational-emotive therapy, proposed that therapists should be direct in pointing out the problems in their client's thinking. He talked about irrational thoughts, unrealistic expectations, and realizing the role of A, B, C, D, and E in the psychological problem.*

✓ If you were a mental health professional, what aspects of the different psychotherapies discussed in this chapter would you use to treat depression? *Depression is a mood disorder that is so common it has been referred to as the common cold of psychological disorders. Possibly for that reason, most approaches have worked with and/or done research on this disorder. Biological therapies include recommendations of specific drugs that can improve the symptoms of depression. However, research suggests that cognitive therapy may be just as effective as drug therapy. Also consider the contributions of the humanistic approach and sociocultural approaches to the disorder.*

✓ Consider this scenario: You have a friend who seems troubled. What kinds of question would you ask him/her to help this friend figure out if he/she needs to seek help from psychotherapist? *In helping a friend to evaluate if he or she needs a therapist, you may ask if he/she has experienced any of the following recently: feels sad frequently, has a very low self-esteem, feels like others are always out to get him/her, has a hard time concentrating on school work, feels so anxious he/she can hardly function, has a tendency to alienate people inadvertently, is frightened of things that should not be fear provoking, hears voices that tell him/her what you should do, and/or is unable to share problems with anyone.*

## Correcting the Incorrect

1. Drug therapy is often administered to patients by their *medical doctors or psychiatrists.* (p. 562)
2. *Lithium is the drug most commonly* used to treat bipolar disorder. (p. 564)
3. Drug therapy for a person with schizophrenia includes the use of a neuroleptic. (p. 566)
4. There *are* significant side effects to electroconvulsive therapy. (p. 567)
5. The *psychodynamic theories of Freud* were important in developing psychoanalysis. (p. 570)
6. Freud believed that problems could be traced back to childhood conflicts about sexuality. (p. 570)
7. In *free association*, the person is asked to say whatever comes to mind even if it is trivial or embarrassing. (p. 570)
8. The *latent content* of a dream refers to its underlying, symbolic meaning. (p. 571)
9. Psychoanalysis *tries to work through* resistance. (p. 572)
10. In client-centered therapy, the therapist creates an atmosphere with *no conditions of worth*. (p. 573)
11. The therapist's role in client-centered therapy is *nondirective*. (p. 573)

12. Perls developed Gestalt therapy to help people focus *on here and now.* (p. 574)

13. Behavior therapies are based on *learning theory.* (p. 574)

14. In systematic desensitization, the person *learns to relax increasingly anxiety-provoking situations.* (p. 575)

15. Aversive conditioning associates some undesirable behavior with aversive stimuli. (p. 577)

16. An example of a procedure based on operant conditioning is *token economy.* (p. 577)

17. A cognitive therapist focuses on *how thoughts influence her client's behavior.* (p. 578)

18. Ellis argues that irrational and self-defeating beliefs play a role in psychological problems. (p. 579)

19. Beck's approach to therapy is *much less directive and confrontational than Ellis's.* (p. 581)

20. Group therapy takes advantage of relationships that may hold the key to an individual's problems. (p. 584)

21. Hans Eysenck provided evidence that psychotherapy is *ineffective.* (p. 589)

22. A meta-analysis examines *the results of many studies.* (p. 590)

23. Cognitive therapies seem to be most successful with depression and anxiety. (p. 591)

24. The integrative therapy approach *is compatible* with the biopsychosocial model of abnormal behavior. (p. 592)

## Practice Test 1

1. a. no; biological therapies are designed to change symptoms directly by altering how the body works.
   b. no; this is a type of biological therapy.
   c. no; this is a type of biological therapy.
   d. YES; psychotherapy is often used in conjunction with biological therapy.
   p. 562

2. a. no; neuroleptics are antipsychotic drugs and depression is a mood disorder
   b. YES; neuroleptics are antipsychotic drugs
   c. no; neuroleptics are antipsychotic drugs and bipolar disorder is a mood disorder
   d. no; neuroleptics are antipsychotic drugs and this disorder is a dissociative disorder
   p. 565

3. a. no; this is not a conclusion of the study presented in the textbook
   b. YES; it is comparable to cognitive therapy and drug therapy in effectiveness
   c. no; this ECT is not more effective than cognitive therapy or less effective as drugs
   d. no; this is not a conclusion of the study presented in the textbook
   p. 567

4. a. no; antipsychotic drugs are used to treat schizophrenic disorders
   b. no; lithium is generally used to treat bipolar disorder
   c. no; ECT is not used to treat multiple personality
   d. YES; it is used to treat depression
   p. 566

5. a. no; the correct term for a dream's symbolic content is the latent content
   b. YES; the manifest content refers to the dream's conscious, remembered aspects
   c. no; the latent content refers to the unconscious, unremembered aspects
   d. no; this concept is not used in psychoanalysis
   p. 571

6. a.   YES; resistance refers to unconscious defense strategies
   b.   no; this is the person's relating to the analyst in a way that resembles another relationship
   c.   no; in free association the person says aloud whatever comes to mind
   d.   no; this is the release of emotional tension when having an emotional experience
   p. 572

7. a.   YES; this is the release of emotional tension when having an emotional experience
   b.   no; resistance refers to unconscious defense strategies
   c.   no; in free association the person says aloud whatever comes to mind
   d.   no; this is acceptance of another person without any strings attached
   p. 570

8. a.   no; conscious thought is a focus of humanistic therapy
   b.   YES; humanists tend to focus on the here and now
   c.   no; humanistic therapy emphasizes personal growth
   d.   no; self-fulfillment is a focus of humanistic therapy
   p. 572

9. a.   no; this is required in client-centered therapy
   b.   no; this is required in client-centered therapy
   c.   YES; this is not required in client-centered therapy since it is nondirective
   d.   no; this is required in client-centered therapy
   p. 573

10. a.   YES; this is an assumption of both Gestalt therapy and psychoanalytic therapy
    b.   no; the client cannot finds solutions without the assistance of a therapist
    c.   no; Gestalt therapy makes no requirement on resistance and transference
    d.   no; psychoanalytic therapy makes use of dream analysis in understanding a person
    p. 573

11. a.   no; behavior therapy does not use insight
    b.   YES; both therapies assume the client needs to gain insight and awareness
    c.   no; insight is not required for the biomedical therapies
    d.   no; in this therapy a behavior is paired with some unpleasant stimulus
    p. 568

12. a.   no; this is not a technique in psychoanalysis
    b.   no; the humanistic therapies would not be so active in confronting individuals
    c.   YES; the therapist often confronts individuals
    d.   no; client-centered therapy would not be so confrontational
    p. 574

13. a.   YES; the person is gradually exposed to the feared object while remaining relaxed
    b.   no; this is not systematic desensitization
    c.   no; this is not systematic desensitization
    d.   no; this is not systematic desensitization
    p. 575

14. a.   no; psychoanalysis stresses the importance of the unconscious mind
    b.   no; this therapy includes challenging and confronting the client
    c.   no; these principles are not extensively used in group therapy
    d.   YES; behavior therapy is based on the idea that maladaptive behaviors are learned
    pp. 575, 577

15. a. no; in this technique, behavior is reinforced with tokens that can be later redeemed
    b. no; the technique uses relaxation and anxiety-producing situations
    c. YES; this is the definition of aversive conditioning
    d. no; this focuses on irrational and self-defeating beliefs as causes of problems
    p. 577

16. a. YES; cognitive therapists focus on irrational beliefs and faulty thinking
    b. no; this is a concept from client-centered therapy
    c. no; the manifest content of dreams would be determined in psychoanalysis
    d. no; psychoanalytic therapy would emphasize unconscious motives
    p. 578

17. a. no; even though Beck does focus on cognitions and the therapy is less directive
    b. YES; Ellis believed that our self-statements are often irrational and self-defeating
    c. no; the technique uses relaxation and anxiety-producing situations
    d. no; operant therapy primarily focuses on the use of reinforcement
    p. 579

18. a. YES; this is a characteristic of the rational-emotive behavioral therapy of Ellis. While there are a number of similarities between the approaches of Ellis and Beck, Beck's cognitive therapy is not as confrontational.
    b. no; this is one of the characteristics of Beck's cognitive therapy.
    c. no; this is one of the characteristics of Beck's cognitive therapy.
    d. no; this is one of the characteristics of Beck's cognitive therapy.
    p. 579

19. a. YES; by expressing understanding to a person, their views are validated
    b. no; this is not validation
    c. no; this is not validation
    d. no; this is not validation
    p. 585

20. a. no; while this could be an advantage, it is not the main one
    b. no; this is not an advantage
    c. no; in fact, the psychotherapist must be competent in several diverse therapies
    d. YES; this is the main advantage of integrative psychotherapy
    p. 592

## Practice Test 2

1. a. no; this refers to expressing understanding to a person to validate his or her views
   b. YES; this is reframing
   c. no; in structural change, the therapist attempts to change relationships in the family
   d. no; this technique is used to direct attention from a child to the parents
   p. 585

2. a. no; this technique refers to the therapist attempting to change relationships
   b. YES; this technique is used to direct attention from a child to the parents
   c. no
   d. no; this is teaching family members to view individual problems as family problems
   p. 586

3. a. no; behavior therapy uses principles of learning to address maladaptive behaviors
   b. no
   c. YES; the development of social skills is facilitated in group therapy
   d. no; this therapy creates an atmosphere in which the person can gain insight
   p. 585

4. a. YES; different therapies are more effective for specific types of problems
   b. no; this is not correct
   c. no; there are psychotherapies that are effective for certain types of disorders
   d. no; other disorders can be effectively treated using psychotherapy
   p. 590

5. a. no; an ethnic match would probably not result in professional similarity
   b. YES; cultural commonality may make the therapy more effective since the client is likely to be more comfortable with the therapist and be less likely to drop out early
   c. no; this is not likely to occur
   d. no; an ethnic match would probably not result in socioeconomic commonality
   p. 588

6. a. no; a negative correlation would indicate that the more therapy sessions the less the improvement as in the disorder.
   b. YES; in a study by Anderson and Lambert (2001) it was found that the more therapy sessions the person attended the higher the rate of improvement, as rated by the individuals undergoing therapy.
   c. no; there is a correlation, as indicated in Figure 14.13.
   d. no; there is a relationship, and it is a positive correlation.
   p. 590

7. a. no; this would be sensible advice
   b. no; this is an appropriate thing to do
   c. YES; this is not a very good way to pick a psychologist
   d. no; seeking professional psychological help would involve setting specific goals
   pp. 594–595

8. a. no; managed care has attempted to eliminate long-term psychotherapy
   b. YES; this is a criticism of managed care
   c. no; this is not a criticism
   d. no; however, managed care has been criticized for increasingly using mental health professionals with less experience and constraining the services offered by psychiatrists and clinical psychologists
   p. 593

9. a. YES; a psychiatrist is a medical doctor who specializes in psychological disorders
   b. no; clinical psychologists do not engage in graduate medical training
   c. no; social workers may work as mental health providers but do not have medical training
   d. no; counselors have at least a master's degree in psychology but do not have medical training
   p. 562

10. a. no; Xanax is a benzodiazepine used to treat anxiety disorders
    b. no; Xanax is a benzodiazepine used to treat anxiety disorders
    c. YES; Prozac is a selective serotonin reuptake inhibitor used to treat mood disorders
    d. no; buspirone is a nonbenzodiazepine used to treat generalized anxiety disorder
    p. 563

11. a.  no; these drugs have the side effect of drowsiness
    b.  YES; these drugs have been linked to abnormalities in babies born to mothers who were taking these medications during pregnancy
    c.  no; these drugs have the side effect of fatigue
    d.  no; these drugs can be addicting
    p. 563

12. a.  no; antipsychotics are used to treat schizophrenia
    b.  no; MAO is associated with mood regulation
    c.  YES; Nardil is an example of an MAO inhibitor; these drugs are used less that tricyclics because they are more toxic and have dangerous side effects
    d.  no; personality disorders are not usually treated with drug therapy
    p. 563

13. a.  no; MAO inhibitors are used to regulate mood
    b.  YES; schizophrenia is characterized by an excess of dopamine
    c.  no; this is what tricyclics, the antidepressants, do
    d.  no; this is what benzodiazepines do in the process of relieving anxiety disorders
    p. 565

14. a.  no; dream analysis is the technique of interpreting dreams to figure out their unconscious content
    b.  YES; this is a behavioral therapy approach
    c.  no; this is the technique of asking the person to share freely whatever comes to mind
    d.  no; this is the technique of liberating pent-up emotions and issues
    p. 575

15. a.  no; catharsis is another psychoanalytic issue
    b.  no; resistance is when the person starts interrupting the therapeutic process
    c.  YES; the person has transferred his issues with his mother to the therapist
    d.  no; free-association is asking the person to share whatever comes to mind
    p. 571

16. a.  no; this is one of the issues Kohut emphasizes in his therapy
    b.  no; this is also one of the issues that Kohut emphasizes in his therapy
    c.  YES; Kohut focuses more on being empathic and understanding and encouraging people to strengthen their sense of self; this would be inconsistent with a therapist figuring out the meaning of dreams
    d.  no; this is also one of the issues that Kohut emphasizes in his therapy
    p. 572

17. a.  no; the psychodynamic approach, at least in the original version, tended to be more "therapist-centered," because the therapist was the one making all the interpretations
    b.  YES; this type of therapy was developed by Carl Rogers
    c.  no; behavioral therapy assumes that the therapist is more knowledgeable than the person about how to solve the problems
    d.  no; this therapy came out of the humanistic approach
    p. 573

18. a. no; systematic desensitization is used with phobic disorders
    b. no; the person is not being offered a token as a reward
    c. YES; classical conditioning is being used to have the person stop doing the undesirable behavior
    d. no; actually, aversive conditioning is a type of classical conditioning
   p. 577

19. a. no; this is the therapy that focuses on unconscious influences and early life experiences.
    b. no; this is a cognitive therapy, but it focuses on facing irrational beliefs.
    c. YES; these methods are used to teach the client to manage his or her own way of thinking.
    d. no; this is the term used by Rogers to refer to his humanistic approach to therapy.
   p. 581

20. a. YES; this is the definition of primary prevention
    b. no; secondary prevention involves the screening for early detection of problems and early intervention
    c. no; tertiary prevention involves efforts to reduce the psychological disorders
    d. no; this is too broad a concept
   p. 587

21. a. no; this is one of the expectations that according to Ellis tends to lead to irrational expectations and beliefs about life.
    b. YES; this is a negative expectation and inconsistent with the basic demands that Ellis proposed.
    c. no; this is also one of the basic demands proposed by Ellis.
    d. no; this is also one of the basic demands proposed by Ellis. According Ellis we also expect all others to treat us kindly.
   p. 579

## Practice Test 3

1. a. YES; tricyclics actually increase the level of serotonin
   b. no; this is correct about tricyclics such as Elavil
   c. no; this is correct about certain types of antidepressants, an example is Nardil
   d. no; this is a new type of drug being researched to use as an antidepressant
   p. 563

2. a. no; this is incorrect, the symptoms return when the drugs are not used
   b. no; the use of drug therapy actually reduces the hospital stay time
   c. YES; tardive dyskinesia is a very disruptive side effect of neuroleptic drugs
   d. no; the excess dopamine is what causes the undesirable symptoms
   p. 566

3. a. no; this is what used to be referred to as prefrontal lobotomy
   b. YES; small and precise lesions are made in the amygdala or another part of the limbic system
   c. no; these were extreme measures that are not currently performed
   d. no; this is the area in charge of higher processing and it is not lesioned or removed in psychosurgery to treat psychological disorders
   p. 568

4. a. YES; a psychoanalyst assumes that the statements of a person always have some unconscious or latent meaning
   b. no; behavioral therapists focus only on behaviors and don't explore anything beyond what the person shares in therapy
   c. no; a humanist expects the person to be the better one to figure out what the issues are
   d. no; a Gestalt therapist also assumes that the person may be saying honest things and not necessarily that they mean something else
   p. 570

5. a. no; this would be more consistent with behavioral therapy
   b. no; this would be more consistent with psychoanalysis
   c. YES; by inducing the panic attack the therapist can help the person realize that his or her thoughts are irrational
   d. no; this is a simplistic statement unlikely to be used by a psychologist, not even a rational-emotive behavioral therapist
   p. 582

6. a. no; these drugs are used to treat anxiety disorders
   b. CORRECT
   c. no; these drugs are used to treat schizophrenia
   d. no; psychoanalysis and cognitive therapy have not been compared in terms of their effectiveness treating depression (at least such research was not presented in the chapter)
   p. 582

7. a. no; actually, the sociocultural approach argues that the person will benefit from exploring the problem in a social context
   b. YES; these approaches consider exploring the problems with the people who are involved
   c. no; on the contrary, sociocultural approaches are based on the assumption that being in a social setting encourages effective therapy
   d. no; even in collective therapies, the credentials of the therapist are important
   p. 584

8. a. no; this refers to the sympathy and support groups provide
   b. no; this refers to receiving information about the disorder from a therapist as well as from others with the disorder
   c. no; this refers to viewing the group as a family
   d. YES; this helps people deal with some of the fears associated with having the disorder
   p. 584

9. a. no; in family therapy it is not common for all family members to be peers in the psychological problem; in other words, they don't go to family therapy because they all have depression
   b. no; this is an individual therapy, thus the role of peers is irrelevant
   c. YES; another person who has the same problem has credibility when he or she shares experiences
   d. no; this is an individual therapy
   p. 586

10. a. no; this is one of the practices that started with this movement
    b. no; prevention is considered a priority in the community mental health approach
    c. YES; the community mental health approach emphasized that psychological problems can be targeted at many other levels in the community
    d. no; this is the transfer of mental health care from institutions such as mental hospitals to community-based facilities
    p. 587

11. a.   no; primary prevention involves reducing the numbers of new cases, and this is not being targeted at this facility
    b.   no; secondary prevention involves early screening for disorders, and the people using this facility have already been diagnosed with a disorder
    c.   YES; daytime facilities such as the one described here are designed to help the person reintegrate into society and prevent future crisis based on the disorder
    d.   no; the question does not address the use of behavioral therapy.
    p. 588

12. a.   YES; a culturally sensitive therapist should realize that Christmas is not celebrated by everybody and that some of his clients may be offended by such a greeting, regardless of how well intentioned it was
    b.   no; this is a good idea, because the therapist will be better able to understand the concerns of people from other parts of the world
    c.   no; while being completely bilingual may not be necessary, showing an effort to learn can go a long way in making the client feel comfortable and understood; a simple greeting in the native language of the client can go a long way
    d.   no; this is a very important task for the culturally sensitive therapist, because gestures and communication styles may be different and relevant to the therapy.
    p. 588

13. a.   no; this is recommended for male clients
    b.   YES; women are more concerned with relationships and thus therapy should consider these female interests
    c.   no; this is a recommendation for male clients
    d.   no; this is not a recommendation
    p. 588

14. a.   no; this is one of the common elements of effective psychotherapies
    b.   no; this is one of the common elements of effective psychotherapies
    c.   no; this is one of the common elements of effective psychotherapies
    d.   YES; this is the approach in behavioral therapies, but not all effective approaches focus on changing behaviors
    p. 591

15. a.   no; this is not how this concept is used
    b.   no; this is not how this concept is used
    c.   YES; when the therapist considers different types of therapies and applies them depending on the needs of the client, he or she is engaging in therapy integrations
    d.   no; this may fall under group therapy
    p. 592

16. a.   no; this is a specific type of cognitive therapy, and the question does not address this specific approach
    b.   YES; Ling is being treated with more than one type of therapy
    c.   no; while managed care may play a role in the type of care Ling may have available, this question does not address those issues
    d.   no; this is an issue that pertains to psychoanalysis
    p. 591

17. a.  no; this is one of the criticisms of managed care, basically hiring people with less training to be able to pay them less
    b.  no; this is one of the criticisms: psychotherapists don't get to decide if the person receives therapy or not
    c.  YES; this is incorrect; extended individual therapy can usually be afforded only by the affluent
    d.  no; this is one of the criticisms of managed care, which may also be controlled at the point of hiring mental health care providers, by hiring more individuals who are trained in the brief treatment options

    p. 593

18. a.  no; this is recommended, particularly the licensing and certification information; well-trained and honest therapists should have no problem sharing this information
    b.  YES; this is not recommended; once you have chosen a therapist, it is recommended that you give it some time before moving on, because therapy usually takes time to show effects
    c.  no; this is recommended
    d.  no; this is recommended

    p. 595

19. a.  no; this is one of the symptoms that may indicate that professional help could be useful
    b.  no; this is one of the symptoms that may indicate that professional help could be useful
    c.  YES; walking around at night in urban areas is fear-provoking for many people; therefore, it is not necessarily a sign of an anxiety disorder
    d.  no; this is one of the symptoms that may indicate that professional help could be useful

    p. 594

20. a.  no; the research in the critical controversies section is on drug therapies, not on psychotherapies
    b.  YES; a meta-analysis revealed that placebos were 75% as effective as the drugs
    c.  no; the research in the critical controversies section is on drug therapies, not on psychotherapies
    d.  no; the research in the critical controversies section is on drug therapies, not on psychotherapies

    p. 565

# Chapter 15—Stress, Coping, and Health

## Learning Goals

1. Describe the scope of health psychology and behavioral medicine.
2. Define stress and identify its sources.
3. Explain how people respond to stress.
4. Discuss links between stress and illness.
5. Outline strategies for coping with stress.
6. Summarize how to promote health.

*After studying Chapter 15, you will be able to:*

- Describe the scope of health psychology and behavioral medicine.
- Define *stress*.
- Discuss the personality factors associated with stress, such as behavioral patterns, hardiness, and personal control.
- Describe the environmental factors associated with stress.
- Understand the sociocultural factors associated with stress, including acculturative stress and poverty.
- Explain how people respond to stress and explain the role of biological and psychological factors in the process.
- Define *psychoneuroimmunology*.
- Understand how the immune system works.
- Understand how stress plays a role in cardiovascular disease and cancer.
- Discuss the association between positive emotions and physical well-being.
- Define coping.
- Distinguish between problem-focused coping and emotion-focused coping.
- Discuss how coping is enhanced with optimism, positive thinking, social support, assertive behavior, religion, and stress-management programs.
- Describe the role of exercise in physical and mental health.
- Explain what proper nutrition is and how it affects health.
- Describe the health effects of smoking as well as strategies for quitting smoking.
- Discuss sexual knowledge, contraception, and sexually transmitted diseases.

## CHAPTER 15: OUTLINE

- With few exceptions, historically, physical illness was viewed in biological terms alone, not in terms of mental factors. Health psychology is a field of psychology that specializes in promoting and maintaining health and preventing and treating illness.

- As an interdisciplinary field, behavioral medicine focuses on developing and integrating behavioral and biomedical knowledge to promote health and reduce illness. Psychological and social factors play important roles in chronic illnesses.

- One of the main areas of research in health psychology and behavioral medicine is the relationship between stress and illness. *Stress* is the response to circumstances and events that threaten us or tax our coping abilities.

- To understand stress we must consider personality, environmental, and social factors. Among the personality factors are behavior patterns, such as Type A and Type B.

- *Type A behavior* is a cluster of characteristics such as competitiveness, hostility, and impatience; *Type B behavior* refers to characteristics such as being calm and easygoing.

- The Type A behavior cluster was thought by many psychologists to be related to the incidence of heart disease; however, it is hostility that is most associated with coronary disease. Another personality factor is *hardiness*, which refers to a personality style characterized by a sense of commitment, control, and a perception of problems as being challenges. Having a sense of personal control reduces stress.

- Environmental factors that can produce stress include life events and daily hassles. Another environmental factor, conflict, occurs when we must decide between options, and it can be of these types: approach/approach conflict, avoidance/avoidance conflict, and approach/avoidance conflict.

- Overload occurs when stimuli become so intense that we can no longer cope with them; this can lead to burnout. People experience work-related stress when their jobs don't meet their expectations. Sociocultural factors include acculturation stress and poverty.

- *Acculturation stress* is the negative contact between two distinct cultural groups. People can adapt to acculturation in four ways: assimilation, integration, segregation, and marginalization.

- Marginalization and separation are the least adaptive responses to acculturation. Poverty can also cause considerable stress and is related to threatening and uncontrollable life events. Ethnic minority families are disproportionately represented among the poor.

- According to Selye, the body's reaction to stress is called the *general adaptation syndrome* and consists of the alarm stage, the resistance stage, and the exhaustion stage. Selye also described *eustress* as the positive features of stress.

- The neuroendocrine-immune pathway describes the relationship between the endocrine system and immune system; cortisol can have a negative effect on the immune system. The sympathetic nervous system pathway describes how the release of hormones during the fight-or-flight response can be harmful over time.

- According to Lazarus, how we respond to stress depends on how we cognitively appraise and interpret events in our lives. As we interpret a situation, we go through primary appraisal and secondary appraisal.

- The field that explores the relationship between psychological factors, the nervous system, and the immune system is called *psychoneuroimmunology*.

- The immune system is similar to the nervous system in the following characteristics: both have a way of receiving information from the environment, both can carry out an appropriate response, and both engage in chemically mediated communication.

- Research supports the connection between the immune system and stress. Acute stressors can produce immunological changes. Chronic stressors are associated with a compromised immune system. Positive social circumstances and low stress are associated with increased ability to fight cancer. Chronic stress is associated with high blood pressure, heart disease and early death, and smoking, overeating, and avoiding exercise.

- The relationship between stress and cancer can be best understood by exploring how cancer treatment can negatively affect a person's quality of life, by recognizing that a diagnosis of cancer can cause some people to engage in damaging behaviors, and by studying the biological ways in which stress can contribute to compromising the immune system of people with cancer.

- Positive emotions have been associated with keeping colds at bay and overall facilitating the ability to cope with problems.

- *Coping* refers to managing taxing circumstances, expending effort to solve life's problems, and seeking to master or reduce stress.

- In problem-focused coping, individuals squarely face their troubles and try to solve them. When we use emotion-focused coping, we respond to stress in an emotional manner, especially using defensive appraisal. Depending on the context, either approach may be adaptive.

- *Cognitive restructuring* refers to modifying the thoughts, ideas, and beliefs that maintain a person's problems. *Self-talk* is mental speech we use when we think, plan, or solve problems. *Illusions* are related to one's sense of self-esteem. The ideal overall orientation may be an illusion that is mildly inflated. Sometimes defensive pessimism may actually work best in handling stress; however, optimism is the best overall strategy.

- *Self-efficacy* is the belief that one can master a situation and produce positive outcomes; self-efficacy can improve an individual's mental health and ability to cope.

- Social support provides information and feedback from others that one is loved and cared for, esteemed and valued, and included in a network of communication and mutual obligations. The benefits of social support include tangible assistance, information, and emotional support.

- Assertive behavior illustrates how we can deal with conflict in social relationships. Stress management programs teach people how to appraise stressful events, how to develop skills for coping with stress, and how to put these skills into use in everyday life.

- Other ways to cope with stress include meditation, relaxation, and biofeedback. Multiple strategies for coping with stress work better than any one single strategy.

- Exercise is one of the most effective ways of promoting health. Aerobic exercise, even to a moderate degree, can reduce the risk of heart attacks and provide positive benefits for self-concept, anxiety, and depression.

- Proper nutrition is vital in maintaining good health. Many of us are unhealthy eaters. There is a link between fat intake and cancer. A sound diet includes fat, carbohydrates, protein, vitamins, minerals, and water.

- Smoking has significant effects on health. Although the adverse consequences of smoking have been widely publicized, smoking is still widespread because it is addictive and reinforcing. Five methods have been developed to help smokers quit: nicotine substitutes, taking antidepressants, stimulus control, aversive conditioning, and going "cold turkey."

- Making healthy decisions with regard to sexuality is important. Making the correct decisions is dependent on having accurate knowledge about sex, contraception, STDs, and AIDS.

# Building Blocks of Chapter 15

## Clarifying some of the tricky points in Chapter 15
## and
## In Your Own Words

*To respond to the questions and exercises presented in the "In Your Own Words" section, please write your thoughts, perspectives, and reactions on a separate piece of paper.*

### Health Psychology and Behavioral Medicine

*Health* psychology is a field of psychology that specializes in promoting and maintaining health and preventing and treating illness. *Behavioral medicine* develops and integrates behavioral and *biomedical* knowledge to promote health and reduce illness. Behavioral medicine focuses on *behavioral* and *biomedical* factors, whereas health psychology focuses on *cognitive* and *behavioral* factors.

### Stress and Its Sources

The experience of stress is caused by *personality, environmental,* and *social factors.* A cluster of characteristics, such as being excessively competitive, hard-driven, impatient, and hostile, that are thought to be related to the incidence of heart disease is called *Type A* behavior pattern.

The component of Type A that is especially related to heart disease is *hostility.* A personality style characterized by a sense of commitment, control, and a perception of problems as being challenges is called *hardiness.* Personal *control* has also been associated with the development of problem-solving strategies to cope with stress. *Environmental* factors include life-events, hassles, conflict, overload, and work-related stress. Significant *life events* have been proposed as a major source of stress. A widely used scale to measure life events and their possible effect on illness is the *Social Readjustment Rating Scale.* People who experience clusters of life events are more likely to become *ill.*

Psychologists are increasingly considering the nature of daily *problems (hassles)* and their effects on stress. A hopeless, helpless feeling brought on by relentless work-related stress is called *burnout.* Burnout usually occurs as a result of a *gradual accumulation* of stress rather than from one or two incidents. Burnout is also a problem with *college* students.

Conflicts in which an individual must choose between two attractive stimuli or circumstances are called *approach/approach* conflicts. Conflicts in which individuals must choose between two unattractive stimuli or circumstances are called *avoidance/avoidance* conflicts. A conflict in which a single stimulus or circumstance has both positive and negative characteristics is called *approach/avoidance* conflict.

*Sociocultural* factors that contribute to stress include *acculturative* stress and poverty. *Acculturative stress* refers to the negative consequences of continuous, first-hand contact between two distinct cultural groups. *Assimilation* occurs when individuals relinquish their cultural identity and move into the larger society. In contrast, *integration* implies the maintenance of cultural integrity and the movement to become part of the larger culture. A self-imposed withdrawal from the larger culture is called *separation,* but when it is imposed by the larger dominant society, it is referred to as *segregation.* The term that refers to the process in which groups are out of contact with both their traditional society and the dominant society is *marginalization.* Two adaptive outcomes of acculturative stress are *integration* and *assimilation.* Poverty creates considerable stress for individuals and families; *ethnic minority* families are disproportionately among the poor. Poverty is also related to threatening and uncontrollable *life events* such as crime and violence.

## In Your Own Words

*Please write your thoughts, perspectives, and reactions on a separate piece of paper.*
✓ *Develop some examples that you have experienced for each of the types of conflict presented in the chapter.*

## Stress Responses

The response of individuals to the circumstances and events that threaten them and tax their coping abilities is referred to as *stress*. According to Selye, the body's reaction to stress is called the *General Adaptation Syndrome*.

The GAS consists of three stages: (1) the body enters a temporary state of shock in the *alarm* stage, (2) an all-out effort is made to combat stress in the *resistance* stage, and (3) wear and tear on the body increase in the *exhaustion* stage. *Cortisol* is a steroid that, over time, can suppress the immune system; it is part of the neuroendocrine-immune system.

A term suggested by Lazarus that describes individuals' interpretations of their lives and their determination of whether they have the resources to cope is called *cognitive appraisal*. According to Lazarus, in *primary* appraisal, people interpret whether an event involves harm, threat, or challenge. In *secondary* appraisal, they evaluate their resources and determine how to cope with the event.

## Stress and Illness

The field that explores the relationships between psychological factors, the nervous system, and the immune system is called *psychoneuroimmunology*. Stress affects the immune system in the following ways: acute stressors produce *immunological* changes, chronic stressors impair the functioning of the *immune* system, and *positive* social circumstances and low *stress* are associated with increased ability to fight cancer.

Chronic emotional stress is associated with high *blood pressure, heart disease,* and early *death*. Also, people who live in a chronically stressed-out condition are more likely to start *smoking, overeating,* and avoiding *exercise.* It has been argued that to better understand the relationship between stress and cancer, researchers must explore the roles of *quality of life, behavioral factors,* and *biological pathways.*

Positive emotions have been linked to the release of secretory immunoglobulin A, the antibody that is believed to be the first line of defense against the *common cold.*

## Coping Strategies

The process of managing taxing circumstances and seeking to master, minimize, reduce, or tolerate stress and conflict is called *coping*. According to Lazarus, individuals who cope with stress by facing their problems and trying to solve them engage in problem-focused coping, whereas those who cope with stress in an emotional, defensive manner engage in emotion-focused coping. Over the long term, it is best to use problem-focused coping more.

## In Your Own Words

*Please write your thoughts, perspectives, and reactions on a separate piece of paper.*
✓ *Do you use problem-focused coping and/or emotion-focused coping as you are assigned papers and projects and face exams? In these contexts, what are the advantages and disadvantages of each?*

The process of modifying the thoughts, ideas, and beliefs that maintain an individual's problems is called *cognitive restructuring*. The soundless, mental speech we use, called self-talk, is often helpful in cognitive restructuring. Although mental health professionals have long recommended an accurate view of reality, recent research has demonstrated the value of positive self-illusion. In other situations, a strategy of imagining negative outcomes, called *defensive pessimism*, is best for handling stress.

Seligman recommends that individuals who wish to develop an optimistic outlook should consider cognitive therapy. Cognitive therapists suggest avoiding self-pity and disputing negative thoughts. The belief that one can master a situation and produce positive outcomes is called self-efficacy.

Information from others that one is loved, esteemed, valued, and included in a network of others is called *social support*. The benefits of social support stem from tangible assistance, information, and emotional support. With stress-management programs, individuals learn how to appraise stressful events and develop skills for coping.

A system of thought designed to attain bodily or mental control, as well as enlightenment, is called *meditation*. The most popular form of meditation in the United States is transcendental meditation.

Researchers disagree as to whether the benefits of meditation are superior to those derived from relaxation. A process of monitoring an individual's muscular or visceral activities and providing the information to individuals so they can learn to control the physiological activities is called *biofeedback*. When a person is facing stress, multiple coping strategies are often better than using a single strategy.

### Healthful Living
Sustained exercise, such as jogging, swimming, or cycling, that stimulates heart and lung activity is called *aerobic exercise*. Researchers generally agree that even moderate exercise can reduce the risk of heart attack. Exercise also provides positive benefits for depression, anxiety, and self-concept. A well-balanced diet provides more energy and can decrease blood pressure, cancer risk, and tooth decay. Although the adverse consequences of smoking have been highly publicized, smoking is still widespread because it is pleasurable and reinforcing.

Five methods can be effective in helping smokers to quit: nicotine substitutes, stimulus control, taking an antidepressant, aversive conditioning, and going cold turkey.

Age influences the choice of contraceptive method, and it has been shown that the minority of adolescents use contraception in their first intercourse. Also, older adolescents and young adults are more likely to rely on the pill or diaphragm while younger adolescents rely more on condoms or withdrawal, which are less reliable methods of contraception. AIDS is caused by HIV, which destroys the body's immune system.

### In Your Own Words

*Please write your thoughts, perspectives, and reactions on a separate piece of paper.*

✓ *Of those ways described in the chapter on methods to cope with stress (e.g., optimism, self-efficacy, social support, assertive behavior), which one is your greatest strength? Which one do you need to develop further?*

## Correcting the Incorrect

Carefully read each statement. Determine if the statement is correct or incorrect. If the statement is incorrect, make the necessary changes to correct it. Then check the answer key at the end of the chapter for the correct statement and page reference in the textbook.

1. Stress is defined as the response of individuals to circumstances and events that threaten them and tax their coping abilities.
2. Bandura developed the General Adaptation Syndrome.
3. The General Adaptation Syndrome consists of three stages: alarm, resistance, and marginalization.
4. Being competitive is directly associated with cardiovascular disease.
5. The components of hardiness are commitment, control, and challenge.
6. Cognitive appraisal refers to the individual's interpretation of events.
7. In primary appraisal, individuals evaluate their resources and determine how effectively they can be used to cope with the stressor.
8. An approach/approach conflict occurs when the individual must choose between two unattractive stimuli or circumstances.
9. The life events checklist provides important information about a person's psychological makeup.
10. Separation and marginalization are the most adaptive responses to acculturation.
11. Acculturative stress refers to the negative consequences of the third stage of the General Adaptation Syndrome.
12. Poor women are more likely to experience crime and violence than are middle-class women.
13. Denial is an example of problem-focused coping.
14. Self-talk is a sign of serious psychological disturbance.
15. Seeing reality as accurately as possible is the best path to mental health.
16. A strategy of defensive pessimism is never a good way to deal with stress.
17. Pessimism can be overcome through cognitive therapy.
18. Assertiveness is the belief that one can master a situation and produce positive outcomes.
19. The more diverse the social support is, the less effective it is in helping us cope with stress.
20. One way to become more assertive is to state problems in terms of their consequences for others.
21. Stress-management programs teach us how to avoid stress.
22. Biofeedback is effective at reducing an individual's muscle tension.
23. Nicotine is a stimulant that relaxes the smoker.
24. A minority of adolescents do not use contraception during their first sexual intercourse experience.
25. HIV destroys the immune system.
26. The majority of cases of AIDS in the United States are injection drug users.

## Practice Test 1

1. A model that is used in the field of health psychology emphasizes a combination of influences on health. This model is called the _____ model.
   a. psychodynamic
   b. general adaptation syndrome
   c. hardiness
   d. biopsychosocial

2. Dr. Livingston is interested in studying the relationship between the degree to which people follow doctor's orders and health care outcomes. Of the following, Dr. Livingston most likely works in which field?
   a. clinical psychology
   b. behavior modification
   c. psychoanalysis
   d. behavioral medicine

3. _____ is the response of individuals to the circumstances and events that threaten them and tax their coping abilities.
   a. Frustration
   b. General adaptation syndrome
   c. Stress
   d. Appraisal

4. Which of the following is the best example of a stressor?
   a. taking a vacation
   b. talking to a friend
   c. getting an A on an exam
   d. being fired from a job

5. If you were a psychoneuroimmunologist, you would be most likely to read which fictitious journal?
   a. *Journal of Humanistic Psychology*
   b. *Journal of Motor Skills*
   c. *Journal of Dream Analysis*
   d. *Journal of the Behavior and Health*

6. Which of the following cancer patients would you predict to have the weakest immune system?
   a. Donesha: she is a college graduate, has a good job, and a loving family
   b. Charles: he is homeless, sleeps and eats at shelters whenever he can, and is generally alone
   c. Anita: she has raised three children and enjoys spending time with her grandchildren
   d. James: he owns a business, has many friends, but lives by himself

7. Selye's three-stage pattern of reaction to stress is known as the
   a. cognitive appraisal scale.
   b. social readjustment scale.
   c. personality adjustment system.
   d. general adaptation syndrome.

8. According to Selye, the immune system effectively fights off infection in the _____ stage of the general adaptation syndrome.
   a. alarm
   b. resistance
   c. exhaustion
   d. none of the above

9.	Eduardo always feels like he is running out of time. He rarely takes a vacation and finds it hard to relax at home. He demands perfection of himself and is competitive in all arenas of his life. Eduardo can be described best as a(n)

a.	avoidant personality.
b.	Type A personality.
c.	Type B personality.
d.	bulimic personality.

10.	Each of the following is characteristic of the Type A behavior pattern except

a.	hostility.
b.	competitiveness.
c.	impatience.
d.	a general sense of satisfaction with life.

11.	If you have a sense of commitment, control, and perceive problems as challenges, then you have the personality factor of

a.	appraisal.
b.	Type B.
c.	hardiness.
d.	self-talk.

12.	According to Lazarus, in primary appraisal, people assess whether an event involves each of the following except

a.	fear.
b.	harm.
c.	threat.
d.	challenge.

13.	Lazarus suggests that in secondary appraisal individuals

a.	evaluate their resources for dealing with stress.
b.	unconsciously recall other similar stressful events.
c.	engage in the use of defense mechanisms.
d.	experience resistance and then exhaustion.

14.	What do primary appraisal and secondary appraisal have in common?

a.	They both take about the same amount of time.
b.	They both are cognitive activities.
c.	They both occur at the same time.
d.	They both are basically passive activities.

15.	Burnout appears to be a widespread phenomenon among college students. In order to avoid this situation, a college student should do all of the following except which one?

a.	take well-balanced class loads
b.	avoid class overloads
c.	use available campus support resources
d.	plan to graduate in three years

16.	The negative consequences that result from contact between two distinctive cultural groups is called

a.	burnout.
b.	hardiness.
c.	acculturative stress.
d.	diversity.

17. Jane is experiencing stress. Both of her boyfriends have asked her out for the same night. Assuming she is equally attracted to both, which source of stress is Jane experiencing?
    a. approach/avoidance conflict
    b. approach/approach conflict
    c. avoidance/avoidance conflict
    d. none of the above

18. Kenneth can't decide whether or not to ask Debra to marry him. He really loves her, but he knows his parents will object if he marries her before he finishes college. Kenneth's situation exemplifies which type of conflict?
    a. active/coping
    b. approach/avoidance
    c. avoidance/avoidance
    d. approach/approach

19. You take a break from studying and find yourself staring into the refrigerator. The only thing you see is an old piece of leftover pizza and some old jello. You would rather not eat either, but you are very hungry. The stress you are experiencing is called
    a. approach/approach conflict.
    b. avoidance/avoidance conflict.
    c. approach/avoidance conflict.
    d. burnout.

20. Sangrita feels that she does not fit within any cultural group and that she has lost her identity. Sangrita is experiencing
    a. assimilation.
    b. separation.
    c. marginalization.
    d. integration.

## Practice Test 2

1. In the research of the relationship between psychology and health, the difference between health psychology and behavioral medicine is that while behavioral medicine focuses on behavioral and biomedical factors, health psychology focuses on
    a. physical factors.
    b. psychodynamic factors.
    c. cognitive and behavioral factors.
    d. genetic factors.

2. Which of the following characteristics of the Type A behavior pattern has been associated with incidence of heart disease?
    a. competitiveness
    b. being hard-driven
    c. impatience
    d. hostility

3. Which of the following is not one of the characteristics of hardiness?
    a. making and honoring commitments
    b. feeling empowered
    c. feeling threatened by problems
    d. dealing with problems as challenges

4.    The type of conflict that involves choosing between two "evils" is referred to as
    a.      approach/approach conflict.
    b.      avoidance/avoidance conflict.
    c.      approach/avoidance conflict.
    d.      the evil conflict.

5.    Which of the following situations is likely to lead to burnout?
    a.      being in a serious car accident
    b.      having a loved one die
    c.      having to deal with house, school, and work and facing challenges in all these settings
    d.      being in a car accident in which a loved one dies

6.    What is the current average of hours an American works each week?
    a.      30
    b.      40
    c.      47
    d.      70

7.    Which of the following is not one of the common characteristics of the nervous system and the immune system?
    a.      They both receive information from the environment.
    b.      They both carry out an appropriate response.
    c.      They are both centralized in the body.
    d.      They both use chemical mediators for communication.

8.    According to the text, the healthiest, least stressful adaptation to acculturation is
    a.      integration.
    b.      marginalization.
    c.      separation.
    d.      assimilation.

9.    Emotion-focused coping involves
    a.      using defense mechanisms.
    b.      facing your troubles and trying to solve them.
    c.      a rational approach to solving problems.
    d.      none of the above

10.   Imagining potential problems as a strategy for dealing with or preventing negative outcomes is used in which of the following?
    a.      problem-focused coping
    b.      biofeedback
    c.      defensive pessimism
    d.      self-efficacy

11.   The process of changing the thoughts and beliefs that maintain one's problems is referred to as
    a.      self-efficacy.
    b.      self-talk.
    c.      cognitive restructuring.
    d.      positive self-illusion.

12.   Hideo is one of those people who always sees "the glass as half empty." His thoughts are dominated by negative themes and pessimism. What method could be used to improve Hideo's negative thoughts about himself and the world around him?
    a.   biofeedback
    b.   cognitive restructuring
    c.   behavior modification
    d.   psychoanalysis

13.   Individuals who have high self-efficacy are least likely to do which of the following?
    a.   persist in the face of obstacles
    b.   expend effort in coping with stress
    c.   experience less stress in challenging situations
    d.   perceive that they have no control over the situation

14.   Tangible assistance, emotional support, and information are potential benefits derived from
    a.   assimilation.
    b.   self-efficacy.
    c.   social support.
    d.   biofeedback.

15.   Assertive coping has beneficial effects on mental health because it
    a.   is a method of active and effective coping that reduces stress.
    b.   relies on defense mechanisms.
    c.   requires the internalization of anger.
    d.   makes others feel guilty for not meeting their responsibility.

16.   What is the best way to cope with stress?
    a.   positive self-talk
    b.   problem-focused coping
    c.   biofeedback
    d.   multiple coping strategies

17.   A process involving the use of instruments to learn to control physiological activities is called
    a.   behavior modification.
    b.   meditation.
    c.   biofeedback.
    d.   the relaxation response.

18.   Most experts recommend that adults engage in _____ minutes or more of moderate-intensity physical activity on most days of the week.
    a.   5
    b.   15
    c.   30
    d.   60

19. The best nutritional plan consists of a
    a. diet high in fibers.
    b. low-fat and low-cholesterol diet.
    c. well-balanced diet that includes all nutrients we need.
    d. high-vitamin and high-mineral diet.

20. The best predictor of getting an sexually transmitted disease is
    a. being homosexual.
    b. having sex with multiple partners.
    c. living in a large urban city.
    d. being between the ages of 16 and 22.

## Practice Test 3

1. A person studying the relationship between how a person perceives a problem and how it affects her ability to cope with stress is likely to be
    a. a health psychologist.
    b. engaging in behavioral medicine.
    c. a psychoneuroimmunologist.
    d. a personality psychologist.

2. Which of the following personality patterns is not strongly related to stress and/or illness?
    a. Type A behavior pattern
    b. anxiety and worry
    c. hostility
    d. hardiness

3. Marianne just finished medical school and the corresponding internship. Now she wants to do a residency in pediatrics. She has been accepted in a residency in pediatrics, but it is in a hospital she does not like and this creates a conflict for her. What type of conflict is Marianne facing?
    a. approach/approach conflict
    b. avoidance/avoidance conflict
    c. approach/avoidance conflict
    d. the medical student conflict

4. Jo Ann is experiencing work-related stress. She has a number of expectations about the workplace that are not being met. Jo Ann is a typical American in terms of what she wants from her job. Which of the following expectations is Jo Ann unlikely to have about her job?
    a. She expects to have a long-term job that offers security.
    b. Jo Ann wants to be able to work at her level without worrying about moving up in the organization.
    c. She wants to get along with co-workers and have a sense of community in the workplace.
    d. Jo Ann wants to be able to solve problems and be creative.

5. Jose is a Mexican immigrant. He moved in with family members and is working in the Mexican community. Jose speaks only Spanish and has made no efforts to move beyond the boundaries of the Mexican community. The community is large enough that Jose can engage in all normal activities, such as working and socializing within this community. According to John Berry, Jose is engaging in
   a.  assimilation.
   b.  integration.
   c.  separation.
   d.  marginalization.

6. Minerva is Puerto Rican. Minerva is also the head of the family, as she is the single mother of three children. Considering the statistics, Minerva is also likely to
   a.  live in poverty.
   b.  avoid burnout.
   c.  have a Type A behavior pattern.
   d.  have a Type B behavior pattern.

7. Cortisol is released during the alarm stage of the general adaptation syndrome. Which of the following is not one of the effects of cortisol?
   a.  It increases appetite.
   b.  It suppresses the immune system.
   c.  It promotes brain cellular functioning.
   d.  It causes glucose to move to the muscles.

8. Jennifer is at the ATM when a young man comes in, threatens her with a weapon in his pocket, and asks for her to take out $1000 and give it to him. Jennifer is likely to deal with this fight-or-flight situation by
   a.  spraying mace on the eyes of the assailant.
   b.  trying to talk the young man out of the assault, telling him that he does not want this kind of trouble, and to please consider that she does not have that kind of money and also has a family to take care of.
   c.  using karate to attack the assailant.
   d.  running away as fast as possible.

9. Muzafer was fired last week from his job. He went through a stressful time of realizing the different ways in which this job loss would hurt him. Now, he has decided to take a few computer classes at the community college in order to get a different type of job that might offer him more security. This decision to continue education may be considered an example of
   a.  primary appraisal.
   b.  stress.
   c.  secondary appraisal.
   d.  tertiary appraisal.

10. Where in the brain is corticotropin, the hormone that unites the stress and immune responses, produced?
   a.  cerebral cortex
   b.  temporal lobe
   c.  thalamus
   d.  hypothalamus

11. Which of the following is not true about the relationship between stress and the immune system?
    a. Divorce has been associated with reduced immune system responsiveness.
    b. People with life-threatening conditions who experience a sudden one-time life event, such as a tragic car accident, tend to have poorer immune system functioning than do people with the life-threatening conditions who did not experience a tragic event.
    c. A low degree of stress is often associated with a lower NK-cell levels.
    d. Having social support is often linked with higher levels of NK-cell.

12. Henry is constantly and chronically under stress. He is likely to
    a. start a new exercise program.
    b. start smoking.
    c. start a diet.
    d. engage in behaviors that protect him from cardiovascular disease.

13. A person who is more likely to get a cold is a person who
    a. uses humor frequently.
    b. watches comedy sitcoms.
    c. watches sad dramas.
    d. experiences positive emotions frequently.

14. Krystina's parents often yell to her and bark out orders. In response, she usually laughs at them. Which coping strategy is Krystina using?
    a. cognitive restructuring
    b. positive self-illusion
    c. problem-focused coping
    d. emotion-focused coping

15. Defensive pessimism may be an effective coping strategy
    a. by focusing on the positive aspects of the problem.
    b. if the person needs to develop some negative expectations about a situation.
    c. when thinking of the negative consequences motivates the person to act.
    d. because the person does not take responsibility for the problem.

16. In terms of social support, which of the following individuals is least equipped to cope with stress?
    a. A widow who has one sister who visits her once a week and who can't get along with her two daughters-in-law.
    b. An alcoholic person who has co-workers that offer help and family to support her in the process.
    c. A person who treats neighbors very nicely, as if they were family.
    d. A person with depression who has friends to tell her that they love her and will be there for her as she gets therapy and improves her condition.

17. Lately, Sean has been overwhelmed by extreme demands from his boss. He has been complaining and gossiping about the boss. By doing this, he has managed to have others do some of the work for him. The way Sean is dealing with the conflict is by
    a. acting aggressively.
    b. acting manipulatively.
    c. acting passively.
    d. acting assertively.

18. If Sean (from question 17) decided to act assertively, which of the following behaviors would not be recommended?
   a. making an appointment with the boss to talk about the problem
   b. letting the boss know that if things don't change this could reflect badly on both of them
   c. telling the boss exactly how he feels about the situation
   d. asking the boss directly and specifically for the changes he wants

19. When people are meditating, their brains show activity similar to the brain of a person who is
   a. dead.
   b. hypnotized.
   c. sleeping.
   d. schizophrenic.

20. The delicate balance between physical and psychological well-being is demonstrated by the fact that psychological benefits result from engaging in
   a. a high-intensity aerobic program.
   b. a moderate-intensity aerobic program.
   c. a light-intensity aerobic program.
   d. no exercise.

## Connections

*Take advantage of all the other study tools available for this chapter!*

## Media Integration

| NAME OF CLIP | DESCRIPTION | KEY CONCEPTS AND IDEAS |
|---|---|---|
| | | **Health Psychology and Behavioral Medicine** |
| | | **Stress and Its Sources** |
| Type A Behavior | This interactivity includes an assessment of type A personality and discusses the relationship between Type A and heart disease. | Type A<br>Heart disease |
| Stress and Life Events | The interactivity "Stress & Life Events: Nothing is so certain as change in a person's life" includes the original SRRS by Holmes and Rahe. Participants are asked to consider a list of change/stressful events and mark if they happened within the last year. In the posts-activity analysis, participants are asked to consider why the correlation between events and illness may not always be positive. Mediators of stress on health are listed: biological, personality, cognitive, environmental, and sociocultural. Participants can print their results. | Stress<br>SRRS<br>Health<br>Mediators |
| | | **Stress Responses** |
| | | **Stress and Illness** |

| | | **Coping Strategies** |
|---|---|---|
| Social Ostracism | Kipling Williams, an expert in social ostracism, discusses how humans need to belong, to have a sense of control, self-esteem, and a meaningful existence. Ostracism is a metaphor for death. Experiments that simulate ostracism are presented. Physiological arousal is experienced in those being ostracized. A response to ostracism may be frustration, leading to aggression. The case of the killers at Columbine High School is discussed. At the end of the video clip, Elliot Aronson discusses how the Jigsaw classroom, by encouraging cooperation, also has positive effects on intelligence, cognition, and motivation. | Social ostracism<br>Experimental method<br>Jigsaw classroom<br>Cooperation |
| | | **Healthful Living** |
| Exercise and Mental Illness | In this video clip, Garry Martin's published review of the effects of exercise on mental illness is discussed. This review concluded that exercise itself can be an effective treatment for mental illness. Exercise can be used to treat mild to moderate depression. James Blumenthal compared effects of exercise and drug therapy in elderly patients with depression. One third of them do not respond to medication. He found that exercise alone was as effective as medication or a combination of exercise and medication. Those treated with exercise had lower rates of relapse. The effects could be due to neurochemical or self-esteem changes. | Exercise<br>Therapy<br>Depression |

**Online Learning Center (www.mhhe.com/Santrockp7u)**
- Interact and make learning fun!
    - **Interactive Exercises**
        - Type A Behavior
        - Stress & Life Events
    - **Interactive Reviews**
        - Level of Analysis: Stress
        - Coping Strategies
- Brush up on the Key Terms for this chapter by first reviewing the electronic **Glossary** (in English or Spanish) and then testing your retention using the **Flashcard** feature.

- **"Notes"**—This feature allows you to use the website as you would your text, inserting your own study notes and highlighting areas of particular importance.

**In Your Text**

- Found throughout each chapter, the **Review and Sharpen Your Thinking** feature breaks the text into logical chunks, allowing you to process, review, and reflect thoughtfully on the information that you've just read. When going back to *study* the chapter, try reading the feature *before* the section of text to which it relates. In doing so, you will be able to focus your attention on important concepts *as* you encounter them. In this chapter, this feature can be found on the following pages: pp. 604, 612, 616, 620, 631, and 639.

**Practice Quizzes**

- Test your knowledge of stress, coping, and health by taking the different practice quizzes found on your text's **Online Learning Center** and on the **In-Psych Plus CD-ROM** packaged with your text.

## ANSWER KEY

## In Your Own Words

✓ Develop some examples that you have experienced for each of the types of conflict presented in the chapter.

*There are three types of conflicts presented in the chapter: approach/approach conflict, avoidance/avoidance conflict, and approach/avoidance conflict. Approach/approach conflict involves making choices between two desirable options. Avoidance/avoidance conflict involves making choices between two undesirable options. Finally, approach/avoidance conflict refers to dealing with one choice that has both positive and negative characteristics.*

✓ Do you use problem-focused coping and/or emotion-focused coping as you are assigned papers and projects and face exams? In these contexts, what are the advantages and disadvantages of each?

*Problem-focused coping is the cognitive strategy of facing the challenge and figuring out ways to deal with it. Coming up with a schedule to work on each of the tasks would be a problem-focused coping strategy. An emotion-focused coping strategy involves responding to stress in an emotional manner, especially by using defensive mechanisms. Calling home and crying about all the work that you have been unfairly assigned would be using an emotion-focused strategy.*

✓ Of those ways described in the chapter on methods to cope with stress (e.g., optimism, self-efficacy, social support, assertive behavior), which one is your greatest strength? Which one do you need to develop further?

*Optimism refers to an explanatory style in which people explain bad/stressful events in a manner in which they protect themselves. They may explain the bad event with external, unstable, and specific attributions. Self-efficacy refers to the expectation a person has to be capable to deal with a situation. There are many types of social support, but the more diverse and emotionally supportive your network is, the more effective it will be. Being assertive involves a series of approaches and skills. Overall, an assertive person engages in problem-focused coping by addressing the problem directly but not in a confrontational or aggressive manner.*

## Correcting the Incorrect

1. Stress is defined as the response of individuals to circumstances and events that threaten them and tax their coping abilities. (p. 604)

2. *Selye* developed the General Adaptation Syndrome. (p. 612)

3. The General Adaptation Syndrome consists of three stages: *alarm, resistance, and exhaustion.* (p. 612)

4. Being *hostile* is directly associated with cardiovascular disease. (p. 605)

5. The components of hardiness are commitment, control, and challenge. (p. 605)

6. Cognitive appraisal refers to the individual's interpretation of events. (p. 615)

7. In *secondary* appraisal, individuals evaluate their resources and determine how effectively they can be used to cope with the stressor. (p. 615)

8. An approach/approach conflict occurs when the individual must choose *between two attractive stimuli or circumstances.* (p. 608)

9. The life events checklist *does not* provide important information about a person's psychological makeup. (p. 607)

10. Separation and marginalization are *the least adaptive* responses to acculturation. (p. 611)

11. Acculturative stress refers to *the contact between two distinctive cultural groups.* (p. 610)

12. Poor women are more likely to experience crime and violence than are middle-class women. (p. 612)

13. Denial is an example of *emotion-focused coping.* (p. 621)

14. Self-talk *is helpful in cognitive restructuring.* (p. 622)

15. *Having positive illusions may be helpful for mental health.* (p. 622)

16. A strategy of defensive pessimism *may be a good way* to deal with stress. (p. 623)

17. Pessimism can be overcome through cognitive therapy. (p. 622)

18. *Self-efficacy* is the belief that one can master a situation and produce positive outcomes. (p. 624)

19. The more diverse the social support is, the *more effective* it is in helping us cope with stress. (p. 626)

20. One way to become more assertive is to state problems in terms of their consequences for *you.* (p. 626)

21. Stress-management programs teach us how to *cope with stress.* (p. 629)

22. Biofeedback is effective at reducing an individual's muscle tension. (p. 630)

23. Nicotine is a stimulant that *increases the smoker's energy and alertness.* (p. 635)

24. *A majority* of adolescents do not use contraception during their first sexual intercourse experience. (p. 637)

25. HIV destroys the immune system. (p. 638)

## Practice Test 1

1. a. no; this option emphasizes unconscious causes
   b. no; this model describes the effects of stress
   c. no; hardiness is a personality trait that influences how we cope with stress
   d. YES; you can see in the term a reference to several types of causes
   p. 603

2. a. no; she may be working in clinical psychology, but there's a better option given her interest
   b. no; she may be using behavior modification, but this is not a field
   c. no; she is the least likely to be working in psychoanalysis since there's no reference to unconscious or therapy
   d. YES; she is integrating behavioral and biomedical knowledge
   p. 603

3. a. no; frustration is the response
   b. no; this syndrome describes the biological factors involved in stress
   c. YES; this is the definition of stress
   d. no; this refers to interpretation of events
   p. 604

4. a. no; a vacation can threaten or tax some people's coping abilities; but there is better example of a stressor
   b. no; this probably does not threaten or tax coping abilities
   c. no; this probably does not threaten or tax coping abilities
   d. YES; being fired from a job is threatening and taxes our coping abilities
   p. 604

5. a. no; humanistic psychology is probably of not much interest to you
   b. no; more than likely you don't have a high interest in motor skills
   c. no; more than likely you don't have much interest in analyzing dreams
   d. YES; since you are interested in the relationships among psychological factors, the nervous system, and the immune system
   p. 616

6. a. no; Donesha seems to have adequate resources, such as close relationships
   b. YES; these characteristics put Charles' immune system at risk
   c. no; she has a social support and close relationships
   d. no; he has social support
   p. 617

7. a. no; this is not Selye's approach
   b. no; this is a scale that measures how much stress has been experienced
   c. incorrect
   d. YES; the GAS consists of three stages
   p. 612

8. a. no; there is often a temporary state of shock when resistance drops
   b. YES; hormones that reduce inflammation are released
   c. no; there may be exhaustion, and vulnerability to disease increases
   d. no
   p. 614

9. a. no
   b. YES; Type A personality consists of competitiveness, impatience, and hostility
   c. no; Type B personality refers to people who are relaxed and easygoing
   d. no
   p. 605

10. a. no; this is a characteristic
    b. no; the Type A behavior pattern does include competitiveness
    c. no; impatience is a characteristic of the Type A behavior pattern
    d. YES; a general sense of satisfaction with life does not characterize the Type A behavior pattern
    p. 605

11. a. no; appraisal refers to interpretation of events
    b. no; Type B personality refers to people who are relaxed and easygoing
    c. YES; these three components characterize hardiness
    d. no; this is the soundless mental speech we use as we think or plan
    p. 605

12. a. CORRECT; we do not appraise an event as fear, fear is a response
    b. no; we may appraise an event as harmful
    c. no; we may appraise an event as a threat
    d. no; we may appraise an event as a challenge
    p. 615

13. a. YES; we also determine how to use our resources to cope with stress
    b. no; this is not what happens in secondary appraisal
    c. no; secondary appraisal does not include the use of defense mechanisms
    d. no; these are two stages of the general adaptation syndrome
    p. 615

14. a. no; obviously, primary appraisal occurs before secondary appraisal
    b. YES; interpretation is a cognitive activity
    c. no; obviously, primary appraisal occurs before secondary appraisal
    d. no; interpretation is a very active process
    p. 615

15. a. no; doing this would reduce the risk of burnout
    b. no; doing this would reduce the risk of burnout
    c. no; doing this allows the student get the needed support, reducing burnout
    d. YES; graduating in three years is difficult and not likely, which could lead to burnout
    p. 609

16. a. no; burnout is an experience of overload and is not associated with bicultural experiences
    b. no; hardiness is a personality factors that buffers the negative effects of stress
    c. YES; this is a type of stress that results from bicultural experiences
    d. no; diversity, let it be cultural or of any other type is not a negative consequence
    p. 610

17. a. no; this refers to a single circumstance, and Jane has two boyfriends
    b. YES; Jane must choose between two equally attractive options
    c. no; this is a conflict that involves two unattractive circumstances
    d. no
    p. 608

18. a. no; this is not a type of conflict
    b. CORRECT
    c. no; this is a conflict that involves two unattractive circumstances
    d. no; this conflict involves two attractive circumstances
    p. 608

19. a. no; this conflict involves two attractive circumstances
    b. YES; this is a conflict that involves two unattractive circumstances
    c. no; this conflict involves a single circumstance with positive and negative characteristics
    d. no; this is not a type of conflict
    p. 608

20. a. no; assimilation occurs when individuals give up their cultural identity and move into the larger society
   b. no; separation is self-imposed withdrawal from the larger culture
   c. YES; marginalization occurs when groups are put out of contact with both their traditional and the dominant society
   d. no; integration is when the group becomes an integrated part of the larger culture but still maintains its cultural integrity
   p. 611

## Practice Test 2

1. a. no; physical and biomedical factors are equivalent concepts
   b. no; health psychology is not as concerned with unconscious factors
   c. YES; this is the focus of health psychology
   d. no; genetic factors can be categorized as biomedical factors
   p. 603

2. a. no; this is one of the characteristics of the Type A behavior pattern, but it has not been directly linked to heart disease
   b. no; this is one of the characteristics of the Type A behavior pattern, but it has not been directly linked to heart disease
   c. no; this is one of the characteristics of the Type A behavior pattern, but it has not been directly linked to heart disease
   d. YES; hostility has been consistently associated with coronary risk
   p. 605

3. a. no; a sense of commitment is one of the characteristics of hardiness
   b. no; a sense of control is one of the characteristics of hardiness
   c. YES; perceiving problems as threats is not one of the characteristics of hardiness
   d. no; perceiving problems as challenges instead of threats is one of the characteristics of hardiness
   p. 605

4. a. no; this would involve choosing between two good things
   b. YES; this involves choosing between two bad things
   c. no; this involves choosing to pursue something that involves both positives and negatives
   d. no; this is not one of the conflicts discussed in this chapter
   p. 608

5. a. no; this is one traumatic event, but burnout usually results because of a gradual accumulation of everyday stresses
   b. no; this is one traumatic event, but burnout usually results because of a gradual accumulation of everyday stresses
   c. YES; this scenario suggests a gradual accumulation of everyday stresses
   d. no; even two traumatic events are not as likely to cause burnout as the accumulation of everyday stresses
   p. 608

6. a. no; the number is higher than this
   b. no; while this is the equivalent of 8 hours 5 days a week, Americans work more than that
   c. YES; 47 is the current average; the number has gone up 8% in one generation
   d. no; considering the stress effects, our society would be in great trouble if Americans worked an average of 70 hours a week!
   p. 609

7. a. no; this is one of the common characteristics
   b. no; this is one of the common characteristics
   c. YES; the immune system is decentralized, with its organs located throughout the body, while the nervous system is localized in the brain, spinal cord, and fixed pathways
   d. no; this is one of the common characteristics
   p. 609

8. a. YES; integration is the healthiest, least stressful response
   b. no; marginalization and separation are the least adaptive responses
   c. no; marginalization and separation are the least adaptive responses
   d. no; assimilation can be a healthy response, but there is some cultural loss
   p. 616

9. a. RIGHT; defense mechanisms are used in emotion-focused coping
   b. no; this sounds more like problem-focused coping
   c. no; this sounds more like problem-focused coping
   d. incorrect
   p. 611

10. a. YES; in problem-focused coping, we are squarely facing our troubles and trying to solve them
    b. no; biofeedback allows people to learn control over physiological activities
    c. incorrect
    d. no; self-efficacy is the belief that one can master a situation and produce positive outcomes
    p. 621

11. a. no; self-efficacy is the belief that one can master a situation and produce positive outcomes
    b. no; this is the soundless mental speech we use as we think or plan
    c. YES; this attempts to modify the thoughts, ideas, and beliefs that maintain a person's problems
    d. no; this refers to one's options about self, work, and events
    p. 622

12. a. no; biofeedback allows people to learn control over physiological activities
    b. YES; this attempts to modify the thoughts, ideas, and beliefs that maintain a person's problems
    c. no; this focuses on using principles of learning to modify behavior
    d. no; psychoanalysis focuses on unconscious conflicts and motives
    p. 622

13. a. no; high self-efficacy allows people to persist in the face of obstacles
    b. no; those with high self-efficacy are likely to expend effort
    c. no; people with high self-efficacy experience less stress in these situations
    d. YES; in fact, high self-efficacy will lead to a sense of control
    p. 624

14. a. no; this is a type of adaptation to acculturative stress
    b. no; self-efficacy is the belief that one can produce a desired outcomes
    c. YES; social support provides effective ways to cope with stress
    d. no; biofeedback refers to a technique to learn control over physiological activities by using instruments
    p. 624

15. a. YES; assertive coping is a way to deal with conflict in relationships
    b. incorrect
    c. incorrect
    d. no; this is not a benefit
    p. 624

16. a. no; while this can be effective, it is not the most effective
    b. no; while this can be effective, it is not the most effective
    c. no; while this can be effective, it is not the most effective
    d. YES; multiple coping strategies give individuals more choices
    p. 621

17. a. no; this is the use of the principles of learning to modify behavior
    b. no; even though meditation can help control physiological activities, it does not use instruments
    c. YES; biofeedback involves learning to control processes such as heart rate by receiving feedback from instruments
    d. no; this does not use instruments
    p. 630

18. a. no; this is too short a time
    b. no; this would be good, but more is better
    c. YES; half an hour seems to be effective in promoting health
    d. no; this might be excessive
    p. 632

19. a. no; while a diet high in fibers is good, it may ignore other nutrients
    b. no; while a low-fat diet is good, a well-balanced diet is even better
    c. YES; this is the best nutritional plan
    d. no; this diet may not include other important nutrients
    p. 635

20. a. no; while this is a risk factor, it is not the best predictor of getting an STD
    b. YES; having sex with multiple partners is the best predictor
    c. incorrect
    d. incorrect
    p. 639

**Practice Test 3**

1. a.    YES; health psychologists study the cognitive and behavioral factors associated with health and illness
   b.    no; behavioral medicine does not focus as much on mental processes such as on perception
   c.    no; a psychoneuroimmunologist focuses more on the relationship between psychological factors and the nervous and immune systems
   d.    no; the issue might be of interest to personality psychologists, but their focus is not on stress and other health and illness issues
   p. 603

2. a.    YES; recent research has shown that the whole pattern of Type A is not associated with coronary problems; however, one of its elements is
   b.    no; anxiety and worry have been associated with cardiovascular disease
   c.    no; hostility is the one element of the Type A behavior pattern that is strongly associated with heart problems
   d.    no; hardiness has been associated with lack of illness; therefore, it has been associated with illness (just because the correlation is negative does not mean that there is no relationship)
   p. 605

3. a.    no; she does not have to choose between two good things
   b.    no; she does not have to choose between two bad things
   c.    YES; she has to make a decision about a single option that involves both positive and negative elements
   d.    no; there is no such conflict in psychological theory
   p. 608

4. a.    no; Americans want jobs that are secure
   b.    YES; Americans actually prefer jobs that offer advancement opportunities
   c.    no; Americans want a workplace that offers a sense of community
   d.    no; Americans want jobs that allow them to use their creativity and problem-solving skills
   p. 609

5. a.    no; assimilation would occur if Jose relinquished his Mexican identity and tried to blend into the mainstream American culture
   b.    no; Jose is not trying to move into the larger American culture
   c.    YES; Jose has self-imposed a withdrawal from the larger culture
   d.    no; Jose is clearly grounded in his native Mexican culture, and in marginalization there is a loss of the native culture and lack of the new culture
   p. 611

6. a.    YES; Puerto Rican families headed by a woman are fifteen times more likely to live in poverty than are families headed by White men
   b.    no; considering the number of daily hassles Minerva is likely to encounter, she is a good candidate for burnout
   c.    no; the question does not address any of the characteristics of this behavior pattern
   d.    no; the question does not address any of the characteristics of this behavior pattern
   p. 611

7. a. no; this is one of the effects of cortisol, which is why it can also contribute to weight gain
   b. no; this is one of the long-term effects of cortisol
   c. no; this is also one of the long-term effects of cortisol
   d. YES; this helps the body to react to stressful situations
   p. 613

8. a. no; this question is making reference to gender differences in the fight-or-flight response, and women are less likely to act aggressively
   b. YES; Jennifer, as a female, is more likely to "tend and befriend" in a stressful situation
   c. no; see reply to item a
   d. no; females are also less likely to "flight" the situation; in terms of evolution, it has been argued that running away from danger could put the female's offspring at risk
   p. 614

9. a. no; this occurred back when he realized how losing this job would affect him
   b. no; he experienced stress, but that is not the answer to the question
   c. YES; continuing his education is the strategy Muzafer chose to deal with the stress of losing his job
   d. no; Lazarus did not propose a third type of cognitive appraisal
   p. 615

10. a. no; hormones are not produced in the cerebral cortex
    b. no; the temporal lobe is a subdivision of the cerebral cortex
    c. no; this is the part of the brain that relays sensory information to the cerebral cortex
    d. YES; the hypothalamus generates corticotropin, a hormone shared by the nervous system and the immune system
    p. 617

11. a. no; this is correct
    b. no; this is correct about acute stressors
    c. YES; this is incorrect, high stress is associated with low levels of NK-cell, which can attack tumor cells
    d. no; this is correct
    p. 617

12. a. no; Henry is likely to avoid exercising
    b. YES; Henry is likely to pick up smoking
    c. no; Henry is likely to start overeating
    d. no; Henry is likely to engage in behaviors that will put him at risk of cardiovascular disease
    p. 618

13. a. no; humor has been associated with higher levels of secretory immunoglobulin (S-IgA), the antibody that defends the person from getting a cold
    b. no; in an experiment, watching a happy video resulted in higher levels of S-IgA
    c. YES; in the same experiment addressed in reply b, others who watched a sad video showed a drop in S-IgA
    d. no; positive emotions have been linked to the release of S-IgA
    p. 619

14.  a.  no; in this scenario, Krystina is not considering her self-talk
     b.  no; in this scenario, Krystina is not taking advantage of a positive self-illusion to cope with the stress of her strained relationship with her parents
     c.  no; Krystina is not seeking strategies to solve the problem
     d.  YES; Krystina is responding to stress in an emotional manner
     p. 621

15.  a.  no; in defensive pessimism the person focuses on possible negative consequences
     b.  no; defensive pessimism means that the person already has the negative expectations about the situation
     c.  YES; defensive pessimism, worrying about negative expectations, can serve as a motivator to avoid the negative consequences
     d.  no; in defensive pessimism the person does take responsibility for the problem; that is partly what motivates him or her to act and do something to solve the problem
     p. 623

16.  a.  YES; this woman has a weak social support system, which places her at higher risk of being unable to cope with stress
     b.  no; this person has the benefit of information and emotional support
     c.  no; this person has a diverse social support network
     d.  no; this person has emotional support
     pp. 624–625

17.  a.  no; Sean is not being hostile or aggressive
     b.  YES; Sean has been making other people feel sorry for him and manipulating them to get them to do things for him
     c.  no; Sean has been expressing his feelings
     d.  no; Sean is not going directly to the boss and facing the problem
     p. 626

18.  a.  no; this is a good recommendation, unless the person needs to be assertive on the spot
     b.  YES; Sean should state the problem in terms of the consequences for him, not including the boss; telling the boss that this could also reflect badly on him could be considered acting aggressively
     c.  no; this is a good recommendation; if not, a solution may be delayed
     d.  no; being assertive includes demanding specifics, so this is a good recommendation
     p. 626

19.  a.  no; the brain of a dead person shows no activity!
     b.  YES; the brain waves are mainly of the alpha variety, regular and rhythmic (go back to the chapter on states of consciousness to refresh your memory)
     c.  no; while sleeping, the person shows beta, theta, and delta brain waves
     d.  no; the brain of a schizophrenic shows irregular activity (go back to the chapter on psychological disorders to refresh your memory)
     p. 630

20.  a.  no; while engaging in such a program reaps the best physical benefits, it does not result in psychological benefits
     b.  YES; people who walk or jog to elevate their heart rate to 60% of the maximum are more likely to get positive psychological benefits such as reduced tension and anxiety
     c.  no; the light program was not as effective as the moderate program
     d.  no; the control group in this study did not show psychological benefits
     p. 633

# Chapter 16—Social Psychology

## Learning Goals

1. Describe how people think about the social world.
2. Identify how people are influenced in social settings.
3. Discuss intergroup relations.
4. Explain how aggression and altruism characterize social interaction.
5. Understand the nature of relationships.

*After studying Chapter 16, you will be able to:*

- Define social psychology.
- Understand social thinking.
- Describe our tendencies in making attributions.
- Understand social perception, including the processes of perceiving others, perceiving oneself, and presenting oneself to others.
- Explain what attitudes are and their relationship to behaviors.
- Understand how cognitive dissonance theory and self-perception theory explain attitude change.
- Discuss social influence including conformity, obedience, group influence, and leadership.
- Explain the factors that increase and decrease conformity in a group.
- Understand issues of intergroup relations such as group identity and prejudice.
- Describe ways of improving intergroup relations.
- Describe the biological and environmental/psychological influences on aggression, as well as gender differences.
- Discuss altruism including biological, psychological, and sociocultural foundations.
- Describe the bystander effect.
- Discuss the factors that contribute to interpersonal attraction.
- Describe the three types of love: romantic, affectionate, and consummate.
- Discuss the factors that contribute to loneliness, including life's transitions and technology, as well as strategies for reducing loneliness.

## CHAPTER 16: OVERVIEW

- *Social psychology* is the study of how people think about, influence, and relate to other people. The areas of study in social psychology may be classified into social thinking, social influence, intergroup relations, social interaction, and relationships.

- *Social thinking* or *social cognition* involves how we encode, store, retrieve and use information about other people. How we think about social stimuli (e.g., a friend) is different in some ways to how we think about other stimuli (e.g., a chair).

- Three areas that distinguish social thinking are attributions, social perception, and attitudes. People are motivated to make sense of their world, and attribution theorists suggest that as part of that effort we continuously explain why people do the things they do.

- *Attributions* vary along three dimensions: internal versus external, stable versus unstable, and controllable versus uncontrollable. Weiner argues that the types of attributions we make affect our emotions and motivations. For example, if a bad thing happens and we make an internal, stable and/or uncontrollable attribution, that is likely to have a negative affect on our self-esteem. Making attributions is not a completely rational process, because we are subject to a variety of cognitive biases such as the fundamental attribution error and the self-serving bias.

- The *fundamental attribution error* is the tendency to overestimate the importance of traits and to underestimate the importance of the situation in explaining another's behavior. The *self-serving bias* involves attributing our success to internal factors and attributing our failures to external factors.

- *Social perception* involves the process of perceiving others, perceiving ourselves, and presenting ourselves to others. When we meet another person for the first time we tend to be influenced by the primacy effect, which in social psychology refers to the tendency for first impressions to have a long-lasting effect.

- We also have an implicit personality theory, which is our conception of how personality traits go together in an individual. This implicit theory leads us to make assumptions and arrive at conclusions about other people based on a few pieces of information.

- Another social perception phenomenon is the classification of people into groups as a way of simplifying social information. One of the ways in which we perceive ourselves, or think about ourselves, is by comparing ourselves to others in a process called *social comparison*. One of the interesting tendencies in social comparison is that we are more likely to compare ourselves with people who are similar to us than to people who are different from us, possibly because it is more informative to do so.

- Another area of social perception is *impression management* or *self-presentation*, which is the process of individuals striving to present themselves as a certain sort of person. Effective impression management involves using the right nonverbal cues, conforming to situational norms, showing appreciation for others, and matching the behaviors of others.

- Some people are more concerned about the impressions they give to others; these individuals are high in self-monitoring.

- The last topic on social thinking discussed in the chapter is attitudes. *Attitudes* are beliefs and opinions about a people, objects, and ideas. Attitudes can predict how a person will act when the attitudes are strong, when the person is aware of his or her attitudes, and when attitudes are relevant to the behavior. Behaviors can also influence attitudes, as suggested in the theory of cognitive dissonance.

- *Cognitive dissonance* refers to a person's motivation to reduce the dissonance or discomfort caused by two inconsistent thoughts or inconsistent thoughts and behaviors. For example, if a person smokes and has a negative attitude about smoking (e.g., smoking is bad for the health), the person is likely to experience dissonance, an uncomfortable experience resulting from the inconsistent thought and behavior. In such a situation, the behavior could prompt a change in the attitude. Since the behavior is harder to change, the person is more likely to modify the attitude. We also have a strong need to justify our actions, particularly if we put effort into what we do and our self-esteem is involved. This process is called *effort justification*.

- Another approach to the issue of the effect of behavior on attitudes is the self-perception theory of Daryl Bem. Bem suggests that people look at their own actions to figure out what their attitudes are.

- To change attitudes, we must consider the four main elements of the communication process: characteristics of the communicator, characteristics of the message, the medium of the message, and the characteristics of the audience.

- Communicators who are credible, powerful, attractive, likeable, and similar to the audience tend to be persuasive. Messages that include emotional appeals can be persuasive, especially if the audience is not well informed.

- The elaboration likelihood model proposes that there are two ways to persuade: the central route (using data and relevant information) and the peripheral route (using superficial cues such as the attractiveness of the communicator). The central route is persuasive if the audience is informed, interested, and motivated to pay attention to the facts, while the peripheral route is persuasive if the audience is paying close attention to the message.

- The order in which arguments are presented in a message also influences the extent to which it may be persuasive. For example, the foot-in-the-door strategy involves asking for a small request followed by a large request. The door-in-the-face strategy also works; it involves asking for an extreme request first followed by a large but in comparison lesser request.

- Regarding the communication medium, it has been found that television exposure enhances persuasion. Finally, two characteristics of the audience that play a role in persuasion are age and strength of attitude.

- Conformity, obedience, group influence, and cultural and ethnic influences are all instances of *social influence*. *Conformity* is a change in an individual's behavior to coincide more with a group standard.

- Solomon Asch found that the pressure to conform is strong even when individuals conform to something that they objectively know is wrong. Among the factors that contribute to conformity are normative social influence (social influence because we seek approval) and informational social influence (social influence because we want to be right).

- Conformity increases if there is unanimity in the group, if there is no prior commitment to an attitude inconsistent with the group's position, if the person has low self-esteem, if the group members are perceived as experts and attractive, and if the culture is collectivistic.

- *Obedience* is behavior that complies with the explicit demands of the individual in authority. Milgram's experiments demonstrated the power of obedience. In the famous shock study, Milgram found that close to two-thirds of the participants delivered the highest level of shock. The research procedure used by Milgram has raised questions about the ethics of psychological research.

- Social influence in groups involves structure, performance, interaction and decision making, and leadership. Two aspects of group structure are norms (rules specific to the group) and roles (define how different people in the group should behave). Performance in a group is different from performance in isolation, as shown by the research on social facilitation, social loafing, and deindividuation.

- When making decisions in groups, a risky shift tends to emerge, such that the decisions of the group tend to be riskier than the average decision made by individual group members. This is consistent with group polarization, which occurs when the group members are already biased in a direction.

- Group polarization involves the additional strengthening of the position the members share. *Groupthink* is the impaired decision making that takes place in groups that overestimate their power, think of themselves as morally superior, are close-minded, and are pressured toward uniformity.

- Various strategies may be used to avoid groupthink, including involving people outside the group in the decision-making process and having impartial leadership. In groups, the minority can still have influence through informational pressure.

- Two theories that attempt to explain effective leadership are the great-person theory (certain personality traits are associated with effective leadership) and the contingency model of leadership (personality and situational factors determine who is an effective leader).

- Conflicts among ethnic and cultural groups are common around the world. Social psychology studies these conflicts by researching group identity, prejudice, and ways to improve interethnic relations.

- *Social identity* is how we define ourselves in terms of our group memberships. According to Tajfel's social identity theory, we are motivated to feel good about ourselves and feel good about the groups that we belong to.

- Tajfel found that we engage in in-group/out-group thinking even when people are divided into groups based on meaningless criteria, such as overestimating the number of dots on a screen. As soon as participants were assigned to a group, they engaged in favoring the members of the in-group.

- *Ethnocentrism* is the tendency to favor one's own group over other groups. While ethnocentrism can foster a sense of pride in the in-group, it can also encourage in-group /out-group thinking.

- Studying prejudice, stereotyping, and discrimination helps in understanding why groups become so antagonized. *Prejudice* is an unjustified negative attitude toward an individual based on the individual's membership in a group. Adorno argued that people with the authoritarian personality are more likely to be prejudiced. Prejudice may also be caused by competition between groups.

- Based on social identity theory, it can also be argued that people engage in prejudice to enhance their self-esteem. Our social cognitive processes also contribute to prejudice, as we have a tendency to categorize people into groups to simplify social information. Social learning may also contribute to prejudice, because we learn our beliefs from family, friends, and social structures.

- The cognitive root of prejudice is the *stereotype*, a generalization about a group's characteristics that does not consider any variations from one individual to the next. We tend to perceive the out-group as more homogeneous than the in-group. Once stereotypes are acquired, they influence our social cognition such that we are less likely to modify them. Emotions can influence the intensity of our stereotypes.

- *Discrimination* is an unjustifiable negative or harmful act toward a member of a group simply because the person belongs to that group. While in America overt discrimination is not acceptable, a number of subtle forms of discrimination have emerged. Two approaches have been effective in improving intergroup and interethnic relations: task-oriented cooperation and intimate contact.

- Sherif found that task-oriented cooperation is effective in bringing groups of people together to cooperate in reaching some goal. A strategy devised by psychologists to encourage cooperation instead of conflict between groups is called the *jigsaw classroom*. An example of intimate contact is living in integrated housing, which can diminish in-group/out-group distinctions.

- Two extremes of social interaction are aggression and altruism. Aggression has been extensively explained in terms of biological influences including evolutionary views, instinctual explanations, genetic basis, and neurobiological factors. Among the neurobiological factors, stimulation of the limbic system has been associated with aggression, and levels of serotonin have been found to be low in aggressors.

- The frustration-aggression hypothesis states that frustration leads to aggression; the hypothesis was later revised to show that other responses to frustration do occur. Aversive circumstances can lead to aggression and may include environmental variables (e.g., noise, weather). The cognitive factors of expectations, equity, intentions, and responsibility influence whether we respond aggressively.

- Aggression can also be learned through observational learning and reinforcement; consistent with the learning hypothesis is the observation that different cultures have different levels of aggression. A number of studies have demonstrated the negative effects of children viewing violence and aggression on television. In terms of gender, males tend to be more aggressive than females; however, both biological and cultural factors influence the male-female differences in aggression. According to psychodynamic and ethological theories, catharsis is an effective way to reduce aggression, but social cognitive theorists argue that acting aggressively only fosters more aggression.

- Teaching conflict management skills and having students serve as peer counselors are two of the aggression-reduction strategies used in schools.

- *Altruism* refers to an unselfish interest in helping someone else. The evolutionary psychologists view some forms of altruism as being important in perpetuating our genes. Some psychologists have suggested that altruism has never been demonstrated among humans. Others suggest an important distinction between altruism and egoism.

- In social psychology, the bystander effect occurs when individuals who observe an emergency are less likely to help or are delayed in helping when others are present than when they are alone. While in the past several decades college students showed a decreased concern for the well-being of others, in recent years there seems to be a shift toward more interest in altruism. In terms of gender differences, females and males are both likely to show altruism; however, the context also influences who will help: females are more likely to help when the context involves nurturing, but men are more likely to help if the situation seems dangerous.

- Psychologists have studied the factors that are involved in our attractions to each other. Familiarity, similarity, and physical attraction have been implicated in interpersonal attractions. Love can take the form of romantic love, affectionate love, or consummate love.

- Sternberg's triangular theory of love proposes the following three elements: passion, intimacy, and commitment. Studies on gender differences show that females tend to have stronger interest in relationships than males. Males tend to prefer report talk, while females prefer rapport talk.

- Loneliness is more likely during life's transitions; this is why college students are especially prone to loneliness. The increased use of television and Internet technology also contribute to isolation and loneliness.

**Building Blocks of Chapter 16**

**Clarifying some of the tricky points in Chapter 16**
**and**
**In Your Own Words**

*To respond to the questions and exercises presented in the "In Your Own Words" section, please write your thoughts, perspectives, and reactions on a separate piece of paper.*

### Social Thinking

We are motivated to discover the causes of behavior as part of our interest in making sense of the behavior, according to *attribution theory*. One important distinction relating to attribution is whether we attribute the causes of our behavior to the environment, called *external attribution,* or to our personality, referred to as *internal attribution*. Our explanations can also focus on whether a cause is permanent or temporary, which is *stable/ unstable*. The third dimension of causality is controllable/uncontrollable causes.

Our tendency to overestimate the importance of traits and underestimate the importance of situations in seeking explanations of an actor's behavior has been called the *fundamental attribution* error. In the *self-serving* bias, we attribute our success to internal factors, while *failures* are attributed to external factors. When we think about our social world to try to make sense of it, we engage in *social* perception. When we form impressions of others, those impressions are both *unified* and *integrated*.

### In Your Own Words
*Please write your thoughts, perspectives, and reactions on a separate piece of paper.*
✓ *In the past 24 hours, what attributions have you made about the people around you? Have you committed the fundamental attribution error? Have you experienced the self-serving bias?*

We also have a notion of how personality traits go together in an individual; this is referred to as *implicit personality* theory. First impressions are often enduring; psychologists refer to this as the *primacy* effect. A process in which individuals evaluate their thoughts, feelings, behaviors, and abilities in relation to other people is called *social comparison*. The process in which individuals strive to present themselves as a certain sort of person is called *impression management*. Individuals' awareness of the impression they make on others and the degree to which they fine-tune their performance accordingly is called *self-monitoring*.

Beliefs and opinions that predispose individuals to behave in certain ways are *attitudes*. Two strategies for persuasion are the foot-in-the-door and the door-in-the-face. The *foot-in-the-door* strategy suggests presenting the larger request later in the presentation; the *door-in-the-face* strategy, however, suggests presenting an extreme request first followed by a large but in comparison lesser request.

Psychologists have been interested in the relationship between attitudes and *behavior*. Psychologists have found that a stronger association of attitudes and behavior occurs when attitudes are based on *real* experiences and when we think about our *attitudes*. Evidence also shows that changes in behavior sometimes precede changes in *attitudes*. One explanation is that we have a need for cognitive *consistency*. This motivation is what Festinger referred to in his theory as *cognitive dissonance*. This concept suggests that we develop *justifications* for our actions and in the process may change our *justifications* to be consistent with our behaviors. We also have a need to justify the effort we put forth in life, termed *effort justification*. The most intense effort justification occurs when our *self-esteem* is involved. Some psychologists believe that the dissonance view relies too heavily on *internal (cognitive)* factors. Bem's theory, called self-perception theory, suggests that individuals make inferences about their attitudes by perceiving their own *behaviors.*

## In Your Own Words

*Please write your thoughts, perspectives, and reactions on a separate piece of paper.*

✓ *Compare cognitive dissonance theory and self-perception theory. Offer an example to illustrate how each theory can predict how behaviors influence attitudes.*

### *Social Influence*

When individuals change their behavior to coincide more with a group standard, they experience conformity. The power of *conformity* was demonstrated by Asch's study on judgment of line lengths. *Normative social* influence refers to the influence that other people have on us because we seek their approval or avoid their disapproval. In *informational social* influence, other people influence us because we want to be right. People are more likely to conform when group opinion is *unanimous.* Conformity also increases for those with low *self-esteem* and if group members are experts, attractive, or *similar* to the individual. Conformity rates have been found to be lower in *individualistic* cultures.

Behavior that complies with the explicit demands of an individual in authority is *obedience.* In Milgram's classic experiment, subjects obeyed even though they believed they were *hurting* (*shocking*) someone. Milgram's research raises important questions regarding *ethics* in psychology experiments.

All groups have rules that apply to all members; these are called *norms.* Some rules govern only certain positions in the group; these are *roles.* Our performance on well-learned tasks usually improves in the presence of others; this is labeled *social facilitation.* In some groups, we can reduce our effort and not be detected. The lessened effort exerted in a group because of reduced monitoring is called *social loafing.* In some groups, we lose our individual identity and take on the identity of the group; this is known as *deindividuation.*

When decisions are made in groups, there is often a tendency to make a riskier decision than when we are alone; this has been called the *risky shift.* Although group decisions are not always riskier, group discussion usually strengthens the position we initially held; this is termed the *group polarization* effect. Sometimes group members seek to maintain harmony and unanimity among the group members; this may lead to *groupthink,* in which individual differences of opinion are stifled. Although in most group decision making in the majority wins, when the minority presents its views consistently and confidently, its views are more likely to be heard; this has been labeled *informational pressure.*

Some individuals have certain traits that are best suited for leadership positions, according to the *great-person* theory. A contrasting view that takes into account both personality characteristics and situational influences is called the *contingency model* of leadership. According to this model, if a group is working under very favorable or very unfavorable conditions, a *task*-oriented leader is best. However, if the conditions are more moderated, a *relationship* -oriented leader is better.

## In Your Own Words

*Please write your thoughts, perspectives, and reactions on a separate piece of paper.*

✓ *Have you ever done group work in which there was social loafing? Was anything done to reduce it?*

## Intergroup Relations

An unjustified negative attitude toward an individual because of the individual's membership in a group is called *prejudice*. An oversimplified generalization about a group's characteristics is a *stereotype*. The tendency to favor one's group over other groups is referred to as *ethnocentrism*. *Social identity* theory suggests that when individuals are assigned to a group, they invariably think of the group as an *in-group*.

### In Your Own Words
*Please write your thoughts, perspectives, and reactions on a separate piece of paper.*
✓ *What stereotypes exist for individuals who share your appearance, gender, ethnicity, religion, and major?*

Other theories of prejudice contend that prejudice will increase if groups have to *compete* over valued resources, or if a person has an *authoritarian* personality and is motivated to increase his or her *self-esteem*. Prejudice may also be culturally *learned* and promoted by social cognitive processes. *Discrimination* is an unjustifiable negative or harmful action toward a member of a group simply because the person belongs to that group. Sherif found that promoting the in-group/out-group thinking at a summer camp for boys created *conflict (competition)* between two groups. Positive relations between the two groups were created when the groups were required to carry out *task-oriented* cooperation. This cooperative strategy was applied in a classroom setting called the *jigsaw classroom*. Research has also suggested that interethnic relations can be improved by *intimate* contact.

### In Your Own Words
*Please write your thoughts, perspectives, and reactions on a separate piece of paper.*
✓ *Describe prejudice and explain the factors that contribute to it.*

## Social Interaction

According to ethologists, certain stimuli release *innate aggressive* responses. According to evolution theory, the most aggressive individuals were probably the survivors. Freud believed that aggression was related to the *death* instinct. One part of the brain that has been associated with aggression is the *amygdala*, which is part of the *limbic* system.

The *frustration-aggression* hypothesis states that when we are frustrated we will become aggressive. The psychological factors of *equity*, *intentions*, expectations, and responsibility are used to determine if we respond aggressively in an aversive situation. Bandura would argue that *observational* learning plays an important role in aggression. Most psychologists would agree that TV violence *induces* aggressions or antisocial behavior. Catharsis is the release of anger or aggressive energy by directly engaging in anger or aggression. With regard to gender, *males* tend to be more aggressive than females.

An unselfish interest in helping someone else is called *altruism*. According to evolutionary psychologists, some types of *altruism* are important in perpetuating our genes. These psychologists emphasize the importance of altruistic acts that encourage the survival of *offspring*. An important psychological aspects of altruism is *reciprocity*. Some psychologists argue that altruism has never been demonstrated. Others suggest an important distinction between altruism and *egoism*.

The degree of altruistic motivation is influenced by characteristics of the *situation*. Individuals who observe an emergency are less likely to help when someone else is present; this is called the *bystander effect*. Bystanders are less likely to intervene when the situation might lead to *personal harm*, when helping takes time, when a situation is *ambiguous*, when struggling individuals are *related*, when a victim is drunk, and when bystanders have no history of being victimized themselves. Males are more likely to help when a perceived *danger* is present and they feel *competent* to help. Females have a stronger orientation than males toward *caregiving*.

### Relationships

We like to associate with people who are *similar* to us. Forming close relationships with others similar to ourselves is rewarding because it provides consensual *validation* of our own attitudes and behaviors. Physical *attraction* is an important factor in determining that we like someone. Research suggests, however, that we choose as a mate someone who is close to our level of attractiveness, a process referred to as the *matching hypothesis*.

*Romantic* love is also referred to as passionate love or Eros. It often predominates in the *early* part of a romantic relationship. Affectionate love is also called *companionate* love. It is characterized by a desire to have the other person near and by a deep, caring affection for the other person. *Consummate* love is experienced when the couple shares passion, intimacy, and commitment, the three elements of Sternberg's *triangular* theory of love.

*Rapport* talk refers to language of establishing connections and is preferred among *women*. Report talk is talked designed to give *information*, for which *men* have a strong preference.

Loneliness is associated with life's *transitions*. Men tend to blame loneliness on *internal* factors, while women attribute loneliness to *external* factors. Men are socialized to *initiate* relationships, while women are socialized to *wait*. To become better connected to others, one might want to draw a diagram of the *social networks*.

## Correcting the Incorrect

Carefully read each statement. Determine if the statement is correct or incorrect. If the statement is incorrect, make the necessary changes to correct it. Then check the answer key at the end of the chapter for the correct statement and page reference in the textbook.

1.  Attributions focus on the causes of behavior.
2.  There are three dimensions of causality: internal-external, stable-unstable, and optimistic-pessimistic.
3.  An external attribution would be a person's intelligence or attitudes.
4.  The fundamental attribution error describes how we attribute success to internal causes and failures to external causes.
5.  The recency effect describes the enduring quality of initial impressions.
6.  In the foot-in-the-door strategy, the strongest point or request is made first, followed by a weaker point or request.
7.  Cognitive dissonance is experienced when we have two consistent thoughts.
8.  Self-perception suggests that we are motivated toward consistency between attitude and behavior and away from inconsistency.
9.  Conformity is when a person changes behavior in response to an explicit demand of one in authority.
10. Milgram studied conformity by using a real subject and several accomplices.
11. When we seek the approval of others, or when we avoid their disapproval, we are experiencing normative social influence.
12. In the Milgram study, two of every three subjects stopped at 100 volts.
13. Roles are rules that apply to all members of the group.
14. Social loafing improves the group's performance.

15. Individual members of a group that is rioting probably experience risky shift that makes them more likely to engage in irresponsible behavior.

16. Group polarization refers to impaired decision making and avoidance of realistic appraisal to maintain group harmony.

17. A person believes she has the necessary traits best suited for a leadership position; this is most consistent with the contingency model of leadership.

18. Prejudice is an unjustified generalization about a group's characteristics that does not consider any variation from one individual to the next.

19. Noncompetitive contact between groups is effective in reducing prejudice.

20. According to ethologists, aggression is learned.

21. Altruism is an unselfish interest in helping someone else.

22. The more people who witness an emergency, the more likely someone will help.

23. Consensual validation involves validating our attitudes because other people hold them as well.

24. We end up choosing someone who is close to our own level of attractiveness; this is called *affectionate love.*

25. The triangular theory of love includes the dimensions of passion, affection, and trust.

26. Men prefer rapport talk.

27. Loneliness is related to a lack of compassionate love and altruism.

## Practice Test 1

1. What are the three dimensions that are used in the attributions people make?
   a. internal or external, stable or unstable, and controllable or uncontrollable
   b. internal or external, primary or secondary, and chronic or acute
   c. stable or unstable, controllable or uncontrollable, and primary or secondary
   d. stable or unstable, primary or secondary, and interpersonal or intrapersonal

2. Which of the following most clearly illustrates an internal attribution?
   a. John believes his sister plays the piano to make a good impression on others.
   b. Larry believes that his father is hostile because of the difficulties at work.
   c. Maria believes Rob gossips about others because of a mean and spiteful streak.
   d. Diane believes her son lies to her to avoid possible punishment.

3. Which of the following is not a component of social perception?
   a. developing impressions of others
   b. gaining self-knowledge from our perceptions of others
   c. presenting ourselves to others to influence them
   d. trying to persuade somebody to change their attitudes

4. Suppose you are interviewing for a job. Based on what you know about the primacy effect, you should
   a. present yourself honestly so that the interviewer does not expect too much from you.
   b. make sure that the interviewer first notices your positive traits.
   c. present your positive and negative qualities at the same time.
   d. use the foot-in-the-door technique.

5. You have a friend who is very much aware of the impressions she is making on others. You would say that this person has a high level of
   a. self-promotion.
   b. self-monitoring.
   c. cognitive dissonance.
   d. self-serving bias.

6. Which of the following is true of individuals experiencing cognitive dissonance?
   a. They show an inability to make up their mind.
   b. They have lost their sense of self and the ability to make decisions.
   c. They are preoccupied with how they are perceived by others.
   d. They are experiencing a conflict between their attitudes and behavior.

7. "Start small and build" best describes the
   a. door-in-the-face strategy.
   b. face-in the-door strategy.
   c. foot-in-the-door strategy.
   d. foot-in-the-face strategy.

8. Conformity is lowest
   a. when group opinion is unanimous.
   b. among individuals with low self-esteem.
   c. if group members are experts.
   d. when there are dissenters in the group.

9. The type of social influence that involves seeking approval or avoiding disapproval is called
   a. obedience.
   b. social facilitation.
   c. informational social influence.
   d. normative social influence.

10. In Milgram's research, it was discovered that obedience decreased
    a. as people were paid more to participate.
    b. when the authority figure was perceived to be legitimate.
    c. when the authority figure was close by.
    d. when the victim was made to seem more human.

11. Paula is a good racquetball player whose performance seems to improve as the crowd watching her gets larger. The best explanation for this pattern is
    a. the bystander effect.
    b. deindividuation.
    c. social facilitation.
    d. egoism.

12. Omar is frustrated because there are people in his committee who are just not pulling their weight and doing their assigned tasks. This lack of effort is called
    a. social loafing.
    b. social facilitation.
    c. deindividuation.
    d. groupthink.

13. The historical examples of the space shuttle Challenger, the Bay of Pigs invasion, and the Watergate cover-up illustrate the consequences of
    a. rapport talk.
    b. groupthink.
    c. altruism.
    d. foot-in-the-door.

14. The fifth-grade teacher was surprised when her Japanese-American student, Hiroko, performed poorly in math. The teacher's reaction was due to
    a. polarization.
    b. stereotyping.
    c. groupthink.
    d. deindividuation.

15. Tajfel's social identity theory provides an explanation for
    a. prejudice.
    b. the risky shift.
    c. group leadership.
    d. social loafing.

16. Research on improved interethnic relations in shared facilities disregards placing importance on
    a. task-oriented cooperation.
    b. the jigsaw classroom.
    c. intimate contact.
    d. competition.

17. According to Dollard, what triggers aggression?
    a. pain
    b. culture
    c. socioeconomic status
    d. frustration

18. Which of the following statements about research on gender differences in aggression is incorrect?
    a. Males are more aggressive than females in all cultures.
    b. More aggression by males than females is found in animals as well as humans.
    c. Males are found to be more aggressive than females as early as two years of age.
    d. In verbal aggression, no differences are found between adult males and females.

19. Dan spends all day volunteering with others to pick up roadside garbage. That evening, he confides to a roommate that his motivation to volunteer was to impress his girlfriend. Dan's behavior is an example of
    a. reciprocity.
    b. social exchange.
    c. altruism.
    d. egoism.

20. The matching hypothesis of attraction states that
    a. individuals prefer a person more attractive than themselves.
    b. individuals are uncomfortable around attractive people.
    c. individuals choose someone close to their level of attractiveness.
    d. in enduring relationships, physical attractiveness becomes more important.

21. When it comes to relationships, women tend to emphasize
    a. independence.
    b. autonomy.
    c. connectedness.
    d. focus on self.

## Practice Test 2

1. People are interested in discovering the causes of behavior, according to
    a. cognitive dissonance.
    b. self-perception theory.
    c. attribution theory.
    d. catharsis.

2. "Whenever I do well on an exam, it is because I studied hard. Whenever I do poorly on an exam, it is because the test was unfair." This demonstrates
    a. the fundamental attribution error.
    b. implicit personality.
    c. prototypes.
    d. the self-serving bias.

3. Another name for impression management is
    a. attribution formation.
    b. self-perception.
    c. self-presentation.
    d. risky shift.

4. "First impressions are lasting impressions" according to
    a. the primacy effect.
    b. the latency effect.
    c. attribution theory.
    d. the social comparison theory.

5. _____ are beliefs or opinions about people, objects, and ideas.
    a. Attributions
    b. Altruisms
    c. Stereotypes
    d. Attitudes

6. If Simone changes her behavior to better fit with a group standard, then _____ is said to have occurred.
    a. obedience
    b. conformity
    c. groupthink
    d. ethnocentrism

7. Cansas changed her plans and decided to go on a trip because she thought that her sister was going to pressure her to go. Cansas was influenced by
   a.    deindividuation.
   b.    foot-in-the-door.
   c.    conformity.
   d.    door-in-the-face.

8. In Milgram's classic study, the "teacher" was
   a.    a confederate.
   b.    shocked by the "learner."
   c.    the subject.
   d.    afraid of the "learner."

9. Which of the following is true regarding Milgram's research on obedience?
   a.    Milgram found lower levels of obedience than he had predicted prior to conducting the research.
   b.    Milgram's research failed to debrief participants.
   c.    Milgram found surprisingly high levels of obedience.
   d.    Milgram found vastly different results when he conducted his research in a more natural environment.

10. When individuals make decisions on their own, their decisions tend to be more conservative than the decision they will agree to in a group. The tendency for a group's decision to be more daring is called
    a.    deindividuation.
    b.    emergent boldness.
    c.    disinhibition.
    d.    the risky shift.

11. According to the great-person theory of leadership,
    a.    a good leader in one circumstance will not necessarily be a good leader in another circumstance.
    b.    leaders have certain traits that are best suited for leadership positions.
    c.    a combination of personality characteristics and the situation helps determine who will become a leader.
    d.    leaders use informational social influence.

12. Why does intimate contact tend to facilitate interethnic relations?
    a.    It allows people to discover their similarities.
    b.    It allows people to confirm their stereotypes.
    c.    It encourages people to re-categorize others.
    d.    It reinforces ethnic and cultural differences.

13. Ethologists say that aggression is _____ based.
    a.    cognitively
    b.    culturally
    c.    biologically
    d.    psychologically

14. What do behavioral and social cognitive theorists argue about the cause of aggression?
    a. Aggression is biologically based.
    b. Aggression is the result of unconscious needs that go unmet.
    c. Aggression is learned through observational learning and reinforcement.
    d. Aggression is the result of frustration.

15. What is the unselfish interest in helping someone else called?
    a. agonist
    b. egoism
    c. altruism
    d. catharsis

16. Don was in need of help on a very busy highway. No one stopped to help. No one accepted responsibility since everyone assumed that someone else would stop. This is best explained by
    a. the bystander effect.
    b. risky shift.
    c. groupthink.
    d. the matching hypothesis.

17. Our own attitudes and behavior are supported when another's attitudes and behavior are similar to ours, according to
    a. the matching hypothesis.
    b. consensual validation.
    c. altruism.
    d. cognitive dissonance.

18. Ken and Barbie have a love relationship characterized by passion, intimacy, and commitment. According to Sternberg, this is called
    a. a temporary situation.
    b. romantic love.
    c. consummate love.
    d. affectionate love.

19. In explaining loneliness, women tend to attribute it to _____ factors.
    a. external
    b. internal
    c. psychological
    d. unconscious

20. Which of the following individuals is most at risk for loneliness?
    a. Vera: she and her family are moving into a new house
    b. Rod: he was promoted to manager within his company
    c. Jennifer: she just broke up with her boyfriend
    d. Allen: he is moving to a new city where he knows no one

**Practice Test 3**

1. It's the first day of classes and your professor just fell flat on her back as she was walking into the classroom. Considering the fundamental attribution error, which of the following attributions is most likely to be shared by the students in the class?
   a. "The floor must have been slippery."
   b. "It's the first day of classes, these things happen."
   c. "The professor is clumsy."
   d. "Someone must have startled her."

2. According to Weiner, which of the following attributions for our success in completing a project would enhance our self-esteem?
   a. The project was easy.
   b. I was lucky to finish it on time.
   c. I did it because I am intelligent.
   d. I finished this one, but I am not so sure about the next one.

3. If we asked each member of a married couple what percentage of housework each does, and one says 75% and the other says 60%, we are seeing evidence of
   a. prejudice.
   b. the self-serving bias.
   c. stereotyping.
   d. romantic love.

4. Raoul is a young African-American college student. According to Leon Festinger's theory of social comparison, when Raoul evaluates himself, he is more likely to compare himself to
   a. a young causasian college student.
   b. an older African-American female.
   c. another African-American male.
   d. an adult college student.

5. Jonathan is going on a first date, and he really wants to make a positive impression. Which of the following would be a bad idea for Jonathan?
   a. He should show appreciation of his date by complimenting her.
   b. He should match her behaviors; for example, if she leans forward he should lean forward.
   c. He should be different. Maybe he should wear a Hawaiian shirt and shorts to a fine restaurant!
   d. He should engage in eye contact.

6. Esther is a college student, and like most people she believes that the cost of tuition is simply too high. As part of a psychology class exercise, Esther is asked to write an essay supporting an increase in tuition. In this assignment she has to come up with ten good reasons to increase tuition. Based on cognitive dissonance theory, we can expect that after writing the essay, Esther
   a. will have an even more negative opinion about the high cost of tuition.
   b. will moderate her attitude about the cost of tuition and start thinking that maybe the cost is not so bad.
   c. will feel compelled to write an essay against a raise in tuition.
   d. will organize people to protest the high cost of tuition.

7.	You work for an ad agency and you have been assigned the task of designing an advertising campaign for "Tab," the popular soda drink of the 1970s. You decide to use an attractive communicator like an actress because you expect the audience to be persuaded via
	a.	the central route.
	b.	the peripheral route.
	c.	the factual route.
	d.	the close attention route.

8.	Alissa has very long hair that gives her terrible headaches because of the weight. Everybody compliments her on her beautiful hair, particularly her boyfriend and close friends. While she would like to cut it, she does not because
	a.	of normative social influence.
	b.	of informational social influence.
	c.	she has high self-esteem.
	d.	she is from an individualistic culture.

9.	Which of the following situations is more likely to lead to conformity?
	a.	a group that has dissenters
	b.	a group in which some members established a commitment to their attitudes before joining the group
	c.	if there is a lot of diversity in the group
	d.	if the group members are from a collectivistic culture

10.	If you were a parent and you wanted to use the studies of Milgram to make your kids more obedient, which of the following things would you do?
	a.	give orders to the kids over the phone on a regular basis
	b.	legitimize your position as a parent and authority figure
	c.	allow one of the kids to be disobedient
	d.	allow one child to enforce obedience on other kids

11.	When the man is expected to open the door for a woman, this is referred to as
	a.	the norms of the group.
	b.	the roles in the group.
	c.	consummate love.
	d.	affectionate love.

12.	According to social facilitation theory, when we are good at something, our performance is _____ in the presence of others. Also, when we are not so good at something, our performance is _____ in the presence of others.
	a.	impaired; impaired
	b.	enhanced; enhanced
	c.	enhanced; impaired
	d.	impaired; enhanced

13.	Which of the following individuals is least likely to engage in social loafing when assigned to a group project in a class?
	a.	a Chinese female
	b.	an American female
	c.	a French male
	d.	a Japanese male

14. Terrorist organizations are likely to attract individuals who share a common bias, such as dislike of government. Once these individuals join a group, their ideas become more extreme. Which of the following social factors better explains this tendency?
    a. impression management
    b. group polarization
    c. minority influence
    d. leadership

15. According to social identity theory, prejudice occurs because
    a. people identify the other group as evil.
    b. people have a hard time connecting to their groups.
    c. people want to achieve self-esteem through their group identity.
    d. people do not trust the members of their own group, therefore they trust even less those in another group.

16. Prejudice
    a. is less likely in a person with an authoritarian personality.
    b. can be caused by competition between groups.
    c. is limited by our social cognitive processes.
    d. is innate.

17. Stereotype is to _____ as discrimination is to _____.
    a. attitude; cognition
    b. cognition; attitude
    c. behavior; cognition
    d. cognition; behavior

18. A good strategy to promote collaboration is
    a. assigning different tasks to each group member that he or she must share with the group.
    b. bringing people of different backgrounds to work together in a project.
    c. creating a social-oriented situation, in which the group members first have to get along before they can proceed with the task.
    d. discouraging intimate contact between the group members.

19. Agression is less likely if
    a. an undesirable stimulus is unexpected.
    b. an undesirable stimulus was intentionally delivered.
    c. receiving an undesirable stimulus is perceived as unfair.
    d. an undesirable stimulus was caused by a source that was not completely in control.

20. Which of the following clichés has been supported by the research in interpersonal attraction?
    a. opposites attract
    b. birds of a feather flock together
    c. killing two birds with one stone
    d. time flies

## Connections

*Take advantage of all the other study tools available for this chapter!*

## Media Integration

| NAME OF CLIP | DESCRIPTION | KEY CONCEPTS AND IDEAS |
|---|---|---|
| | | **Social Thinking** |
| Fundamental Attribution Error | Lee Ross discusses the fundamental attribution error, comparing internal versus external explanations and the tendency to pay more attention to personality than to social factors. Ross presents a variety of examples that illustrate the power of the situation. | Fundamental attribution error<br>Attribution |
| | A dramatization illustrates the fundamental attribution error. Lee Ross discusses factors associated with this tendency, including: perceptual, motivational, cultural, and language. | Fundamental attribution error |
| Self-Enhancing Bias | This exercise demonstrates the problems associated with self-report bias in surveys. Participants are asked to rate the degree to which they are concerned about a series of social issues and to rate the degree to which others are concerned about those same social issues. The tendency for self-enhancing bias is illustrated. | Self-report bias<br>Self<br>Self-enhancing bias |
| Impression Formation | This interactivity simulates an online chat room. This realistic simulation asks participants to rate their impressions of others in the chat room based on the limited information they have. The process of impression formation is discussed. | Impression formation |
| Persuasion | Richard Petty explains the research on routes to persuasion (central and peripheral) and the processes that produce long-lasting versus short-term attitude change. The role of motivation in persuasion is discussed. Robert Cialdini discusses the | Persuasion<br>Central route<br>Peripheral route<br>Principles of influence<br>Self-persuasion<br>Cognitive dissonance |

| | six principles of influence in the peripheral route: reciprocation, liking, consistency, social validation, authority, and scarcity. These principles of influence cause people to be persuaded for reasons other than the merits of the case. Elliot Aronson discusses self-persuasion. In certain situations, people feel compelled to persuade themselves. Research on cognitive dissonance is discussed. The central route to persuasion is more powerful and permanent than the peripheral route. | |
|---|---|---|
| | | **Social Influence** |
| Culture and Self | This video clip starts with insights into what people in a conversation are thinking about themselves. The effect of culture on self-concept and how that definition of the self influences individual psychology are discussed. Experts Markus and Kitayama are interviewed and present their perspective on the role of culture in the definition of self, comparing American and Asian cultures. They discuss how we pass our cultural understandings through interactions. The video clip also presents a discussion of the relationship between the motivation for achievement and the definition of the self. The topics of conformity and persuasion and their relationship with definition of self are discussed. | Self-concept<br>Culture<br>Social psychology<br>Cross-cultural psychology<br>Independent vs. interdependent self<br>Achievement motivation |
| Conformity and Obedience | This video clip discusses social influence and group pressure. Video of the classic Asch study of conformity is presented. Anthony Pratkanis discusses conformity in contemporary society. Pratkanis's replication of the original Asch study is showed. Video of the original | Conformity<br>Obedience<br>Asch conformity study<br>Milgram's obedience study |

|  | Milgram study of obedience is presented. The consequences to the obedience are discussed. |  |
|---|---|---|
|  |  | **Intergroup Relations** |
| Learning Prejudice | This audio clip discusses the work of Jerlean Daniel, a child development researcher who studied prejudice in preschoolers and found evidence that preschoolers tend to engage in prejudice on the basis of the name of another child. Children at that age are aware of prejudice and can act on it. Daniel suggests adults need to model appropriate behaviors and attitudes. | Prejudice<br>Developmental psychology<br>Modeling |
| Stereotype Threat | This video presents Claude Steele discussing his research in the area of stereotype threat. Performance can be influenced by negative stereotypes. The anxiety of being concerned with stereotype results in detriment of performance. The studies presented explored the impact of gender and racial stereotypes. Stereotypes can shape identity and have long-term effects on society. | Stereotype<br>Stereotype threat<br>Experimental method |
| Social Ostracism | Kipling Williams, an expert in social ostracism discusses how human need to belong, to have a sense of control, self-esteem, and a meaningful existence. Ostracism is a metaphor for death. Experiments that simulate ostracism are presented. Physiological arousal is experienced in those being ostracized. A response to ostracism may be frustration, leading to aggression. The case of the killers at Columbine High School is discussed. At the end of the video clip, Elliot Aronson discusses how the jigsaw classroom, by encouraging cooperation also has positive effects on intelligence, cognition, and motivation. | Social ostracism<br>Experimental method<br>Jigsaw classroom<br>Cooperation |

| Prisoner's Dilemma | In the "Prisoner's Dilemma" the participant is placed in a situation of a burglar who has been arrested with his partner. The participant is asked to choose between confession and denial. Research shows that most people choose to confess, thus engaging in a competition strategy with their partner. A second interactivity presents the prisoner's dilemma in the context of earning money. | Prisoner's dilemma<br>Cooperation<br>Competition |
|---|---|---|
|  |  | **Social Interaction** |
| Genocide | Irving Staub discusses his studies on the antecedents of genocide. Genocide is the outcome of ordinary psychological processes and their evolution. Staub studied genocide in Rwanda. Some of the starting points of genocide are severe economic problems, political turmoil, elaborate social changes, and conflict between groups over territory or economic power. A history of conflict can lead to an ideology of antagonism—in other words, the other group is seen by the first group as antagonistic to reaching their ideal. Dehumanization is an element of genocide. A more obedient society is less likely to stop the process leading to genocide. Psychological processes leading to aggression are discussed. | Genocide<br>Aggression |
| Bystander Effect | The video dicusses the research on the bystander effect by John Darley and Bibb Latane. In an interview, John Darley discusses the classic study. The Kitty Genove case is presented. A reenactment of the bystander effect experiment is presented. How people tend to take cues for actions from others and the diffusion of responsibility effect are discussed. Latane offers | Bystander effect<br>Diffusion of responsibility |

| | | |
|---|---|---|
| | recommendations for potential victims on how to decrease the bystander effect and diffusion of responsibility. | |
| | | **Relationships** |
| Attraction | This video clip explores the relationship between biology and culture in determining mating preferences, including a discussion of the role of hormones in animal mating. Clip includes interviews with Alice Eagly and Davis Buss, presenting the sociocultural and evolutionary perspectives on interpersonal attraction and mating. | Evolutionary perspective<br>Sociocultural perspective |

**Online Learning Center (www.mhhe.com/Santrockp7u)**

- Interact and make learning fun!
    - **Interactive Exercises**
        - Self-Enhancing Bias
        - Impression Formation
        - Prisoner's Dilemma
        - Nuts
        - Till Death Do Us Part
    - **Interactive Review**
        - Levels of Analysis: Aggression
- Brush up on the Key Terms for this chapter by first reviewing the electronic **Glossary** (in English or Spanish) and then testing your retention using the **Flashcard** feature.
- **"Notes"**—This feature allows you to use the website as you would your text, inserting your own study notes and highlighting areas of particular importance.

**In Your Text**

- Found throughout each chapter, the **Review and Sharpen Your Thinking** feature breaks the text into logical chunks, allowing you to process, review, and reflect thoughtfully on the information that you've just read. When going back to *study* the chapter, try reading the feature *before* the section of text to which it relates. In doing so, you will be able to focus your attention on important concepts *as* you encounter them. In this chapter, this feature can be found on the following pages: pp. 657, 667, 675, 685, and 693.

**Practice Quizzes**

- Test your knowledge of social psychology by taking the different practice quizzes found on your text's **Online Learning Center** and on the **In-Psych Plus CD-ROM** packaged with your text.

## ANSWER KEY

### In Your Own Words

✓ In the past 24 hours, what attributions have you made about the people around you? Have you committed the fundamental attribution error? Have you experienced the self-serving bias?
*Attributions are explanations about the behaviors of others and our own behaviors. The fundamental attribution error involves our tendency to make internal attributions before considering external attributions. The self-serving bias involves a tendency we have to think more positively about ourselves that we think about others.*

✓ Compare cognitive dissonance theory and self-perception theory. Offer an example to illustrate how each theory can predict how behaviors influence attitudes.
*Both of these theories deal with the issue of the relationship between attitudes and behaviors. Cognitive dissonance argues that we match our attitudes and behaviors through an internal process of coping with the uncomfortable psychological experience of realizing that two aspects of one's psychology are inconsistent. However, self-perception theory takes a more behavioral view on the issue and argues that we simply consider our actions as clues of what our attitudes are and that we change our attitudes to match our behaviors.*

✓ What stereotypes exist for individuals who share your appearance, gender, ethnicity, religion, and major?
*The question here is basically what are the stereotypes for your in-groups. Stereotypes are generalizations that we make about group characteristics that do not consider individual variations. If you understand how the self-serving bias and social identity theories work, you'll realize that you will come up with stereotypes that are relatively more favorable that the stereotypes of your out-groups.*

✓ Have you ever done group work in which there was social loafing? Was anything done to reduce it?
*Think of group projects and consider how the teacher structured the task and how that may have contributed to the effectiveness of the group in working on the project. Consider how anonymity, gender, and culture could have played a role in social loafing.*

✓ Describe prejudice and explain the factors that contribute to it.
*Prejudice is a negative attitude about an individual based on the group that the person belongs to. It is an attitude based on a stereotype (cognition) of a group. Prejudice is not a simple phenomenon, and many different factors contribute to it. Among those factors are personality characteristics such as the authoritarian personality and self-esteem, social identity, intergroup competition, social cognition, and cultural learning.*

### Correcting the Incorrect

1. Attributions focus on the causes of behavior. (p. 647)
2. There are three dimensions of causality: *internal/external, stable/unstable, and controllable/uncontrollable.* (p. 647)
3. An *internal* attribution would be a person's intelligence or attitudes. (p. 647)
4. The self-serving bias describes how we attribute success to internal causes and failures to external causes. (p. 649)
5. The *primacy* effect describes the enduring quality of initial impressions. (p. 649)
6. In the foot-in-the-door strategy, *the weaker point or request is made first, followed by a stronger point or request.* (p. 657)
7. Cognitive dissonance is experienced when we have *two inconsistent* thoughts. (p. 653)

8. Cognitive dissonance theory suggests that we are motivated toward consistency between attitude and behavior and away from inconsistency. (p. 653)

9. *Obedience* occurs when a person changes behavior in response to an explicit demand of a person in authority. (p. 660)

10. *Asch* studied conformity by using a real subject and several accomplices. (p. 659)

11. When we seek the approval of others, or when we avoid their disapproval, we are experiencing normative social influence. (p. 659)

12. In the Milgram study, two of every three subjects *went all the way up to 450 volts, the maximum level.* (p. 661)

13. *Norms* are rules that apply to all members of the group. (p. 663)

14. Social loafing *decreases* the group's performance. (p. 663)

15. Individual members of a group that is rioting probably experience *deindividuation*, which makes them more likely to engage in irresponsible behavior. (p. 664)

16. *Groupthink* refers to impaired decision making and avoidance of realistic appraisal to maintain group harmony. (p. 665)

17. A person believes she has the necessary traits best suited for a leadership position; this is most consistent with the *great-person model of leadership*. (p. 667)

18. *A stereotype* is an unjustified generalization about a group's characteristics that does not consider any variation from one individual to the next. (p. 672)

19. *Intimate* contact between groups is effective in reducing prejudice. (p. 674)

20. According to ethologists, aggression is *innate*. (p. 676)

21. Altruism is an unselfish interest in helping someone else. (p. 682)

22. The more people who witness an emergency, the *less* likely someone will help. (p. 684)

23. Consensual validation involves validating our attitudes because other people hold them as well. (p. 686)

24. We end up choosing someone who is close to our own level of attractiveness; this is called the *matching hypothesis*. (p. 687)

25. The triangular theory of love includes the dimensions of *passion, intimacy, and commitment*. (p. 689)

26. Women prefer rapport talk. (p. 690)

27. Loneliness is related to *life's transitions*. (p. 691)

## Practice Test 1

1. a. YES; these are the dimensions of attributions
   b. no; these concepts do not correspond to the dimensions of attributions
   c. no; these concepts do not correspond to the dimensions of attributions
   d. no; these concepts do not correspond to the dimensions of attributions
   p. 647

2. a. no; John is attributing his sister's playing to some external factor
   b. no; Larry is attributing his father's hostility to some external factor
   c. YES; Maria is attributing Rob's behavior to a personality or disposition
   d. no; Diane is attributing her son's lying to an external factor
   p. 647

3. a. no; this is part of social perception
   b. no; this is part of social perception
   c. no; this is part of social perception
   d. YES; this is another aspect of our social behaviors but does not fall under social perception
   pp. 649–651

4. a. no; this is a good idea, but it does not have to do with the primacy effect
   b. YES; the primacy effect refers to the tendency to remember initial information
   c. no; this may be persuasive but it does not have to do with the primacy effect
   d. no; this is a technique used to change people's attitudes
   p. 649

5. a. incorrect
   b. YES; being high in self-monitoring means that the person pays much attention to the impression she makes on others
   c. no; this is the motivation to reduce the discomfort caused by inconsistent thoughts
   d. no; this is the attribution of our success to internal factors and our failures to external factors
   p. 652

6. a. no; cognitive dissonance contributes to their making up their mind
   b. no; cognitive dissonance is a normal phenomenon not associated with losing a sense of self
   c. no; this sounds like a very high level of self-monitoring
   d. YES; we are motivated to reduce the dissonance caused by inconsistency
   p. 653

7. a. no; this is when the strongest demand is made first, followed by a weaker one
   b. no; this is just moving around the words from item a
   c. YES; start with a small request then follow with a stronger one
   d. incorrect; this is not a strategy
   p. 657

8. a. no; this contributes to conformity
   b. no; this contributes to conformity
   c. no; this contributes to conformity
   d. YES; when the opinions are not unanimous, conformity decreases
   p. 660

9. a. no; obedience is behavior that complies with an authority figure's explicit orders
   b. no; this describes an individual's performance that improves in the presence of others
   c. no; this is social influence that involves the desire to be right
   d. YES; we conform in order to be liked and accepted by others
   p. 659

10. a. no; this was not an issue in the experimental procedure
    b. no; this tends to increase obedience
    c. no; this tends to increase obedience
    d. YES; this encouraged disobedience
    p. 661

11. a. no; this effect has to do with helping behavior
    b. no; deindividuation refers to a loss of identity when in the presence of a group
    c. YES; social facilitation occurs when individual performance increased in the presence of others
    d. no; egoism describes helping behavior that provides benefits to the person helping
    p. 663

12. a. YES; social loafing occurs when individuals do not expend much effort when in a group because of reduced monitoring
    b. no; this describes how an individual's performance improves in the presence of others
    c. no; deindividuation refers to a lost of identity when in the presence of a group
    d. no; this describes how groups make poor decisions
    p. 663

13. a. no; this is a style of talking that establishes connections and negotiates relationships
    b. YES; in groupthink there is impaired decision making and avoidance of realistic appraisal to maintain group harmony
    c. no; altruism is an unselfish interest in helping someone else
    d. no; this is a method to change people's attitudes
    p. 665

14. a. no; this describes the solidification of a group's position
    b. YES; a stereotype is a generalization about a group's characteristics that ignores individual variation
    c. no; in groupthink there is impaired decision making and avoidance of realistic appraisal to maintain group harmony
    d. no; deindividuation refers to a loss of identity when in the presence of a group
    p. 672

15. a. YES; we tend to think of our group as an ingroup and other groups as outgroups
    b. no; social identity theory does not address this social phenomenon
    c. no; social identity theory does not address this social phenomenon
    d. no; social identity theory does not address this social phenomenon
    p. 669

16. a. no; this contributes to interethnic relations
    b. no; the jigsaw classroom requires that all individuals make contributions, which aids interethnic relations
    c. no; intimate contact allows others to see people as individuals and contributes to interethnic relations
    d. YES; competition does not contribute to interethnic relations
    p. 673

17. a. incorrect
    b. incorrect
    c. incorrect
    d. YES; Dollard developed the frustration-aggression hypothesis
    p. 677

18. a.   no; this is a correct statement
    b.   no; this is a correct statement
    c.   no; this is a correct statement
    d.   YES; the type of aggression is important to consider when examining gender differences in aggression (females tend to display more verbal aggression)
 pp. 680, 682

19. a.   no; he is not returning a favor to her girlfriend
    b.   no; he is not doing this for a direct exchange with the girlfriend
    c.   no; altrusim is the unselfish interest in helping someone else
    d.   YES; Dan helped because he wanted to gain something
 p. 683

20. a.   no; this may be true in the abstract, but it is not the matching hypothesis
    b.   no; this may be true, but it does not summarize the matching hypothesis
    c.   YES; we choose others who are close to our own level of attractiveness
    d.   no; in fact, attractiveness becomes less important
 p. 687

21. a.   no; this is emphasized by men
    b.   no; this is emphasized by men
    c.   YES; women prefer to engage in rapport talk, which stresses connectedness
    d.   incorrect
 p. 690

## Practice Test 2

1. a.   no; this is the motivation to reduce the discomfort caused by inconsistent thoughts
    b.   no; this theory says that we make inferences about our own attitudes by perceiving our behavior
    c.   YES; attributions are explanations for behavior
    d.   no; this is the release of anger by directly engaging in anger or aggression
 p. 647

2. a.   no; this is the tendency to overestimate the importance of traits and underestimate the importance of the situations when explaining someone's behavior
    b.   no; implicit personality refers to how a layperson understands how traits go together
    c.   no; these are abstract categorizations of traits that describe a particular personality type
    d.   YES; we attribute successes to internal factors and failures to external factors
 p. 649

3. a.   no; attribution refers to the causes that we give to explain behavior
    b.   no; this theory describes how we infer attitudes from behavior
    c.   YES; in self-presentation we try managing the impression others have of us
    d.   no; this describes the tendency of groups to make more risky decisions
 p. 651

4. a.   YES; the primacy effect refers to the tendency to remember initial information
    b.   no; the latency effect refers to the tendency to remember information that is presented later
    c.   no; attribution theory describes how we explain behavior
    d.   no; this theory describes how we compare our thoughts and behaviors to other people's
 p. 649

5. a.    no; attributions are the suspected underlying causes of behavior
   b.    no; altruism is an unselfish interest in helping someone else
   c.    no; stereotypes are generalizations about a group's characteristics that ignore individual variation
   d.    YES; this is the definition of attitudes
   p. 653

6. a.    no; obedience is behavior that complies with explicit demands of an authority
   b.    YES; this is the definition of conformity, and it can take many different forms
   c.    no; groupthink is the tendency of groups to make impaired decisions
   d.    no; this refers to the tendency to favor one's own group over other groups
   p. 658

7. a.    no; this refers to losing a sense of one's identity
   b.    no; this is a technique to change attitudes
   c.    YES; Cansas changed her behavior to fit her sister's standard
   d.    no; this is a technique to change attitudes
   p. 658

8. a.    no; the "learner" was the confederate
   b.    no; the "teacher" believed that was shocking but did not really shock the "learner"
   c.    YES; the "learner" was a confederate
   d.    incorrect, there is no data to suggest this
   p. 660

9. a.    no; Milgram found just the opposite
   b.    no; Milgram conducted extensive debriefing of the subjects
   c.    YES; over 60% of the "teachers" (i.e., subjects) did not stop before arriving at the maximum level of shock
   d.    no; in different settings, there were still high levels of obedience
   p. 661

10. a.    no; deindividuation refers to a lost of identity when in the presence of a group
    b.    incorrect
    c.    incorrect
    d.    YES; this is the definition of the risky shift
    p. 664

11. a.    no; the great-person theory says that the situation is not relevant
    b.    YES; the great-person theory says that some people have certain traits that are best suited for leadership
    c.    no; this sounds like the contingency model of leadership
    d.    no; while this might be true, the great-person theory does not say this
    p. 667

12. a.    YES; we discover that there is more similarity with the outgroup than difference
    b.    no; this would tend to deteriorate interethnic relations
    c.    no; this would reinforce our perceptions of an ingroup and outgroup
    d.    no; this could reinforce stereotypes and encourage prejudice
    p. 675

13. a.   no; ethologists do not focus on cognitive factors
    b.   no; ethologists do not focus on cultural factors
    c.   YES; ethologists believe that certain stimuli act as innate releasers of aggressiveness
    d.   no; ethologists do not focus on psychological factors
    p. 676

14. a.   no; this sounds like the view that ethologists take.
    b.   no; a psychoanalyst would adopt this argument
    c.   YES; social learning focuses on the role of observational learning and reinforcement
    d.   no; this is most consistent with the frustration-aggression hypothesis
    p. 678

15. a.   no; this is a type of drug (from Chapter 3)
    b.   no; this is selfish
    c.   YES; altruism is unselfish, no gains are expected
    d.   no; this is a way of releasing aggression
    p. 682

16. a.   YES; the presence of others reduces the chance that any one person will help
    b.   no; groups tend to make more risky choices
    c.   no; groupthink refers to impaired decision making in a group
    d.   no; this refers to the tendency we have to choose someone who is close to our own level of attractiveness
    p. 684

17. a.   no; this refers to the tendency to select others who have similar level of attractiveness as we do
    b.   YES; others' attitudes and behaviors validate our attitudes and behaviors
    c.   no; altruism is unselfish interest in helping others
    d.   no; cognitive dissonance refers to differences in attitudes within the person, not between people
    p. 686

18. a.   no; this is not a type of love
    b.   no; Ken and Barbie seem to share more than romantic love
    c.   YES; consummate love includes passion, intimacy, and commitment
    d.   no; affectionate love includes intimacy and commitment
    p. 688

19. a.   YES; women consider the role of others and circumstances
    b.   no; this is more likely to be done by males
    c.   no; this is too general a concept
    d.   no; women as a group do not consider unconscious influences when explaining loneliness
    p. 691

20. a.   no; Vera has others to rely on
    b.   no; Rod still falls back on relationships that are already established
    c.   no; Jennifer can still interact with her other friends for support
    d.   YES; Allen is in a new city where there is no social support network for him
    p. 691

# Practice Test 3

1.  a.  no; this is an external attribution
    b.  no; this is also an external attribution
    c.  YES; this is an internal attribution for the professor's behavior
    d.  no; this is an external attribution
    p. 647

2.  a.  no; this is an external attribution for success
    b.  no; this is an uncontrollable attribution for success
    c.  YES; this is an internal and stable attribution for success
    d.  no; this is an unstable attribution for success
    p. 647

3.  a.  no; the opinions of married couples about house chores do not involve prejudice
    b.  YES; clearly both partners believe that they are doing more than what they are in fact doing, since 75% and 60% add up to a lot more than 100% of the housework; they are exaggerating their positive beliefs about themselves
    c.  no; this scenario does not involve stereotyping
    d.  no; this question is not addressing the level of love that this married couple is experiencing
    p. 649

4.  a.  no; the ethnic difference would probably make this comparison not very informative for Raoul
    b.  no; as in item a, there are many differences between Raoul and this person, therefore the comparison would not be as informative
    c.  YES; while age or education have not been specified, this is the one option that presents most similarity with Raoul and thus he is more likely to obtain an accurate appraisal from that comparison
    d.  no; this person may not share much in common with Raoul
    p. 650

5.  a.  no; this is a good recommendation because it is a good technique of impression management
    b.  no; this is a good recommendation because it is a good technique of impression management
    c.  YES; this goes against the rules of impression management; it is better to conform to situational norms (unless he is trying to make a point about Hawaiian shirts, and then that is another issue)
    d.  no; this is a good recommendation because it is a good technique of impression management, along with other effective nonverbal cues
    pp. 651–652

6.  a.  no; this may lead to more dissonance
    b.  YES; a way of solving the cognitive dissonance is by changing the attitudes to be more consistent with the behavior
    c.  no; this may be more effortful than changing attitudes
    d.  no; this may be more effortful than changing attitudes
    p. 653

7. a. no; the attractive communicator is irrelevant for the person who wants facts and is paying attention to the advertisement
   b. YES; you expect people to be superficially attentive to the ad
   c. no; this is a made-up name but, in any case, in terms of meaning it is more consistent with the central route
   d. no; this is also a made-up name but, in any case, in terms of meaning it is more consistent with the central route
   p. 657

8. a. YES; Alissa keeps the long hair because she seeks the approval of others
   b. no; this is not about being right or wrong, it is about being liked
   c. no; if she did, she would be less likely to conform
   d. no; if she was, she would be less likely to conform
   p. 659

9. a. no; this means that there is not unanimity and this reduces conformity
   b. no; being committed to an attitude makes it harder for people to conform to a different attitude in the group
   c. no; the more similar the group members, the higher the conformity
   d. YES; collectivistic cultures encourage conformity
   p. 660

10. a. no; this qualifies as being an authority from a distance, and this reduces obedience
    b. YES; being a legitimate authority figure is one of the main contributors to obedience
    c. no; this is the same as having a dissenter
    d. no; this reduces the legitimacy of the parent as the authority figure
    p. 661

11. a. no; norms are the rules that apply to all group members
    b. YES; this question presents roles for the man and the woman that are different within the group/couple
    c. no; the question does not address love
    d. no; the question does not address love
    p. 663

12. a. incorrect
    b. incorrect
    c. YES; when we are good and skilled at something, doing it in the presence of others actually facilitates and enhances our performance; however, if we are new at what we are doing, having to do it in front of others actually impairs our performance
    d. incorrect; the opposite is true
    p. 663

13. a. YES; this person has two characteristics that make her less likely to engage in social loafing: she is a female and she is from a collectivistic culture
    b. no; while this person is a female, she is also from an individualistic culture
    c. no; this is the most likely to engage in social loafing, a male from an individualistic culture
    d. no; while this person is from a collectivistic culture, he is also a male
    pp. 663–664

14. a. no; impression management is not a group dynamic
    b. YES; group polarization is the tendency for an original bias to become strengthened and in some cases more extreme
    c. no; in groups where people share a bias, it is not likely for there to be a minority influence; basically, there is no minority in such groups
    d. no; while leadership can play a role in the development of terrorist organizations, this question does not address that factor
    p. 664

15. a. no; social identity theory did not address such attributions
    b. no; actually identifying with a group seems to be very easy
    c. YES; this is the main postulate of this theory
    d. no; actually, people favor the people in their group, even when the reasons they are together in a group are meaningless
    p. 669

16. a. no; the opposite is true
    b. YES; competition over valued resources tends to breed prejudice
    c. no; actually, some of our social cognitive processes tend to contribute to prejudice, such as our tendency to categorize people into groups to facilitate our management of social information
    d. no; prejudice is an attitude and attitudes are learned; however, the roots of prejudice may have some innate/evolutionary basis
    p. 671

17. a. no; prejudice is an attitude, and stereotypes are cognitions
    b. no; while stereotypes are cognitions, discrimination is not an attitude
    c. no; the opposite is true
    d. YES; stereotypes are thoughts and discrimination is an action
    p. 672

18. a. YES; this is the basic idea in the jigsaw approach to cooperation and integration in classrooms
    b. no; diversity will not by itself lead to collaboration
    c. no; creating a task-oriented situation may be better to foster collaboration
    d. no; on the contrary, intimate contact should be encouraged
    p. 674

19. a. no; when we don't expect an aversive action, we tend to react more aggressively
    b. no; if we perceive that the person intended to harm us, we do tend to respond more aggressively
    c. no; if receiving an aversive action is perceived as not fair or justified, that increases aggression
    d. YES; if the source is not perceived as completely responsible or not in control of the undesirable stimulus, our aggression is lowered
    p. 678

20. a. no; the opposite is true
    b. YES; similarity says that we tend to associate with people who are similar to us
    c. incorrect
    d. incorrect
    p. 686